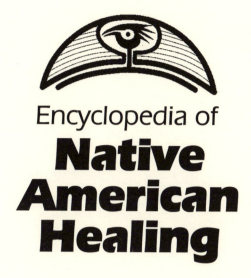

Encyclopedia of
Native
American
Healing

Encyclopedia of
Native American Healing

William S. Lyon

ABC-CLIO

Santa Barbara, California
Denver, Colorado
Oxford, England

Library of Congress Cataloging-in-Publication Data

Lyon, William S., Ph. D.
    Encyclopedia of Native American healing / William S. Lyon.
      p. cm.
    Includes bibliographical references and index.
    1. Indians of North America—Medicine—Encyclopedias. 2. Indians of North America—Religion—Encyclopedias. 3. Indians of North America—Rites and ceremonies—Encyclopedias. 4. Healing—North America—Encyclopedias. 5. Shamanism—North America—Encyclopedias.
    I. Title
    E98.M4L96   1996
    615.8'82'08997—dc20   96-26860
                                          CIP

ISBN 0-87436-852-9

02 01 00 99 98 97 96 95   10 9 8 7 6 5 4 3 2 1

ABC-CLIO, Inc.
130 Cremona Drive, P.O. Box 1911
Santa Barbara, California 93116-1911

This book is printed on acid-free paper ∞.
Manufactured in the United States of America

To those Native American healers whose legacies still remain with us today, to those healers whose lives are now likewise dedicated, and to those who the healers and the spirits will come to teach. May understanding, respect, and peace come your way. It is long overdue.

And to Ken Wagnon of Wichita, Kansas, for saying the right thing at the right time that led me down the right path, all of which made the eventual production of this work possible.

Contents

Illustrations . . . . *ix*

Preface . . . . *xiii*

User's Guide . . . . *xvii*

Maps . . . . *xix*

Encyclopedia of Native
 American Healing 3

Bibliography *335*

Ethnobotany Bibliography *349*

Illustration Credits *353*

Index *355*

Illustrations

The decorative illustrations on the first page of each chapter for letters A–L are from the following publications: *Decorative Art of Indian Tribes of Connecticut*, Anthropological Series, no. 10, Memoir no. 75 (Canadian Department of Mines Geological Survey, 1915); *Navajo Medicine Man Sandpaintings* by Gladys A. Reichard (New York: Dover Publications, Inc., 1977); *Quill and Beadwork of the Western Sioux* by Carrie A. Lynford (Washington, D.C.: Bureau of Indian Affairs, United States Department of the Interior, 1940); *Iroquois Crafts* by Carrie A. Lynford (Lawrence, K.S.: U.S. Indian Service, 1945); *Southwest Indian Designs* by Caren Caraway (Owing Mills, M.D.: Stemmer House Publishers, Inc., 1983); *Southwestern Indian Designs* by Madeleine Orban-Szontagh (New York: Dover Publications, Inc., 1992). The illustrations on the first page of each chapter for letters M–Z are from *Decorative Art of the Southwest* by Dorothy Smith Sides (New York: Dover Publications, Inc., 1961).

Each illustration, listed by chapter and position on the page, is briefly described below. The publication from which the art was taken is noted following each description in letters A–L, together with the original source of the art whenever possible. Only the original source of the art cited by Sides is noted following each description in letters M–Z.

A

Top — Apache basket design [Orban-Szontagh 1992: Museum of the American Indian, Heye Foundation, New York]

Middle — Body designs from Mohegan painted baskets [Canadian Department of Mines Geological Survey, 1915]

B

Top — Mimbres design on bowls

Middle — Wildschut-Ewers: Crow beadwork, Fig. 42-0

Bottom — Iroquois design used on metallic ornaments and brooches [Lynford 1945]

C

Top — Mimbres design on pottery

Middle — Iroquois Celestial Tree design

Bottom — Apache basket design [Orban-Szontagh 1992: Museum of the American Indian, Heye Foundation, New York]

D

Top — Iroquois design used on metallic ornament [Lynford 1945]

Middle — Sacaton design

Bottom — Apache basket design [Orban-Szontagh 1992: Museum of the American Indian, Heye Foundation, New York]

E

Top — Hopi, Kachina design [Caraway 1983]

Middle — Apache basket design [Orban-Szontagh 1992: Heye Foundation, New York]

F

Holy man, Navajo medicine man, Shooting Chant sandpainting [Reichard 1977]

G

Top — Quill work, Western Sioux [Lynford 1940]

Middle — Classic Mimbres bowl design

Bottom — Quill work, Western Sioux [Lynford 1940: U.S. Department of the Interior Bureau of Indian Affairs]

H

Top   Quill work, Western Sioux [Lynford 1940]

Middle   Hopi, Kachina design [Caraway 1983]

Bottom   Quill work, Western Sioux [Lynford 1940]

I

Top   Mohegan painted baskets [Canadian Department of Mines Geological Survey 1915]

Middle   Hopi, pottery design [Caraway 1983]

J

Top   Sacaton design [Canadian Department of Mines Geological Survey 1915]

Middle   Crow, beadwork [Lynford 1940]

Bottom   Scatticook, painted design [Canadian Department of Mines Geological Survey 1915]

K

Top   Hopi, kachina design [Caraway 1983]

Middle   Mohegan painted design [Canadian Department of Mines Geological Survey 1915]

Bottom   Quill work, Western Sioux [Lynford 1940]

L

Feathered snakes, Navajo sandpainting [Reichard 1977]

M

Top   Painted pottery decoration from a Sikyatki ruin, Arizona [Fewkes 1901]

Middle   Pottery decoration, American Southwest [Chapman 1916]

Bottom   Pottery decoration from a Sikyatki ruin, Arizona [Fewkes 1901]

N

Top   Pima basket design, Arizona [Russell 1908]

Middle   Hopi pottery decoration, Arizona [Chapman 1916]

Bottom   Pima basket design, Arizona [Russell 1908

O

Top   Pima basket design, Arizona [Russell 1908]

Middle   Pottery design from Acoma, New Mexico [Stevenson 1883]

Bottom   Pima basket design, Arizona [Russell 1908]

P

Top   Pottery design from San Ildefonso, New Mexico [Chapman 1933]

Middle   Bird design on painted pottery, Pecos Pueblo, New Mexico [Kidder 1936]

Bottom   Pottery design from Sikyatki ruin, Arizona [Fewkes 1901]

Q

Top   Papago basket design, Arizona, Sonora [Kissell 1916]

Middle   Stylized bird on painted pottery, Zuni Pueblo, New Mexico [Chapman 1916]

Bottom   Papago basket design, Arizona, Sonora [Kissell 1916]

R

Top   Painted ceramic decoration, Sikyatki ruin, Arizona [Fewkes 1901]

Middle   Pottery decoration from Sikyatki ruin, Arizona [Fewkes 1901]

Bottom   Pottery decoration from Four Mile Run, Arizona [Fewkes 1904]

S

Top   Pottery design from Homolobi Ruin No. 1, near Winslow, Arizona [Fewkes 1904]

Middle   Pottery decoration from Santo Domingo, New Mexico [Southwest Museum specimen]

Bottom   Design on painted pottery, Homolobi Ruin No. 1, Arizona [Fewkes 1904]

T

Top   Painted snake design on pottery, Shongopovi ruin, Arizona [Fewkes 1904]

Middle   Pottery decoration from Pecos Pueblo, New Mexico [Kidder 1931, 1936]

Bottom   Prehistoric pottery decoration from the Mimbres River Valley, New Mexico [Southwest Museum specimen]

U

Top   Pottery design from Zuni, New Mexico [Stevenson 1883]

Middle Pottery decoration from Chevlon (Shakwabaiyki) ruin, Arizona [Fewkes 1904]

Bottom Pima design, Arizona [Russell 1908]

V

Top   Stylized bird on painted pottery, Zuni, New Mexico [Stevenson 1883]

Middle Pottery design from Sikyatki ruin, Arizona [Fewkes 1901]

Bottom Decoration on painted pottery, Zuni, New Mexico [Stevenson 1883]

W

Top   Decoration on painted pottery, San Ildefonso, New Mexico [Chapman 1933)

Middle Papago basket design, Arizona, Sonora [Kissell 1916)

Bottom Navajo rug design, Arizona, New Mexico [Southwest Museum specimen]

X

Top   Pottery decoration from Four Mile Ruin, Arizona [Fewkes 1904]

Middle Bird design on Hopi painted pottery, Arizona [Bunzel 1930]

Bottom Painted pottery decoration from Four Mile Ruin, Arizona [Fewkes 1904]

Y

Top   Navajo rug design, Arizona, New Mexico [Specimen from collection of Mrs. Kenneth Worthen]

Middle Pottery decoration, Homolobi Ruin No. 1, Arizona [Fewkes 1904]

Bottom Navajo rug design, Arizona, New Mexico [Southwest Museum specimen]

Z

Top   Geometric pottery design from Four Mile Ruin, Arizona [Fewkes 1904]

Middle Pottery design from Shongopovi ruin, Arizona [Fewkes 1904]

Bottom Pima design, Arizona [Russell 1908]

Preface

From our very first contacts, our relationships with Native American healers has continually been a love-hate affair. This unusual dichotomy stems from the fact that Native Americans have always seen external reality through different eyes. They inhabit a world in which the Creator is known only as a "Great Mystery." Such a view negates any possible discussion concerning the nature of God (a "mystery power") and also imbues the lives of Native Americans with mystery. And as any good anthropologist will tell you, where there is mystery in a culture, there is bound to be magic begotten from the "mystery powers."

The use of such powers is central to all Native American healing. Despite centuries of missionary work and other acculturative forces such as mandatory education, these mystery powers remain very active to this day, though they are secreted away on Native American reservations spread across this land. It is the use of these mystery powers by Native American healers that constitutes the hate side of the love-hate affair. As non-Native Americans, we tend hate anything we cannot rationally explain, and healing among Native Americans certainly operates, for the most part, in a realm of reality totally foreign to the Western mind. During our initial encounters with Native Americans, in the early 1600s, we were certainly not prepared for the concept of a physician's "spirit helper" effecting a human cure. Furthermore, if such cures did exist, we reasoned they were certainly the "work of the devil." And when it came to "the infernal, terrible shrieking" of their medicine men and women, that is where most of us drew the line. Since then, more than 300 years have passed yet our attitude remains much the same. If anything, we are even more skeptical of Native American healers for no longer is the devil given blame—now we simply deny they have any powers at all. Unfortunately, our tendency to simply dismiss the mystery powers of Native American doctors only serves to obscure any real understanding on our part of the actual efficacy of their healing techniques.

Recently it has been made clear that Native American healing practices cannot be separated from Native American religious beliefs [Hultkrantz 1992]. That is, for Native American healers spirituality is a necessary aspect of medicinal treatments. This fact has long been known by anthropologists, who for over a century have been equating the Native American meaning of the word "medicine" with "mystery," "holy," and "sacred." However, anthropologists have largely avoided this mystery-power aspect of Native American healing by artificially creating rational and irrational categories for treatments. Irrational treatments are those procedures that involve the use of mystery powers, while rational treatments include their medicinal herbal knowledge, message techniques, methods for setting broken bones, and other such procedures that can be rationally explained. The result of this artificial division is that Native American irrational therapies have, for the most part, been ignored by ethnographers, while at the same time such information is usually held in secret by their doctors and not discussed with outsiders.

For rational treatments, this is not the case. For example, the enthnographic data reveal that Native American's medicinal herbal knowledge was, and still is, astounding. It is not unusual for a skilled "doctor" (medicinal herbalist) to know the medicinal uses of 300 to 400 different local plants, including mixtures thereof. Because this knowledge also differs from area to area, their total plant knowledge is phenomenal. For example, Vogel's classic work on medicinal plants, which is limited to "remedies used by both Indians and whites" [1970:9], lists over 500 known botanical drugs. In fact, there have been only "a bare half dozen, at most" [Vogel 1970:6] plant drugs ever listed in *The Pharmacopoeia of the United States of America* since its inception in 1820 for which Native American uses have not been documented. On the other hand, there are several hundred Native American plant remedies that have never even been listed in our pharmacopoeia. As such, it is safer to assume that these few undocumented cases are simply missing field notes rather than to assume no Native Americans ever knew of their uses.

But even these "rational" therapies often contain irrational components—a plant harvested improperly, such as breaking its root, can easily lose its "power" to heal; a certain type of moss must be gathered only from the north side of the tree truck; a certain root must be selected according to its shape; while plant concoctions must be administered to patients only when singing the proper "medicine" songs. As such, over years of inquiry we have found that many of their plant formulas, stripped of their mystery aspects, simply do not work in our laboratory settings. Nevertheless, plant healing remedies are relatively easy for our minds to accept, and many an early settler skirted death through their usage. Today many people continue to seek out Native American herbal remedies.

Native American ethnobotany (the study of plant use) includes their medicinal uses of plants. As such, this "rational" aspect of Native American healing is more frequently documented than the "irrational" component, even though the latter is most often used for the more serious cases of illness. Because of this and also because the entire scope of Native American healing cannot be adequately represented in a single volume, the role of the Native American herbalist and other "rational" therapies are largely ignored in this work. Instead, the focus here is on the little-known, "irrational" aspects of Native American healing—what has been termed for decades now in anthropology as *shamanic healing*. However, for those readers interested in the medicinal uses of plants by Native Americans a special ethnobotany bibliography has been appended to the bibliography. In addition, most Native American ethnographies include a small section on the medicinal uses of plants.

Unfortunately, many a contemporary scholar or physician who has never set foot on a Native American reservation, let alone ever attended an authentic shamanic healing, will be quick to inform you that shamanism is mere trickery and deception. This encyclopedia contains ample evidence to the contrary. Furthermore, my own fieldwork over the past two decades has documented several cases in which Native American shamanic treatments succeeded after Western medicine had failed [Lyon 1996].

It eventually became clear to me that even the Native American healers themselves do not understand these mystery powers, they simply know how to wield them. They do what they do because it works for them. At the same time, they experience no anxiety whatsoever in knowing that fundamentally their healing treatments are a mystery even unto themselves. In fact, it is the shaman's "trickery" at the onset of a healing ceremony that enables the minds of the participants to witness these mystery powers in action.

So what has been shrugged off in the past as primitive superstition is better regarded as a viable system of healing that we know very little about. And, in spite of its irrational nature, this Native American system of healing operates totally within the view of the general public, whereas our own physicians keep their successes and failures secreted away. For example, I do know that Native American techniques are much more efficacious than Western medicine with respect to the diagnosis and prognosis of ailments. One rarely reads of misdiagnosis by a shaman, while, on the other hand, prescribing several different drugs in the course of a treatment is common among Western physicians.

This is the first scholarly work to survey the mystery powers of Native American shamans with respect to healing. It is long overdue. Herein lies a wealth of rarely seen documentation concerning various aspects of shamanic healings as they have been observed and recorded over the past 350 years. In sifting through this evidence one sees that shamanism has very definite, cross-cultural patterns. That is, it is an organized system with definite rules of operation. For example, one rule is that the presence of a single menstruating woman at a healing almost always causes the treatment to fail. Why this should be the case remains a mystery. Nevertheless, the existence of such rules validates shamanic healing as an operational system that extends beyond mere human imagination. That is, shamans are not just in their heads when it comes to treating patients.

Prior to the 1960s most shamans were written off by anthropologists and others as simply mental cases. One of my Lakota "relatives," Wallace Black Elk, was turned in by the local priest on the Rosebud Reservation in South Dakota during the late 1940s for publicly supporting traditional Lakota healing. When he began speaking about the spirits who come to heal, they had him institutionalized and subjected to electric shock "treatments."

More recently, however, anthropologists have reversed this view, causing the professional study of shamanism to come into vogue. For the most part, these studies have been limited to the psychological studies of shamans per se. That is, interest is focused mainly on the shaman's altered states of consciousness, the various techniques used for inducing trances, the general nature of shamanic trances, EEG readings of shamans, and other such psychological aspects of shamanism.

Blatantly absent are theories, hypothesis, and research regarding the actual physics of shamanism. The scant data we have tend to indicate that the two aspects cannot be treated separately. That is, we need to look at the interplay between psychology and the physical theories now emerging from the fields of special relativity, general relativity, quantum theory, and quantum field theory. Such studies constitute the future of research on shamans and their healing abilities. The first noteworthy attempt to this end was made only recently by physicist Fred Alan Wolf [1991]. In his ground-breaking work, Wolf sets forth nine hypotheses that attempt to interrelate the laws of modern physics with the known psychology of shamanism.

Because our understanding of shamanic healing is currently rudimentary at best, it is hoped that this encyclopedia will serve not only to better inform the reader of the depth and efficacy of this aspect of Native American healing, but also serve as a tool for further research into this little understood realm of human ability.

User's Guide

Entry Format

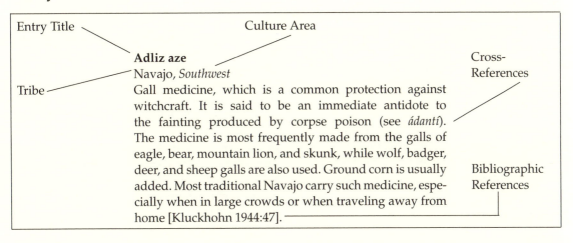

Entry Title — Culture Area — Cross-References

Adliz aze
Navajo, *Southwest*

Tribe — Gall medicine, which is a common protection against witchcraft. It is said to be an immediate antidote to the fainting produced by corpse poison (see *ádantí*). The medicine is most frequently made from the galls of eagle, bear, mountain lion, and skunk, while wolf, badger, deer, and sheep galls are also used. Ground corn is usually added. Most traditional Navajo carry such medicine, especially when in large crowds or when traveling away from home [Kluckhohn 1944:47].

Bibliographic References

Entry Title: Every entry in the encyclopedia is headed with a word or phrase that is intended to most fully and accurately reflect the content. Because of the diversity and complexity of the information in many entries, an adequately representative title is not always possible. To provide readers access to the significant information in entries not adequately reflected in the titles, I provide entries under other significant titles that direct the reader, by means of cross-references, to these entries. Many of the entry titles are in Native American languages. I recognize that many of these terms will be unknown to most users of this work. Still it is by this means that I am able to retain cultural identity and integrity of the information presented. The information in these entries is intended to be accessible through other entries with more familiar entry titles by following the cross-reference suggestions. Often users of this work will want to follow a series of cross-references, even chains of cross-references, to find the information they seek. I also hope that, for many users, this cross-referencing technique will stimulate a process of exploration. I hope that readers will be interested in compar-

isons, compilations, and connections among the entries in the encyclopedia.

Tribe and/or *Culture Area:* Entry titles are followed by the identification of the tribe and/or culture area where relevant. Typically a tribe, a list of tribes, or a tribal grouping (Algonquian, Teton, Pueblo, etc.) is listed first followed by the culture area (identified in italic type) in which this tribe, list of tribes, or tribal grouping is located. The culture areas are in turn keyed to a set of detailed maps, as explained on p. xviii.

Unfortunately, the division of Native American culture areas has not been standardized in anthropology, and several different systems have been devised throughout this century. In this work, the division into culture areas as set forth by Murdock (1975) has been adopted, except that I use the phrase "Canadian Eastern Woodlands" for Murdock's "Eastern Canada" area.

Cross-References: These are terms found in the text of the entries that are also the titles of other entries where related information is presented.

These terms are cross-referenced using the phrases "see" or "see entry."

Bibliographic References: Because the information in this encyclopedia represents only a small fraction of a veritable mountain of available material, bibliographic references are provided for most entries. This feature, along with the extensive bibliography, enhances the usefulness of this encyclopedia for scholars and specialists, as well as for the general reader.

Maps

Maps are provided for the 15 culture areas to assist in locating tribes. Tribe and/or culture area designations are given in entries where relevant. Maps 1–15 present the culture areas in detail.

Bibliography

The bibliography is in alphabetical order by the last name of the author. Works by the same author are organized chronologically by the year of publication. Multiple publications for the same year for a given author are arranged alphabetically by title or by date published and an alphabetic character is appended to the year. References to the bibliography are made throughout the encyclopedia by reference to the author's last name and the year of publication.

Index

An index to the entries has been provided to facilitate research on specific tribes or tribal groupings. It is a standard subject index that includes tribes or tribal groupings, culture areas, and key concepts germane to Native American healing.

Native American Languages

More than 150 Native American languages are represented in the titles of entries in this encyclopedia. Native American languages have come to be written primarily through the introduction by linguists and others of orthographic systems that assign a symbol or alphabetic character to the phones (the distinguishable sounds) of a language. For many Native American languages several different orthographies have been used. Further complexity is introduced by the abilities and eccentricities of various persons who have recorded these Native American terms. Some hear a "b" sound where others hear a "p" sound; some hear "ts" where others hear "s." The linguistic and orthographic complexities of any Native American language are fully understood only by the specialist in that language. Though ideally every Native American word used in the dictionary would be presented so that the orthography would most closely reflect Native American pronunciations, this is not even possible, much less practical, and it would require readers to engage a mini-course in phonetics to use the dictionary. I have decided to do all I can to avoid misrepresentation and confusion, yet I recognize that it is essential for the encyclopedia to be "user-friendly." Native American words are presented either in the most commonly used Anglicized forms, where known, or exactly as they appear, plus most diacritical markings, in the sources I have used. Readers should be aware that pronunciations of the terms based on the simplified presentation likely only generally resemble how the word would sound if pronounced by a speaker of the language. Many of the ethnographic documents contain discussions of language and orthography. Readers interested at this technical level are encouraged to consult these works, as well as dictionaries on the relevant languages.

Maps

1

Arctic Coast
(Adapted from Murdock 1975)

2

Mackenzie-Yukon
(Adapted from Murdock 1975)

3

Northwest Coast
(Adapted from Murdock 1975)

4

Oregon Seaboard
(Adapted from Murdock 1975)

5

California
(Adapted from Murdock 1975)

6

Peninsula
(Adapted from Murdock 1975)

7

Basin
(Adapted from Murdock 1975)

8

Plateau
(Adapted from Murdock 1975)

9

Plains
(Adapted from Murdock 1975)

10

Midwest
(Adapted from Murdock 1975)

11

Eastern Canada
(Adapted from Murdock 1975)

12

Northeast
(Adapted from Murdock 1975)

13

Southeast
(Adapted from Murdock 1975)

14

Gulf
(Adapted from Murdock 1975)

15

Southwest
(Adapted from Murdock 1975)

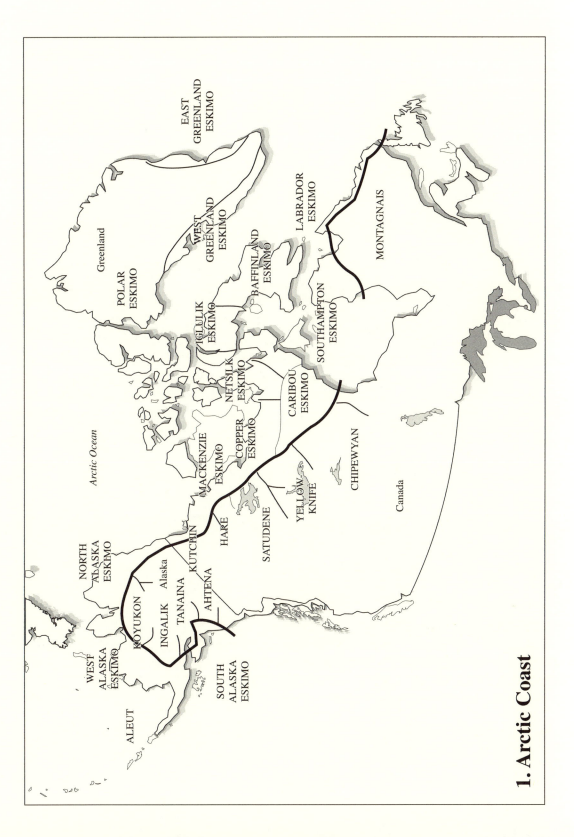

1. Arctic Coast

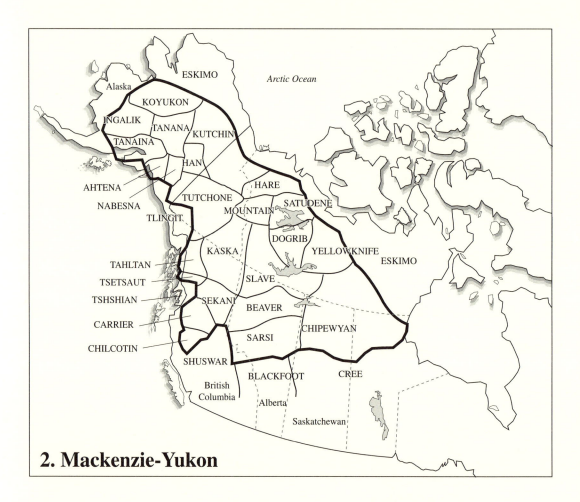

2. Mackenzie-Yukon

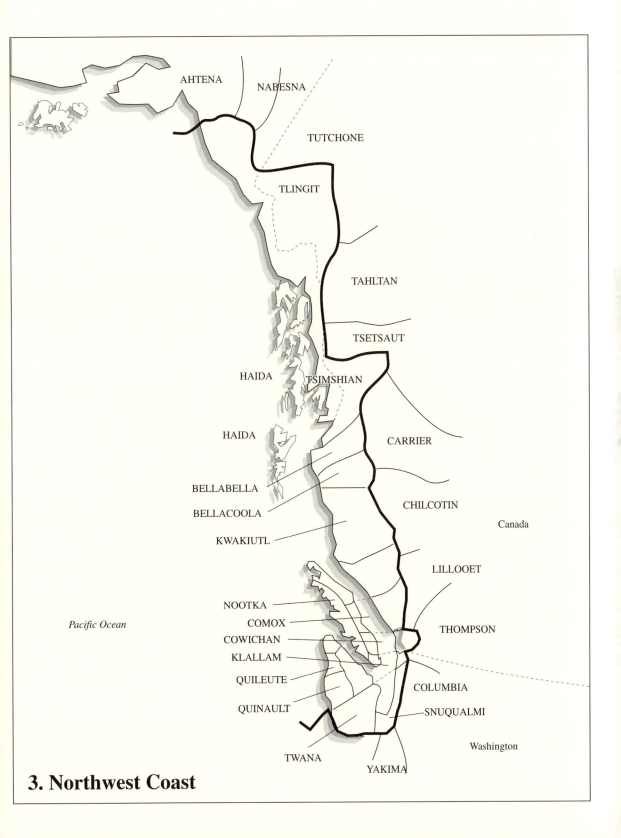

AHTENA

NABESNA

TUTCHONE

TLINGIT

TAHLTAN

TSETSAUT

HAIDA

TSIMSHIAN

HAIDA

CARRIER

BELLABELLA

BELLACOOLA

CHILCOTIN

KWAKIUTL

Canada

LILLOOET

Pacific Ocean

NOOTKA

COMOX

COWICHAN

THOMPSON

KLALLAM

QUILEUTE

COLUMBIA

QUINAULT

SNUQUALMI

TWANA

YAKIMA

Washington

3. Northwest Coast

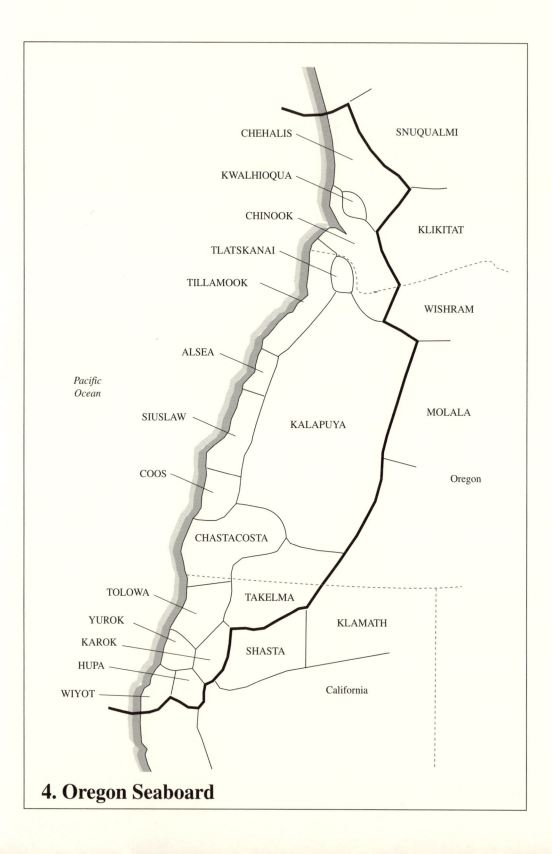

CHEHALIS

SNUQUALMI

KWALHIOQUA

CHINOOK

KLIKITAT

TLATSKANAI

TILLAMOOK

WISHRAM

ALSEA

Pacific Ocean

MOLALA

SIUSLAW

KALAPUYA

COOS

Oregon

CHASTACOSTA

TOLOWA

TAKELMA

YUROK

KLAMATH

KAROK

HUPA

SHASTA

WIYOT

California

4. Oregon Seaboard

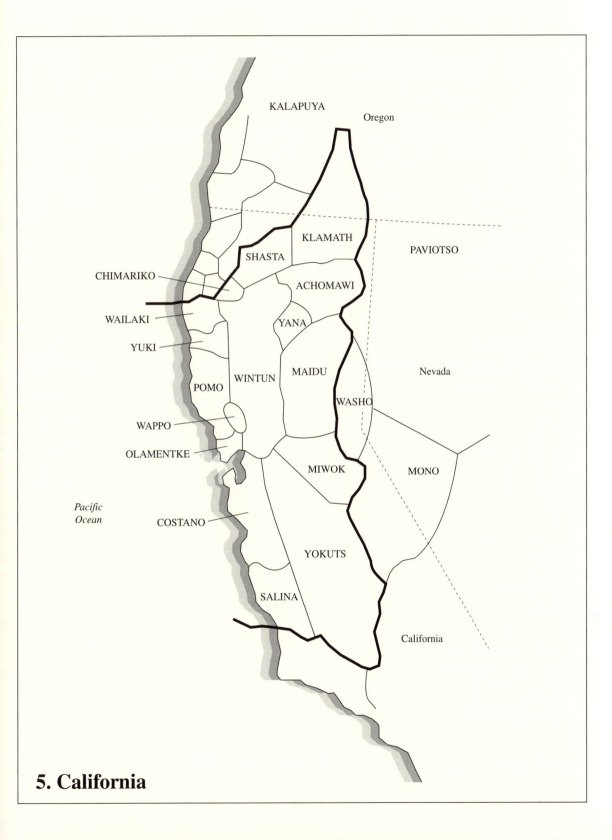

KALAPUYA

Oregon

KLAMATH

SHASTA

CHIMARIKO

ACHOMAWI

PAVIOTSO

WAILAKI

YANA

YUKI

WINTUN

MAIDU

POMO

Nevada

WASHO

WAPPO

OLAMENTKE

MIWOK

MONO

*Pacific
Ocean*

COSTANO

YOKUTS

SALINA

California

5. California

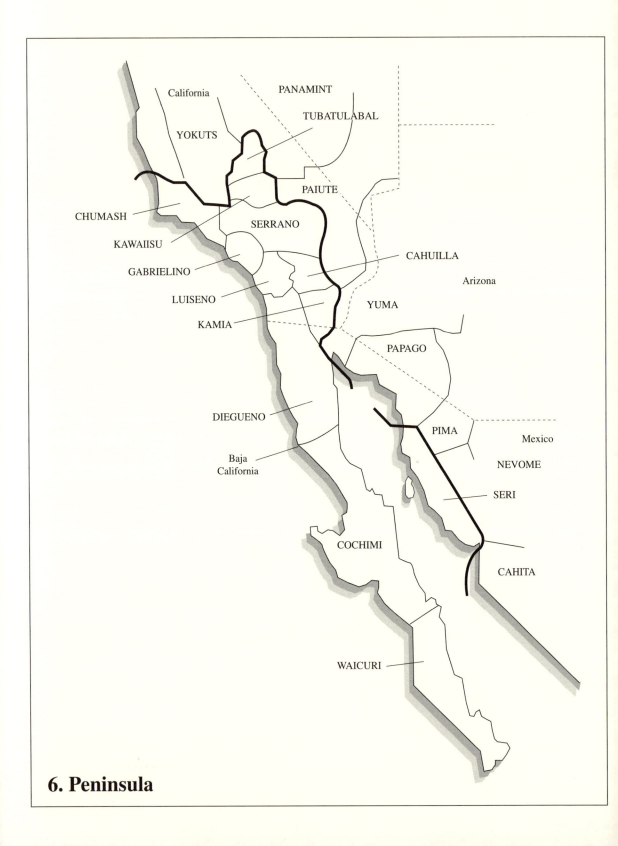

6. Peninsula

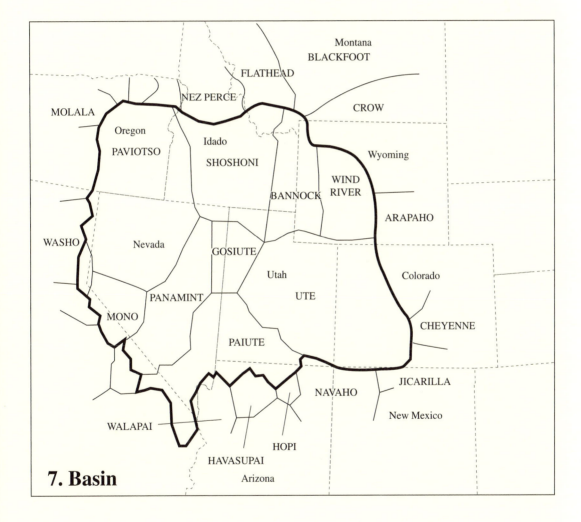

7. Basin

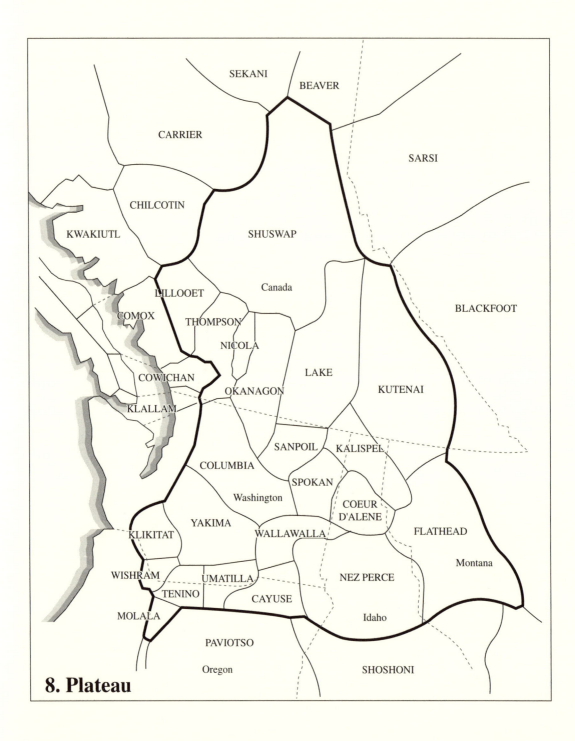

SEKANI

BEAVER

CARRIER

SARSI

CHILCOTIN

KWAKIUTL

SHUSWAP

Canada

LILLOOET

BLACKFOOT

COMOX

THOMPSON

NICOLA

LAKE

COWICHAN

KUTENAI

OKANAGON

KLALLAM

SANPOIL   KALISPEL

COLUMBIA

SPOKAN

Washington

COEUR
D'ALENE

YAKIMA

KLIKITAT

WALLAWALLA

FLATHEAD

Montana

WISHRAM

UMATILLA

NEZ PERCE

TENINO

CAYUSE

MOLALA

Idaho

PAVIOTSO

Oregon

SHOSHONI

8. Plateau

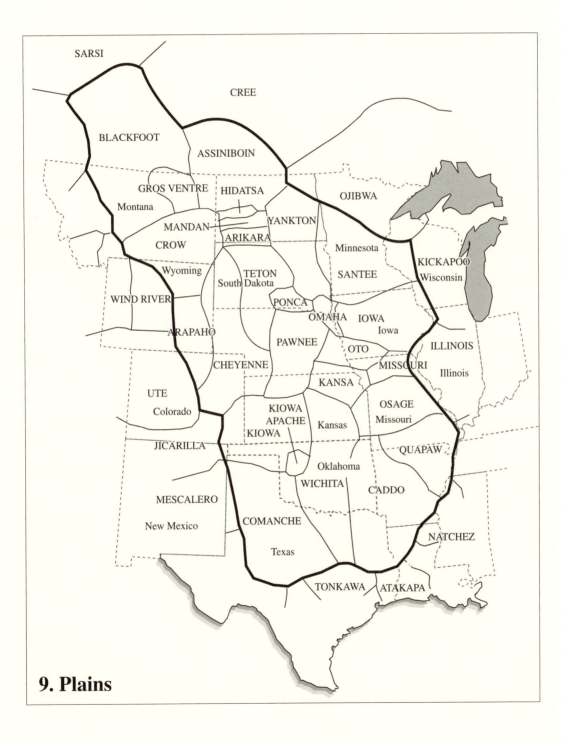

SARSI

CREE

BLACKFOOT

ASSINIBOIN

GROS VENTRE   HIDATSA

OJIBWA

Montana

MANDAN

YANKTON

CROW

ARIKARA

Minnesota

KICKAPOO

Wisconsin

Wyoming

TETON

SANTEE

South Dakota

WIND RIVER

PONCA

OMAHA   IOWA

Iowa

ARAPAHO

PAWNEE

OTO

ILLINOIS

CHEYENNE

MISSOURI

Illinois

KANSA

UTE

KIOWA

OSAGE

Colorado

APACHE

Missouri

KIOWA

Kansas

JICARILLA

QUAPAW

Oklahoma

MESCALERO

WICHITA

CADDO

New Mexico

COMANCHE

NATCHEZ

Texas

TONKAWA   ATAKAPA

9. Plains

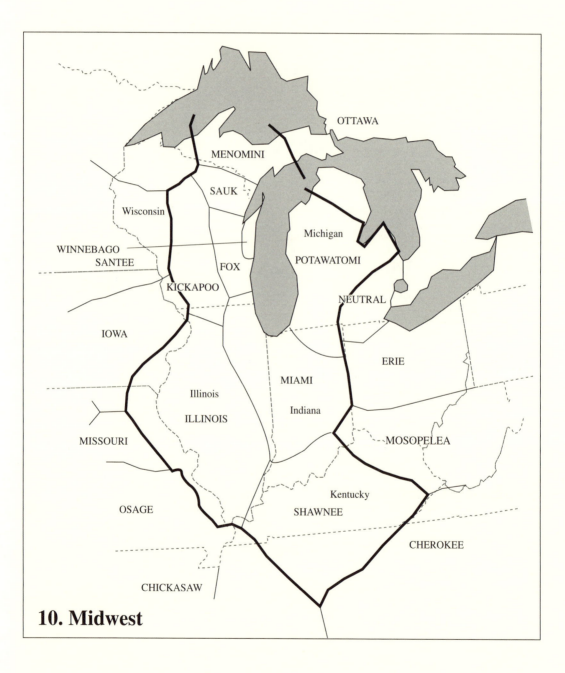

10. Midwest

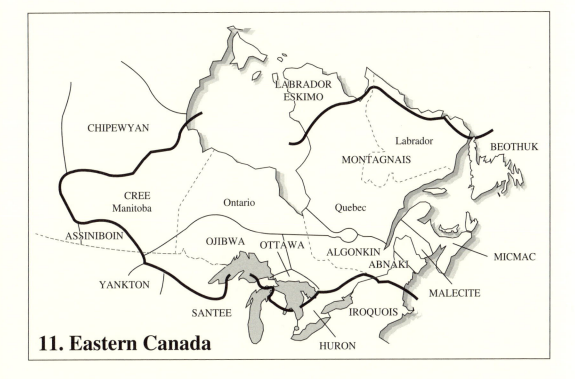

CHIPEWYAN

LABRADOR
ESKIMO

Labrador

BEOTHUK

MONTAGNAIS

CREE
Manitoba

Ontario

Quebec

ASSINIBOIN

OJIBWA

OTTAWA

ALGONKIN

ABNAKI

MICMAC

YANKTON

MALECITE

SANTEE

IROQUOIS

11. Eastern Canada

HURON

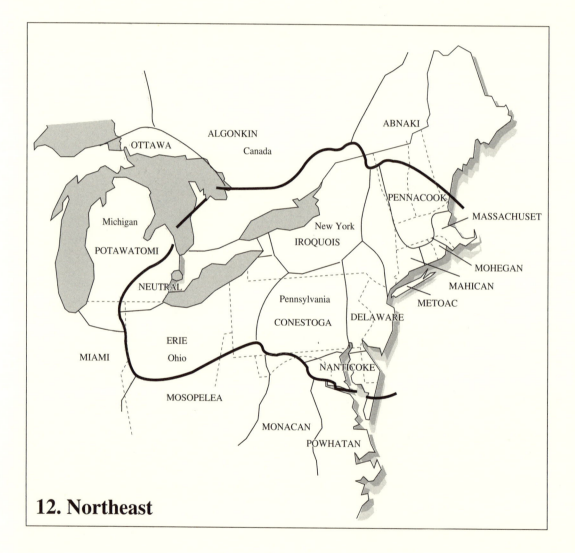

12. Northeast

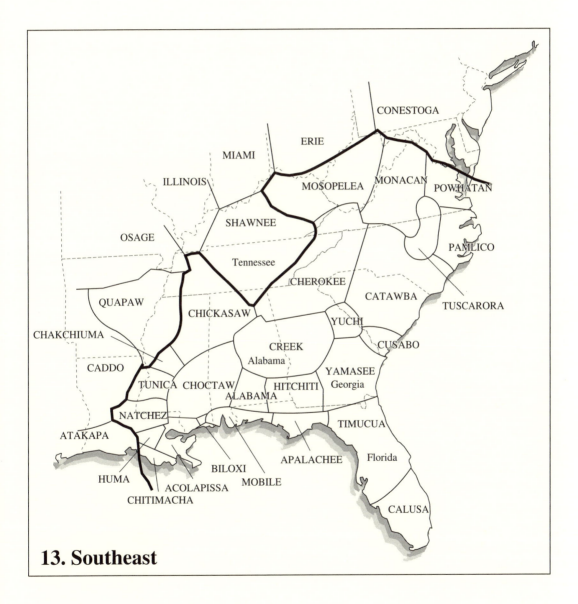

13. Southeast

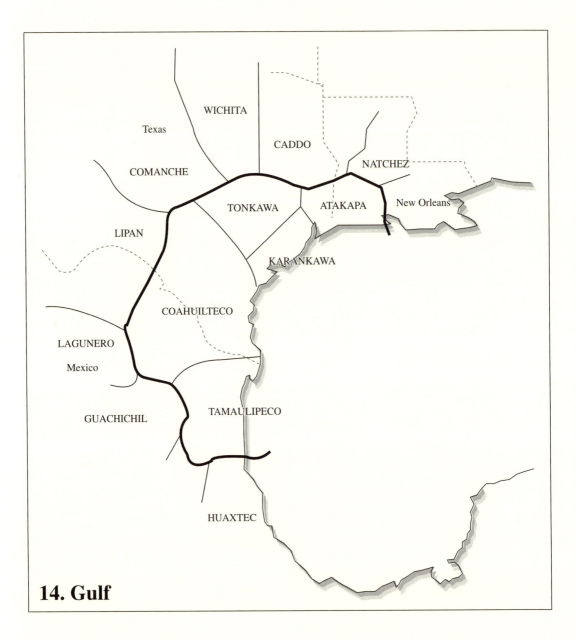

14. Gulf

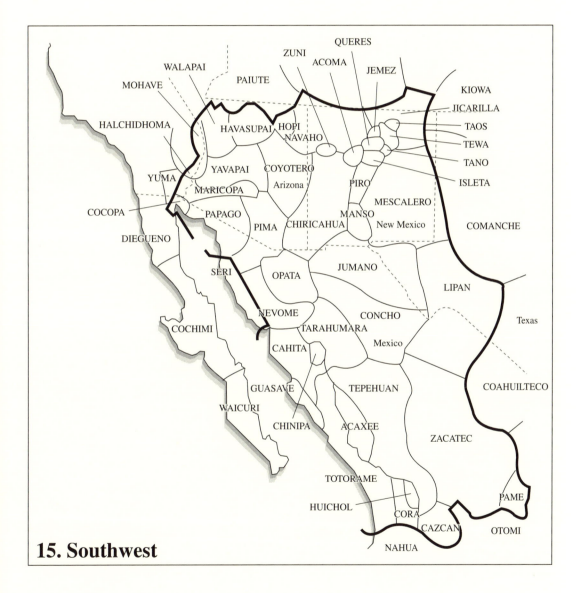

QUERES
ZUNI
WALAPAI
PAIUTE
ACOMA
MOHAVE
JEMEZ
KIOWA
JICARILLA
HALCHIDHOMA
HAVASUPAI
HOPI
NAVAHO
TAOS
TEWA
YAVAPAI
COYOTERO
TANO
YUMA
Arizona
PIRO
ISLETA
MARICOPA
MESCALERO
COCOPA
PAPAGO
MANSO
COMANCHE
DIEGUENO
PIMA
CHIRICAHUA
New Mexico
SERI
JUMANO
OPATA
LIPAN
NEVOME
CONCHO
Texas
COCHIMI
TARAHUMARA
CAHITA
Mexico
COAHUILTECO
GUASAVE
TEPEHUAN
WAICURI
CHINIPA
ACAXEE
ZACATEC
TOTORAME
PAME
HUICHOL
CORA
CAZCAN
OTOMI
NAHUA

15. Southwest

The Honorable Lewis Cass commenting in
1826 on Native American culture:

"Eyes have not been wanting to see, tongues to
relate, nor pens to record, the incidents which
from time to time have occurred. The eating of
fire, the swallowing of daggers, the escape from
swathed buffalo skins, and the juggling incantations and ceremonies by which the lost is found,
the sick healed, and the living killed, have been
witnessed by many, who believed what they
saw, *but who were grossly deceived by their own
credulity, or by the skill of the Indian wabeno.*"

[Cass in Schoolcraft 1857:570; italics added to
separate fact from fiction]

Subsequently, anthropologist Walter James
Hoffman commenting in 1896
on the Honorable Lewis Cass:

". . . as Mr Cass is said to have observed an old
Ojibwa medicine woman, who had come up at
each dance to actively participate in the exercises, he asked someone near by why this old
woman took such an active part, as she appeared
rather uninteresting and had nothing to say, and
apparently nothing to do except shake her
snake-skin medicine bag. The woman heard the
remark and became offended, because she was
known among her own people as a very powerful mitä´kwe. In an instant she threw the dry
snake-skin bag toward the offender, when the
skin became a live serpent which rushed at Mr
Cass and ran him out of the crowd. The snake
then returned to the medicine woman, who
picked it up, when it appeared again as a dry
skin bag."

[Hoffman 1896:105]

Finally, contemporary Lakota wicasa wakan
Wallace Black Elk
commenting in 1990 on American culture:

"But we kind of blanked out. Our mind's eye is
blank, so we rely just on our naked eyes. So we
cut off the hearing. So we lost that communication."

[Black Elk and Lyon 1990:85]

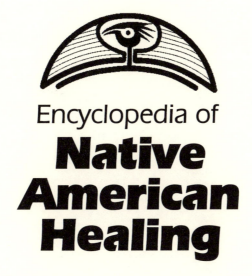

Encyclopedia of
Native
American
Healing

Aaskouandy

Iroquois, *Northeast*

Iroquoian magical charms that are small in size but contain great powers and are mystical unto themselves. For instance, the *aaskouandy* "sometimes change their shape or appearance, and . . . a man who has put away the stone or snake found in the entrails of a deer will be astonished, next day, to find in its place a bean, or a grain of corn, or sometimes the beak of a Raven, or the talons of an Eagle" [JR 1897–1905:33:213]. The Iroquois treat these charms as living persons that need to be fed, listened to, talked to, and so forth. Charms that are not treated well can turn on their holders and become dangerous.

Áata

Papago, *Southwest*

A shamanic healing ceremony designed to drive an evil spirit from the body of a patient; also used to negate the power of evil charms. Literally, the term means "sending away," and the ceremony consists of singing the proper sending-away songs. During the singing, the shaman uses his crystal to look for the exact location of the evil charm. Once it is located, he leaves the ceremony and proceeds to the charm's burial place alone. "Its 'tail' stuck up above ground, and on this he pulled, while the charm wriggled frantically under the earth, pulling the shaman to and fro. In some legendary cases the shaman was pulled underground and never came back. But the strong shaman ultimately dragged out the charm. . . . After it was pulled up the charm was burned, and this burned the sorcerer's heart (the culprit) so that he died" [Underhill 1946:282].

Aatirh

Gitksan, *Northwest Coast*

Special objects that represent a shaman's power source and are used in healing. As a shaman dreams of different power sources, such as otter, mink, canoe, sweat house, or moon, he acquires an object to represent that power. The object is then placed on the body of the patient during a healing ceremony [Barbeau 1958:44].

Aaum sumatc

Mojave, *Southwest*

Also: *hipom sumatc*. A specialist among Mojave shamans called the burn doctor. He "treated burns by blowing on them and cooling them off" [Stewart 1974:10].

Adälön
Cherokee, *Southeast*

The beads used in a divinatory method known as examining the beads. Their use is considered the best method for determining the diagnosis and prognosis of a patient. The original meaning of this word was probably seed, but it evolved to bead and, subsequently, came to mean money, then finally dollar [Mooney and Olbrechts 1932: 11]. For details, see *adanöwiski* and *Doctor Mink*.

Adanöwiski
Cherokee, *Southeast*

Plural: *didanöwiski*. Translates to "he cures anyone" or "he cures people" [Mooney and Olbrechts 1932:84]. There is no special word in Cherokee for medicine man. Although *adanöwiski* is often used to refer to medicine men, they are, for the most part, individually named by words that describe their particular specialties. In 1888 James Mooney began his work on the now famous Swimmer manuscript (see *Swimmer*), a booklet containing the medical formulas of the Cherokee. This work and that of subsequent investigators have provided a detailed account of Cherokee healing.

Most Cherokee healers are men, although women doctors do exist. When healing a patient, the first activity of a medicine man is to diagnose the cause of the ailment—the "seat of the pain." To this end, the medicine man questions the patient regarding his or her dreams and possible taboo violations. The diagnosis is very thorough and often investigates dreams from two or three years earlier. Diagnosis is an individual matter, and some medicine men rely more on physical symptoms, such as headaches or rings around the eyes, than on the patient's dreams. In any event, it is most important to discover the real cause of the disease so that the medicine man can work against it and force it to release its hold on the patient. Almost all diseases are caused by human ghosts, animal spirits, or witches (see *asgina* for details).

If there is a problem making the diagnosis, the medicine man resorts to a divination method known as "examining the beads." To do this, "the medicine man holds a black bead (called *adälön*; see entry) between thumb and index finger of the left hand, a white or red bead between forefinger and thumb of the right hand, and, reciting an appropriate formula, examines what are the chances of the sick man. The brisk movements of the right-hand bead gives an affirmative answer; its sluggish movements, or its remaining motionless, a negative answer" [Mooney and Olbrechts 1932: 133, 41]. These beads were considered the preeminent instrument for determining a true diagnosis and prognosis. (For an example of bead diagnosis, see *Doctor Mink*.)

Once the diagnosis is complete, the medicine man prescribes the proper formula. Each ailment has its own formula that outlines a specific healing ritual, and different medicine men own different formulas. If the medicine man making the diagnosis does not own the particular formula needed, the owner of the proper formula is called for. These formulas have been recorded by the Cherokee shamans in various ways over the years. For instance, the Swimmer manuscript contains 137 formulas written in Sequoyan syllabary. Each formula usually involves the use of plants, spirits, and message techniques, coupled with certain taboo observations. There are also prescribed songs or recitations to be given by the medicine man at specific points in the healing ceremony.

Although specific plants are called for in each formula, what is most important in determining their efficacy is the plant's physical appearance. For instance, the formula might call for the plant to have only one stem, or inverted roots, or branches that incline in a certain way. The time of collecting, such as during a rainstorm, and the place, such as bark obtained from the sunny side of a tree, are also all part of the formula. Furthermore, plants are not considered to be efficacious unless they are used in a prescribed number— usually four or seven, the two most sacred numbers to the Cherokee. Once gathered, the plants are generally either pounded and steeped in water, or boiled before use. All these "sacred" rules in the formulas have led scholars to conclude that the choice of a certain plant as an antidote for a given ailment is based on occult rules rather than the natural chemical properties of the plants selected. Thus, Cherokee shamans cannot be considered knowledgeable herbalists merely because they use plants.

The spirits that are called upon to treat a disease are those that are in opposition to the spirits that have been determined to cause it. For instance, "if a disease is held to be caused by worms, various kinds of birds that are known as worm eaters are called upon to wage the fight. If the disease is thought to be of an unusually tenacious and obstinate nature, such animals as beavers, rats, weasels, the dogged stubbornness of which is proverbial, are commanded to gnaw and tug at it until no trace of it is left. Should the most striking feature of the 'important thing' be its cunning, its evasiveness, such a sly and wary individual as the otter is commandeered to effect the relief" [Mooney and Olbrechts 1932:43].

The plant mixtures are usually administered to the patient by a family member. Often the formula calls for a gourd dipper to be used. In some formulas, however, the medicine man must give the drink to the patient, or he may blow the medicine onto the afflicted part through a blowing tube, usually made from the stem of a trumpet weed *(Eupatorium purpureum)*. Sometimes he blows the medicine over the entire body of the patient or simply sprinkles the patient with it. At other times he may blow his breath on the patient instead of blowing the medicine. In all cases, the patient faces east during this blowing process. In former times, the patient was often taken to a sweat lodge, where the medicine mixture was poured over the hot stones in the lodge.

Massage is frequently mentioned in Cherokee healing methods, especially in formulas for sprains, aches, and swellings. Before massaging the patient, the medicine man warms his hands on some live coals gathered by his assistant. Massaging usually involves the use of only the right hand pressed on the bare skin of the patient.

Taboos are often included in each formula. The two most common taboos are no salt and no hot food in the patient's diet. Taboos differ from formula to formula and are often quite specific and extensive. For example, "when treating anyone who has been wounded by a bullet or an arrow, the medicine man should not chew tobacco for four days; this same taboo has to be observed by

the patient" [Mooney and Olbrechts 1932:65]. Some taboos extend beyond the end of a healing ceremony, ranging in time from a month to a year to a lifetime.

During the nineteenth century, Cherokee formulas also included the use of a stamper, made from the wood of a persimmon tree, in massaging techniques. However, the stamper has been out of use for so long that there are no details about it. Another item no longer in use is the gourd rattle that once accompanied the medicine songs.

As a rule, healing ceremonies are conducted over either four or seven days. If bead divination indicates that the patient will not recover, the medicine man still completes the required four or seven days of doctoring. In serious cases when there is no hope for the patient, the patient is given a new name. The treatment then continues on this "new" person. (For an example, see *Doctor Mink*.)

Today, if one wants to become a medicine man, one approaches someone who is well versed in the formulas. The shaman examines the beads to see whether the requester has a vocation for it. In earlier times, the Cherokee had initiation ceremonies for a beginning practitioner. These are no longer remembered, except for the fact that they were conducted in the sweat lodge.

Ádantí
Navajo, *Southwest*

Witches. In his classic study on Navajo witchcraft, Clyde Kluckhohn [1944] described the practice by creating four technical terms: witchery, sorcery, wizardry, and frenzy witchcraft. Witchery includes all phenomena that the Navajo call *ántí*. For example, *ántízi* means "Witcheryway."

"The classic Witchery Way technique is that mentioned in the emergence legend. A preparation (usually called 'poison' by English-speaking informants) is made of the flesh of corpses. The flesh of children and especially of twin children is preferred, and the bones at the back of the head and skin whorls are the prized ingredients. When this 'corpse poison' is ground into powder it 'looks like pollen.' It may be dropped into a hogan from the smokehole, placed in the nose or mouth of a sleeping victim or blown from furrowed sticks into the face of someone in a large crowd. 'Corpse poison' is occasionally stated to have been administered in a cigarette. Fainting, lockjaw, a tongue black and swollen, immediate unconsciousness or some similar dramatic symptom is usually said to result promptly. Sometimes, however, the effects are less obvious. The victim gradually wastes away, and the usual ceremonial treatments are unavailing" [Kluckhohn 1944:25].

Sorcery is one aspect of those activities that the Navajo refer to by the -ndzin stem. Sorcery, called inzid, is essentially an enchantment by spell. Most informants regard it as a branch of witchery way, but unlike witcheryway, the sorcerer need not personally encounter his victim. Instead, the sorcerer obtains a personal item from the intended victim such as a piece of clothing, a fingernail, or a lock of hair. This is "buried with flesh or other material from a grave or buried in a grave or under a lightning-struck tree" [Kluckhohn 1944:31]. The sorcerer then recites the proper incantation, which consists of a prayer, a song, or both. There are also rare instances of sorcerers making images of their victims from clay or carving them from wood and then killing or torturing the victims by sticking pins into the effigies or shooting projectiles into them.

Wizardry refers to those practices that the Navajo call adagash. "The central concept here is that of injecting a foreign particle (stone, bone, quill, ashes, charcoal) into the victim. The projectiles are often described as 'arrows.' English-speaking Navajos will occasionally refer to this kind of witchcraft as 'bean-shooting,' but the majority of informants stated that actual beans were never used. . . . The shooting was apparently believed by a few informants to be carried out through a tube, but the majority opinion was that the objects were placed in a special sort of red basket or on a cloth or buckskin and made to rise through the air by incantation. According to some informants, shooters removed their clothes and rubbed ashes on their body before shooting" [Kluckhohn 1944:34].

Frenzy witchcraft refers to one of several classes of behavior that the Navaho designate as ajile. It is associated with azite, the Prostitutionway chant. Information on this chant is extremely hard to come by due to the Navajo's great reluctance to discuss anything about it. However, it includes the use of certain plants, gathered in a prescribed manner, for "love medicine" and luck in trading and gambling. Also, divination by ingesting Datura (Jimson weed) is a form of frenzy witchcraft. Such divinations are used mainly to locate stolen goods and trace thieves rather than to diagnose illness. These practitioners reportedly never behave as were animals. Father Bernard Haile held the opinion that frenzy witchcraft was originally a technique for obtaining foreign women.

Adelaghadhíya
Cherokee, *Southeast*

A shaman who was born near Jay, Oklahoma, around 1896, and died on 3 July 1938. The name is translated to "he watches over the bead(s) [money]." Nothing is known of the person or persons who taught him his shamanism. As was the custom of most nineteenth-century Cherokee shamans, he wrote many of his sacred formulas down in the Cherokee alphabet. He converted to Christianity but continued to practice his traditional healing methods. Although his reputation was not awesome, it was solid. His medicine was "alive," as the Cherokees say. Following his death, some of his formulas were translated and studied by Kilpatrick and Kilpatrick [1970].

Adisokanag
Ojibwa, *Canadian Eastern Woodlands*

A term meaning spirits [Black 1977:n.2:143].

Adliz aze
Navajo, *Southwest*

Gall medicine, which is a common protection against witchcraft. It is said to be an immediate antidote to the fainting produced by corpse poison (see *ádantí*). The medicine is most frequently made from the galls of eagle, bear, mountain lion, and skunk, while wolf, badger, deer, and sheep galls are also used. Ground corn is usually added. Most traditional Navajo carry such medicine, especially when in large crowds or when traveling away from home [Kluckhohn 1944:47].

Aenichit
Clayoquot, *Northwest Coast*

A shaman during the latter part of the nineteenth century. His name freely translates to "our only help" [Densmore 1939:293]. He treated the sick and was known to be a powerful shaman. He could lift water out of a bucket as though it were frozen and had the power to "harden the salt water and walk on it" [Densmore 1939:293]. He received his healing songs from the wolf and wore a wolf skin when treating patients; he could "make it come to life and walk in a natural manner" [Densmore 1939:293]. He also used a rattle made of elk horn. When he was using both hands to treat the patient, his assistant shook the rattle for him.

His daughter, Sarah Guy, told Densmore that "a new doctor had to have lots of singers to help him but an old doctor did not need them; he asked only the people who lived in the house to sing with him" [Densmore 1939:294].

Agotkon
Iroquois, *Northeast*
Shamans who use their powers to cast harmful spells on people; sorcerers [Lafitau 1974].

Aguain
Caddo, *Plains*
Disease. Little is known about how this eastern Texas culture treats diseases. "One method of combating disease was to drive it out by smoking the affected part with the fumes of buffalo fat and tobacco" [Bolton 1987:168]. For the most part, however, their shamans are sucking doctors.

In treating a patient, the first step is to divine to see whether the disease is curable and determine the cause and the necessary treatment. In former times the shaman drank a concoction of mescal beans. "A whole school of healers grew up around this type of medicine. But just prior to the beginning of the First World War, these practices came to an end . . . Caddo society no longer practices this traditional form of healing" [Newkumet and Meredith 1988: 80–81]. For additional details, see *konah*.

Ahma Humare
Mojave, *Southwest*
Described in 1932 as a "good-natured elderly shaman," he reported on his healing technique as follows:

"I see things only at night. As a child of seven or eight, I saw Mastamho (insane Mojave god) in my dreams, and he, who came to me in my dreams, told me about hiwey lak (anus pain), gave me the power to cure this sickness, and described its symptoms to me. He came only at night and taught me from sunset to sunrise. He said to me, 'It is fine from sunrise to sunset. Therefore, let your right arm be like the day (the day too, being a dream-bringing "person") and your left arm like the night—for with the left arm you will be able to cure. The power will be in your left arm when you touch people who claim to have this sickness. And if the illness they have is really *this* one, the touch of your left arm will cure them.' Thus, if the patient is not cured by the time I am through with the fourth song of the curing rite, he does not have this disease. . . .

"When they bring me a patient who claims to have hiwey lak, I ask him to tell me his dreams, so that I may be sure that he does have hiwey lak and not some other disease. If I discover that he does not have this illness, I will advise him and tell him which shaman he should consult. I must take into account that a patient's bad dreams may be balanced by his good dreams. I can cure not only Mohave Indians, but also whites who have this disease.

"I forbid the patient to eat any kind of watermelon or pumpkin, other than the grayish-white variety of pumpkin. The rest of his food will be prepared as usual. I prescribe a diet only in very serious cases. No other taboo of any kind need be observed. The patient, his relatives, and the shaman are neither painted nor dress in any special way. The ghost who appeared in the patient's dreams is not contacted and has no connection with the cure. The patient is treated at some convenient place, that is, generally at the house of the shaman. . . .

"An audience, as numerous as possible, is useful. The audience just sits around and says, 'Yes, yes,' whenever I sing. I press the patient's abdomen with my left hand, blow on it, and sing my four songs.

"I know the traditional songs while some other shamans don't. However, the fact that they do not know these songs does not affect their healing powers in any way. What matters are not the songs themselves but the power to cure, which one receives in a dream" [Devereux 1961: 161–162].

Ahutru
Yokuts, *California*
The first degree in medicine attained by men or women among the Yokuts doctors. Most use some form of herbal remedy for their cures [Latta 1949].

Ahwe sumach
Mojave, *Southwest*
Stewart [1974] uses *awhe sumatc* in his later publications on Mojave shamanism, whereas in his earlier work [Stewart 1970] he uses *ahwe sumach*. Thus, *awhe sumatc* is most likely the more proper form. See *awhe sumach*.

Ai sumatc
Mojave, *Southwest*
A specialist "in treating club wounds, or any other wounds made by wooden objects, such as slivers, or 'anything that sticks you'" [Stewart 1974:8].

Aixagidalagilis
Kwakiutl, *Northwest Coast*
A shaman from around the turn of the twentieth century. The following is a rare account of a double healing ceremony conducted by Aixagidalagilis in which he doctors two patients in sequence. Firsthand, detailed accounts of multiple healings are rare because, as a rule, shamans treat only one patient at a time. This account was written by Giving-Potlatches-in-the-World sometime between 1895 and 1900. In this case, the writer was also a Kwakiutl shaman (although Tlingit by birth), and, as is often the case, his skepticism toward the ability of a rival healer is visible in this account:

"Then we went into the house of Aixagidalagilis. We were told to sit down in the middle of the right hand side of the house. Now the four Kwakiutl tribes were all inside with their women and children. Now I saw that I was alone, the last one to enter the house, for immediately the door was barred after I had come in and I sat down with my wife. I had not been sitting for a long time when Aixagidalagilis came out of his room holding the shaman's rattle in his right hand. He had on his head a ring of rough red cedar bark and spread out was the neckring of red cedar bark. He stood up in the rear of his house in front of the song leaders. Then he spoke and said, 'This was my dream last night; the shaman-maker said to me that you should come into my house here, friends. If I should not obey what he said to me I should have bad luck. Therefore I thank you that you have all come to my house,' said he and swung his rattle. Now he went around the fire in the middle of the house and he came up near to the door. Then he sang his sacred song. Now the supernatural power came to him. He continued going around the fire in the middle of the house. After he had gone around four times he stood still in the rear of the house. Then he said, 'I am very hungry, I am very hungry,' said he swinging his rattle. Evidently all the men did not understand what he meant by being hungry, and therefore nobody spoke. Then he said again, 'I am very hungry, I am very hungry, I am very hungry,' said he. Then his daughter, whose name is Inviter-Woman, arose at the right hand side of the rear of the house. 'You fools, don't you understand why my father here, the shaman, says he is hungry? This is what he means by being hungry, it is your sickness. Go on, take off your clothes, you who are sick, so that he may take pity on the one who will do so; for there is nothing to be feared this night, for that is his dream. Therefore, you will not pay my father, this shaman,' said she. Immediately undressed one man, whose name was Wawengenol, for he was consumptive. And when he had done so Inviter-Woman came and put on the floor a basin containing water and spread under it a new piece of white calico while the shaman was still standing there on the floor and did not move in the place where he was standing in the rear of his house. Then Inviter-Woman finished after she had put down the basin on the floor and she told the shaman her father. Now the shaman turned to the right and he went and sat down at the right hand side of Wawengenol. For a long while he felt of the middle of the chest. I heard Aixagidalagilis say that there was no sickness in the middle of the chest. Then he felt of the right hand side of the chest. He had not been feeling long before he felt of the left hand side of the chest. Then he pointed with his first finger to the place where the heart of Wawengenol was beating. Then the shaman spoke and said, 'I have now found the place where the sickness is,' for I heard all the words of the shaman, for there was only one man between myself and him. Then he rinsed his mouth with the water in the basin. After he had done so he put his mouth to the place where was beating his heart. Four times he blew at it and then he sucked. He was sucking at it for a long time, then he lifted his head. He pressed his mouth with his right hand and then he blew out of his mouth into his hand something really white. Then the shaman said that it was pus sucked out, and mixed with it was what he referred to as the sickness. Then he washed off what he called pus and he squeezed the sickness in his left hand. Then with his right hand he took his rattle and arose on the floor and shook his rattle, then he sang his sacred song. Then he went around the fire. When he came in front of Wawengenol the shaman put down his rattle on the floor and he took off his rough head ring of red cedar bark. Then Aixagidalagilis spoke and said, 'Now all you friends, now I will show you the strength of the sickness for I shall put the former sickness of this our friend into my head ring,' said he as he tucked what he called the sickness into its front part. After he had done so he took his rattle and he told the song leaders to go on and beat fast time. Then the shaman shook the rattle and sang his sacred song, as he walked towards the post of the ridge pole on the right hand side of the door. Then he put the red cedar bark on a smooth place on the post. He said that the sickness had bitten the post. He came walking and went around the fire in the middle of the house. He went straight up to the post and took off the head ring and he pinched off what was referred to as the sickness. He put it into his mouth and swallowed it. He does that way for he says that he puts the sickness into his stomach after he has obtained it. He sucked just once on Wawengenol for the shaman said that he had taken out the sickness. The shaman never showed the sickness to Wawengenol and to all the spectators. As soon as he had finished another man whose name was Made-to-Give . . . took off his shirt. Then Made-to-Give spoke and said, 'Indeed, you my tribe, now we are told by this great shaman to come to this house to be pitied by him. Now I came to beg you to have mercy on me and to pity me and to try to save me, you, great shaman,' said he. Immediately Inviter-Woman took the wash basin and

poured out the saliva and water that was in it where the rain drops from the roof on the right hand side of the house. The reason why Inviter-Woman poured out the water in the wash basin for wetting (the mouth) is that her father tried to guess whether it might be attempted to take the saliva mixed with water; for Inviter-Woman said to me that, when she poured on the ground what her father had sucked out, that she stepped over it four times to take away its supernatural quality, so that her father should not feel the witchcraft of the witches, said she to me. She came carrying the wash basin and put it on a new piece of cotton goods which she spread down on the right hand side of Made-to-Give. Then she put on it the wash basin and she drew fresh water and poured it into the wash basin. As soon as she had done this she called her father who was just standing still in the rear of the house. Immediately her father, the shaman, started, still carrying the rattle. Then he sat down at the right hand side of Made-to-Give. He felt of each side of his neck. Then he said that there was no sickness there. Then went down what was being felt by him on each side of the chest. It arrived what was being felt by him down at the lower end of the sternum and the upper end of the stomach. Then the shaman spoke and said, 'Now I have found what does this to you, for it is this sickness which stops up the mouth of your stomach,' said he. Now the shaman pressed his right hand in the water in the wash basin and he scooped up the water and put it in his mouth and rinsed his mouth. As soon as he had done so he applied his mouth. Now he blew four times and sucked at the upper part of the stomach. When he had been sucking a long time, then finally he lifted his head. He said that he had not succeeded in getting the sickness, 'for it is rooted, therefore I find it really difficult to get it. Now go on, please help me, you song leaders, go on and beat fast time that this great sickness may jump out of our friend,' said he. As soon as the shaman applied his mouth the song leaders beat fast time; but it was not long before the shaman lifted his head. Then the song leaders stopped beating fast time. Now the shaman spit out the saliva into his left hand and he squeezed it when he put it into the water in the wash basin and he squeezed it so that all the saliva came off from what he referred to as the sickness.

Then he arose and squeezed with his left hand what he called the sickness. Then he held in his right hand his rattle and he said that he got the 'mother of the sickness.' As he said this he walked around the fire in the middle of the house. When he arrived at the rear of the house he lifted his hand in which he held his rattle, and looked at his rattle. Then the shaman spoke looking at his rattle. He said to his rattle, 'You say that you are hungry?' Evidently his rattle answered him saying that it was hungry. I only guess that this was what the rattle said because the shaman said, 'Go on, take care that you swallow this great sickness,' said the shaman, as he told the song leaders to go ahead and beat fast time. As soon as the song leaders beat fast time the shaman put the beak of the raven carving on his rattle nearest to the knuckle of his second finger and of his first finger. Then his rattle hung down from there while he went around the fire in the middle of the house. When he arrived at the rear of the house he took the handle of the rattle and pulled it off. Then said the shaman to the spectators, 'Did you see my rattle as it bit the palm of my hand after it had swallowed the great sickness?' said he. Now also had never seen one of the men what was referred to by the shaman as the sickness. Now he finished after this. And now he sang his sacred song. Then he told the song leaders to sing after him the words of his sacred song. . . .

"Now the shaman danced around the fire in the middle of the house and all the shamans started to sing, for that was meant by the words of the sacred song, for Aixagidalagilis said to the shamans that only he was a real shaman. He said that they all only pretended to be shamans, therefore he said this in the last words with which he had danced. . . .

"As soon as the sacred song was at an end the shaman sang again, dancing with the sacred song. . . . As soon as the dance with the (last) sacred song of the shaman ended, he sat down. Now he finished" [Giving-Potlatches-in-the-World in Boas 1930:2:24–28].

Aiyakokiyiu
Blackfoot, *Plains*
The Shaking Tent Ceremony (see entry); literally means "putting up a small tepee."

Aiyicks
Seminole, *Southeast*
See *hilleeshwa*.

Ajasowin
Chippewa, *Canadian Eastern Woodland*
Tattooing; used in the treatment of rheumatism, dislocated joints, and backaches. Practitioners use prescribed procedures and ingredients in tattooing, and it is done to both adults and children on the afflicted part of the body. There is no pattern, and the tattoos resemble blueberries in size and color. The tattooing instrument, called a *djabonigan*, is made from the twig of a tree, such as a hazelnut. Three or four needles are placed into one end of the twig, dipped into a powdery substance, and applied to the patient. One woman, who had been cured of a goiter, had many marks on her chest and neck [Hilger 1951:93].

Akaka
Yavapai, *Southwest*
See *basamacha*.

Akbaalía
Crow, *Plains*
A shaman who heals [Frey 1987:59]; it translates to "one who doctors." In his work on the Crow, Lowie [1935:238] uses the term *batse maxpe* (see entry).

Akbaria
Crow, *Plains*
A person who cures others with herbal medicines without the use of supernatural aid. Recently, however, Frey [1987:59] rendered this term as *akbaalía*, "one who doctors." In his usage of this term, he includes shamans who are doctors, whereas Lowie uses the term *batse maxpe* (see entry) for shamans who doctor. *Akbaria* is also the term used for white physicians [Lowie 1922:373].

Akeutit
Copper Eskimo, *Arctic Coast*
Incantations that are handed down from generation to generation and used to either appease or drive away spirits, which are one of the major sources of illness. "The incantation is usually sung by all the people, with one of their shamans standing in the centre of the ring; and as they sing their

bodies sway from side to side, though their feet remain stationary. At the conclusion of the refrain the shaman invokes his familiars (spirits), and with their aid produces the desired result" [Jenness 1922:187].

Akicita
Lakota, *Plains*
Members of several societies that are responsible for maintaining camp order. Shamans who misuse their authority or spiritual powers are punished by these individuals even to the point of death [Blish 1926].

Akme
Kutenai, *Plateau*
The stem of the verb meaning "to call a guardian spirit." For example, *nakmente* translates to "he asked for the help of the manitous (spirits)" [Boas 1918:8].

Akua
Hawaiian, *Pacific*
Singular form of the term for spirits. See *aumakuas*.

Akuwacdiu
Crow, *Plains*
A wound doctor [Lowie 1935:64]. Wound doctors are usually shamans who received healing powers from the bear during their vision quests.

Akúwecdìu
Crow, *Plains*
A special class of doctors who specialize in the treatment of wounds. These practitioners are usually men who had buffalo visions [Lowie 1922: 373]. See *Dapic* for an example.

Alikchi
Choctaw, *Southeast*
A doctor [Edmonson 1958:69]; however, Gardner [1973:38] translates the same term to the verb "to doctor."

Alini
Miwok, *California*
West Central Sierra Miwok shamans who doctor illnesses. Informants Tom and Suzie Williams reported to Gifford that "the word *alini* also denotes mana and some people who possess it. Thus, white people are spoken of as *alini* because of their

superior equipment and ability to accomplish things the Indian cannot" [Bates 1992:114]. See *koyabi* for details.

Altar
The display of sacred items used in a healing ceremony. Every shaman has his own personal altar, so no two altars are alike. Initially, all items to be displayed on the altar are smudged to purify them. Most often this involves burning sweet grass, sage, or cedar. In some cases the items are steamed over hot rocks with water. Persons setting up the altar—the shaman or his assistants—must be purified either by smudging or in a sweat lodge ceremony before handling any of the items.

In setting up an altar, one must follow strict rules for the placement and position of each item. The rules are set forth by the shaman's helping spirits, and often change over time. If one item is missing, out of place, or handled improperly, it can cause the healing ceremony to fail and bring harm to the shaman. Often these altars are so complicated and contain so many items that it takes longer to set up the altar display than to conduct the healing ceremony.

An altar should not be thought of as a small platform on which the shaman's items are placed. Rather, it is the space—often a large amount of space—used by the shaman in the room, tepee, or lodge in which the ceremony is conducted. This space becomes sacred space once the altar display is completed, thus providing a locality for the manifestation of the shaman's spirits. For example, the Lakota *yuwipi* (see entry) altar is an approximately ten-foot square that is demarcated on the floor by a long string of tobacco offerings (ties). Within this square the *yuwipi* shaman places rattles, a sacred pipe, a small mound of mole dirt, and a bed of sage, among other items used in the ceremony. During the ceremony, the participants must remain outside of the square, sitting around its perimeter. There may be only two feet between the wall and the string of tobacco offerings, so participants must be careful in the dark not to touch the string. If they do, they get a good smack from the spirits for violating sacred space.

How the shaman displays his altar also determines which spirits will be called in. It is not unusual for different spirits to require different altars. Therefore, a shaman's altar can be seen essentially as a spirit calling device. This helps explain many shamans' reluctance to allow their altars to be photographed or drawn. They are concerned that a person could copy the altar, call in a spirit, and then be unprepared to handle the situation.

Ambelan

Tsimshian, *Northwest Coast*

The special medicine apron worn by shamans in this region during healing ceremonies. It is made from bark fiber—or sometimes of leather—and is tied around the waist of the otherwise naked shaman. The apron usually has a fringe across the bottom to which deer-hoof rattles are attached, thus the nickname "rattling apron." In addition, the apron usually has a design on it [Barbeau 1958:4].

Amnaa

Cahuilla, *California*

See *maiswat*.

Anááji

Navajo, *Southwest*

The Navajo healing ritual called Enemyway; classified in the Navajo chantway system as belonging to the Evilway (or Ghostway) chants. In the nineteenth century, Enemyway was used to cure sickness caused by contact with non-Navajo in the context of war. Today the ceremony is used to treat any infection believed to be caused by foreign contact. In either case, the source of the malevolence is the ghost of a dead foreigner. The ceremony is performed over a four-day (five-night) period. Like all Navajo rituals, the Enemyway Ceremony is modeled on the original ritual of the ceremony, as told in an origin story. The exact details of the ritual may vary among different ritualists, but they all contain the same basic elements: the emetic rite, the litany intonement of prayer, the unraveling rite, and the blackening rite [Gill 1987:100]. For example,

"In the emetic rite the medicine is prepared in a Navajo basket, an object that in ritual is associated with unity, beauty, and health. The basket is placed on a figure of Ripener, a female insect figure who is strongly associated with fertility, that

has been drawn on the floor at the rear (west side) of the hogan. On the surface of the medicine is drawn, in pollen, the figure of Big Fly, who serves as a messenger between human beings and the holy people who seldom come personally to the world of humans. Big Fly is a protector and informer. Pollen, of course, is invariably connected with health, life, fertility, and plenty. The emetic is drunk by kneeling with one's hands and knees on those of the figure of Ripener drawn on the floor. One drinks the medicine from the very center of the Big Fly figure drawn on its surface" [Gill 1987:100].

The emetic is also applied to the body of the patient.

The prayer recitation is known as the "Prayer to the Shoulder Bands and Wristlets." It consists of a set of twelve different prayers of identical constituents with two much shorter prayers appended. The songs of Changing Woman are sung before the prayers are recited. These songs describe the achievement of a new order and happiness in the world because things have been put back into their proper places.

During the unraveling rite, medicine and pollen are applied to slip-knotted strings. Each string is held to a certain part of the patient's body while the knots are pulled out. Specific songs accompany these actions. When the unraveling is finished, an unraveling medicine and pollen are applied to the patient's body.

In the final blackening rite, the patient is dressed as Monster Slayer to protect him. His body is then blackened with tallow that has been mixed with the ashes of specific plants associated with the killing of monsters. Thirty-four songs accompany this procedure.

Anaana

Hawaiian, *Pacific*

One of several types of evil sorcerers. The *anaana* always performs his rituals in secret, and generally at night. Before attacking a victim, he procures something that belonged to that person such as a lock of hair or a fingernail clipping. The item procured is referred to as the *maunu*, meaning "bait," and this item is usually buried or burned following the ceremony. Although these sorcerers are capable of acting out of revenge, most work for pay.

Anaidjuq

Netsilik Eskimo, *Arctic Coast*

An unusual, early-twentieth-century shaman. He apparently had problems controlling one of his helping spirits named Orpingalik. This spirit would suddenly attack Anaidjuq from behind and pull out the shaman's genitals, which Anaidjuq would then recover during a trance, after much yelling [Balikci 1963: 383]. One rarely finds reports of a shaman's spirits attacking the shaman outside of ceremony, meaning while the shaman is not in a trance.

Anakua

Iglulik Eskimo, *Arctic Coast*

The spirit-given ability to see shamanically. From this term comes the general term for shamans among the Eskimos, *angakut* (plural form of *angakoq*). The *anakua* is a particular personal experience that manifests for the shaman as "a mysterious light which the shaman suddenly feels in his body, inside his head, within the brain, an unexplainable searchlight, a luminous fire, which enables him to see in the dark . . . for he can now, even with closed eyes, see through darkness and perceive things and coming events which are hidden from others. The first time a young shaman experiences this light, while sitting upon the bench (calling) his helping spirits, it is as if the house in which he is in suddenly rises; he sees far ahead of him, through mountains, exactly as if the earth were one great plain, and his eyes could reach to the end of the earth. Nothing is hidden from him any longer; not only can he see things far, far away, but he can also discover souls, stolen souls, which are either kept concealed in far, strange lands, or have been taken up or down to the land of the Dead" [Rasmussen in Beck and Walters 1977:121].

Angakoq

Eskimo, *Arctic Coast*

Plural form: *angakut*. A widespread term for shaman used by the inland North Alaskan, Iglulik, Baffin Island, Labrador, Polar, West Greenland, and East Greenland Inuit. Other Eskimos use *angatkoq* (see entry). Among the Diomede Islanders, it appears as *angutkok* or *ahngutkok*. The Mackenzie and Netsilik Eskimos use both pronunciations.

Some Bering Sea Inuit use *angalsqoq*, and others use *tunghak, tunghalik, or tunralik*. Other dialectic variants include *tunerak* on the north Alaskan coast, *tonngag* among some of the bands of Copper Eskimos, and *torngevok* among some of the Labrador Eskimos. In every case, the term means "one who has a spirit," indicating that it is used for those shamans who have acquired and use helping spirits [Merkur 1985:41, 267].

Weyer [1932:421, 437] uses *angakok* in describing the general nature of Eskimo shamans:

"He is a strange soul, the Eskimo medicine man, a compelling and absorbing personality, both to his people and to the investigator, who sees in him the embodiment par excellence of primitive religious expression.

"What powerful force galvanized him when he is in the throes of an ecstatic trance. . . . Call it what you will, when he enters into a state of trance he becomes as a man possessed. . . . Now we see him transported in his fanatical ardor into an inspired trance; but shortly, in a different mood, he may shamelessly bamboozle whomsoever he can, performing sideshow miracles to gain profit or prestige. . . . But on psychological grounds it must be insisted that the angakok cannot be denounced as an utter charlatan. Beneath his superficial artifices there stirs a tremendous spiritual force that is incontestably real. . . . His art as a magician is but accessory to his acknowledged alliance with the spirits. We must not be too critical, therefore, lest perceiving nothing but palpable sham in the magic art of the angakok we fail to grasp the more important phase of his operation."

Most often the *angatkok* is male, but females can also acquire great prestige as healers and are less feared for sorcery than are male shamans. Power is usually acquired by a novice through various means rather than being inherited from his father. Inheritance of shamanic power appears only among the far western Eskimos, with an exception occurring among the Eskimos of St. Lawrence Island and the nearby Diomede Islands.

The prestige of an *angatkok* rests on his demonstrated possession of supernatural powers. These powers are applied mainly to finding and procuring game, predicting the weather, finding lost items, and healing, but their applications are considered limitless. Healing often involves driving out an evil spirit from the body of a patient. For example, an inordinately skinny shaman from the Point Barrow region was known to be very effective at such cures. "By virtue of his paper thinness he was reckoned a good doctor, for he could get into places where larger men could not go, so that the 'evil spirit' had a hard time to conceal himself from this doctor. He was very successful in driving out the devil from the innermost recesses of the Eskimo heart, soul, and body" [Weyer 1932: 423].

Shamans generally train under an elder shaman, who teaches them how to communicate with the spirit world. Among the Angmasaliks of eastern Greenland, two novices often undergo training together, and this usually entails some form of vision questing in isolation. The quester rubs two small stones together over the course of several days, which causes a spirit to come forth from the stone. Training also includes certain taboos and dietary restrictions. When a spirit is forthcoming, in almost all cases the novice shaman undergoes a traumatic death and rebirth initiation during his encounter with it. Often a novice keeps his training secret until he has gained sufficient power to practice. Then he makes a public announcement of his abilities. If he acquires power and does not announce it, he is forced by his power to become a sorcerer.

Among the Copper Eskimos, both males and females are shamans. They lead regular lives and wear no distinctive mark or dress of any kind. During their shamanic rituals they become possessed by their helping spirits and do not remember what transpires. If they speak, it is often in a voice other than their natural speech, and it is often a torrent of wild gibberish. It is the spirit who diagnoses the illness and performs the cure.

Their general method of healing has been summarized by Spenser [1959:306–307] as follows:

"When a man was ill, he usually waited for a time before summoning a shaman, trying any ways of curing or remedies that were at hand. When the case proved stubborn, the patient often being in extremis, the shaman was summoned. He either worked in the house of the patient, or, if it ap-

peared that a larger audience could be commanded, in the karigi. If he did his work in the house, he most often had the patient laid out on the floor boards. He then walked about the patient, examining him from all angles. Then he might touch the patient about the spot where the 'pain' lay. He licked his hands, then rubbed them over the painful area. Some shamans blew on the affected part, occasionally sucking at it tentatively at first if the case was diagnosed as one of (object) intrusion. With duck wings, the shaman might sweep the affected area. When these preparations were completed, the shaman began to sing.

"He stood over the kataq, the round door which was located in the floor of the house, straddling it, his feet either firmly planted or kneeling. Then he began to talk with his familiar (helping spirit). He stood with his back to the room, facing the door in the floor. The people assembled in the house could hear the voices of his spirit helpers coming from the hall. Then he lifted his tambourine before his face and began to sing. The tambourine, it is said, was just a bit smaller than the trapdoor itself. The shaman would sing for some time. Sometimes, in the course of singing, he threw mittens belonging to the patient or to any of his kin, tied to a cord, into the hallway and struggled to make them return. Here, the concept was that the mittens would go out to seize the errant soul (in accordance with a diagnosis of soul-loss). Another method was to place the tambourine on his head after singing and lapse into a trance. At this point, the shaman might announce that his own soul was leaving his body to fetch that of the patient. The trance followed. Such a trancelike state might last indefinitely, often for several days. During this time, no one present dared go into the hallway, and no one entered the house. At the end of the trance, the shaman moaned a little, and as he moved, it was said, 'His soul is coming back now.' On coming out of his trance, the shaman drummed again and made a formal announcement to the effect that he had succeeded in restoring the soul, or was having a hard time getting it back from whatever being had it. . . .

"The shaman stripped to the waist, sang his measured songs, often gradually stepping up the tempo to a frenzied pitch. He perspired freely, his eyeballs turned inward, and the ritual was punctuated by the voices of his familiars, with their wolf howls, their bear growls, or other sounds coming from the hall. His pounding and stamping shook the floor of the house and, working in darkness or semidarkness as he often did, the effect must have been wholly dramatic. Certainly the contrast between the frenzied singing and moving of the shaman and his sudden lapse into a wholly silent, trance-like state was striking. Even while he was in a trance, however, his spirits continued to speak from the dark hall."

The Canadian ethnographer D. Jenness became ill during one of his visits to the Copper Eskimos around 1914 and submitted to treatment by a female shaman named Higilak. The following is a brief account of that ceremony:

"I was taken very ill shortly after this, and my condition remained serious for several weeks. Ikpakhuak and Higilak became greatly alarmed, and the latter held a 'consultation' over me. She used my coat to divine with, though she made a pillow for it out of her foot-gear. First she orated about the disagreeableness of being ill, how it made everyone unhappy, with other remarks in the same strain. Then, addressing the kila (in this case the tied up coat), she enquired whether my system was out of order of its own accord, and the kila replied 'No.' 'Who caused it then? Was it a white man?' 'No.' 'Some one from Great Bear lake?' 'No.' 'A Western Eskimo?' 'Yes.' I was told to enquire his name, and suggested Aiyakak. The kila answered 'Yes.' 'What are you doing here,' said Higilak, 'Jenness is not here, he's a long way away. What do you want here?' [Jenness notes here: "Apparently a malignant shade (soul of a deceased person) may be fooled or deceived as well as propitiated or intimidated. Why the human breath should drive it away I did not discover."] And Ikpakhuak, at her signal, struck the kila with the edge of her knife. This disposed of one shade, but almost immediately the kila became heavy again through the entrance of another, Alak, as I suggested. Ikpakhuak tried to evict it in the same manner, but failed. Then a man suggested that Higilak should breathe on the bundle, and this was successful. 'It's heavy again,' she said a mo-

ment later. Ikpakhuak caught hold of the cord (binding the coat) and said, 'No, it's light.' 'Heavy, surely,' she replied, not too well pleased, I fancied, at her husband's interference. 'Go on,' said a woman spectator. Higilak did not trouble to enquire the name of the shade this time, but merely said, 'Go away,' and struck the kila with her knife and breathed on it. The bundle at once became light; all the malignant shades had been disposed of, and nothing remained presumably to prevent my recovery. A year later Higilak reminded me of this ritual, and claimed that she had been instrumental in curing me of my illness" [Jenness 1922:214–215].

Variations on this weight-testing method of divination occur among the Copper Eskimos. In other cases, "the shaman's familiar (helping spirit), instead of entering the body and taking possession of him, is supposed to exert its power extraneously by forcing the shade (soul) of some dead man or woman to enter the *kila* and manifest itself and give answers by its weight. The *kila* may be either the head or the foot of a patient, his clothes, or the clothes of the shaman himself" [Jenness 1922:217].

Among the Copper Eskimos, illnesses were often attributed to activities of an evil *tarrak* (spirit of a dead person) or *tornrak* (spirit controlled by a shaman). In such cases, "the diagnosis alone is considered sufficient to arrest the evil, especially if it is reinforced by an abstinence from such articles of food as the shaman may ordain" [Jenness 1922:171]. In other cases, illnesses were attributed to object-intrusion, with the cure coming by removal of the object, which the shaman would display. However, healing might be as simple as the shaman spitting on his hands and rubbing them on the afflicted part "to lend some of his vital force to drive away a disease" [Jenness 1922:172].

Angatkok
Eskimo, *Arctic Coast*
Dialectical equivalents: *angakoq* (see previous entry), *angakok, angalsqoq.* Plural form: *angatkut.* A Central Eskimo term often found in the literature referring to Eskimo shamans in general, where shamanism constitutes the highest aspect of Eskimo religious expression. In those cultures

where there are categories of shamans, this term is usually used for the most powerful shamans. For example, the Tikerarmiut use the term *ibrukok* (see entry) for a lesser *angatkok* [Rainey 1947:275]. This form of the word appears among the coastal North Alaskan, Copper, Caribou, Mackenzie, and Netsilik Eskimos. The latter two groups also use *angakoq* for shaman. Some Bering Sea Inuit use *angalsqoq* [Merkur 1985:267]. The word seems to be purely an Eskimo term, and its etymology is no longer understood.

Angatkungaruk

Netsilik Eskimo, *Arctic Coast*

A class of shamans much less powerful than the *angatkok*. "This class of shamans received no special training, practiced very rarely the *krilaq* technique, and was incapable of foreseeing future events" [Balikci 1963:385]. Because of their lack of power over the helping spirits, their treatments often had to be repeated.

Angelica

A plant *(Angelica atropurpurea)* whose aromatic root has widespread use in North America as a purification herb. Its aroma is used to attract a shaman's helping spirits. For example, in California it is commonly burned during a shaman's prayers in a healing ceremony [Keeling 1992:131]; in Arkansas it is "always carried in their medicine bags" and added as an ingredient in their smoking mixtures used in their sacred pipes [Vogel 1970:272]. Its scent resembles that of the anise seed. It is also used as an herbal medicine. For example, among the Creek in the Southeast, it is used for "stomach disorders, dry bellyache, colic, hysterics, worms, and pains in the back" [Vogel 1970:273]; among the Menomini in the Great Lakes area it is added to a poultice used for the reduction of swelling.

Ant Father Ceremony

Tiwa, *Southwest*

See *toyide*.

Antelope Shaman

See *deer shaman*.

Antuw

Yokuts, *California*

Shaman [Edmonson 1958:70]; also referred to as *mets antuw* (power shamans).

Aoutmoin

Micmac, *Canadan Eastern Woodlands*

Also: *aoutem*. Used by Marc Lescarbot in 1606 for Micmac shamans. Today the term is rendered as *buówin* (see entry).

Aperfat

Iglulik Eskimo, *Arctic Coast*

The shaman's helping spirit. Such spirits appear to their shamans in unsolicited dreams. The shaman must show no fear of such spirits if he wants to use them [Beck and Walters 1977:122].

Aperksaq

Netsilik Eskimo, *Arctic Coast*

A weak helping spirit used mainly in the *krilaq* (head lifting) divination or curing technique. The term means "one that exists to be questioned." Dialectical variants of the other word for the shaman's helping spirit are *tornaq, tornat*, and *torngat*.

Apo leo

Hawaiian, *Pacific*

An art of sorcery known to some kahunas in which the victim loses his ability to speak. These kahunas call upon Uli, god of sorcery, and Hiiaka, sister to Pele, goddess of fire, to bring about this condition in the victim. Prayers and offerings are made during a night ceremony, and the following day the kahuna seeks out his victim and enters into conversation with him, at which time the kahuna causes the victim's vocal cords to become paralyzed.

Apuluq

Chugach, *Arctic Coast*

Historically, the most famous shaman on Montague Island in the Prince William Sound area of Alaska. He lived there before the Russians arrived and was the chief of his village. Apuluq was renowned for being an especially good weather prophet. He and another shaman named Tutyiq were the only shamans to use rattles in their healing ceremonies, and he had an assistant who drummed for him. During his healing ceremonies, Apuluq routinely circled the central fire five times while carrying each patient on his back and singing sacred songs. Throughout his life he trained many shamans on Montague Island.

Arctic Shamanism
Åke Hultkrantz's term denoting an ecologically conditioned, special form of general shamanism that developed in the Arctic areas (the Eskimo) and parts of the Northwest coast. Hultkrantz believes that these shamans had connections to the forms of shamanism found west of the Bering Strait. In Arctic shamanism, the trance is an integral part of the shamanistic ritual, whereas in general shamanism, ecstasy is not always a prevailing factor [Hultkrantz 1967b: 35].

Arnägneq
Netsilik Eskimo, *Arctic Coast*
The newly born who have allowed other souls to reincarnate within them. These are usually the souls of deceased human beings that choose to live on in other bodies. When such a soul comes into the body of a newborn, that person receives special powers and protection in gratitude for allowing the soul to incarnate, and will most likely become a shaman [Rasmussen 1931:220].

Artgeist
A species-specific spirit protector. The term is derived from German and literally means "species *(art)* spirit *(geist)*." In many Native American cultures, this is the spirit of a certain animal that appears to a shaman during a vision.

Asatchaq
Iñupiaq Eskimo, *Arctic Coast*
The last great *kikituk* shaman at the village of Tikigaq (Point Hope), Alaska. He was prominent during the 1870s and 1880s. The *kikituk* is an ivory or wood carving that symbolizes the shaman's animal power-object. Asatchaq kept his *kikituk* on the drying rack above the oil lamp in his igloo to keep it warm. "Otherwise, it traveled under the shaman's parka or 'inside his body,' entering and leaving through the mouth or armpit when magically animated" [Tukummiq and Lowenstein

1992:149]. "When he intends using his kikituk he has somebody to sing and drum for him. He goes around in a circle and rubs his belly. His belly swells, he turns down his pants and kneels facing the audience as though he were having a baby, the old way. He puts his hand between his legs, and holds it up: there is blood there. Now he calls for a new fawn-skin parka, and somebody brings it; then he just shows the head of the kikituk sticking out of the fawn-skin parka sleeve. He always works with someone in the group who is ill when he performs with the kikituk: he has the kikituk bite the place that is sick and it heals. . . . The creature (kikituk) had the curative power of 'biting' the spirit that was causing a client's illness" [Tukummiq and Lowenstein 1992:140, 149].

Asgina
Cherokee, *Southeast*
Plural: *anisgina*. A human ghost. The ghosts of both animals and humans are a source of sickness. In fact, "the diseases sent by these human and by the animal ghosts are so multifarious as to include practically the whole of known illnesses and ailments" among the Cherokee [Mooney and Olbrechts 1932:28]. Human ghosts cause, for the most part, psychopathic illnesses. An animal ghost is called *ûntali* (see entry). Another source of illness is the *tsikili* (see entry), or witch.

Atayohkanak
Plains Cree, *Plains*
The spirit powers that are intermediaries between humans and the Creator [Mandelbaum 1940:251]. Everything in the natural world contains such a potential—there is horse spirit power, hawk spirit power, rock spirit power, maple tree spirit power, thunder spirit power, and so forth. In some cases, shamans call upon strange forms of spirit powers such as Iron Capped Eagle or Two Legged Buffalo. Each power confers specific supernatural abilities to whoever procures it. This comes in the form of a helping spirit, or *pawakan* (see entry).

"The spirit powers resided in their namesakes, but were not confined to them. The spirit power of bear dwelt in every bear, but was also present somewhere on high, where lived all the powers. Moreover, there was a concept of a greater bear power, overlord of the other bear spirit powers, who was called 'Great Parent of Bear.' The greater spirit powers were never seen, but they controlled those which did reveal themselves. Similarly there were masters of Moose, Horse, and all other spirit powers" [Mandelbaum 1940:251].

Ätchin
Keres, *Southwest*

The slat altar that is an integral part of the total altar display for healing and other ceremonies at the Sia Pueblo. During a healing a sand painting is normally drawn on the ground in front of the *ätchin*.

Atci sumatc
Mojave, *Southwest*

A specialist among the Mojave shamans known as the fish doctor. These shamans treat illnesses caused by fish and water animals. "If a person gets a fishbone caught in his throat, the doctor touches the throat with his fingers and sings, and the bone goes out" [Stewart 1974:10]. They also treat rheumatism and arthritis, as these illnesses are caused by the beaver.

Atcigamultin
Lenni Lenape, *Northeast*

The Otter Ceremony of the Unami (a branch of the Lenape also called the Delaware). Harrington [1921:176] reports that the term means "compulsory hog-eating." Central to the ceremony is a sacred otter skin (called *Kununxäs*) that confers good health on the ceremony participants. To maintain good health, the otter skin is "fed" every two years in this special ceremony, which is conducted in the spring and lasts from dusk until noon of the following day.

The otter skin has a slit down the middle of the neck. During the ceremony, the owner of the skin places his head through the slit such that the otter's nose is under his chin and the body and tail hang down the middle of his back, thus impersonating the otter spirit. This person "would open the ceremony by walking about the fire, chanting and shaking the turtle rattle . . . while the audience kept time to his song. . . . When he had finished, another man put on the skin and took up the chant, and so on until noon the next day, when the ceremony was brought to a close" [Harrington

1921:180–181]. In this manner the otter spirit is "fed," and good health is gained. Following the ceremony, a sacrificial pig is consumed in its entirety.

Atiasxw
Tsimshian, *Northwest Coast*

Any object, mental or physical, that a shaman receives from his spirit helper to aid in using supernatural powers. Its actual nature is somewhat ambiguous. In most cases, it is a mental object focused on by the shaman while in a trance. "It is a spirit because it has power, though being a mental image, it is not visible; it is an object because it can be manipulated; and it is a helper because it generates the power to intervene on behalf of the clients" [Guédon 1984:200]. It is not unusual for a shaman treating a patient to dream of a new *atiasxw*, as evidenced in the following statement by Tsimshian healer Isaac Teens:

"When later I attended a patient for the first time, on my own, I had a new vision. The *halaait* doctors were still training me, teaching me. For this reason I was invited to all the *swanassu* activities. As soon as I was able to go out by myself, I began to diagnose the cases by dreaming (*wawq*: sleeping, or *ksewawq*: dreaming), with the help of my instructors. I acquired charms (*atiasxw*), that is, things I would dream of: the *Hoqwest* (snare for the bear), *Hlorhs* (the Moon), and *Angohawtu* (Sweathouse). And besides, I had also dreamed of charms: the Mink (*nes'in*), the Otter (*watserh*) and Canoe (*mal*). I acquired charms when I attended a patient" [Barbeau 1958:44].

The shaman uses the *atiasxw* to bring healing power into proper focus. Thus the methods used are more important than the object per se. The following account, recorded in 1975, is of a female healer whose *atiasxw* is a rope; it is an example of how the *atiasxw* is more a point of view:

"If she is looking at a sick person in a normal way, she knows she cannot get through (not only to the sick person but also to herself), that there is nothing she can do to help the person. Her idea is to shift the point of view: she would imagine herself as a rope, 'a big rope of light going from way, way

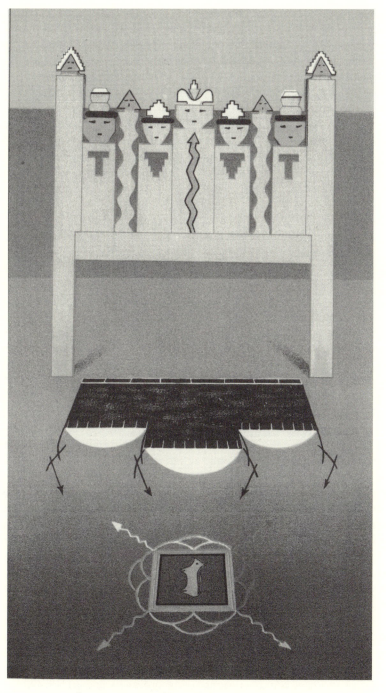

Ätchin and sand painting of the Sia snake society.

back to way, way in the future. As a rope I can do something. I can be there as a rope and there would be that other rope (the patient) with a big knot (the disease).' She can get close to the other rope and rub her own against it until the knot is let loose. We may note that she is not actually transformed into a rope; the question whether something else is at work does not occur. The ati-asxw is simply used as a point of view" [Guédon 1984:204].

Aua
Iglulik Eskimo, *Arctic Coast*
A shaman of the early twentieth century. His life was documented by Rasmussen, and in the following passage, Aua tells of becoming a shaman and subsequently obtaining two spirit helpers:

"Then I sought solitude, and here I soon became very (sad). I would sometimes fall to weeping and fell unhappy without knowing why. Then for no reason, all would suddenly be changed, and I felt a great joy, a joy so powerful that I could not restrain it, but had to break into song, a mighty song, with only room for the one word: joy, joy! And I had to use the full strength of my voice. And then in the midst of such a fit of mysterious and overwhelming delight I became a shaman, not knowing myself how it came about. But I was a shaman. I could see and hear in a totally different way. I had gained my enlightenment, the sha-man-light of brain and body, and this in such a manner that it was not only I who could see through the darkness of life, but the same light also shone out of me, (unseen) to human beings, visible to all the spirits of earth and sky and sea, and these now came to me and became my helping spirits.

"My first helping spirit was my namesake, a little Aua. When it came to me, it was as if the passage and roof of the house were lifted up, and I felt such a power of vision, I could see right through the house, in through the earth and up into the sky; it was the little Aua that brought me all this inward light, hovering over me as long as I was singing. Then it placed itself in a corner of the passage invisible to others, but always ready if I should call it. . . .

"My second helping spirit was a shark. One day when I was out in my kayak, it came swimming up to me, lay alongside quite silently and whispered my name. I was greatly astonished, for I had never seen a shark before; they are very rare in these waters. Afterwards it helped me with my hunting, and was always near me when I had need of it. These two, the shore spirit (Aua) and the shark, were my principal helpers, and they could aid me in everything I wished" [Rasmussen in Beck and Walters 1977:126–127].

Aumakuas
Hawaiian, *Pacific*
Spirits. Most disease is believed to be caused by displeasing the *aumakuas*. Although healing ceremonies include the use of herbal remedies, the herbs' efficacy comes directly from the goodwill of the *aumakuas*.

Autmoin
Micmac, *Canadian Eastern Woodlands*
The term used by eighteenth-century French explorer Charlevoix for the shamans he observed performing at Nova Scotia and New Brunswick. Among his observations is an early description of a Shaking Tent Ceremony (see entry). However, in his account, he refers to the shaking tent as a stove. He writes, "There are some who, before they enter the stove, take a draft of a composition very proper, they say, for disposing them to receive the divine impulse, and they pretend that the advent of the spirit is made manifest by a rushing wind, which suddenly rises; or by a bellowing heard under the ground; or by the agitation and shaking of the stove" [Charlevoix 1761:177].

Ave sumatc
Mojave, *Southwest*
A shaman specializing in the treatment of venomous bites from rattlesnakes, scorpions, Gila monsters, black widow spiders, and tarantulas. According to Stewart [1974:8]:

"He just sings around. People run up and call him, and he starts to sing. A heavy wind comes up. He sings and walks around in a circle. He tells the family not to drink water until he says that he knows that the patient will be alive.

"He gets some kind of clay and wets it in his mouth, and then makes marks around the bite, so that the poison won't go beyond the bite. It stays where it is, and he drains it out."

In addition, these specialists can bring rain and find water in the desert.

Avgo
Angmagsalik, *Arctic Coast*
During the latter part of the nineteenth century, believed among the East Greenland Eskimos to be a truly great shaman. Thalbitzer [1914:98] reports "that once during the performance of his arts he was seized by a bear, who dragged him down to the shore, where a walrus fastened its teeth in him, dragged him out to the horizon, and devoured him there. The skeleton returned and met on its way the pieces of flesh, which little by little grew up around it, and finally the eyes, so that the man returned whole." However, this account sounds like a classic shamanic initiation rather than a ritual.

Avi sumatc
Mojave, *Southwest*
A specialist who treats cuts or bruises caused by rocks [Stewart 1974:12].

Awahokshu
Pawnee, *Plains*
The abode of supernatural powers; the holy place where spirits dwell. This is a composite word: *awa* comes from *Tiráwa*, the "supernatural powers," and *hokshu* means "sacred, holy" [Alexander 1910:44].

Awhe sumach
Mojave, *Southwest*
A healing specialist commonly called a scalper [Stewart 1970:20]; the name translates to "enemy dream(er)." Only a warrior who has dreamed the appropriate power can take an enemy scalp. Warriors who scalp an enemy without this power dream are vulnerable to the "enemy sickness," called *awhe hahnok* [Stewart 1974:6], which causes them to go insane. The healer, or scalper, can cure this illness, and one scalper accompanies each war party.

One prescription for treating this illness is for the warrior to fast and bathe for eight consecutive days away from the camp and to clean his fingernails. When bathing, he first rubs his body with a soapy plant (a yucca?). After the fourth day of the scalp dance, the warrior has to go four days without eating any salt [Stewart 1970:20–21]. "The scalper cleaned the scalp with mud to 'tame' it, or purify it. . . . Even the scalper had to undergo purification lest he fall ill with 'enemy sickness'" [Stewart 1970:21].

"Enemy sickness" is also caused by marrying, having intercourse with, or even smelling a foreigner. "It's what they call 'the smell of an enemy.' It causes sickness, *awhe hahnok*. They go crazy from it sometimes. They get pretty sick, and get poorer and poorer until they lay down and die. The *awhe sumatc* treats it. They get it from the White people mostly, but the colored are the worst. Sickness from them sure hurts. It's hard to cure, too" [Stewart 1974:7].

This specialist also treats other types of illnesses, such as *itcimava hahnok*, a sickness caused by eating foreign food that usually results in an upset stomach. Perhaps most unusual, however, is sickness caused by feathers: "Feathers are very dangerous. They can make people sick, make them faint or maybe pass away. You couldn't keep eagle or chickenhawk feathers in the house. It gives you nightmares. You have to take it easy on waking up, or you'll get a stroke and go. If you keep eagle feathers in the room, you'll get sick and cry all night. If you get sick from eagle feathers, the *awhe sumatc* treats you" [Stewart 1974:7–8].

Stewart [1974:6] reported that "some Mojave informants said that the *awhe sumatc* had the strongest power of any of the shamanistic specialists." (Note: In his 1970 publication, Stewart uses the spelling *ahwe sumach*, whereas in his 1974 article, he uses *awhe sumatc*; the latter is assumed to be the more correct form.)

See *kwathidhe* for more details on Mojave healing.

Awonawilona
Zuni, *Southwest*
A class of spirits that includes such individuals as the sun, earth, corn, and gods of war. The term literally means "the ones who hold our road." These

spirits have gifts for humans that must be secured through ritual offerings, songs, and prayers.

Awusua
Crow, *Plains*
Sweat lodge. In former times, the sweat lodge was used only when a shaman was prompted to do so by a dream. Thus, because of the Crow's nomadic lifestyle, sweat lodges were seldom used more than once. Their use in healing seems to be a rather recent innovation. They differ from most sweat lodges in that the fire is placed to the right of the doorway rather than being in the center. The frame is usually built from 12 willows but may consist of any multiple of 4 up to 100 poles. The leader sits in the first seat to the left of the door, and all enter in a clockwise fashion. Stones, heated on a fire in front of the door, are brought in one at a time. No one is allowed to speak until four rocks have been brought in. Thereafter, individuals can state their wishes. Unlike in most other sweat lodge ceremonies, there seems to be no reckoning of the number of stones to be used. The ceremony normally consists of four rounds of songs and prayer, with the lodge door being opened at the end of each round.

Axèki
Shasta, *California*
Supernatural beings that appear to every Shasta who has a vision. Usually they are described as being very small men carrying tiny bows and arrows. Although considered to be human, they come in many different forms, and many animals are also regarded as *axèki* [Holt 1946:326]. When the *axèki* appears, he sings a song for the vision-quester; this song becomes the one that the shaman will use in her healing practice (Shasta shamans are usually women). The vision-quester must learn the song upon threat of immediate death if she fails to do so. After the vision-quester successfully repeats the song, the *axèki* reveals his name and gives the vision-quester a "pain"—some object, usually a short, sharpened splinter of some material such as glass or stone. The shaman must then set about gathering the proper paraphernalia that goes with this particular "pain." Once the correct paraphernalia is gathered, the shaman may attempt to perform a healing cere-

mony. Since each aspiring shaman normally obtains three "pains" in the first year, it is usually several years before their collections are complete. When all the items are on hand, a special dance is held that lasts for five consecutive nights; this is the final rite of passage to becoming a fully recognized shaman.

"Though all the *axèki* could be seen by any shaman, a given one was the friend and guardian of only one shaman and was hereditary in the family. Occasionally, however, one deserted a family, going over to another shaman, and there were also numerous unpledged *axèki*, one or more of which a shaman might attract to herself and which might be more powerful than her inherited guardian" [Holt 1946:328]. The more powerful a shaman's *axèki*, the greater the shaman's feats.

One of these spirits lived in a mountain in back of Applegate towards Grants Pass, Oregon, and was known as The-Rawhide-Basket-up-on-Something. This spirit had the power to treat people who had been struck by lightning. Another one looked like an eagle and lived near Lake. He was known for treating anyone who choked on a fishbone in the throat. The *axèki* who lived in some rocky cliffs at the head of Horse Creek Canyon called himself Wild Pigeon, but looked like a man and could treat any sickness.

The *axèki* can also cause sickness, and each one has specific illnesses that he can induce. A shaman is unable to treat any sickness caused by her own *axèki*.

Axikiye
Biloxi, Ofo, *Southeast*
The treatment of a patient by a shaman; translates to "treating him" [Dorsey and Swanton 1912:221].

Ayañkxiyan
Biloxi, Ofo, *Southeast*
Doctor or shaman [Dorsey and Swanton 1912:220].

Ayelkwi
Luiseño, *California Peninsula*
The concept of power generally referred to in anthropology as mana. *Ayelkwi* is omnipresent, imperishable, and immutable. Every detail of existence and every event in nature throughout time

is an expression of *ayelkwi* in some form. *Ayelkwi* must be used specifically and unvaryingly according to a set procedure, and it must always be used on an appropriate occasion [White 1976: 361]. Violating the rules for the use of *ayelkwi* results in some form of misfortune.

Ayelkwi manifests itself in many different forms. For example, the term is often translated as "knowledge," which is one of its manifestations, although "knowledge-power" is a better translation of the term. White [1976:361–362] groups these different manifestations into four general categories: "(1) 'Common' knowledge is that cultural and physical nature common to the Luiseño as distinguished from all other creatures and their respective forms of 'common' knowledge; (2) 'innate' ayelkwi is the differential powers with which individuals are born and that marks some of them as unusual and powerful persons; (3)

'residual' ayelkwi comprises virtually all the unknown and unusual features of the Luiseño environment—a potentially procurable residuum of powers 'thrown away' by Wiyot, the Luiseño culture hero; (4) 'formulated' ayelkwi is represented by ritual forms and procedures considered to have been promulgated in decisions made either in cosmogonic times or later."

Ayikcomí
Seminole, *Southeast*

Medicine maker; specifically, those who use plants to heal their patients. The healing ceremonies also include the use of sacred medicine songs that go with each plant and usually some form of massaging the patient's body. In addition, the healers suck through cane tubes on the afflicted parts of the body to remove objects causing illness.

Baaheamaequa
Crow, *Plains*

A vision, the main source of a shaman's ability to heal; translates to "something you see." However, shamans also receive power through dreams called *bashiammisheek*, which literally means "he has a medicine" [Wildschut 1975:6]. In both cases, a supernatural being appears. With a vision, the person is awake, and with a dream, the person is asleep. Power received in visions is not necessarily greater than power received in dreams.

Baaxpàak
Crow, *Plains*

Translates to "one who has *baaxpée* (power)" [Frey 1987:130]. It sometimes refers to shamans who doctor.

Baaxpée
Crow, *Plains*

See *maxpe*.

Bacóritsi'tse
Crow, *Plains*

A sacred or power rock that one acquires, similar in concept to the Sioux *tunkan* (see entry). It is characterized primarily by its shape, which frequently suggests the head of some animal, but may resemble some other body part, such as the hoof. Although such stones may be acquired in visions, they are most often found on the ground. According to some informants, they are found by the odor they emit. They are kept wrapped in a cloth or skin along with other offerings such as beads, elk teeth, sweet grass, and so forth. Their owners treat them with great respect, "feeding" them, singing to them, kissing them, and addressing prayers to them. These stones have a tendency to multiply like living beings. It is customary to unwrap them when the first thunder is heard in the spring. Normally these sacred stones are passed from generation to generation, but they can also be sold. Different stones have different medicines. For example, Looks-at-a-Bull's-Penis had stones that became light in spring and heavy in summer. In the coldest winter there would be frost on them, for they breathed. These stones told Looks-at-a-Bull's-Penis where the Crow should go to avoid a bad winter and have plenty to eat. Thus they avoided hard times [Lowie 1922: 390–391].

Bad Bad Bull
Gros Ventres, *Plains*

A powerful shaman who lived during the latter part of the nineteenth century. After his death, his ghost passed on his power song to his wife, Woman. She used this song not only to call her husband, but also to doctor. Woman died around 1907 [Cooper 1944]. The following account of one of Bad Bad Bull's healing ceremonies is told by a woman named Singer:

"There was a man who had power to cure this stomach-eating sickness. His name was Bad Bad Bull. In his lodge he had little willow back-rests with fringes along each side, and on each piece of fringe he had these little animals that cause this sickness. . . .

"Bad Bad Bull's nephew's wife had this stomach-eating sickness. It was making her poorly and she was sick all the time. The old fellow said: 'Oh I will pity my nephew. If his wife dies and he has to go out and cry. I guess I will pity him and doctor his wife.'

"So they fixed the lodge in readiness for the doctoring. Iron Bucket, my husband, was present there for the doctoring. They all sat around, and Bad Bad Bull told them to sing and said: 'When you get through singing I will pick away all the stuff that the animal has eaten. And then I am going to suck this thing out. I want you to catch hold of my back locks of hair and hold my head up.'

"He had them heat two rocks and these rocks were still in the fire while he was doctoring. So they watched him when he was throwing that bad stuff out. When he had his mouth ready to suck, they pulled his head up, and he had that animal in his mouth. So, as they always do, they all looked at it. When Iron Bucket saw it, it was round and most of it was mouth. After they had all seen it, Bad Bad Bull had them pull the two red-hot rocks out of the fire, and he put the animal on them and burned it up. The woman got well. She came out of her sickness and lived a long time. Bad Bad Bull's animals used to be of all different colors—green, yellow and black, the black ones were not quite so bad" [Cooper 1957:345–346].

Bàkumbírio
Crow, *Plains*
Public displays in which shamans "duel" each other with their powers. These ceremonies are enthusiastically attended, and people gamble on their favorite shaman. The supernatural feats are quite spectacular and include a wide variety of shamanic abilities, such as swallowing large stones, completely disappearing, manifesting objects, handling fire, "killing" and then resuscitating victims, and other such common shamanic activities.

Baltadak
Skagit, *Northwest Coast*
The Spirit Canoe Healing Ceremony. See *sbatatdaq* for details.

Baohigan
Penobscot, Abenaki, *Canadian Eastern Woodlands*
Dialectical variants: *puhigan* (Malecite and Passamaquoddy); *buohigan* (Micmac); *powhigan* (Natick). The shaman's helping spirit, most often coming in the form of an animal. Speck [1919:249] translates this term as meaning "instrument of mystery."

Barbeau, Marius
A Canadian ethnographer and folklorist born on 5 March 1883. He was a Rhodes scholar at Oxford and earned a B.Sc. degree in anthropology in 1910. His career was spent in the Division of Anthropology at the Geological Survey of Canada (now the Canadian Museum of Civilization). Most of his Native American work was among the Tsimshian and the Huron-Wyandot. He published nearly 1,000 articles during his career. Germane to the topic of this book is his *Medicine-Men of the North Pacific Coast*. He died on 27 February 1969.

Basamacha
Yavapai, *Southwest*
Shaman—either male or female. The term translates as *ba*, "person," and *samacha* (actually *sumacha*), "medicine power" [Gifford 1932:234]. Shamans receive their power during trance visions in which a spirit teaches them songs and the procedures for healing the sick.

Healing ceremonies are conducted at night. A shaman first enters into a trance to diagnose the case. A spirit informs the shaman whether the patient will live or die and how to treat the person if he or she is to live. The shaman begins by singing over those who are to be treated. "While singing the shaman saw a flash of lightning (widaukam) to the most painful spot" [Gifford 1932:234]. Once the seat of pain is discovered, the shaman incises a cross on the skin with a flake of flint or a piece of glass. The shaman then sucks on the marked area until the disease-causing object has been removed from the patient. The object is shown to those present.

During his treatment, the shaman doctors the patient with four eagle feathers, a gourd rattle, a bullroarer, and sometimes hawk feathers. When eagle feathers are used, they are usually the whitish axillaries. At the point in the ceremony when the feathers are to be used, the patient's head is placed facing eastward, and the four feathers are stuck in the ground near the patient in the four cardinal directions. Then the shaman sings and picks up each feather, one by one, and touches it to the seat of pain on the patient's body.

If the shaman uses a bullroarer, he first circles the house of the patient many times while swinging it. If his spirit instructs him to use it during the treatment, he swings it in a vertical direction, sometimes before singing and sometimes during his songs. Not all shamans use a bullroarer. For instance, the rattlesnake shaman makes no use of it.

If the treatment is not successful, other shamans may be called to doctor the patient. If the patient dies, all the property given to the shaman for his treatment is returned to the family of the patient.

In addition to healings conducted by individual shamans, the Yavapai call forth spirits called *akaka* by performing a spirit impersonation dance. The *akaka* reportedly have more power than a shaman. Usually there are eight men who dress as *akaka* and are led by a shaman. Each dancer wears a mask that "consisted of a white buckskin bag with holes for eyes, nose, and mouth. This was inverted, drawn down over the head, and tied about the neck. The body was covered with white clay and two small weed aprons, front and behind, suspended by a belt. . . . Each carried two sticks painted white, one in each hand, and a cane whistle in his mouth" [Gifford 1932:236].

The healing ceremony with the *akaka* is conducted at night in a specially constructed, diamond-shaped enclosure about 50 feet in diameter. Once dressed, the shaman uses his bullroarer to call the *akaka* to the enclosure, where the patients await them. At this point, the *akaka* are considered

sacred, and if anyone touches them they become cramped. The *akaka* begin their treatment by dancing around the sick, who are at one edge of the enclosure, in a counterclockwise direction. The shaman and his singers stand in the middle of the enclosure. "Each akaka made a cross of tule pollen on top of the shaman's head before going to treat the sick, and another after treating the sick. All eight akaka visited each patient four times during the night. They kept close together, so that all eight treated each sick person in quick succession. . . . Each akaka pressed four times at the seat of pain, made tule pollen crosses on the top of the head, on each shoulder, on the chest, and on the seat of pain, and put a pinch of pollen in each patient's mouth" [Gifford 1932:237–238]. During their treatment, the *akaka* do not sing, but they frequently sound their whistles. The ceremony ends before daylight. If the treatment is not successful, it is repeated. The *akaka* receive no payment for their services.

Basbatadaq
Twana, *Northwest Coast*
The Spirit Canoe Ceremony; translates to "soul-loss curers in a group soul recovery." See *sbatatdaq* for details.

Batse maxpe
Crow, *Plains*
Shamans who have received great powers and have fully demonstrated their abilities to use them [Lowie 1935:238]. The term *maxpe* means "sacred" or "mysterious." More recently, Frey [1987:130] gave the term *akbaalía*, which translates to "one who doctors," which is a more appropriate term for those shamans who use their powers to heal. "To designate someone as *akbaalía* is in many ways vague and misleading. Simply possessing *medicine* is not synonymous with being a *medicine* man. Many who are not *akbaalía* regularly use a medicine bundle. For some, 'medicine' means knowledge of the medicinal properties of a particular leaf, which, when made into a tea and taken regularly, may prevent a cold or cure bleeding ulcers. The power to stop a hemorrhage has been given to certain young men. Certain women have the skill to treat colicky babies or to rid a

child of an earache. In all of these cases, however, *xapáalíia* (power object) is applied for a specialized purpose and only for that purpose. The tea, for instance, cannot treat arthritis or a backache. Although some people have a *xapáaliia* that can treat a particular problem more effectively than anyone else, they cannot be considered *akbaalía* simply because they have *xapáaliia*" [Frey 1987:130–132].

Crow shamans, both males and females, acquire their powers through personal vision quests on isolated mountain peaks. In rare cases, supernatural power comes unsought, without the hardship of fasting for a vision. These revelations are usually in the form of visionary dreams. For example, Bull-All-the-Time "gained a doctor's powers while asleep in his tipi" [Lowie 1935:246]. Often the supernatural helper first appears in human form and then later reveals his true form, which is most often an animal. However, dwarfs, thunderbirds, lizards, ants, bees, and other creatures are also potential sources of power. It is common for a shaman to have more than one spirit helper, especially if he has performed many vision quests.

Although shamanic powers come to Crow shamans mainly through visions, acquired powers can also be transferred to other persons, usually through inheritance or by purchase. The shaman does not own the medicine, he is only its caretaker. It is owned by his helping spirit. Therefore, the shaman's helping spirit ultimately decides who, if anyone, is to receive his medicine. When transfers occur, they usually involve some sacred object, such as a feather, arrow, or rock, that symbolizes the power that has been given to the vision-quester. "By teaching the relevant rules the owner could therefore bequeath or transfer it [the sacred object] to a close relative, who thus became a beneficiary without himself enjoying direct spiritual contacts" [Lowie 1935:248]. Such objects are incorporated into a person's sacred bundle, which is always kept close at hand by its owner. If a shaman dies without transferring his medicine bundle, it may be left with the family for safekeeping or it may be weighted down with rocks and thrown into a river.

On rare occasions, "the natural son of an *akbaalía* (shaman) has been the recipient of *xapáaliia* (power object) even though he had not antici-

pated such a gift. . . . Even when a gift of medicine has not been received through a vision, *baaxpée* (power) still resides in the *xapáaliia*. The Iilápxe (helping spirit) may convey to their new son or daughter the specific intentions and responsibilities associated with the subsequent application of the medicine. Dreams eventually will be sent. During future fasts the son or daughter will share in their spiritual power by participating in a dialogue with the Iilápxe" [Frey 1987:95].

For purposes of healing, shamans acquire specific powers to treat specific aliments. For example, those who have visions of the bear often become wound doctors, called *akuwacdiu* [Lowie 1935:64]. Thus, shamanic healers become specialists according to the powers they have received. It is not unusual for a shaman to have several helping spirits, and therefore a number of different treatments available.

Doctoring is often associated with prayer meetings in which the sacred medicine bundles are opened. During one part of the prayer meeting, those who need doctoring come forth and are treated. In more serious cases or between prayer meetings, the patient is brought to the home of the shaman, or, if the patient is unable to make the journey, the shaman goes to the home of the patient to provide treatment. However, some shamans possess the ability to doctor at a distance. In such cases, the shaman sends his helping spirit to doctor the patient. "Because they can 'travel by lightning,' the Iilápxe (helping spirits) are able to 'touch up' a sick person immediately, no matter where that person is" [Frey 1987:141].

Most illnesses are diagnosed as being caused by some foreign object in the body, and the cure is to suck on the part of the body where the object is lodged. This is often done through the stem of a sacred pipe. For example, Goes-ahead would treat pneumonia by sucking on the patient's body with a pipe stem. He would draw out blood through the pipe stem and then spit it out. "Such suction left no mark in the place where the blood was extracted" [Lowie 1935:64]. Other illnesses are diagnosed as being caused by a breach of taboo or the activities of a ghost or spirit. In some cases, the treatment entails blowing on the patient's body rather than sucking on it. Various herbs are often incorporated into the treatments.

Some shamans doctor sick persons with their eagle feather fans. "After a prayer during a prayer meeting or while standing in front of the center pole at the Sun Dance, the *akbaalía* (shaman) 'touches up' an afflicted person with his fan of Eagle feathers. As the feathers gently brush over the person, the *akbaalía* feels the *baaxpée* (power) 'pulsate' into the fan through his fingers and arm and then into the patient's body. *Baaxpée* is transferred from 'head to foot.' The patient feels a 'cooling' sensation. With his hands and fan held over the afflicted area, the *akbaalía* feels the 'pulse' working. The throbbing continues for a while, and when it begins to cease, the *akbaalía* jerks the fan away from the patient's body, and the ailment is 'tossed to the east, letting it blow away.' The *baaxpée* has entered the patient's body and removed the illness" [Frey 1987:74–75].

Today, Crow shamans work closely with the local Indian Health Service and make regular visits to hospitals. The following is an account of a shaman doctoring a man who was hospitalized for two bullet wounds he received in a bar fight:

"Because the man has lost a lot of blood and because the two bullets are lodged dangerously near his heart, the (white) doctors are reluctant to operate. A specialist is brought in. The parents of the boy, knowing that help is available now, seek out an *akbaalía*. That evening the *akbaalía* goes to the man's hospital room. As it's a late hour, few will be around to disturb them. Standing at the man's bedside, the old man pulls back the bandages very carefully so as not to cause any discomfort. The powder of a particular root is all he has with him. It's part of his *xapáaliia*, given to him by his Iilápxe. He gently pours some of the powder into each of the wounds and places the bandages back in their proper position. Praying, the *akbaalía* stays with the young man through the night and into the early morning. It's all he can do. The next morning the nurses come into the room to change the dressings, but what they find as they pull back the sheets are the two bullets lying beside the man; 'they'd come out the same way they'd gone in.' X-rays are taken, finding no sign of the bullets, and as soon as the boy regains his strength he's allowed to go home" [Frey 1987:127].

In all treatments, the sincerity of the patient and the depth of his belief in the shaman's power are critical to a successful cure. In addition, some form of payment to the shaman is necessary.

Batsirápe
Crow, *Plains*
A shaman's helping spirit [Lowie 1922:340–341]. More recently, Frey [1987:65] used the term *Iilápxe* (see entry). During visions or during visionary dreams, when power is received from a spirit, this spirit often enters the shaman's body, where it resides thereafter. For example, Muskrat, a female shaman, reported to Lowie [1922:340]:

"I also got weasel medicine. . . . I went to the mountains to fast, and could not sleep all night. A cloud came up. I went to the rocks for shelter and lay down to sleep. A weasel appeared and came on my neck, causing a queer feeling. He went into my stomach. . . . Then he gave me a whistle (sound to make). He sang a song. . . . Both a horse and a weasel are inside of my body. . . . When I was out fasting, a gray horse came up to me and went into my stomach. He told me he should enter me. After the *batsirápe* once gets in, it does not go out. I doctor horses if they can't make water (urinate). I chew something and put it in their mouth. Then they can make water. I use chewing tobacco. Tobacco is one of my main medicines, I always have plenty on hand to doctor with."

Bear Butte
See *mato tipi*.

Bear Doctors
A special class of shamans in central California who receive their power from the grizzly bear. This often takes the form of the shaman entering the bear's abode, where the bear appears in human form. It is reported that these shamans can assume the form of a grizzly bear at will to inflict harm on their enemies. Furthermore, if the shaman is killed while in the form of a bear, he can return to life. Of the Pomo bear doctors, Barrett wrote: "The Pomo bear doctor never performed any cure, practiced his magic with the greatest secrecy and only for his own satisfaction and aggrandizement" [Barrett 1917b:463]. If their

practice is discovered, these shamans are usually put to death.

Bear, Tom
Peigan, *Plains*
A shaman who practiced until the 1950s. He reported that his spirit helper was the ghost of a former Native American police officer who had been killed around the turn of the century.

Beast Gods
Zuni, *Southwest*
The group of spirits used by shamans for healing. See *we'mawe*.

Berdache
The anthropological term for a Native American transvestite. They often become powerful shamans. The following is an account of a Plains Cree *berdache*:

"They were called *a·ya hkwew*. It happened very seldom. But one of them was my own relative. He was a very great doctor. When he talked his voice was like a man's and he looked like a man. But he always stay among the women and dressed like them. . . .

A shaman, who was a berdache (transvestite), wears a hat, trade bead and coin necklace, and dance apron, all of which are considered female apparel.

"He had another name, *oskas·ewis*, Clawedwoman. He wanted to be called *piecuwiskwew* (Thunder-woman), because Thunder is the name for a man and *iskwew* is a woman's name; half and half just like he was.

"He never took a wife, nor did he bother the women or the men. We never teased him or made fun of him. We were afraid to, because he was a great doctor.

"Once an old man brought him some clothes and a horse to doctor a boy who had fallen from a horse. He took them right away. He called for my father to sing with him. Again he made a big fire. He took his dress off, just wore a breechclout. I heard the sound from the outside as he stood on the fire. He blew at the side of the boy and called for a wooden bowl. 'He has got matter inside of him, but not in his lungs.' He sang again, he held his hands over the sweetgrass and tapped one hand over the other. Suddenly, you could see bearclaws sticking from his palm. He laid the boy on his belly. He stuck the bearclaw in the boy's neck. Then he sucked out a lot of matter and spit it into the bowl. He rubbed his hands over the wound and though it was daylight we couldn't see any marks on the boy where he had been stuck. 'I've got pretty nearly all the matter out. But there is some left. I don't want to take it all for fear that I'll hurt the boy. I'll take the rest out this evening.' In the evening he went back and took more out. He saved that sick boy.

"He saved a lot of people. Sometimes he would doctor them only once and they would be well. He got lots of horses that way. Even those who had only one horse would give it to him so that he would doctor" [Fine-Day in Mandelbaum 1940:256–257] .

Betil
Dwamish, *Northwest Coast*
A class of spirit beings who live under the ocean and take the form of "sea people." Some informants describe them as "meremen" [Waterman 1930a:310].

Betsaki
Atsugewi, *California*
Shamans who doctor. Atsugewi doctors can be either male or female. These shamans acquire their

spirit helpers through *wes comi* (vision quests) at known power spots. Successful quests are often marked by the shaman bleeding from the nose or mouth or both. They are never formally trained by older shamans but have to get the powers on their own. As one informant stated: "A person cannot learn from others how to be a doctor. They must get their own powers" [Grant in Park 1986:34]. These powers can come from animals, insects, lakes, mountains, springs, rocks, and dwarflike beings. When such a spirit appears, he gives the shaman healing songs to be used in curing specific illnesses. Therefore, the more numerous their helping spirits and thus their songs, the more power shamans command over healing. Healing ceremonies are usually conducted over the course of several nights, the number being determined by the seriousness of the case and instructions from the helping spirits. Among the best doctors are the *mache da* (Coyote) and the *tchi can ama* [Park 1986:39].

Some informants use the phrase *pats hage char ra* for male shamans and *iter char ra* for female shamans [Park 1986:5].

Beuski

Atsugewi, *California*

Supernatural powers a shaman acquires from his helping spirits [Park 1986:n.5:5].

Biisänoxu

Arapaho, *Plains*

Insect medicine. The name comes from a plant called *biisänoxi*, whose red seeds are the primary ingredient in this mixture. Kroeber obtained a sample of this medicine from the Arapaho. It was contained in a small leather bag to which were attached a mole skin and a catlinite (see *Catlin, George*) ring. Kroeber [1907:422] reported: "To touch a mole, or even the earth thrown up by one, gives the itch. The medicine kept with this mole-skin is used to cure this itch, as well as the bites of insects, or diseases supposed to be caused by them." In addition to the red seeds, "the medicine in the bag consists of scented leaves called tcaax-uwinan, of charred tobacco, . . . of the dust, probably the spores, of small mushrooms, which are supposed to fall from the sky with the rain, and of powdered bone of hiintcäbiit, the water-monster.

. . . The small bag containing this mixed medicine has the shape of a mushroom, it is said. Four small pits have been bored in the catlinite ring, giving this the appearance of a world-symbol" [Kroeber 1907:422–423].

Bilisshíissanne

Crow, *Plains*

To fast from water and food [Frey 1987:77]. Fasting usually takes place during a Sun Dance or a vision quest and is the primary means by which shamans, both male and female, acquire their healing powers.

Billie, Josie

Seminole, *Southeast*

Josie Billie was born around 1887. He was a member of the Mikasuki band of Seminole and lived on the Big Cypress Reservation at the tip of the Florida peninsula. His Seminole name, which he received at the age of 15, roughly translates to "crazy spherical puma" [Sturtevant 1960:508]. He became increasingly interested in the Seminole medicine ways and asked many different shamans about their healing songs and medicines. At the age of 17, he began formal training under a shaman named Old Motlow. He went on a four-day fast, during which Old Motlow came each day to teach him. At the beginning of each day, Old Motlow prepared two emetics for Josie to drink that would enable him to absorb the teachings. On the first day, Old Motlow spoke of various sicknesses and sang the songs for curing them. On the second day, he spoke of their origins as a people and about the theory that sickness is caused by the wandering of the soul during dreams. On the third day, he reviewed the songs of the first day and added more songs. On the fourth day, Old Motlow taught Josie some of the more powerful songs and spells, including magical formulas for personal protection and power.

The next year, Josie returned for another round of teachings from Old Motlow. The following year, he completed a fast with Tommy Doctor as his teacher and then began to apprentice with him, learning how to collect and prepare various herbs, learning healing songs, learning how to diagnose cases, and so forth. His apprenticeship with Tommy Doctor lasted four years, after which

Josie began doctoring, although he was still too young to be fully trusted by his people. Around 1920, Tommy Doctor died, and Josie took over his practice. When visited by botanist John K. Small in 1921, Josie had approximately 30 plants he was using in his treatments.

During his training, Josie was imbued with a special medicine that gave him extra curing powers. He was asked to find a particular plant, the name of which he would not reveal, and bring it to his teacher. "The teacher prepared the plant into a medicine by singing a special song and transferring the power of the song to the medicine by blowing through a cane tube in the usual way. When Josie drank the potion it came alive in his body. It is still living there—perhaps in his heart, he told me—and when he prepares medicine it churns about and gives off a magical 'smell' which enters the patient and helps effect a cure. To keep this medicine alive and strong, every month or two Josie must fast for a day and take an emetic concocted with a special 'medicine eater's song.' Should he fail to cure a patient, he concludes that his 'living medicine' has become weak, and he fasts and takes the emetic to restore it" [Sturtevant 1960:513–54].

On 2 January 1945, Josie Billie was baptized, but he continued to doctor. That year he made the first of what were to become annual visits to Oklahoma, where he learned several medicines from the Creek and also learned to read and speak the Creek language. In 1946, he entered the Florida Baptist Institute, and by July 1948, he had become an assistant pastor in a new church opened on the Big Cypress Reservation.

In September 1958, an article appeared in *Time* magazine about Josie's abilities as a maker of medicines. This was followed by his work in Kalamazoo, Michigan, with the Upjohn laboratories on a tranquilizer made from several plants. By this time, he was reputed to be the most skilled and powerful of the Seminole healers, having about 225 different plants in his repertoire.

Biricísande
Crow, *Plains*
The vision quest ritual in which the shaman seeks healing or other supernatural powers; translates to "not drinking water." With regard to healing,

Lowie [1922:334] received the following account concerning visions from White-Arm sometime between 1907 and 1916:

"Sometimes the Sun himself appeared to the visionary, but mostly animals came. Those I do not think are related to the Sun at all. When men are praying, the Sun is first thought of, but generally other beings appear. After returning from a quest, the faster made a sweat lodge and all the famous people were called in; while they were assembled in the sweat lodge the visionary told his vision, and the audience afterwards told the other people. Snake visionaries are mostly doctors, e.g. Flatdog; the snake tells them how to treat the sick. Some would smell the incense in a vision and thus know what weed to use for medicine."

Birket-Smith, Kaj
A Danish anthropologist born in Copenhagen on 20 January 1893. He is known for his extensive ethnographic work among the Inuit in Greenland and Alaska. In 1921–1923 he worked as an ethnographer on Knud Rasmussen's Fifth Thule Expedition. In 1933 he studied the Chugach Eskimos on the Pacific Coast. He was a member of the Department of Ethnography at the Danish National Museum in Copenhagen from 1929 until his retirement. For his work on the Eskimos, he was awarded honorary doctorates from the Universities of Pennsylvania, Oslo, Basel, and Uppsala. He also founded the Department of Anthropology at the University of Copenhagen in 1945. He died on 28 October 1977.

Black drink
Southeast
A ritual emetic made from boiling the parched leaves and stems of the yaupon holly (*Ilex vomitoria*). In the anthropological literature, it is often referred to as cassina, an Anglicized version of a Native American (probably Timucuan) name for this tea [Hudson 1979:1]. The black drink is used throughout the southeastern United States and is one of the defining cultural traits of this geographical area. Its use also extends into eastern Texas. The active ingredient is caffeine, and it is the only holly plant in North America known to contain it. Although used as a social beverage, its

Eastern Timucua Indians consuming black drink. Utilized for both ceremonial and healing, the caffinated drink was served in large marine shells. Ritual vomitting occurs after consuming the drink.

primary role is the attainment of ritual purity and as a medicine. As such, some of the southeastern nations call it the white drink. Its role as an emetic is not clear and is probably restricted to cases of its being consumed in large quanities.

Little is known of its history, except that it was often drunk from large marine shells (lightning whelk, emperor helmet, and horse conch) found on the Atlantic and Gulf Coasts. These shells were traded throughout the Southeast and have been found in archaeological sites of considerable antiquity. For instance, they are found in some of the burials of the Hopewellian period between 200 B.C. and A.D. 500. Stronger evidence for use of the black drink appears by the beginning of the Southern Cult (or Southeastern Ceremonial Complex) after A.D. 1000. It was certainly in use at the time of the earliest European contacts. For example, members of the 1564 French expedition to the mouth of the St. Johns River, where Fort Caroline was built, noted its use by the local Timucuan in-

habitants. Eventually, the colonists adopted its use under several names, including yaupon tea, Carolina tea, and Appalachian tea. For a time, it was even marketed in England under the name South-Sea tea.

The historical use of the black drink is best known among the various members of the Creek Confederacy, where it was known as *assi* [Fairbanks 1979:123], one of four great medicines used in the annual busk or green corn ceremonial. It was also used to purify individuals before they undertook certain ritual performances; in this case, only males drank it. The drinking of it was often accompanied by the smoking of tobacco. It was also known to be administered during curing ceremonies [Merrill 1979:41].

Among its medicinal benefits, it was recommended as a cure for diabetes, gout, kidney disorders, and smallpox. It was also used as a diuretic and to calm the nerves. Some accounts prescribed its use for purifying water.

Black Elk, Sr., Nicholas
Lakota, *Plains*

Nick Black Elk, although not particularly re-nowned among his own people, is the most well-known Native American shaman in the world as a result of John Neihardt's *Black Elk Speaks*, which has been translated into more than 20 languages since 1960. Black Elk was born in December 1863

Lakota holy man Black Elk.

near the Little Powder River in Wyoming and died on 19 August 1950 at Manderson, South Dakota. He received his healing powers in a vi-sion from a helping spirit named Eagle Wing Stretches [DeMallie 1984:116], "a little blue man," and his power to cure from the bear. "Although I was not able accurately to verify the actual num-ber of medicines known to him, many Oglala said that he knew over 200 distinct herbs. Along with songs and prayers, these herbs were used in heal-ing ceremonies" [Brown 1992:32]. The first herb used by Black Elk was obtained from the power of the north in a vision. He reported:

"As I looked down upon the people, there stood on the north side a man painted red all over his body and he had with him a lance (Indian spear) and he walked into the center of the sacred nation's hoop and lay down and rolled himself on the ground and when he got up he was a buffalo standing right in the center of the nation's hoop. The buffalo rolled and when he got up there was an herb there in his place. The herb plant grew up and bloomed so that I could see what it looked like—what kind of an herb it was from the bloom. After the buffalo's arrival the people looked bet-ter and then when the buffalo turned into an herb, the people all got up and seemed to be well" [De-Mallie 1984:128–129].

Soon thereafter, Black Elk, at 19 years old, lo-cated the herb and performed his first healing. He recounted the event as follows:

"That evening was to be my first performance in medicine. While eating supper a man by the name of Cuts to Pieces came over and was saying: 'Hey, hey, hey! I have a boy of mine and he is very sick and I don't expect him to live, and I thought since you had so much power in the horse dance, heyoka, etc. that you might have the power to cure my son.' I did not know how to go at it, but I had seen other medicine men so I thought I'd follow their way. So I sent him back and told him that if he wanted me to go there and do a little curing that he should bring me a pipe with an eagle feather on it, which would mean that I was really wanted. The fellow went back and brought me the pipe back with him. I told him to come around the left side as he came in, and to put the pipe with the ea-gle feather on it facing me, and then he should walk out on the right side. I took the pipe and lit it and offered it to the four quarters, Great Spirit, and mother earth. I recalled the vision and asked for power. Then I began to smoke. My father, my mother and a man were there so I had to pass it around to them also. I just figured out how to go at this. . . . And so now I used the drum to make the rumbling sound which represented the power of the west. Of course I had never received any instructions from anyone, but I just fixed a way for my curing. . . .

"Then I went to get One Side and brought him to my tipi. We went out now to the sick boy and when we got there Standing Bear was there too. Medicine men usually use several medicines but I only had the one herb now. . . .

"We went into the tipi, left to right, and sat ourselves on the west side. The patient was on the northeast. The boy was about four years old and was very sick. The child seemed to be just skin and bones. He had been sick a long time. The parents presented me with a horse first, because the horse is about the only property that we had and we were to stay here until the child had been cured. This was my first experience so I had to borrow the drum, the eagle bone whistle, and a wooden cup which I told them to put some water in. They set the cup right in front of me with water in it. From here on I had to think awhile, because I had a little bit of doubt about whether or not I could do this. I gave the eagle bone whistle to One Side and told him how to use this. I filled my pipe with kinnikinnick and there was a pretty girl here too and I gave the pipe to her and told her to hold it just as in the vision (I had received). Then everything was in readiness and I sent up a voice (prayed). The power I had to use was in the pipe, cup, drum, and the chief power was in the herb. The eagle bone whistle represented what the eagle had told me in the vision.

"Everything was now ready so now I beat the drum in time while sending up this cry: 'Hey-a-a-hey' four times. It seemed that while I was doing this a feeling was coming over me from my feet up. I was still beating this drum in time while sending a voice. . . .

"And then I prayed to the powers of all the other quarters as I had been taught in my vision. One power might have been enough, but I was so eager to cure the child that I used all the powers of my vision. . . .

"I was of course facing west, standing, and then I went to the right and stopped at the south, showing that I should walk the good road with my people (live a sacred life). The song I sang:

In a sacred manner I have made them walk
A sacred nation lies low.
In a sacred manner I have made them walk.
A sacred two-legged, he lies low.
In a sacred manner I have made him walk.

"When I sang this I could feel something queer in my body and I wanted to cry. At first I was in doubt but I was in earnest now. After singing this song I walked toward the west where the cup of water was and I saw the little sick boy looking up and smiling at me (in the cup of water). Then I knew that I had the power and that I would cure him. The next thing I made an offering and took a whiff at the pipe. Then I drank part of the water and started toward where the sick boy was and I could feel something moving in my chest and I was sure that it was that little blue man (from my vision) and it made a different sound from anything else. Then I stamped the earth four times standing in front of the boy. Then I put my mouth on the pit of the boy's stomach and drew the north wind through him. At the same time the little blue man was also in my mouth, for I could feel him there. I put a piece of white cloth on my mouth and I saw there was blood on it, showing that I had drawn something out of his body. Then I washed my mouth with some of the water of the cup. And I was now sure that I had power.

"This was the first time that I had ever conjured. I took some of the herb, powdered it, and put it all over the top of the hot water in the cup. I mixed it up and put some of it in my mouth and blew it over the boy to the four quarters and gave the rest of it to the boy to drink. I did not give this to the boy, but I let the virgin carry it to him. We ordered the virgin to help the boy stand up. We made him walk from the south to the four quarters. Of course, the boy was very poor and it would take some time for him to get perfectly well again, but he was cured and grew to be a young man and died before the age of thirty. I was not there, and if I had been I would probably have cured him again, for he was sick another time after this.

"Always when I was doctoring I could tell whether or not I could cure the patient, for if I could cure him, I would always see him smiling in the cup of water" [DeMallie 1984:236–239].

Black Road
Lakota, *Plains*

A powerful shaman who founded the Sacred Bow (or Medicine Bow) Society among the Oglala and Minneconjou divisions of the Sioux. The Sacred Bow Ceremony was used to prepare for war. Oral tradition reports that Black Road dreamed of the Thunder Beings while suffering from smallpox. He returned after the vision to ceremonially organize the Sacred Bow Society and become a powerful healer among his people. "He truly possessed medicines that healed and protected. His snake medicine was especially potent; when he used it on snake bites they did not even swell; and people came to him from far and near for help. His personal charm was the long-tailed deer, apparently one source of his power; and in his role as medicine man he always carried a hoop" [Blish 1934:180].

Black Wolf
Ponca, *Plains*

During the late nineteenth century, "Black Wolf was one of the most successful medicine men and prophets in the Indian Territory" [Draper 1946: 13]. A reporter named William Draper witnessed Black Wolf's suicide and reported the incident in the *Christian Herald*:

"While we stood there on the front porch of the agency, talking, I saw a crowd gathering in front of Black Wolf's wigwam. There was something afoot, said the agent, so we walked down that way. As the redskins swarmed around the tent and shouted for him to come out, the squaws lashed them back with whips.

"And then Black Wolf came forth, bleeding from fresh cuts on his arms and legs. His face, dark and sullen, was drawn with pain. He lifted his arms and began to talk, making a farewell speech

reciting all the good things he had done for his people. . . .

"The medicine man stopped talking. He was approaching his God, and it was time to be silent. Crossing his left hand over the right hand and holding them both to the front, he turned and marched slowly toward the river bank. Humming a song of death, as indicated by the position of his hands, he did not stop on the sandy bar, but waded into the swirling waters, and was soon lost to view.

"When his body was recovered, a few hours later, the Indians wailed, and mourned, and gave the old man a stylish funeral" [Draper 1946: 19–20].

Blue Back, Walter
Ponca, *Plains*

Sometimes known as Black Eagle, his Sun Dance name, Blue Back was a bear shaman (see *matógaxe*). Later he abandoned this practice to become a leader in the Peyote religion. He was one of the last of his generation to practice the traditional medicine ways. He died in 1955 at the age of 66 [Howard 1965:xi].

Boas, Franz

Franz Boas was born in Minden, Germany, on 9 July 1858. He was a linguist and one of the founders of Native American ethnography, specializing in the Northwest Coast cultures. He came to the United States in 1887 as an editor of *Science* and began his academic career the following year as an instructor at Clark University. He joined Columbia University in 1896 as an instructor and became a professor of anthropology in 1899. He remained at Columbia for the rest of his life.

From 1901 to 1905, Boas was also curator of anthropology at the American Museum of Natural History. During this time, he directed the Jesup North Pacific Expedition, which sought to investigate the cultural relationships between the Native Americans of Alaska and their Siberian counterparts. As an ethnographer, he was more interested in the documentation of facts than theoretical interpretations. He collected voluminous data on Native American languages, religion, and material culture—perhaps more information than any other Native American ethnographer. He was a prolific writer throughout his life, publishing one of his major works, *Race, Language, and Culture*, in 1940 at the age of 82. He died in New York City on 21 December 1942.

Bob-Tailed Wolf
Cheyenne, *Plains*
A shaman who recorded some of his healing songs for anthropologist Frances Densmore during the early twentieth century. He received all his healing songs directly from spirits and was powerful enough to treat all forms of sickness.

"Power has come to him in many dreams, but the first manifestation was connected with an experience in a thunderstorm. He was traveling on horseback when the storm arose. A bolt of lightning knocked him unconscious and killed his horse. On the fourth night after this occurrence he had a dream in which he was told how to treat the sick. The day was clear when he recorded that song for the writer, but within an hour the rain was falling heavily. He said this always happened when he sang this song. . . . With his songs he uses a rattle made of stiff rawhide; a face is painted on one side, the handle is wrapped with deerskin, and formerly a buffalo tail was attached to it.
    "Bob-tailed Wolf says that when he is treating sick babies they tell him where they feel bad. He received his power with them (babies) in the following manner: One day he came upon a covey of little plovers hardly old enough to walk. He was about to take them away when the mother came and said, 'Indian, don't take them; I love them and they are so pretty. If you will spare them I will give you power to treat sick babies.' He accordingly refrained from taking the tiny birds and their mother told him to use water in treating sick babies, instructing him to apply it to their bodies and to use it without herbs" [Densmore 1952:449].

Body soul
The force that keeps the body alive. This term is associated with the concept of "soul loss" found in many Native American cultures. Soul loss generally presupposes a belief in at least two independent soul systems: the body soul and the free soul. The body soul animates the breath while the free soul travels to the spirit world, land of the dead, or other supernatural realms. Other terms for body soul are life soul and breath soul, while another term for free soul is dream soul [Hultkrantz 1992:32, 74].

Booöinwadagan, Booöwinode
Micmac, *Canadian Eastern Woodlands*
See *buówinudi*.

Braided Tail Bundle
Crow, *Plains*
A medicine bundle used by shamans to diagnose illness. The existence of this bundle among the Crow has been traced back to pre-1780.

Brave Buffalo
Lakota, *Plains*
One of the most powerful shamans on the Standing Rock Reservation in South Dakota at the turn

Brave Buffalo

of the twentieth century. He was born near Pollock, North Dakota, around 1840, the son of Crow Bear, who was also an important medicine man. Brave Buffalo's power to heal came in a dream in which he was surrounded by a pack of wolves. He noticed that each of them had their nostrils and paws painted red. Then he fainted. When he regained consciousness, the wolves took him to a den on top of a high hill. There the wolves gave him a song that he used in healing.

In diagnosing his patients, Brave Buffalo used a 4- by 6-inch mirror encased in a flat, wooden frame. On the surface of the mirror were drawn a new moon and a star symbol. He reported: "I hold this mirror in front of the sick person and see his disease reflected in it; then I can cure the disease." He reported that his healing powers were the strongest during the full moon, "and when the moon dies my strength is all gone until the moon comes back again" [Densmore 1918:249].

Speaking of his treatment of the sick in general, Brave Buffalo reported:

"Some diseases are affected by the day and others by the night. I use this song (obtained in his wolf dream) in cases which are worse at night. I composed it myself and always sing it at night, whether I am treating a sick person or not. I offer smoke to the four winds and sing this song.

"Some people have an idea that we medicinemen, who get our power from different sources, are the worst of human beings; they even say that we get our power from the evil one, but no one could disregard such dreams as I have had, and no one could fail to admire the sacred stones (*tunkan*). Wakan tanka (Creator) is all-powerful, and if we reverence his work he will surely let us prove to all men that these things are indeed his doing. It is a very strict requirement that a medicine-man shall act out his dream (or vision), and that he maintain absolute integrity of character. If he fails to do this he will be punished and will not live long. I am not required to fast, only to smoke, showing that I am at peace with all men. Dreams come to me now in a natural way. Often during the day when I am alone on a journey, and my mind is on many things, I stop to rest awhile. I observe what is around me, and then I become drowsy and dream. Often I see the sacred stones in my dreams" [Densmore 1918:248–249].

In his treatment of the sick, Brave Buffalo was a sucking shaman. Once he located the disease-causing agent, he would suck the object from the patient using a hollow bone tube. The object would then be spat into a wooden bowl containing water and properly disposed of.

Breath soul
An anthropological term for the soul that animates one's breath. In many cultures, a human being is believed to have several souls. In most Native American cultures, the breath is thought to be under direct supernatural control. In fact, the name Breath-Maker or Breath-Giver is often used for Supreme Being or God. When a shaman makes an out-of-body journey, it is the breath soul that sustains his life, and it is his free soul that journeys. See *body soul.*

Buaxantï
Southern Paiute, *Basin*
See *puaxantï.*

Buffalo Chip Woman
Blood, *Plains*
A medicine woman who performed a variant of the Shaking Tent Ceremony. In 1953, Harry Under Mouse gave this account of a ceremony she had performed:

"She next asked her guests to partition her off in the corner by stretching a blanket between the two adjacent walls. She said, 'After I'm ready, I will sing some songs. You must then turn down the lamp low so that the room is nearly dark.' The medium now started to sing. Soon the sound of a galloping horse could be heard outside. It was heard circling the house and approaching the door. Next came the sound of a person jumping off. At this point the seeress asked that the lamp be turned low. Then she spoke again, 'Now he is coming in!' The company heard a thud at the door, which caused a rattling noise in the stovepipe. The conjurer now spoke to the spirit, 'Don't frighten these people! I sent for you to ask something. There's food for you under the stove. (An offering had been placed there prior to the start of the ceremony.) When you have finished eating, I want to talk to you.' In a moment the rapid pecking sounds of the ghost eating from the shell could be heard. When they ceased, the conjurer asked that the lamp be turned up. The food receptacle was brought out and found to be empty.

"A spectator named Running Sun then spoke to the medium. 'My wife went for rations two weeks ago. Upon her return, she lost the key to our house. Can your spirit locate it?' Now the ghost was heard to speak. None but the seeress could understand the peculiar, humming sounds he made. . . . As the spirit spoke, she interrupted. 'I'm going out again! Each of you take a smoke from the pipe!'

"Middle Bird Woman lighted the pipe at the stove and passed it among those present. The conjurer explained, 'This is the way I meet the spirit. Take this buffalo robe and be ready! Pull me from the corner and cover me with the robe so the hair side is out! My husband will then sing the song to bring me back.' The company continued to smoke. Soon the spirit could be heard returning. The cry of an owl was now heard. Again a thud at the door marked the guest's re-entry. Then the sound made by a bunch of keys striking the floor was noticed. The spirit asked, 'Are those the missing keys?' Running Sun identified them as such" [Schaeffer 1969:11–12].

Bull Lodge
Gros Ventre, *Plains*

A famous shaman who died around 1886. A woodpecker feather was one of his main doctoring implements. In addition to healing, he was also well known for his magical transforming abilities, such as turning dirt into sugar. The following is an account of one of his healing ceremonies conducted on his granddaughter, who "had an attack of some kind of sickness and blood just poured out from underneath":

"The old man (Bull Lodge) got there and felt around and said: 'Oh there is a big lump in there that busted your blood. Instead of cutting you open I am going to work it the other way. I will give you the medicine I use to help a woman in labor. I will work it off that way. I don't know what it is but it is a big lump.' So he told his wife: 'Take that frying pan, heat water quick.' So she did. He put three or four kinds of medicine in this water

and told her: 'Boil it quick.' Of course it didn't take long, and he said: 'Take two cups (of the infusion) and put it in there and cool it quick, so she can drink it.'

"They did this, and after the medicine was cool enough, the patient's husband raised her up so she could drink this medicine. She took it, and Bull Lodge said: 'All right. Just hold her up like that.' Bull Lodge took the black handkerchief (another one of his doctoring implements) and balled it up, prayed and sang, and put it right on top of the patient's head and shook it back and forth quick, and when he did that, she said: 'Grandfather, something dropped.'

"When she said that, he lifted her to another place, and here (where she had been) was what looked like a rock, as big as a man's fist and it was blue. What it was I do not know, but that it was what this woman had in her and it must have busted that blood. The blood was just running all over. The blood was still coming, and Bull Lodge said: 'Well, I have to heal that wound inside.' So he told Curly Head: 'Run to the creek and take a cup with you, and when you dip it in the water, dip it upstream.' So Curly Head did that and brought the water and said: 'Here is your water.' Bull Lodge put some medicine in it, stirred it up, and said to the patient: 'Drink this. This is going to heal that wound inside and is going to make blood. You lost too much blood.' So she drank that, the whole cupful, and when she got through drinking it the blood quit flowing.

"After Bull Lodge cured her, of course they took that thing that came out of her and built a great fire outside of buffalo chips. He said: 'Make a big fire and put it (the blue rocklike lump) in and see what is going to happen.' So they put it in the fire, and it rolled out. They would throw it in again, and it would roll out, the other way. It was a long time before they could stop it (from rolling out), but finally they got it to stay in the fire, and it broke open and was just like a shell. I did not see this fire myself but that is what they told me (happened). This woman whom Bull Lodge doctored lived to be an old, old woman" [Garter Snake in Cooper 1957:348–349].

Bull Lodge would use his woodpecker feather to cut open the body of the patient and then remove the disease-causing object with his hands, in much the same manner as the famous "psychic surgeons" of the Philippines. In Bull Lodge's case, however, a permanent scar would remain where he made the cut. The following account details his use of this feather:

"The sick woman was named Wind Woman, and she had trouble with her stomach, as if something were traveling around in there, and she was awfully sick. Her man went and gave a pipe to Bull Lodge to come and doctor this woman. She was just skin and bones and ready to give up the ghost (her spirit, meaning 'to die'). So Bull Lodge said: 'I will operate on her. I will have to cut her open and in that case I have to have seven men singers and six women to sing.' The men sat on one side of the lodge and the women on the other. . . . They all got seated there and she (Wind Woman) said: 'Father-in-law, I am about to die anyway, so don't be ashamed to doctor me. If you doctor me I know you will cure me and I want to live.' Bull Lodge said: 'All right. I will do what I can.'

"So this woman of course was stripped from her waist up and when she was lying on her back they could see this thing beating like in her abdomen. Bull Lodge called: 'Son, Otter Robe, come and give me charcoal.' And after Otter Robe had given him just a little piece of charcoal, he said: 'Son, put your hand on where the most pain is.' Otter Robe said: 'I don't know anything about it.' But anyway Otter Robe put his hand there and you could see his hand jumping, and right from there downward Bull Lodge made a mark with the charcoal.

"Then Bull Lodge took his woodpecker feather and prayed and talked and passed it sideways from each corner of his mouth twice, four times in all. I was looking to see what he was going to do. I was curious to know all about it. So he smudged the feather, spat on it, and at the upper end of the charcoal mark wiggled it as if working it in, and after he got it half way in he started to cut right along that charcoal line he had made, and at the lower end of the line took the feather out and the skin opened up. Bull Lodge smudged his hand and he put his hand in that cut, and he pulled something out and put it on the ground. It was as big as a fist and green on one side and white on

the other. It was a wano:'wa, a kind of bug that grows in a person, or a stone. So Bull Lodge said: 'Well, light that pipe,' and he put the handkerchief over that cut. So Otter Robe took the pipe and brought it around and gave it to his father and the old man lit it. After he lit it he smoked and blew that smoke on the handkerchief, and the fourth time he took away the handkerchief and the cut was gone,—there was nothing but a little scar. And the woman got well and lived to be an old woman" [Garter Snake in Cooper 1957: 349–350].

Bull-all-the-time
Crow, *Plains*
Sometime between 1907 and 1916, Lowie [1922: 328] received the following unusual account about Bull-all-the-time, a shaman who had received unsolicited healing powers:

"Bull-all-the-time, who secured a martial vision through torture and fasting, was also blessed with another for doctoring while he was asleep in his tipi. He saw a horse fastened to a rope, which was lengthened up to him. He heard a person sing. The horse was a sign that my informant would get horses as fees for his cures. He was told that if anyone fell sick he was to doctor him. He saw an old man decorated with red paint and holding a pipe in his hand. This man was standing over the recumbent patient and blew through a pipe stem over him. The sick man rose and then sat down. Bull-all-the-time saw all the sickness come out of the patient's blood and saw him get well. Bull-all-the-time showed me the pipe stem he had dreamt of; it had a horse's track incised near one end."

Gray-bull told Lowie [1922:375] of a time that his son, White-hip, had been doctored by Bull-all-the-time:

"[White-hip] had eaten some food and something stuck in his throat, and though he drank water he could not get rid of it. Bull-all-the-time was summoned and ordered everyone out of the lodge except the patient and Gray-bull, whom he asked to look at him. The doctor rubbed some substance on White-hip's breast, abdomen, and neck. He sang some songs, sucked at the patient's throat with his

mouth, making a popping sound, and produced a morsel of meat which had lodged in White-hip's throat. . . . On another occasion a big crowd were ready to mourn over a man who had swallowed a fish bone that stuck in his neck. They offered Bull-all-the-time a gun and other presents, and he drew forth the bone, curing the patient. Still another time a woman had a swollen leg and my informant sucked at it with his pipe and made the swelling go down. He also knew how to doctor spider bites, but did not treat snake bites or wounds."

Bulletproof Medicine

A form of preventive medicine found among the shamans of North America. The great warrior Crazy Horse is said to have had such a medicine made for him by Old Man Chips (see *Horn Chips*), the famous Lakota *yuwipi* (see entry) shaman. This power was imbued in a sacred *tunkan* (stone) that Crazy Horse wore in a small pouch around his neck. It is said to have protected both him and his horse during battle.

Lowie [1924:292–293] gives the following first-hand account of witnessing such medicine:

"Panayús told me of a Comanche boy raised among the Ute who developed into a great shaman with a reputation that bullets could not harm him. He received his powers from an old Ouray Ute chief who had this gift of invulnerability. One spring the people were camping by a mesa near the site of Ignacio. The Comanche shaman would doctor sick people, but there was always the discharge of guns accompanying the treatment since the medicine man had other men shoot at him. Panayús had always been skeptical of the man's power. On this occasion the medicine man rose early and said to my informant, 'Friend, you have never believed me. When the sun shall rise, I will give you an exhibition, then you'll believe.' When the sun was nearly up Panayús's son was still asleep. The Comanche said, 'Wake up the boy and bid him stand in the door. Put him behind the door, standing toward the sun.' Panayús was a policeman and had a revolver with all its chambers loaded. The shaman asked for it, whistled a tune, snapped the cock, walked toward the boy and then round the fireplace, then cocked the gun and

shot at the boy. The boy was scared but not hurt; in the door no bullet hole was to be seen. 'Do you believe me now? I'll show you again.' He asked for a blanket and let the boy lead him. The informant's mother was cooking while his father was outside and also saw it. The shaman covered himself with the blanket and stretched it out, led by the boy. Panayús shot him between the shoulders. There was a little ripple on the blanket but no hole. He shot again with the same result. Close by the door, only a few feet away, he shot again: there were marks on the blanket but no hole. Then Panayús believed in the shaman's power."

Lowie [1924:295] gives two more examples of such powers: "The idea that there were bullet-proof men also obtained among the Wind River Shoshoni, the one-time war chief Pitu being cited as an example of one through whom bullets would not pass. Another Man, called Big New Percé, was often knocked down by bullets but would get up with nothing worse than a blue spot on his body."

Lowie [1910:45–46] provides another example among the Assiniboin, but in this case, the shaman also included a power display:

"The next performer was a man dressed in a bear-skin, holding a big knife in one hand, and a muzzle-loader in the other. He said, 'Anyone may take my gun and shoot me.' One man took the gun, which was (then) loaded. 'Put powder in the barrel, and drop a piece of lead in there.' The man obeyed. Then he was told to stand about ten yards off. The bear-man growled like a bear, and imitated a bear in his movements. The man pointed the gun at him, then the bear rushed on him, seized the gun, and with his knife, split it in two. Then he put the two halves together again, and the gun was as good as ever. Next, the performer again ordered the man to take the gun and shoot at him from the same place. He stripped, and began growling like a bear. He walked up to the man and bade him shoot at the fourth dash. When the bear-man rushed at his opponent the fourth time, he was shot above the navel. The barrel of the gun dropped. The blood began to ooze. The other shamans covered the performer with robes, and began singing over the prostrate form, saying that he was merely displaying his power. They danced around. Suddenly, the dead man made a movement. One man raised his robe. A fire was burning near-by. The bear-man rose, pointed at his wound, growled like a bear, jumped around, picked up a handful of fire, rubbed it on his wound, and fell to coughing, until he coughed up the bullet shot into him. They kept singing for a while, finally the performer walked off."

Bullroarer

A sound-making device used by shamans that consists of a flat board tied to the end of a string. The unattached end of the string is held in one's hand while the device is swung around the head. The sound emitted resembles a rush of wind. They are often used in rain-making ceremonies. Also called a rhombus (see entry), whizzer.

Buówin

Micmac, *Canadian Eastern Woodlands*
Also: booöin. Shaman. By the early twentieth century, shamanism had fallen into disrepute among the Micmac, and all *buówin* were considered evil-doers; even to speak of their activities was considered evil. This term is also used to refer to anything that cannot be explained, but this may be a recent linguistic development. The word probably stems from *bu(o)*, meaning "mystery," and *in*, meaning "person." Another term for shaman known to contemporary Micmac is *gínap*.

Little is known about how Micmac shamans acquired their powers. Contemporary informants from the Micmac report that the power comes from self-induced dreams [Johnson 1943:63]. Hagar [1896:172] reports that shamans obtain their powers in three ways:

"It may be imparted by the little people . . . or by the discovery of a certain mystic herb. . . . But generally, when a Micmac wished to gain this power, he must, while keeping his object a secret, go into the woods alone and dwell there. His camp must be constructed to shelter two, and in all his equipments [sic] he must likewise provide for two. Even at his meals he must set apart an equal share for an expected visitor. At length he will find his food already cooked, upon his return

to camp, and soon after he will begin to observe a faint and shadowy being flitting in and out of his wigwam. Gradually he will see this being more and more clearly, until it grows as plainly visible as any man. Then the two will become friends and companions, and the Micmac will receive the gift of magical power."

Buówinudi

Micmac, *Canadian Eastern Woodlands*
Variations: *booöinwadagan, booöwinode.* The shaman's supernatural powers.

Busk Ceremony

Seminole, *Southeast*
An annual ceremony held each spring to renew the sacred medicine bundles. There are six such medicine bundles among the Seminole, and each one is cared for by a different medicine man. The existence and proper treatment of these bundles are considered essential for the existence and continued well-being of the Seminole themselves. Thus, the Busk Ceremony is their most important religious ceremony as well as their main social event. Each person in the nation is associated with a certain bundle through his or her membership in a clan, and each person attends the Busk Ceremony for his or her particular bundle.

Each bundle contains a collection of power objects, most of which are associated with curing wounds and attaining superiority in warfare. The keeper of the bundle displays the contents during each Busk Ceremony. When the keeper dies, a new keeper, often a relative, is appointed as the new guardian of the bundle.

The famous medicine man Josie Billie was the keeper of one such bundle, the Tiger (puma) clan bundle, from 1937 to 1944, but he gave it up when he was baptized a Christian [Sturtevant 1960].

Buxantï

Southern Paiute, *Basin*
See *puaxantï.*

Buyabu'ú

Tewa, *Southwest*
An informal healing ceremony. It is conducted in cases of minor illness and requires only one sha-

man, called the *Ke* (meaning Bear man, although a woman can also become a Bear). The ceremony requires no formalized request on the part of the patient and no special preparations, such as setting up an altar. The treatment is brief and simple. The Bear begins by touching the patient to "feel" the sickness. This is often followed by massaging the patient with circular motions while the Bear recites sacred prayers. Sometimes the Bear also chews herbs and then spits them on the afflicted part of the patient's body. The procedure may also include sucking out a stone or some other object from the patient's body. The treatment is repeated four times over a period of four days.

Cadekwcrache kaihweyoni
Cayuga, *Northeast*
The eight-day midwinter ceremony. The third and fourth days of this ceremony are reserved for treating illnesses by the various Cayuga medicine societies. See *eyondwanshgwut* for details.

Calumet
Sacred pipe. On first contact, the French used this term to refer to the sacred pipe, but over time, it was used in the literature to refer to any pipe. Springer [1981:n.1:230] states that the word comes from the medieval French *chalemel* and later *chalumeau*, meaning "reed"; Hultkrantz [1973:24] states that it is a French word taken over from the Latin word *calamus*, also meaning "reed." When these pipes were first reported by the Jesuits among the Miami in 1667 and the Illinois in 1673, the priests observed pipes that were made from a hollow cane decorated with feathers and the heads and necks of various birds. See *sacred pipe* for more details.

Can hotidan
Dakota, *Plains*
Tree dweller; a supernatural elf who lives in a hollow stump. Skinner obtained from the Wahpeton branch a sacred bundle containing the wooden image of this elf housed in a boxlike hollow cottonwood tree. These wooden images are used during the Wahpeton (Dakota) Medicine Dance Society rituals, where the "owners of these images are able to make them dance magically during the rites of the society" [Skinner 1925a:71]. Painted near the top of the hollow tree, "in red, is a conventional figure of the thunderbird, inverted, which recent information says symbolizes the Medicine Lodge Society; beneath is shown the incised and painted head of a buffalo bull, symbolic of courage; and under that, a coiled serpent, incised and colored with yellow ocher. These undoubtedly have reference to the various supernatural powers granted the owner by his dream guardians" [Skinner 1925a:69].

Cangcega
Lakota, *Plains*
Drum. Shamans use drums to accompany their medicine songs during healing ceremonies. Often a ceremonial assistant does the drumming. The drums are usually small in size and have a skin stretched over both sides of a wooden frame. They are beaten with a rattle or a drumstick, called *cangcegaicabu* [Buechel 1970:115].

Canli wapahta

Lakota, *Plains*

Tobacco ties or tobacco offerings. They are found at nearly every Lakota ceremony and represent the prayers of the participants. Each offering consists of a small, colored piece of pure cotton cloth that is about 1 inch square. The colors used and the order in which they are used differ from ceremony to ceremony and from individual to individual. Most often, the only colors used are those representing the four cardinal directions (red, yellow, white, and black) and earth (green) and sky (blue). A small pinch of tobacco is placed in the square of cotton cloth as one says a prayer. The four corners are then pinched together, forming a small packet for the tobacco. This

A "tree dweller" (left) and "hollow tree."

packet is finally tied to a cotton string, and the process is repeated. The number of ties placed on the string also differs from ceremony to ceremony. For a sweat lodge purification ceremony, one might make 7 ties on a string, whereas for a vision quest, one usually makes 405 ties. However, the ceremonial number required may differ from shaman to shaman. For example, "for doctoring meetings, Kills Ree prescribes fifty packets in the short string and 250 in the long string; for other meetings he prescribes respectively twenty and 96. Felix Green prescribes respectively 125 and 650 packets. Other supplicants in the meeting may bring strings of four, seven, or ten *canli wapahta* as offerings to the spirits and to indicate their desire to ask or speak in the meeting" [Kemnitzer 1970:68].

The main purpose of preparing these offerings is to focus one's mind and heart on the ceremony. The preparation of a string of 405 ties requires several hours of concentrated effort. The person making them should be by himself in a quiet place and should not speak to others during this time. Most often, the person sponsoring the ceremony makes the necessary number, but others may help the sponsor. During the ceremony in which the offerings are used, the spirits read the prayers contained in them. Thus, the strings are often referred to as a rosary.

Cantojuha

Lakota, *Plains*

The skin bag in which a sacred pipe is stored. Such containers are about 18 inches in length, depending on the length of the pipe stem, and are usually decorated with beadwork or porcupine quills. The term translates to "heart bag."

Catches, Pete

Lakota, *Plains*

A prominent medicine man during the mid-twentieth century. When ritually addressed, his name was *Petaga Yuha Mani*, "He Walks with Coals of Fire" [Amiotte in Gill 1983:91]. He was a Sun Dance leader during the 1960s and 1970s. His medicine for healing was from the Eagle, and he held regular Eagle Power night-sings. During the 1970s, he also began to conduct peyote ceremonies, although he had formerly disapproved of its use.

Pete Catches was most unusual in that he was raised in an orphanage and attended a Catholic mission school. Afterward, he became a catechist for the church for five years. Eventually, he acquired his shamanic powers and abilities through the tutelage of two older shamans named Good Horse and Frank Good Lance. Over the years, he gradually became more and more traditional. He ceased being a catechist and began to change white practices to Lakota ones. He stopped allowing recordings and observations to be made of his ceremonies and even began to refuse to ride in automobiles [Lewis 1980a].

One of his healing ceremonies was the Eagle Pipe or Eagle Medicine Ceremony. He used it to cure tuberculosis, gallbladder problems, and many other ailments [Zimmerly 1969:53].

Catlin, George

George Catlin was born in Wilkes-Barre, Pennsylvania, on 27 July 1796. He trained as a lawyer but later abandoned that career to take up painting. By 1830 he had begun traveling in remote regions to paint Native Americans and eventually became an amateur ethnologist. He feared the extermination of native people and feverishly sought to record their lifeways. In 1836 he became the first white person to see the singular site in Minnesota where many different Native Americans gathered to quarry a particular red stone for their pipe bowls. Later, this mineral was named catlinite after him, and the site was named Pipestone. He traveled throughout the Midwest and Pacific Coast regions over the years and even traveled to South America to paint. His obsession with painting caused him to become bankrupt by 1846, but he continued his work until his death on 23 December 1872. Many of his paintings are the only records of Native American ceremonies. His best-known written works are *Letters and Notes on the Manners, Customs, and Condition of the North American Indians* (1841), *Life among the Indians* (1861), and *O-kee-pa: A Religious Ritual* (1867).

Cecene

Wailaki, *California*
See *keteu*.

Ceseko

Menomini, *Great Lakes*
A class of shamans referred to earlier as Jugglers. They conduct their ceremonies, often referred to as the Shaking Tent Ceremony, in a small birch-bark lodge. Payments are made to the shaman prior to conducting the healing ceremony. When disease is attributed to soul loss, the shaman tries to coax the patient's soul to return to the shaman, who catches it in a small wooden cylinder. The cylinder is then attached to the patient's body for four days, giving the soul time to reenter the body. In other cases, when the illness is diagnosed as the intrusion of some foreign object into the body, it is removed by sucking. These objects can take all sorts of forms, with a witch's arrow being one of the more common ones.

Hiram Calkins, a visitor to the Menomini in 1851, reported his observations on a typical *ceseko* ritual:

"He usually performs after dark, in a wigwam (shaking-tent lodge) just large enough to admit of his standing erect. This lodge or wigwam is tightly covered with mats, so as entirely to exclude all light and the prying curiosity of all outsiders. . . . He first prepares himself in his family wigwam by stripping off his clothing. Then he emerges singing, and the Indians outside join him in the sun with their drums, and accompany him to the lodge, which he enters alone. Upon entering, the lodge commences shaking violently, which is supposed by the Indians outside to be caused by the spirits. The shaking of the lodge produces a great noise by the rattling of bells and deer's hoofs fastened to the poles of the lodge at the top, and at the same time three voices are distinctly heard intermingled with this noise. One is a very hoarse voice, which the Indians are made to believe is that of the Great Spirit; another is a very fine voice, represented to be that of a Small Spirit, while the third is that of the medicine man himself . . . the Great Spirit converses in a very heavy voice to the lesser spirit, unintelligibly to the conjurer, and the lesser spirit interprets it to him (the shaman), and he communicates the intelligence (what the spirit said) to his brethren without. The ceremony lasts about three hours … (the shaman) comes out in a high state of perspiration" [Spindler 1970:189–190].

Chalchihuitl

Apache, *Southwest*
Ground turquoise, used by all Apache shamans. It marks the carrier as a qualified healer and is sprinkled on the patient during a healing ceremony.

Chantways

Navajo, *Southwest*
Ceremonies of the Navajo Nation. With regard to human health, there are over 60 chantways for blessing, curing, and purification. The blessing ceremonies are used to safeguard individuals and their material world. They serve as a form of preventive medicine. Central is the Blessingway, which sets the pattern for all other rituals. The

Amateur ethnologist George Catlin traveled throughout the Pacific Coast and Midwest regions documenting Native American ceremonies in his paintings. He painted this Blackfoot medicine man, draped in a bearskin, in 1832.

curing ceremonies form the core of Navajo healing. They are known as the Holyway rituals and form the largest group of chants. They are used to treat illness traced to offenses against various supernaturals and holy people (spirits). In some classification systems, a second set of curing ceremonies is called Lifeway chants. These ceremonies are usually conducted to treat cases of bodily injury. Finally, the purification ceremonies, known as Evilway or Ghostway chants, purge beings, places, and objects of contact with dangerous beings (ghosts) and things (lightning, dreams of ghosts, taboo violations, and so forth). In cases of ghost illness, the Evilway rituals are employed to cure the patient. This is most prevalent in cases of witchcraft, when a disease has been projected into the body of a patient by an evil sorcerer or witch. In cases of ghost sickness, the Upward-reachingway, the original Ghostway, is used. The idea behind Evilway ceremonies is that it is necessary to avoid the dead, because contact with them can lead to disease or premature death.

Of these healing ceremonies, Gill [1983:108] states:

"It must be recognized that the ceremonials are primarily religious acts which serve to reveal the power and knowledge of a way of life to the Navajo people. I believe that the therapeutic and prophylactic effects of a ceremonial on a person are not actually most central and in many cases not even expected. It is common practice to perform a ceremonial for a person long after the physical aspect of their illness has been cured. It is increasingly common to perform a ceremonial for a person who has gone first to a hospital to receive treatment by European-American scientific medical practices. It is common to perform trial versions of ceremonials to see if a person responds. The full ceremonial must still be performed for him at a later time. Certain sicknesses if contracted in the summer may not be treated immediately because of seasonal restrictions on ceremonial ritual. Were the person to regain his health before the proper season, he still will have the ceremonial. There is mounting evidence that the ritual of the ceremonial is not solely tied to the cure of a physical or mental illness even though that is the stated motivation for many ceremonial performances."

The patient is first diagnosed by a medicine person. Once the diagnosis is made, the proper chantway to cure that particular illness is called for.

Chanunpa
Lakota, *Plains*
Sacred pipe. All Lakota shamans have such a pipe, which plays a central role in every healing ceremony. Once a pipe is made, it becomes activated only via a special ceremony in which the spirits take the pipe and touch it to the original sacred pipe brought to the Lakota by the White Calf Buffalo Woman. This original pipe, called the *Ptehincala Chanunpa*, is still in their possession and is currently being held by the Looking Horse family. The original pipe is made from the leg bone of a buffalo calf; pipes currently in use consist of a stone bowl, usually made of catlinite, and a wooden stem, usually made of alder. Because the bundle in which the original pipe is kept also contains other pipes, there has been some confusion in the literature about what it looks like. For instance, one published report erroneously contended that the original pipe was a T-shaped bowl with a quill-covered stem.

Charisma
The power manifest in a shaman. In its disembodied and impersonal form, supernatural power is called mana, but when mana manifests itself through a shaman, it is often referred to as charisma. The greater the supernatural power of the shaman, the greater his or her charisma. There are many theories concerning the nature of the shaman's charisma. For example, Aberle [1966:229] contends that "variations in amount of charisma . . . are correlative with amounts and kinds of unpredictability and uncontrollability."

Cherry Necklace
Hidatsa, *Plains*
An early nineteenth-century shaman who received his healing abilities from the otter. The following account from around the 1840s is of a healing ceremony performed by Cherry Necklace on Four Bears—one of the war chiefs at Knife

A dancer holds the sacred items used in the Nightway chant. Ceremonies of the Navajo Nation, called chantways, play an integral role in maintaining and restoring both physical and spiritual health.

River after 1837—who had been shot in a battle with the Assiniboin:

"Then One Buffalo went to Cherry Necklace with the pipe and asked him to doctor Four Bears. Cherry Necklace instructed One Buffalo to bring in four of the round hand-drums. Then he dressed in his medicine objects, the otter, and went to Four Bears' lodge where all the people were gathered. He said to the people, `Do not let any dogs into the lodge for that is a rule when I doctor. If a dog gets in, my patient will die.' The Waterbusters (clan) selected one of their members to sit at the door and keep the dogs out.

"Four young men were selected to use the round hand-drums and sing the holy songs with Cherry Necklace. Then he said to the people, 'Go over to the river bank and see how I am going to do this.'

"Cherry Necklace and Four Bears were naked with only an otter skin on Cherry Necklace's head. They went to the river where Four Bears was led into the water until they were in the water to the depth of Four Bears' belt where he was wounded. Cherry Necklace took down the otter skin and wet it all over and said to the people, 'I am not holy at all; I can't do anything by myself. But the otter is the one I get my powers from.'

"Cherry Necklace spoke to the otter saying, 'It is you who has the powers. You should cure this man so the people can see with their own eyes what you can do.' Then he sang the Otter song.

"He dipped the otter skin under the water and when he took his hand away the second time the otter came up on the other side of Cherry Necklace and swam over to Four Bears, touching the spot where he was wounded. When the otter backed away from the wound, blood came out. Then the otter swam to Four Bears' back and did the same thing. The otter did that four times and then Cherry Necklace said, 'I am glad that this wounded man is going to be healed.'

"Cherry Necklace instructed Four Bears to wash his head in the river and drink a little water. Then the clansmen helped him back to his lodge where Cherry Necklace continued to sing the holy songs. It was not long until he was walking about again. Cherry Necklace was highly re-

spected, for he had succeeded in saving the life of a great war leader" [Bears Arm in Bowers 1965: 256–257].

Chgalyic
Kato, *California*
One of three classes of doctors. Although not healers per se, they restore victims of "outside people." The "outside people," known as *taikehañ*, are spirits that are black and of small stature. When encountered, most often in the night, they scare people.

The *chgalyic* are also adept at predicting the future. They obtain their information via dreams.

The other two classes of doctors are the *etien* (see entry) and the *nachulna* (see entry) [Loeb 1934a:38–39].

Chitina Joe
South Alaska Eskimo, *Arctic Coast*
An Ugalakmiut shaman who lived around the turn of the twentieth century in the village of Eyak along the Copper River delta near the entrance of Prince William Sound. Because he had died by the 1930s, when ethnographic data about the Ugalakmiut (also called the Eyak Indians) were being recorded, only secondhand accounts of his activities are available. He was described as being "a great big fellow" that everybody liked, although he was "kind of goofy." He was known to have cured many people. One such account is as follows:

"Nick Chimowitski was sick. He had some kind of pain or cold. His mother-in-law wanted to call in Chitina Joe. Nick finally agreed and Joe was sent for. He came in and said: 'Nobody laugh now!' Silvester and some other young fellows were sitting around, nearly bursting with suppressed laughter. Joe had a basin of water brought and had a hot fire made in the stove. He walked around the patient four or five times with the beer glass (one of his power objects) full of water. Then he set the beer glass on the floor and placed his forked alder stick (one of his power objects) beside it. He placed his hands on Nick's head, then wiped them together. He blew on them clasped together over the fire. He stroked Nick's back from his head down to the end of his spine, then repeated the motions of blowing on his hands over the fire. Then he stroked Nick's sides from his head down to his ribs, and repeated the motions over the fire. Then he danced five times around the beer glass with the eagle feather (one of his power objects) in his hand, while he sang. Then he took a sip out of the beer glass and made Nick drink some. This was repeated five times. Nick recovered completely next day and gave Joe $5. Joe never asked payment in advance" [Birket-Smith and Laguna 1938:224].

It is reported that Chitina Joe passed his shamanic powers on to Johnny Stevens, who used the same beer glass, forked alder stick, and eagle feather in his healing ceremonies.

Cicigwan
Otchipwe, *Canadian Eastern Woodlands*
A rattle used to accompany the singing of the shaman. The rattle is made from thin strips of wood that are bent around to form the shape of a tin can. Each end of the hollow cylinder is then covered with another piece of thin wood, and a 5/8-inch-diameter stick is inserted through the center of both ends, projecting out one end by about 5 inches to form the handle. The rattle is painted half blue and half red along the perpendicular axis [Cooper 1936:25], that is, its right and left sides.

Cicigwun
Montagnais, *Canadian Eastern Woodlands*
A disclike rattle used by Naskapi shamans. It is made by sewing a double covering of caribou-skin parchment over a circular hoop made of maple. The hoop is about 1/2 inch wide and 6 inches in diameter. A handle is formed by allowing an extension of the hoop to project straight out. The handle may be carved on its margins, painted red, or decorated with ribbons. Sometimes this rattle is substituted for a drum, or it can be used as a drumbeater [Speck 1935:175].

Cigigwan
Chippewa, *Canadian Eastern Woodlands*
The drum used by a shaman during a healing ceremony. He uses it to accompany his medicine

songs sung over the patient [Hilger 1951:88]. The drum is made by stretching an untanned deer skin over both sides of a 2-inch-wide circular band of wood about 7 inches in diameter. Inside the drum are placed two sections of a long bone—any bone that contained marrow—of an animal. During the ceremony, the shaman either beats the drum with two small drumsticks or uses it as a rattle.

Coffee Charlie
Paviotso, *Basin*
A shaman. The following account was given to Lowie [1924:294] by Annie Lowry:

"Coffee Charlie was once doctoring his own boy, four years old, who was very sick and had been given up. The boy suddenly said, 'Do you see a little bird on my head?' Coffee Charlie told him there was nothing there, but the boy insisted that a bird was there, chirping, and the bird was saying to him, 'Little boy, you won't die, you will live.' Coffee Charlie doctored him, and he lived. On another occasion Coffee Charlie doctored Annie Lowry's son, who had been given up by the white physician. Coffee Charlie used a stick about four feet long, carefully smoothed, and sprinkled with white clay, and with an eagle (?) feather at one end. This was set at the patient's head; the idea of the clay was that it would cause moisture all over the patient's body. The shaman went into a trance, then the boy was placed on him so that the pits of their stomachs were together, then the boy was taken away by his mother. Before this he shook his rattle; at first the sound seemed far away, but gradually it got closer and closer. The boy at first did not recognize his mother, but did a little later. He recovered."

Common Faces
Iroquois, *Northeast*
Spirits that live everywhere in the forest and are either hunchbacked or crippled below the waist; one of the two main classes of False Faces. Their disability is emulated by dancers wearing masks during healing ceremonies. The dancers usually carry either a hickory bark or turtleshell rattle, but some carry only a staff or stick. The Common Faces have their own dance and healing song, but

like the other False Faces, they cure by picking up hot coals and blowing the ashes on the patient. The other class of False Faces is the False-Face Company.

Conjurati
Medicine men; a term used in the early literature on Native Americans.

Conjuring
Prior to the twentieth century, used in the literature to refer either to the activities of a shaman or to the Native American method of healing and treating the sick [Riggs 1893:216].

Conjuring complex
Another name for the Shaking Tent Ceremony (see entry) that is widely practiced in many different forms throughout the Great Lakes and Plains areas.

Conna
Caddo, *Plains*
See *konah*.

Corn pollen
Navajo, *Southwest*
Corn pollen is central to all Navajo ceremonies. Every shaman carries corn pollen, and no shaman would undertake a healing ceremony without it. Corn pollen is associated with Changing Woman, who created the Navajo and gave them corn pollen as a means of contacting her. In drawings of Changing Woman, she is dressed in corn pollen. There are six corn pollen spirits that act as intermediaries between Changing Woman and the Navajo people.

As with healing herbs, corn pollen is gathered in a ritualistic manner and is considered to be a powerful element. "It (corn pollen) is inherently powerful.... It is so powerful that we don't let just

Ernest C. Becenti, a Navajo medicine man, holds corn pollen taken from his pouch above his head as he performs a blessing. Many shamans of the southwest believe corn pollen to be the most powerful medicine.

anybody collect it. It has got to be collected by an unwed maiden . . . usually it is a virgin. . . . She goes out very early at the break of dawn. . . . During the course of the time she is collecting it, usually they will have a 'medicine man' singing . . . maybe at the dwelling, and maybe right among the corn. He sings the Corn Pollen song and the Talking God song. This is because even though it has power of itself, this will give it more strength. And also it gives the girl that much more strength" [Raitt 1987:524–525].

Corn pollen is often used during prayers. In fact, the act of strewing pollen without any accompanying words is considered a prayer by the Navajo. Traditional Navajo use pollen on a daily basis, sprinkling it during morning and evening prayers—usually at sunrise and dusk. Corn pollen is sprinkled on persons as a blessing and to empower them. For example, newborns are sprinkled with pollen. Corn pollen is used to purify ritual objects much in the same way that sage smoke is used by other Native American cultures. For example, corn pollen is applied to the four directions of a hogan before it is used for a ceremony. In fact, it is applied to almost everything connected with a ceremony, as Wyman [1970:31] points out: "It is applied to everything for consecration and sanctification, to the hogan, to the patient, to prayer sticks, to dry paintings and ceremonial paraphernalia, to the suds of the bath, to cornmeal mush to be eaten ceremonially, to the spectators."

Navajo healing is based on the premise that a person's illness is caused by the individual's being out of harmony with life, and sprinkling a person with corn pollen helps reestablish that harmony. In their ceremonies, corn pollen is said to be pure and immaculate. As such, this substance has the power to drive off the forces that produce disharmony. In fact, it is so powerful that it is often carried by individuals simply for good luck. Within the context of healing, many Navajo shamans claim that corn pollen is their most powerful medicine—not in the sense of a plant used for healing, but in the sense of its ritualistic power. For example, during the Blessingway Ceremony, the application of corn pollen to the hogan being used for the ritual transforms that structure into the original hogan

in which Changing Woman first experienced Blessingway. All the beauty (blessing) that comes into the hogan during the ceremony is attributed to corn pollen. Corn pollen also serves as a bridge between humans and spirits; it is spoken of as "the door path of Talking God." Finally, it is seen as a food for spirits and as a healing food for humans.

Cornmeal
Pueblo, *Southwest*

Cornmeal is used in many different ritual ways in these corn-centered, agricultural cultures, including (1) to draw lines that represent paths along which spirits travel or paths that lead people to places where the presence of the spirits is actualized, (2) to draw lines on the ground to demarcate sacred spaces, (3) to accompany prayers to the rising sun, (4) as a reinforcement for prayers in general, (5) to consecrate sacred objects such as prayer sticks and kachina masks, and (6) to place it in the mouth of a corpse before burial [Raitt 1987].

Coyote Woman
Mandan, *Plains*

A shaman around the turn of the eighteenth century. Good Bear, her granddaughter, gives the following account of her healing procedures:

"She (Coyote Woman) began doctoring the sick people the way she had formerly been instructed by the bear (clan). She examined her patients first to learn what caused the illness. Some were made ill by snakes or bugs in their bodies; others from the influence of evil spirits; others from the loss of god (soul-loss?). She had a medicine song and a medicine root. If she found the pain was in one spot, she sucked with her mouth or a hollow horn, sometimes drawing out long slim worms or maggots of different colors. She pressed the stomach for pains located in the stomach or bowels and blew chewed-up cedar bark over the patient; when a person had a headache, she let out blood from the forehead. . . .

"Certain doctors were called upon to help women laboring in childbirth. Some of the women of the house would fill a pipe and place it before the woman they wished to act as midwife or doctor (i.e., make a formal request). The doctor gave instructions which must be carried out and set the price which was for the number of days she would serve. If she failed to help the patient in that time, she left to give another a chance to cure the patient. If the doctor failed to cure the patient in the time designated, the relatives might again place the pipe before her, and she was obliged to remain longer. Extra goods were then paid for the additional time. When the doctor entered the lodge where the woman in labor lived, she ordered all the men and small children out, and women then in their menstrual period were asked to stay away from the lodge. Should any woman during her menstrual period come into the lodge, sage was immediately burned in four places in the lodge, two fires being made of sage painted red and two of white sage. If this was not done, it was believed that the patient might die. A special song was sung during the burning of the sage, for which the doctor received an additional fee. The doctor called in two young girls while the four fires were burning and asked them to doctor the patient in her stead by singing the medicine songs and dancing around the sick person. At the end of the songs, the two girls walked to the sick person and said, 'You are well now,' and left the lodge. The doctor then continued to administer to the sick woman" [Good Bear in Bowers 1950:176].

Cupping instrument

A device used by sucking shamans to extract the disease (or disease object) from a patient's body. It is usually a tubelike device, often made from a buffalo horn. One type is from the Arapaho and was made from a buffalo horn and incised with symbols. When used by Arapaho shamans, "in case of rheumatism or similar ailments, a hole is cut in the skin, and the hollow horn set over the cut. The horn is then supposed to suck the wound of itself, dropping off . . . when full of blood" [Kroeber 1907:439]. Among the Arapaho, the hole at the top end is sometimes plugged with medicine.

Curtis, Natalie

Natalie Curtis was born in New York City on 26 April 1875. She trained for a career as a concert pianist but became interested in Native American music during a visit to her brother's home in Arizona in 1900. She began recording Native American songs, which resulted in her 1905 publication *The Indians' Book*, which contained 200 songs from 18 Native American cultures. She eventually persuaded President Theodore Roosevelt not only to lift the ban on Native American music and language but also to enact the policy of preserving and encouraging Native American music, art, and poetry. She lectured extensively on the preservation of Native American culture. She was killed when a car struck her in Paris on 23 October 1921.

Cushing, Frank Hamilton

Frank Cushing was born in Northeast, Pennsylvania, on 22 July 1857. In 1875 he was hired as an assistant in ethnology at the Smithsonian, and the next year he was made a curator in ethnology. He was a protégé of John Wesley Powell, head of the Bureau of American Ethnology. In 1879 he traveled on a museum expedition to the Southwest and stayed with the Zuni for the next two and a half years; in 1881 he was initiated into the first order of the Priests of the Bow. He was the first anthropologist to conduct among the Native Americans what is known as participant observation, in which one becomes accepted in another culture and lives its lifeways to better understand it. As such, Cushing became an advocate for Zuni interests, which eventually resulted in his termination on the study. He also instigated a change in the meaning of the word "culture" in American anthropology: from civilizations or societies as entities to an integrated and internally consistent social and material whole. Cushing died at the age of 42 on 10 April 1900, before publishing his complete findings on the Zuni. However, Cushing remained faithful to the Zuni for the rest of his life and never published the secret ritual knowledge learned from the Zuni priests, nor did he leave behind any such field notes. His *Zuni Folktales* (1901) and *Zuni Breadstuff* (1920) were both published after his death.

Cusiyaes

Diegueño, *California.*
See *kwisiyai.*

Cuwaha

Zuni, *Southwest*
A form of purification called "wiping off" that is used in healing ceremonies. The shaman

expectorates on a piece of cedar bark, a corn husk, or a prayer stick. It is folded and the packet is waved around his head four times in a counter-clockwise direction. It is then taken outside toward the east for burial.

Cxwneam
Lummi, *Northwest Coast*
Shaman [Stern 1934:75]. Shamans, both male and female, acquire their healing powers through spirit helpers. A shaman often has more than one spirit helper, giving him or her more power to cure patients. In this manner, shamans become specialists at curing certain types of illnesses.

Illnesses are most often diagnosed as being due to either the harmful actions of a sorcerer or soul loss. A shaman begins by using his or her spirit to find the illness. Then the shaman proceeds as follows:

"When the cause of the illness is discovered, the medicine man becomes violent and frenzied, crawling rapidly and jerkedly along the ground as if animated by some unseen force with which he is struggling. He indicates where the force is to be found and when he becomes more composed, if he feels equal to the task he tries unaided to break up its influences. As this is considered a very difficult task for a single person, the help of other medicine men is often solicited. . . . The medicine man having this spirit, falls into a trance while the other medicine men watch over him fearing that he might die. As he lies on the ground he mutters an account of what his spirit is doing in its effort to destroy the influence of the whirlpool or other forces, telling how or why it affected the family. When he finally gets the force entirely under control, the person is healed and the family is free from its evil influence. . . . At times he places the (disease-causing) spirit in a bundle of cedar-bark and shoots an arrow through the bark, piercing the spirit in the same manner. At other times he destroys the spirit by placing it in a rock which has been heated and then breaking the rock by pouring water on it. Sometimes he holds the spirit in his hands and twists it as if he were breaking a long object after which he throws the parts in opposite directions or reunites them in a reverse position, returning the spirit to the medicine man who caused the illness. . . . The medicine man sometimes holds the spirit he has discovered over the fire, after which he releases it so that it goes back to its master and makes him ill, occasionally even bringing on blindness" [Stern 1934:76–77].

In treating cases of soul loss, the shaman travels with his helping spirit in search of the patient's lost soul, called *selee* by the Lummi. Then he proceeds as follows:

"After a medicine man identifies the soul, he returns it to the patient. He sings his spirit song, and rubs his hands over the patient's body, as if caressing it, preparing the latter for what is to follow. He then places hands upon the patient's head and repeatedly breathes forcefully through an opening between the thumbs and palms of his hand, causing a warm feeling to suffuse the patient, making him sense that he is under the influence of the medicine man. The medicine man may also massage the back and the breast of the patient, vibrating the latter to the rhythm of his song or he may vibrate the patient's head with his hands or rub his thumbs or palms over the eyes of the patient. He then takes the soul in his cupped hands and sings a song especially sung for the return of souls. While the song is continued by others, he approaches the patient and when he reaches him he lifts his hands over the latter's head and, slowly bringing them down, places the soul either over the breast of the patient or over one of his shoulders or on one of his sides. He then sweeps his hands over the patient in a soothing way and when the song is finished the work is done" [Stern 1934:79–80].

Dadahnesesgi
Cherokee, *Southeast*
Evil shamans or sorcerers [Kilpatrick and Kilpatrick 1967b:4]; translates to "putter-in and drawer-out of them."

Daitino
Caddo, *Plains*
Also: *daitono*. Mescal-bean doctor [Parsons 1941:34]. (See *konah* for additional details.)

Damaagome
Achomawi, *California*
A shaman's helping spirit. Shamans obtained their helping spirits through vision quests in the nearby mountains along the Pit River. Jamie de Angulo [in Beck and Walters 1977:103] presents the following account of a healer who misused his *damaagome:*

"Yes, some of them *damaagome* is mean. When I started doctoring I tried a trick. I tried bringing my poison (power) to a hand-game. Now a doctor is not supposed to use his poison for gambling. It's against the rules. But I thought I was smart, see. I thought to hell with the rules. I do like white man, see. Well, in the middle of the game I got awful thirsty, and I get up and go to the spring, and I take a long drink of water, and I got awful dizzy and sick. I got cramps, I puke. . . . See, my *damaagome* he do that, he mad because I bring him to hand-game, not supposed to do that."

Dapic
Crow, *Plains*
The most famous *akúwecdìu* (wound doctor) of recent historical times, who practiced during the latter part of the nineteenth century. He acquired his powers during a three-day vision quest at a hot springs located near Thermopolis, Wyoming. A spirit took him into this spring, sang medicine songs for him, and gave him the name of Dapic. He returned to use the spirit of the water bull and the long otter to treat wounds. Lowie [1922:377–378] provides some details of a healing ceremony performed by Dapic on a warrior who had been brought back to camp with a bullet wound to the navel:

"In the morning the people formed two lines of spectators. They made the patient rest on a high pillow and several men sang for him. No person or dog was permitted to pass in front of him. The doctor had his wife and daughter wear a robe and with them he approached the door of the lodge, where the singing was going on continually. Dapic transformed himself into a bull and made a snorting noise over the patient, who rolled over. Then he bade the wounded man seize his tail and forthwith he was able to stand up as though well. Dapic led him to the water, re-assuming human shape on the way. He took him where the water reached up to his chest and then dived down alone. Before so doing, he whistled upstream, then downstream. The patient's blood flowed downstream, and he stood there for a long time awaiting the leech's return. His wound healed. Only the wounded man saw the doctor in buffalo shape."

Dapic always doctored wounds by treating the patient in chest-high water. If the patient needed to have a bullet or an arrowhead removed, he often used his otter spirit. He would hold "an otter in his hands, showing its teeth," then dive under the water with the patient, and after "four breaths he came out again and the otter had the bullet . . . [or] the arrow-head in its mouth" [Lowie 1922:377].

In preparation for a healing, Dapic would paint his body in accordance with instructions revealed to him by his spirit helpers. "Dapic alone was able to cure wounded men immediately; he hardly ever failed. However, in his later years he was smitten with blindness for breaking one of his spiritual patron's rules" [Lowie 1935: 66].

Dark Dance Ceremony
Seneca, *Northeast*
This ceremony, termed *Dewanondiissondaikta* in Seneca, is performed by one of their medicine societies—the Pygmy Society [Parker 1909:167]. The ceremony is conducted in total darkness and consists of 102 songs, divided into four sections. A water drum and a horn rattle are used for keeping time to the songs. The spirits of this medicine society join in the singing. The purpose of the ceremony is to transfer the power of the spirit members (called *hotcine'gada*) to charms, which are kept by people. The most important class of these spirits is the little people, called *Jongä'on*—sometimes translated as "elves" or "pygmies." These *Jongä'on* are thought to be "next to the people" in importance. Other spirit members of the society

include Blue Panther, the herald of death; Exploding Wren; White Beaver; Corn-bug; Sharplegs; Little Dry Hand; and Great Naked Bear [Parker 1909:168-169]. Some of the charms obtained from these spirits are for benevolent purposes, and others are used for evil.

Dasan
Pomo, *California*
A *dja minawan* (see entry), or outfit doctor, around the turn of the twentieth century. These healers specialized in treating sickness caused by becoming frightened by seeing a spirit. Dasan's costume "consisted of a stiff basketry cap, with little feathered sticks extending in all directions from it. The basket extended down over the face. The performer's body was naked and painted with red, white, and black stripes. He wore no belt. In his mouth he carried a large elderberry wood whistle, which he blew constantly" [Loeb 1934a:11]. Of his curing technique, Loeb [1934a:11] reports:

"Dasan came running chased by four singers. He entered and backed out four times. Then he went around the patient four times counterclockwise and four times clockwise. As he did this he kept blowing his whistle and shaking his throat with his hand, singing, 'Ah ah ah ah, hu u u u.' Dasan doctored with the stick (*hai detoi*), by laying it on the patient. Then he went around the patient four times and ran off. The people of the village threw dirt and sticks at the retreating figure, hissing, 'Sh-h-h.' By doing this they threw off disease from the village."

Dävéko
Kiowa-Apache, *Plains*
A renowned shaman who was born around 1818 and died in 1897 or 1898. Nothing is known of his early years other than that his father was also a shaman. He received his powers during a four-day vision quest during which "some medicine, something, like rattlesnake, like owl, like little whirlwinds, came toward him, causing the ground to tremble like an earthquake. . . . Dävéko could not recognize it. It was like the approach of a great storm; rains were coming, and there was a

great black cloud with a tail touching the ground. This was the small, soft turtle with the long tail that took pity on him" [McAllister 1970:37]. Thus he acquired powers from the snake, owl, and turtle. Thereafter he wore the rattles of a rattlesnake tied to his scalp lock. A typical account of his healing follows:

"Dävéko first sang his medicine song. Then his stepson, Sam, who was assisting him, sang. . . . When they sang it became foggy over the man who was sick. There was something in him. Dävéko put his mouth in the regions of the man's navel and sucked out a piece of tough skin as tough as that from a man's heel. The young man had not moved, but after Dävéko took that out the young man stirred. They sang again and the sick man wanted to be raised up. It was after sundown and getting dark. . . . They had been singing all day and he (Sam) was tired. He (Sam) went to bed. After he left, the sick man sat up and asked for water. They gave him a drink. Dävéko sang a *Klintidie* song. The sick man was sitting up and his friends were feeling good, so they all sang. . . . The next morning he was up and walking around in the tipi" [McAllister 1970:42].

In addition to sucking, Dävéko doctored by blowing water from his mouth onto his patients, a technique he had learned from his turtle spirit helper. He also used a deer-hoof rattle with the wing feathers of a swift hawk tied to it. He would use the feathers to clean out wounds. When looking for a disease object within a patient's body, he would use a black handkerchief; this enabled him to locate the object, which he then sucked out. In curing snakebites, he sucked out snake teeth from the wound. For horses that had been snakebitten, he would draw a circle with white clay above the wound and then rub white clay below this to take away the swelling. He was also versed in the use of certain herbs and roots.

In addition to his healing abilities, Dävéko was well known for the many power feats he could perform, including the ability to stand in the rain without getting wet, materialize objects

such as plumes and then eat them, and find lost persons or objects. He was rarely defeated in the bean gambling game, in which his opponents would try to guess in which hand he held a bean.

Dävéko was well paid for his services and was, for the most part, greatly feared. Many accused him of shooting sickness into people so that he could collect a healing fee.

Dawando
Seneca, *Northeast*
The Society of Otters, whose members are female. The purpose of the society is to appease the otter, which is the chief of the small water animals (including the fish) and is believed to be a powerful medicine animal. The society seeks to procure good health from this spirit. The society has no songs or dances; the women are organized simply to give thanks to the water animals and to retain their favor. However, when a person becomes ill as a result of abusing one of the water animals—such as killing a beaver without offering tobacco or being wasteful with fish—the women of the society go to the sick person's home and perform healing ceremonies on the patient. One aspect of the ceremony involves the ritual procurement of fresh water from a spring, which is then sprinkled on the patient [Parker 1909:171].

Day, David
Lakota, *Plains*
A shaman who practiced during the first half of the twentieth century, noted for his ability to cure paralysis. His helping spirit was a well-known Lakota elder spirit known as *Hunkala*. He used special herbs in his healings as well. His altar was made of ashes in a crescent shape, and he held his healing ceremonies in a lighted room, both unusual traits for a Lakota shaman.

Debwawendûnk
Ojibwa, *Canadian Eastern Woodlands*
A shaman described in 1910 as "an old member" of the *Midewiwin* (see entry) at the Bois Fort Reservation. His name translates to "eating noisily" [Densmore 1910:25]. Members of the *Midewiwin* were ranked into eight different grades, according

Debwawendûnk

to their healing powers. Powerful shamans were included in the last four "sky" grades, and Debwawendûnk was a member of the sixth degree. As such, he was considered to be a powerful healer.

Deer shaman
Term used by scholars for California Indian shamans. These shaman specialists are usually associated with animals and are responsible for controlling large game in the hunting territory. They are also associated with the ability to transform their shapes into other forms and are generally known to be skillful medical practitioners [Bean 1976].

Degiyagon oäno
Seneca, *Northeast*
The Buffalo Society, one of several Seneca medicine societies. During their ritual, the members dance in imitation of buffalo stamping off flies. This dance "stamps out" illness. A water drum and horn rattles are used to accompany the singing [Parker 1909:177].

Dek Setskéha
Cayuga, *Northeast*
The Chicken Dance, one of the Cayuga healing ceremonies in which anyone can participate. See *eyondwanshgwut* for details.

Deswadenyationdottu
Seneca, *Northeast*
The Woman's Society, one of several Seneca medicine societies. The purpose of the society is to procure good fortune and health for women. During the ceremony, the women dance and the men are singers. Horn rattles and water drums are used to accompany the singing and dancing [Parker 1909: 178].

Dewanondiissondaikta
Seneca, *Northeast*
See *Dark Dance Ceremony*.

Didahnvwisgi
Cherokee, *Southeast*
Also: *dinadahnvwisgi*. Medicine man among the Cherokee living in Oklahoma [Kilpatrick and Kilpatrick 1967b:4]; translates to "curer of them" or "those who cure them" [Kilpatrick and Kilpatrick 1967a:29]. Because the Cherokee were the only nation to develop writing (called Sequoyan, after its inventor), they are also the only Native American medicine men to have written down their sacred activities. Every medicine man had a small library of such manuscripts. "The literary motivation of them all is the same: magical sayings abound in archaisms, and tricky wording, and they are hard to remember" [Kilpatrick and Kilpatrick 1967b:4].

Disease
Disease is conceived of in a variety of ways throughout North America. Generally, it is believed to occur due to a lack of protection (that is, not using charms), the presence of some material object that has intruded into the body (usually via sorcery), or the absence of the free soul from the body. Disease is seen as being natural to human beings, and without the spirits' protection, one

will assuredly become ill on numerous occasions throughout one's life. An exception to this general view is found among the Winnebago, who believe that a spirit named Disease-Giver is the source of diseases.

In all Native North American cultures, disease is associated with the religious aspect of the society. This is due mainly to the fact that supernatural powers are, for the most part, associated with the causing and curing of diseases.

Disease-Giver
Winnebago, *Midwest*
The spirit who deals out life-giving powers from one-half of his body and death-giving powers from the other half. He also disseminates disease. Disease-Giver is a literal translation of the Winnebago word, but this probably does not convey the exact meaning [Radin 1923:168]. This spirit seems to be particular to the Winnebago; it is not found among other Siouan cultures nor among the Algonquin.

Dismemberment
Dismemberment is a common theme in Native American and other shamanism. Often, during a vision quest, a novice shaman experiences bodily dismemberment before encountering his spirit helper for the first time. This is tantamount to the novice facing his own death—a fear that he must overcome to succeed. For this reason dismemberment is most often associated with shamanic initiations. However, this theme is also often played out in shamanic rituals, especially among the Eskimo, where the shaman often cuts off his own head or that of the patient during a healing ceremony. The head is then reattached, and the cure is effected.

Diyi
Apache, *Southwest*
Doctor. Both males and females can become healers. To become a doctor, most young men and women seek supernatural helpers via fasts and vision quests at known power spots. In addition, some seek out successful shamans and pay to be trained by them. Such training usually entails at least a year of instruction. In the end, however,

each follows the instructions dictated by the spirits that come to them.

Unlike many of their neighbors, Apache shamans are not known to use any intoxicants during their rituals, and they are not formed into societies, as neighboring Navajo and Pueblo shamans are. One or two shamans are called upon to conduct a healing ceremony, and they are paid by the patient or his friends at the time the request is made. Each shaman has a sacred bundle, which is brought to the healing ceremony. The relatives and friends of the patient attend to the fire and help with the singing. When there is only one sick person, the ceremony consists exclusively of drumming and singing; in cases of epidemics, dancing is added. "There are allusions by several authorities to the necessity of confession by the patient before the efforts of the medicine-men can prove efficacious" [Bourke 1892:465].

During the ceremony, the shaman uses a special language known only to him. The patient is usually placed on a couch. The singing employs a trance induction and monotonous intonation, which often puts the patient to sleep [Bourke 1892:464]. In some cases, herbal remedies are administered to the patient, but most shamans rely on the healing songs given to them by their helping spirits. During the ceremony, the shaman applies cattail pollen, called *hoddentin* (see entry), to the patient's body. Typically, the "medicine-men in the intervals between chants applied this yellow powder to the forehead of the patient, then in the form of a cross upon his breast, then in a circle around his couch (upon which he laid), then upon the heads of the chanters and of sympathizing friends, and lastly upon their own heads and into their own mouths" [Bourke 1892:500]. In cases of object intrusion, the shaman sucks on the patient's body. If the patient dies, the shaman risks death at the hands of the patient's relatives unless he can demonstrate that a witch afflicted the patient.

Diyinne
Carrier, *Mackenzie-Yukon*
Shaman. In earlier times, they were called *nilkin* [Jenness 1943:564]. Initially, potential shamans

A Diyi medicine shirt.

are seized by a sickness known as medicine song sickness, in which the afflicted person lies inert and listless "in a state of dreamy phthisis" [Jenness 1943:559]. A knowledgeable shaman has to make a shamanic journey on behalf of the victim to recover his lost soul—that is, to stabilize the novice and imbue him with additional power. Thereafter, the novice is able to control the supernatural forces and becomes a shaman after a two- to three-month training period, which is usually spread out over one to two years. The shaman who cures the novice is not necessarily the same one who trains the novice. If the medicine song sickness is not treated, the victim will die.

From this account, it is obvious that by the twentieth century the Carrier had lost the older notion that a youth could obtain a helping spirit through a vision quest. That is, a person can no longer be the active agent in procuring a spirit helper but is chosen by the spirits themselves. If, after having a spirit dream, the person does not display the usual medicine song sickness, his spirit experience is considered to be too weak for him to become a shaman.

Because the Carrier differ among themselves as to the exact nature of this medicine song sickness, there are three different approaches to curing an afflicted novice. "One group of practitioners claimed to recover the shadow from its supernatural prison house; another to open the patient's eyes to his dreams and release his pent-up medicine song; while a third sought to discover and extract the incubating shadow (spirit), then either to reinsert it, if the patient was fitted to receive it again, or else to dispose of it in some other way" [Jenness 1943:560]. These various treatments result in differences in subsequent rituals as shamans.

Carrier shamans adorn costumes for their rituals. A costume includes "a coronet of grizzly-bear claws, a bone or skin image (bea) of his guardian spirit, animal or fish, to suspend from his neck, and a skin cloak, usually the hide of a bear or wolf" [Jenness 1943:560].

Once a shaman begins his practice, his first and foremost ability is to heal soul-loss illness and to cure patients whose sickness is caused by the same spirits possessed by the shaman.

Because different spirits cause different illnesses, Carrier shamans become specialists, and many different specialists are needed within a single community to cover all the possibilities. In earlier times, they treated object-intrusion sicknesses, but they eventually abandoned that concept. Today, sorcerers are said to steal the victim's shadow rather than sending an object into the victim's body.

When healing a patient, the shaman first makes a diagnosis. He seats himself beside the patient and proceeds according to the following account:

"[He] demanded a bowl of water, sipped up a mouthful and blew it out again to lubricate the passage of the 'sickness.' He then shook his rattle and chanted one of his dream, or medicine songs, in which the audience joined. Sipping up more water he chanted a second song, sometimes a third. Finally, he sat silent with his eyes closed, but with his mind searching out the innermost recesses of his patient's body to discern, if possible, the shadow. . . . If this was the doctor's diagnosis, he returned home, and during the night sent forth his own shadow to secure the release of the captive, or to regain it by force and lodge it for safekeeping in his body. In the morning he visited the patient again, proclaimed his success, and, dipping up a little water from a basin, sipped it into his mouth and spouted it over the sick man. The audience then drummed and chanted the doctor's medicine song while he shook his rattle and danced vigorously round the room. After several minutes he stopped, rapped himself from stomach to chest, vomited the errant shadow into his cupped hands, and, laying them on the patient's head, blew it into his body. Thus he restored the vital spark, dispelled the cause of the sickness, and set the patient on the road to health" [Jenness 1943:560–561].

The diagnosis is often better arrived at if the patient admits to some breech of taboo. To this end, the shaman thoroughly questions the patient before his introspection on the matter. Also, the shaman's healing abilities are thought to increase in accordance with the payment made by the patient's family.

Diyunanda kwa

Cayuga, *Northeast*

The Snow-Snake healing ceremony, in which any-one can participate. See *eyondwanshgwut* for details.

Diyúsodáyego

Cayuga, *Northeast*

The Dark Dance or Little Water Society, the members of which perform healing ceremonies. See *eyondwanshgwut* for details.

Dja minawan

Pomo, *California*

A special class of healers called outift doctors; translates to "person walk-over." These healers wear special costumes called *gula cuna*, which translates to "tool boat." According to Loeb [1934a:9–10],"the outfit doctor was peculiar to the Pomo. He cannot be described as a shaman in the proper sense of the word, either of the inspirational or non-inspirational variety, since he had no special contact with the supernatural." Outfit doctors, both males and females, inherit their outfits from their uncles or fathers. They receive instructions on the costume from their relatives but are also trained by the Pomo Kuksu cult. Their main function is the impersonation of spirits, and they are most frequently used to treat "frightsick" people—those who have been frightened by seeing a spirit. During their healing ceremonies, they use a special pole called *hai detoi* ("stick striped") made of madrona wood. "With his pole he pointed four times at the place in the patient's body where the pain was located. Then he laid the pole on the patient's body four times. Next he removed the feathers from the pole and left it standing upright by the sick man's house for four days. Then the ghost left" [Loeb 1934a:11]. When a person is frightened by thunder, these doctors treat the patient by whirling a bullroarer over the patient's head and then touching the patient's body with it in four places.

Djasakid, Djessakid

Ojibwa, *Canadian Eastern Woodlands*

See *jessakkid*.

Djesikiwinini

Otchipwe, *Canadian Eastern Woodlands*

Shamans who specialize in performing the Shaking Tent Ceremony (see entry). The tent is cylindrical in shape, with the top remaining open. Captain Edwards, the Indian agent at Kenora during the 1920s, witnessed one ritual in which the upright tent poles, which were about three inches in diameter, "bent at the top about one foot from the perpendicular during the shaking" [Cooper 1936:9–10].

Djigamágan

Micmac, *Canadian Eastern Woodlands*

Drum [Speck 1919:n.1:241]. S. T. Rand, in his *Micmac Dictionary,* also gives the word *bepkwejedaak* for drum.

Djutidro

Cayuga, *Northeast*

The healing ceremony performed by members of the Otter Society. See *eyondwanshgwut* for details.

Doctor Charley

Twana, *Northwest Coast*

A powerful Skokomish healer during the early twentieth century. He lived at the Twana village at the head of Hood Canal. He acquired his shamanic powers from the otter. His brothers Tenas Charley and Tyee Charley were also shamans who healed.

Doctor Mink

Cherokee, *Southeast*

The alias used by Olbrechts for the nineteenth-century shaman who wrote manuscript II of the Cherokee medicine formulas obtained by James Mooney. He died sometime prior to 1920. While doing fieldwork in 1926–1927, Frans Olbrechts received an account from her main interpreter of a typical healing procedure performed by Doctor Mink, called for by his half sister. This account shows the complexities involved in the diagnosis and prognosis of a patient (also see *adanöwiski*):

"Many years ago (1913) my cousin, Charlie, Je's son, was very ill; he was very poorly; he was just about to die. My mother was very sorry for her daughter and for her grandson, and she sent after Doctor Mink, asking him to come down to see what he could do. An evening, soon after, Doctor Mink came to our house and said he would spend the night. But my mother was anxious to know something about her grandson's illness and prepared the cloth and the beads (*adälön; s*ee entry). Mink examined with the beads, but he found that nothing could be done. My mother cried and was sorry because of her grandson; she got some more white cloth and two more white beads, and asked the medicine man to try again. He did, but again he said the boy could not recover. And again my mother put some more cloth and two more beads down, but still there was no hope. A fourth time she got cloth and beads and the medicine man examined once more; but again he found that the boy was very poor, and that he would die.

"I then proposed to go over the mountain to where the sick boy lived, and to go and see him anyway. We all went, and when we got there we found the boy unconscious.

"I asked the doctor if he would come to the river with me; we took a dipper which we filled with water, and when we got back to the house, we sprinkled some of it on the boy's face; I then went back to the river and poured the rest of the contents of the dipper away exactly where we dipped it from. When I came back, I asked Doctor Mink if he would examine with the beads again to see if the boy could be cured. I prepared cloth and the beads and I went with Mink to the edge of the river. He examined with the beads, but found there was no hope. I put down some more cloth and beads, but again the doctor found there was no help. I then suggested to change the boy's name. Charlie could die, but we would give him a new name; we would call him Alick. Mink then again examined with the beads, and he found that Alick was going to get better. They tried a fourth time, and again there was hope. I then got Mink to examine to see if he would be able to cure him; but he found he couldn't. Then he examined for another medicine man, and then for another, and another, and finally he found that Og could cure him. We then sent for Og to cure him. In the sick boy's house nobody was allowed to sleep that

night. Doctor Mink kept busy about the fire, working against the witches.

"Og came down every morning and every night; he did the curing, and Doctor Mink did the examining with the beads. Four days afterwards I went down to the river once more with Doctor Mink, and we found that in seven days Alick would be about, hunting. And so it was" [Mooney and Olbrechts 1932:67–68].

Dodd, Bobby
Northern Paiute, *Basin*
A shaman around the turn of the twentieth century who lived at Pyramid Lake. The following account was given by William Paddy of a healing ceremony in which Dodd retrieved the lost soul of a sick patient:

"Bobby Dodd's way of doctoring was good. He had the waterbabies for his helping spirits. . . . If a person was pretty sick, Bobby Dodd would go to heaven to try to bring the spirit back. First he would instruct the interpreter for two or three minutes. Then the interpreter would tell everybody what's going to happen and to start singing a special song the doctor used when he wanted to go after a spirit. Four or five men were told to stand in a circle, holding a rope. I held the rope one time. Bobby Dodd took his rattle and shook it, moving it up the middle of the sick person. Then he started singing and walking in a circle inside the rope from left to right. Every time around he'd stop where he planned to fall. He wasn't going to fall by the sick person because he figured if he fell and people didn't catch him, he wouldn't fall on the sick person. The rope was so he couldn't get out. If you are sick or dying, you can't catch your breath. Your spirit is going. Bobby Dodd walked around for about thirty seconds, then he'd start losing his breath. He breathed heavily until he couldn't get any more air. Then he stopped, raised both hands over his head, and rang his rattle against his left hand, so the people knew he was going to fall. His power made him stiff as a log. He'd fall into the men's arms. Somebody grabbed him around the arms, somebody else around the knees, and laid him on the bed right next to the sick person, with his arm across the sick person like he told them. . . . Then everybody would be quiet while the doctor was asleep (in trance). The doctor's spirit flew up after the spirit of the sick person, leaving his body behind. . . . When Bobby Dodd came back, he'd start to shake. This showed that his power was strong. He'd be singing real low when he came down. The people would start singing with him and make him feel good and give him more power. People would give him a song so he could come along good. Then the interpreter would take the eagle feather and sprinkle water from a can just on its black tip end. He'd brush that on the doctor's head. When the doctor opened his eyes, the sick person would open his eyes at the same time and look around. The people would be surprised and amazed. Everybody would feel good. The interpreter would tell the people to help the doctor up. He'd be all stiff. Two guys would lift him and set him on his feet, still stiff as a log. Then the interpreter would take the stick with the feathers on it and give it to him. The doctor would put it behind his knees and kneel with it there in front of the sick person. Then he'd be all right and start to sing again" [Olofson 1979:21].

Doha

Kiowa, *Plains*

Medicine man [Nye 1962:223]. Kiowa medicine men obtain their powers through vision questing accompanied by their sacred pipes. Also see *Toneakoy.*

Dokulungkili

Tewa, *Southwest*

The act of offering white cornmeal; translates to "I (scatter) corn grains": *do,* "I" or "it"; *kulung,* "corn"; and *kili,* "grain" [Robbins et al. 1916:87]. Cornmeal is a common offering given during prayers and plays an important role in all healing ceremonies, where cornmeal is sprinkled on the patient. It is used most often by women as an offering; feathers are used most often by men. It is carried in a special buckskin bag, called *ibikuluk-ilimu,* which is attached to a leather thong and worn around the neck.

Dorsey, George Amos

George Dorsey was born in Hebron, Ohio, on 6 February 1868. In 1894 he received the first Ph.D. in anthropology to be awarded in the United States from Harvard University. After two years as an instructor at Harvard, Dorsey became an assistant curator at Chicago's new Field Columbian Museum. In 1898 he was promoted to curator of anthropology and held that post for the next 17 years. During this period, he published many articles on Native American culture, especially from the Plains area. He resigned from the museum in 1915 and pursued a career in journalism until his death in New York City on 29 March 1931.

Dorsey, James Owen

James Dorsey was born in Baltimore, Maryland, on 31 October 1848. In 1871 he was ordained at the Theological Seminary of Virginia as an Episcopal minister. He spent the next two years as a missionary among the Ponca, where he began a long study of the Siouan-speaking tribes of the northern plains. Eventually, illness forced him to leave the ministry, and he began to work as an ethnographer and linguist for the Bureau of American Ethnology. He is best known for his classification of the Siouan, Athabascan, and Caddoan languages. He worked in no fewer than 30 different Native American cultures and published most of his findings in the annual reports of the Bureau of American Ethnology. He continued his work up until his death on 4 February 1895.

Dorsey, Willie

Northern Paiute, *Basin*

A shaman who lived around the turn of the twentieth century. The following account of him was given by William Paddy:

"When I was a small boy in Owyhee, a little girl about twelve years old who was my niece swallowed the sharp buckle on her bib overall. They got Willie Dorsey right away. The girl about died but she got all right. He showed the people the buckle sticking out under her skin and above her navel. He said to us, now I'll sing and take it out. He had the bear for his power and called for it. He stood by the door and hollered like a bear. He spit the buckle out of his mouth into his hand" [Olofson 1979:17].

Dream soul
See *free soul.*

Drops in the Fire
Gros Ventre, *Plains*
A shaman during the latter part of the nineteenth century. The following account, given by Coming Daylight, is of a healing ceremony conducted by him for Crow Bull, who had been wounded by a bullet in battle:

"My mother and grandmother and my uncle with his wives were sitting on the west side in the lodge. The four men singers were on the opposite side. Crow Bull, to be doctored, was at the place opposite the door, with the doctor there too.

"The doctor started to sing and then he gave two drums there to the singers. He said: 'You all look at me. You all look at me good.' Then he said: 'Give me a gun. This thing (the gun) is the main thing. Look at it. If I don't make this work, he (Crow Bull) is going to leave you (to die), and if it works as I want it to work he is going to get well.' There is a wild rhubarb which is called 'gun' and when a person is going to eat it he runs his thumb up the stalk to eat the inside of the rhubarb stalk. The doctor said: 'Now you see this gun (the real gun).' And he ran his thumb up the barrel, and it made a sound like that made when a person opens a wild rhubarb stalk. And it looked as if the real gun was laid apart. They all looked at it. And the doctor said: 'We are going to have good luck.' Then they all cheered like they were thanking him. Then he ran his hand along the gun (barrel) and when they looked again the gun was just as good as ever. Then he laid the gun up. I used to think he was a wonderful man because I saw him do this with a real gun.

"After this, the doctor took the bandage off Crow Bull and started doctoring him. He took a snake-skin which was just flat and wrapped it around the wound. All this time he was talking and praying. All this time he held the tail and head of the snake-skin together at the back of Crow Bull's head. He would kind of move his hand, quivering it at the back of Crow Bull's head where he was holding the two ends of the snake-skin together. The bullet had lodged there. The head of the snake was inside (nearest the scalp) and the tail was laid over it. He just quivered his hand about four times and at the same time told the singers: 'Not yet. Keep singing.' He was trying to work the bullet out. Finally, he grasped the snake-skin by the middle and shook it, and the bullet dropped out. That is why I thought he was wonderful" [Cooper 1957: 341– 342].

Drums
Most of the early accounts of Native American healing ceremonies include some comment concerning all the noise made during the ritual. In terms of communication theory, noise consists of sounds that interfere with the meaningful message being transmitted and is therefore a non-message. However, this is not the case with Native American ceremonies.

Nearly every known Native American healing ceremony includes singing accompanied by drums or rattles or both. These drums come in many different forms. Some are merely dried pieces of skin or bark; more frequently, they consist of animal skin stretched over a wooden frame on one or both sides. Drums may be used by either the shaman or the shaman's helpers.

Early observers such as Wilken [1887] noted the presence of drums whenever a shaman set forth to call his helping spirits. Later, Eliade [1964:179] wrote that "there is always some instrument that, in one way or another, is able to establish contact with the 'world of the spirits.'" By the 1930s, anthropologists such as van der Leeuw [1933:ch. 26, 2] began to note that drumming and dancing induce a state of ecstasy in the shaman. This notion was solidified when Andrew Neher [1962] showed that the rhythmic aspect of drumming plays a key role in altering human consciousness. Prior to Neher's paper, researchers had already noted that "rhythmic stimulation of the organ of hearing as a whole can be accomplished *only* by using a sound stimulus containing components of supra-liminal intensity over the whole gamut of audible frequencies—in effect a steep fronted sound such as that produced by an untuned percussion instrument (e.g., drum) or an explosion" [Walter and Walter 1949:82]. Since that time, anthropologists have agreed that there is a connection between percussion and the states of consciousness attained by shamans [Needham 1967]. That is, drumming is essential in helping the shaman make the transition from an ordinary state of consciousness to the shamanic state of consciousness (SSC). Thus, quiet healing ceremonies are almost unheard of.

The rhythmic stimulation of the drum plays a key role in assisting a shaman's transition from an ordinary state of consciousness to a shamanic state of consciousness.

Dúajida
Pima, *Southwest*
A diagnostic ceremony conducted by shamans; translates to "the vitalization." A shortened form of this ceremony is called *kúlañmada*, which literally means "the application of medicine."

Duhisa
Hopi, *Southwest*
The art of the sorcerer or witch; black magic. Sorcerers are called two-hearts, because they think with their head as well as their heart. *Duhisa* comes from the sorcerer's helping spirit. The extent of the sorcerer's *duhisa* depends on which being is his helper. Little black ants are the most powerful helping spirits; others include coyotes, wolves, owls, crows, bull snakes, cats, and dogs [Titiev 1956:53].

Duklij
Apache, *Southwest*
Turquoise and green malachite, which contains supernatural qualities. It is worn to ward off evil spirits and to bring rain. A small bead of it attached to a bow or gun makes the weapon shoot accurately. Because all medicine men use it, Bourke [1892:589] called it "the Apache medicine-man's badge of office, his medical diploma . . . without it he could not in olden times exercise his medical functions."

Duride
Tiwa, *Southwest*
Used at the Isleta Pueblo to refer to a light—the form taken by a witch—that comes in the night. The term was also applied to train engines because of their flashing head light. When this light appears, it jumps from place to place [Parsons 1932:243].

Duxuda'b
Coast Salish, *Northwest Coast*
Shaman. Literally it means the person with the *xuda'b* type of guardian spirit. These are the shamans who conduct the Spirit Canoe healing ceremony. "This xuda'b alone makes it possible for a shaman to visit the land of the dead" [Haeberlin 1918:250]. See *sbatatdaq* for more details.

Dyaguna gaut
Cayuga, *Northeast*
The healing ceremony conducted by members of the White Buffalo Society. See *eyondwanshgwut* for details.

Eagle Shield

Dakota, *Plains*

A shaman who lived on the Standing Rock Reservation in South Dakota during the latter part of the nineteenth century. He began healing in the 1870s and was best known for his treatment of bone fractures and wounds. He received his healing powers and knowledge of herbs from the bear and the badger. His bear medicine was used mostly for adults, and his badger medicine for children. When interviewed around 1912, he allowed his bear claw to be photographed; he had been using it in his healing ceremonies for 48 years.

In treating wounds, he used "herb for the wounded," which was later identified as yarrow (*Achillea lanulaosa* Nutt.). The yarrow was prepared by drying the entire plant. During the healing ceremony, the patient was required to chew on the remains. The following describes one of his successful healings:

"Eagle Shield said that he had treated men shot through the body and they had recovered. One man thus treated was personally known to the writer. The man had attempted suicide by shooting himself in the left side, the bullet passing through the body and breaking the edge of the shoulder blade. As a result of the wound his arm was paralyzed, and two doctors of the white race said that it must be amputated. Eagle Shield undertook the treatment of the case and did his work so effectually that the man appears to have as free use of one arm as of the other" [Densmore 1918:254].

For treating loss of appetite, he used locoweed (*Astragalus carolinianus* L.). Another species of locoweed was used for treating heart trouble and pain in the stomach. For treating headaches, he used dried Colorado sage (*Artemisia frigida* Willd.), which was dried and placed on hot coals; the patient would inhale the vapor. For treating diseases of the kidneys, he prepared a decoction from wild lettuce (*Lactuca pulchella* DC.). For a pain in the side, he made a tea from the leaves and stalks of coneflower (*Ratibida columnaris* (Sims) Don.); for earaches, a drop of a decoction made from the root was put into the ear. For diarrhea in children, wild columbine (*Aquilegia canadensis* L.) was steeped in hot water and administered to the child in a small spoon made of white bone. For fever and headaches in children, he steeped dock (*Rumex* sp.) and then administered it internally or rubbed the child's entire body with the liquid. All these herbal remedies had come to him through visions of either the bear or the badger. Each remedy also entailed the singing of a specific

69

medicine song during its administration to the patient. When gathering the herbs, tobacco offerings were made to the appropriate animal spirit for each plant taken.

Eagle Shield was also a specialist in the treatment of broken bones. First the bone was set; then he would rub his hands with the dried leaves and root of wild four-o'clocks (*Allionia nyctaginea* Michx.) that had been mixed with grease. He would hold his hands over the fire until the mixture warmed and then apply it to the skin of the patient just above the fracture. The fracture was then wrapped in a splint made from parfleche.

Ecstasy, Ecstatic trance

"Almost every writer on the subject singles out ecstasy as the inescapable ingredient of shamanism. But the meaning ascribed to it is often diffuse and at times contradictory. Some authors have proposed that true shamanic ecstasy implies possession by spirits [Loeb 1929]; others take an alternative view, believing that the true shaman experiences only magical flight [Eliade 1964; Heusch 1962]. Lewis [1971:49] argues against interpreting shamanic ecstasy as being exclusive to either phenomenon. His definition includes both magical flight and spirit possession, and he notes that they can exist separately or coexist in various degrees [see also Reinhard 1976]. In the 42 cultures surveyed (in our study), 18 reported spirit possession only, 10 magical flight only, 11 both; and in 3, neither concept was used to explain the shaman's trance" [Peters and Price-Williams 1980:398].

Eliade [1964] established ecstasy as an integral aspect of shamanism. This ecstasy is seen as being controlled by the shaman—that is, the shaman begins and ends his trance state at will. Further control of the shaman's ecstatic trance is rendered by the audience participating in the ceremony. They help keep the shaman within cultural limits and out of uncontrolled frenzy.

Eehyom

Cheyenne, *Plains*

Shamans who are able to harm over long distances [Schlesier 1987:16]. Included in this category are shamans who possess an *oxzem* (spirit

lance) and the keeper of the *nimahenan* (sacred arrows).

Elik

Copper Eskimo, *Arctic Coast*

Shaman; translates to "one who has eyes." It designates the shaman as one who can see where others cannot [Beck and Walters 1977:121].

Endorphins

Commentators on shamanic trance often equate it with hypnotic trance. However, recent studies of acupuncture indicate that analgesia is produced by endorphins. It was found that the stimulation of muscle, joint, and tendon sensory endings is largely responsible for the production of acupuncture-induced analgesia. (This fact was noted by the Chinese before the discovery of endorphins.) Studies of hypnosis indicate that hypnotic analgesia is not blocked by naloxone (a narcotic antagonist). Thus, the endorphin-mediated analgesia of acupuncture and transcutaneous stimulation operates by a different mechanism than analgesia produced by hypnosis. Shamanic trance analgesia and euphoria are more likely to be of the endorphin type, where vigorous motor activities—dancing and drumming—produce these effects. In addition, shamanic trance is nearly always accompanied by rapid muscle tremor; this twitching could act as an endorphin pump, which in turn produces the well-known shamanic ecstasy [Prince 1982]. It is interesting to note that early on, Radin [1914:336] noted in his study of Native Americans that certain muscular responses "performed at certain propitious times, do actually call forth religious feeling."

Ènti

Chiricahua, *Southwest*

The harmful aspect of supernatural power; those who direct it or lend themselves to it—sorcerers, witches, etc. Supernatural power is seen as being either good or evil; this term applies to harmful supernatural power [Opler 1935:69, 1946:88].

Erinaliut

Eskimo, *Makenzie-Yukon, Arctic Coast*

A collective term used mainly by Canadian anthropologists to refer to any words—spoken (spells), sung (power songs), or thought—that bear the power to bring about supernatural events. In Greenland the term is *serrat*. Healing songs and chants used by shamans all fit into this category. The mental direction of the shaman's thoughts in controlling his helping spirits is also included, as well as the songs or thoughts that bring forth these spirits. Of course, throughout Alaska, Canada, and Greenland, there are many different ways in which magical words are brought into action [Merkur 1990:50].

Eskimo
The people who inhabit the northernmost regions of North America or the Arctic region. The word is a Cree term meaning "eaters of raw meat" [Jenness 1963:405]. In Canada in anthropology the Eskimo are divided into five regions: (1) Labrador Eskimo inhabiting the eastern side, (2) Central Eskimo living to the north of Hudson Bay, (3) Caribou Eskimo occupying the central region to the northwest of Hudson Bay, (4) Copper Eskimo living above Great Bear Lake and Great Slave Lake, and (5) Mackenzie Eskimo living along the western border of Canada. To the west of the Mackenzie Eskimo are the Alaska Eskimo. Another general term for the Eskimo is Inuit.

Estufa
Pueblo, *Southwest*
See *kiva*.

Etien
Wailaki, *California*
Sucking shamans; one of three classes of healers found among the Kato branch. The *etien* were extinct by the beginning of the twentieth century [Loeb 1934a:35]. In all cases of illness, the *etien* was always called in first to make a diagnosis and, if possible, to treat the patient. He did this by making a small incision with a flint knife in the skin at the location of the disease and then sucking on it. Any blood he sucked out was spit into a waiting basket. The disease object, usually an insect, was also spit into this basket. The basket was then removed and the disease disposed of.

The other two classes of healers among the Kato are the *nachulna* (see entry) and the *chgalyic* (see entry).

Etowe
Zuni, *Southwest*
Fetishes used in healing and other ceremonies. These objects are usually carved animal figures made of stone, but they may be as simple as a small pebble. The *etowe* of the Zuni shamans correspond to the medicine bundles of other North American cultures.

Ewil letimk
Yuki, *California*
A Huchnom singing doctor; translates to "poison doctor." These shamans hold six-day healing ceremonies called *ewil wokask*, or "poison dance." The ceremony includes removal of disease objects [Loeb 1934a:62].

Exhastoz
Cheyenne, *Plains*
A cosmic power that permeates and maintains the world; the Cheyenne equivalent of *orenda* (see entry) [Schlesier 1987:7].

Eye yomta
Patwin, *California*
See *yomta*.

Eyondwanshgwut
Cayuga, *Northeast*
The curing rites performed by the different medicine societies among the Cayuga; translates to "wish or request to go by." According to one informant:

"The society dances and songs are not regarded as the sole agencies of relief. But they are provided to act upon spiritual causes of ailment in conjunction with herb medicines which produce an effect upon the body. Only in rare cases are the rites of the societies called for or prescribed as cures without resort to other medicinal means. The underlying principles of pneumatism, as the use of the spiritual appeals through dances and song rituals may be denoted, are that the curing ceremonies, addressed to spirits who may be hindering the successful action of the medicines administered to the patient, should coax away the obstacle of the spirit's ill-will. They work on the idea that every time a native medical prescription (or for that matter one propounded by a white practitioner)

A Cayuga Iroquois False Face dances and shakes his rattle as part of a healing rite to frighten off harmful spirits that cause illness. The mask's distorted facial features represent a disease spirit. It is only in rare cases that the healing rites of the societies are called for or prescribed as cures without resorting first to other medicinal means.

fails to produce relief it is because of an obstacle in the guise of some spirit, animal, dwarf, ghost, or some other of the panphantasia standing in the way of the cure. The rites performed to effect the removal of the spiritual obstacle appeal to the unseen agency to cease, through the supplication of the people who attend the rites and who take part. The feast which is part of the event is in homage to the spirit" [Deskáheh in Speck 1949:58].

The Cayuga medicine societies fall into two broad categories—restricted and unrestricted. The rites of the restricted societies are performed by members only; in the unrestricted societies, nonmembers may participate in the ritual of various rites. All rites are referred to as dances. Full rites are performed within the home of a patient, and partial rites are done for longhouse and public rituals. A patient who is cured by a restricted society is eligible to become a member of that society, and most individuals do so to ensure that their sickness will not return. If the patient does not join, he or she must request the ritual of the rite periodically to satisfy the spirit invoked and to avert recurrent illness. Members of the society who are of the opposite moiety to that of the patient conduct the ceremony. If the healing ceremony of a certain society calls for ceremonial foods or objects, the person requesting the dance provides the necessary items.

Following is a list of the different Cayuga medicine society rites and their functions:

Restricted Societies (Members Only)

1. Midwinter Ceremony. The annual eight-day New Year's festival. It is referred to as the *cadekwcrahe kaihweyoni*, which translates to "midyear ceremonial mark." On the third and fourth days of this festival, the different medicine societies perform healing ceremonies on all those who have requested a healing. This usually entails the ritual of 30 or more different rites or dances. Patients are treated collectively. If a patient's healing is not completed during these two days, additional rituals are conducted in the home of the patient.

2. Bear Society Rite. The bear dance or *nyagwékya*. The members sing and dance counter-clockwise around the patient, using a short shuffle-step in a single file, to the accompaniment of the water drum and horn rattle. (In former times, folded hickory bark or cylindrical elm bark rattles were used.) Members take berry juice in their mouths and spray it on the patient, who is seated on a bench. Herb tea is also used, because the bear likes herbs. Those treated in this rite must not wash off the berry juice and herb tea. The dance continues until all the members have had an opportunity to blow the medicine on the patients. The society is known to treat attacks of dementia in which the victim crawls on the ground like a bear.

3. Otter Society Rite. The society is also referred to as the Fish Eating Society. Individuals afflicted by the spirit of the otter become nervous and out of control. Everyone present consumes a feast of fish chowder and bread to appease the spirit of the otter. There is no dancing or singing during this ceremony (called the *djutidro*). After the feast, the members sprinkle water, procured in a specific sacred manner, onto the patient by dipping tied bundles of corn husks into the water. The members also splash one another on the head and shoulders. One member of this society, named Levi Baptiste, is known to have cured a child who developed St. Vitus's Dance. This occurred around 1944. Three white physicians had given up on the girl, but Levi repeated his sprinkling ceremony over a three-day period, and the child was cured.

4. White Buffalo Society Rite. This society is referred to as *dyaguna gaut*, which literally means "those who have horns." Afflictions attributed to the spirit of the white buffalo cause one to bellow continually and wallow around on the ground. Such persons cannot eat and, therefore, become very weak. For the healing ceremony, a cornmeal mush is prepared and placed in the center of the room on the floor. The members dance around this bowl facing one another. They are accompanied by two singers who sit on a bench and use a water drum and a horn rattle. They usually sing seven or eight songs. At a certain point, the members face outward from the circle and begin imitating a buffalo bull, bellowing and pushing one another aside. At the conclusion of the dance, each

member dips his hand in the mush and licks it off. Between rituals of this dance, the members eat cornmeal mush. The members also blow herb tea onto the patient's head. In one case, an Oneida woman was treated around 1910 for dementia, convulsions, and bellowing hysteria. She was treated by the Bear Society but had a relapse during the ritual. She was then referred to the White Buffalo Society, which cured her.

5. Wooden False-Face Society. This society is called *okísot hanatuí*. Okísot means "grandfather," but the term refers to the wooden masks used by this society. These masks, called false faces *(gagósa)*, are spiritual forces that have "the same power as the medicines that grow on earth" [Deskáheh in Speck 1949:72]. Different faces represent different spirits, and the form of the mask is revealed to the carver during a prayer and tobacco offering ceremony. Like in most other Iroquois societies, these masks are first carved into a living tree, then removed and decorated with paint and hair. Long horsetail hair is now used, but in former times, corn husks were used for the hair on the masks. They are made from poplar, basswood, maple, and occasionally white pine. They are painted in four solid colors: red, black, red and black, and white. These masks are treated with great respect; otherwise, their power turns on the user. New masks are consecrated on the hot coals of a longhouse fire. During this ceremony, a tiny cloth bag of native tobacco is tied near the forehead to feed the spirit of the mask and keep it appeased. This tobacco is renewed periodically, and the old bags are often left attached. In addition, the masks are fed, in a form of the False-Face traveling rite, by rubbing them with sunflower oil mixed with animal grease.

The False-Face Societies perform only in cases of serious illness. They are called in when the rites of other societies have failed. The performance of their ritual is restricted to society members. It may be performed at any time of day or night. Each masked dancer carries a large turtleshell (snapping turtle) rattle, and some carry staffs of untrimmed hickory branches. The patient is placed on a bench in the center of the room, and the members dance around the bench using only gestures, never speech. During the dance, some of the dancers go to the fire and

scoop up hot coals in their hands and rub the ashes on the patient's head. Near the end of the ceremony, the dancers feed the patient with False-Face mush, which is made from parched cornmeal to which maple sugar and berries have been added. The dancers also partake of this mush. When the patient recovers from his illness, he is a member of this society. The patient must request the ritual of this rite at least once a year, usually during the midwinter festival, to prevent any recurrence of illness.

During an informal longhouse (public) ritual of this rite, the dancers do not wear their masks. The informal or partial ritual of the rite is called *djosi dadi has*. The members of both moieties dance collectively, and they sing 12 songs. The cornmeal mush is not served at this ritual.

6. Corn-Husk Mask Society. Members of this society include both females and males; some of them are only 8 to 12 years old. The are called upon to cure sickness of almost any nature and perform in the home of the patient at any time, wearing corn-husk masks and burning tobacco. The performers frequently handle ashes and rub them on the patient's head while also blowing on it.

7. Medicine Men's Society. The Cayuga call this society hanaitus, but it is an ancient term no longer translatable. Two other names are also used: "big rattles" (odjistauwedrowa nes), because its members carry large pumpkin rattles when performing; and "keeper of the bones of an animal" *(onatcinákeso)*, which refers to the bones of a mythical animal that had horns. The medicine from these bones is called *kanuda*, or "hunter's medicine," and is reported to be very powerful, especially in healing wounds. It is also used to doctor injuries from violence, falls, or accidents.

During the ritual of their healing ceremonies, no outsiders are permitted. In addition, no meat can be cooked in the house while the patient is there, no salt can be added to the cornmeal mush that is ritually consumed, and the ritual room must be kept as dark as possible.

Part of the medicine used in this ceremony is a pig-head mask. To appease the spirit of this mask, a cooked pig's head is ritually consumed by society members. No utensils are used, only their teeth, and when partaking of the head, they croak like ravens. The pig-head mask is used on victims of serious accidents and for "hopelessly ill" persons, so it must be kept in constant readiness.

8. Dark Dance Society. This society is also referred to as the Little Water Society. The Dark Dance is called *diyúsodáyego*, meaning "in the dark(ness)." It is performed in private homes to cure sickness in general, in conjunction with medicine prescribed by a shaman. It is also used to treat weakness and a decline of strength. The patrons of this society are the *djigá*, which translates to "dwarfs." The dance also serves as an invocation to spirits of the departed.

The ceremony begins with the filling and lighting of a new clay pipe, which is first smoked by the patient and then passed clockwise to each member. After this, the lights are extinguished and there are three rounds of singing and dancing. Between rounds, the lamps are relit. During the dancing, all members blow their breath on the patient at intervals as they dance about him. At the end, there is a feast of cornmeal mush and a pig's head. In former times, the head of a bear or deer was used.

9. Eagle Dance Society. The healing ceremony of this society is called *kanrugwae*, meaning "making a noise with a stick." It is performed for those who are afflicted by the spirit of the eagle. The symptoms are nervousness or general debility, and it is a difficult illness to diagnose. The ceremony is conducted with four dancers and two assistants. One assistant uses a water drum and the other keeps time with a horn rattle. Each dancer carries a horn rattle in one hand and a feather wand in the other. The wands are hardwood sticks approximately 10 to 14 inches in length to which six feathers are attached about 1 inch apart, beginning with the outer end. The feathers are not necessarily from an eagle; both hawk and pheasant feathers have been observed. The wands are used only once and must be made new for each ritual.

Unrestricted Societies

1. Snow-Snake Rite. This rite is actually a game and is called *diyunanda kwa*, meaning "playing sticks." The sticks are long and thin,

with a thick, rounded head that has a notch in the end for the forefinger of the player; the sticks are referred to as snow snakes. The rite is used for sickness in general. In one case, it was used to treat sores on a woman's leg. Tobacco is burned on the fire, and a prayer is directed to the snake spirits. Afterward, two or three men form two teams and go outdoors to engage in the snow-snake game. The cure is not affected by which team wins the game.

2. Chipmunk Rite. This rarely performed ceremony is called *ngak saga nii*, meaning "rubbing the bowl." It is used for relief in general, but one specific application is to treat the compulsion to steal and hide objects. The ceremony is performed by a circle of men with one man standing in the center of it. This man sings the chipmunk rite song while playing a rasp that is about 2 feet long and made of hickory. One end is set on the floor, and a stick is drawn over the notches in it. After finishing the song, the singer tries to escape the circle. If he is successful, the ceremony is over. If not, he must repeat his ritual.

3. Thunder Rite. The principal part of this rite is playing a game of lacrosse, called *gatci kwae*, meaning "beating the mush." Before the game, the players take an emetic, a medicine "to clean them out." A fire is built outside the longhouse, and the ceremonial leader prays to the Great Spirit and the Seven Thunderers for the patient's relief. At a certain point in the prayer, he throws a small, corn-husk basket containing tobacco into the fire as an offering to the Seven Thunderers. The game is then played, but the cure is not dependent on which side wins. Afterward, the players sing the thunder song and dance into the longhouse, where they begin the *Wasáse*, or "war dance song." Following this, tobacco and corn mush are distributed among the players. The rite is used for the relief of any illness when prescribed.

4. War Dance. The *Wasáse* ("Osage"), or War Dance, is usually a social dance but may also be requested for curative purposes. When it is performed for curing, the requester brings a basket of gifts that are distributed to the dancers at the conclusion of the rite. During the ritual, the ceremonial leader strikes the floor with his walking stick to interrupt the singing, which is

accompanied by the water drum and horn rattle. He then speaks on behalf of the patient. If there is more than one patient, he repeats this process until all have been spoken for. When a medicine man prescribes "need of a friend" to give relief to a patient, this rite is performed to make the ceremonial friendship.

5. Chicken Dance. This dance is known as *dek setskéha* and is used to cure sickness in general, especially when a chicken is seen in a dream or a vision as a premonition of sickness. The water drum is used, and each of the dancers has a horn rattle. The men sing, and the women stand in a group near and around them. After singing a number of verses, the men take women partners and continue the dance side by side with them. At about the middle of the dance, the men face their partners and continue in a single file in a quick shuffle in time with the drum.

6. Striking Stick Dance. This is called *kanhyae,* "stick beating." Its purpose is to cure disease of almost any character, according to the condition of the individual requesting it. It resembles the War Dance in that both sexes line up in opposite formation, beating time with their feet. At certain intervals they pass and change sides. The dance is rarely called for.

7. Ghost Dance. The *okiwe*—"ghost" or "dead people"—dance is performed to prevent and cure illness by satisfying the spirits of the dead. It is performed when an ill person dreams of dead people dancing. Specifically, it is used for relief from convulsions and weakness or from paralysis that is caused by ghosts seen in a dream or a vision. It is also used for general recovery in the case of obstinate sickness. When the dance is performed in private homes, it consumes the entire night. Only women dance, and the males sing. The women move counterclockwise in a circle while holding their arms horizontally doubled outward, with hands closed in front of their chests. There is a lead singer with a water drum and an assistant with a horn rattle; they sit on a bench. During the ceremony, they sing approximately 100 songs. It is performed in winter or fall after the harvest has been gathered or in the spring before planting time, lest cold weather or frost be brought about by the presence of the ghosts invoked. The conclusion of the ceremony is marked by the ritual of the Kettle Dance.

8. Dream Guessing Rite. This ceremony is called *ságodiwenha gwus*, "her word (dream) taken off." It is performed for a person who has been harassed by a persistently recurring dream of evil portent or whose trouble has been brought about by mask spirits, causing a mental disturbance in the patient. The ritual takes place on the third or fourth day of the midwinter ceremony. Shamans are asked to use their powers to guess the nature of the dream. The patient answers only "yes" or "no" to the questions put to him until the dream has been correctly determined. Guessing the dream is the cure. Whoever guesses the dream makes a miniature mask that is given to the patient as a medicine. The mask is kept in the home of the relieved dream-sufferer. If the patient is a member of the Wooden False-Face Society, the miniature mask is tied to the hair near the forehead of that person's large mask.

9. Dreamer Rite. Also called the fortune-teller rite, this ceremony is performed by "dreamers" to diagnose illnesses that have baffled practitioners in the various medicine societies. The male dreamer is known as *hadrauta*; the female as *hodrauta*. In cases of serious illness, someone puts tobacco in a piece of the sick person's clothing and wraps it up. He takes this to a dreamer and tells him of the person who is ill. The dreamer puts the small parcel under his pillow, and that night he dreams. He has a secret medicine that he drinks before going to bed. The next morning, the dreamer tells this person what he has seen in his dream vision, returning the clothing and keeping the tobacco. The dreamer tells whether a certain medicine must be prepared and administered or whether one of the medicine societies should be called in.

10. Pulling Rite. Also called the tug-of-war rite, this ceremony is termed *tadi nyac,* "they (both sides) grab the stick." The last known ritual was in 1915. It is performed to cure a seizing compulsion—an urge to grab hold of something. It is also used to alleviate trembling. The ritual takes place on the third day of the Midwinter Ceremony. The

rite is performed when the malady appears in the community, when prescribed as a remedy by a medicine man, or when called for by a patient who becomes conscious of its need.

The person who requests this ceremony provides a 2-foot stick, which is given to two men—one from each moiety, as representatives of the group. These two men face each other in the middle of the longhouse on each side of a dividing line drawn on the floor. They firmly grasp the stick—hands alternating, one palm up and the other palm down. Eight other men line up on each side behind the stick holders. They form an interlocking chain on each side by placing one arm over the left shoulder and the other arm under the right shoulder of the person in front of them. A signal is then given to pull, and whichever team pulls the other across the line wins. If one of the stick holders loses his grip, his team loses. As in other such rites, the efficacy of the cure is not dependent on which team wins. The cure develops from the symbol of the pulling act. In some cases, women are team members.

11. Football Rite. This is called *wesatwas gatcikwai,* meaning "kicking game." When requested via a dream or a vision or prescribed by a medicine man, it is played on the third day of the Midwinter Ceremony. It is frequently performed for mild illnesses. Its purpose is to coax the withdrawal of unfriendly spirits who are standing in the way of the successful action of the medicine administered. Therefore, it is not directed toward any specific form of illness.

The game is played on the north side of the longhouse. There are five men on each side from the two moieties. Two goals are formed by placing upright sticks 8 feet apart; the two goals are placed about 150 feet apart. The ball, provided by the ceremony requester, is made of canvas stuffed with rags and is about 6 inches in diameter. The person requesting the game furnishes a portion of cornmeal mush for each player—a symbol of feeding the spirits by proxy to satisfy them. The same person tosses the ball up to start each play. To score a point, one of the players must kick the ball between the two upright sticks. Hands can be used only to knock the ball to the ground; otherwise only the feet are used. One man stands guard at each goal. The first team to score three points wins. Some groups play this game at night, in which case the ball is soaked in oil and ignited.

See Speck [1949] for details on any of the above ceremonies.

False-Face Society
Iroquois, *Northeast*

This society is based on the "false faces," or wooden masks, used by various nations for healing. The Seneca word for mask is "face" (*gagohsa'*), the Onondaga word is "hunchback" (*hadu'i'*), and the Mohawk word is "face" (*gagu-'wara*). Skinner [1916:500–505] observed that the easternmost group of Ojibwas, the Mississaugas, adopted the False-Face Society from the Iroquois for use in healing. The masks are wooden portraits of several types of mythical beings that wander about in the forests. According to Fenton [1941:406]:

"The Faces of the forest also claimed to possess the power to control sickness. They instructed the dreamers to carve likenesses in the form of masks, saying that whenever anyone makes ready the feast, invokes their help while burning Indian tobacco and sings the curing songs, supernatural power to cure disease will be conferred on human beings who wear the masks."

The masks are carved from a single block of basswood or other soft wood such as willow. In former times, each person carved his own mask on a living basswood, but today, craftsmen most often carve the masks for society members. Because each mask reflects the visions or dreams of the person for whom it is carved, and because the craftsmen also give in to their artistic whims, Henry Redeye, an old Seneca, reports that there are as many false-face types as there are different people. The Iroquois themselves have no formal classification of mask types. Local tradition determines the forms of faces that come in visions, so there are some similarities in the masks. Although the face portrays the spirit being, the wearer must dramatize the actions of that particular spirit, such as a slouching gait or an unintelligible nasal speech, all of which is accompanied by a shaking rattle. These masks are used for other purposes as well as healing, but the older masks inevitably become "doctor" masks. The actions of the wearer are more important than the form of the mask in determining its use. Members of the society often possess more than one mask.

These masks are treated as sacred objects and are handled with great respect. If a man happens to drop his mask, he makes an offering by burning tobacco and ties a little bundle of sacred tobacco near the ear or forehead of the mask. Also, when a mask is passed on or purchased, the new owner ties a bundle of sacred tobacco to it. Thus, older masks often have many such bundles tied to them. When not in use, the mask is wrapped in a cloth or hung on a wall; the mask is hung facing the wall, or its face is covered if it points outward. A person's mask can be used by any member of the society.

The most variable feature of such masks is the mouth, and the Iroquois tend to name the masks according to the expressions of the mouth, except when they are named for the spirit helpers they represent. Examples would be: "his mouth is twisted," "his mouth is straight," "the corners of his mouth are hanging," "he is smiling," and so forth. In general, the masks have deep-set eyes and large, often bent noses. The brows are arched and usually deeply wrinkled. The face is usually painted red or black and is framed by a wig of black hair from the tail of a horse. In earlier times, corn-husk braids, shredded basswood bast, or buffalo mane was used for the hair. Such masks were observed by Jesuit priests among the Huron during the first quarter of the seventeenth century.

The False-Face Society has two main classes of false faces, each with a different healing ritual for patients. One is the False-Face Company, whose masks represent the greatest doctor—known to the Seneca as "our defender the doctor" and to the Onondaga as "the great humpbacked one." Other masks from this group represent his underlings, "the common forest people whose faces are against the trees." The other class is the Common Faces, who live in the forests and are deformed—either hunchbacked or crippled below the waist. The members of the False-Face Society are, for the most part, people who have been cured by the society's healing ceremonies. Other members are admitted as a result of their dreams. In both healing rituals, the

Two Iroquoise wear carved wooden False-Face masks used in healing ceremonies, and a third (standing, right) wears a braided corn-husk mask.

mask wearers handle hot stones and coals while curing the patient by blowing on him/her.

When a person becomes ill, he or she is first attended to by a shaman known to be clairvoyant, who diagnoses the case. Ailments of the head, shoulders, and joints are usually referred to the False-Face Society. Thus, the masks are used to cure swellings of the face, toothaches, inflammations of the eyes, nosebleeds, sore chins, earaches, and so forth. There have been reported cases of hysterical possession among Iroquois women when the masked men approach: "On hearing the rumpus of whining and rattles, which marks their approach, one woman would fall into spasms, imitate their cry and crawl toward the fire, and, unless she was restrained, plunge her hands into the glowing embers and scatter the fire as if she were a False-face (spirit) hunting tobacco" [Fenton 1941:422]. The masked men would restore her to normal by blowing hot ashes on her.

A typical description of one of these longhouse healing ceremonies is as follows:

"They (False-faces) have entered. The singer straddles the bench to beat out the tempo for their dance, which they energetically commence, scattering ashes (from the fire) everywhere. They hasten to finish curing the patient, their host who stands before the fire, since they crave tobacco and hunger for the kettle of mush (a sacred offering) which he has set down for them. A tall, red-faced (red mask) fellow vigorously rubs the patient's scalp before blowing the hot ashes into the seat of pain. A dark one moans anxiously while rubbing hot ashes between his palms prior to pouncing on his victim's shoulder and pumping his arm. Across the fire, a red face stoops to scoop live coals, while another impatiently shakes a turtle rattle. They are naked above the waist, but wearing the masks is said to protect their bodies from cold and their hands from the burning embers" [Fenton 1941:428].

In addition to curing individuals, members of the False-Face Society go through the settlement twice a year, in the spring and fall, to rid it of

Customarily painted black or red, Iroquois' masks are identified by the arched brows, bent noses, and a wig of black horsehair.

sickness. They shake their rattles and use brushes of pine boughs, accompanied by loud cries, to drive sicknesses away. They visit every room in a house, sweeping under the beds and peering into every nook and corner for disease spirits. If they happen upon a sick person, they blow ashes on him.

Harrington [1921:161] reports that "a vague tradition exists to the effect that the False Face Company of the Cayuga once put a stop to an epidemic of cholera among the Minsi (branch of the Lenni Lenape or Delaware)." Among the Seneca, Parker [1909:179] terms the society *Jadigonsashono* and reports that there are three divisions of the false faces that employ four classes of masks—doorkeeper or doctor masks, dancing masks, beggar masks, and secret masks.

The secret masks are never used during public ceremonies. Their principal ceremonies include the Marching Song, the Doctors' Dance, and the Doorkeepers' Dance.

Familiar

In the anthropological literature, a shaman's personal spirit helper or guardian spirit.

Fasting

Abstention from food. For the most part, fasting is used by Native Americans as a basic purification ritual, and is often performed as a lead-in to other religious ceremonies. For instance, shamans often fast before undertaking a healing ceremony. Although fasting is used primarily for individual purification, it can also be seen as a means of coming into contact with the spirit world. For example, the Central Algonquian "believed that by fasting the suppliant underwent such suffering, made himself so weak, that the spirits were overcome with pity, and so granted him whatever he desired" [Blumensohn 1933:451]. Among the Plains cultures, fasting for a vision is a common undertaking among males. Here again is the notion of the spirits taking pity on the faster. Also, it is seen as a form of sacrifice throughout the Plains area. However, in most cases, fasting is used to prepare individuals for success in hunting, warfare, and other such undertakings.

Fishpeople

Tewa, *Southwest*

See *pa towa*.

Fletcher, Alice Cunningham

Alice Fletcher was born in Cuba on 15 March 1838. She did brilliant fieldwork among the Plains cultures, especially with regard to music and religious ceremonies. She was an advocate of Native American policy and was one of the principals behind the Dawes Act of 1887, which was a failed attempt to release Native Americans from being wards of the government. In 1890 she was awarded a lifetime fellowship at the Peabody Museum at Harvard and became the first woman to join the Harvard faculty. Her classic works are *The Hako: A Pawnee Ceremony* and *The Osage Tribe*. She wrote the latter in conjunction with a young

Osage named Francis LaFlesche, whom she formally adopted as her son in 1891. She was also one of the founders of the School of American Research in Santa Fe, New Mexico. She died in Washington, D.C., on 6 April 1923.

Flint Society

Keres, *Southwest*

One of the medicine societies at Santo Domingo Pueblo. Densmore [1952:445] gives the following account:

"The members of the society, usually 15 or 16 in number, go to the house of the sick man, arriving early in the evening. They shake their black gourd rattles and sing until about midnight, with pauses for relaxation and smoking at intervals of about eight songs. . . . There is much ceremonial procedure, including the making and effacing of a meal-painting (altar) on which certain ceremonial articles are placed. The medicine men 'call on the birds and animals,' whose voices are distinctly heard. They look in a crystal ball and make use of a special song with these words:

I am fighting to cure you.
I will suck out what is hurting you, to cure you.
The things I shall take out are the things that are causing your sickness
Now I shall take Mother-bear and put her under my arm
As I get ready to look in the crystal, and I will help you.
Help us all.
Thank you.

'Mother-bear' refers to the 'bear-paws' or 'mittens' which the medicine man puts over his hands. They consist of the skin of the forelegs of the bear, with the paws. It is said that the people 'never deny what a medicine man says he sees in the crystal.'"

Flounder, Fanny

Yurok, *Oregan Seaboard*

One of the last of the powerful *kegeyowor* (shamans) in the twentieth century. She died during the 1940s at close to 100 years of age. She "ultimately acquired five pairs of *telogel* ('pains' or dis-

Alice Fletcher, seated third from the left, with Native American and white women at a Presbyterian mission on the Omaha Reservation in Walthill, Nebraska, in 1883–1884. Fletcher, an anthropologist and a pioneer in the study of Native American music, was the first woman to join the Harvard faculty in 1890.

eases), making her one of the most powerful, famous, and wealthy doctors in memory" [Buckley 1992:140]. She was a sucking doctor and had the ability to move objects at will. Florence Shaughnessy reported witnessing one of her rituals:

"We sang and sang and she (Fanny) danced. Finally she spewed up a bloody mess (the *telogel*) into a basin *(keyom)* we had there. It looked just like a small swallow all covered with bloody slime. I looked and I could see its little beak, the gold stripes on its shoulder. It was *breathing* there—I saw it clearly, sitting there breathing.

"George put the bowl on the mantle (storage ledge of the semi-subterranean house). Then she drew on her long pipe. There was a *thud!*—I can still hear it, like flesh hitting flesh. Then the basin came swirling down to the floor, empty. She got up. . . . That bird was a new pain for her, and they said it gave her power over tumors" [Buckley 1992:141].

Another informant, Harry Roberts, who had spent time with her as a young man, reported:

"When Fanny was curing I used to see a blue light coming off the back of her head, and I could see it at the end of her fingers. You see that in a dim room. She'd create a low-keyed hum—'hmmmmmmmm'—and click sticks together, or clap her hands lightly. She'd go on like that for a long time, like a beehive: keep it up for hours. Then suddenly she'd touch a tension spot on her patient's body and lead the tension off. Then she'd (wipe her hands vigorously). . . . Once I asked Fanny how she got those baskets *(keyom)* off the (ledge). 'I just think them off' is what she said" [Buckley 1992: 143].

Free soul

Anthropological term for one of several types of souls. In many cultures, humans are believed to have more than one soul. The free soul is that part of the being that leaves the body to travel elsewhere, such as the land of the dead or the spirit world. This is the extracorporeal form of the sha-man that takes flight in shamanic journeys. Loss of the free soul is often diagnosed as the cause of an illness. It has its basis in dreams and ecstasies. In some cases, the free soul is referred to as the dream soul. The force that keeps the body alive while the free soul travels is known as the body soul [Hultkrantz 1992:32].

Gahoya
Atsugewi, *California*

A disease object in the body that is the source of illness. It is called a poison, although other cultures in this area refer to it as a pain. It is usually described as being a small, sharp, needlelike point. One informant described it as looking "like a diamond but it has a little black point on it" [Grant in Park 1986:32]. Healing involves sucking the poison from the patient's body.

Gahuni manuscript
Cherokee, *Southeast*

One of several manuscripts obtained by James Mooney in the summer of 1888 that contains the sacred formulas of Cherokee shamans written in Cherokee syllabary. Gahuni, the writer of the manuscript, had died during the mid-1850s. The book contains only eight formulas, although they are "of a character altogether unique" [Mooney 1891:314].

Gajisashono
Seneca, *Northeast*

The Husk-Faces Society, one of several Seneca medicine societies. Its members act as water doctors and cure diseases by spraying and sprinkling water onto patients [Parker 1909:182].

Ganegwäe
Iroquois, *Northeast*

The Eagle Dance, which is widespread among the different Iroquois nations. It is a healing ceremony that is conducted by members of the Eagle Society. Historically, it was known as the Big Bird Dance (or Striking Stick Dance) and was a ritual for boasting of scalp records. Two birds that never come to the ground and live beyond sight—one red (the most powerful one) and one white—are associated with the dance. Over the years, it evolved into "a medicine society of persons whom the Big Birds had accepted for membership by making them sick" [Fenton 1953:33]. Having been cured of his eagle sickness by the society, the patient becomes an eligible member. Membership may also come through appropriate dreams or when a diviner sees that membership is appropriate for a person. In some of the Eagle Societies, such as the Seneca, membership "carries an annual obligation or renewal, else the person becomes sick" [Fenton 1953:35].

The dance has a basic pattern: (1) a greeting and thanksgiving to the Creator by the dance leader; (2) a tobacco invocation followed by three introductory songs

in which eagle feather fans (four or six feathers per fan), horn rattles, and striking sticks (canes) are given to the dancers (this assigns the ceremonial roles) and the patient's illness is described; (3) the dancing, which begins with the fourth song and is followed by 9 to 13 more songs, during which the patient is treated; (4) a closing speech by the dance leader; (5) the last song during which the dancers lay down the eagle feather fans; (6) a feast, which in former times required a boiled pig's head. All the songs are accompanied by a high-pitched water drum.

Sarah Snow of the Bear Clan at Allegany described an illness for which the Eagle Dance is performed:

"It is good for a cough and high fever, 104°, this is sometimes accompanied by nervousness; or the patient may be afflicted by a general weakness and lassitude which the Eagle causes; sometimes they fever, sometimes they cough, and sometimes they merely have violent headaches; sometimes it takes the form of lumbago.The patient gets well when he puts up the Eagle Dance" [Fenton 1953:129].

Gatci kwae
Cayuga, *Northeast*
The thunder rite, which involves playing a game of lacrosse to treat illness. Literally means, "beating the mush." Anyone may participate in its ritual. See *eyondwanshgwut* for details.

Gatigwanasti manuscript
Cherokee, *Southeast*
One of several manuscripts containing the medicine formulas of Cherokee shamans that were obtained by anthropologists during the nineteenth century. Gatigwanasti was a prominent shaman during the mid-nineteenth century, and James Mooney obtained the 122-page booklet from his son in July 1888. Mooney [1891:313] reported that "these papers of Gatigwanasti are the most valuable of the whole (collection of sacred formulas), and amount to fully one-half the entire collection, about fifty pages consisting of love charms. The formulas are beautifully written in bold Cherokee characters (Sequoyan syllabary), and the directions and headings are generally explicit, bearing

out the universal testimony that he was a man of unusual intelligence and ability."

Gauk burakal
Pomo, *California*
Bear doctors. Translates to "human bear." Both men and women can become bear doctors, and this usually occurs in middle age or later. Thus, most people learn this medicine from an old person. Barrett [1917b:452] reported that "even a woman so old and feeble that she could hardly walk would acquire great powers of endurance and swiftness through this magic." Each bear doctor has a secret hiding place, such as a cave, in which they teach the novice the proper songs and use of their ritual paraphernalia, which includes a bearskin suit. Each bear doctor has an assistant, usually a woman, who sings the ritual songs and prepares the special foods needed by the bear doctor. The actual healing ceremonies are conducted near the hiding place where the bear suit is kept. This suit, called *gawi*, is usually made from a grizzly-bear skin, but in some cases, a net covered with shredded soaproot fibers is used. An openwork basket made of white oak twigs is woven to fit the head of the bear doctor. Disks of abalone shell with small holes for vision are placed over the eye openings in the basket. The eyeholes of the bearskin are then made to fit over the shell eyeholes. This basket serves as the foundation over which the bearskin is placed and allows the shaman to move violently without losing the bearskin suit. The skin is fashioned such that it covers all visible parts of the body. This leads to the possibility of hunters attacking this "bear," so the shaman usually wears an armor of shell beads underneath the skin. This armor takes the form of four 6-inch-wide belts that are placed around the abdomen. Sometimes, however, they simply use the standard wooden rod body armor that is commonly used in warfare. Two small round baskets filled with water are usually attached inside the suit. When the shaman dances, the water splashing around in the baskets imitates the sound of a bear's viscera as it moves along. Persons who are attacked by bear doctors can neutralize their power by pulling off the shaman's basket helmet. Although these shamans are generally thought of as evil, they are called upon to cure bear bites and

to avenge wrongs done to their community. However, the bear doctors believe that if they kill more than four persons in one year they will lose their powers.

Gebegabau
Ojibwa, *Canadian Eastern Woodlands*
A visionary *mide* ("mystic") shaman prominent on the Manitou Reserve during the 1930s. His brother, Naugumig, was also a *midewiwin* officer / shaman, however "they always acted seperately, perhaps because one refused to subordinate himself to the other" [Landes 1968:79].

Geesick, John Ka Ka
Ojibwa, *Canadian Eastern Woodlands*
A shaman who lived on Muskeg Bay at Lake of the Woods, Minnesota. He was born in 1844 and lived to be 124 years old. His name is derived from *gaagige giizhig*, which means "forever" and "day," or "everlasting day."

Gemiwûnac
Ojibwa, *Canadian Eastern Woodlands*
A shaman, described as an aged man, who recorded sacred songs for Frances Densmore in 1907; his name literally means "bird that flies through the rain." He was one of the *Midewiwin* (see entry) leaders who lived in the Leech Lake community. "His name was known on all the reservations (in northern Minnesota) and he was held in the same high esteem everywhere" [Densmore 1910:95].

Ghost
Often used in the literature on shamanism as a substitute for spirit. Within any shamanic culture, there are usually many terms applied to the phenomenon of a spirit or a ghost. For example, among the Blackfoot, the ordinary term for spirit is *istaau*, or simply *staau*, which means "fearing something unseen." This particular term is taboo and is never used in the presence of a shaman for fear of insulting his helping spirit. Another taboo term for spirit is *soxkataksapini*, which means "large hollow eyes." Some of the safe terms for spirit include *ksistapssiu*, meaning "nothing"; *sipiapo*, meaning "going around at night"; *tsiktumspikoan*, meaning "fleshless person"; and *akasapikitsoksatsi*, meaning "wearing many rings." The Blackfoot word for the shaman's spirit helper is *aiyikinon*, which means "human bone." This refers to the Blackfoot tradition whereby a person who seeks a spirit helper often carries a bone from a deceased relative in the hope that the spirit of that relative will come to teach and assist him [Schaeffer 1969:13–14].

With arms outstretched, four Arapaho women perform the Ghost Dance, a religious ceremony designed to bring back their ancestral lands and traditional way of life.

Ghost Dance
A general term applied to many of the different religious revitalization movements that occurred mainly during the latter half of the nineteenth century throughout North America. These new religious ceremonies were designed to bring back the old way of life that was rapidly disappearing. All such movements were greatly feared for their potential to encourage Native Americans into warfare with the United States. The most dramatic movement was begun during the 1890s by a Paiute prophet in Nevada named Wovoka (see entry) ("The Cutter"), whose English name was Jack Wilson. Although the Ghost Dance was not a ceremony for healing, Mooney [1896:786] reports that "it is held that frequent devout attendance on the dance conduces to ward off disease and restore the sick to health."

Ghost Midewiwin

Ojibwa, *Canadian Eastern Woodlands*

A ritual held for a patient who dies during a *mide* cure. Because the patient has become a "shadow," another person is chosen to represent the deceased during the ceremony. It is conducted to help the patient's ghost reach the land of the dead, and in so doing "cures" the patient. Thus, for the Ojibwa it is possible to cure even a patient who has died [Landes 1968:50].

Ghost sickness

General term for any illness caused by coming into contact, even in dreams, with the spirit of a deceased person. Some of the symptoms include: long periods of crying; nightmares; afraid of the dark; unable to sleep.

Gicelemûkaong

Lenni Lenape, *Northeast*

The Great Spirit in the Unami dialect of the Lenni Lenape (also called Delaware). Literal meaning is "creator."

Gilya

Tikerarmiut, *Alaska Eskimo*

See *tungat.*

Gínap

Micmac, *Canadian Eastern Woodlands*

A shaman who is always trying to help people in whatever way he can and is reported to be more powerful than the *buówin*—the standard word for shaman. This term is thought to be derived from *gín*, meaning "great or strong," and *ap*, meaning "man." However, it is not clear whether this term applies to a certain supernatural being or to various quasi-mythical, unnamed people. No *buówin* can harm the *gínap*, and the *gínap* can prevent the *buówin* from doing anything.

Gisamá

Havasupai, *Southwest*

Doctor or medicine man [Spier 1928:276]. These doctors are always men, and specialize in the treatment of fractures, wounds, and snakebites. Although sometimes referred to as shamans, they have no helping spirits. Those shamans who do have helping spirits are called *githiye* (see entry).

Githie

Walapai, *Southwest*

Shaman or doctor [McKennan in Kniffen et al. 1935:185]. Shamans can be either male or female, but most are male. They receive their powers in a dream or a series of dreams. The following account describes the *githie*:

"There was little specialization among the Walapai shamans. . . . The profession was not strictly hereditary, although in practice it seems to have been largely so. Of all the recent doctors only two were not sons of shamans, and one of these had a maternal grandfather who was a shaman. On the other hand it was not mandatory for a son to follow in his father's footsteps, although there was a strong likelihood that the son of a dead shaman would be asked in a dream by the spirit of his father to take up the profession. Such calls when received could not be denied. Often a man became a doctor late in life. . . .

"His patron spirit would furnish him with the power to heal disease. In particular cases this power might not be sufficient. In such crises the doctor, through his own spirit (helper), would communicate with the spirit of Wikame (Newberry Mountain, north of Mohave valley). . . . Before the spirits from Wikame arrived, the doctor had swallowed dirt and had been stretched out as dead in the sweathouse. Once the spirit of Wikame arrived, however, it brought him to life again. Miraculously, he escaped from his buckskin bindings and burst through the sweatlodge, leaving no hole. The spirit lodged in his throat and, speaking through the doctor's mouth, diagnosed the case, indicating the trouble. After such a treatment the patient usually got well" [McKennan in Kniffen et al. 1935:185, 186].

The primary item used in doctoring is a gourd rattle in which the shaman's helping spirit resides. In fact, in former times, only shamans possessed rattles. The shaman begins his treatment by shaking his rattle and singing over the patient. The diagnosis is usually that of object intrusion. Once located, the disease-causing object is removed by the shaman's sucking on the patient's body. The removed object is displayed for all to see, after which the shaman most often swallows it. Unlike in most other cultures, the object removed by the Walapai shaman is often a sacred stone that has been given to him by his helping spirit. This stone is used over and over, being swallowed after each healing ceremony.

"Shamans on occasions took their patients into the sweathouse, although this was not primarily a shamanistic institution. At such times they would leave their rattles behind and resort to singing, together with blowing or sucking upon the afflicted part" [McKennan in Kniffen et al. 1935:187].

Most healing treatments are conducted at night. The shaman treats the patient as long as necessary, sometimes a month or more. Other shamans are called in if the treatment is not successful. In former times, payment was made most often in buckskins, horses, and blankets, but today, shamans are paid with money.

Githiye
Havasupai, *Southwest*
A shaman who cures [Spier 1928:277]. Only men are shamans, and they acquire their powers either through inheritance or by dreaming; they are the only ones who have helping spirits. "Each shaman has one (spirit) within his chest. When he wants to discover something he sends the spirit traveling, perhaps for a day and night. The shaman goes out into the darkness; his spirit is heard hollering and whistling to him from a distance. It re-enters his mouth, makes noises, and talks. The shaman shuts his eyes and apparently sings, but in reality it is the spirit telling what it saw" [Spier 1928:276].

Havasupai shamans are sucking doctors. For instance, "Doctor Tommy treated Lina for aches, particularly for fever in the head. He sucked her forehead directly with his lips. His spirit drew out the trouble which he showed her; little white worms like threads, about a centimeter long. He also instructed her husband to cut her hair short; this cured her somewhat" [Sinyella in Spier 1928:279].

Shamans conduct their healing ceremonies at night, often over the course of several nights. If the cure is not successful, another shaman is usually called in. In some cases, several shamans work simultaneously on the patient. "Whatever their opinion of the shamans they believe in the efficacy of their cures. Possibly we may suppose the shamans share the belief, for they are said to cure members of their families as well as themselves" [Spier 1928:281].

Giwire
Keres, *Southwest*
A shamanic healer who belonged to the Shikani Society, one of the medicine societies at Laguna Pueblo. Elsie Parsons, who witnessed one of his ceremonies, first reported it in 1920:

"The altar is set up in the house of the patient, preferably facing east toward the Sun's house. At the back there is a ridge of moist clay, about two inches high, in which a row of prayer-sticks is set. Parallel is a line of meal on which the corn fetishes stand. Up to them leads a line of meal with four cross-lines, the 'road.' Near by are the medicine bowl and a bear's paw, and farther out lie four eagle-wing feathers on a piece of buckskin.

"Giwire, the doctor, is nude save for breech-cloth. Across his nose are two lines of red and two more across his lips. There are four vertical lines on each side of his face. He is painted like Ma´sewi (son of Earth Mother), 'because it is through Ma´sewi he hopes for success.' His hair is tied in a top knot, and over the fontanelle is painted a red cross 'to keep away witches.'

"An assistant holds a crystal to the light, and Giwire goes about the room in a daze (trance), as if searching for the patient's heart which has been stolen by a witch animal. The ceremony itself is called 'going after' (the patient's heart). As his assistant sings, Giwire sucks the patient in different places. Then, having rubbed ashes on his body against the witches, and on the calves of his legs so as not to tire, with the bear paw on the left hand and a flint knife in the right, Giwire rushes outdoors, slashing in the air with his flint, against the witches. To protect him, two War captains with bows and arrows follow, also a kinsman with a gun. Giwire is an old man, but he runs so fast that his companions can hardly keep up with him. He may go to the river for the heart—a stolen heart is usually found in the riverbank, or he may dig somewhere else, with his bear paw. In one notable case Giwire dug up his patient's heart under a cedar.

"Returning to the house of the patient, Giwire creeps in on hands and knees, clasping the 'heart' in the bear paw. The War captains take the 'heart' from him, his behavior being so violent that they have to hold him down. Then he stiffens into a kind of catalepsy, and his kinswomen have to massage him back to consciousness. They rub him with ashes. No matter how distressing his condition, his people may not cry; if they cry he might die.

"After Giwire comes to, he is given warm water to drink, and he goes out and vomits. Returning, he takes from the altar the eagle feathers and with them rolls up to the patient the 'heart,' three or four grains of corn (yellow, blue, red, and white) wrapped, one by one, in red cloth, bound with cotton. He undoes the tangle, searching out the thickly wrapped grains. If there are three grains only, the patient will die, if four, the patient will recover. In the latter case Giwire would say, 'There are enough.' He places the four grains on the palm of his right hand and blows as if blowing them back into the body of the patient. He blows toward the left arm of the patient, then toward the right arm, toward the left knee, and the right knee. After this, in a shell, he gives the patient the four grains of corn to swallow together with medicine from the bowl on the altar. In conclusion, the kinswomen of Giwire wash the head of the patient" [Parsons 1939:711–712].

Glacier Bull
Blackfoot, *Plains*
A shaman around the turn of the twentieth century who was renowned for being able to call upon his helping spirits night or day. Whenever a skeptic was present at one of his ceremonies, Glacier Bull's spirit would enter the darkened lodge and tie up the skeptic so tightly that the person could not get loose. The spirit would then instruct Glacier Bull to throw a robe over the doubter, and the latter would emerge untied.

Goda'ensiyus'ta'kwa
Seneca, *Northeast*
The shaman's medicine bundle [Parker 1923].

Goes Back
Gros Ventre, *Plains*
A female sucking shaman who doctored during the first part of the twentieth century. It was not unusual for Gros Ventre shamans' helping spirits to put limitations on the number of cases they were allowed to cure. In the following account, Coming Daylight tells of Goes Back's doctoring of her husband, Little Man, who had a pain near his heart accompanied by intermittent hemorrhaging as the result of medicine put on him by a sorcerer. Goes Back's treatment was conducted in a sweat lodge, and in this case, it seems as though she was exercising the one cure given to her for this particular illness:

"I called a woman doctor named Goes Back. I got a nice horse and hitched it at this woman's place as payment. This woman doctor said: 'I am going to doctor you (Little Man) once.' Other doctors had been trying to cure Little Man but they could not succeed because the one who had put the medicine on him was extremely powerful. Goes Back talked to the one (helping spirit) who had given her her power and said: 'You (the spirit) told me that I could use this medicine work just once, and that then I would get a particular person well.' This is what had been promised to this woman.

"So she said: 'I will ask for a sweat-lodge, like a man.' Only medicine men used to ask for a sweat-lodge. She said: 'I am going to doctor in this sweat-lodge.' Several people went into the sweat-lodge. I attended to the opening and shutting (of the door thereof). There were only certain rocks that they used and these were heated until red. Someone else (the 'fireman') attended to this. The patient (Little Man) was inside the sweat-lodge and the medicine woman invited some others to go in there. Except for the medicine woman, only men went in. I sat beside the door, but on the outside."

"They sang, and I heard the woman praying (to her spirit): 'My nephew has suffered a long time. Please listen to me. You promised that I would get some one person well by doctoring just once, and I want this to be that one time.' When she got through doctoring, that is, sucking, she said: 'Lift up the curtain.' So I lifted it up and opened the sweat-lodge, and one of the men there said: 'I too never believed these things. I am going outside to see for myself.' He asked the old woman doctor for the thing she had drawn out of the patient.

"So she gave it to him in his palm. It was just a little round thing. He took it, fingering it and smoothing it out. It turned out to be a little piece of white rag. It had been all balled up. On that little piece of white rag were seven marks, like needle-pointed writing, and at the end right in that rag was a piece of blood clot. The man saw this and said: 'Now I have seen something for myself with my own eyes.'

"They handed this around so that everybody could see it. Then they handed it back to the medicine woman. She said to this rag: 'I don't want you to ever come back again. You go out to where you belong.' So she wrinkled it up again and threw it in the flaming hot fire. As soon as she did that it burned up quickly.

"As soon as she had drawn it out of Little Man he felt much better. He got well because he knew that this thing was out of his system, and he quit having hemorrhages" [Coming Daylight in Cooper 1957:340–341].

Following the cure, Goes Back told Little Man who had put the evil medicine on him and why the person had done so: the sorcerer had convinced himself that Little Man was going after his wife and wanted to get even with Little Man. In response to being healed, Little Man promised to go on a vision quest, which he did.

Good Lance, Frank
Lakota, *Plains*
A shaman who practiced on the Pine Ridge Reservation during the first half of the twentieth century. He was an eagle doctor who held healing ceremonies in a darkened room in which he set up an altar. During his ceremonies, eagles could be heard flying around the room. He demanded that only Indian food such as boiled dog, fry bread, and *wojapi* (berry dessert) be used for the feasts following his ceremonies.

Good Singer
Gros Ventre, *Plains*
A female shaman who doctored during the first part of the twentieth century with the aid of an ancestral spirit helper. As were most Gros Ventre shamans, she was a sucking shaman. The following account of one of her healings was given by the wife of the patient:

"Once the man I was living with was very ill, almost dead. One of his wives—he had several besides myself—called in this medicine woman, Good Singer. The one that called her in made a smudge, with fire of buffalo chips on which some kind of medicine—sweet pine, or sweet grass—was sprinkled. Good Singer then smudged herself, putting the smoke up to her face four times and then rubbing it on her breast. Then she sang her song, the burden of which was: 'My pipe is lying here!' Then she was ready to doctor.

"She hit herself on the chest, and a bead came out of her mouth. She put the bead on the top of her foot and extracted it from the sole thereof. She next smudged the bead four times by putting it to her mouth, and then laid the bead down.

"Next she went to the patient and worked on him, sucked at the spot where his pain was, and after showing the people what she extracted from him swallowed it, and named the one who had caused the sickness. Then she swallowed her own medicine (the bead) and smudged her mouth four times. They gave her a lot of things for doing that—horses and blankets and such things" [Singer in Cooper 1957:343–344].

Gowäli
Cherokee, *Southeast*
The shaman's formulas; the word means "paper," "book," "that which has been written" [Mooney and Olbrechts 1932:145]. Each disease or ailment calls for the application of a specific formula. In addition, there are formulas for long life, gathering medicine, hunting and fishing, love attraction, using tobacco, examining the beads (see *adälön*), protection, and so forth. Each formula contains the proper prayers, songs, recitations, plants, and animal spirits that are needed to effect a cure. The appropriate order and timing of their use are also included in the formula. Each formula is thus a detailed account of how to conduct the proper healing ceremony for a particular ailment.

The origin of these formulas is unknown, but they are usually attributed to people who lived a long time ago or, less frequently, to some form of revelation on the part of the *adanöwiski* ("shaman"; see entry). The formulas for healing are sold from shaman to shaman; less powerful formulations, such as those for protection or for long life, are often sold to anyone. The most famous set of formulas is the Swimmer manuscript, obtained by James Mooney during the latter part of the nineteenth century from a shaman by that name. It contained 137 formulas. The document was brought back to the Smithsonian Institution but mysteriously disappeared.

In general, some of the formulas are recited, and others are sung. "When the formulas are recited the medicine man mumbles them under his breath, and at a very fast tempo, so that neither the patient nor any one of his household manages to catch a single word" [Mooney and Olbrechts 1932:155]. When they are sung, it is with a high-pitched falsetto voice accompanied by a peculiar nasal twang. In applying a formula, great attention is given to detail, because its efficacy lies not in the meaning of the words recited or sung but in the strict adherence to wording and form. For example, the shaman must be careful not to omit a single syllable of a recitation. In addition, there are many things that go along with the successful use of a formula, such as the proper gathering and preparing of medicinal plants, the proper administering of the medicine, and the proper attitude (unwavering belief) of the patient.

See *igawésdi* for related details.

Goyò

Takelma, *Oregon Seaboard*

Term for medicine man among the people living around the Rogue River valley in southwestern Oregon [Sapir 1909:185]. Spirits are attributed to mythical beings; inorganic objects such as sun, moon, wind, whirlwind, snow, and rain; locations such as definite rocks, mountains, and trees; animals; and half-human beings that inhabit the woods and waters. The spirit of the wind is particularly efficacious in driving sickness out of the body.

A disease or illness is caused by a disease spirit or pain that has become lodged in some part of the victim's body. This pain is a material object that must be removed by the shaman through a sucking technique. Most often the object is believed to have been sent by a sorcerer. A powerful sorcerer or spirit can cause an illness by merely wishing a person to be ill or by mentally poisoning him. The coyote is often blamed for this, sending his sickness through the hummingbird or whirlwind. In the case of a sorcerer, if the culprit is determined, he is forced to cure the victim upon threat of death.

Shamans often obtain several helping spirits, and each one has its own song that the shaman sings. For the most part, these spirits are associated with different animals such as wolf, rattlesnake, eagle, woodpecker, and mountain lion, but they can also come from the moon, wind, and so forth. The spirit of the sun is not desirable because shamans who have that power usually lose their children. Spirits are obtained most often during vision quests. Both men and women become shamans.

Healing ceremonies most often involve the shaman locating the disease object through his spirit helper, and then catching it and removing the object. Participants join in the singing while the shaman dances, but conspicuously absent is the use of a drum, which is unknown in Takelma healing ceremonies. During the ceremonies, an assistant, known as the shaman answerer, explains the unintelligible language being used by the shaman, which, for the most part, is inaudible to the participants. Healing ceremonies are performed during the day as well as at night. Fees for a healing ceremony vary greatly and are determined by the seriousness of the case. Sapir [1907:43] reports that sometimes women are given as payment.

In addition to the *goyò*, the Takelma have a second class of less powerful shamans known as *somlohólxaes* (see entry). These latter shamans appeal to an entirely different set of helping spirits.

Grand Medicine Society/Lodge/Ceremony

See *Midewiwin*.

Grant, Samson

Atsugewi, *California*

Samson Grant was a renowned shaman—a "big doctor with very strong (supernatural) powers" [Park 1986:ix]. He was born around 1850 in northeastern California among the Atsuge branch of the Atsugewi. Although he adopted Christianity, he continued to practice traditional medicine among his people. He was interviewed in the 1950s by Susan Park, then a student of Alfred Kroeber. Around the age of 15, Grant went on his first vision quest and acquired his traditional name, Walle ta mela. Shortly after he married, at around the age of 22, he began to have visions of two small boys, about a foot high, who called themselves Morning Butterfly. They gave him healing songs and told him to burn feathers during his healing ceremonies. Later he received power from two spirits called Morning Boy and Morning Girl. His third power was from Coyote. Of this power, he said, "He is not really Coyote but he says he is" [Park 1986:32–33]. He used these spirits to diagnose illnesses and to render the healing, but he did not begin doctoring until around the age of 50.

Grant said that his powers had come through vision quests at a particular lake where power resides. He said:

"These powers come to me. They like me. But I had to go to the big lake to get those powers (to come to me). If anyone wants to be a doctor, he has to go to the lake first before he can get his power. That's what all the Indians did; that's what the lake is for. . . . In this big lake that's where all the power stays. I'll go to the big lake and jump in the water. I might find something there. I might find a bow and arrow. I might find feathers there. If I find any feathers there I am going to be a doctor. . . . Then the powers would talk to me while I was lying there" [Park 1986:33].

Grant insisted that one could not learn healing from others but had to get one's own powers through dreams of spirits at the lake. Sometimes his lake visitations entailed swimming under the waters in search of sacred objects. Of such underwater encounters, he reported that "it is just as if I went to sleep and the waters just washed me out. I have been there and I stayed there ten or fifteen minutes or maybe twenty minutes" [Park 1986:33].

The following is a brief account, given by Grant, of his curing:

"I went behind the sick woman and everyone went. I was ready when I got there (meaning Morning Boy had already diagnosed the case for him). I went inside the house. Oh! That sick person was pretty bad. Lots of doctors gave her up.

"When I got through smoking I began to sing. I sang about five times before my powers said something. They said in my ear, 'We know what is the matter with that woman. That woman ate meat when she was menstruating. She ate meat and that is what makes her sick. Something has grown in her stomach,' my power said. 'We can cure that easy. We'll tell you what to do. Just do what we tell you.'

"So I doctored and doctored and they told me what to do. The woman had appendicitis. So I doctored her.

"I told the people, 'I'm going to doctor two nights, no more.'

"So I only doctored two nights, and I cured her and all the people went away. Now we drew out the appendicitis. We had the power in our hands to draw it out. Sometimes you have to suck it (the poison) out by your mouth.

"A poison looks like a diamond but it has a little black point on it. The poison goes in through the point; it just slides in.

"After I cured this woman they called me a good doctor.

"I have cured pneumonia. The power knows what is wrong. He knows how to cure sickness and tells me what to do" [Park 1986:31–32].

In addition to giving him healing powers, the power he called Butterfly also showed him how to swallow fire and eat flint. "At dances I swallow fire to show the people my power. I can put fire under my arms or on my belly and it won't burn me. I know how to hold it" [Park 1986:32].

Green, Joe
Northern Paiute, *Basin*

A famous shaman during the 1930s who received considerable attention from ethnographers. He resided on the Pyramid Lake Reservation in Nevada. Joe Green was unusual in that he not only followed traditional Paiute beliefs but was also an active member of the Native American Church (peyotists) and the Episcopal church. At one point, he was selected as the most devout Christian among Nevada Indians at an all-state interdenominational conference of Christian missionaries. However, having acquired his healing abilities from spirits, he was forced to continue responding to requests for healing under the threat of becoming ill or losing his life. His reputation as a shaman was widespread, and he became one of the wealthier healers in the area [Stewart 1956].

Grizzly-Bear Dance
Winnebago, *Midwest*

A dance given by those individuals who have been blessed (received power) during a vision quest by the grizzly bear. It is common for different individuals to receive different blessings or powers from the grizzly bear. Bear medicine is particularly powerful with regard to healing, as the following account illustrates:

"Little Priest had been wounded in so many places that he was practically dead. He was, of course, entirely unconscious when his relatives arrived. They decided to perform the grizzly-bear dance for him. He himself had been blessed by the grizzly bears when he was young.

"The dance was to be given at the lodge of an Indian named Good Soldier. They carried Little Priest to the lodge in a blanket so that they could sing for him and permit him to show the powers he possessed. He was unable to move on account of the wounds and the bruises he had gotten. The man who sang for him at that time was South-Wind. There were all in all ten Indians, entirely naked, except for their breechclouts. Little Priest had told South-Wind that he was a grizzly bear and that he could heal himself (no matter how badly he had been wounded).

"As soon as the songs and dancing commenced Little Priest began to move his little fingers. Soon he was able to move his arm as far as his forearm, and gradually he regained the power of moving the entire arm. Finally he sat up and began to keep time on the drum. Then he tried to stand on his feet, but owing to his weakness it was only with the greatest difficulty that he could straighten out

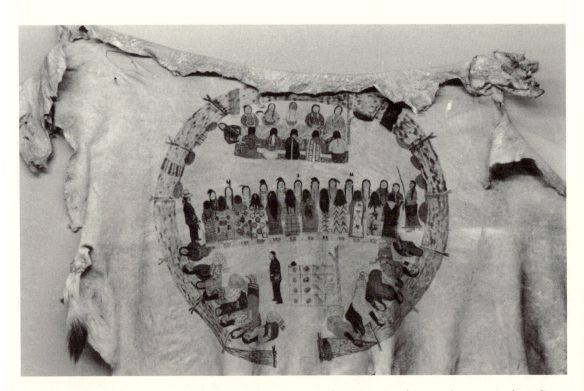

A bear dance scene painted on buckskin depicts spectators watching 12 pairs of men and women in dance lines as people at the table (top) play monarchs.

his body. Finally he stood erect. Then he started to walk around the lodge very slowly. The second circuit he made more easily, and by the time he had made the fourth circuit he was dancing just as the other dancers were with all his strength restored. Then he walked to the maⁿwarup'uru (ceremonial, earth-mound altar representing a bear's cave), took some earth, rubbed it on his wounds, and they were healed immediately. There was only one wound that he could not heal, which was situated on a part of his back that he could not reach with his hands.

"He sang many songs while dancing. These songs were the ones that the spirits had taught him when they blessed him" [Radin 1923:348–349].

If there are sick people at a Grizzly-Bear Dance, they place some tobacco on the maⁿwarup'uru and ask for life during the dance.

Guisiyag
Diegueño, *California Peninsula*
Alternative spelling of *kwisiyai* that appears in the *Respuesta of 1812* [Engelhardt 1920:181].

Guksu Ceremony
Pomo, *California*
An initiation ceremony that lasts for six days and includes scarification of selected children. The Pomo have six different supernatural beings living at the ends of the world (in the six cardinal directions). Guksu is the supernatural being who lives in the south, the direction most associated with the powers of healing by the Pomo. The children being initiated, both boys and girls, range in age from about 5 to 10 years old. The children are made to lie down on the ground, and each child has two 1-inch cuts made across the small of the back with a broken shell. The ceremony is also used to remove all illness from the village. In the 1870s, Powers first observed a variation of this dance among the Gallinomero that he referred to as a spear dance. He describes the mystical aspect of this dance.

"A woman as nearly nude as barbaric modesty will permit is placed in the center, squatting on the ground. Then some Indian intones a chant, which he sings alone, and the sport, such as it is, begins. At the bidding of the prompter, the clown makes a furious sally in one direction, and with his spear stabs the empty air. Then he dashes back in the opposite direction and slashes into the air again. Next he runs some other way and stabs again. Now perhaps he makes a feint to pierce the woman. Thus the prompter keeps him chasing backward and forward, spearing the thin air toward every point on the compass, or making passes at the woman, until nearly tired out, and the patience of the American spectators is exhausted, and they begin to think the whole affair will terminate in 'mere dumb show.' But finally, at a word from the prompter, the spearman makes a tremendous run at the woman and stabs her in the umbilicus. She falls over on the ground, quivering in every limb, and the blood jets forth in a purple stream. The Indians all rush around her quickly and hustle her away to another place, where they commence laying her out for the funeral pyre, but huddle around her so thickly all the while that the Americans cannot approach to see what is done. Thus they mystify matters and hold some powwow over her for a considerable space of time, when she somehow mysteriously revives, recovers her feet, goes away to her wigwam, encircled by a bevy of her companions, dons her robe, and appears in the circle as well as ever, despite that terrible spear-thrust" [Powers 1877:179–180].

The Guksu dancers also form a class of medicine men. When they are called upon to doctor, they adorn their Guksu ceremony attire. These medicine men never speak or sing over their patients; rather, they constantly blow on a special double-bone whistle during the healing procedure. They approach the patient the same way they approach the ceremony house during the dance—that is, by coming in from the woods impersonating the supernatural Guksu. Following the healing ceremony, the shaman "ran rapidly out of the village and into the hills, where he stopped and turned his head toward the left four times. He then disappeared and was supposed to have returned to his supernatural abode in the south, carrying with him the ailment of the patient" [Barrett 1917a:431].

Hächamoni

Keres, *Southwest*

The Sia Pueblo term for special offerings presented to a shaman as part of a formal request for healing. These offerings are also used in the altar displays for the ceremonies of their different religious societies. The offerings consist of notched and painted wooden sticks, usually willow, to which plumes are attached. "The hächamoni are symbolic of the beings to whom they are offered, the messages or prayers being conveyed through the notches upon the sticks. These symbols frequently have herrotuma (more slender sticks representing official staff) bound to them with threads of yucca" [Stevenson 1894:76]. Thus, the hächamoni can take many different forms.

There are ritual procedures to be followed in the gathering of these sticks as well as in their preparation. Once the sticks have been properly carved, they are painted with black, yellow, and turquoise ground pigments mixed with water. Stevenson [1894:91–92] provides the following details of ceremonial preparation:

"While the hächamoni were being colored the ho'naaite (shaman) was busy sorting plumes. He first laid thirteen turkey plumes separately upon the floor, forming two lines; upon each plume he laid a fluffy eagle feather, and then added successively to each group a plume from each of the birds of the cardinal points, turkey plumes being used instead of chapparal cocks'. A low weird chant was sung while the ho'naaite and his vicar tied each pile of plumes together with native cotton cord, the ho'naaite waving each group, as he completed it, in a circle from left to right before his face. The woman at the same time made four rings of yucca, 1 1/4 inches in diameter, some two dozen yucca needles having been wrapped in a hank and laid in a bowl of water. The child brought the hank from the farther end of the room to the woman, who, taking a needle of the yucca, wound it four times around her thumb and index finger; then wrapping this with an extra thread of yucca formed the ring. When the four rings were completed the child took them to the paint stone, which the woman had removed to the far end of the room, and dipped them into the yellow paint and laid them by the woman, who tied three of the piles of plumes together and afterwards handed the rings to the ho'naaite, who added to each ring a plume from the wing of a humming bird.... In attaching the plume offerings to the hächamoni, the latter are held between the large and second toes of the right foot of the men and woman."

Hadaho

Kwakiutl, *Northwest Coast*

A shaman from the Koskimo village around the turn of the twentieth century. The following is a description, provided by the shaman Giving-Potlatches-in-the-World, of a healing ceremony conducted in part by Hadaho on princess Woman-Made-to-Invite of the house of Beginning-to-Give-Potlatches. Hadaho was treating the patient for a sickness "at the lower part of the chest at the upper end of the stomach" and was being assisted by three other shamans, Place-of-Getting-Rich, Great-Dance, and Post-of-World:

"Now Great-Mountain asked me to go with him and his wife, and we went into the house of Beginning-to-Give-Potlatches. Then we were asked to sit down at the right hand side of the door of the house. Now I saw Woman-Made-to-Invite lying down on a new mat in the middle of the rear of the house. When all the men and women who did not menstruate and the children had come in Beginning-to-Give-Potlatches arose and spoke. He said, 'Welcome, supernatural ones, for you have come to fight for my child with the Evil-Bringing-Woman. I mean this, supernatural ones, now you will really suck it out,' said he. Now none of the shamans of the Koskimo went near Woman-Made-to-Invite, the sick woman, for they kept together sitting down in the middle of the right hand side of the house. They do not act in the way as is done by the Nakwaxdaxu, for the song leaders beat fast time four times before the shaman comes into the house. And so the first to stand up was Hadaho, and he sat down at the right side of Woman-Made-to-Invite. Then they took off the shirt of Woman-Made-to-Invite and immediately Hadaho pressed his right hand on the lower end of the chest, not making a sound. Then Beginning-to-Give-Potlatches took a small dish and poured fresh water into it. After he had done so Beginning-to-Give-Potlatches called the four late shamans, old women, to go and pray that the shaman might cure her. The name for the four women is 'Those-who-Pray-for-the-Shaman.' Now two women sat down on the right hand side of Hadaho, and two sat down on his left. And when the four who pray for the shaman were ready, Hadaho put his right hand into the water in the small dish and he put the water into his mouth and took it in his hand. Now he rinsed his mouth. As soon as he had finished, he bent his mouth to the upper end of the stomach of the sick woman. As soon as he began to suck the women began to pray speaking together, the four praying-women of the shaman. They said, 'Go ahead, go ahead, curer, curer, curer, who begs for our true friend. You, supernatural power, supernatural power, go ahead, go ahead! Now have mercy of her, use your supernatural power that you may make her alive with your true life-bringer of your supernatural power. Supernatural power, go ahead, go ahead, curer, curer, curer.' As soon as the shaman lifted his head, for this is referred to by the Indians as lifting the head, when he stops sucking the sick woman, then again the four women said together, 'Now it has come, now it has come, now it has really come. You have obtained what made sick our friend,' said they. Then the shaman pressed with his right hand his mouth and he took out of his mouth saliva and put it on his hand. He squeezed the saliva which is called by the shamans of the Koskimo 'mixed with sickness.' He put his hand into the water in the small dish and he squeezed it in the water so that all the saliva should come off. Hadaho just squeezed what was referred to as the sickness with his right hand. Then he lifted his hand and he opened his hand and blew upon it once. Then he blew upward what is referred to as the sickness. This was all that Hadaho did" [Boas 1930:15–16].

Hadigadjisashooh

Seneca, *Northeast*

The Husk-Faces, who belong to the Husk-Face Society of shamans. These shamans doctor their patients in the same manner as the False-Face Society shamans, except that they use water instead of ashes in effecting their cures [Skinner 1925b:197].

As with the False-Face Society, Husk-Face Society members wear carved wooden masks during their healing ceremonies. These masks imbue the dancer with the supernatural qualities of the spirit face represented in the carving. The masks are treated as living beings and contain supernatural powers. Skinner [1925b:201–202] offers the following description:

"Some masks know in advance when they are to be used in doctoring, and beads of sweat are seen upon them. Others perspire when disaster is about to befall their owners; they also refuse to hang straight under these circumstances, or when they have been offended in some way. One mask is reputed to have had the power to sweat blood as a warning of impending peril. Some fall from the wall under such circumstances, and some drop down to announce to the family of the owner the death of that individual, should it occur away from home. One noted antique mask at Cattaraugus was supposed to have been able to instruct other and newer masks, and was in demand to put under cover with them so that it might impart its knowledge and virtue to them."

Hadntin
Apache, *Southwest*
See *hoddentin*.

Hadrauta
Cayuga, *Northeast*
Male dreamers; female dreamers are *hodrauta*. These people have the ability to see into things, like fortune-tellers. They are used to perform the dreamer rite, which is used to diagnose illness. See *eyondwanshgwut* for details.

Hai detoi
Pomo, *California*
A stick of madrona wood used by the *dja minawan* (outfit doctors; see entry) during their healing ceremonies; translates to "stick striped." It has feathers attached to one end and a flint on the other end [Loeb 1934a:11].

Hakan
Keres, *Southwest*
The Fire Society at Acoma Pueblo, one of four known medicine societies from this pueblo. See

Hictiani for an elaboration on their healing ceremonies [White 1932:107].

Halaait
Gitksan, *Northwest Coast*
One of two terms for shaman. See *swanassu* for details.

Halaidm swanaskxw
Tsimshian, *Northwest Coast*
A shaman who has aquired the power to heal. See *swanaskxw* for details.

Halait
Tsimshian, *Northwest Coast*
Shaman; Boas [1916:562] translates the term to "Chief Mountain." This is the general term for shaman. A more specific term is *swanaskxw* (see entry).

When doctoring a sick patient, the shaman called upon to perform the healing ceremony usually invites other male and female shamans to assist in the cure. The following is an account of the general nature of their healing ceremonies:

"When a person is sick, then the wife or the husband of the sick one will offer much property to

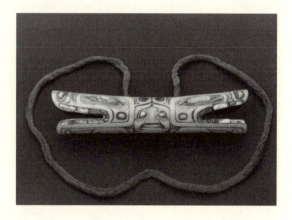

In service of the halait, or shaman, this Tsimshian amulet, carved of bone and inlaid with bright abalone shell in ca. 1860, depicts a human figure between two spirit heads, which appear to be wolves. Amulets, such as the one pictured, are worn around the neck during healing ceremonies and bring back the patient's wandering soul.

H the male shaman to treat the patient. Then the male shaman assembles all his shaman friends, sometimes ten or eighteen, and they all go to the house where the sick person is. One of them carries a large bag in which the shaman's implements are kept, and another one carries a round skin drum consisting of a hoop over which a drumhead is spanned on one side, while on the opposite side two crossing skin straps are spanned which form a handle. Then they all enter, and sit down on one side of the house, the shaman at the head of the patient. He opens his bag containing the rattles and takes out his rattle and dancing-apron first, the crown of grizzly-bear claws, and the figures of various kinds of animals made of bone or stone, also a small leather bag containing red ocher, which he puts on his face; and he hands the ocher to his companions, and all paint their faces. The shaman also puts eagle down on his head, and hands it to his companions, and they all do likewise. Then he puts on his apron and his crown of grizzly-bear claws, hangs the figures of animals around his neck, and takes his rattle in his right hand. Then he takes out his small vessel, and some one pours cold water into it. The shaman, who is naked, dips the fingers of his left hand into the cold water, puts the fingers into his mouth, and blows the water on the bare body of the patient. He only wears his apron. Then he begins to work. He calls upon all his supernatural helpers, saying, 'Save him, save him!' and his companions repeat what he has said. They all beat time with the batons which they have in their hands, and the drummer beats his drum. The shaman repeats this four times, and the singers do the same. Again he dips his fingers into the cold water and blows it over the body of the patient. Then the shaman sings his first song, and his partners sing with him. They beat their batons, and the drummer beats his drum. While the first and second songs which the shaman has given out are being sung, he works around the patient, shaking his rattle, which he holds in his right hand. His eyes are closed, and his left hand is raised, with the palm toward the patient. Thus he dances around the fire. A female shaman is seated at the foot of the patient, wearing her crown of grizzly-bear claws. She also wears a necklace of carved figures of an-

imals, has a rattle in her right hand, which she shakes lightly. Her eyes are closed, and she also holds her left hand raised toward the patient. Thus they continue through six or seven songs. Then the shaman rests and tells his vision. If he tells the people who called him that the patient will get well, they are glad; or if he has to say that he can not be cured, the relatives of the sick one give him more property. Thus he comes with his party every day.

"If the patient dies, the shamans return everything that they have received from the relatives of the sick one.

"If in his vision the shaman saw the soul of the patient close to a body in the graveyard, the relatives of the sick one invite more than eight or ten shamans to come with the principal one, and also two or four female shamans. They start to work early in the evening. All the male shamans put on their crowns of grizzly-bear claws and wear their dancing-aprons and their necklaces, and have the rattles in their right hand. Thus they march around the fire in the house where the sick person lies. The four female shamans sit down, two on each side of the patient—one on each side of the head, and one on each side of the feet. They also wear their crowns of grizzly-bear claws, and each has a rattle in the right hand. While the male shamans are marching around the fire, the female shamans shake their rattles which they hold in their right hand, and hold a white eagle tail in the left hand with which to fan away the disease. Thus they try to bring back the soul of the sick one from the dead body in the grave. The ten male shamans have their faces blackened with charcoal. They are dressed only with their dancing-aprons. After they have finished marching around the fire, all the male shamans go out; but the singers remain in the house, singing, and the four women continue to fan away the sickness. Then the male shamans go to the graveyard, leading four lads, each of whom holds a torch to light the way. When they reach the graveyard they stand around the place where the corpse is. They continue to rattle, and at a given signal they all strike the ground with their rattles. The females remaining in the house also strike the ground with their rattles. The singers keep on singing a tune which moves in a four-part rhythm. Then the principal shaman drops his rattle, takes up the soul of the patient in both of his hands, which he holds close together, and goes back from the grave with closed hands. The second man takes one rattle in each hand, and all the rest march along behind them. The man who has caught the soul gives a signal to the four women before he enters. All those who had been to the graveyard march around the fire four times, as they did before they went out. Then the principal shaman puts the soul of the patient on his own head to give it strength. After four days the soul of the patient gets better through contact with the head of the principal shaman. Then he assembles all his companions. They dance around the patient, and finally the leader takes the soul of the sick one from his own head and puts it on the head of the patient; and he orders all the people who live in the same house where the sick one is to keep silent for four days, else the soul might fly away and the patient might die.

"Sometimes the soul of a sick person is swallowed by a shaman. No one must pass behind or in front of a shaman while he is eating, lest his soul be swallowed by him. Therefore all the people are afraid of both male and female shamans.

"The sign that a person's soul has been swallowed by a shaman is that his nose is bleeding all the time. When a shaman sees in a vision that the soul of a sick person has been swallowed by another shaman, the two are called to sit down by the side of the patient—the one who swallowed the soul at the foot end; the other one at the head. And while the shamans are singing, the one who is to cure the patient strikes the back of the shaman who has swallowed the soul of the sick one with his rattle which he is holding with his right hand, and he strikes his stomach with his left hand. He strikes hard and moves both of his hands upward until the shaman who has swallowed the soul opens his mouth. Immediately the other shaman throws away his rattle, puts both hands into the mouth, and takes out the soul of the sick one. Then the other shaman vomits blood. The shaman who is about to cure the patient puts the soul on his own head, and after four days he returns it to the patient, who then recovers" [Tate in Boas 1916:558–560].

In addition to these healing procedures, the Tsimshian shamans extract disease objects, as described in the following account:

"The instrument used (for incantations) is a rattle, generally in the shape of a bird or a frog, in the body of which a few small stones are placed. This is whirled about the patient while a song is sung. Occasionally the doctor applies his ear, or his mouth, to the place where the pain or disorder chiefly rests. It is also very common, at this stage, to make incisions where the pain is felt, or to apply fire to the place by means of burning tinder made of dried wild flax. If relief follows these measures, the doctor asserts that he has extracted the foul substance that has done the mischief; which substance is supposed by them to be the bad or poisonous medicine some evil-disposed one had silently inserted into the invalid's body" [Duncan in Boas 1916:561].

Haldawit
Tsimshian, *Northwest Coast*
Sorcerer or witch. Such individuals are often diagnosed as being the cause of sickness. The following is a brief account of their practice as found among the Tsimshian:

"They (witches) steal a portion of a corpse, which they place in a small, long, water-tight box. A stick is placed across the middle of the box, and thin threads are tied to this stick. The piece of corpse is placed at the bottom of the box, and part of the clothing or hair of the person whom the witch desires to bewitch is tied to these strings. If it is in immediate contact with the body, the person will die soon; if it is hung a little higher, he will be sick for a long time. If hair is put into the box he will die of headache; if part of a moccasin, his foot will rot; if saliva is used, he will die of consumption. If the person is to die at once, the *haldawit* cuts the string from which the object is suspended, so that it drops right on the corpse. This box has a cover, and is kept closely tied up. It is kept buried under the house or in the woods. After the witch has killed his enemy, he must go around the house in which the dead one is lying, following the course of the sun. After the enemy has been buried, he must lie down on the grave and crawl around it, again following the course of the sun, and attired in the skin of some animal. If he does not do this, he must die" [Boas 1916:563–564].

Witches who were found out were executed.

Hanaitus
Cayuga, *Northeast*
The Medicine Men's Society. The healing ceremonies of this society may be performed only by members. See *eyondwanshgwut* for details.

Hanbloglaka
Lakota, *Plains*
The first aspect of a *yuwipi* ceremony; translates to "he tells of his vision." When the ceremony is ready to begin, all the lights are turned off. The shaman begins by making a statement, speaking in a normal voice, about why the ceremony has been called. This includes the name of the patient and the nature of the illness. There may also be announcements of other healing ceremonies soon to be performed. Following this, the shaman gives "a description of parts of his vision, an assurance to God that the people gathered here were accustomed to using the Pipe, and pleas for treatment of the sick, delivered in a rhythmical, cantorial style" [Kemnitzer 1969:28].

The *hanbloglaka* is not a necessary aspect of every *yuwipi* (see entry) ceremony. The actual form and content of the ritual vary from shaman to shaman, depending on who taught them the ceremony and what instructions they subsequently received from their helping spirits about its proper ritual.

Hanmdepi
Lakota, *Plains*
Literally, "to dream," but the term "is applied almost wholly to the custom of seeking for a dream or revelation" from a spirit [Dorsey 1894:436]. It is related to the Lakota word for vision quest, *hanble ceyapi*, which translates to "crying for a vision" [DeMallie 1984:83].

Hánwahe waci
Iowa, *Plains*
A power ceremony performed by the Medicine Dance Society. It literally means "day dance" but

is called "making friends with the buffalo doctors." Iowa buffalo doctors are adept at treating wounds. The ritual entails the buffalo doctors' causing a buffalo to appear, while the Medicine Dance Society members cause a bear to appear [Skinner 1920:251].

Harav heya
Mojave, *Southwest*
Described as old and nearly blind, this shaman was a specialist in the treatment of *hiwey lak* (anus pain) and *hikupk* (venereal diseases). He reported on his healing technique as follows:

"I use my right hand, because my power comes from the Ancient Ones. I may, however, also use my left hand, as do those whose power comes from Avikwame (the name of a mountain in the Mohave area). . . . Some shamans forbid certain foods, but I don't, even though some foods may pull down the resistance of the patient. I give them whatever food is handy, and should it harm them, I will cure them of that illness too. As to their relatives and myself—we can eat what we want. . . . With my right hand I gently press the abdomen, and the region just below the solar plexus. It is only a sort of massage, because the patient is too weak for me to hurt him. Then the stomach gas goes out either way (eructation or flatus). I blow on the solar plexus first and then immediately press my hand on the same spot, to keep my breath on it. I may also blow on the patient, starting from the upper part of his chest and progressing toward his abdomen, to remove the pains. If the pains are strong, I will also boil the bark of the white mesquite tree, or make a willow bark tea and give it to the patient to drink" [Devereux 1961:157–158].

Hatcamuni
Keres, *Southwest*
The Acoma Pueblo word for prayer sticks. They are always cut from a living bush or tree, usually a willow or cedar. These sticks vary in size and are carved and painted in many different ways. Sometimes feathers are attached to them. While making a prayer stick, the individual isolates himself so that no one else can view his work. Once the sticks have been used, they are usually thrown

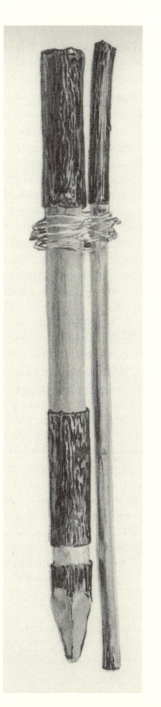

Hächamoni, offerings made of notched and painted wooden sticks, are sacred requests to a shaman from an individual requesting to be healed. Pictured here are the wooden sticks before the attachment of plume offerings.

over the cliff from various locations; however, some are buried at the foot of the mesa.

In cases of minor ailments, usually only one medicine man is called to the home of the patient. In serious cases, the patient is treated by members of a medicine society. When only one shaman is required, a relative of the patient, usually the father, makes a prayer stick and prays for the health of his relative. The prayer stick is then given to the patient, who also prays for recovery with it. This prayer stick is then presented to the shaman on behalf of the patient. When this ritual is performed, the shaman is obligated by his powers to treat the sick person [White 1932:125–126].

Hatcok sumatc
Mojave, *Southwest*
A specialist called the dog doctor [Stewart 1974:9]. They are renowned as powerful shamans who can cure almost anything but are most effective in treating dog bites and epilepsy. They "also treated sickness in infants that was believed to be a consequence of the mother having looked at a dead dog or 'anything ugly' during her pregnancy" [Stewart 1974:10].

Hayoka
Lakota, *Plains*
See *heyóka*.

Heammawihio
Cheyenne, *Plains*
The Wise One Above, the principal god who lives above. In prayer, he is addressed first, and when smoking the sacred pipe, the first smoke is offered to him. The Cheyenne have an equally powerful and beneficent high god living under the ground called *Ahktunowihio* [Grinnell 1923:2:88].

Heliga
Kwakiutl, *Northwest Coast*
Healer [Edmonson 1958:70].

Helika
Kwakiutl, *Northwest Coast*
The supernatural power used by shamans for curing; one form of *tlogwe* (see entry) [Goldman 1975:180].

Hemaneh
Cheyenne, *Plains*

A transvestite shaman; translates to "half-man, half-woman." The last two *hemaneh* shamans died in 1879. These shamans were associated with the blue sky space, one of seven regions of the universe in Cheyenne cosmology. They wore women's clothes and did not use the inverted speech used by other Cheyenne shamans because they were already inverted by their attire. They were renown for their healing abilities [Schlesier 1987:67].

Hematasooma
Cheyenne, *Plains*

The free soul or dream soul. This is the part of the shaman that makes magical flights to the spirit world. "The unconscious separation of three of the four parts of one's *hematasooma* led to sickness and eventually to physical death" [Schlesier 1987:10]. Domesticated plants and animals have no *hematasooma*, but natural (wild) ones do.

Hen fó
Tewa, *Southwest*

Small bundles of prayer plumes referred to as the clothing of the gods. These prayer offerings consist of small, soft eagle plumes and other feathers that are sprinkled with cornmeal, breathed on, and wrapped in corn husks. In former times, everybody made such offerings; today, however, they are most often made by ceremonial dancers and kachina. Such bundles are usually part of the formal request for a medicine man's healing services. After the healing, the prayer offering is placed in a field or buried in the ground.

Herrotume
Keres, *Southwest*

The Sia Peublo term for wooden staffs decorated with plumes that are used by shamans in sacred ceremonies [Stevenson 1894:78].

Hetimwok
Coast Yuki, *California*

The healing ritual performed by sucking doctors. After sucking on the patient, the shaman goes out into the bushes and speaks with spirits. After-

ward, he comes back to the patient and continues to dance and sing [Loeb 1934a:57].

Heyóka
Assiniboin, Dakota, Lakota, Plains-Cree, Plains-Ojibwa, Ponca, *Plains*

The "contraries" or "sacred clowns" who have had visions or dreams of the Thunder Beings called *wakinyan* (see entry). The vision can also take the form of water symbols or lightning. In fact, Lame Deer [1972:241] reports that a Lakota "doesn't even have to see the actual lightning, or hear the thunder in his dream. . . . Every dream which has some symbol of the thunder powers in it will make you into a *heyoka*." Those who have had such dreams are required to participate in ceremonies by acting and speaking backwards, or they will be struck by lightning. They perform such antics as riding their horses backwards, washing themselves with dirt, saying the opposite of what they mean, and expressing joy by sighs and moans. "In the oppressive heat of summer . . . [they] fold around them robe on robe, and lean over a rousing fire, sniveling and shaking with cold" [Pond 1867:45]. They are also known to perform a special dance that involves dipping their arms into a kettle of boiling water to grab pieces of meat. As they perform this dance they splash the hot water on one another. It has been reported that to protect their skin from burns, the dancers apply the juice from either the whip root plant *(Echinacea augustifolia)* or the red false mallow *(Malvastrum coccineum)* to form a mucilaginous coating on the skin [Gilmore 1919:31, 103]. They also wear special costumes during this dance, including a long-nosed mask made of buffalo hide or cloth.

The vision of the Thunder Beings often involves a healing for the recipient, as evidenced in the following account by Raymond Buckley, a Dakota:

"When I was about ten years old I got real sick. I had a fever and was out of my head a lot of the time. My body hurt all over. One evening about sundown I look over west. A big thunderhead was rolling up there. I look in the middle of it and there was *Thunder*. He had a bow and would shoot lightning bolts from it every now and then. He came right down towards me from the thunderhead and said, 'Don't worry. I am going to make you well again.' He told me that when I grew up I would have to dance clown. After that I got better. I didn't dance clown right away. When I was grown up, about age 21, I danced for the first time. I made myself a mask and a costume of gunny sacks and took part. If I hadn't done this, sooner or later I would have been hit by lightning" [Howard 1954:257].

Apart from the special dance they perform, the *heyóka* appear at other ceremonies such as the Sun Dance. Their antics cause the participants to laugh and thus lighten the serious mood. Although no special healing powers are granted to the *heyóka*, many prominent healers were known to be a *heyóka*, such as the powerful Lakota shaman John Fire Lame Deer. According to Lewis [1981:101]:

"The healing powers of *heyoka* maskers were combined with an unwanted but unavoidable power to neutralize or destroy the work of other healers or procedures. The 'backward' (reversed) public behaviors of the *heyoka* were often comic but contained also a connotation of potential disruption or destructiveness, producing uneasy laughter and avoidance from members of the audience at ceremonies and in daily life. The *heyoka* consequently experienced a social alienation, ceremonially and in daily life, in some ways similar to that of a madman. On ceremonial occasions, playing to a larger audience, the *heyoka* was disguised in ludicrous, tattered, unclean apparel. He brought fear, apprehension, and derisive laughter into solemn proceedings. He seemed to strive to arouse anxiety, revulsion, and denial. He personified the unpredictable, the deviant, the unspeakable. He fomented disorder as if to invoke the magic of chaos, leaving its eventual resolution to others."

Hianyi
Keres, *Southwest*
Blessing; a Keresan term meaning "the road by which the Spirits travel" [Parsons 1939:489].

Hictiani
Keres, *Southwest*
The Acoma Flint Society, one of the four known medicine societies from this pueblo. The patient may request to have one of these societies treat him, especially in cases of severe illness. Once treated by this society, the patient is then eligible for membership.

To secure the efforts of a medicine society, the relatives of the patient make some *wabani* (feather bunches). Usually the father of the patient prays for recovery with one of them and then gives it to the patient, who does the same. The *wabani* are then presented to the headman of the society, called the *naicdia*. The headman calls together the doctors of the society, distributes the *wabani* among them, and tells them about the sick patient. If the patient is critically ill, they proceed to him at once.

Generally, the society goes to the house of the patient for treatment. A room is cleared of all furniture, and they set up their altar and lay out all their healing paraphernalia. Each doctor has a *honani* (corn ear fetish; see entry), which is placed in front of the altar. Also included are medicine bowls, small stone figures of animals (the beast gods from which they derive their powers), large flints, a bowl of sacred water with a gourd dipper, a refuse bowl for extracted objects, and a rock crystal to divine the location of the disease. Each medicine man has a black band painted across his face that covers the eyes. Their long hair is tied up in front with a corn husk, and two short turkey feathers are worn at each temple.

When all has been prepared, the patient is brought in and placed on a blanket on the floor. Several relatives may also be in attendance, but the healing ceremony is not open to the general public. The *naicdia* prepares medicine for the patient by mixing herbs with water in a special medicine bowl, called *waititcani*, while singing a song toward each of the four cardinal directions, beginning with the north. Afterward, other shamans sprinkle their own medicines into this bowl.

The diagnosis is begun by using a special quartz crystal, called *macaiyoyo*. Each shaman has such a crystal that is used on the patient. Afterward, all the shamans except for two go behind the altar, where they sit down and begin to sing. The remaining two dance in front of the altar and the patient. They hold an eagle-wing feather in each hand, with which they make cutting and slashing movements away from the patient—to wipe away the disease. When they are finished, the eagle feathers are laid by the altar. Then they massage the patient with their hands. If they find some foreign object in the body, they suck it out and spit it in the refuse bowl. Common items removed are stones, rags, bits of yarn, and sometimes even a live snake. Once the items are deposited in the bowl, the shamans gargle, wash their hands, and go back to the altar. Then two other doctors come out and repeat the process. This is done until all have doctored the patient, with the *naicdia* being the last person to do so.

When the curing is complete, the *naicdia* administers the *wawa* (medicine) to the patient from the medicine bowl. The patient drinks the medicine, and some of it is sprinkled on him. The remaining *wawa* is given to the relatives in attendance to drink. This concludes the ceremony.

The members of the medicine society then depart, leaving two shamans behind to watch over the recovery of the patient. These attending shamans pray and sing a great deal. The altar is left in place for four days, after which it is removed to the society house. The society receives no compensation for the healing but does receive many gifts if the patient subsequently joins the society [White 1932:109–111].

Hila
Eskimo, *Mackenzie-Yukon, Arctic Coast*
See *sila*.

Hilleeshwa
Seminole, *Southeast*
Also: *hilis* [Hodge 1907:549]. The term for medicine among the Cow Creek Seminole. Among the Miccosuki, the word for medicine is *aiyicks* or *aiyickschee* [Capron 1953:162]. From these terms come their terms for shamans. Among the Cow Creek band the shaman is called *hilleesha putschashee* ("looks after"), while in the Miccosuki band he is known as *aiyicks meforsee* ("takes care of") [Capron 1953:162].

A shaman's medicine is carried in a deerskin medicine bundle folded with the hair on the outside. There are three major medicine bundles for the three Seminole bands (Big Cypress Seminole, Cow Creek Seminole, and Tamiami Trail Miccosuki). "Within the outer covering, each kind of medicine is done up in a small piece of buckskin, and wound with a buckskin thong. The private medicine of certain of the Indians is usually wrapped in cloth. The Medicine consists of many different things: pieces of horn, feathers, stones, dried animal parts—some six or seven hundred different items in each Medicine Bundle—but the identical things in each of the three bundles" [Capron 1953:164]. The medicine in these bundles is no longer used for curative purposes.

Little is known of Seminole shamanism, but the medicines contained in a medicine bundle are given to the Seminole by *Este Fasta*, "person-give," who acts as an intermediary between the Creator and the people. When a new medicine is needed, it is *Este Fasta* who brings it to Earth and places it in the shaman's medicine bundle. Thus the concept of a shaman's personal guardian spirit seems to be absent, certainly in the twentieth century.

Hilotca kaiyan
Southern Pomo, *California*
Outfit doctors. These shamans impersonate certain powerful healing spirits by wearing specific costumes during their healing ceremonies. They only give medicine and sing; they never suck on their patients [Loeb 1934a:101].

Hilyulit
Yuki, *California*
A ritual cure performed by a society. "Songs pertaining to the various spirits impersonated by the cult initiates—the Creator and the ghosts—were sung until the patient trembled violently. Thereby it was known which kind of spirit had 'frightened' him into illness. Then the cure was arranged by having the corresponding spirit impersonation—singing, dancing, and touching—made for him. This worked homeopathically" [Kroeber 1940: 213–214].

Hinawa
Zuni, *Southwest*
The word for the sacred white corn flour that is used in all religious rituals. It is most frequently used as an offering during prayers. Every Zuni carries a small bag of it with him wherever he goes [Bourke 1892:507].

Hishämi
Keres, *Southwest*
The Sia Pueblo term for a bundle of two eagle feathers used in sacred ceremonies. During a healing ceremony, the shamans dip their *hishämi* into a bowl of medicine water to sprinkle the patient and also use them to wipe away the disease-causing agent [Stevenson 1894:79].

Hithoitcimai sumatc
Mojave, *Southwest*
A shaman who specializes in treating toothaches. "He puts his finger by the fire and heats it, then puts it on top of the patient's tooth. He does it lots of times, for fifteen or twenty minutes. Then he blows on it and kills the pain" [Stewart 1974:11]. A more common treatment is to heat a stick in a fire and then press it against the tooth to draw out the pain.

Hithorau sumatc
Mojave, *Southwest*
A shaman that specializes in the treatment of sore eyes. Most of them are women. The treatment involves the shaman rolling her tongue on the inside of the eyelids and blowing her breath on them [Stewart 1974:11].

Hiwarau sumatc
Mojave, *Southwest*
A shaman that specializes in the treatment of heart trouble [Stewart 1974:10].

Hiweyi
Central Miwok, *California*
A special dance that was revealed to a sucking shaman named Tciplitcu (also Chiplichu) during the early 1870s in a vision. The dance usually lasts four days, beginning at dusk each day and continuing to midnight. It is used most often in cur-

ing ceremonies to treat illness caused by the sighting of a spirit [Gifford 1926b:402].

Hiweylak sumatc
Mojave, *Southwest*
A shaman that specializes in the treatment of stomach, bladder, and kidney ailments; venereal disease; and blood disorders. "In the case of a man whose 'urine was stopped up,' he 'steps on your back and it starts in an hour or so, because his power goes in through his feet'" [Stewart 1974:9].

Hobbomock
Massachuset, *Northeast*
Dialectical variant: *Hobbamoqui.* Identified in the early literature as an evil deity, but it appears to be a shaman's helping spirit, based on the following:

"This as farre as wee can conceive is the devill, him they call upon to cure their wounds and diseases. . . . This Hobbomock appears in sundry formes unto them, as in the shape of a man, a deare, a fawne, an eagle, etc., but most ordinarily as a snake" [Purchas in Jarvis 1820:94]. Jarvis concludes that *Hobbomock* "is evidently the Oké (see entry) or Tutelary Deity, which each Indian worships" [Jarvis 1820:94].

Hochinagen
Seneca, *Northeast*
Healer or shaman [Hewitt 1918:491]. For an example of their healing practice, see *nikahnegaah.*

Hoddentin
Apache, *Southwest*
Also *hadntin* [Bourke 1892:500]. The yellow pollen taken from cattails (tule) that is applied to a patient's body by the shaman during a healing ceremony. It is also fed to the sick person as a medicine. Buckskin bags of this pollen are carried and used by nearly every Apache. One informant reports, "When we Apache go on the warpath, hunt, or plant, we always throw a pinch of hoddentin to the sun" and say a prayer for the undertaking [Bourke 1892:501]. During their morning prayers, a pinch of it is blown toward the dawn. In fact, it seems to be used with all prayers. Stone [1932:27] reports that "all plains Indians possessed it."

Hodrauta
Cayuga, *Northeast*
See *hadrauta*.

Hohnuhka
Cheyenne, *Plains*
A society of "contraries" (people who do things backwards or not in a normal manner). Members of this society are both male and female shamans. Their major function is to perform during the annual midsummer Massaum ritual, a five-day ceremony "performed in order that the success of a beginning is assured" [Schlesier 1987:72]. Massaum derives its name from *massane*, meaning "acting contrary to normal." The shamans perform spectacular supernatural feats, such as dancing on hot coals, placing their hands in kettles of boiling water, lifting great weights, and jumping great distances. They are related to the *wabeno* (see entry) shamans of the Central Algonquins. They are also renowned for their healing abilities. "When in a contrary condition, Hohnuhka Society members accomplished great feats in healing the sick and disabled, applying inverted techniques that included jumping high over people or tossing people through the air" [Schlesier 1987: 71].

Hokshu
Pawnee, *Plains*
Holy or sacred [Alexander 1910:44].

Holhkunna
Choctaw, *Southeast*
Shaman [Edmonson 1958:69].

Holkkunda
Choctaw, *Southeast*
Witchcraft. This is often believed to be the source of personal illness or disease. About Choctaw witches, Bushnell [1909:29] writes:

"Those having proper knowledge could remove at night their viscera, thus reducing their weight to so great an extent that they could fly through the air to the individual they wished to harm. Accompanying them always were several spirits, otherwise resembling men, but no larger than a man's thumb. On reaching the person against

whom the spell was to be directed the witch would stop and point toward him, whereupon one of the little spirits would go noiselessly and touch him, afterward remaining and doing a great deal of mischief about the place. The spirit was able to pass with ease through cracks, and thus to reach places not accessible to a larger being. After directing the little spirit, which was left to continue its work, the wizard would fly back to his village or house and again assume his natural condition."

Holy Dance, Robert
Lakota, *Plains*
A respected herbalist and shaman from the Rosebud Reservation (Brule Band) in South Dakota who died in 1972. Lewis [1980b:417] reports that "he must have been more than 85 because he remembered well the illegal ghost dances of his childhood." His knowledge of herbs was extensive, but he also had spirit helpers that he used in curing. "He confidently treated fevers, menstrual delays, pelvic inflammatory disease, trauma, asthma, unhappiness, indecision, and crises of confidence" [Lewis 1980b:417]. His efficacy was so well known that he also treated the families of local white ranchers. The wife of one affluent rancher reported:

"Holy Dance treats my kids and the people on this side of Porcupine (South Dakota). He has a baked leaf preparation for sinusitis. It is burned and inhaled. He has absolute cures even in people who go to white doctors when they live in town. He treats everybody. We don't need a doctor when he is around. He treats everybody and they always get better" [Lewis 1980b:418].

Honaaite
Keres, *Southwest*
The presiding officer of each of the eight religious societies of the Sia Pueblo. Because Sia shamans are all members of one or more societies, the *honaaite* is most often an older shaman with well-developed powers. The term *honaaite* may be equated with "shaman," but not all Sia shamans are *honnaites*.

Not all Sia religious societies have ceremonies for healing the sick. Most societies are divided into two or more orders, and it often takes many years before one is initiated into the higher orders of a society. Only the members of the higher orders of certain societies are qualified to perform healing ceremonies, which are quite distinct from other religious ceremonies.

At the beginning of the Sia new year in December, all the societies hold synchronal ceremonials that last four days and four nights. During this time, all those who are ill in the pueblo attend the ceremony of the society to which they belong to receive healing. All other healing ceremonies are called for by the patient or his relatives when the need arises. This is done in a prescribed way that entails sending a notched stick decorated with plumes, called a *hächamoni* (see entry), to the appropriate *honaaite*. The Sia most often use eagle plumes, for which they keep eagles in cages, or turkey plumes from their domesticated turkeys.

Prior to conducting a healing ceremony, the participating members of the society first observe a four-day period of physical purification. During this time, they refrain from sexual intercourse and take an emetic each morning. On the fourth day, all the married members are required to bathe and have their heads washed in yucca suds.

"The cult societies observe two modes in curing diseases: One is by sucking, and the other by brushing the body with straws and eagle plumes. The former mode is practiced when Ka-nat-kai-ya (witches) have caused the malady by casting into the body worms, stones, yarn, etc.; the latter mode is observed when one is afflicted through angry ants or other insects, which are thus drawn to the surface and brushed off" [Stevenson 1894:75].

The healing ceremony is conducted in either the patient's home or the ceremonial kiva of the society. "The honaaite discovers the diseased parts of the body through the instrumentality of ashes, and with the scattering of ashes to the cardinal points, physical and mental impurities are cast from those present and the chamber is also purified" [Stevenson 1894:134]. Upon completion of the healing ceremony, the only compensation necessary is the donation of a sacred shell mixture by the patient or his relatives. This is most unusual, as shamans in other cultures generally require generous compensation.

For details, see *Skoyo Chaiän*.

Honani
Keres, *Southwest*

The Acoma Pueblo term for the sacred corn-ear fetish used by shamans of their medicine societies. *Honani* is the Hopi word for badger. "This is the chief fetish of a medicine man" [White 1932:109]. For a description, see *mile*.

Hoopiopio
Hawaiian, *Pacific*

A form of sorcery in which the shaman makes a magic mark across a road where his victim is sure to pass. In another form of this spell, called *pahiuhiu*, the shaman makes a square with his finger, divides it into four equal squares, and places a stone at the center crosslines. In the *hoopiopio*, prayers are sent to Uli, the god of sorcery, and in the *pahiuhiu*, prayers are sent to Kane, one of the principal gods, both for the death of the intended victim.

Hopá
Hidatsa, *Plains*

Matthews's [1877:149] rendering of *xupá* (see entry), meaning "mysterious" or "sacred." From this adjective comes the noun *hopádi*, meaning "mystery" or "medicine."

Hopaii
Choctaw, *Southeast*

Shaman. There is a brief description of their seventeenth-century healing procedures recorded by a French Jesuit:

"When there is a sick person among them they have the doctor come to the place where he is, who, after having conjured or demanded of their Spirit if the sick person will get well, bleeds him with a piece of flint. Eight or ten incisions are made in the skin in the space of the size of a crown (ècu), as when one cups, over which they place one end of a pierced horn and suck it until the horn is full of blood. As these jugglers sometimes wish to hide their ignorance they say that someone has thrown a spell over them (the patients) and then they adroitly put some bison wool or a little piece of wood into the bottom of the horn, and after having sucked the sick man and poured out the blood which is in the horn, they show this wood or bison wool to the parents of the sick man" [Swanton 1931:228].

From this account, one may deduce that the Choctaw curing shamans were primarily sucking doctors. The French were convinced that shamans were in communication with the devil and provided the following example of a Choctaw shaman's actions as evidence:

"He (the shaman) took his tobacco-pouch which was an otter skin in which he kept his pipe and tobacco, which he threw into the middle of an open place where the people were assembled to judge of his skill; after he had uttered a number of obscurely articulated words and thrown himself repeatedly into the fire, from which he came out in a perspiration, and without being burned, this skin was seen to swell out, fill with flesh, and come to life, and to run between the legs of the Frenchmen, some of whom in the company having caressed it and felt of it, found that it was like a true otter. When each one was satisfied it returned to the same place where it had come to life and was seen to diminish in size and return to the form which it had before" [Swanton 1931:229].

Horn Chips
Lakota, *Plains*
Also Charles Chips; his Lakota name is *Petehe*. One of the most powerful *yuwipi* (see entry) shamans remembered among the Lakota, he lived from 1873 to 1946. His father—known simply as Old Man Chips (Lakota name *Woptuka*), and with whom Horn Chips is often confused in the literature—is remembered as the founder of the *yuwipi* ceremony among the Lakota. He lived from around 1836 to 1916.

Around 1915, the Pine Ridge Reservation superintendent ordered Horn Chips to perform his *yuwipi* ceremony in a lighted room rather than in the total darkness to see if his powers were real. During the ceremony, the spirits appeared as lights on the ceiling, and upon their departure, Horn Chips's hands, which had been bound, were untied.

Horn Chips passed his *yuwipi* powers to his son Ellis Chipps (an additional "p" was added to the family name during this period), and today,

Ellis's youngest son, Godfrey Chipps, continues the family *yuwipi* ceremonies.

Hotcine gada
Seneca, *Northeast*
Charm members or spirits that belong to the Pygmy Society. See *Dark Dance Ceremony*.

Howlish Watkonot
Wallawalla, *Plateau*
The last recognized chief of the Wallawallas; his traditional name translates to "Wolf Charging" [Relander 1956:67]. He was born around 1872 and was eventually given the name Jim Kanine. He was known to have doctor's power and conducted medicine dances in his lodge for many years near Cayuse, Oregon. He died on 17 June 1952.

Hózhó
Navajo, *Southwest*
The Navajo ideal of beauty, harmony, and well-being. This concept is at the core of every Navajo healing ceremony, in which the goal is to bring the patient back into *hózhó*. The patient internalizes the image of *hózhó* represented in the sandpaintings used in healing ceremonies, and experiences their design as a spiritual mandalla in terms of which physical recovery can take place. After the ceremony, the sandpainting is destroyed [Porterfield 1984:280].

Huapsi
Nootka, *Northwest Coast*
A form of preventive medicine known as "breaks up a plan." "This medicine was used when a person was conscious of being near an enemy which meant death. The fresh roots were pounded and rubbed on the body. A man would pay from five to ten blankets for one application of this remedy" [Densmore 1939:321].

Hulkilal
Yuki, *California*
A spirit of a deceased person among the Huchnom branch. During ceremonies, the *hulkilal* are impersonated by dancers who paint their bodies with stripes of black and white and wear blossoms in their hair. Most important is the *hulkilal woknam*, or "lying dance," which is an initiation

Navajo medicine men create a sand painting as part of a healing treatment in Rough Rock, Arizona. During the treatment, the patient focuses on the image of *hózhó*, the Navajo ideal of inner peace and harmony, as symbolized in the sand painting.

ceremony for young boys into the mystery powers [Kroeber 1925:204]. This lying dance is also performed in healing ceremonies, during which a unique form of spirit-disease extraction takes place:

"The patient, naked, was laid supine upon the ground with the limbs widely extended. Four springy twigs were then placed in the ground a short distance from his hands and feet, bent over and tautly tied to the extremities of the invalid. The shaman . . . burnt the string, as he muttered appropriate incantations, with a live coal. As the string parted the branches snapped upright, to the tune of the well coached patient's screams. In this way the evil spirit was twitched forth" [Stone 1932:29–30].

Hunka
Winnebago, *Midwest*
Peyote; translates to "chief." Although the peyote ceremony is not a healing ceremony per se, its use is associated with healing, as evidenced by the following account given by John Rave around 1910:

"Many years ago I had been sick and it looked as if this illness were going to kill me. I tried all the Indian doctors and then I tried all of the white man's medicines, but they were of no avail. 'I am doomed. I wonder whether I will be alive next year.' Such were the thoughts that came to me. As soon as I ate peyote, however, I got over my sickness. After that I was not sick again. My wife had suffered from the same disease, and I told her that if she ate this medicine (peyote) it would surely cure her. But she was afraid, although she had never seen it before. She knew that I used it, but nevertheless she was afraid of it. Her sickness was getting worse and worse and one day I said to her, 'You are sick. It is going to be very difficult, but try this medicine anyhow. It will ease you.' Finally she ate it. I had told her to eat it and then to wash herself and comb her hair and she would get well, and now she is well. . . . From that day on to the present time she has been well. Now she is very happy" [Radin 1923:391–392].

Husikpe
Miwok, *California*
Central Miwok word for shaman [Broadbent 1964:44]. A more common word is *koyabi* (see entry).

Husk Face Society
Iroquois, *Northeast*
The Husk Faces are spirits that dwell on the other side of the earth and, like the Iroquois, grow corn, beans, and squash—the "three sisters." They come from the east every new year during two nights of the Seneca midwinter festival. "Unlike the False-faces, they are mutes and only puff as they run with great leaps. They have their own tobacco invocation, a medicine song, and they dance about the staves which they carry. They also have the power to cure by blowing hot ashes; but in Canada they sprinkle water on their patients" [Fenton 1941:416]. Membership in the society is obtained either through a dream or by being cured by the society.

Iariko
Keres, *Southwest*
Also: *iatiku, iärriko* (Sia Pueblo). The sacred corn-ear fetishes carried by shamans in the Keresan pueblos of the Rio Grande [White 1932:129]. See *mile* and *yaya* for descriptions.

Ibrukaon
Tikerarmiut, *Arctic Coast*
A device used in the widespread, head-lifting form of divination used by the Eskimos. It is a stick to which a looped thong is attached. The thong is placed around the head of a patient who is reclining on the ground on his or her back. The *ibrukok* (shaman) sings his spirit-calling songs. Once the spirit has arrived, the shaman asks a yes-or-no question, then pulls up on the *ibrukaon*. Depending on whether the head is heavy or light, an affirmative or negative answer is assigned to the question. It is often used to determine whether a patient will recover or not.

Ibrukok
Tikerarmiut, *Arctic Coast*
The term used by the Eskimo living in the village of Tikera (also called Tigara) at Point Hope, Alaska, for a shaman who is less powerful than shamans referred to as *angatkok* (see entry). Both types of shamans commune with the spirit world in visions. The differentiation appears to be based on the nature of such communication. An *ibrukok* sings to experience his vision and then speaks with the spirits that appear to him in the vision. An *angatkok* uses his drum to call his power spirit; then, in a trance, he feels his own spirit go down and travel away under the ground. When the *angatkok's* own spirit returned it "grasped the man by his collar bones and pulled itself back in" [Rainey 1947:275]. The *ibrukok* possess many minor powers, such as the ability to change the weather and divine the future.

Ickade
Omaha, Ponca, *Plains*
The power feats of shamans [Dorsey 1894:417]. For example, when treating a toothache, a shaman removes the worm that was causing the pain. Such feats are often referred to ethnocentrically as sleight-of-hand tricks by those who fail to comprehend the shaman's use of their mystery powers.

Idiaxílalit
Wasco, *Oregon Seaboard*
Shaman; translates to "one who doctors" from *-gila-it*, "to doctor." The Wasco were a Chinookan tribe formerly living on the south side of the Columbia River near The

Dalles in Wasco County, Oregon. They were eventually moved to the Warm Springs Reservation in Oregon. Their shamans healed through the use of guardian spirits obtained during personal vision quests.

Idos oäno
Seneca, *Northeast*
Society of Mystic Animals. The members of this society are medicine people who perform the ceremonies that maintain their working relationship with medicine animals. Upon becoming a member of the society, each person receives a song and a rattle, and during ceremonies, each member sings his own particular song. The leader of the society is always a powerful shaman who performs some of the power feats attributed to former medicine men in the ceremonial songs as these songs are being sung. Such feats include taking a red-hot stone from the fire and juggling it in his hands, locating various objects around the house while wearing a wooden mask with no eyeholes in it, and causing a doll to become animated. Parker [1909:172] relates an instance in which a woman was laughing at a medicine man's power during a ceremony. The medicine man approached a doll, and although he was wearing a wooden mask that hid the doll from his view, he adeptly cut the string holding up the doll's skirt, causing it to fall off. Much to the laughing woman's embarrassment, her skirt also fell to the floor at the same instant.

Three wooden masks are used in the various rituals of this society: the conjurer's mask, the witch mask, and the dual-spirit's mask [Parker 1909:174]. They differ from the masks used by the False Face Society in that they have no metal eyes. The healing ceremonies of the Society of Mystic Animals are said to be particularly efficacious for fevers and skin diseases.

Ie yomta
Wintun, *California*
Sucking doctors among the Patwin branch [Loeb 1934b:226].

Iemaparu
Tiwa, *Southwest*
The Isleta Pueblo name for the corn-mother fetish used in healing ceremonies. These specially selected and prepared ears of corn are part of the shaman's altar display during healing ceremonies [Parsons 1932:443].

Igawésdi
Cherokee, *Southeast*
The aspect of a healing ritual that consists of something one says, thinks, or sings; translates to "to say, one." James Mooney coined the term "sacred formula" for the *igawésdi*. "The published literature on Cherokee magic does not recognize a fundamental truth: in any magical ritual all generative power resides in thought, and the *i:gawé:sdi*, which focuses and directs that thought, alone is inviolate" [Kilpatrick 1965:4–5]. The shaman is at liberty to include extraneous elements into the *igawésdi* that "take the form of the repetition of a key word the sacred four times; the interjection of the supremely sacrosanct numeral seven; the insertion of the pronoun *ayv* ('I'); and a hiatus in which the reciter thinks intently upon the purpose of the ritual. These are not introduced with complete freedom, but only at certain junctures approved by custom, and they are usually indicated in manuscript texts by symbols—crosses, numerals, a series of vertical dashes, and the like" [Kilpatrick 1965:7]. However, a shaman can improvise on a text if the spirit moves him to do so.

Although the literature often implies that each saying is to be used for only one specific purpose, in actuality, a saying may be used for any purpose for which its wording qualifies it. As one shaman put it, "If I wished, I could use the same *i:gawé:sdi* for every purpose that there is. It is the intention in the heart, and the knowledge, that really count" [Kilpatrick 1967:187b, n.4]. See *gowäli* for "sacred formula" details.

Igjugarjuk
Caribou Eskimo, *Arctic Coast*
A shaman during the first part of the twentieth century. Accounts of his shamanism were recorded by Rasmussen; the following is an excerpt concerning his healing activities:

"I understood that I had become the shaman of my village, and it did happen that my neighbors or people from a long distance away called me to heal a sick person or to 'inspect a course' if they were going to travel. When this happened, the people of my village were called together and I told them what I had been asked to do. Then I left tent or snow house and went out into solitude; away from the dwellings of man. Now those who remained behind had to sing continuously: just to keep themselves happy and lively. If anything difficult had to be found out my solitude had to extend over three days and two nights, or three nights and two days. In all that time I had to wander about without rest and only sit down once in a while on a stone or a snow drift. When I had been out long and had become tired, I could almost doze and dream what I had come out to find and about which I had been thinking all the time. Every morning, however, I could come home and report on what I had so far found. But as soon as I had spoken I had to return again, out into the open, out to places where I could be quite alone.

"These days of 'seeking for knowledge' are very tiring, for one must walk all the time, no matter what the weather is like and only rest in short snatches. I am usually quite . . . tired, not only in body but also in head, when I have found what I sought. . . .

"True wisdom is only to be found far away from people, out in the great solitude, and it is not found in play but only through suffering. Solitude and suffering open the human mind, and therefore a shaman seeks his wisdom there" [Rasmussen in Beck and Walters 1977:124].

Igvnedhi
Cherokee, *Southeast*
The physical procedure required to be performed by a shaman during a ceremony [Kilpatrick 1965:5]. Translates to "to do, one." Not every ceremony has such a requirement.

Iikháah
Navajo, *Southwest*
Ceremonial sandpaintings; translates to "they enter and leave." During a healing ceremony, the sandpainting is aligned with the entryway of the ceremonial hogan, which always faces east. It is through this sandpainting that the *yéii* (spirits) enter and leave the ceremony [Gill 1983:75].

Iilápxe
Crow, *Plains*
Shamans' helping spirits [Frey 1987:65]. Translates to "his Father." Spirits that appear to the Crow in their vision quests are seen as mediators of *Akbaatatdía* ("Maker" or "Creator") and most often appear in the guise of an animal such as an eagle, otter, or buffalo. However, the spirit may also appear as a rock, bird, star, *Awakkulé* ("little people" or "dwarfs"), and so forth. In addition, the vision-quester often receives some object that is a tangible image of his *Iilápxe*. "The distinction between Akbaatatdía and Iilápxe is fundamentally one of degree; each has a different level of transcendence from the material world. The Iilápxe are thus the immediate and personalized mediators for the more pervasive and transcendent Akbaatatdía" [Frey 1987:66].

The medicine powers acquired from spirits usually contain the characteristics associated with the particular form of a spirit. For example, one shaman "acquired the power of the Mole or, specifically, of the dirt that the mole pushes as it tunnels its way into the earth. This dirt was once a barrier to free movements. By administering the 'Mole's dirt,' one with the power of the Mole curtails the flow of internal bleeding, nosebleeds, or hemorrhaging. . . . One who has Elk medicine can elicit the strength of the Elk. The quality that an object or animal manifests in the natural world parallels the power of the medicine represented by the Iilápxe" [Frey 1987:67–68].

Medicine powers and medicine objects received from spirits are always treated with great respect. In the case of objects, this often led early observers to mistake them for idols. Such objects are generally kept wrapped and then encased in a medicine bundle. Medicine powers often come with associated taboos. For example, a shaman is usually not allowed to eat the flesh of the animal from which the power comes. This restriction is sometimes limited to one specific part of the animal, such as the heart. In treating the sick, such consumption taboos are often extended also to the patient during the course of treatment.

In speaking of his helping spirit, a shaman often simply refers to his spirit as *Iilápxe*. One shaman referred to his helping spirit by the English name "Medicine Father"; others are more glib, "simply applying the term *xapáaliia* (see entry) to this agent (spirit)" [Frey 1987:67].

In his writings on the Crow religion, Lowie [e.g. 1922, 1935] uses the term *batsirápe* (see entry) for a shaman's helping spirit.

Ikhareyev
Karok, *Oregon Seaboard*
See *wogey*.

Iksivalitaq
Netsilik Eskimo, *Arctic Coast*
The last Netsilik shaman of the twentieth century who was of great importance to his people. He died around 1940. At the height of his power, he held seven *tunraqs* (helping spirits), one of which was called "Big Mountain." This spirit was described as being "about 3" long and 1" high, with black and red spots. The shaman could remove this *tunraq* from his mouth, where it was in the habit of staying, and make it run on his hand" [Balikci 1963].

Ilisiniq
Netsilik Eskimo, *Arctic Coast*
A form of magical hexing that uses some manipulative technique; it usually involves connecting something associated with the victim to the dead or to menstrual blood. For example, animal bones brought in by the victim may be stolen and placed in a graveyard, or menstrual blood may be mixed in with his seal meat. The simplest form of *ilisiniq* is merely spitting in front of the victim. The most important aspect of hexing is to keep one's attention focused on the specific calamity one has in mind while performing these techniques. In doing *ilisiniq* against another person, the hex can backfire if the victim's protection is strong enough, sending the hex back to the sender.

Ilisitsut
East Greenland Eskimo, *Arctic Coast*
Sorcerer among the Angmagsalik, who can steal a person's soul and cause illness. The *angakok* (shaman) must retrieve the soul to effect a cure.

Ilitkosaq
Tikerarmiut, *Arctic Coast*
One of several words for "spirit" among the North Alaska Eskimo; it refers to the free soul or dream soul, that is, the spirit that leaves the shaman's body to travel to the spirit world, where it visits with *tungai* (spirits) [Rainey 1947:275].

Ilyesa sumatc
Mojave, *Southwest*
Shamans, called bone doctors, who specialize in the treatment of broken bones and arthritis. One bone doctor named Peter Dean, now deceased, was always present on the sidelines at the Needles (Nevada) High School football games to treat Mojave players who might be injured: "He puts his breath on it and takes the pain away. Then it doesn't pain him [the injured player], and he could walk home on it" [Stewart 1974:10].

Imitative shamanism
A phrase used by some scholars to refer to ceremonies in which the participants imitate the act undertaken by the shaman. For example, among the Salish of the Northwest Coast, any illness diagnosed as soul loss requires a journey to the land of the dead to retrieve the lost soul. During this healing ceremony, the participants imitate a journey in a canoe to the land of the dead. The phrase is used to distinguish this type of act from pure shamanism, which involves the shaman entering into an ecstatic trance. However, many of the participants in such imitative ceremonies do indeed enter into ecstatic trances.

Inâli manuscript
Cherokee, *Southeast*
One of several manuscripts obtained by James Mooney in the summer of 1888 that contains the sacred formulas of the Cherokee shamans written in Sequoyan syllabary (Cherokee characters). Inâli, whose name translates to "Black Fox," "had died a few years before at an advanced age, and ... was universally admitted to have been one of their most able men and the most prominent literary character among them" [Mooney 1891:314].

In addition to being a traditional shaman, Inâli also became a Methodist preacher in 1848.

Inikagapi
Lakota, *Plains*
The sweat-lodge ceremony of purification; the term means "with it they make life." See *inipi*.

Inipi
Lakota, *Plains*
Also *initi* [Feraca 1963]. The sweat lodge, a small, domed-shaped structure usually consisting of 12 to 16 willow poles that are placed in the ground in a circle and then bent over and tied together. The structure is usually around 8 feet in diameter. It is covered with blankets or canvas until it is light-tight when the door flap is closed. Stones, called "grandfathers," are heated on a fire in front of the entry and brought into the lodge when they are glowing red. Between the fire pit and the lodge is placed an earth altar, called *makakagapi* (see entry), upon which are placed sacred pipes to be used during the ceremony and any articles one wants blessed. Contrary to popular belief, the Lakota are shy about nudity, so all the participants cover themselves with towels when entering the lodge. Also, it is traditional for men and women to attend lodge ceremonies separately.

The sweat lodge is used before a healing ceremony or any other ceremony that requires purification of the participants, such as the Sun Dance Ceremony. The ceremony usually has four "rounds," that is, four times in which the door flap is closed. When the flap is closed, water is poured over the hot rocks, and the resulting steam envelops the participants. Sacred songs and prayers are recited at this time, the purpose being to focus one's mind on the ceremony that is to follow. The sweat lodge is also often used by itself to pray.

Initiatory sickness
A technical term used by Eliade [1964:33] to refer to behaviors during an illness that indicate that the patient is to become a shaman. Because such telltale behavior often involves bizarre actions from a Western perspective, many scholars mistakenly claimed that all shamans were psychotic.

This attitude was in vogue from the 1930s to the 1960s, but has since been put to rest.

Inkoze
Chipewyan, *Mackenzie-Yukon*
Shaman [Edmonson 1958:69].

Inua
Eskimo, *Arctic Coast*
The soul of any object or person. The word comes from the noun *inuk* (plural, *inuit*), which translates to "man, person; inhabitant; possessor, owner." The possessive form of this noun is *inua* (plural, *inuat* or *inue*). Literally, it means "its man" but is better translated as "its owner," since it can refer to the soul of an animal or object. Merkur [1985:225–226] reports:

"The term *inua* has generally been translated as 'owner' of nature, but I have demonstrated that the metaphysical conception pertains instead to the second sense. The Inuit conception of the indwellers in nature may be characterized, in Western philosophic terms, as a variety of metaphysical idealism. An *inua* is an idea that indwells in and imparts individual character to a physical phenomenon. As one Nunamiut put it, an *inua* is the 'essential existing force' of a physical phenomenon, that causes it to be what it is. An indweller has, employs, and is a power. As they indwell in physical phenomenon, indwellers are ordinarily invisible. However, like breath-souls, indwellers are anthropomorphic, regardless of the phenomena in which they indwell, whenever they can be seen. In all cases, indwellers are personal beings that think, have emotions, and act with motivation . . . indwellers are also anthropopsychic and social beings, who are capable of communication . . . indwellers are also the ideas with which the mind thinks."

As such, an *inua* may have a personality.

The other term for a shaman's helping spirit is *torngak* (see entry) or *tornaq*. This is a different type of helping spirit that is thought to be more powerful than an *inua*.

There are many cognates for this term. For example, among the Iglulik Eskimo, the word is

inusia, which literally translates to "appearance as a human being." Among the Eskimo of Point Hope in northwest Alaska, the *inyua* (*chua* and other variants) is conceived of as the "owner" of the river, tree, drum, and so on, whereas the souls of men and animals are called *inyusaq* or *chuchik* [Lantis 1950:321].

Inugwak
Labrador Eskimo, *Arctic Coast*
Small wooden magical dolls worn by Koksoagmyut shamans. The doll is a material image of the shaman's helping spirit. During his rituals, the doll is normally worn around the shaman's waist and dangled from a polar-bear-skin belt. The face of the doll always points outward, away from the shaman, so that the spirit can be on the alert [Turner 1894:198].

Inyan wakan
See *tunkan*.

Inyuin tarrak
Copper Eskimo, *Arctic Coast*
Plural: *inyuin tarrait*. Shades (spirits) of the dead [Jenness 1922:185]. Among the Copper Eskimo, almost all illnesses and misfortunes are believed to be the direct result of *inyuin tarrait* or *tornrait* (spirits). This is certainly the case if one breaks an *aglenaktok* (taboo).

Ipa sumach
Mojave, *Southwest*
Also: *ipa kusumanya, ipa sumatc*. A specialist known as the arrow wound doctor. One of these shamans always accompanied war parties. He pulled out the arrows and sucked on the warriors' wounds. He never doctored during battle, but during the camp on the first night of the return, he washed the wounds and sang [Stewart 1970: 19–20]. This shaman also made special medicine

on the way to a raid to debilitate the enemy. There were often several wound doctors in a society, but only one would go on a raid; the others remained behind. For more details on Mojave healing, see *kwathidhe*.

Itcuthau sumatc
Mojave, *Southwest*
A specialist who treats children's ailments. They treat children who become sick by breaking food taboos, such as eating rabbit, quail, or duck, and those who become sick from handling dead animals. "A person would get sick if he ate anything killed by a bird or dog, and the *itcuthau sumatc* would have to treat him" [Stewart 1974:11].

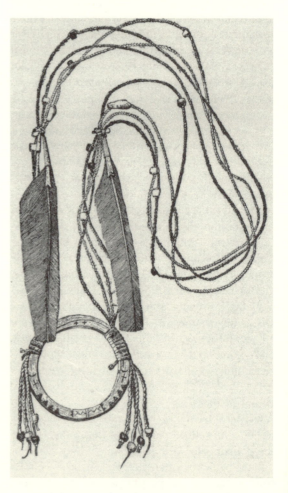

Medicine cord used by Apache shamans.

Ithaethe

Ponca, Omaha, *Plains*

The power to heal acquired by a shaman. Dorsey [1894:367] reports that the literal translation of this term is "to pity him on account of it, granting him certain power." However, he elaborates that "its primary reference is to the mysterious animal, but it is transferred to the person (shaman) having the vision, hence, it means 'to receive mysterious things from an animal, as in a vision after fasting; to see as in a vision, face to face (not in a dream); to see when awake, and in a mysterious manner having a conversation with the animal about mysterious things'" [Dorsey 1894:367–368].

Izzekloth

Apache, *Southwest*

Medicine cords used by shamans [Bourke 1892: 550]. These cords are used only for the most sacred and important occasions; otherwise, they are never seen. When used, they are worn hanging from the right shoulder over the left hip. Because they are considered so sacred, Bourke could not persuade anyone to tell him about their use. He did determine, however, that they are made only by advanced shamans and are used, among other things, for curing the sick. In addition, he reports:

"A bullet will have no effect upon the warrior wearing one of them . . . the wearer can tell who has stolen ponies or other property from him or from his friends, can help the crops. . . . If the circle attached to one of these cords is placed upon the head it will at once relieve any ache, while the cross attached to another prevents the wearer from going astray no matter where he may be" [Bourke 1892:552–553].

Jackson, Jimmy

Ojibwa, *Canadian Eastern Woodlands*

A traditional medicine man who was interviewed during the late 1980s when he was 76 years old. He began to practice medicine ways at the age of 32, and during his early years, he was taught through dreams. He stated that his powers came from the Great Spirit, but that "all the medicine I know, I had to pay for that, I had to pay the price to know that medicine" [Aitken and Haller 1990:57]. He also learned from his elders. Of them he said: "They were the ones who taught me and they were the ones who helped so I could recognize when I had discovered my gift. . . . When I first started out I had to ask often from the old medicine men here how to do something. And I was told to do everything exactly the way the spirits showed me in my dreams" [Aitken and Haller 1990:56, 60].

His link to his spirit helpers was through prayer with tobacco. "But you have to remember to use tobacco all the time. You've got to carry it always, and every time you put it out, you're sacrificing. The tobacco is a link to the spirits, they will get it, and they will listen to what you have to say or for what you're asking" [Aitken and Haller 1990:58]. With regard to these helping spirits he said: "All these spirits can communicate. This aspect of spirituality is an important component of medicine, it is a real part of the effectiveness of the practice of medicine and of the treatments that are used. . . . You know I'm a medicine man. I go out there in the woods and I don't go along with all this imaginary stuff. I'm out there to think and to listen and to hear the spirits. . . . When I go out there in the woods, I say a prayer, and I offer my tobacco, and I talk to the spirits in the woods. If there's a true spirit for me to see, I'll see it" [Aitken and Haller 1990:60, 64–65].

Concerning his patients he said: "The spirits know right away when a person comes to me. Or I might have known it two or three days ahead of time that this person would be coming. It might be someone from far away, and sometimes I'm told what's ailing the person who will be coming to see me. Well, that makes it all the easier for me to find what the spirits have been telling me about, and so I will first look for those signs of illness" [Aitken and Haller 1990:65].

Jessakkid

Ojibwa, *Canadian Eastern Woodlands*

Also: *jeesuhkon, jossakeed.* One of the three classes of shamans identified by Hoffman [1891]. Most often these shamans exercise their power to reveal hidden truths, but they are also involved in healing practices, most often involving sickness caused by spirit possession. Sucking tubes are commonly employed by these shamans to remove the evil spirits from the patient's body. The power of these shamans is said to come from Animiki, the god of thunder.

Not all scholars follow Hoffman's classification. For example, Densmore [1910:119] states that the "Chippewa (Ojibwa) word *djasakid* is applied to two classes of people—doctors and jugglers." In her classification, doctors are shamans who perform healing ceremonies, and jugglers are those who perform the Shaking Tent Ceremony (see entry). Densmore [1910:119–120] describes the healing ceremony as follows:

"The Chippewa doctor treats the sick by singing, shaking his rattle, passing his hands over the body of the patient, and apparently swallowing one or more bones, which are afterward removed from his mouth. Each of these phases is considered indispensable to the treatment. . . .

"The sick person lies on the ground, the doctor kneeling at his right side. The doctor holds his rattle in his right hand and at his left hand is a pan or bowl of water in which lie the bones to be swallowed. The doctor opens his mouth, protrudes his tongue, places the moistened bone on it, and 'swallows' it quickly. After shaking the rattle a while he 'swallows' another of the bones; usually this procedure is continued until four or five bones have been disposed of in this manner. One doctor stated that the bones lodge in the chest near the shoulder. It is also said that there is a spirit inside the doctor which takes the bones.

"After 'swallowing' the bones the doctor strikes his breast with the rattle; then he leans over the sick person and strikes his back between the shoulders with the rattle. It is claimed that this enables him to see where the disease is located in the patient."

Once located, the shaman removes the disease by sucking on the patient's body in the appropriate area, accompanied by the proper medicine songs.

Jish
Navajo, *Southwest*
Collective term for medicine bundle, medicine pouch, medicine bag, and ceremonial bag; it can also mean ceremonial mask. Reichard [1944:38] states that the term *jish* is also "used to name a medicine bundle with all its contents, the skin (quiver) in which the contents are wrapped, the contents as a whole or each part of the contents." Thus, smaller bags within the main bag are also referred to as *jish*.

To an outsider, medicine bundles are tangible in form, but to the Navajo, the medicine bundle is a source and repository of sacred power. During healing ceremonies, it is used to attract good and transfer it to the patient.

Once a *jish* is assembled, it is usually inherited by some family member. In some cases, however, the *jish* is sold. Because there are many different types of Navajo ceremonies, there are many different types of *jish*—Blessingway *jish*, Shootingway *jish*, and so forth. As a general rule, the more items contained in a bag, the more powerful and valuable the *jish*. For example, a singer's reputation and the amount he charges are often dependent on his *jish* [Frisbie 1987].

John-Paul
Ojibwa, *Canadian Eastern Woodlands*
A shaman from the Birch Island Reserve located just north of Manitoulin Island. He was born around the turn of the twentieth century and was the grandson of the renowned nineteenth-century shaman Shaw-wan-oss-way. John-Paul's shamanic calling came when he was in his twenties; he was on a boat during a thunderstorm, and a vision was induced by a flash of lightning. Paper [1980:199] contends that later in his life, sometime between 1940 and 1950, John-Paul underwent a transformation from shaman to mystic.

Jones, Flora
Wintu, *California*
A renowned healing shaman who was born in 1909. She received her first spirit—a star spirit—at the age of 17. Following is a descripton of one of her typical healing ceremonies:

"The arrival of the spirit-helpers is marked by the shaman's sharp inhalation; the group falls silent as the spirits begin to speak through the shaman's

A Chippewa *djasakid* shaman holds a rattle in his right hand and a sucking tube in his left hand. Shamans often used sucking tubes to rid the patient's body of disease-causing objects.

voice, offering advice or prophecies and some-times quarreling or joking among themselves.

"The shaman drinks clear water, then a solu-tion of acorn water from a small container—an of-fering to the helping spirits. With the diagnostic powers of the spirit-helpers acting through her hands, she begins to move her fingers carefully across the patient's body sensing unseen, internal injuries or abnormalities. Flora explains, 'I feel for the sores, the aches, and the pains. When I put my hand over the body I can feel every little muscle and every little vein. I can feel the soreness. It hurts me. If they have heart trouble, my heart just beats. Any place they are hurting I hurt. I become part of their body.'

"If the spirits (find) the source of the sickness, they prescribe for the patient's care, speaking through the shaman. Remedies may be offered for both physical and psychological ills and often in-clude traditional herbal medicines, which Flora collects and stores.

"Upon awakening from the trance, the shaman learns of the spiritual diagnosis from the inter-preter and proceeds to treat the patient accord-ingly. In the past, a patient's family would present the shaman with a tiny, hand-made basket of char-acteristic striped design following a successful treatment. Now the transaction usually involves money and takes place regardless of the outcome of the therapy.

"Only in the most dire cases, when a patient is unconscious and death emminent [sic], does Flora perform the Soul Dance—a final attempt to recapture the victim's wandering soul. This ritual is performed at midnight. As the shaman dances to the rhythmic beating of sticks she waves a staff wearing a miniature basket in which to catch the lost soul. If the shaman's search is successful, the soul is brought back to its owner and placed over his heart, its natural resting place" [Knudtson in Beck and Walters 1977:139].

Because Flora does not remember what she says during her trances, she began to tape-record her sessions. This innovative technique was initially criticized by her helping spirits, but she reported that they eventually got used to it.

Jossakeed
Ojibwa, *Canadian Eastern Woodlands*
See *jessakkid* [Hoffman 1888].

Juggler
Also: *jugler, jongleur.*
A term used in nineteenth-century and earlier lit-erature to refer to Native American shamans. Most of the early accounts of Native American healings were written in highly prejudiced and derogatory terms. The following is one such ex-ample, given in 1703 by La Hontan (in his *New Voyages to North America*), describing the healing practices among the Algonquian cultures:

"When they are sick, they only drink Broth, and eat sparingly; and if they have the good luck to fall asleep, they think themselves cur'd: They have told me frequently, that sleeping and sweating would cure the most stubborn Diseases in the World. When they are so weak that they cannot get out of Bed, their Relations come and dance and make merry before 'em, in order to divert 'em. To conclude, when they are ill, they are always visited by a sort of Quacks (*Jongleurs*); of whom 't will now be proper to subjoin two or three Words by the bye.

"A *Jongleur* is a sort of *Physician*, or rather a *Quack*, who being once cur'd of some dangerous Distemper, has the Presumption and Folly to fancy that he is immortal, and possessed of the Power of curing all Diseases, by speaking to the Good and Evil Spirits. Now though every Body rallies upon these Fellows when they are absent, and looks upon 'em as Fools that have lost their Senses by some violent Distemper, yet they allow 'em to visit the Sick; whether it be to divert 'em with their Idle Stories, or to have an Opportunity of seeing them rave, skip about, cry, houl [sic], and make Grimaces and Wry Faces, as if they were possess'd. When all the Bustle is over, they de-mand a Feast of a Stag and some large Trouts for the Company, who are thus regal'd at once with Diversion of Good Cheer.

"When the Quack comes to visit the Patient, he examines him very carefully; If the Evil Spirit be here, says he, we shall quickly dislodge him. This said, he withdraws by himself to a little Tent made on purpose, where he dances, and sings houling [*sic*] like an Owl; (which gives the Jesuits Occasion to say, That the Devil converses with 'em.) After he has made an end of the Quack Jargon, he comes and rubs the Patient in some part of his Body, and pulling some little Bones out of his Mouth, acquaints the Patient, *That these very Bones came out of his Body; that he ought to pluck up a good heart, in regard that his Distemper is but a Trifle; and in fine, that in order to accelerate the Cure, 't will be convenient to send his own and his Relations Slaves to shoot Elks, Deer, &c., to the end they may all eat of that sort of Meat, upon which his Cure does absolutely depend.*

"Commonly these Quacks bring 'em some Juices of Plants, which are a sort of Purges, and are called *Maskikik*" [La Hontan in Hoffman 1891:151–152].

Kabina
Keres, *Southwest*
One of four medicine societies at Acoma Pueblo. The word is no longer translatable, although one informant from Santo Domingo said that it referred to a person "who ate too much" [White 1932:107]. The society became extinct during the winter of 1926–1927. Its major function was to heal illnesses caused by sorcerers.

Kachina
Pueblo, *Southwest*
See *koko.*

Kaetcine
Zuni, *Southwest*
A bundle of individual sacred prayer sticks. Selected individuals are designated to offer them up to the spirits. The bundles are usually buried or deposited in cornfields, in river mud, in shrines in the mountains, in springs, in excavations, and in or near the village.

Kagske
Netsilik Eskimo, *Arctic Coast*
Large ceremonial snowhouse used for shamanic rituals. Usually the ceremonies are conducted in the dark.

Kahsatsenhsera
Iroquois, *Northeast*
A property that is inherent in all matter; for example, one might speak of the "spirit" of a medicine, food, mineral, and so forth. The term means "power" or "strength" and refers to the power of nature. This power has no consciousness, volition, or will but is simply an inherent power. For instance, when sacred foods are brought to a ceremony, the spirits consume this essence, but the food itself remains physically unchanged. The word contains the root *sera*, which means "to be born of" [Blanchard 1982:220]. A synonym in Iroquoian is *tsiniiakoianorenhseraten*, which also contains the *sera* root.

Kahuna
Hawaiian, *Pacific*
Although this term is often used to refer to a Hawaiian shaman, it is better translated as "master" or "expert." For example, the *kahuna kalaiwaa* is a master canoe builder, the *kahuna hookelewa* is a skilled navigator of canoes, and the *kahuna lua* is a master of muscles and hence skilled in boxing and wrestling. See below entries for several types of masters associated with healing.

Kahuna anaana
Hawaiian, *Pacific*
A kahuna "who prayed people to death" [Larsen in Handy et al. 1974:261]. These kahunas have great powers of suggestion over people and are well versed in the use of three primary poisons: *akia*, a plant poison; *auhuhu*, a plant that poisons fish; and *oopuhue*, a deadly fish poison. "Very frequently all the Hawaiian medical lore is confused with the activities of the kahuna anaana, but these were in reality only one part of Hawaiian medical practice" [Larsen in Handy et al. 1974:261].

Kahuna ha ha
Hawaiian, *Pacific*
A shaman that specializes in diagnosis. "He felt the patient to determine what was wrong. If he could determine no bodily ailment, he might send the patient to the kahuna nui for spiritual aid. Otherwise, the patient was sent to the kahuna lapaau laau" [Larsen in Handy et al. 1974:262]. On rare occasions the patient would *ha ha* the diagnosis.

Kahuna hoonoho
Hawaiian, *Pacific*
A shaman that specializes in trance mediumship. Before beginning a session, the shaman drinks a narcotic made from the root of the awa plant. In this state, the shaman becomes the *kahu* or *ips* of the spirit. Such spirits are often called *makani*, meaning "wind." Once possessed, the shaman determines the cause of the patient's illness, and if sorcery is indicated, the sorcerer is named. These shamans are also used to locate lost objects and find stolen goods.

Kahuna hoonohonoho
Hawaiian, *Pacific*
One of several varieties of sorcerers. Although the main god of sorcery is Uli, different sorcerers call upon different lesser gods and demons in their practice. They are usually classified according to which gods they call upon. Other varieties include the *kahuna hoounauna, kahuna hookomokomo,*

and *kahuna hooleilei*. When illness is diagnosed as having been caused by an evil spirit, one of these sorcerers is brought in to dispense with it. The *kahuna hoounauna* are skilled at sending their helping spirits on errands. They are particularly skilled in sending back evil spirits to attack their source.

Kahuna kahea
Hawaiian, *Pacific*
A master of psychotherapy. Through prayer and the power of suggestion, patients are cured. "To whatever cause we ascribe it, it is a fact that suffering and pain can be relieved through 'suggestion' or whatever we choose to call this power. These powers were made very effective in the old days because the patient believed implicitly in the skill of the kahuna, whom he had respected and looked up to from his earliest years" [Larsen in Handy et al. 1974:266].

Kahuna lapaau
Hawaiian, *Pacific*
The class of shamans that conducts healing ceremonies. The tutelary gods of these practitioners are Maiola and Koleamoku. The shaman diagnoses an illness by calling upon his helping spirit, his *akua*, to which prayers and sacrifices have been made. In most cases, the illness is diagnosed as being caused by displeased spirits, *aumakuas*, and a sacrifice to the spirits is deemed necessary to cure the patient. Perhaps the most common sacrifice is a bird, but shamans also use squid, dogs, or even humans when the patient is a chief and the illness is very serious [Alexander 1899:66]. Sometimes the treatment includes a sweat bath for the patient. The patient is seated upon a pile of heated rocks covered with wet leaves, and the patient is also covered with leaves. Following the steaming, the patient is dipped into the ocean.

Nils Larsen translates the term *kahuna lapaau laau* as "herb doctor" [Handy et al. 1974:262]. "Very careful training was given to the young men who were to be the herb doctors of that day. While they were very young, they were taken into the family of a specially trained kahuna and carefully instructed in the appearance of the different herbs, in their uses and effects, in the way to find them and gather and prepare them for use. The student remained in the home of the kahuna for fifteen or twenty years, and when he left this home, his training was complete and he was ready to enter upon his life work as a kahuna, expert in what was then known of drugs and medicines" [Larsen in Handy et al. 1974:257].

Kahuna lomilomi
Hawaiian, *Pacific*
A master of massage [Larsen in Handy et al. 1974:262]. "They knew just how to manipulate and massage and pound sore and stiff muscles, and to bring relief. They were skilled in the arts of what is known as physio-therapy today" [Larsen in Handy et al. 1974:265–266].

Kakini
Maidu, *California*
Spirit. Both the *yomi* (sucking doctor; see entry) and the *oye* (singing doctor; see entry) have such spirits.

Kakinpe
Maidu, *California*
See *Yukbe*.

Kalalik
South Alaska Eskimo, *Arctic Coast*
Shaman. It comes among the Chugach, from the word *kalagät*, meaning "spirit." As such, the term literally means "a person who has spirits" [Birket-Smith 1953:120]. The *kalagät* are reported to be evil-minded for the most part and are visible only to shamans.

Kalangi
Miwok, *California*
The term used by the Central Miwok at Bald Rock for dance doctors. See *koyabi* for details.

Kalullim
Carrier, *Makenzie-Yukon*
A society of assistants to the *kyanyuantan* society (see entry for details). These individuals had all experienced the *kyan* dream-sickness, called *kyanilkyot*, and were therefore deemed fit to assist in curing an illness considered to be highly contagious.

Kamantocit
Montagnais, *Canadian Eastern Woodlands*
Shamans whose helping spirit is the snake; the literal translation is "one who deals with snakes." The animal helper of this type of shaman is known as *kamadzit*, "one who does evil" [Speck 1919:254].

Kan
Apache, *Southwest*
The general term for spirit. Each shaman has his own *kan* from which he obtains supernatural power [Bourke 1892:581].

Kangalik
West Alaska Eskimo, *Arctic Coast*
A Nunivagmiut shaman practicing during the mid-twentieth century. Kangalik was a cripple and the son of a powerful shaman. Around the age of 12, he began seeing strange things in his dreams. When he told his father of this, his father told him not to mention it to anyone. He eventually developed the ability to see spirits not only in his dreams but also while awake. He would see objects being moved by the spirits within them, and he could see tiny spirit people and even their dogs. At night, he would stay awake to see many spirit people on the ceiling of the men's sleeping house. Often he heard a loud noise that would make him tremble. Because he never talked of these things, he did not know that others were not having similar visions.

Finally, his strange nature became known to others, and he was asked to cure a sick man. Although he did not know how to do this, he undertook the healing. When he did this, he found that he heard healing songs coming to him from everywhere—from a lamp, from the rim of his drum, and so forth. Thereafter, he became a healer [Lantis 1950:313].

Kanhyae
Cayuga, *Northeast*
The Striking Stick Dance healing ritual, which may be performed by anyone. See *eyondwanshgwut* for details.

Kanouga
Cherokee, *Southeast*
A scratching instrument used by Cherokee shamans in their healing ceremonies. This instrument was used during the latter part of the nineteenth century, but today, other items such as briers, pieces of flint or flint arrowheads (preferably black), and bunches of laurel leaves are used instead.

The original comblike device was made from seven splinters of turkey leg bone. These splinters were set into a small, rectangular frame (about 4 centimeters by 5 centimeters) made from a turkey feather quill. The quill was bent around the bone splinters to form the frame such that the tips of the splinters projected slightly beyond the edge of the quill along one side. Set in such a way, it was impossible to inflict a deep wound on the patient.

During the healing ceremony, the shaman recites the scratching formula and lightly scratches the patient's skin in the afflicted area. Then an infusion of very pungent plants is applied to the scratched area, because "the pungent smell puts the disease demon to rout" [Mooney and Olbrechts 1932:53]. The intention of the scratching is not to draw blood but to condition the skin so that the infusion is more readily absorbed into the patient's body. "It is undeniable that this treatment is often efficacious to allay the pains caused by neuralgia, nervous headache, and similar complaints" [Mooney and Olbrechts 1932:71]. It is also a standard treatment for rheumatism.

Kanrugwae
Cayuga, *Northeast*
The Eagle Dance Society, one of the Cayuga medicine societies. Its healing ceremonies may be per-

formed only by members of the society. See *eyondwanshgwut* for details.

Kapay
Karok, *California*
See *kuwi.*

Katagara
Pomo, *California*
A small whistle used by the *dja minawan* (outfit doctors) to locate sickness in the body. The whistle is concealed in a chipmunk hide that is passed over the patient's body until the whistle sounds, indicating the location of the disease [Loeb 1934a:10].

Katsa tala
Pomo, *California*
The "ash-devils" or fire-eaters who perform during the Pomo Devil Dance Ceremony; sometimes referred to as *no' xahluigak*. "The actual dancing lasted for perhaps half an hour, after which the ash-devils sat down and began to 'eat fire,' jump into it, and perform other miraculous feats with it. They, to all appearances, actually picked up live coals, which they call *bu* (Pomo for 'potatoes'), and devoured them, preferring the coals of manzanita wood, as these were the strongest and hottest" [Barrett 1917a:419]. During the dance, the ash-devils wear only a headdress, and their bodies are painted. They each carry a ceremonial staff that has the head of a crane attached to the top. This is their sign of absolute authority to do as they please during the Devil Dance.

Ke
Tewa, *Southwest*
Term used by the Tewa of San Juan Pueblo to refer to the Bear shamans, who specialize in healing ceremonies. The Bear shaman is one type of Fish-people—those who are involved in the ceremonial life of the people. Bear men and women are initiated into power through a ceremony that lasts eight days and eight nights. "It is indeed dangerous to become a Bear, dangerous and frightening, because you have to get the power and you have to fight the witches and the evil spirits. You

must be strong and your heart must not tremble" [Laski 1958:100].

If a person wants to become a Bear, he or she has to gain entry into the *Ke* Society. The only people qualified are those who have been cured by the Bears or those who are sick and want such a cure. The one exception to this rule is a person who has been called by "the departed ones themselves."

For minor illness that can be handled by a single Bear, the *buyabu'ú* (see entry) is performed. In more serious cases requiring the services of several Bears, much more elaborate preparations are necessary. Laski [1958:113–116] provides excellent details of this ritual, which she calls "The Great Healing Ceremony":

"A very formal request is made to obtain the combined services of the Bears. The father, or another male relative of the patient, who knows the ancient, formal language for such occasions, carries a small corn husk package to one of the Bears. This package is filled with sacred cornmeal upon which the patient has blown his breath. In presenting it to the medicine man, the messenger addresses him in the ancient, respectful way:

Poor, humble me,
Will you forgive me
If by my humble presence
I am disturbing the peace
Of your most beautiful home?

"After receiving some friendly encouragement from the Bear, the visitor asks, 'May I state my business?'

"When he has received permission to go ahead, he explains: '(name of patient) has become ill and has decided that the goddess Yia·kwiyó· may be of help to him. . . .'

"The Bear eventually agrees to see the patient and notifies two or three other medicine men. After the necessary preparations, they will go together to the patient's home, which has already been prepared for the special event. The largest room of the house has been completely emptied of all furniture. Sheepskins are placed on the floor along the four walls. The patient's relatives and friends, who have been asked to come, squat on these sheepskins along three of the walls. The

medicine men and the patient are seated on sheepskins along one of the shorter walls. They wear nothing but G-strings, and no face or body paints are used. The ceremonial corn painting, built around the bowl of holy medicine water, is right in front of them. . . . There are also lightning stones, eagle feathers, anthropomorphic and animal shaped stone fetishes, and several well polished but unsculptured small stones which might be kept in little pouches.

"Immediately in front of each Bear (that is, between the Bear and the corn painting) is his Bear paw, the symbol of the Bear Society to which the medicine man belongs. Each medicine man carefully unwraps his reed container to take out the yia· kwiyó·, the perfect ear of white corn which is the image of the White Cornmother. The Bear lifts the yia· kwiyó· and displays it to the people by moving it slowly around and giving his blessing to all those present: 'May you be loved and liked through the Great Goodness of Yia· kwiyó· and through myself who am only a poor human being.'

"The father of the patient has, in advance, prepared ceremonial cigarettes of homegrown tobacco wrapped in corn husk leaves. These are now smoked by the Bears and by the 'learned' men who formerly requested their help. The Bears may also be seen chewing certain herbs which, in the opinion of some Indians, might help to bring about the forthcoming trance.

"The ceremony begins with a weird singing which has a suggestive, almost hypnotic quality. Sometimes a medicine man dips one of the large eagle feathers into the holy water and pulls the feather through the mouth of another shaman to help him 'become a Bear.'

"On the floor near the participant onlookers, small plates with cornmeal have been placed at intervals. When the medicine men begin to sing, everybody takes a little cornmeal in his hand, blows his breath upon it, and throws it towards the altar, saying . . . 'Be a man and be a woman.'

"As the ceremony progresses, and especially when the medicine men are beginning to fall into trance, the corn throwing and the ceremonial phrase are repeated with increasing emphasis, as an encouragement to the Bear to become magical, and as an encouragement to the patient to be receptive to the magical powers to which he is exposed. The ceremonial phrase, 'be a man and be a woman,' is used in many Tewa ceremonies whenever supernatural powers are about to break through.

"As soon as a medicine man has become magical, he puts the long glovelike Bear paw over his arm, and with it he touches everybody within reach while he moves around and continues to roar his wild 'xa·axa·, xa·axa·.' When all shamans have become Bears, they get up from their seats one by one, and all but the chief Bear Dance before the cornmeal altar. They take a deep look into the lake in the center of the corn painting to see the... 'evil spirits' or witches which they will have to fight in order to cure the patient. . . .

"Before approaching the patient, the medicine men touch the images of the White Corngoddess, and with their hands, seem to draw strength from the sacred Cornmothers. Sucking at the sick parts of the patient's body, they finally succeed in taking out rags and stones which are believed to have caused the illness. The Bears also approach other people in the room whom they try to cure, but their efforts are concentrated upon the patient for whom they were originally called.

"Stones, rags, and fibers, pulled or sucked from a patient, are thrown into the family urinal which was held in readiness somewhere in the back, and which has now been placed by one of the women in the center of the room near the altar.

"While still in a trance, two medicine men leave the house to fight the witches in the dark and to catch the witch which has caused the illness. They return with a rag doll referred to as the witch. When the witch doll has been passed around and everybody has seen it, it is held at the rim of the urinal. . . . Two lightning stones are rubbed against each other to produce a spark which is supposed to burn the witch. Actually, there is no fire; the burning is symbolized by the sparks from the lightning stones. Eventually, the witch is torn to shreds and thrown into the urinal, which, if still intact, is now intentionally broken.

"The broken pieces, as well as the sucking stones, rags, and torn up witch doll, are all swept together into a shawl and bundled up into a bag. After sprinkling cornmeal on this bag and swinging it in the four directions above the cornmeal altar, two Bears carry it out of the kiva and the pueblo to throw it into a canyon. While they are gone, a male relative of the patient expresses to the remaining medicine men his formal thanks for their service.

"After their return, the medicine men awake from their trance, and a melodious, soothing chant is heard while the Bears wash their hands and later pass around a bowl of holy water from which everybody takes a sip. The patient is given a fetish, usually a bear shaped rock, which he keeps for four days before he returns it to the shaman.

"At the very end of the ceremony, the patient's relatives, who were invited, bring their gifts—usually baskets of flour—to the Bears who divide them among themselves. The patient's immediate family serves food to all who are present, and, after the usual offering is made to the departed ones, all feast together."

A similar healing ritual is performed at Santa Clara, San Ildefonso, and Tesuque pueblos. The Taos pueblo no longer has a Bear Society. Until about 1930, a communal curing ceremony was held for the entire population every fourth spring in the large kiva of San Juan.

Ketcima Netowani
Fox, *Midwest*
"The Great Manitou who made this earth, who made everything" [Michelson 1921:25]. It is the Fox variant of the widespread Algonquian term *Kitchi Manitou*. Under the influence of Christianity, it has become the term for God.

Kegey
Yurok, *Oregon Seaboard*
Also: *kegei, kegeior, kégei, kay-gay.* Plural: *kegeyowor.* The Yurok (also Tolowa) term for shaman. It comes "from the verb stem *key(chek'in-)* 'to sit,' through an infixed *-eg-*, a nominalizing element signifying intensive, repeated action: a practice. Thus, 'One who sits as a practice'" [Buckley 1992:n.19:160]. This probably refers to shamans' common use of redwood stools during their rituals. They sit on such stools smoking their pipes while diagnosing the patient's illness. They also

have such seats during their training periods in the mountains.

Most Yurok shamans are women. It is not unusual for them to work with shamans from adjacent cultures, in this case, Karok and Tolowa shamans. Shamans usually acquire their powers through vision quests at known power locations. Others inherit their abilities through the family lineage, most often from mother to daughter. In the latter case, they are earmarked by having special types of dreams; inheritance is thus only a potential, not an absolute. In addition, the shamans all go through a stringent training process called *hohkep*. This training is usually carried out during the summer in the high mountain areas. The actual spot in the mountains is called the prayer seat. Informant Dewey George [in Buckley 1992:134–135] reports on one such site:

"The doctors used to walk up to Doctor Rock. They had power, so they walked up. They'd go up with their relations to dance. Up on Doctor Rock there were different parts of the rock for each (power). I've seen four places where there have been fires. They'd go up there and they'd dance for ten days, ten nights. Then they'd come back and they'd dance in the sweathouse for another five or six nights. That's if they wanted to be good doctors."

These training sessions are intense. Buckley [1992:135] reports, "I have twice been told that doctors dance with such concentration that their feet entirely leave the ground, and they levitate. The dancer listens for the right voices among the many she hears. . . . When she hears the right voices she falls into trance and runs back down the mountain to her village sweathouse, unconscious and 'crazy,' protected by her male relatives who have accompanied her and her trainer and who may restrain her with a long strap, lest she injure herself." They speak of this training as the novice having "made her path into the mountains."

After the novice has acquired the ability to suck out pains (diseases), called *telogel*, they apprentice themselves to an established shaman for a period of time, usually at least one year. Their entire training, including the time spent in the mountains, usually takes from two to three years.

In healing sessions, the shaman begins by smoking her pipe and singing and dancing to determine the cause of the illness. This initial divination usually results in the shaman detecting some breach of taboo that has been committed by the patient. It might be "a memory in the family, some terrible secret they'd hidden, a 'skeleton in the closet' that was affecting that person—and when it was stated, then it would go away and the person would get better" [Florence Shaughnessy in Buckley 1992:138]. Any family members present who know of the deed are required to make a public confession, termed *pahsoy*, at this point in the ceremony. In former times, there were specialists—usually males, called *pegahsoy*—who conducted this initial divination.

The shaman then locates the source of the illness and sucks it from the patient's body. "I saw her take things out of people, sucking them with her mouth. Then she'd spit it out in her hand. I saw her spit out eyes, eggs, lizards, arrows. That was real. I saw those things breathe and move" [Aileen Figueroa in Buckley 1992:140]. The object is put into a basket or bowl provided for that purpose.

Kein
Karok, *Oregon Seaboard*
The Karok equivalent of the Yurok *kegey* (see entry).

Ketaltnes
Wailaki, *California*
A Kato doctoring stick used during healing ceremonies. It translates to "sharp heels," which is also the nickname given to Nagaitco, the chief spirit called upon during healing ceremonies. The stick is stripped of bark, and condor feathers are attached to one end and a stone blade to the other end [Loeb 1934a:36].

Ketanitowet
Lenni Lenape, *Northeast*
Also *Kacheh Munitto*. One of two terms used in the Minsi dialect of the Lenni Lenape (also called Delaware) to refer to the Great Spirit. The second term, *Patumawas*, translates to "He who is petitioned."

Keteu
Wailaki, California
Dialectical variant: *cecene*. Sucking doctor. It was not unusual for a *keteu* to also be a *naitulgai* (dreamer). Young male novices and married females, most often those who had dreamed of or seen a spirit, were taken up into the mountains each spring by three or four male and female sucking doctors for an eight-day training session. They were brought back each night to dance and sing in the village. During this time, the novices received no food and little water. The last time this training ritual was conducted was around 1885–1890.

Their overall schooling lasted a year, but most candidates failed to complete the entire training. In addition, some of them repeated this training over several years before becoming sucking doctors. "It is important to note that among the Wailaki the sucking doctor had both to carry the 'pain' in his body and also have a guardian spirit. The 'pain' was powdered obsidian spat into the mouth of the neophyte (during initiation) by the instructor. Here we have a combination of the Northwest Californian concept, where the 'pain' was the essential requirement for a sucking doctor, and the Central Californian concept, where the guardian spirit alone was necessary" [Loeb 1934a:80].

Sucking doctors diagnosed sickness among the Wailaki, so they were always called in first. Normally, they treated a patient over a four-day period, sucking on the patient each day. During this time, the shaman would refrain from eating meat and sometimes drank no water. They had a secret language they used during their healing ceremonies.

One of the most important spirits for the sucking doctors was the eagle. During treatment, the sucking doctor would wave an eagle feather over the patient in imitation of the flight of an eagle. Sometimes he also made passes with his arms in the same manner. In addition to the eagle, most sucking doctors had other spirits that came to their aid. During a typical sucking ceremony, the shaman would locate the seat of the patient's pain and suck on that area of the body several times. Each time, the shaman would spit into a basket provided for that purpose and drink water from

another basket. Between the suckings he would sing. When the disease object was finally removed, the shaman would display it to those present. Usually it was some form of insect. This object would then be held in his hand for about 15 minutes while he sang over it. Finally, he would crush it between his hands and drop it into the basket, whereupon it would be taken outside and the contents burned in a fire. Upon completion of the ceremony, he would be paid in deerskins, baskets, and so forth.

Bear shamans occurred throughout California and usually used their abilities to kill enemies. However, among the Wailaki, there were Bear shamans who used their powers for curing. These were the *keteu* whose guardian spirits had appeared in dreams as grizzly bears. These doctors became possessed by bears and would imitate their behavior, such as biting people. In these possession states, the spirit of the bear would speak through the shaman.

In other cases diagnosed by the sucking doctor, the singing doctor, called *naitulgai*, was called in to complete the cure with his songs [Loeb 1934a:75–82].

Keyugak
Mackenzie Eskimo
The shaman's helping spirit [Jenness 1922:191]. It is possible among these people to purchase such a spirit from a shaman [Stefansson 1914:368]. "However, (this) is only partly true, for all that the owner can impart is his good-will, and a knowledge of how to approach and summon the particular spirit that he has sold; the rest depends on the spirit itself. The aspirant must go out to some lonely place and summon the spirit, which may or may not appear" [Jenness 1922:191].

Khichikouai
Montagnais, Canadian Eastern Woodlands
The term used by the French Jesuit missionary Father LeJeune during the 1630s to refer to the spirits that came during a Shaking Tent Ceremony he observed. He reported that the word comes from the stem *khichikou*, which he translated to "light"

K

or "the air." LeJeune referred to these spirits as "Genii."

Although LeJeune did not refer to the ceremony as a Shaking Tent rite per se, his description confirms that it was:

"He (the shaman) shook this edifice (the tent) gently; but, as he continued to become more animated, he fell into so violent an ecstasy, that I thought he would break everything to pieces, shaking his house with so much force and violence, that I was astonished at a man having so much strength; for, after he had once begun to shake it, he did not stop until the consultation was over, which lasted about three hours . . . he commenced to whistle, in a hollow tone, and as if it came from afar; then to talk as if in a bottle; to cry like the owls of these countries . . . then to howl and sing, constantly varying his tones . . . after a thousand cries and howls, after a thousand songs, after having danced and thoroughly shaken this fine edifice (the conjuring tent), the sorcerer consulted them (the spirits). . . . These Genii, or rather the juggler (shaman) who counterfeited them, answered . . . always disguising his voice" [JR 1897–1905: 6: 165–167].

Khichikouai is also spelled *kichikouai* and *khichekouai* on different pages of LeJeune's writings.

Khmungha
Lakota, *Plains*
To cause sickness or death through the actions of a sorcerer or witch [Dorsey 1894:499].

Kichil woknam
Northern Yuki, *California*
The obsidian ceremony, in which older shamans trained their novices [Loeb 1934a:99].

Kikituk
North Alaska Eskimo, *Arctic Coast*
A Tikerarmiut carved wooden or ivory animal effigy used by Alaska Eskimo shamans. It represents their helping spirit and can be used for both good and evil. When used for healing, the *kikituk*

is animated by the shaman and proceeds to bite the afflicted area of the patient's body to effect a cure. In so doing, the *kikituk* bites the spirit that is causing the illness. When used by sorcerers, the *kikituk* is made to burrow into the victim's body until it reaches the heart, causing death. Rainey [1947:277] describes one found in 1939 as "a carved wooden figure of a strange looking beast about 2 feet long. It was equipped with very sharp teeth; the lower jaw was loose so that it could be manipulated up and down. All the old people recognized the creature . . . and it was obvious that there was still an ill-concealed horror of the effigy." For an example of a *kikituk* shaman, see *asatchaq*.

Kilokilo uhane
Hawaiian, *Pacific*
A class of shamans that specializes in dream interpretation and reports on the condition of the soul.

Kilpatrick, Jack Frederick
Cherokee, *Plains*
Jack Kilpatrick was born at Stilwell, Oklahoma, in 1915 and died in the same area in 1967. His formal education was in music, and he held a doctorate in music from the University of Redlands. Leopold Stokowski called him America's greatest composer, and during his lifetime he produced 168 compositions. However, he also made extensive contributions to the ethnographic knowledge of his own people and, with the assistance of his wife Anna, published extensively on the Cherokee culture in Oklahoma. His best work, published in the same year as his death, was *Run toward the Nightland: Magic of the Oklahoma Cherokees*.

Kitche Manitou
Ojibwa, *Canadian Eastern Woodlands*
The Great Mystery [Johnston 1982]. Coleman [1937] gives other renditions of this term: *Kimie manido*, *Kitci manitu*, and *Gitci manitu*. Brown [1977:104] uses *Kitchi Manitou* and translates it as

"Great Spirit." Vizenor [1981:84] uses *gichi-manidoo*. For the Otchipwe of Lake of the Woods and Rainy Lake in western Ontario, the equivalent term is *Kije Manitu* [Cooper 1936:26]. The dialectical variant among the Northern Cree is *Kisci manitu*. There is evidence that prior to European contact, *Kitche Manitou* referred to a whole class of spirits; under the influence of Christianity, it became a synonym for God [Paper 1983].

Kiva
Pueblo, *Southwest*
A ceremonial room within the pueblo. Usually there are several kivas within a pueblo, each being used by different medicine and other ritual societies. Sometime they are round, and sometimes they are square. Some of them are halfway underground. Some are covered, and others are open. Those that are covered usually have a hole in the middle of the roof—called *sipapu*—for entry. This opening symbolizes the place from which the first humans emerged from the earth's interior. It is also believed to lead down to the realm of the dead. Another word for *kiva* is *estufa*.

Kixunai
Hupa, *Oregon Seaboard*
See *wogey*.

Kluckhohn, Clyde Kay Maben
Clyde Kluckhohn was born in Le Mars, Iowa, on 11 January 1905. He studied at the University of Vienna in 1931–1932, where he also underwent psychoanalysis. This experience led him to become one of the founders of psychological anthropology. In 1932 he was a Rhodes scholar at Oxford and received his Ph.D. in anthropology from Harvard in 1936. He subsequently joined the Harvard faculty, where he remained for the rest of his career. Kluckhohn is best known for his brilliant work on the Navajo, both as an ethnographer and as a linguist. His work is among the best produced by any American anthropologist concerned with Native American cultures. He first encountered the Navajo while recuperating from rheumatic fever at the Vogt family ranch in New Mexico in 1923 and was so impressed with them that he returned many years later as an anthropologist. He died in Santa Fe, New Mexico, on 29 July 1960 at the age of 55.

Klukwalle
Makah, *Northwest Coast*
Also known as *tlu'qali* among the Makah, *tlu'kwana* among the Nootkan, and *tlu'gani* among the Kyoquot. The Wolf ritual or the winter ceremonial. This ritual appears in various forms for various purposes. When the *klukwalle* is an initiation ritual (its most common use), it is a four-day ritual called *Qua-ech'*. Occasionally it is used for healing when a patient cannot be cured by one of the less powerful shamanic healing ceremonies. The Wolf ritual is considered to have final power over healing and can be performed only with the permission of the shaman conducting the healings.

Kohota
Mojave, *Southwest*
Also: *kwaxot*. The *kohota* has been variously described as a dance director, manager of entertainments, and festival chief. However, some *kohota* are also shamans who have dreamed certain powers of curing. Such persons are designated *sumach* (dreamer) *kohota*. Such power dreams are often in accordance with the *kohota*'s role as custodian of enemy scalps that have been taken in warfare. As such, they are usually skilled at treating "enemy sickness," which is caused by coming into contact with the enemy. Such shamans also decontaminate any enemy captives brought back to camp after a war raid to prevent camp members from contracting enemy sickness. He bathes the captives, first rubbing them with soaproot and then smudging them with arrowweed. This is repeated over four consecutive days.

In his role as scalp keeper, he is known as *ahwe kusumanya*. He knows how to handle scalps without becoming sick. He washes and prepares them for ceremonies; otherwise, they are kept in a gourd sealed up with greasewood or arrowweed gum in the corner of the house where he sleeps.

When he dies, the scalps are burned [Stewart 1970:22–23].

Kohuyoli
Southeastern Pomo, *California*
Term used by the Clear Lake Pomo to refer to a shaman's medicine bag or the doctoring of a patient with it [Gifford 1926a:331].

Koiahpe
Miwok, *California*
See *koyabi*.

Kokkothlanna
Zuni, *Southwest*
The Great God Society, one of several medicine societies at Zuni. Members are called upon to treat any illness that results in the swelling of any part of the body. However, they are called only after all other efforts at healing have failed. During their healing ceremonies only the patient and society members may be present. The healing ceremonies usually begin at dusk. During the ceremony the powers of certain spirits are called forth by the shamans, who wear the appropriate masks for each spirit used in the ceremony. Lines are drawn on the patient with cornmeal, and these lines are traced over with yucca that the shamans hold in their hands. Herbal medicine is also administered to the patient.

One unusual aspect of this healing ceremony involves the use of bread. "Kwelele (masked shaman), who remains, stands with a foot on each side of the sick man's head, holding the fire stick in his left hand and the drill in his right hand. He also holds in his left hand four cakes of bread strung on a yucca ribbon, three of which are in ring form while the fourth is a perforated disk. Holding his hands close together Kwelele, bending forward, moves them over the patient from the head down the center of the body to the feet" [Stevenson 1904:489–490]. This process is repeated over the patient's extremities, and when the shaman is finished, the bread is placed over the patient's heart. Then the patient "eats three pieces and throws the fourth to a dog which has been brought into the room by his mother-in-law for the express purpose of receiving the bread. The dog's eating the bread that has been laid upon the heart of the invalid is supposed to absorb the disease from the invalid" [Stevenson 1904:490].

Following this ritual action, the society members present the patient with four sacred corn ears, a prayer plume to Sun Father and one to Moon Mother, "and a calico shirt or some such gift. Each member present dips a handful of (yucca) suds and deposits them on the head of the invalid, after which the head is thoroughly washed" [Stevenson 1904:490]. Following this cleansing, the ceremony is concluded with a feast given by the patient's relatives at which gifts, most often cornmeal and flour, are distributed to the members of the medicine society as payment for their services.

Koko
Zuni, *Southwest*
Also: *Ka-ka*. The word for *kachinas*—a class of spirits that are impersonated through the use of masks and costumes. They serve many purposes, one of which is to bring health to the people. Hultkrantz [1987:104] reports that "the Zuni *kachina* cult is the most conspicuous example of ancestor worship in North America."

Konah
Caddo, *Plains*
Also: *conna* [Bolton 1987:168]. A curing doctor or shaman [Parsons 1941:32]. Both males and females become shamans following an eight-day, vision-inducing, initiation ceremony in which the participants consume a concoction prepared from the psychoactive mescal bean. One of the earliest observations on the Caddo reports that their shamans wear "special insignia of office, in the form of peculiar headresses, or curious necklaces of highly colored snake skins and other articles. They are also said to have always carried bows and arrows" [Bolton 1987:86].

Illnesses are often attributed to object intrusion, the cure of which is to remove the disease-causing object. Often, the object—horsehair, an insect, a bit of cloth, an arrow—has been sent by a witch or a sorcerer. If the shaman determines who sent it and knows that the sorcerer has more power, the shaman will not take the case, since the sorcerer could send the sickness back and into the curing shaman.

To procure a healing ceremony, the requester gives the shaman a gift of tobacco. If he accepts the tobacco, it indicates that he will undertake the cure. The form taken by the cure depends on instructions from the shaman's helping spirits. The shaman goes to the patient's house for the treatment and conducts the healing over the course of six days. If the patient is not cured, another shaman is usually called in. The shaman normally doctors the patient alone, with the assistance of a man or woman from the household. No one is allowed to enter the patient's room during the healing without first being smudged with cedar or sage. Early observers of the Caddo report that patients were often taken to the sweat lodge for treatment.

Among the various types of shamans, the most powerful healers are the Beaver shamans, called *tao* [Parsons 1941:34]. They are also usually mescal-bean doctors, called *daitino* (also *daitono*), although informants claim that each type is grouped into a different society, called "bands" by the Caddo. Another type of shaman is the *yuko* (also *yoko, yuku*). These shamans treat wounds but are best known for their ability to foretell the future and find lost objects.

The only recorded account of an actual treatment is an eighteenth-century Spanish one:

"To cure a patient they make a large fire under the bed, and *palillos* provide flutes and a feather fan. The instruments are manufactured [sticks] with notches resembling a snake's rattle. This palillo placed in a hollow bone upon a skin makes a noise nothing less than devilish. Before touching it they drink their herbs boiled and covered with much foam and begin to perform their dance without moving from one spot, accompanied by the mu-sic of Inferno, or the song of the damned. . . . This ceremony lasts from midafternoon to nearly sunrise" [Bolton 1987:168].

Konäpämik
Menomini, *Midwest*
"The cowrie shell contained in every medicine-bag and used during the shooting ceremonies of the lodge" [Skinner 1920:336]. However, Skinner uses this term interchangeably with *megise* (see entry), the more common name for this shell.

Koo bakiyahale
Pomo, *California*
A shaman who specializes in handling *koo*, which translates to "poison" but refers to illness caused by a sorcerer. A *koo bakiyahale* is thus a "performer for the poisoned." In their healing ceremonies, these shamans sing their power songs and use rattles and objects from their medicine bags. They are taught this form of healing from an older shaman, usually a relative; their knowledge is not obtained from spirit helpers. This tends to make their healing ceremonies more ordered and predictable [Kroeber 1940:214].

Koo detul
Pomo, *California*
The object removed from a patient by a sucking doctor that is the source of the patient's illness; translates to "poison standing-up." Among the Pomo, this object is most often some form of live insect [Loeb 1934a:9].

Koyabi
Miwok, *California*
Also: *koiahpe*. The term used by the East Central Sierra Miwok for shamans who doctor using their helping spirits. Supernatural power is gained either through heredity, with the novice being trained by a parent or grandparent, or through a visionary dream of a guardian spirit. Both males and females can become shamans, and as a rule, they all go through at least three years of special training. Most of them become sucking doctors. In treating a patient, they often use a small bone whis-

tle made of a red-tailed hawk or owl wing bone, which is blown or sucked over the affected part of the patient's body. When the whistle becomes plugged up, it signals that the disease has been removed. The shaman then sucks the disease from the whistle. Others simply make a small cut in the skin over the afflicted area and then suck on it.

Some shamans become singing doctors. They cure a patient by rubbing and pressing their hands over the patient's body while singing and blowing an elderberry whistle.

Other shamans, called *kalangi* by the Central Miwok at Bald Rock, become dance doctors [Bates 1992:100]. These shamans neither suck on the patient nor administer herbal remedies. Prior to treating a patient, these shamans observe a four-day mandated fast in which they abstain from eating meat and having sexual intercourse. During a typical healing ceremony, the dance doctor "would circle the patient, singing and dancing to each of the four directions. He would shoot at the seat of pain (source of illness) with a medicine bow and arrow and shake a cocoon rattle filled with small quartz pebbles. Often he would also use an 8" obsidian knife smeared with medicine, and four sticks. He would set one stick on each side of the patient, one at the head and the other at the foot. The poison or evil that the doctor blew off the patient passed out through the sticks" [Bates 1992:100].

The shamans also have special costumes that they wear during their healing ceremonies. "Among the Central Miwok at Groveland, the sucking doctor's outfit consisted of a flicker quill band, hairpins, hair plumes, a 10-inch baton-like cocoon rattle, feather wand, abalone shell necklace, two strips of buckskin covered with crow feathers (one passing along the outside of the arm from the wrist across the shoulders to the other wrist, and another passing from wrist to wrist across the chest), a belt of buckskin, buckskin clout, necklace of small perforated stones, a double whistle, eagle or hawk down stuck to the face and hair, red paint stripe from ear to ear across the upper lip, vertical bars of red, black and white paint on the chest, and similar horizontal rings of

paint on the arms and legs" [Hudson in Bates 1992:100]. In contrast, the dance doctor's outfit consists of a woodpecker-tail head plume, head net filled with eagle down, abalone necklace, eagle-claw necklace, back cape of hawk tails, baton of hawk pinions or roadrunner tails, and a double-bone whistle.

Shamans are paid in advance for their services, usually with fresh deer meat and yards of shell money. If the patient is not cured, the payment is returned. If the shaman loses several patients, he is suspected of sorcery and is sometimes put to death.

Krilaq
Netsilik Eskimo, *Arctic Coast*

The head-lifting divination technique used by less powerful healers. It is said that powerful shamans never practice *krilaq*. The technique is generally performed using the wife of the practitioner, his own leg, or a stone. A thong is tied around the wife's hooded head, and the healer allows questions to be asked. The answers are determined by pulling on the thong—an easy pull is a negative response, and a heavy pull is a positive response.

Kroeber, Alfred Louis

Alfred Kroeber was born in Hoboken, New Jersey, on 11 June 1876. He studied under Franz Boas at Columbia University, where in 1901 he received a Ph.D. in anthropology—the first such degree awarded at Columbia. The following year he began his career at the University of California. In 1909 he became the head of the department at Berkeley, where he remained until his retirement in 1946. He is often cited as the father of California anthropology, and following the death of Boas in 1946, many referred to him as the dean of American anthropology. He published extensively in all areas of anthropology—ethnology, linguistics, archaeology, and physical anthropology—but is best remembered for his ethnographic fieldwork among the Yurok, Mojave, Zuni, and Arapaho. He was an innovator in many areas, such as historical approaches to ethnography, statistical methods, kinship, culture-area theory, and the area distribution of cultural elements. Much of his research focused on problems in historical linguistics, and he was among the first to study speech varieties within a culture, such as Yurok ritual speech. He died in Paris on 5 October 1960.

Ktahándo
Penobscot, *Canadian Eastern Woodlands*
The shaman's magical power; translates to "spiritual power" or "witch power." Among the Malecite and Passamaquoddy, the same term is rendered as *ktahánt* [Speck 1919:240].

Kuksu
Pomo, *California*
See *Guksu Ceremony.*

Kuksu Cult
California
The anthropological term for a widespread religious complex among a number of California cultures, especially the Pomo, Kato, Yuki (Northern, Southern, and Coast), Huchnom, Wailaki, Miwok, Maidu, Wappo, and Patwin. In his analysis, E. M. Loeb [1934a, 1934b] divided the complex into a western *Kuksu* cult and an eastern one. He subdivided the western cult into northern (Sherwood Pomo, Huchnom, Kato, Yuki) and southern (Pomo, Wappo, Lake and Coast Miwok) halves because of certain cultural differences.

The *Kuksu* cult proper was a secret shamanistic society for certain men and women. The central theme of the cult was the impersonation of *Kuksu* or Big Head, the doctor god from the south. In the western area, there were two aspects to the cult: the Ghost Ceremony (not to be confused with the widespread Ghost Dance movement), which served as an initiation ceremony for boys; and the *Kuksu* Society, which operated a training program for neophyte shamans who showed potential for becoming healers. Among the Patwin and Maidu, the *Hesi* cult arose along the Sacramento River and put an end to the two original subdivisions in the western cult. In the eastern area, the cult was of more recent origin. Although the origin of the *Kuksu* cult is unknown, it seems to have spread

northward along the California coast among the western aspect of the cult and then eastward.

Kúlañ o'odham
Pima, *Southwest*
One of two words for shaman. *Kúlañ* is from the Spanish verb *curar,* "to cure." It is used only as a noun meaning "medicine." *O'odham* means "man" [Bahr 1977].

Kúlañmada
Pima, *Southwest*
See *dúajida.*

Kulkuli
Maidu, *California*
Stone pipes, usually made of slate or soapstone. They are used by shamans during healing ceremonies to blow tobacco smoke on their patients. The pipes are usually 5 to 8 inches in length and bulge at the mouthpiece.

Kumnakànikitnámu
Kutenai, *Plateau*
See *uwámu.*

Kuni Ceremony
Hawaiian, *Pacific*
Kuni means "to burn" and refers to a fireplace that is connected with this ceremony. The ceremony is performed by a sorcerer to determine who caused a person's death. It is also used to detect and kill thieves. These ceremonies are always performed in public and during daylight. Following a prayer to Uli, the chief god of sorcery, "a fireplace was then made, and four sticks with flags of white kapa set up at the corners, surrounded by the plant called *auhuhu,* fish poisons, and green gourds. A fire was kindled by rubbing the firestick *aulima* on a stick of *akia,* a poisonous shrub, and a large quantity of wood was burned. If his object was to punish a thief, the *kahuna* took several kukui-nuts and threw the oily kernels one after another into the fire, chanting the 'fire-prayer' or imprecation in the name of Uli" [Alexander 1899:70].

K

Kunque
Pueblo, *Southwest*
The term used by Bourke [1892:507] to refer to the sacred white cornmeal that is used in all sacred ceremonies. Each pueblo has its own term for it.

Kununxäs
Deleware, *Northeast*
See *atcigamultin*.

Kuseyaay
Diegueño, *California*
See *Kwisiyai*.

Kusi
Diegueño, *California*
The plant *(Datura meteloides)* known as Jimson weed in the United States and devil's weed in Europe and Mexico; in Spanish it is called *toloache*, from the ancient Aztec name for the plant, *toloatzin*. A decoction of the plant is used for the initiation ceremony of shamans and is ingested by shamans prior to some healing ceremonies.

Kusiut
Bella Coola, *Northwest Coast*
Shaman; literally, "a learned one." The acquisition of full shamanic powers takes many years, and it often takes 30 years of training before one has the ability to cure illness. Power is accumulated through solitary vision quests and fasts that are repeated over the years. Often the quester scrubs himself in cold water with stems from the devil's club *(Echinopanax horridum)* as part of his prequest purification ritual. Others ingest an emetic made from the root of false hellebore for the same purpose.

One of the most common means of obtaining power is through the appearance of a powerful supernatural woman named *Tlitcäplitäna*. This woman has to ability to travel through space at phenomenal speeds and always appears wearing a blanketlike cape decorated with dyed and undyed cedar bark. Often she appears to sick persons, male or female, and grants them powers. Her approach is always signaled by a whistle; one often hears her whistle over the course of several days before she actually appears. When she does appear, she teaches the quester one or more songs. Once the shaman acquires sufficient power, he announces it to the community at large. Prior to that, all is kept secret.

Tlitcäplitäna has the ability to cure many different diseases and is known by many different names among the Bella Coola. Which name is used depends on which malady is being cured. Following is a list of names that different shamans received from *Tlitcäplitäna*:

Sexsexqwalxelasoslaix: "The Strengthener of the Breath." This shaman had the ability to heal patients who have difficulty breathing.
Nexnäxmälosaix: "The Dancer Near the Fire."
Änolximdimut: "The Dancer Who Makes Noise Only with His Body." A shaman with this name does not use a rattle when curing.
Änuxelnimut: "Quivering to and fro." This refers to the dance movements of a shaman.
Qpänpäntiktnimlaiz: "The Revolver." This term comes from *qpäntiktnim*, meaning to revolve sunwise, which is an aspect of many healing ceremonies. The name really signifies "The One Who Restores to Strength."

Sometimes other supernatural beings about whom little is known appear to cure an illness. Since these spirits function in the same manner as *Tlitcäplitäna*, it is probable that they are the same being under other names. Some of these names are:

Ninitsamlaix: "The Restorer." He is able to cure even those who are at the point of death.
Änuskieknim: "The Savior." He can rescue persons who have been injured by other supernatural beings.
Nunutsnimikmem: "The One Who Is Thought of." He has such powerful curing abilities that people often concentrate on him when they are ill.
Änotäbäkmots: "The Open-Mouth One." His mouth is always open to suck out sickness.
Nustkäkstämidjut: "He Whose Basin Is in His Own Body." A person who receives the ability to

cure from this being does not use the customary basin (discussed below).

Although healing power usually comes from such supernatural beings, animals also carry a form of healing power and often come to the aid of shamans. For example, salmon, especially the coho and early spring salmon, are extremely potent curers. The same holds true for plants. One man was cured by a tree that gave him a yodel-like shaman's song, imitating the creaking and waving of its branches.

Shamans who receive their power through a spirit visitation during an illness do not always reveal the power songs they learn. They often wait until they have accumulated more power (that is, songs) before making their ability publicly known. One man was known to have waited until he acquired 10 songs. When the announcement is made, the shaman gives away goods to validate his shamanic name. Afterward, his future status as a shaman depends on his healing efficacy. In such close-knit societies, a shaman's ability is always common knowledge.

Shamans actually carry this potent supernatural power within their bodies. Thus, it is dangerous for them to be around others, so shamans are socially isolated and often spend time in the woods alone. They wear distinctive collars, consisting of alternate rows of dyed and undyed cedar bark. The collar is a signal to menstruating women and others who are unclean to remain at a distance. Although this collar is not worn at all times, it is worn whenever a shaman undertakes a healing ceremony.

When a person is ill, one of his relatives goes to the shaman to request a healing. The shaman usually replies as though he were his spirit helper, saying something to the effect, "I will help the mortal." No fee is spoken of, but it is implicit if the cure is successful. The shaman then calls for his singers and proceeds to the house of the patient, along with anyone else who wishes to attend.

The shaman first examines the patient by feeling him, often throwing himself upon the patient. He kneads the flesh, pounds the patient, leaps on him, and pummels him. The aim of this procedure is to bring the disease-causing object to the surface of the skin, where it can be extracted. Several forms of extraction exist. In former times, shamans often carried a life-stick, with which they could cure by simply touching the afflicted area with the life-giving end of the stick. In simple cases, the shaman presses his head near the afflicted area and, while making growling sounds, ejects a flow of saliva over the sick person. In so doing, he inserts his own power into the patient, who at once begins to imitate this sound and shake his hands. Then the shaman proceeds to recall his power back into himself by scooping it up with half-cupped hands. The sickness accompanies this returning power, but the shaman is immune to it. If the shaman fails to recall his power, he loses his ability to heal. In serious cases, the shaman uses a specially constructed basin, the design of which is often dictated by his helping spirit. The basin is filled with water, which the shaman sprinkles on the patient while kneading him in the manner already described. This is often a lengthy procedure.

During this time, the participants are lined up in two rows facing each other between the door and the central fire. Each person carries a beating stick, and a sounding board is placed in front of each row. To the accompaniment of a drum, the two rows beat against the sounding board. There is a dance leader who orchestrates this beating; for instance, leaning toward one row indicates that that row is to beat louder. This elaborate beating is repeated four times, on each occasion concluding with a double jump by the dancers. If a dog barks during the stick-beating, it nullifies the effects and may cause the healing to fail. Eventually, the shaman arises with the sickness cupped in his hands. He then walks to the door, opens it, and blows the sickness from his hands.

Some powerful shamans cure by the use of dyed and undyed cedar bark. A roll made of these two items is placed among glowing embers until it is aflame. Then the shaman takes it from the fire and places it in his mouth. While the shaman has it in his mouth, the participants dance to rapid and loud stick-beating. The shaman then takes the bark roll, still burning, from his mouth and returns it to the fire. This procedure is repeated four times. The shaman then thrusts the burning bark into the patient's mouth and leaves it there for some time before pulling it out. This, too, is repeated four times. By the fourth retrieval, the patient's sickness has been attracted to the burning bark. The shaman disposes of the sickness by disposing of the burning bark.

During most healing ceremonies, the sickness is extracted by the shaman's sucking it from the patient. In recent years, some shamans have taken to displaying the sickness in visible form. Although common elsewhere, this practice among the Bella Coola seems to be a recent innovation adopted from the Bella Bella. These disease objects take many different forms, such as toads, snails, sticks of wood, and so forth. Those shamans who doctored with life-sticks would have these objects appear at the end of the stick when they touched the afflicted area of the patient's body. Often the shaman ties the sickness up in a bundle of four pieces of dyed and four pieces of undyed cedar bark. Then he sprinkles eagle down over the whole bundle. Finally, the bundle is disposed of by throwing it into a nearby river.

The Bella Coola understanding of shamanic healing is that the shaman inserts his supernatural power into the patient to effect the cure. The more serious the sickness, the more power that needs to be inserted. Sometimes the patient is so sick that an enormous amount of power must be inserted to help him, and he dies from its receipt. In such cases, the patient is subsequently revived by *Änunitsektnim*, a male supernatural being whose sole function is to restore those whom *Tlitcäplitäna* has slain. This return to life frequently occurs when relatives have been mourning the death of the patient [McIlwraith 1948:547–564].

Kuwi
Yana, Karok, *California*
Shaman. Most often shamans are men, but women can also become healers. Allen [1982] uses the term *kuwi* for "medicine man or doctor" and the term *ka-pay* for "medicine woman or doctor."

A man who wants to become a shaman goes to one of several known medicine men's water pools to swim. In one such pool, there is a rock beneath the water with a hole through it. If he is to receive power, the hole remains open, otherwise, it closes. While in this hole, he gropes about for black crane feathers. If the swim is a successful quest for power, this is indicated by his bleeding from the mouth and nose upon coming out of the water. Afterward, he goes on a six-day power quest alone in the woods. If contact is made with the supernatural, the successful shaman returns with a power song. Although the shaman calls upon power from rocks, trees, birds, and the like for supernatural aid, there is no indication that he addresses specific spirits. (Early ethnographic notes on the Yana make no mention of spirit helpers.)

Yana shamans are concerned primarily with curing, but there is no record of any of their healing ceremonies. We do know that in the past, shamans were enticed with payments of beads, preferably white ones, to undertake a cure. We also know that once a shaman accepts an invitation to heal, he returns to bathe in the pool from which he obtained his power before beginning the healing ceremony. Ceremony participants aid in the singing during a healing. Disease is caused by a foreign object in the body, which the shaman sucks out and normally throws into a fire. In successful cases, the shaman is paid his fee five days after the conclusion of the healing ceremony. Healing is often conducted by the shaman over the course of several days, the length of which is revealed to the shaman in dreams.

Of the shaman's regalia we know only of a ceremonial net cap with feathers, called *batski*. In addition, shamans seek at least two different types of power stones. One, called *onunuipa*, can be recognized by peculiarities of color, marking, and shape. Particularly sought are small, round stones with light-colored bands. The other type of stone is called *kulmatsi*—small, white, prismatic stones, generally of quartz. One informant translates this term as "diamonds," hence they were probably crystals [Sapir and Spier 1943:279–282].

Kwacmin
Coast Salish, *Northwest Coast*
The rattle-stick carried by shamans during the Spirit Dance healing ceremonies. It is a clublike staff of wood with an animal or human head carved at the top. It is decorated with individual

designs and deer-hoof pendants that rattle. The *kwacmin* is obtained after four years of active participation as a dancer, and thus signifies a mature shaman who is well in control of his spirit helpers [Jilek 1982b:138].

Kwaipai
Diegueño, *California Peninsula*
The shaman who heads the *awik* ("from the west") ceremonies. Certain aches in the bones are attributed to the nonobservance of the *awik* ceremonies. "These aches are called *awik wutim* or 'sickness from the West.' The only way to prevent the experience of these evils, including snake-bites, is to hold the ritualistic dances" [Waterman 1910:276].

Kwashapshigan
Eastern Cree, *Canadian Eastern Woodlands*
The conjuring lodge used in the widespread Shaking Tent Ceremony (see entry). The term literally translates to "conjuring house." Their lodges are typically 10 feet high and 5 feet in diameter and are made from six vertical poles tied in place by two horizontal hoops—one at 4 feet above the ground, and the other hoop near the top of the lodge. (Among other Native American cultures, these lodges are usually conical vs. cylindrical in shape.) The upright poles have their branches remaining on the tips. Some of the older shamans use twelve upright poles in their lodges. Upwards of five different trees are used to build one lodge, and they are arranged in such a way that no two poles of the same species stand adjacent to each other. These poles are covered with canvas to complete the lodge.

The ceremony begins only after nightfall, and there are no lights allowed in the area. In this variation of the Shaking Tent Ceremony, the shaman is not bound, but simply enters the lodge by lifting up the bottom of the canvas cover. Within the lodge, he kneels on a cushion and is hailed by his *mistabeo* (helping spirit) simply as *kaowtstibit* (the one who is kneeling there) [Preston 1970:39].

Kwashaptum
Eastern Cree, *Canadian Eastern Woodlands*
Shamans who have learned to perform the Shaking Tent Ceremony. As in other nations, this ceremony is almost always performed by a man.

Kwasiyai
Diegueño, *California Peninsula*
See *kwisiyai.*

Kwathidhe
Mojave, *Southwest*
Shaman. Power is obtained through dreaming. "The (power) dreams were believed to be first experienced while the unborn Mojave was yet in his mother's womb, only to be forgotten on birth. Later in life the dreams were remembered or dreamed over again. In a typical Mojave power dream the 'shadow' (*matkwesa*, soul) of the dreamer was impelled back in time to the beginning of the world, when the 'shadows' of the future Mojaves were with the deities at the sacred mountain *Avikwame* (Spirit Mountain). At Avikwame the culture hero Mastamho built a sacred house, and, according to Kroeber, 'it is of this house that shamans dream, for here their shadows were as little boys in the face of Mastamho, and received from him their ordained powers'" [Stewart 1970:17].

Mojave shamans are usually men, although women can also become shamans. Their shamans are usually specialists, and each shaman is able to cure only certain illnesses, depending on the nature of his power dreams. For example, one informant reports of a specialist in rattlesnake bites:

"While the doctor is on his way to the victim he sings so the man won't suffer. Meanwhile, the victim's family won't drink water. I heard that the doctor sang around until the victim didn't suffer. He didn't suck the bite and didn't blow on it (two common forms of Mohave doctoring), but just sang. I saw one man who got bit. His arm was swollen all the way up to his neck. The doctor came and put his hands over the arm and the swelling disappeared. I don't know how he did it" [AL in Stewart 1970:20].

Powerful shamans dream the power to cure more than one type of illness. For example, "if a doctor dreamed three or four cures, and on top of that had a dog dream, he could cure anything" [Stewart 1974:12]. Those shamans who doctor any sickness are called *naiyu sumatc, matcupeik sumatc,* or *kwathidhe tahan* [Stewart 1974:12].

When called upon to conduct a healing ceremony, the shaman first diagnoses the patient by feeling all over his body. "Mojave conceptions of the causation of disease included soul loss (the most common explanation), dream poisoning, contamination by contact with enemies, and object intrusion" [Stewart 1970:17]. If the shaman diagnoses an illness that he is not able to cure, he refers the patient to another shaman who has dreamed the power necessary to cure that particular illness. When the diagnosis is object intrusion, the sucking shaman does not remove a material object, as is most often the case in this form of healing, but rather sucks out the blood that has been poisoned as a result of the object intrusion.

"In the most usual method of curing the shaman sang the songs that he had dreamed, describing how he had acquired his power. He blew tobacco smoke over the patient to drive away evil or bring back the patient's soul. Sometimes a shaman sprayed saliva over a patient. Other curative procedures included massage or brushing with the hand, and the prescription of bathing and food taboos. Some doctors sucked on the bodies of their patients to draw out evil influences, but they did not suck out disease objects. Nor were Mohave shamans possessed by spirits while curing" [Stewart 1970:18]. The shaman is paid a fee only if the cure is successful.

Kwaxot
Mojave, *Southwest*
See *kohota.*

Kwisiyai
Diegueño, *California Peninsula*
Also: *cusiyaes, kuseyaay.* Shaman. *Kuseyaay* is the term given by Shipek [1992:89–90] for the Southern Kumeyaay, also known as the Diegueño-Kamia or Ipai-Tipai. (The Diegueño are so named because of their close approximation to the San Diego Mission, but they prefer to refer to themselves as the *Kumeyaay.*) They believe that illness stems from three major causes: witchcraft and other supernatural causes, which entails object intrusion; natural causes, such as accidents and infirmities of age; and outside illnesses such as smallpox or measles [Almstedt 1977:2]. A good healer can merely look at a patient without touching him and know what is wrong. The most serious cases are associated with supernatural causes.

The efficacy of their shamans was noted by Boscana in 1831: "oftentimes they performed cures, when the patients were apparently fast verging into eternity, and in the space of twenty-four hours, by their extravagances and witchcraft, they have enabled them to rise from a bed of sickness" [Boscana 1970:54].

There seems to be no clearly defined method for a person to become a shaman, although Strong [1929:212] reports that individual dreams or physical peculiarities usually lead a person to become a shaman. Another method is for males to participate in an initiation ceremony that uses Jimson weed *(Datura meteloides),* termed *kusi* (see entry). The initiate, especially if predisposed to shamanism (having a propensity for dreaming and an interest in doctoring), often has a power dream in which he learns certain healing songs. There seems to be no formal training given by adept shamans to novices. However, most shamans receive their power through visionary dreams and are also assisted in their training by established elder shamans. They also use herbal remedies in their cures. Once power is acquired, they often become specialists in curing, such as the *wikwisiyai,* or rattlesnake shaman. For example, "Upon arriving at the side of the bitten man, the *Kuseyaay* began singing a slow chant and slowly stroking the injured man with a feather. This was the only treatment given, and in a few days the person recovered" [Shipek 1992:94]. Blatantly missing, however, are the bear doctors that are so common to other California cultures and the weather shamans [Rogers and Evernham 1983:108].

The shaman's diagnostic and healing techniques often involve the interpretation of his patient's dreams as well as his own. Particularly dangerous to one's health are dreams of dead relatives. When this occurs, the person often consults a shaman, whether he is ill or not. Other dreams such as "sex dreams accompanied by apathy, loss of appetite, and other atypical behavior indicated specific problems" [Rogers and Evernham 1983:109]. Shamans usually make their own diagnosis before performing a healing ceremony.

The most common forms of healing include rubbing, blowing, breathing, sucking, and the use of herbs, although Forde [1931:198] mistakenly reported that "doctors never gave herbs to cure disease." The Diegueño do have herbalists, especially among older women, who have no shamanic powers. Most shamans are sucking doctors, and healing includes the use of the sweat lodge, after which the participants jump into the ocean. Shamans also use singing and dancing in their curing techniques. "The shaman's manipulatory procedures were dexterous and impressive. He would massage, fan, and blow upon the patient's body. His preeminent technique was ostensibly sucking or blowing from the patient's body an object, such as a pebble or thorn, which he claimed to be the cause of the disease. Sucking was done either directly with the mouth or with the aid of a tube of hard black stone through which the doctor sucked or sometimes blew, on the theory that the disease was either sucked out or blown away. The tube was sometimes filled with wild tobacco and lighted, the smoke being blown over the patient. As a purported result of the sucking or blowing, the disease-causing object was produced—with dramatic ceremony—and displayed to the patient and onlookers" [Rogers and Evernham 1983:110].

A typical account from a shaman is as follows:

"Sometimes I blow and sometimes I rub, but I do not use herbs much. I have been given the power to cure with my hands. I spit and blow on my palms and cure with these. I feel with my hands: if the patient's body is cold, I rub it until it is warmed. Then when I feel that he is warm I let him go" [McCarty in Spier 1923:335].

In addition, Waterman [1910:280] noted "a belief that disease may be charmed away. When a man for example was taken ill, they stretched him out on the ground and gathered around him. Then they motioned upwards three times with the hands, expelling the breath each time. They then danced around him from left to right, stepping sideways and singing. . . . At the conclusion of this song, they sat about the patient in a circle. The oldest woman present (representing long life), taking a small *olla* or pottery cup provided for the purpose, urinated in it. The patient was then sprinkled with an eagle feather, the company chanting:

awisi awisi awisi sprinkling sprinkling sprinkling" [Waterman 1910:280]. On other occasions, "tobacco smoke was blown three times in the air to prevent disease . . ." [Waterman 1910:336].

Kyan
Carrier, *Makenzie-Yukon*

The term is difficult to translate, but people who dream of a *kyan* become sick. Some informants speak of the *kyan* as a mysterious, "formless, indefinite but living force . . . a devouring sickness that travels invisible, though just as much alive as a man or animal" [Jenness 1943:570]. Others speak of it as a definite animal spirit, of which there are many and of unequal power. Possession by *kyan* is always evidenced by intense hysteria on the part of the victim. It is a dream sickness called *kyanilkyot*, "caught by *kyan*" [Jenness 1943:569]. This violent hysteria "recurred every few hours or days" and "induced in the subject cannibalistic cravings that made him a menace to his fellow men, even his own kin" [Jenness 1943:567]. The cure often takes from one to three years and can be accomplished only by a *kyanyuantan* (see entry), a man who has suffered a similar affliction and succeeded in controlling the *kyan* that seized him. The most violent form of *kyanilkyot* is said to be caused by the otter. Victims of any form of *kyanilkyot* who are not treated most often die.

Kyanyuantan
Carrier, *Makenzie-Yukon*

An accredited member of the loosely organized society that specializes in the treatment of *kyanilkyot* (see *kyan*). The term *kyanyuantan* is also used to refer to the society itself, which is often called the cannibal society because the victims of *kyanilkyot* frequently display cannibalistic cravings. If an ordinary *diyinne* (shaman) diagnoses a patient as having *kyanilkyot*, a *kyanyuantan* must be called in to cure the patient. All such doctors are recovered victims of the *kyanilkyot* dream sickness. The *kyanyuantan* doctor is always assisted by society members. Thus, their healing ceremony is a rare example of a medicine society that specializes in group psychotherapeutic treatment of the victims of a singular form of mental illness—namely, a particularly acute form of hysteria.

In the winter of 1924–1925, Jenness observed the ritual of Old Sam, a *kyanyuantan* doctor, treating his wife, who had been stricken with *kyanilkyot*. The ritual lasted for two hours and included three other female patients. A partial account of the healing follows:

"Suddenly a whistle shrilled, blown by Old Sam, though none of us saw it. To the Indians it blew kyan into the room. The Chinaman's wife (one of the patients) flung her head to the floor with a shriek and beat a wild tattoo with her hands on the bare boards, while her two companions sighed loudly 'hu hu hu,' and swayed their bodies up and down and from side to side. Old Sam from his chair began to shout his medicine-song, and his assistants joined in, beating the tambourine and pounding the planks (two 4-inch-wide boards laid horizontally side by side, each 7 feet long, struck with sticks). The three women in the middle were seized with violent hysteria; their eyes were staring and dilated, their bodies swayed, their hands quivered as with palsy. Old Sam's wife, holding her long stick before her in both hands, raised it up and down jerkily; the woman in black swung her shorter (18 inches) stick first to one side, then to the other; while the Chinaman's wife, more violent than either, shuffled along the floor, her head down and her hands beating the boards or clawing the air rhythmically in front of her. Occasionally this woman raised her head and faced the singers in an attitude of wild adoration, trying, like her companions, to join in the song, but, like them, able to utter only shrieks, or whistling sounds, or loud sighs of 'hu hu hu.'

"The song, repeated over and over again, louder and with more frantic drumbeats and pounding of sticks whenever the women's frenzy threatened to break out into greater violence, lasted some 15 minutes. . . . Suddenly it stopped, and there was an interval of about 10 seconds during which the women sighed loudly and repeatedly 'hu hu.'

"Old Sam now started another song. . . . The music stirred up the women again, causing them to resume their frantic gestures. Sometimes they faced the drum and executed a kind of squatting dance in front of it, their waving arms and swaying bodies reminding me strongly of Malayan dances. The extreme paroxysm of their first frenzy, however, had passed over, and their movements seemed more controlled by the rhythm of the chant. As the song continued Mrs. Old Sam began to 'hu hu' vigorously again, and Mrs. Felix (one of the society assistants), who herself had caught the infection and 'hu hued' once or twice while pounding her plank, rose and slowly danced on her toes toward her. Stretching out her hand, she raised Mrs. Old Sam to her feet, braced her arm with her own, and led her round the room in a slow rhythmic dance, during which the patient continued to bow her head over her horizontally held stick and toss it backward again. The woman in black danced on her toes behind them, flinging out her short stick first on one side, then on the other. Last of all, after two or three futile efforts, the Chinaman's wife struggled to her feet and danced in their train, with her head lowered, her face almost concealed by her hair, and her hands waving gracefully to right and left alternately. As they passed me, so close that I had to move back my chair, I could see their fingers quivering as if palsied; but both their feet and their hands kept perfect time with the song and the drumbeats.

"At the close of this song, which also lasted about a quarter of an hour, Mrs. Felix retired to her seat, the three patients sank slowly to the floor, breathing heavily 'hu hu,' and Old Sam hobbled over to them to shout the same cry 'hu,' in their ears, one after another. His wife, only half-conscious apparently, pushed back the hair from her forehead, then pulled out a pan of water from beside the stove and mechanically washed her hands, while the other two women squatted in an attitude of exhaustion. In less than half a minute Old Sam started a third song. . . .

"Old Sam, by 'hu huing' in the women's ears, had expelled some of the kyan from their bodies into the air and was now driving it into the pan of water. (His song went, 'Something goes into the water.') The three women remained squatting, swaying their bodies as in the earlier songs, but less violently; and when the song ended Mrs. Old

Sam pushed the basin of water under the stove again.

"The fourth song was in the Carrier language also, being, like the three preceding, one of Old Sam's own medicine songs. It ran: 'Many wolves come for something to eat.' The women continued to squat throughout its repetition, but the Chinaman's wife shuffled a little around the floor.

"The fifth song was wordless; the sixth a song of the kalullim society, in the language of the Haida Indians of the Queen Charlotte Islands, which my interpreter could not understand. As soon as it commenced, Mrs. Felix rose and slowly hopped in front of Mrs. Old Sam to lead them in another dance. They stood in line one behind the other, Mrs. Felix facing them and moving her arms like a band conductor to make their feet and bodies keep time with the slow music. Mrs. Old Sam waved her stick up and down in front of her, the woman in black swung her stick from side to side, and the Chinaman's wife waved her arms gracefully to left and right alternately. The dance was perfectly timed. . . . When it ended Old Sam again hobbled forward to 'hu' in each woman's ears, even in Mrs. Felix', since she also seemed to have become infected and cried 'hu hu' occasionally with her patients.

"The last song, also a chant of the kalullim society, was in the Gitksan language. It ran: 'The strong man afflicted by kyan is eating something.' The women still breathed 'hu' occasionally as they repeated their dance, and Mrs. Old Sam emitted one or two whistling sounds. So when the song ended and they squatted to the floor again, Old Sam hastened over to 'hu' into their ears, and to beat them upward on chest and back with a bundle of eagle feathers in order to expel any kyan that still remained in their bodies. Each woman gave a long-breathed 'hu' as it left her and Old Sam blew it away from the crown of her head. But from the woman in black it seemed very reluctant to depart; even though Old Sam beat her vigorously with his eagle feathers and shouted 'hu' in her ears, she still 'hu hued' hysterically. At last he dropped his feathers and rubbed her vigorously with his hands, when with one dying shriek 'hu-e-e' she subsided and sat quiet. The performance was now over" [Jenness 1943:574–575].

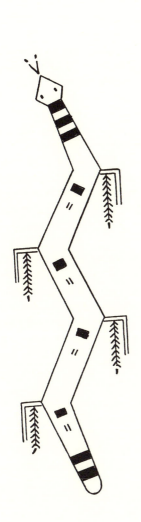

La Barre, Weston

Weston La Barre was born in Uniontown, Pennsylvania, on 13 December 1911. He received an A.B. degree from Princeton, where he graduated summa cum laude in 1933, and received his Ph.D. with honors from Yale University in 1937. His doctoral dissertation, *The Peyote Cult*, has been published at least 13 times by five different publishers. His first fieldwork was with the Kiowa under the auspices of the Santa Fe Laboratory of Anthropology. Much of his work centered around psychological anthropology. During his career, he was a Sterling fellow at Yale, a Guggenheim fellow, and a National Science Foundation fellow in London, Rome, and Paris. He was the James B. Duke professor of anthropology at Duke and also a Rutgers faculty member. His best-known work is *The Ghost Dance: Origins of Religion*.

La Flesche, Francis

Francis La Flesche was born on the Omaha Reservation in Nebraska in 1857. His father was an Omaha chief. In 1880, he became a clerk with the Bureau of Indian Affairs, and the following year he began work as an assistant to Alice Fletcher of the Bureau of American Ethnology. Fletcher legally adopted La Flesche in 1891, and together they published the classic *The Omaha Tribe* in 1911. From 1910 through 1929, La Flesche was a full-time ethnologist for the Bureau of American Ethnology. During the 1920s, most of his activities were focused on the Osage, about whom he published extensively in the annual reports of the bureau. He died near Macy, Nebraska, on 5 September 1932.

Lagekwa

Kwakiutl, *Northwest Coast*

Dyed red cedar bark worn by shamans during their rituals. It is ritually referred to as "the great happy maker, the long life giver" [Boas 1930:68]. Gathering and preparing the cedar bark often takes several days. The bark is fashioned into headbands and neck collars that indicate the wearer's status as a shaman.

Lainaitelge

Wailaki, *California*

Singing doctors, one of several classes of shamans among the Wailaki. When a person is ill, the *keteu* (sucking doctor; see entry) is first called in to diagnose the sickness. Then the *lainaitelge* is called in to locate the seat of pain (the intruding object) in the patient. These two types of shamans work together, splitting the payment received. Both types of shamans are able to see spirits, talk to them, and receive aid from them. Both have guardian spirits and have been trained by older shamans in a formalized school for shamans. The major difference between the two is that during their initiation, some of the neophytes were unable to swallow the "pain" (consisting of powdered obsidian) spat into their mouths by one of their instructors. That is, they did not bleed from the mouth and nose, which was the indication of a successful initiation of a sucking doctor. Those who swallowed the pain and carried it in their bodies became sucking doctors. The other initiates became singing doctors [Loeb 1934a:78].

Another type of healer found among the Wailaki is the *naitulgai* (dreamer; see entry).

Lakota Night Cult
Lakota, *Plains*
See *yuwipi*.

Lamcem
Yuki, *California*
Also: *nunnun letim,* translates to "sucking doctor" [Loeb 1934a:61]. Huchnom sucking doctors, who can be either male or female. They obtain their power from helping spirits acquired either through dreams or in visions. Once an individual is informed by a spirit that he or she is to become a healer, other shamans conduct a special four-day dance, called *lamciwok,* as a form of initiation. Often the novice bleeds from the mouth or nose, which is taken as an indicator of doctoring powers.

Lamshimi
Yuki, *California*
Medicine man or shaman. Most of the Yuki healers are sucking doctors. They go into a trance during a healing ceremony and use their spirit helpers to effect a cure. These shamans, unlike most shamans, use no rattle and sing little, if any, during ceremonies. Usually they are male, but on rare occasions a woman might become a sucking doctor, but not until much later in life. They obtain their powers through dreams and visions. Once a boy has a proper dream, which often occurs when he is around 12 years old, the older shamans hold a special dance known as *lamci wok,* in which the novice is grasped by the hair and whirled until

dizzy. His face is then held toward the sun as he slips into unconsciousness, which is seen as a favorable condition. Similar, but less rigorous, rituals are held for females who want to become sucking doctors [Loeb 1934a:70].

Le Clair, John
Puyallup-Nisqually, *Northwest Coast*
A shaman from a branch of the Coast Salish who was interviewed by Marion Smith during the winter of 1935–1936. He was described as "the only living man in this region who claims doctoring power" [Smith 1940:83]. Speaking of his healing powers, he reported to Smith [1940:84–85] as follows:

"Later I went to see my mother. She was sick. I took off my collar and shirt and doctored her. I got the power and [it] said it was devil fish, *sqálatc,* and that it belonged to *takédab,* the same one [old man] who had made me sick before. I said I was going to kill him so I stirred up the fire and threw it in. Now he would get hot sick and die. A few days after, the old man took a high fever and he soon died.

"People don't believe I have power because I'm half white. But I have a curing power, not a killing one.

"Once I came along and met Tommy Lane. He wanted me to come and doctor his wife. He said also that Jimmy Cross was blind and wanted me to go there. I said, 'No, I've never tried eyes.' But Tommy said, 'He's your friend, you try.' Cultus Jim had sucked his eyes but they weren't any better. So I went. I sang a little, then I said, 'No, I'll come back. I'm going to Mrs. Lane now.' I went there but she had consumption and you can't do much for that. I brought a lot of people to Jimmy Cross' and sang, sang. I found that Cross' power had been scared away by people with a grudge against him. So I sang to get it back. Then Jimmy said, 'I can see a little bit.' He started to sing. I told him, 'Go on and sing.' As his power came back he wanted to sing and Jimmy and his wife gave a big sing after that. He was all cured.

"After that I and an old man, *citoládtu,* worked together over Mrs. Tommy Lane. I got tired and went out to walk around. While I was out the old man told the people I was no good, that I was a breed who had picked up a song and pretended to have power. When I came in again an old woman who had a daughter she wanted me to marry told me about it. We doctored together again. I got the power out and told the old man to kill it. He poured water on it from his hands but nothing happened. I told him again. Still no harm came to it. So I said, 'You're no good.' And I let the power go. Then I sat down and while the old man was singing I took a little stick and just shook it at him a little and he fell right down. I thought, 'If he's any good this won't hurt him.' He came crawling to me and said, 'I will die. Fix me up.' I knew he wouldn't so I just walked off. He came crawling again, he couldn't stand. So the people called out, 'Fix your partner.' I said to some men to hold him up. I took the power out and let it fly. The old man said, '*He, he,*' and was well. Nobody knew what ailed him. So I said, 'The old woman told me what he said. I did it and he isn't strong enough to resist even a little hair from a coyote which I shot in him.'"

Legerdemain

A French term often used in the early literature on Native Americans to refer to the power feats of shamans. It is an ethnocentric term, in that it implies trickery on the part of the shaman.

Life soul

See *body soul.*

Lifietoynin

Tiwa, *Southwest*

A general term used at Isleta Pueblo to refer to any ceremony conducted by the different medicine societies in which the special root *lifiewah* is ingested by the chiefs. The term translates to "root medicine men."

Parsons [1932:339–340] provides a glimpse into such a four-day ceremony:

"On the fourth morning in the same house the two groups set their ground altars, the Town Fathers setting theirs first. Each chief has chewed the root lifiewah, which gives power. Moved by this, with his power, the chief calls in from all the directions the *ke'chu* (fetish animals). Over the bowl of water from the river the chief makes a cross with his eagle-wing feathers, stirring the water. Sounds of bear, mountain lion, coyote, snake, eagle, come from the bowl. When the iridescent feathers of the duck are put into the bowl, after the cross is made over the water, sounds of ducks playing and flapping their wings also come from the bowl. Meanwhile the assistants are sitting in line behind the altar, behind the Mothers, shaking their gourd rattles and singing. For each ritual incident there is, as usual, a special song. Power has been given the assistants through the line of meal sprinkled from the door by the chief to the altar. . . . With his stone point in his right hand, in his left his whistle, the chief now whistles into the bowl to call all the powerful animals—mountain lion, bear, rattlesnake, eagle, badger.

"Now the chief will call lightning and thunder. He tells the people present to cover their heads lest they be frightened. Thunder is heard and flashes of lightning may be seen. . . . The chief now takes his seat in the middle of the line of assistants, and the war chief gives him a lighted cigarette to smoke in all five directions and on the line of the Mothers. . . . With his power the chief calls the moon and the morning star. . . . All the assistants circulate among those present and with his two eagle feathers each brushes out from everybody whatever noxious thing may be inside his body—stick, rag, stone. . . . The assistants again brush the people, putting everything they take out of their bodies in a large bowl by the door. The bowl is carried out by two assistants to the ash pile, where they sprinkle its contents with water taken in a shell from the medicine bowl and bury them in a hole. They ask Waeide ('He is the head of all') to take it all away."

Liföla

Tiwa, *Southwest*

A term used at Isleta Pueblo for small thorns sent into the body of a victim by a sorcerer or witch to cause sore eyes. The cure consists of a sucking doctor removing the thorns [Parsons 1932:242].

Lightning Shaman

Apache, *Southwest*

A shaman who has lightning power and is able to perform the lightning ceremony. There are three classes of shamanic ceremonies among the

Apache: (1) the lightning ceremony, (2) the 30 to 40 traditional ceremonies that must be learned verbatim, and (3) an addition to a traditional ceremony. In the latter case, the shaman may be instructed by an advanced shaman who has mastered the addition, or the addition may be revealed to him in a dream or vision. Sometimes a shaman dreams an addition to a particular ceremony without knowing the ceremony. In such cases he must then learn the full ceremony, because the addition cannot be used without it.

The lightning ceremony is the only ceremony that is derived entirely from personal experience through a dream or vision. Thus, only the most mystical minded become lightning shamans. According to Goodwin [1938:31]:

"Most of the men who have the lightning ceremony are the imaginative, mystic kind, relying more on their own intuition than the average Apache, who is a stickler for exactness and fact in all information not gossip. Working with several such men proved this. . . . The sources of the power have observed the individual in question; notice that he is deserving; and single him out as their recipient. They present themselves to him while he is alone in the hills, or while asleep at night, bestowing on him a holy name. Later he is taken into the sky with them, traveling from place to place. This period of instruction may continue for several days, even weeks. Following it he dreams songs, putting words to them when awake. When a sufficient number are acquired, he reveals himself as a holy man. Men who have only traditional curing rites are sharply distinguished from those who have the lightning ceremony. The latter alone are spoken of as 'holy' and are considered so, i.e., invested with supernatural power of high quality. They are addressed in prayer, just like sources of power, for protection against lightning, etc. People also pray with pollen to the shaman conducting a lightning ceremony."

Little Dickey
Paviotso, *Basin*
A shaman around the turn of the twentieth century. An example of his doctoring was given by

Henry William, who attended a healing ceremony Little Dickey conducted on a girl in Smith Valley:

"The mother thought the girl was dead. She cried. The doctor told her to stop crying so he could bring the girl back. He had a little bullet-shaped thing like lead that his power gave him. He put it in the girl's hand and closed her hand tightly. Then he said, 'I am going to sing five songs.' He walked around the fire twice while he sang each song. Then Little Dickey announced, 'I can feel her coming back through the hole in the lead. It is coming nice and cool now.' People then felt a wind start blowing. The girl opened her eyes and the shaman told them to give her some water. He started another song and sang until morning. Little Dickey lost the piece of lead after that. He never found it again. He died very soon. Nothing could help him" [Park 1934:106].

Little Man
Gros Ventre, *Plains*
A shaman during the first part of the twentieth century who received his curing powers from a bear, an old man, and a coyote. When doctoring, he would paint his body in a manner that had been described to him by his helping spirits. His power to cure illness was limited by his spirits to seven cases. During his life, he used only four of his seven opportunities. The following is a brief account of these four healings as given by Al Chandler, Little Man's adopted son:

"Little Man said that long ago when he first started out in medicine work there was a woman who was already given up for dead. . . .

"So they went over there and he (Little Man) took his medicine bag. He looked at the sick woman and she was still breathing but was pretty close to the edge. He told her folks who were all sitting around ready to see her go at any time: 'I pity this woman. I am going to try my medicine the first time. I guess you heard my story (of acquiring powers). Now I am going to try it. All get out of the way, sit back. Just four men and three women stay in here (to sing). The men sit on the left coming in and the women on the right.' So he fixed up like he was shown (by coyote) and started in. He kind of felt this woman to see how far gone she was and told them: 'Well, I am going to doctor her three times today, and the third time we will know for sure whether I fail or whether I succeed.' He hit the drum just lightly while he prayed. Then he sang and beat the drum harder. He sang the song until the men got on to it. Then he gave one of them the drum and the others sang to his drumming while Little Man was doctoring the woman.

"He had a powdered root and chewed it and blew it on the patient like they do for one who is this far gone, that is, they blow it here and there over the body because being so far gone they couldn't tell where the sickness was. He went through that. He was going to doctor at intervals twice more that night. At the third doctoring when it was just coming daylight he would know whether she would live or not. That was a long time to allow until the third doctoring because the woman could have easily died before then. He didn't rush or get excited but did according to what he had been told when out crying and praying (vision questing). So the third time he doctored her, the woman started to fuss and look around at everybody. . . . He told them: 'She is going to be all right. In the morning if she wants to eat, feed her, give her anything she wants. She will be hungry.' He had boiled medicine for her and asked: 'Can you sit up and drink this?' She sat up and drank it and he said: 'She is going to be all right. She will be thirsty after this. In the morning give her all she wants to drink.'

"So Little Man and his wife went home, and close to noon, say about ten o'clock, they went back to the patient and he said: 'I am going to doctor her four more times. I have to do it seven times in all. You don't have to do anything else. If these other medicine men want to give her something to drink, it is all right. It will help her that much more to take medicine, whatever they give her.' So he doctored her again and said: 'This afternoon I will come and that will be the fifth time.' He came and did the same thing as before. In the evening just before sundown he did it again and that was the sixth time. He told them he wouldn't be back until midnight for the seventh and last time.

"These folks asked him if they needed him could they call him in the meantime. He said: 'I

don't know. I don't think you need to worry about that. After I have done it seven times I am through. Just let her do what she pleases. Leave it to her. She is all right. She is cured.' And sure enough, in a few days she was up and around.

"The second case of critical illness he cured was Al Plumage, then a boy. . . . He had t.b. of the stomach and was just black and had a big bloated belly.

"Paul, the boy's father, had come to get Little Man. . . . So Little Man went down there and cured this boy just the same as he had cured the woman, telling them the number of times they should expect to hear news and so on.

"Little Man didn't go around and brag and say he could have cured this or that. He had told the story of his power and if any wanted to call on him it was up to them. He was young when he got his power and old when he died. He only used this power four times. The other two cures he made with this medicine were Cora's mother and my son Jimmy, who was Little Man's pet.

"The mother of my wife, Cora, had pneumonia. They had already covered her up but I went to see the old woman and sized up her situation. I saw that she was still breathing and I said I was going to call my father. I told him just how things were. Little Man had just got back from some place and had his wagon still loaded. I didn't have a pipe (for making the formal request for healing), but my father would do anything for me, pipe or no pipe. . . . So he told me to get the horses and I went over home and pretty soon he came along. They just stopped by the house and didn't unhook the team but went in to see how the old woman was. He came back out and got his medicine bag and told these folks just how he was going to doctor. The third time he doctored her she wanted to eat. . . . Little Man said, 'Let her eat if she wants to eat. It won't hurt her. She will be well.' So they did. She got well and lived a long time after that.

"Jimmy was the fourth one cured. At first he had summer complaint. Neither the agency doctors nor Indian doctors could do a thing for him. The only thing Jimmy lived on was soda crackers. . . . Jimmy was just skin and bones and was getting black. He was only about two and Cora had another little baby at that time. They had given him up for sure.

"This is a sample of the way Little Man would do. He doctored Jimmy just a little at first. There was nobody there to sing then. Little Man said: 'Up there where I live there are some plants we call shoestrings in the brush. . . . You go up there and pick a good handful.' . . . So I got busy (picking) and then rushed back over there (with them). In the meantime Little Man had picked seven purple flowers—just the flower part.

"So when I got there, he said to put on water in a big dishpan to warm it, not to boil it. When the water got warm he broke the flowers and the shoestrings up in it and stirred and stirred the water. Then he got his wife to hold Jimmy standing in that water and bathed him all over from head to foot, especially his stomach, but didn't give him any to drink. Then he said: 'That is all. Put him in bed and cover him up.' And he told Cora: 'Watch what he passes and let me know.' So she look every little while. Finally he passed and Cora told me, so I told the old man who came and looked for himself. They beheld a wonderful sight to see. They saw these shoestrings were whole, just like I had picked them, and they were covered with excrement. Now you might be able to understand it if he had given the child these things to drink. But he didn't and besides they had been all broken up in the water and not whole like that. After that Jimmy wanted to eat. He ate from then on and began to pick up.

"The next time Jimmy got sick he had typhoid. . . . Little Man wasn't around when Jimmy got sick. . . . So Little Man got back and I came after him and told him that Jimmy was sick again. He came over and looked at him and doctored a little bit like he does at first. He doctored him twice that same day and the next morning was when he used that bear claw. He told Jimmy: 'Tell me wherever it hurts and I will work on it.' Jimmy said: 'Here on my right side.' The old man said: 'That's a bad place. I don't like to suck there because it might hurt your guts. But I will do something else. I will use this bear claw now.' So he asked the boy, showing him the bear claw, 'Do you think you can stand this?' Jimmy said he could and Little Man said, 'Well make sure you can stand it.' He told the old lady to hold Jimmy's hands down and me to hold his feet down. But first he told me to get hot coals and just put a lit-

tle of the sweet pine on the coals and smudge the end of the bear claw. He took some paint and painted himself like the bear had showed him that time when he was out crying (vision questing). So after he did that, I held Jimmy and the old man sang first himself. He sang that song four times and then got busy. He put the claw right where it should be, and you could see just the claw going in. The boy wriggled and made faces. The claw went right in at the side and he jerked it out and you could hear something drop. I saw where it dropped. . . . Little Man told me: 'Pick it up. Let us see it.' I took it and give it to him. He worked it around in his palm. It was a whole cherry seed and Jimmy's gut, kind of rotten, was stuck on it and that is what was blocking his gut. Right after that he was well.

"The claw was a big one but it didn't even make a scar because I looked to see if there was any blood coming out. As soon as he jerked the claw out, he rubbed his hand just a little bit over the place and that is all there was to it" [Chandler in Cooper 1957:351–355].

Little Warrior
Lakota, *Plains*
A well-known medicine man from Kyle, South Dakota. He practiced into the 1940s. Hurt [1960:52] assigned him to the ghost doctor class of shamans—the class that used herbs, the sacred pipe, and helping spirits to cure but were not *yuwipi* (see entry) men. Little Warrior was usually given a horse for his rituals. He died around 1950.

Little Water Society
Seneca, *Northeast*
A medicine society that met four times a year to perform the rites that were necessary to preserve the potency of a secret medicine called the "little-water powder" [Parker 1909:165].

Liwa wenenapi
Coast Miwok, *California*
A shaman who administers herbal medicines during his cures; translates to "water doctor." However, the term is used by the southern Coast Miwok for their outfit shamans. Among the

Northern Coast Miwok, the same shaman is called *walimitca* (see entry) [Loeb 1934a:114].

Lohau sumatc
Mojave, *Southwest*
A specialist "in treating birth defects, children's diseases, and respiratory ailments such as colds, influenza, and pneumonia" [Stewart 1974:8].

Lokoala
Kwakiutl, *Northwest Coast*
The act of obtaining magical gifts from spirits [Boas 1897:396].

Looks Twice, Willie
Lakota, *Plains*
A shaman who practiced on the Rosebud and Pine Ridge Reservations up until his death in 1965. He was a bear doctor and was much sought after for his ability to treat wounds and burns [Kemnitzer 1976:263].

Lopez, Walter
Ute, *Basin*
A Towaoc (or Ute Mountain) sucking shaman and sheepman who was also a member of the Native American Church (peyotism; see entry). He was observed during the 1950s by anthropologist Omer Stewart treating a Navajo patient who had been unsuccessfully treated by his own people.

Lopez reported to Stewart that he often took his patients into peyote meetings to "double the efficacy of his sucking cures" [Stewart 1956:75].

Lowanpi
Lakota, *Plains*
A healing ritual performed by a medicine man; translates to "they sing." The form of the ritual is determined by the helping spirits of the medicine man. Different forms are used for different situations. Often the ritual involves the singing of sacred songs, use of the sacred pipe, and an altar display by the medicine man. As in other Lakota healings, the patient must perform the *opagi* (see entry) ritual to secure the services of the medicine man.

Luirh
Gitksan, *Northwest Coast*
A special red cedar collar placed around the neck of a shaman who is undergoing treatment for an illness by other shamans. During the ceremony, the other shamans take hold of this collar and raise the sick shaman [Barbeau 1958:54].

Lycanthropy
A term used in the anthropological literature to refer to shamans' ability to turn themselves into wolves. It is often applied to the general ability of shamans to turn themselves into an animal form.

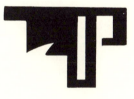

Macaiyoyo
Zuni, *Southwest*

A divining crystal used by shamans. Every shaman possesses one or more such crystals, which are used to see "anything, anywhere" [White 1932:110]. During the healing ceremonies of medicine societies, the shaman uses this crystal to locate an object in the patient's body that is causing the illness or to locate the sorcerer who is responsible for projecting the object into the victim. One procedure is for the shaman to dip the crystal into the ceremonial *wait-itcani* (medicine bowl) and then rub his eyes with it.

Mache da
Atsugewi, *California*

A Coyote doctor among the Atsuge branch; considered to be one of the best types of healers [Park 1986:39]. See *betsaki* for details.

Mad Bear
Iroquois, *Northeast*

The name of a contemporary Tuscarora shaman who is a member of the Bear Clan. His grandmother was a medicine woman, and she initiated him—gave him his name and his medicine—when he was only nine years old. From her he learned many plant remedies for specific diseases. One mixture he prepares to help people in certain situations is "medicine smoke."

During a conversation with Doug Boyd, he responded to a question concerning his diabetes by stating, "Oh that. That diabetes didn't belong to me. From time to time I've been doing that. I was only hanging on to that for somebody else" [Boyd 1994:238]. He uses his medicine mainly to perform as a mediator.

Boyd documented a successful healing conducted by Mad Bear and Peter Mitten, a shaman from Oklahoma, on Richard Oakes. Oakes was in a coma and dying in a San Francisco hospital. After considerable controversy with the attending physicians, they were allowed to treat the patient unobserved in the hospital room. Mad Bear reported, "I got a couple of birds in the room and while I was doing that, Peter Mitten brought back the normal color in Oakes's chest" [Boyd 1974:242]. The patient fully recovered, even though the Western physicians had given up all hope.

Madatcan
Montagnais, *Canadian Eastern Woodlands*

Naskapi sweat lodge. The lodge is a low, dome-shaped structure into which heated rocks are passed; water is then sprinkled on them. Persons may sing or rattle during this

time. One Mistassini man said that "the water ex-
torts pain from the stones which causes them to
cry out and finally give forth their power for his
services" [Speck 1935:212]. Afterward, the people
go outside and gradually cool off rather than
plunging into a lake or stream, as is often done in
other cultures. The sweat lodge is used as a means
of strengthening one's body and spirit as well as
removing bodily pains. In some cases, it is used in
the treatment of wounds. However, the most common use is to gain control over game.

Madockawando
Penobscot, *Canadian Eastern Woodlands*
A renowned shaman and chief, was born
around 1630 and died in 1697 or 1698. The
French called him Matakanto, and the English
used this name. The Penobscot remember him as
Matakwanto and translate the name as "wonder
worker."

Madodoson
Chippewa, *Canadian Eastern Woodlands*
The sweat bath ritual. Before a shaman conducts
a healing ritual, he purifies himself in the sweat
lodge [Hilger 1951:88]. Sweat lodges are also used
for the treatment of aching or stiff muscles and for
rheumatic pain [Hilger 1951:96].

Madstone
Comanches, *Plains*
Sometimes called a medicine bone, it "was a small
piece of the leg bone of the giant prehistoric mam-
moth, believed by the Comanches to be bones of
piam3mpits—the cannibal owl. Placed over the
affected spot, it was supposed to draw out the poison" [Wallace and Hoebel 1952:171]. It was most
often used for wounds, infections, boils, and
pains.

Madu
Pomo, *California*
Sucking or dream doctor who acquires powers
from a guardian spirit.

Maheonhetan
Cheyenne, *Plains*
Plural: *maheonhetaneo*. A shaman that has served
as a priest in one of the great ceremonials. The
more common term for shaman is *zemaheonevsz*
(see entry) [Schlesier 1987:14].

Mahopá
Hidatsa, *Plains*
Matthews's [1877:184] rendering of *maxupá*. See
xupá for details.

Mahwee, Dick
Paviotso, *Basin*
A shaman who was born around 1885 and lived
on the Pyramid Lake Reservation. He received his
power when he was about 25 years old during a
vision quest at a sacred cave south of Dayton,
Nevada. His spirit helper appeared to him as a
tall, slender man. This spirit came to him in subsequent dreams and taught him to heal. He used
eagle feathers to bring back the lost soul of a patient [Park 1934:102–103].
    When this spirit helper first appeared to him,
the spirit had the tail feather of an eagle in his
hand. Mahwee said that the spirit told him:
"When you doctor, you must follow the instructions that the animals give you. They will tell you
how to cure the sickness. I have this feather in my
hand. You must get feathers like it. You are also to
find the things that go with it. Get dark beads. Put
them on the quills of the feathers and tie a strip of
buckskin to the quills. Also get a hoof of a deer,
and down from the eagle. With these you can go
to people to cure them. These are your weapons
against sickness. You must get three rolls of
tobacco. You can use them to tell your patients
what made them sick and then you can cure them.
The tobacco will also help you if you are choked
with clots of saliva when you suck out the disease.
With this you are beginning to be a doctor. You
will get your songs when you doctor" [Park
1938:28].
    Later, he acquired as spirit helpers an eagle, a
crow, and the ghost of a Pit River Indian.

Maickuriwapai

Keres, *Southwest*

The Sia Pueblo term for a cluster of plumes that represents the four cardinal directions, the zenith, and the nadir. The fetish is used as part of an altar display for healing and other religious ceremonies [Stevenson 1894:78].

Maiswat

Cahuilla, *California Peninsula*

Ceremonial bundle [Bean 1972:88]. Each Cahuilla lineage possesses one such sacred bundle. "The *maiswat* was a reed matting of four or five feet in width, fifteen to twenty feet in length, and enclosed ceremonial objects such as feathers, shell beads used in ceremonial exchange, a bone whistle, a curved stick, tobacco, and other ritual items" [Bean 1972:88]. The bundle is kept in a secret hiding place by its keeper and is brought out only for ceremonies. The bundle contains great power and is handled only by "those who through their personal worth had achieved high status and recognition by their use of supernatural power" [Bean 1972:89]. The power within the bundle is called *amnaa*, and it communicates directly with the handlers of the sacred bundle.

Maiyun

Cheyenne, *Plains*

Spirits; in Cheyenne cosmology, "the spirits who work in the seven regions of the universe" [Schlesier 1987:7]. During ritual and prayer, these spirits are addressed only by their personal spirit names.

Mákai

Papago, *Southwest*

Shaman. Shamans are primarily diviners and prophets, but they also conduct healing ceremonies. Some shamans are specialists. For example, the *síiwanyi* is a rain shaman. He can "spit on a crystal, hold it toward the sun, and cause drops of water to fall out" or "spit on a stick, twist it, and wring out water" [Underhill 1946:263–264].

The shaman's function is more often as a seer and diagnostician than as a healer. This is because the Papago have diverse explanations of disease, each demanding its own form of cure and its own practitioner. The supernatural influence that causes a disease is revealed to the shaman in a vision. Treatment is then a matter of routine.

There are three supernatural causes of disease, and all are treated on the principle that like cures like. One cause of disease is the breaking of a ceremonial taboo—some error or disrespect committed at a ceremony. In these cases, the shaman is powerless, and the cure is in the hands of the ritualists who managed the ritual. A second cause is the ill will of animals. Each animal controls some particular disease, sent as punishment on human beings who have offended it. Again, the shaman is powerless in effecting a cure unless he has dreamed of the animal in question. Only one kind of disease is usually treated by the shaman himself—the kind caused by the intrusion of a foreign object into the patient's body. This intrusion is caused by a sorcerer, and the shaman is the proper person to remove it. His remedy is to suck out the object.

Papago shamans receive their powers from dreams and are rarely aided by other individuals in their quests for shamanic powers. Often these power dreams come unsolicited by the individual. Shamans are most often men, but women can also become shamans, usually later in life, after childbearing age. Because of their late start, women rarely achieve the status obtained by male shamans. They often become herbalists.

In the past, men would often kill an eagle in the hope that its spirit would come to them in a dream, bringing shamanic power. During the period of acquiring power, the shaman usually keeps his intentions secret. Once he has attained sufficient power, he normally tests his healing abilities on his relatives. Once his kinsmen attest to his power, patients begin to flock to him to use his power while it is new and strong.

The shaman's most precious possession is his divining crystal, which he uses to find the seat of disease within the patient or the hiding place of the sorcerer who sent the disease. Generally, a shaman possesses four (a ceremonial number) crystals, which are said to be kept in his heart (possibly in a leather bag around the neck). In fact, these special crystals grow in the shaman's body, but some shamans are led to them on the outside by their helping spirits. They empower the shaman's saliva, which is blown onto the patient during a healing ceremony.

When a shaman is called upon to perform his services, the requester places a bit of cornmeal in the shaman's hand. If the requester plans to pay for the shaman's services with a horse or a cow, he might bring a bit of manure as a symbol. The shaman conducts his ceremonies after dark, seating himself near the patient, with eagle feathers in his left hand and a gourd rattle in his right hand. This eagle feather plume, called *mátcuitak*, consists of the two top feathers of an eagle's wing and is used for divining. Each feather has a small stick cemented into the quill end that projects beyond the quill tip by about six inches. These are wrapped together with a buckskin thong.

During the ceremony, the shaman sings the songs taught to him by his helping spirits. Often he sings only the tune, and not the words. When words are sung, the shaman uses a special, hoarse-croaking voice, known as *kuátkua*. The rattle is shaken horizontally when there are no words, and vertically with words. Each shaman has his own particular pattern of song singing. The songs also serve the purpose of trance induction.

After four songs have been sung, the shaman cleans the patient by touching him with the *mátcuitak*. Each shaman has his own method—some shake it directly at the patient, and others shake it in the air. Afterward the shaman smokes tobacco, sometimes blowing it over the patient. The shaman then sets a crystal on the ground next to the patient. The crystal casts a ray of light on the patient's body, revealing the seat of disease or the presence of an intrusive object. The ray might not strike clearly for some time; meanwhile, the shaman fortifies himself by singing and smoking. In difficult cases, the shaman might go outside to induce a vision that will reveal the disease to him. In especially difficult cases, the entire ceremony might have to be repeated over the course of four nights.

Usually before dawn the shaman announces which curing singer must be sent for, or else he sucks out the disease object himself. However, some shamans do not suck because "they did not have it in their dreams." They merely recommend that another shaman be called. The ceremony is concluded with a feast being served by the patient's family.

If the shaman's diagnosis or his treatment fails, he is open to the charge of murder by sorcery. In former times, this often resulted in the shaman being clubbed to death or shot by a surreptitious arrow, with the consent and sometimes the thanks of the village elders. (See Underhill 1946 for details.)

Mákai
Pima, *Southwest*
Ancient term for shaman. A synonymous term is *kúlañ o'odham* (see entry), which literally translates to "medicine man," meaning that it is a loan translation. The Pima word for a curing shaman is *síatcokam* [Underhill 1946:263].

Makakagapi
Lakota, *Plains*
The small earth altar that appears in every *yuwipi* (see entry) ceremony; in Lakota, the term translates to "they make it of earth" [Kemnitzer 1970:54]. Earth, taken from a molehill, is placed on a red square of cloth placed on the floor. Mole dirt is considered pure because it comes from below the ground. It also symbolizes the relationship between animals and the earth. The dirt is shaped into a small, circular mound about 15 inches in diameter. Tobacco offerings are placed around the circumference, and sacred symbols are drawn on the earth by the quill end of an eagle feather. Different symbols are used for different purposes; one symbol is used for doctoring, and another is used if the purpose of the ceremony is to find a lost object. In addition, each shaman has his own set of symbols. When not in use, the earth is stored in a gallon can and can be used any number of times. It should be noted that not all shamans use earth for these mounds. For example, Fools Crow used sand, emphasizing the connection between water and earth.

Makan athinma
Ponca, Omaha, *Plains*
Root doctors who use herbal medicines [Dorsey 1894:417].

Making-Alive
Kwakiutl, *Northwest Coast*
A renowned shaman during the latter part of the nineteenth century. The following is an account of a healing ceremony conducted by Making-Alive for a patient named Place-of-Home-Coming, the son of Potlatch. Making-Alive is assisted in the ceremony by four other shamans, Fool, Cause-of-Falling-Down, Bring-Life-out-of-Woods, and Life-Owner. They all wear the traditional Kwakiutl shamanic costume, which consists of red cedar bark around their heads, red cedar bark tied around their necks, faces blackened with charcoal, and belts of flat red cedar bark. The account is given by Giving-Potlatches-in-the-World and is most unusual in that the narrator receives shamanic power from Making-Alive at the end of the ritual:

"Now we went out of the house and we went into the house of Potlatch. Then we were asked by Fool to sit down in the middle of the left hand side of the house. Then came in all the men and all the women and children and not even one of them was smiling as they came in and they did not talk loud. Only they did not come in, the menstruating young women. As soon as they were all inside the four shamans took a board for beating time and put it down in the rear of the house in front of the song leaders. And also this, the shamans took batons and distributed them among the song leaders. That one also, Fool, took eagle down and feathered all the song leaders and all the spectators. As soon as he had finished the song leaders beat fast time. They had not been doing so very long when they lifted their batons. It was not very long before they again beat fast time. Then it was not very long before they lifted their batons. Then the shaman came singing his sacred song on the right hand side of the house. Now the four shamans went out of the door of the house and the song leaders beat fast time again. Again they lifted their batons. Now came singing his sacred song

the shaman, at the seaside of the house. Again beat fast time the song leaders. It was Fool who was leading, coming into the house at the door. Then the new shaman (Making-alive) came next to him, singing his sacred song. Behind him came the three shamans like the attendants of the cannibal dancer, whom we call, 'those upon whom he leans.' Now they went around the fire in the middle of the house. They went around four times as he was singing his sacred song and swinging his rattle. Then he sat down in front of the place where Place-of-Home-Coming was sitting, the sick one. The four shamans went by twos standing on each side of Place-of-Home-Coming, who was naked. Now Making-alive felt of the chest of Place-of-Home-Coming while he was just all the time singing his sacred song; but not for a long time had Making-alive been feeling of the chest of Place-of-Home-Coming when Fool asked Skin-dressing-Woman, the mother of Place-of-Home-Coming to take a new dish with fresh water in it as a dish for wetting (the mouth) of the shaman. Now Skin-dressing-Woman took a new dish, which was ready on the floor, to give to Fool. Then Fool put down the dish, the receptacle for wetting (the mouth), at the right side of Making-alive. Then Making-alive put his right hand into the water that was in the dish, the receptacle for wetting (the mouth), and he scooped up the water and put it into his mouth while he was pressing with his left hand on the chest of Place-of-Home-Coming. As soon as he had the water in his mouth he blew it on the place that was being pressed by him. Then the shaman sucked it. And so he was sucking for a very long time when he lifted his head and took out of his mouth the blood in his right hand, and he squeezed the blood so that it dripped into the water in the dish, the receptacle for wetting (the mouth). When the blood was all out, he stood up and sang his sacred song, going around the fire in the middle of the house. Then he stretched out his left hand, opening out his fingers and something stuck, (that looked) like a worm, in the middle of the palm of his hand. That was referred to by Fool as the sickness. Then he went around (the fire) and threw upward the sickness. He sat down near the sick man and blew on his chest; but not really for a long time had he been blowing when he stopped. He sucked only once, for he obtained right away the sickness. When they do not get the sickness when they suck the first time, then they only get the sickness when they have sucked four times. Then Making-alive arose. Around him were standing the four shamans and I saw that they secretly talked to one another. Now they probably finished their talking. Then Making-alive sang again his sacred song and walked out from among the four shamans. He walked around the fire in the middle of the house, swinging his rattle while the song leaders were not beating fast time. As soon as he came to the place from which he had started and where were standing the four shamans, he gave his rattle to Fool. Fool told the song leaders to go ahead and beat time on the boards. Then Making-alive pressed both his hands against his stomach as he was going around the fire in the middle of the house, then he vomited blood and he caught it with his left hand. Now there was among it what was referred to by Fool as quartz, among the blood when Making-alive opened his fingers. Then Fool dipped a cup into the water and poured it into his hand in the middle of the quartz crystal so that the blood came off. Then it was shining. Now he held on the palm of his hand the quartz crystal, as he stretched out his left hand. Then Fool and the three other shamans followed him as he went around the fire in the middle of the house and Fool said as they walked following Making-alive, 'Do you not wish to become a shaman and to let this great shaman go ahead and throw this quartz crystal into the stomach of the one who wishes to become a shaman?' said he. Then not one man answered him. Now Fool told the song leaders to go ahead and beat fast time on the board. As soon as the song leaders were beating fast time on the board Making-alive pressed together his hands and threw the quartz crystal. Fool who was following (him) looked upward watching the quartz crystal. Then he said it was flying about in the house. Now Fool came and stood still in front of the place where I was sitting. He said, 'Oh shamans, important is what has been done by the supernatural quartz for it went into this our friend here, into this Giving-Potlatches-in-the-World,' said he, naming my Indian name.

'Now this one will be a great shaman,' said he. Then all the men turned their faces looking at me where I was sitting. As soon as he finished all went out, the men and women and children, out of the house. Now we all went into our houses for it was late at night" [Boas 1930:2:2–4].

Mali Yomta
Wintun, *California*
Patwin singing doctors [Loeb 1934b:226].

Mamaqa
Kwakiutl, *Northwest Coast*
A powerful spirit being that "has the power to catch the invisible disease spirit, which is constantly flying through the air in the form of a worm. He is able to throw it into his enemies, who die from its effects at once" [Boas 1897:394]. The term means "thrower" [Boas 1897:485]. The power of this spirit is emulated in a special dance in which the *mamaqa* impersonator wears special cedar bark head and neck ornaments.

Mani micami
Fox, *Midwest*
Sacred packs or medicine bundles used by shamans. Each pack normally contains a catlinite pipe and the medicines used by the shaman; thus, the contents differ from pack to pack. Each pack is given a name, such as owl sacred pack or nighthawk (which is also the name of the spirit of sickness) sacred pack, or it is preceded by the owner's name, such as Lucy Lasley's sacred pack or Kwiyama's sacred pack.

Truman Michelson obtained Alfred Kiyana's sacred owl pack in the spring of 1914 for Franz Boas, who subsequently transferred it to the Berlin Museum für Völkerkunde. The proper use of this pack included knowing the proper songs that go with each of the medicines it contained. With regard to healing, Kiyana reported that "one who knows this sacred pack practices doctoring. He doctors one that is shot, who has a broken bone, or what not, even if he has many wounds, even those who are severely wounded, if they have broken bones—yet he doctors them all" [Kiyana in Michelson 1921:29].

The owl sacred pack (bottom) and the fiber bag in which the owl sacred pack is wrapped (above). The proper use of this pack includes knowing the sacred songs for each specific medicine(s) it contains.

According to Kiyana, the shaman would treat wounded patients in a wickiup that was set up "in a place far away." He wore only a breechcloth and would begin by facing the east and singing a medicine song while offering tobacco. During the course of the cure, other medicine songs were sung. The treatment usually took eight days, during which the patient was not allowed to drink water but was given food that had been ceremonially prepared. "And after he had cured them he gave them a smoke. Those just cured used this catlinite pipe. . . . Only after they had smoked were they given medicine to eat. Then, it is said, they separated. Then at any time they began drinking water" [Kiyana in Michelson 1921:31–33].

Manitou
Algonquin, *Northeast*
Also: *manitu, manidoo, mannittos, manito, manittoes.* This term has been popular with missionaries for well over 300 years, and appears written in many different forms besides these five. A medicine man's helping spirit, which most often takes human form when it appears. There are many different types of manitous, but there is also Kitchi Manitou, who is the Creator or Supreme Being. The Creator supervises the activities of the other manitou bosses. For the most part, the Great Manitou is unapproachable, but the "rule is that the Supreme Being is actualized in crisis situations and at great annual thanksgiving ceremonies. He then appears also as a giver of fish and other animals. On other, normal everyday occasions the annual (lesser) bosses (*manitous*) take over" [Hultkrantz 1983:7].

Manitowak
Potawatomi, *Midwest*
A shaman's helping spirit. It is also the general term for spirits [Clifton 1977:50].

Manitowi
Algonquian, *Northeast*
The mystical potency or potentiality to do or effect results. It is the Algonquian cognate of the

Anglicized term *orenda*. Among the Central Algonquian tongues, it appears as *mánitu;* in Montagnais, the form is *meníto;* for the Natick, it is *múndu* [Johnson 1943:58–59].

Manitowuk
Lenni Lenape, *Northeast*
The Lenni Lenape (also called Delaware) term for spirits.

Mankan
Winnebago, *Midwest*
Medicine [Radin 1923:265]. Each medicine is given a specific name, such as white medicine, medicine of the water, round medicine, medicine that spreads over the ground, and so forth.

Mankani
Winnebago, *Midwest*
Medicine man or shaman [Radin 1923:282]. To secure the services of the shaman, a tobacco offering is made to him. Sickness is most often diagnosed as being caused by the presence of some object in the body. The object is removed by a sucking shaman to effect a cure. In most cases, the shaman uses a bone tube, placed on the afflicted part, to suck out the object. "Among the Winnebago the shaman before applying the tube squirts some water upon the afflicted person and breathes upon him" [Radin 1923:171].

The Winnebago shamans also use elaborate medicine mixtures for some of their cures, consisting of plants, animals, and insect parts. For example, the rattlesnake is used in a mixture given to a woman in labor, leeches are used in a mixture to relieve pain, and the bear liver is used in various mixtures for burns, boils, dysentery, chills, nosebleeds, and pains in the stomach. One powerful medicine made from an undetermined plant was known as the "stench-earth medicine":

"A man who was blessed (obtained a spirit helper) was told of all these things. He cured all diseases. If a person had been shot and one blessed with the stench-earth medicine was called, he could be cured. In the same manner, if one is stabbed in what would generally be considered a fatal way and if a man blessed with stench-earth was called in time he would save him. The same cure is effected in cases of broken arms and of patients who are on the point of death. It is for this reason that those blessed with the stench-earth medicines are always praised, and that the people say 'They surely are in charge of life; for their blessings really come from the spirits, just as they claim'"[Radin 1923:264].

Mankánye Waci
Iowa, *Plains*
The Medicine Dance Ceremony, which is a variant of the Ojibwa Medicine Lodge Society Ceremony. In earlier times, it took a candidate four years to enter the society, but now one can enter in two to four days. The Medicine Dance is usually held in the spring and the fall. The major function of the society is to conduct healing ceremonies.

Mantu
Montagnais, *Canadian Eastern Woodlands*
The Naskapi shaman's power. Items that have been revealed in dreams are represented graphically or by symbols so that their *mantu* can be used to gain success in undertakings. This pictorial or symbolic representation of the plant or animal whose aid is being secured, or has been secured, is equivalent to the creature or object itself [Speck 1935:190].

Maraidi
Northern Paiute, *Basin*
The various power feats displayed only by the most powerful shamans; translates to "trick." For example, there is the *nabagappi maraidi*, the power to deflect bullets, as well as the power to make lightning, the power to bring rain or wind, the power to bring water babies to be seen, and so forth. The great shaman and prophet Wovoka is said to have brought about clouds for shade, to have freed himself from jail by causing lightning

to rip open the jailhouse, to have predicted the future, and other such *maraidi*.

Masked-Dancer Ceremony
Apache, *Southwest*
A Chiricahua healing ceremony that can also ward off evil and epidemics. It is also used during a girl's puberty rite. The masked dancers are men dressed and decorated to represent mountain-dwelling spirits. The dancers themselves have no power, but the ceremonial leader is a shaman who fashions the masks they wear and paints or directs the painting of their bodies [Opler 1941:87].

Maskiki
Ojibwa, *Canadian Eastern Woodlands*
Medicine. There are three major classes of medicine: curing medicine, protection medicine, and bad medicine. Bad medicine includes love medicine, hunting medicine, gambling medicine, and other medicines designed to produce individual success. These are seen by the Ojibwa as bad simply because they cause others to do things they would not normally do. The term was used as early as 1703 by Baron Lahontan [1703:47–48], who was the lord-lieutenant of the French colony at Placentia, Newfoundland.

Maskikiwinini
Otchipwe, *Canadian Eastern Woodlands*
Herbalists; the literal translation is "medicine man" [Cooper 1936:9].

Masta
Atsugewi, *California*
Ghost, which usually refers to a dead person. Such ghosts are a source of illness. For example, "A *masta* will go to people's houses. They look around, and if they drink the water that is in the house, and if the people do not know that a *masta* has been there and drunk of the water, and they drink of it, the person drinking the water that has been drunk of by a *masta* will become sick. . . . The person a ghost has attached himself to does not

have any pain but he feels weak and lazy. If no doctor finds out what is wrong with the person, he dies. . . . If the doctor does find out what the sickness is, he makes a big smoke. Towards daylight the sick person sits next to the doctor, and the doctor blows the ghost away" [Park 1986:35].

Mataka libu
Pomo, *California*
Mud whistle, which is molded from clay and has a stick support attached to it. It is used by the *dja minawan* (outfit doctors; see entry) to locate the seat of disease in a patient's body [Loeb 1934a:10].

Matakanto
Penobscot, *Canadian Eastern Woodlands*
Also: *Matakwanto.* The French version of the English name Madockawando (see entry).

Matcupeik
Mojave, *Southwest*
See *kwathidhe.*

Matkothau sumatc
Mojave, *Southwest*
A specialist called a witch doctor. These shamans can bewitch people or "cure those who had been victimized by other witches" [Stewart 1974:9].

Matnonaltcigan
Montagnais, *Canadian Eastern Woodlands*
Dialectical variants: Mistassini, *matoneitcigan*; Eastern Naskapi, *matonentcigan*. This is a Naskapi term difficult to render in English, but it means to cause things to happen by the use of one's will, sometimes referred to as "wish power." It is the process by which shamans cause things to happen. For instance, a shaman named Napani came with his family to a river and had no way to cross it. "Having no canoe he told them to sit in a circle and close their eyes. This they did, and he proceeded to wish and commune with his *nictut* (helping spirit). When he was finished he told them to open their eyes—and behold—they were all across on the other side" [Speck 1935:185]!

Mato tipi
Lakota, *Plains*
Bear Butte, located 8 miles from Fort Meade, South Dakota. For many years, it has been the favorite vision-questing site of the Lakota and other Native American cultures.

Mato wapiye
Lakota, *Plains*
Bear doctors who have bear medicine. Bear medicine is one of the most widespread and powerful Native American healing medicines used by shamans. Bear shamans are among the oldest type of shaman known to the Lakota. They usually perform their healing ceremonies in a totally darkened room. Any herbs that are used are dug with bear claws. These shamans often live as bears live, washing themselves every morning in a creek, throwing water on themselves with pawlike movements, grunting bear sounds, and so forth. "And when one of these doctors kicks on the ground there is heard something within him, singing in a beautiful voice; and so the people believe what the doctors say about diseases" [Dorsey 1894:495]. Currently, there are no Lakota bear shamans practicing, but a bear doctor could emerge at any time via a visionary revelation.

Matógaxe
Ponca, *Plains*
The Bear Doctor Society; also the Bear Dance. Its members are shamans who derive their curing power from the bear. They deal primarily with herbal remedies. Howard [1965:117] reports that they are "the physicians of the tribe."

In addition to healing, they are well known for their spectacular power displays during the Bear Dance ritual. The following is a typical example given by Skinner [in Howard 1965:118]:

"Before performing, a cedar tree was pulled up by the roots and set up in the center of the lodge. During the dance one of the participators would go up and break off a branch and scrape off the bark. Then he would circle the lodge four times, show it to the members, and announce that he would run it down his throat. He would then thrust it in until the tip barely showed. After a moment he would pull it out, and the blood would gush forth. One shaman had the power of thrusting the cedar through his flesh into his abdomen. After he pulled it out he merely rubbed the wound and it was healed. Still another would swallow a pipe, cause it to pass through his body, and then bring it out and lick it.

"Big-goose once saw a man, who was performing in the bear dance, take a muzzle-loading rifle and charge it in everyone's presence. Another man circled the tent singing, and on the fourth round he was shot by the Indian with the gun; everyone thought he was killed, but he soon sprang up unhurt. Another performer took a buffalo robe, had a third man re-load the magic gun, and fired it at the robe. There was no hole visible, but the bullet was found in the center of the robe."

Matovara sumatc
Mojave, *Southwest*
A specialist in difficult childbirths. "He helps to deliver the baby. He sings and blows on her head. He helps to straighten the baby's body out, so it comes out . . . the baby's legs may be in the wrong position, feet first. He sings and tells a story to make the baby behave and listen. Sometimes he blows on the woman's head, and blows the baby right out" [Stewart 1974:11].

Mattahando
Penobscot, *Northeast*
A shaman who died in 1676. The ending *-hando*, according to anthropologist Frank Speck, "is a cognate of the Central Algonquian *manitou* (see entry) and seems to mean mysterious, magical, powerful, miraculous, enabling things to be done supernaturally" [Speck 1919:240].

Matu
Pomo, *California*
Sucking shaman. These shamans can be either male or female. They obtain their healing powers through visions, usually unsought ones. After

such power visions, the novice shaman is assisted by other sucking shamans in a four-day dance ceremony known as *matu ke*. "The ceremony lasted four days. The novice doctor abstained from meat and fish, and ate acorn bread and pinole. He was allowed to drink water. . . . The doctors danced at night and slept in the daytime. . . . The test as to whether or not the novice was to become a doctor occurred in the course of the dancing" [Loeb 1934a:9]. This test consisted of the novice spontaneously bleeding from the nose and/or mouth during the dance. The novice was to swallow the blood; later, during his healing ceremonies, after he had sucked on the patient, blood would be vomited by the shaman as the seat of pain (illness).

Maunetu
Natick, *Northeast*
One term for shaman; another is *pauwau* [Speck 1919:254]. The Natick are a division of the Massachuset Nation.

Maxpe
Crow, *Plains*
Also: *baaxpée* [Frey 1987:61]. The term translates to "mysterious," and it refers to the supernatural aspect of power—that is, power transcending the ordinary. The Crow apply it not to designate particular supernatural beings but to convey the idea that a person or object is possessed of extraordinary qualities. For example, *maxpe* objects (called *xapáaliia*; see entry) are received during visitations from spirits; *maxpe* power is the generic principle of which spirits are the personified, concrete manifestations; and *maxpe* dreams are equated with visionary experiences. *Maxpe* is "more than the power to alter a path, effect a cure, or obtain a job. It is also the power to know which path should be taken . . . expressed through a dream or a vision, (it) can offer wisdom" [Frey 1987:62]. Therefore, this is an abstract notion to which concrete experiences are or are not assimilated. "The man who superintended the driving of deer into a corral is thus described in a text: 'The one who did it was a *maxpe* man, it is said'" [Lowie 1922:315]. The term is equivalent to the widely used concept of

orenda (see entry) among the Iroquois and *wakan* (see entry) among the Sioux.

The term "has an additional connotation in that it can refer to an individual 'on the right side,' i.e., a member of the political faction currently controlling the tribal government and thus a recipient of 'all the benefits'" [Frey 1987:61].

Maxupá
Hidatsa, *Plains*
See *xupá*.

Mayáthle
Clayoquot, *Northwest Coast*
See *oóshtakyòu*.

Meda
Ojibwa, *Canadian Eastern Woodlands*
Ojibwa shamans are classified according to the different techniques they use to heal or divine. "The isolated family shamans are called *meda* for the sound of their drum or rattle, with which they contact their guardian manitou (spirit)" [Grim 1983:113].

Medassoguneb
Ojibwa, *Canadian Eastern Woodlands*
A Manitou Reserve *mide* shaman who was well-known during the 1930s [Landes 1968].

Medéoulino
Penobscot, *Canadian Eastern Woodlands*
Male shamans; translated by the Penobscot as "spiritual men" or "witch men." The word comes from *mede*, meaning "sound of drumming." Among the Penobscot, the shaman is considered a superior individual, and often the greatest shaman also becomes the most important chief. Another Abenaki form of the word is *medeolinu*, which also means "supernatural or spiritual men." Female shamans are designated by the term *medeolinaskwe*. The characteristics of Penobscot shamanism are shared by the Abenaki, Wawenock, Malecite, and Passamaquoddy Nations.

Penobscot shamans derive their power from the spiritual and animal world. They use their powers to heal, cause illness, foretell events, protect hunting territories, and compete with other shamans. Little is known of the shaman's acquisition of power, but it is assumed to be some form

of vision questing. One informant reports that the method for securing a spirit helper is "to go out in the woods or by the shore of a lake according to the home of the animal and sing to it. Gradually it would appear and then the witch-man (shaman) would stroke it with his hand in order to bind the animal to him as a servant" [Newell Lion in Speck 1919:252]. As a rule, these shamans have only one spirit helper, most often some animal form that they have never killed, eaten the flesh of, or mentioned the name of. There are no indications that shamanism is hereditary or acquired through means of training. Thus, shamanism is more than likely an individual matter. Shamans come together for power displays, but not as a society.

Mede'wegan
Ojibwa, *Canadian Eastern Woodlands*
Hoffman's [1988] rendition of *Midewiwin* (see entry).

Medicine
With regard to Native American cultures, this term has come to mean "supernatural power" rather than something that is used for medication. From this usage we get "medicine man," "good versus bad medicine," "medicine bag," "medicine dog" (for the horse), "medicine water" (for whiskey), and so forth. Mooney [1896:980] defined it as "anything sacred, mysterious, or of wonderful power or efficacy in Indian life or belief."

Medicine Lodge (Society)
See *Midewiwin*.

Medicine man
The most popular term applied to Native North American healers. Of course, its usage overlooks the fact that many healers are women. The origin of the term can be traced at least to the time of the French Jesuit missionaries during the seventeenth century. Among the Huron, Montagnais, Ottawa, and other inhabitants of New France, the missionaries wrote of the healers, the *hommes-médécins* (*médecin* is the French word for "doctor") [Underhill 1965:82].

In North America, the terms *medicine man* and *shaman* have become interchangeable in much of the professional literature. However, not all sha-

A Mandan shaman holds a buffalo skull as part of a ritual to ensure a successful hunt. In addition to healing, medicine men often performed rites to protect hunting territories.

mans use their supernatural powers for healing, so this usage can lead to confusion. In Europe, the term *shaman* is generally reserved for those practitioners who enter into an altered state of consciousness to gain access to their power, and the term *medicine man* is used for other healers. These differences have caused North American scholars to use the term *medicine* more in terms of "power," whereas European scholars tend to use it more in terms of its Latin meaning, "physician's art."

Compounding the problem is the reticence of many scholars to use *medicine man* at all, because they believe it to be derogatory, reminiscent of the medicine shows that traveled throughout the country in the nineteenth century and were renowned for their fakery. Others do not like to use it because it provides an inadequate description of a particular practice. For example, among the Navajo, the ritual leader of a healing ceremony is referred to as a singer, whereas among the Lakota, he is referred to as a holy man. Thus, one can only conclude that most shamans are medicine men, but not all medicine men are shamans.

Medicine pipe

Used in the literature to refer to the sacred pipe (see entry).

Mednanenwek

Potawatomi, *Midwest*
The *mide* priests who conducted the Potawatomi variation of the *Midewiwin* (see entry) ritual obtained from the Ojibwa [Clifton 1977:264]. Historical records indicate that the Potawatomi began their practice of the *Midewiwin* in the winter of 1666–1667. Healing during the ceremony was based on object intrusion and thus called for a sucking doctor to remove the disease-causing object.

Meges

Yurok, *Oregon Seaboard*
Herbalist. These individuals are called on to perform simple cures and are not attributed with spiritual powers, but some possess esoteric knowledge. White doctors are also referred to as *meges* [Buckley 1992:123].

Megise

Menomini, *Midwest*
Sacred shells. Dialectical variant of the Ojibwa *migis*. Skinner [1920:336] uses this term for "the bead that is taken in the draft by the candidate when he is initiated into the medicine-lodge" and also refers to it as a "medicine shell or seed." The other Menomini term for the medicine shell is *konäpämik*.

Mehkwasskwan

Woods Cree, *Canadian Eastern Woodlands*
The medicine name of Russell Willier, a shaman residing in northern Alberta on Sucker Creek Reserve near Grouard; translates to "Red Cloud." During the 1980s, he was involved in the Psoriasis Research Project with Professor David Young from the University of Alberta. Russell agreed to treat psoriasis patients by using traditional healing techniques in a downtown Edmonton clinic, where the results could be observed and documented. It was one of the first research projects ever designed to test the efficacy of Native American healing techniques. The results of this collaborative effort produced one of the best insights to date concerning Native American healing.

Russell specializes in the use of what he terms "combinations," which are mixtures of herbs. He uses about 40 different herbs in his work. Some of the combinations were learned from elders, and others were given to him by his helping spirits. Of these he says: "You have to know your herbs in order to put the combination together. Once you get the combination you pretty well have it for the rest of your life until you pass it over to somebody else. And the ones that have been lost, if the medicine man didn't pass them over to someone before he died, they can sometimes be given back by the spiritual world. For example, the spirits might give back a combination to someone by telling them about it in a dream" [Young 1989:62].

Around the age of 18, Russell was given the medicine bundle of his great-grandfather, Moostoos, who had been a renowned healer in his time. Russell reports: "At that time I was just getting into life so I just sort of put it aside; I didn't want to use it because it's something that's sacred. There are two kinds of bundles among the Cree; one (medicine bundle) has herbs in it and another, the spiritual bundle, would have things like rattles, pipes, a bear claw or porcupine hide in it. Medicine bundles are very powerful. In the past they sometimes buried them in the forest until the right person came along and was recognized as being the right kind of person to get that bundle. He would find it" [Young 1989:60].

Once Russell began to use his great-grandfather's medicine bundle, he found that it contained herbs tied together in small bundles. Each bundle was a combination, which he had to learn about from his elders. In healing, fresh herbs would be gathered and combined according to his known combinations. Of these he reports: "A combination consists of herbs that are selected and prepared as medicine. Sometimes you only combine a few herbs, but other combinations may require quite a number of herbs and perhaps an animal part as well. I learned some of my combinations from the medicine bundle. The herbs that were tied together to show the combinations were very old. I didn't actually use those herbs but just looked at them to know what they are, and then I got fresh, new herbs from the ground. Other combinations I have learned from elders who have passed them over to me, but sometimes they're hard to get because they don't want to pass combinations over and often you either have to give a four-legged animal or pay a heavy price. You don't just get it; you have to earn it. You have to earn the trust, the love from them, and they can refuse you any time" [Young 1989:61].

Concerning the animal parts required in certain combinations, Russell reports: "Yes, we use animal. For example, we use bear, beaver, weasel, wild geese, moose, deer, coyote, horse, and there are some wild ducks that are used for medicine. The bear gall-bladder, for instance, will get rid of a lot of poison. You either drink it or you could use it by rubbing it on, anointing yourself. The way you would use it depends on the illness source. . . . The bear and the buffalo are used in doctoring patients with back problems, and you can also use one herb we call the backbone herb. All these different animals, and there are lots of them, have a spirit. If you go and get a skunk you'll ask the Skunk Spirit for help in the cure. These animals, according to our Indian religion, walk on this earth for that purpose. A lot of different animals are on the earth for man to use. Like the wild geese; we use their grease for doctoring, God has put them here for that purpose. So if I use the bear, say the gall-bladder, then I'll have to ask the Bear Spirit first. Most people get it all so confused, they figure the Indian is just praying to the animals, but that's not the case. . . . A certain animal will actually come to you. Sometimes you obtain their help if you fast for four days and nights all by yourself. A certain animal will come, and you will either see him or hear him. He'll be there, and you'll know that that's the one that will help you" [Young 1989:64–66].

Membertou

Micmac, *Canadian Eastern Woodlands*
A renowned seventeenth-century shaman. At that time, the Micmac shaman wore a purse covered with embroidery around his neck that carried his spirit helper. Membertou was also a ruling chief.

Men of Mystery

Throughout the various Native American cultures, the phrase most often applied to their medicine men [La Flesche 1905:10].

Meskwoh

Yurok, *Oregon Seaboard*
Herbal medicines. Among the Yurok, herbal specialists are known as *meges*. Herbal medicines are also administered by shamans [Buckley 1992: 123].

Metèolinu

Montagnais, *Canadian Eastern Woodlands*
Shaman. The term is derived from the Algonquian stem *mede*, which refers to the sound of drumming.

Menomini quilled otter-skin medicine bags.

Meteu

Delaware, *Northeast*

An old Delaware term meaning "one who drums"; it refers to the practice of medicine men beating on a drum to drive away evil spirits. In modern Delaware, the term refers to a turkey cock that drums its wings.

Metewen

Menomini, *Midwest*

Also: *Mitäwin* [Skinner 1920]. The equivalent of the Ojibwa *Midewiwin* (Medicine Lodge Society; see entry) as practiced by the Menomini. This ceremony has been referred to as the Medicine Dance of the Central Algonquin and southern Siouan tribes in the upper and middle Mississippi Valley. It is the oldest and most elaborate ritual of the Menomini connected with shamanic power. The ritual is performed to prolong life and to ensure good health and protection from witchcraft.

Most scholars agree that the ceremony originated among the Ojibwa. The society maintains the medical knowledge of the people, which includes both herbal medicines and shamanic cures. Members of the society in former times zealously guarded any information about their activities, but with the onset of peyotism among the Menomini, competition arose, and they have become more open about their affairs to attract membership. To be initiated into the society, one has to pay a member to impart the necessary teachings. (See Skinner 1920 for details.)

Each member of this society possesses an animal skin medicine bag, giving the shaman the ability to shoot a small, magically endowed cowrie shell, called a *megise* (see entry) or *konäpämik*. The location of the shot *megise* corresponds to the four levels of the society: "When a man is first initiated, a *megise* was shot into his right shoulder; the left shoulder for the second degree; the third time in the right leg; and the fourth time in the left leg. The first *megise* is white, the second black, the third yellow, the fourth is smaller and colored both yellow and black. A man with all four of these objects in him has the highest power that can be given anyone through the *Mitäwin*" [Skinner 1920:164–165]. They also have a medicine for retrieving the shells.

In addition to its medicine functions, the society conducts memorial services for its most important members about one year after burial. The ceremony is conducted to ensure that the spirit of the deceased makes it to the land of the dead.

Metock, Tony

Yuki, *California*

Possibly the last Huchnom sucking doctor among this now extinct culture. He was interviewed in 1930 by E. M. Loeb and was quite old at that time. He received his powers after having a vision of two Thunder Girls. Afterward he ate no fish or meat for two years. From then on, Thunder was his guardian spirit. "He always talks to Thunder now before working a cure, but he never sees him. If he should ever see Thunder he would die" [Loeb 1934a:62].

Micami
Fox, *Midwest*
See *mani micami*.

Midahopa
Hidatsa, *Plains*
Red cedar; translates to "mysterious or sacred tree" [Dorsey 1894:391]. As with many other Native American cultures, the smoke of the burn-ing cedar is used to drive away evil spirits prior to conducting a ceremony, such as a healing ceremony.

Mide
Ojibwa, *Canadian Eastern Woodlands*
One of the three classes of shamans identified by Hoffman [1891]. These shamans are members of the Society of the Mide and are responsible for conducting the Grand Medicine Rite or *Midewiwin* (see entry). As such, they are the principal healers among the Ojibwa who call upon spirit helpers to effect cures. The term *mide* can be used as an adjective or noun and means "mystic" or "mystically powerful."

A view into a Midewiwin lodge during a ceremony at Lac Courte Oreille, Wisconsin, in 1899. A mother holds a child who is being initiated into the Mide Society during a healing ritual. The symbols above the lodge indicate the various helping spirits that enter via the opening in the top.

Midemegis

Ojibwa, *Canadian Eastern Woodlands*

The sacred shell that always appears next to the sacred drum in the course of the *Midewiwin* (see entry). It symbolizes the fact that long life is not sought for its own sake but has to be reclaimed because it was lost by the man who first challenged the Spirit of the Underworld [Johnston 1982].

Midewigun

Ojibwa, *Canadian Eastern Woodlands*

Also: *Mede'wegan.* A rectangular-shaped lodge; the sacred *mide* (shaman) lodge in which the *Midewiwin* healing ceremonies are conducted. Often referred to in the literature as the Grand Medicine Lodge.

Midewiwin

Ojibwa, *Canadian Eastern Woodlands*

One of the oldest Ojibwa societies. It is often referred to in the literature as the Grand Medicine Society, (Great) Medicine Lodge Society, or the Society of Medicine. Johnston [1982:95] gives two other possible meanings for this term: The Society of the Good-Hearted Ones, from *mino* meaning "good" and *dewewin* meaning "hearted"; or the Resonance, from the stem *midewe* meaning "the sound," referring to the drumming and chanting during the ceremony. It is also simply referred to as the *mide* ceremony.

Research indicates that this ceremony came into being among the Chequamegon Ojibwa along the southern shore of Lake Superior around 1700, although Hoffman [1888:211] was told that it originated long ago while they were still living near the Atlantic Ocean. It then spread into Wisconsin, Minnesota, and southwest Ontario. Variations of the ceremony also spread to the Potawatomi, Menomini, Fox, easternmost Dakota, Iowa, Winnebago, Omaha, Ponca, and Kansas tribes [Vecsey 1983:174]. During the 1700s, there was little contact with the Ojibwa, so the first recorded observation of this ceremony did not come until 1804. This ceremony is not found among some of the northern Ojibwa, nor among those who migrated south and east into Michigan and southeast Ontario.

Among the Ojibwa, this ceremony is most often a healing ceremony that usually lasts seven or eight days. Unlike most Native American healing ceremonies, which center around the activities of a single shaman, a *mide* healing ceremony consists of a group of colleagues working together both secretly and publicly. They begin with the secret sessions, usually lasting several days, and then end with a one-day public viewing ceremony.

Before beginning the ceremony, all the participants purify themselves in the sweat lodge. Then, they make four processions around the ceremonial lodge, the *Midewigun*, before entering. During the procession, they use their sacred turtleshell rattles to invoke the spirits of goodwill and to dispel evil spirits while chanting, "Fill our spirits with good. Upright then may be our lives. Defend our hearts against evil. Against evil prevail." During the first procession around the lodge, the participants are met by four fourth-order *Midewiwin* priests dressed in bear robes; they represent good. Farther on, four more bear-skinned priests join who represent evil. These priests try to stop the procession, but the good bears prevail and the participants enter the lodge, each assuming a seat according to which of the four orders of the *Midewiwin* he belongs. The *mide* curing then proceeds for two, three, or four nights and one or two days of secret sessions, followed by a day session in which the public is invited to watch, although casual observers are usually told to leave. Near the end of the ceremony, the patient distributes gifts to each of the ceremony participants according to their rank and office. This is followed by a ritual in which each shaman "shoots" a mystically powerful *migis* shell into the patient to ensure good health. First-grade cures require four shells to be placed on the heart, as the heart is considered the seat of life. The ceremony concludes with a feast and dance. As in other Native American healing ceremonies, the feast often includes the cooking of a sacrificed animal, in this case a dog.

Because the emphasis of this society is on healing, it teaches that every plant has a pharmaceutical use. The administration of herbal remedies is always accompanied by the proper medicine song. Most of these shamans develop their own medicinal knowledge via visions.

Mile (ear of corn covered with plums) insignia of the order of D'naya'na (life givers). During healing ceremonies the mile is swung across the patient's mouth so that the sacred healing breath can be inhaled.

Migis

Ojibwa, *Canadian Eastern Woodlands*

Sacred shells, often called medicine arrows, used by shamans. Each *migi* carries a charge of life, and the smaller the shell, the more powerful it is considered to be. Most often these are small, white shells from the saltwater species *Cypraea moneta*, known as money cowrie [Hultkrantz 1992:42]. These shells are used to send disease into a victim as well as to heal. Every member of the Mide Society has a number of these shells, which were discharged from the hide of some small animal, such as an otter. Each shaman also has one of these mystical hides, called *wayan*. During healing ceremonies, the shaman extracts these shells from the patient's body to effect a cure. In addition, *mide* initiates often hold dueling dances as demonstrations of their powers, in which the dancers try to cause one another to be shot down. The dancer who remains standing the longest is considered the winner of the duel. Landes [1968:75–76] relates one instance in which a drunk white man walked into a *mide* ceremony and began mocking the participants. The chief *mide* lifted his *wayan*, aimed it at the man, and shot him, causing the man to collapse with agonizing pain in his foot and leg. The chief then said, "You are drunk, you come here to mock. We are talking sacredly, all the *manitos* are present, working for the sick one's life, yet you mock. You said you did not believe our power. Now you see: with this *migis* I stopped you!"

Mile

Zuni, *Southwest*

Plural: *miwe, miwachi*. An amulet possessed by every member of the order of Mystery Medicine. The *mile* symbolizes the life-giving or soul power that comes from Awonawilona, the supreme bisexual power who is the breath of life and life itself. The Mystery Medicine *mile* is made by wrapping a specially selected, perfectly formed ear of corn in feathers. This ear of corn—called a *yapota*—must be straight and not have a single grain missing. There is a ritual that must be closely followed in both its preparation and its eventual repair. Four lines are painted lengthwise on the ear to represent the four cardinal directions. The cavity in the heart of the cob is filled with various seeds—corn grains of the six colors, beans, pinon nuts, and seeds from wheat, squash, watermelon, and muskmelon. The cavity is then sealed with earth paste. Cotton cloth is tied over the base of the cob, which symbolizes the apparel of Mother Corn. A rectangular piece of dressed buckskin that has been painted black is fitted over the base of the ear. Holes are punched in the laps of the leather, and a thong is run through them to lace it together. Seeds are placed into this leather base before tying it off. This forms the base of the *mile*. Feathers and plumes are then tied to sticks, which are placed around the ear of corn such that the ear is completely hidden from view. Many different feathers are used—macaw, parrot, dove, duck, and turkey are commonly found on a *mile*. The plumes and feathers are arranged with great precision. Finally, a case is made from wheat straw for the buckskin base of the *mile*, which has bits of shells and beads tied around the top of the straw with a cotton cord.

During healing ceremonies, the shaman draws his *mile* across the mouth of the patient so that he may draw in the sacred healing breath it carries.

The *miwachi* are occasionally repaired, but when they finally disintegrate, all the seeds are taken and given to the members of the order, who plant them in their fields in the coming year.

Mink, John
Ojibwa, *Canadian Eastern Woodlands*
A shaman on the Lac Court Oreilles Reservation in northwestern Wisconsin, who died in 1943. He was born sometime between 1840 and 1850 and was given the Ojibwa name *Shoniagízik* ("Sky Money"). At the time of his death, he was reputed to be the last of the old men on the reservation of 1,700 people who still knew the old medicine ways.

He said of himself, "I fasted all the time when I was young. In the early morning I would paint my face with charcoal and go off into the woods without eating. The spirits came to me in my dreams as I fasted and gave me the power to kill game and to cure people. They taught me songs and charms and how to suck the disease from sick

people and make medicines" [Casagrande 1960: 470].

Over the course of his long life, John Mink became a master of most of the healing arts:

"He was physician, surgeon, obstetrician, pharmacologist, psychiatrist, homeopath, bone-setter, and blood-letter all in one. The treatment he used varied according to the nature and source of the illness, which in the more difficult cases he determined with the aid of his spirit helpers. . . . He had medicines to cure gonorrhea, to staunch bleeding, to reduce fever, and to ease colic. Diuretics, physics, poultices, and tonics were in his repertoire. He had prescriptions to stop menstruation or to start it, and to induce the flow of milk in a new mother. But his favorite medicine was one that he had learned from his paternal grandfather and was used to bring on labor. . . . Some of his medicines were compounded of numerous ingredients, animal, vegetable, and mineral including such substances as pulverized beaver testicles, cloves, bear fat, moss from a turtle's back, and Epsom salts. Other recipes called for rare or exotic plants that were traded from . . . places as distant as South Dakota and Canada. Bundles of dried medicinal plants were stored in the rafters . . . others he preserved in cans and jars. . . . Scarcely a tree or plant grew for which the Old Man did not know a variety of medicinal uses" [Casagrande 1960: 474–476].

In the summer of 1941, John Mink performed a healing ceremony on a patient named Prosper Guibord, for which Prosper paid a bag of tobacco and a pair of tennis shoes. It was an evening ceremony conducted in a room inside Mink's home. Joseph B. Casagrande witnessed the ceremony and reports as follows:

"The Old Man (Mink) began the ceremony with a recitation of his fasting experience. He told how in a dream on the fifth night of his fast he was led to a conjurer's hut by a flock of wild geese. Inside the swaying hut, which he entered through a hole at the top, were a spikebuck and six spirits. Later, her approach heralded by the sound of singing and laughter, these six were joined by a beautifully dressed lady whose home is behind the sun. These were the ones, he said, who taught him how to cure people and told him the songs to sing in summoning their help.

"His recitation finished, he took up his rattle (a quart oil can filled with buckshot), and accompanied by Andrew (his assistant) on the tambourine drum, began to sing. After singing a cycle of songs to call his spirit helpers, the Old Man dropped to his knees at Prosper's side and shook the rattle over him and also around his own body.

"As the drumming continued, he put one of the bone tubes (a 4-inch, polished deer leg bone) into his mouth and after a brief pause, swallowed it, shuddering and jerking his body as the spirits entered it. Still kneeling, the Old Man then regurgitated the tube and, bending close, sucked through it several times in the region of Prosper's lower abdomen. After each sucking he blew through the tube into the pan (pie tin) of salt water. Finally, obviously winded by his exertions, he spat out the tube. The drumming abruptly stopped and Andrew helped the Old Man to his feet.

"After a brief interlude the Old Man sang another song and began a second series of suckings. This time he succeeded in extracting a small piece of whitish substance which was passed around in the pie tin for inspection before Andrew disposed of it. The Old Man said that he had gotten out only a part of the disease, but added that he believed he could get the rest of it the following evening when he would use a stronger spirit. . . .

"We reassembled the following evening at the same hour and with some modifications the ceremony of the previous night was repeated. Prosper, averring that he had slept well for the first night in months, resumed his position on the floor, this time stripped to the waist.

"For the evening's second course of treatments, the Old Man asked Alice to put the bone tube in his mouth and gave Mary the rattle to shake. He did this, he said, because two female spirits were helping him tonight. After sucking a couple of times he asked Andrew to get a larger bone which was secreted under the bed. He swallowed the tube, alarming us all by momentarily gagging on it, then he regurgitated it and sucked again near Prosper's navel. On the first attempt he sucked out a small maggot and several pieces of

the same white stuff, and announced that he had now gotten it all.

"The Old Man said that Prosper had been sorcerized by a woman, immediately identified by Prosper as a former mistress with whom he had lived for two years and subsequently deserted. Prosper thanked the Old Man for saving his life, as he was sure the disease would shortly have killed him, for the woman had never forgiven him" [Casagrande 1956:37–39].

Although he possessed the power to call spirits and had observed the Shaking Tent Ceremony many times, he never performed it, preferring to use his own methods for healing. In addition to his healing abilities, he was the ceremonial leader of the local Medicine Lodge Society (*Midewiwin*).

Miqkä'no
Menomini, *Midwest*
The turtle, the most powerful of their spirit helpers. The turtle is the speaker for others and is consulted in a healing ceremony to diagnose the sickness. When the sickness is diagnosed as being caused by sorcery, the spirit of the offending shaman is called into the ceremony, where *Miqkä'no* "kicks the shade [spirit] of the conjurer almost to death" and makes him promise to return the patient to good health [Hoffman 1896:148].

Mishaami
Shawnee, Sauk, Fox, Kickapoo, *Midwest*
The sacred bundles possessed by shamans [Howard 1981:213]. Only males possess such bundles. Little is known of their content or function, because to speak of a bundle runs the risk of desecrating it. They are all under the control of the Creator, called "Our Grandmother." The *mishaami* are kept in structures resembling doghouses. Different bundles contain different medicines, and the welfare of the tribe is bound up in the proper care and respect of each bundle. "The bundles are a holy mystery that attracts the inarticulate interest of the entire tribe. Immediately preceding the end of the world, it is thought, Our Grandmother will recall the bundles" [Howard 1981:215].

Misinghâlikun

Lenni Lenape, *Northeast*

In the Unami dialect of the Lenni Lenape (also called Delaware), the guardian spirit of all animals. Literally, it means "living mask" or "living solid face." This spirit is represented by a large wooden mask, painted half red and half black. A shaman is the keeper of the mask. When children become sick, the parents call upon *Misinghâlikun* to scare the sickness from the child. The shaman then impersonates the spirit by putting on the mask and covering himself in a bearskin. During the healing ceremony, he uses a turtleshell rattle, a 3-foot-long stick, and a bag made of bearskin. The mask is also used for other shamanic functions, such as finding lost objects and procuring luck in hunting.

Among the Minsi branch of the Lenni Lenape, the mask owners formed a society and had a special meeting house in which they used the mask for healing ceremonies [Harrington 1921:32].

Mistabeo

Eastern Cree, *Canadian Eastern Woodlands*

A shaman's helping spirit.

Mistapeo

Montagnais, *Canadian Eastern Woodlands*

A Naskapi shaman's male spirit helper; translates to "great man." The female counterpart is called *mistapeshkue*. "They are considered the most important supernatural helpers of a Naskapi shaman, who calls them from far away, past many evil lands. They vary greatly in speech and power but always appear in anthropomorphic form" [Webber in Brodzky et al. 1977:119].

Mitakuye oyasin

Lakota, *Plains*

A phrase meaning "all my relations" or "all my relatives." It is said at the end of every prayer in the same manner as "amen" is used. It is said upon entering and leaving a sweat lodge, after smoking the sacred pipe and other such sacred activities. The phrase has been widely adopted and

is one of the few, contemporary, pan–Native American phrases used during their sacred activities. It is intended to remind the one who is saying it that all things in the universe are related, including the nonliving and the living—a Western philosophical division not made by Native American cultures.

Mitä'kwe

Menomini, *Midwest*

A class of shamans. These shamans gather at special meetings to demonstrate their powers to the public at large. Their abilities are believed to come from their spirit helpers, the *manidos*. A shaman whose abilities are greater than another's is thought to possess more powerful "medicine." Hoffman [1896:105] reports one such gathering observed by the Honorable Lewis Cass:

"Mr. Cass is said to have observed an old Ojibwa medicine woman, who had come up at each dance to actively participate in the exercises. He asked someone near by why this old woman took such an active part, as she appeared rather uninteresting and had nothing to say, and apparently nothing to do except to shake her snake-skin medicine bag. The woman heard the remark and became offended, because she was known among her own people as a very powerful mitä'kwe. In an instant she threw the dry snake-skin bag toward the offender, when the skin became a live serpent which rushed at Mr. Cass and ran him out of the crowd. The snake then returned to the medicine woman, who picked it up, when it appeared again as a dry skin bag."

Mitäwäpe

Menomini, *Midwest*

A class of shamans. These shamans are referred to as seers and are used to diagnose illness. The ill person approaches the *mitäwäpe*, offering him tobacco and asking to be diagnosed. The *mitäwäpe* consults his helping spirits that night and gives the patient his diagnosis the next day. The patient then takes the diagnosis to members of the Medicine Lodge Society (see *Midewiwin*) to request a healing. A smaller healing lodge is erected, and within a couple of days, an all-night healing ceremony is conducted on the patient by several shamans who are members of the society. The cure involves the shamans "shooting" the patient with their medicine bags. One shaman "takes his (otter-skin) medicine-bag, holds it before him as though it were a gun, blows on its head to prepare it by loading it with his breath, cries, starts at a trot for the candidate (patient) . . . shoots at the candidate and makes him quiver" [Skinner 1920: 154–155]. The term "candidate" is used here because once the patient has been healed, he then becomes eligible for membership into the society.

Mitäwin
Menomini, *Midwest*
See *Metewin.*

Mitchell, Tom
Paviotso, *Basin*
During the 1930s, Tom Mitchell was considered to be the most powerful shaman among his people. His power to heal came from the eagle, the weasel, a small unidentified bird living in the mountains, and another spirit that was not recognizable by informants at that time [Park 1938:18].

Mitigwakik
Ojibwa, *Canadian Eastern Woodlands*
Water drum used during the Medicine Lodge (*Midewiwin;* see entry) Ceremony; translates to "wooden vessel." It is made from a section of basswood or cedar, cut 16 to 20 inches in length and hollowed out in the center. A piece of pine is sealed in with pitch to form the bottom. A tanned piece of deerskin is held in place over the top by a removable hoop wrapped with cloth. Before it is played, the drum is partially filled with water through a hole in the side. The deerskin is struck with a curved beating stick.

This drum is treated as a living entity, and it is the central icon of the *Midewiwin*. Because it is imbued with supernatural power, it "functioned for the Ojibwa much the same as a medicine bundle" [Vennum 1982:148].

Miwachi
Zuni, *Southwest*
See *mile.*

Miwe
Zuni, *Southwest*
The plural form of *mile.*

Mizinkintika
Lenni Lenape, *Northeast*
The term used by the Minsi branch of the Lenni Lenape (also called Delaware) for the dances of their Mask Society. During the ceremonies, the dancers wear wooden masks, called *mizink* (or *mising* by the Unami branch), that contain copper or brass eyes, a crooked nose, hair, tufts of feathers, and jingling copper cones or deer hooves. When the dancer puts on such a mask, he receives the power of a powerful spirit called *Mizink-hâli'kun*. There are no recorded observations of these ceremonies, but it was reported "that they sometimes put down their rattles, heaped up the ashes from the two fires, then threw the ashes all over the house to prevent the people assembled from having disease. Should any sick person appear, he or she would be especially treated with ashes" [Harrington 1921:159–160]. Harrington obtained one *mizink* from a Canadian Lenape named Isaac Montour *(Kapyu'hum)* that had the decorative lines burnt into the wood instead of the normal painting or carving of such lines. Isaac told Harrington that the *mizink* had been used, at least in part, for healing but revealed no details of its use.

Modesto, Ruby
Cahuilla, *California Peninsula*
An eagle doctor born in 1913 who worked with several anthropologists during the late 1970s. Her guardian spirit was *Ahswit* (Eagle). "*Ahswit* protects me and shows me what to do. He came to me through Dreaming, but he is with me when I'm fully conscious now. He lives in my house" [Modesto and Mount 1980:53]. During her healing ceremonies, she would blow tobacco smoke

on the patient and brush him with an eagle feather as directed by her spirit. She reported that her power to heal came ultimately from *Umna'ah* (Creator), and that *Ahswit* acted as her intermediary. Her specialty was treating psychological illnesses, especially possession.

Moigú
Mohegan, *Northeast*
Shaman [Speck 1919:254].

Moli
Yuki, *California*
Singing doctor. These shamans, unlike the *lamshi-imi* (sucking doctors; see entry), use a rattle during their ceremonies. They are employed mainly to diagnose illness. In addition, the *moli* is caretaker and fire tender of the religious assembly house [Kroeber 1940:213].

Momai yomta
Miwok, *California*
See *yomta*.

Mo'o dedu
Southern Pomo, *California*
Sucking doctors. In cases of illness, these shamans are always called upon first to diagnose and investigate the illness [Loeb 1934a:101].

Mooney, James
Born in Richmond, Indiana, on 10 February 1861, James Mooney received no formal education but developed a keen interest in Native Americans as a youth. In 1885, John Wesley Powell, then the director of the Smithsonian's Bureau of American Ethnology, hired him. He began fieldwork with the Cherokee in 1887 and continued it for many years. He also established a long-term relationship with the Kiowa. Through his work at the bureau, he became one of the leading authorities on Native American culture, also working among the Arapaho, Cheyenne, Apache, Dakota, Plains Apache, Wichita, Comanche, and, to a lesser extent, among the Hopi, Paiute, Shoshoni, and Caddo. He published extensively throughout his career and was a specialist on the Ghost Dance and the use of peyote. In 1913 some members of Congress began to push for antipeyote use legis-

lation. Subsequently, several bills were introduced to prohibit the Native American use of peyote: Thompson Bill (S. 3526), 1915; Grady Bill (H. R. 10669), 1916; H. R. 4999, 1917; and the Hayden Bill (H. R. 2614), 1918. During this period James Mooney, along with Frances La Flesche and Truman Michelsen, led the defense of peyote, which resulted in protecting peyote use via its incorporation as a religion, The Native American Church (see entry), on 10 October, 1918 [Stewart 1987:217-224]. Mooney died in Washington, D.C., on 22 December 1921.

Mosona
Zuni, *Southwest*
Term for the chief of the curing society [Edmonson 1958:70].

M'teoulinak
Penobscot, *Canadian Eastern Woodlands*
See *medéoulino*.

Múdu
Micmac, *Canadian Eastern Woodlands*
The supernatural power inherent in activities of shamans and spirits. It is cognate to the Ojibwa *mide* (see entry).

Mugwa
Shoshoni, *Basin*
Life soul or body soul, the force that keeps one alive [Hultkrantz 1992:74].

Muskrat
Crow, *Plains*
A female shaman who gave Lowie [1922:340] an account of her doctoring around 1907–1916:

"I was fasting on a mountain, having heard that a man had slept there. I put down new bedding. While I lay there, I saw bald-headed hawks (?) but the eagle got ahead of them, jumped towards me, and shook one wing after the other, all in order to scare me. He came up to me and scared me. He shook his wing and one feather fell out. It was the Tobacco. I use Tobacco as one of my main medicines, as a liniment . . . I use chewing tobacco. I always have plenty on hand to doctor with. . . . I also doctor broken bones."

Mxeeom

Cheyenne, *Plains*

One of two terms for the Spirit Lodge Ceremony; it comes from *mxee*, meaning "manifestation from the spirit world," and *om*, meaning "lodge" [Schlesier 1987:59]. The other term for the Spirit Lodge Ceremony is *nisimàtozom*, where *nisimàtoz* means "bringing a spirit ally" [Schlesier 1987:59]. The Cheyenne have four primary uses for this lodge. One is to perform their version of the Shaking Tent Ceremony (see entry), in which the shaman calls forth his spirit helpers to answer questions. Typical of this ceremony, the "helping spirit, traveling with the speed of thought, entered at the top of the *mxeeom* and rushed down to free and revive his shaman associate. The rope (which bound the shaman) slackened. He came with the force of a whirlwind and caused the large lodge to vibrate violently. The whistle sounded, the rattle bounced among the lodge poles, and lightning flashes lit the dark....All arrived with a terrifying display of power. Animal voices approached from below ground and from the night sky" [Schlesier 1987: 60–61].

The three other types of spirit lodge rituals were for: (1) hunting medicines; (2) deaths; and (3) healing the sick. In former times, the *mxeeom* was also used for healing the sick.

Na lakofichi

Choctaw, *Southeast*

Also: *na lakoffichi* [Gardner 1973:250]. A curer [Edmonson 1958:69].

Naarhin

Haida, *Northwest Coast*

A special dancing blanket worn by shamans as part of their shamanic doctoring outfits. The blanket is usually wrapped around the shoulders and hangs down the back like a cape. It is made of dyed mountain goat wool woven on a warp of cedar strings. They are sometimes referred to as Chilkat blankets [Barbeau 1958:65].

Nabu'u

Northern Paiute, *Basin*

Also: *nabuqwi.* A doctoring or healing ceremony. Usually, a healing ceremony consists of the shaman, an assistant who interprets what is going on, the patient, family members of the patient, and a group of singers who strengthen the shaman's powers. Most healing ceremonies are conducted at night and held for four consecutive nights. During the ceremony, the interpreter calls upon the other participants to perform various ritual actions to help the shaman in his cure. For example, "a willow stick is planted in a can of dirt behind the patient's head and the shaman's feathers are attached to it. The shaman instructs the patient (via the interpreter) to concentrate on them as they are visible above him. It is said that if the patient is very sick the shaman can demonstrate his power (and no doubt also strengthen the confidence of the patient in him) by making one of the feathers stand straight up in the air. Then he may ask for this stick to be passed around the group (sitting in a circle around the walls of the patient's room) five times and then be returned to the can; or for the interpreter to roll up five cigarettes and pass them around five times and then return them to the same can or another container; or for the people to line up behind him and follow him in a circle around the fire" [Olofson 1979:18].

Sometimes, a mistake is made during the ceremony. When this happens, the *puha* (power; see entry) of the shaman suffers misuse, and it is the shaman who must pay for the negligent behavior or mistakes of others. Often the shaman falls unconscious to the ground when a mishap occurs. It is then the responsibility of the interpreter to sing the proper sacred songs to revive the shaman so that the ceremony can continue. At other times, the shaman may become sick after the ceremony.

During the ceremony, the shaman calls forth his helping spirits. "Sometimes the doctor's *sonuminu* (mind or thoughts) makes the *tumudainI* (spirit helper) come. A few songs before midnight he tells the interpreter to tell the people that in three or so songs the *tumudainI* will be there. He tells the interpreter to tell the sick person not to be scared of his *tumudainI* when he sees it, that he's bringing it so he can get well. He tells his *tumudainI* what he thinks and it comes. When the people are on the last song they know it is there. Only the sick person can see it. It comes at the foot of the bed, to watch and see how the doctor's doing. When the person is pretty bad off is the time to do this. The *tumudainI* gives the doctor more power and helps him" [Olofson 1979:17].

The shaman then doctors through the spirits, using various techniques such as blowing on the patient, rubbing or merely laying his hands on the patient, sucking on the afflicted areas of the patient's body, and drawing feathers or a rattle across the patient.

Quite often, the illness is the result of improper behavior on the part of the patient. Most healing ceremonies end with the shaman advising the patient how to behave if he wishes to prevent a recurrence.

Nachulna
Wailaki, *California*

One of three classes of Kato healers. These are the singing and dancing doctors who treat outside sickness or fright sickness, which comes to people who have been frightened by the sight of a spirit being. Their healing ceremonies take the form of spirit impersonation, in which one of them dresses in the fashion of the spirit that is to be called upon and then becomes possessed by this spirit. The *nachulna* also treat epidemics and severe illness. In rare cases spirit impersonation is replaced by spirit calling. The chief spirit called upon for curing is Nagaitco. Shamans, who obtain their power through dreams, refer to this spirit as *Ctacuñ*, which translates to "my father of all." Sometimes Nagaitco is not called in personally for

a cure; rather, an effigy of Nagaitco is used, but only in emergency cases.

The following is a brief account of a Nagaitco ceremony:

"Twelve men, called kulcut, went up into the mountains to look for Nagaitco. These men were all doctors, and wore black stripes across their foreheads. Four of these doctors continually kept singing Nagaitco songs, and dancing. . . . The other eight men devoted all their energy to looking for the god.

"Finally Nagaitco answered from far up in the mountains. Then he came down, surrounded by the twelve doctors. He seemed to be walking on air, and he kept revolving and flitting from place to place. Sometimes he turned around so quickly that the wind he created knocked one of his escorts down.

"Upon entering the dance house Nagaitco circled it in the proper manner and then approached the patient. He walked over the patient, straddling him, and going from head to foot four times. After this the god removed the stick from his head, and walked around the patient with this four times. Nagaitco talked in a secret language and made a queer noise, u u u u, in a thin high voice. Finally he retreated to the mountain with his escort of twelve men, who later came back singing. After Nagaitco had taken his departure, the sucking doctor entered the house, and sucked (on the patient). Then the patient was carried home.

"The next day, if the sick man was no better, he was again carried into the dance house, and the sucking doctor sang the Nagaitco song over him. Then he was returned home.

"If the patient refused to recover, after all this treatment, Nagaitco had again to be summoned from the hills. This time he picked up the sick man and danced with him.

"Four days after the final appearance of Nagaitco the patient's family gave a big feast. They then paid the sucking doctor as much as they could afford, there being no set price. They paid the doctor in charge of the case even if, in the meantime, the sick man had died" [Loeb 1934a: 35–36].

The other two classes of doctors among the Kato are the *etien* (see entry) and the *chgalyic* (see entry).

Nàe

Cheyenne, *Plains*

Also: *nàetan*. Plural: *nào*. Healers that cure without the use of personal spirit helpers [Schlesier 1987:14].

Nahneetis

Deleware, *Northeast*

See *Nanitis*.

Nahullo

Choctaw, *Southeast*

The generic term for spirits; translates to "something sacred or supernatural" [Swanton 1931: 199].

Naicdia

Keres, *Southwest*

The head of each of the Acoma Pueblo medicine societies. The term means "father." When a healing is needed, relatives of the patient make a formal request to this person to secure the healing efforts of the medicine society [White 1932:109]. See *Hictiani* for details.

Naitulgai

Wailaki, *California*

Dreamers or dream doctors. They cure by singing healing songs obtained through dreams. They are also called upon to prophesy the future, locate game, and conduct other such shamanic rituals. It is not unusual for a *keteu* (sucking doctor) to also be a *naitulgai*. The dreamers are always used for cases of soul loss, called fright sickness by the Wailaki. During the healing ritual, the dream doctor covers his body with ashes or charcoal before

going out to look for a lost soul. "In the meantime the soul had built a little fire and was sitting down beside it. The doctor saw the fire and he saw the soul, which resembled a miniature person. He plunged forward and caught the soul in his hands. This was evidently the ticklish part of the proceeding, for if the doctor missed the sick person was certain to die. After obtaining the soul, the doctor brought it home and put it over the heart of the patient. Then the doctor bathed the sick man and gave him nourishment, in order to feed the soul and make it aware that it was properly housed" [Loeb 1934a:83].

Some of the dream doctors have no guardian spirits. They merely sing healing songs that they learned in dreams.

Naiyu sumatc

Mojave, *Southwest*

See *kwathidhe*.

Nana ishtohoollo

Cherokee, Creek, Choctaw, *Southeast*

An individual's good helping spirit; translates to "people holy." Bad spirits are referred to as *nana ookproose*, which translates to "accursed people" [Adair in Jarvis 1820:91].

Nanandawi

Ojibwa, *Canadian Eastern Woodlands*

Healing ceremonies that cure by means of the shaman sucking a disease-causing object from the patient's body [Grim 1983:113].

Nanandawiiwe wanini

Ojibwa, *Canadian Eastern Woodlands*

Curer [Edmonson 1958:69].

Nanasuigaint

Shoshoni, *Basin*

Holy; marvelous. "Persons who have shown a faculty for the miraculous or who possess efficient guardian spirits are given the same designation" [Hultkrantz 1967a:14].

Nanitis
Lenni Lenape, *Northeast*
The Minsi term for Doll Being, who is the guardian spirit of health. Doll Beings are represented among the Lenni Lenape (also called Delaware) by wooden sticks about eight inches in length, upon which a head has been carved; the stick is then dressed in clothing. These dolls are used as charms for ensuring good health in a family. They are addressed as "grandmother" or "mother." The dolls are cared for via the Doll Dance, in which they are "fed" and given new clothing. The Doll Dance is held annually in the fall and requires an offering of a fat doe. These dolls are passed down from generation to generation within a family. When they are not in use, they are kept wrapped up in cloth or kept in a special box.

Nantadotash
Apache, *Southwest*
Also: *Nantaditask.* An old, blind medicine man interviewed in 1885 by John Bourke. He belonged to the Akañe or Willow branch. During the interview, Bourke, without the shaman's knowing it, drew a picture of his medicine hat. Later, upon finding out about the drawing, Nantadotash demanded $30 in damages, because his hat no longer worked. The hat was a truncated cone of soft, tanned buckskin with a lobulated tailpiece that fell down between the wearer's shoulders. The tailpiece was symbolic of Nantadotash's spirit helper, the centipede [Stone 1932:12]. The hat had symbols drawn on it in brownish yellow and dirty Prussian blue. It was decorated with downy feathers, black-tipped eagle plumes, pieces of abalone shell, bits of green malachite (turquoise), and a rattlesnake's rattle on the apex. Each of the symbols represented one of the powers to which he called for supernatural help. He named them for Bourke as follows: clouds; rain-

bow; hail; morning star; the God of Wind, with his lungs (to blow away disease); the black *kan* (spirit); and great stars or suns. He wore this hat during his shamanic rituals. It enabled him "to peer into the future, to tell who had stolen ponies from other people, to foresee the approach of an enemy, and to aid in the cure of the sick" [Bourke 1892:580].

In examining the old buckskin hat, Bourke reported: "My suggestion that the application of a little soap might wash away the clots of grease, soot, and earth adhering to the hat, and restore its pristine efficacy were received with the scorn due to the sneers of the scoffer" [Bourke 1892:503].

Nantena
Chipewyan, *Mackenzie-Yukon*
Helping spirits. Hearne wrote of the Chipewyan that they "are very superstitious with respect to the existence of several kinds of fairies, called by them Nant-e-na, whom they frequently say they see, and who are supposed by them to inhabit the different elements of earth, sea, and air, according to their several qualities. To one or other of those fairies they usually attribute any change in their circumstances, either for the better or worse" [Hearne in Jarvis 1820:91].

Narhnorh
Gitksan, *Northwest Coast*
Spirit [Barbeau 1958:42].

Nashie
Tiwa, *Southwest*
At Isleta Pueblo, prayer feathers or prayer sticks. There are many different types of prayer feathers and prayer sticks, many of which are known by specific names. For example, the *to'ai* consists of a joint of cane and two turkey feathers. Prayer sticks are commonly made of willow; they are painted, and feathers are attached with cotton. In former times, homegrown cotton was used. After the *nashie* has been used, it is either placed out of sight

under a bush or rock, or thrown into a spring or river [Parsons 1932:274–275].

Nassassukwi
Shoshoni, *Basin*

A short ritual action found among the Hekandika (Seed-eaters) branch of the Shoshoni, 20 miles east of Pocatello, Idaho. Literally, the term means "blow it away." It is used to get rid of aches and pains in the body. Hoebel observed it being used at a Sun Dance, where "all persons present joined in a deep inbreathing and patting of the joints and muscles of their bodies, following this with heavy exhalations" [Hoebel 1935:572]. These actions, in conjunction with prayer, brought about the desired healing.

Nätanhehi
Gros Ventre, *Plains*

Doctoring shamans [Cooper 1957:325]. Each shaman operates individually, as there is no professional society of shamans among the Gros Ventre. Both males and females can become doctoring shamans, and each has the power to cure only certain illnesses or to heal only in certain circumstances. Thus, they become specialists. "One, for instance, could cure facial paralysis; another, rattlesnake bites; another, venereal disease. Some got special power to foretell the sex of unborn children or to prevent or promote conception" [Cooper 1957:325]. These abilities are acquired through individual vision questing. When the power comes, many shamans keep it a secret—usually for around four years—before beginning their practice of it. Such deferments are required by the shaman's helping spirit, who announces when the recipient of power can begin practicing. A shaman who begins without such permission normally loses any doctoring abilities. When shamans do begin doctoring, they are sometimes limited by their helping spirits as to how many cases of severe illnesses they are allowed to cure. For example, "Goes Back, a medicine woman, was granted power to cure only one case and she used

it to cure Coming Daylight's husband Little Man; Al Chandler's adoptive father, also called Little Man (see entry), got power [from a coyote] to cure seven persons at the point of death, but used it in only three cases" [Cooper 1957:327]. (Cooper subsequently states on page 353 that Little Man's power was used four times instead of three.) There appear to be no limitations on curing minor ailments.

The granting of power by a helping spirit often comes with restrictive taboos. For example, a shaman might be forbidden, upon punishment of death, to eat certain foods, such as buffalo hearts. In the case of Little Man, mentioned above, he was not to allow anyone to pull his hair, which eventually caused his demise. "Actually, Little Man's death, as Al Chandler told it in detail, occurred shortly after a quarrel with his wife in the course of which she pulled his hair. Little Man quit fighting and sat quiet. Two or three days later he was down sick. White and Indian doctors were called in but none could do anything for him. Al Chandler went to stay with him but he did not want Al there. He wanted to die and did not want Al to talk him out of it. In a little while he was dead" [Cooper 1957:327].

If a shaman is not a strong man, an ideal man, he might slip and use his power to harm another individual. In such cases, the shaman pays dearly by the loss of one of his own children or grandchildren.

In addition to the curing powers received from guardian spirits, Gros Ventre shamans incorporate herbal mixtures into their healing ceremonies. There is always a ritual observed in gathering any plant, most of which are taken during the fall. In addition, "not everyone had the right to gather medicinal plants, at least not all kinds. Certain herbal curatives at least could be picked only by those who had been given power, through quest or dream or through transfer" [Cooper 1957:323].

To secure the services of the shaman, one brings him a filled sacred pipe and makes a formal pipe presentation. Accepting the pipe and smoking it is the shaman's confirmation that he will take the case. This formal offering is overlooked in the case of relatives who ask for a healing. In some cases, the shaman requires only that an offering of tobacco be made to him. When a sacred pipe is involved, the requester needs to know exactly how the pipe is to be handed to the shaman.

When conducting a healing ceremony, the shaman is most often accompanied by one or more assistants, usually relatives. The ceremony is private, with only the patient and members of his family being present, along with the shaman and his helpers. To this end, several guards are usually posted at the door of the healing ceremony to prevent anyone from entering. Because a healing ceremony can be ruined by the actions of a single insincere person, it is best to restrict participation to only those individuals who are genuinely concerned about the patient's recovery. Such restrictions are taken seriously. In one instance, "while a doctor was treating a patient, a band chief who was drinking heavily at the time and who had recently killed a relative of the doctor came into the lodge without leave and asked the master of the lodge for whiskey. The doctor packed up his medicines at once, went home, got his rifle, came back and shot the band chief dead on the spot" [Cooper 1957:331–332].

In some cases, the shaman begins his treatment by first taking the patient into a sweat lodge. In most cases, however, the first ritual act in the curing process is praying and smoking the sacred pipe. Often the shaman inquires whether he will be successful in the cure, that is, whether he has the necessary power to return the patient to health. Such inquiries are often accompanied by the display of some power feat on the part of the shaman. For example, in one case, "a doctor, when just about to start treatment, picked up a piece of wood carved in the shape of an arrowhead, and turned it into an iron arrowhead, and so went forward confidently to begin treatment" [Cooper 1957:332].

During the healing ritual, the shaman does not go into a trance or lose consciousness. Those present sing, rattle, and drum during the shaman's treatment of the patient. The shaman quietly drums as he prays, and usually drums louder during the singing of his medicine songs. Eventually he hands his drum off to another person while he doctors. If the shaman uses a rattle in doctoring his patient, it is usually rotated in circles counterclockwise.

During the treatment, the shaman searches out the cause of the ailment. Once located, it is removed by sucking on the patient's body. In difficult cases, the shaman might use a pipe stem to suck the object from the patient's body. The object is then disposed of in some way—by the shaman swallowing it, by burning it, or by some other means.

The following is an account of a treatment given by a shaman identified only as "an old medicine man who was a grandfather to Crow Bull." The treatment was for a woman named Coming Daylight, who was having difficulty nursing her infant daughter. The ceremony took place sometime prior to 1940:

"After he smoked (a sacred pipe) he started to get ready to doctor. He took off all his clothes. He was just stark naked. He went and felt the little infant (girl). . . . So he boiled the medicine herbs in water and let them boil on the coals. He came to me and I was just scared of him, the way he looked. He felt my breasts all over. They were hard and he gave them a good going over, squeezing them and massaging them. Then he told me to take down my dress so he could see my breasts. Next he put the pail of medicine beside me and told me to drink a little of the medicine.

"Then he told me to sit where my husband had been sitting, next to himself. I did not want to sit next to him, but he fixed himself up and knelt down a certain way and told me to kneel the same way and to do whatever he asked me to do. He got ready to doctor me and made me kneel, and then he started to sing a song. He finished the song and then told me, 'Watch close,' and told my husband too, 'Watch close.' Then he prayed to the one (helping spirit) from whom he had gotten his doctoring power, and then said: 'I never used this way of doctoring before. This is the first time. People are always afraid of me but you (addressing my husband) must watch close and see all that I do.'

A peyote specialist, seated third from right (center), accompanies his song with rasping sticks during the peyote ceremony, as the dark blanketed dancer shakes two deer-hoof rattles. This nineteenth-century outdoor ceremony is unusual in that most peyote ceremonies are conducted in a tepee or the room of a house.

After that he sang, and told me: 'Spit twice on each of your hands,' and he did the same to each of his own hands. He put his hands to the ground, palms down, then put his palms to his own breasts and shook them up and down. He repeated this action three times, making four times in all. After the fourth time, his own breasts were big like a woman's.

"Then just that quick,—and you won't believe it but it is true,—although he was a man and it seemed funny to me then, his own breasts started spurting milk which just poured down, and mine did, too, though he did not lay a hand on me (at this juncture). He let this go on for a long time, and then told me: 'You want to watch to see all the bad milk is gone. Right now it is pure flour water and when all that bad stuff is gone it is going to be a bluish color.' And sure enough I then watched it and it began to get a bluish color and kept on gradually until it got completely good. Finally the nipples were just dripping a little with blue milk, and he told me: 'Rinse your breasts from underneath with your hands.' His breasts now became flat and normal, and I was cured.

"After he got through doctoring me, he doctored my baby, every joint of the little girl. He then told me: 'The girl was already full of that stuff (bad milk), but I have drawn it all out.' After that I had all the rest of my children and my milk was never bad. I always nursed my own children" [Coming Daylight in Cooper 1957:338–339].

Native American Church

The Native American peyote church, whose members ingest the peyote cactus, *Lophophora williamsii*, during their ceremonies, known simply as peyote meetings. Peyote (a name derived from the Nahuatl word *peyotl*) is a common, small, gray-green, spineless, napiform cactus, rarely exceeding 15 centimeters (about 6 inches) in length and 5 or 6 centimeters (about 2 inches) in diameter at the top. The narcotic effect of the plant comes

Peyote, *Lophophora williamsii,* a small gray-green cactus is used as a sacred healing plant by Native American Church members. Peyote (called mescal buttons) is consumed dried, powdered and mixed into water, and eaten fresh. Medicinal uses include treatment for snakebites, fractures, paralysis, and rheumatism.

from the four to eight alkaloids that may be present in varying amounts and proportions, with mescaline being the most well known. Peyote is not a habit-forming narcotic, and its intoxication is unique in that consciousness is not lost during its use. Peyote is used as a divine healer and amulet. During a peyote meeting, 4 to 30 mescal buttons (dried peyote) are eaten (some reports give the number as high as 90 per individual). The term mescal button often leads to peyote being confused with the mescal bean (*Agave* spp.),

which is also used by Native Americans in preparing an alcoholic brandy [Schultes 1938:703].

Although the entity is called a church, peyote ceremonies are most often conducted in a tepee or the room of a house. The peyote ceremony is currently the most widespread pan–Native American ritual, but it did not become so until after the collapse of the Ghost Dance and Sun Dance ceremonies at the end of the nineteenth century. Peyote use originated in Mexico and was first noted by Father Bernardino de Sahagun, a Franciscan, in 1560. Its use in the United States began among the cultures living along the Mexican boarder where peyote grows, especially among the Carrizo, Lipan Apache, Mescalaro Apache, Tonkawa, Karaukawa, and Caddo. The Caddo "had used peyote over a long period of time, at least since the early eighteenth century" [Stewart 1987:47]. However, its subsequent spread to Oklahoma and its use there set the standards for the American peyote ceremonies since the late nineteenth century. Slotkin [1958:519], an anthropologist who was a member and officer of the Native American Church, reports that its use among the Kiowa and Comanche in Oklahoma probably originated about 1885. Peyote is not found in the United States except for a small area in southern Texas. Although not designed for healing, the ceremony is often used to that end; patients are brought in to be prayed over by the participants.

Currently, there are two major divisions known as Half Moon and Cross Fire, although no such distinction is made in the church's charter. Both sects incorporate Christian teaching and elements into their ceremonies. The Cross Fire sect uses the Bible, and sermons are preached and texts are read akin to Protestant services. The Half Moon sect does not use the Bible. Each sect is best recognized by the altars they construct. The Half Moon sect has a packed earth, crescent-shaped altar on the floor, whereas the Cross Fire sect builds the same altar but digs a crossed ditch across the crescent and fills it with live coals.

There are four ceremonial leaders—the Road Chief, Fire Chief, Drum Chief, and Cedar Chief. The Road Chief acts as ceremonial and prayer leader. The Fire Chief keeps a fire going within the crescent-shaped altar during the entire ceremony and is assisted by the Cedar Chief, who sprinkles cedar for purification on the fire. The Drum Chief starts the distinctive drumming and singing that is used in this ceremony. The ceremony usually begins at dark and continues throughout the night until dawn. The peyote is taken in a powder form, mixed with water and drunk, or eaten directly, if it is fresh. The participants may ingest as much as they want and may call for more peyote at any point in the ceremony.

The participants bring with them feather prayer fans and rattles to be used during the ceremony. Their drums are most often steel, round-bottom kettles about 8 inches in diameter. They are partially filled with water, and then a skin is stretched tightly over the top. The drums are beaten with wrapped sticks; by tilting the drum, one can vary the pitch, which is often done during the course of a song.

The medicinal properties of peyote seem to be quite limited, and most healing done in peyote meetings must be attributed to other factors. It has been used to treat fevers, rheumatism, and paralysis and as a poultice for fractures, open wounds, toothaches, and snakebites. It has also been used for nervousness and insanity. Despite its limited efficacy, the users of peyote often speak of it as a panacea for many ailments. For example, Schultes [1938:706] found that among the Oklahoma peyotists "there is hardly a disease which is not believed to be curable with peyote. Some of the ills listed as responding to peyote were tuberculosis, pneumonia, scarlet fever, intestinal ills, diabetes, rheumatic pains, colds, grippe, fevers, and venereal diseases."

Slotkin [1958:520–521] reports:

"For sick people Peyote is used in various ways. In a mild illness Peyote is taken as a home remedy. Thus when a man has a cold, he drinks hot Peyote tea and goes to bed. In more serious illnesses Peyote is taken during the Peyote rite. Such an illness is due not only to lack of sufficient power, but also to a foreign object within the body. Therefore a seriously sick person who takes Peyote usually vomits, thus expelling the foreign object which is the precipitating cause of the illness; then more Peyote is taken in order to obtain the amount of

power needed for health. In cases of severe illness, the rite itself is held for the purpose of healing the patient; it is often referred to as a doctoring meeting. In addition to having the sick person take Peyote, as in less desperate cases, everyone else present prays to God to give the patient extra power so he or she will recover."

Spindler [1955:87] reports that, for the Menomini:

"The curative function of Peyote is probably more important (than visions) to the participant, and visions are frequently simply a part of such curing. To the members, 'curing' includes not only relief from or elimination of bodily ills, but therapy for despondency and anxiety, a means of absolution of sins, and a process of salvation. If a 'doctor' is present, the treatment is performed with ritual that is sometimes transparently native in origin but frequently involves surgical notes reminiscent of the operating table. More often, at least with the Menomini, the curing is done simply through the holy power of Peyote and the endeavors of the members to influence the supernatural to aid. . . . Anything from a common cold to arthritis may be benefited by the medicine thus consumed. Many members keep a supply of (peyote) buttons on hand for emergencies and some use it quite casually, like an aspirin."

It was through the efficacy of such cures that peyote use rapidly spread from tribe to tribe around the turn of the twentieth century. Unlike shamanic ceremonies, peyote meetings are not used to call in healing spirits per se.

Natoi
Tiwa, *Southwest*
At Isleta Pueblo, any ceremony of the various medicine societies involved in healing. In many cases, a special root is used, in which case the general term for the ceremony is *lifietoynin* (see entry).

Natugwä
Fox, *Midwest*
Translates to "have a vision." The Fox language differentiates between visions of animate and inanimate objects. A vision of an animate object is

natugwas, and a vision of an inanimate object is *natugw* [Michelson 1930:112].

Natutshikan
Naskapi, *Canadian Eastern Woodlands*
A special charm associated with healing; translates to "necklace." Held in great secrecy to protect their power, the *natutshikans* were not detected by ethnographers until the 1960s. Almost all illness is thought to be caused by supernatural agents, and the *natutshikan* is worn in secrecy around one's neck to "catch" any disease that comes one's way.

"If the shaman consents to treat a patient, his healing vision is depicted by a woman in utter secrecy on a Natutshikan—a necklace. This is given to the patient, who is required to wear it under his clothing for the rest of his life. . . . Five types of Natutshikans are recognized among the Montagnais-Naskapi: two for men, one for women, one for children on which floral symbols are represented in geometrical forms (more powerful symbols being considered harmful for children), and one which can be used by both sexes and all ages. This last is plaited out of strips of skin" [Webber in Brodzky et al. 1977:118].

The *natutshikan* is never made by its user; it is always made under the direction of a shaman. It contains beaded designs and images of the shaman's helping spirits. Wearing it ensures that the shaman's helping spirits are always at hand to help the patient.

Naualak
Kwakiutl, *Northwest Coast*
Term for the widespread concept of *orenda* (see entry), the existence of a magical power that permeates the universe. This supernatural power is inherent in all objects of nature and in spirits. Boas [1897:396] gives the term *naualaku* for "supernatural" and states that the term is used to describe the condition of a person who has received supernatural powers from a spirit helper. In so doing, the person assumes the quality of this spirit.

Navochiwa
Hopi, *Southwest*
A commonly performed cleansing or purification ritual. An account of such a ceremony performed at the end of an Oraibi Snake-Antelope Ceremony is as follows:

"All participants stand around the kiva fireplace in a half-circle, first taking off their moccasins. The chief takes a long buzzard feather in his left hand, a pinch of ashes in his right hand, and all the others some ashes in their right hand. All then hum the *nawuhchi tawi* or discharming song, waving their hands slightly up and down to the time of the singing. Between their left thumb and forefinger the men hold a pinch of ashes, which they have taken from their right hand. This they circle from right to left four times at a certain point of the song and then throw it toward the hatchway, the chief doing the same with the feather and wiping the ashes from the feather toward the hatchway. He sprinkles another pinch of ashes on the feather, the others take a new pinch from the right hand, and the performance is repeated five times, corresponding to the number of verses in the song. After the last stanza all beat off the ashes from their hands and then rub their bodies and limbs" [Parsons 1939:458–459].

Navuzieip
Shoshoni, *Basin*
Dream; also free soul (see entry). Contemporary Shoshoni shamans usually receive their powers through dreams. When the free soul leaves the body, it is identified with dreams [Hultkrantz 1992:86].

Nawalak
Kwakiutl, *Northwest Coast*
Boas originally translated this word as "holy" and then later as "supernatural power." In spoken discourse, *nawalaku* or *nawalak q* translates to "supernatural one" and is used in hailing a spirit [Boas 1921:736–737]. More recently, Goldman [1975:104] defined it as "the power associated with the unusual forms of life." The term can be considered the equivalent of the Iroquoian *orenda* (see entry). To obtain *nawalak*, a shaman simulates or impersonates the actions of the supernatural being from which the *nawalak* is to be obtained. The sky is believed to be the original source of *nawalak* [Goldman 1975:104], but the source of a river is

also a major source of *nawalak*, and shamans commonly go upstream for their quests. Such acquisition also requires that the shaman be in a state of ritual purity, that is, in the particular state of being necessary for receiving such power, which is called *paxa* (see *paxala*). Once a shaman becomes *nawalak*, he possesses the qualities of his supernatural donor. The specific forms taken by *nawalak* are referred to in general as *tlogwe*. For example, one *tlogwe* or form of *nawalak* is the supernatural power *helika*, which is the power used by shamans to cure [Goldman 1975:180].

During ceremonies, the greatest concentration of *nawalak* powers resides in the rings of red cedar bark worn on the head and around the neck, wrists, and ankles. The remainder of the *nawalak* powers is in whistles and in face and forehead masks [Goldman 1975:114].

In general, women have more *nawalak* than men. The principal source of *nawalak* is from animal spirits. Each animal gives a *tlogwe* that is inherent in the nature of the species—fierceness from grizzly bears, industriousness from beavers, and so forth. Red cedar is also considered to be a great source of *nawalak*.

N'dilni'h
Navajo, *Southwest*
A method of divination; it means "hand-trembling."

Ne'moak
Menomini, *Midwest*
A class of shamans referred to as the dreamers. The word *ne'moak* literally means "the dance" and comes from a special dance, the *ni mihe twan* (Dream Dance), that the Menomini adopted from the Potawatomi living in Kansas in the autumn of 1880. (Spindler [1970:198] reports that according to oral tradition, the ceremony was brought to them by a Sioux woman.) They perform this dance six times a year in a specially constructed round enclosure. Although the dreamers do not claim to have healing powers, they believe that the dance ground is sacred during the ceremony, and they bring sick people into the structure to pray over them. The most sacred object of this dance is the drum, the *le we hekan*, into which all the good spirits put some of their power. One can

offer tobacco to this drum and get help from it. Also, misfortune can come from mistreatment of the drum, as illustrated in the following account by Slotkin [1957:36]:

"Some way, this old lady got mad, and took an axe, a sharp axe, and hit the Drum. She was going to bust that Drum entirely. (She) hit that Drum once; couldn't break it. And hit that Drum again twice; couldn't do nothing. So she hits that Drum again third time; no. But the fourth time, then that axe went through.

"Q. What does that show?

"That shows that there's something in the drum, pretty strong. When she bust that Drum (on) purpose—that old lady had a brother—and she lost this brother right away, because she done this wrong."

Netdim maidu
Maidu, *California*
See *oye*.

Newekwe
Zuni, *Southwest*
The Galaxy Fraternity, whose members constitute a medicine society of clowns that specialize in public burlesques of intrusive foreigners and in private shamanic journeys on the Milky Way. The term translates to "gluttons" [Cushing 1974:620]. When they appear in public, they are the most ridiculous of the Zuni clowns, but when they gather for a healing ceremony, "they are the medicine-men *par excellence* of the tribe, whose special province is the cure of all diseases of the stomach—the elimination of poisons from the systems of the victims of sorcery or imprudence" [Cushing 1974:620]. Membership comes when a person with a serious stomach ailment seeks help from the *Newekwe*. After recovery, initiation into the society is necessary for a permanent cure.

Among the shamanic powers gained through membership are the ability to eat any kind or amount of food and garbage (including human excrement) and the ability to engage in shocking sexual displays without feeling shame. These actions are aided by members' ingesting a sacramental medicine, the ingredients of which are unknown but quite possibly include *Datura inoxia*, a variety of Jimson weed. Cushing [1974:621] reports:

"I have seen one of them gather about him his melons, green and ripe, raw peppers, bits of stick and refuse, unmentionable water (urine), live puppies—or dead, no matter—peaches, stones and all, in fact everything soft enough or small enough to be forced down his gullet, including wood-ashes and pebbles, and, with the greatest apparent gusto, consume them all at a single sitting."

As such, they are considered to be the wisest and most fearless people in the entire pueblo.

The founder and patron deity of the *Newekwe* is Payatamu or Paiatuma, the God of Dew, who is the son of the Sun Father. The distinctive costume worn by the *Newekwe* consists of a feathered wooden baton (or jester's bauble), sloppy street clothes, a black overcoat, and a tight-fitting cap painted white, with bunches of corn-husk strips fastened on either side and on top. Wide, alternating, horizontal stripes of black and white are painted on the skin from head to toe.

Nexnox
Tsimshian, *Northwest Coast*
Supernatural beings or spirit helpers of the shaman [Boas 1916:562].

Ngak saga nii
Cayuga, *Northeast*
The Chipmunk healing ceremony; literally, "rubbing the bowl." Anyone may participate in the ritual of this healing ritual. See *eyondwanshgwut* for details.

Niagwai Oäno
Seneca, *Northeast*
The Bear Society, one of several Seneca medicine societies. The ritual of this society consists of 20 songs, accompanied by a water drum and horn rattles, and a dance. The leader of the society is a woman. The healing ceremony is used particularly for fevers and rheumatism, but other illnesses are also treated. Treatment usually consists of blowing on the patient [Parker 1909:176–177].

Nibikiwinini
Otchipwe, *Canadian Eastern Woodlands*
Sucking shaman; translates to "sucking man" [Cooper 1936:8]. These shamans get their curing power through guardian spirits obtained during vision quests. When sucking on a patient, they use hollow bones that are placed against the afflicted area of the body. "The sucking bones are put in a cup of water to clean them. The curer may swallow and disgorge them" [Cooper 1936:8]. Through the sucking procedure, the object that is the cause of the disease is removed and disposed of by the shaman. "In one cure, a child had swallowed a sturgeon bone. The curer swallowed the sucking bones, and through his powers brought the sturgeon bone out direct through the child's breast. In the other case, the *nibikiwinini* cured a child who had swallowed green wild rice, by sucking it out right through the child's skin" [Cooper 1936:9].

Nictut
Montagnais, *Canadian Eastern Woodlands*
A Naskapi shaman's helping spirits.

Níka qùwe
Quapaw, *Plains*
Shaman; translates to "mysterious man" [Dorsey 1894:393].

Nika wakandagi
Kansa, Ponca, Omaha, *Plains*
Shaman; translates to "mysterious man" [Dorsey 1894:367]. The term applies to healing as well as other types of shamans.

Nikahnegaah
Seneca, *Northeast*
A powerful powdered plant medicine known as the Great Bird–medicine [Hewitt 1918:491]; translates to "the small dose." In 1884, only about 20

men on the Cattaraugus Reservation possessed a small portion of it. According to Hewitt [1918: 491–492]:

"When a person who was ill desired to try this medicine, he or some friend was required to give a handful of native tobacco and some other small present to the person who had the medicine. The hochinagen (shaman) could do what he please with the presents. The hochinagen would cast into the fire a piece of the tobacco, at the same time saying to the medicine, which he then held in his hand, 'Take a smell of this tobacco, for I am about to make use of you.' Then he would visit the sick man, and taking a small vessel he would go to a running stream, and after making an offering of tobacco to it in the name of the patient, he would dip up the water with the current, not against it. He took what water he could dip up in this manner.

"Only a minute portion of this medicine, mixed with water, was needed. . . . If all the powder remained on the surface of the water instead of mixing with it, the indication was that the patient must die; but if the powder dissolved completely in the water, this was taken as a sign that the patient would live. When the powder would not mix with the water the latter became of the consistency of sirup; but if it mixed, the water remained clear. When the medicine would not dissolve in the water the hochinagen knew that there was no help for the patient and would not give the medicine to him; but in case the powder dissolved in the water, the solution was given to the sick man to drink.

"If the sick man was not very ill, this one dose would cure him; but if he was very ill other hochinagen who have this same kind of medicine must come to assist in the cure. They must cook a kettle of white beans for themselves and the singers who come to sing that night; they would also give strength to the medicine by the burning of tobacco as directed by the birds.

"When this Nikahnegaah was taken, the smell of burning or broiling meat had a bad effect on its virtues. During her catamenial periods a woman was not permitted to look at a person who had taken this medicine; if she did so he would surely die. Hence it was a standing rule that a patient who had taken this medicine should not be seen by any one for four days except the person who was caring for him.

"If another man came into the patient's presence after having stopped to see a corpse on the way, and looked at the patient, the sick person would immediately grow worse and would die shortly thereafter. For this reason it was customary to hang a skin or a blanket so that the patient should not by any chance see such a person.

"It (the medicine) is so powerful in orenda, or magic potency, that when it was given to the sick by the hochinagen the patient was forbidden to eat anything that was colored; he could eat, however, pure white beans and pure white cob corn. If anything black or in any manner colored was eaten, the taboo was broken, and the man or woman would die, as the medicine's virtue was thus destroyed.

"If the patient recovered his health he must celebrate the event by preparing a feast, the chief dish of which must be a great kettle of hulled corn seasoned with meat or venison cut into small pieces.

"The hochinagen who gave him the medicine must come to sing and dance in honor of the medicine through whose aid they were enabled to cure the patient. . . . Only hochinagen may sing at this feast."

Nilkin
Carrier, *Mackenzie-Yukon*
See *diyinne*.

Nimahenan
Cheyenne, *Plains*
Sacred arrows. The keeper of the sacred arrows is always the male shaman holding the highest position among the *maheonhetaneo* (see *maheonhetan*) [Schlesier 1987:16].

Niniba
Osage, *Plains*
Sacred pipe (see entry). Such pipes are used during healing ceremonies.

Nipikakaka
Kutenai, *Plateau*
Shaman; it comes from nipika (also *nupika*), meaning "spirit." Franz Boas visited the Kutenai in 1888 and observed that a variation of the Shaking Tent Ceremony (see entry) was being performed by their shamans.

Nisimàtozom
Cheyenne, *Plains*
See *mxeeom*.

Nisimon
Cheyenne, *Plains*
A shaman's guardian spirit or personal spirit helper. The general term for powerful spirits is *maiyun* (see entry). The *nisimon* represent "the *hematasooma* [free soul] of a human or an animal" [Schlesier 1987:14].

Noho'o
Yokuts, *California*
Bear shaman [Edmonson 1958:70].

Nomyoh
Wintun, *California*
Powerful spirits from which the shaman acquires healing powers. Sometimes referred to simply as *yoh* (of the west). For example, a great doctor is called *yoh*-old-man [Shepherd 1992:194].

Nonhonzhinga
Osage, *Plains*
Seers, who were considered to be holy men [La Flesche 1921:47]. The term translates to "little old men." At some point, it became the name of one of the Osage societies.

Nooks
Tsimshian, *Northwest Coast*
A Kispiox shaman whose activities were recorded in 1952 by William Beynon from an account given by Robert Wilson, a Gitksan of Kispayaks, on the Upper Skeen River. Nooks's spirit helper was *Ksemhasipk*, Woman of Sickness (also referred to as Medicine-Woman of Sickness).

Nooks was involved in fighting an epidemic of influenza that ravished the community in 1918. He had his nephew, who was a carver for a secret society, carve the effigy of a female medicine woman that was about 3 feet long. Nooks took this carving to a meeting of shamans and announced, "I am in with all my helpers. They have helped me a little, but I must climb by myself into the sky to find out what I can do (about the epidemic)." He then went to a corner of the house, lay down, and went into a trancelike sleep. The others covered him with bearskins and left him there for several days. He could be heard breathing heavily under the skins. When the shamans returned to the corner and lifted the skin, Nooks was not there; in his place was the effigy carving. They put the robes back over the carving, and once again they could hear Nooks's heavy breathing. The next day they uncovered the wooden effigy again and began singing power songs. As they were doing this, the door opened and Nooks walked into the room. Nooks told the assembled shamans about his journey: "When I was taken into the skies, I beheld the sickness canoe in which were several spirits, each with a harpoon. As they saw a person walking about, they threw their harpoon at the victim, who at once became ill. So now the Woman of Sickness shall be my aide. The people will drink oolachen oil and devil's club juice and burn hoohlens (hellebore roots) to disinfect the houses."

It was reported that the assembled shamans went back to their respective villages and used the song of Woman of Sickness and the different medicines to cure patients [Barbeau 1958:75]. This is a clear case of one shaman passing power on to other shamans.

Nossii
Northern Paiute, *Basin*
The special power dream in which a shaman acquires a helping spirit that enables him to cure. Such dreams are not always clear to the recipient. When there is ambiguity, the person places an ea-

gle feather in his pillowcase for five consecutive days. If another such dream comes to him, he then believes that he has received a *nossii*.

Noth
Luiseño, *California Peninsula*
Small, sacred effigy stone heads, with certain shapes and engravings, imbued with power and used by shamans. The term is also used to designate the head of a religious organization [White 1976:364, 368].

Noxkwasagi
Seneca, *Northeast*
A drink made from dried, ground sunflower seeds; translates to "Falseface medicine-water" [Skinner 1925a:193]. In former times, it was carried by the False-Face "performers from house to house and administered to the patients about to be doctored" [Skinner 1925b:193].

Ntiómel
Micmac, *Canadian Eastern Woodlands*
Spiritual agents; the contents of a shaman's medicine bag used in his practice. Father Chretien Le Clercq, an early French, Jesuit missionary saw the contents of one such bag, which contained a stone the size of a nut, a bark figure in the shape of a wolverine decorated with black and white beadwork, a little 1-foot bow, and a 1-foot stick decorated with red and white porcupine quills that had two dozen dewclaws of moose attached to the end (most likely a rattle). Most common are power objects made from animal bones, which can be acquired in two ways. One way is for a person to take the bones from the desired animal and throw them into a stream. The bones that travel upstream have sufficient power to aid the shaman in his activities. The other way is for the likeness of the selected animal to be carved into the bone. The making and using of bone figures by shamans has not been reported for any other Algonquin people [Johnson 1943:69]. The shaman sends forth his *ntiómel* to do his bidding. From such descriptions, one can assume that these objects

are representations of the shaman's helping spirits.

Nukatem
Cahuilla, *California Peninsula*
Shaman's helping spirit [Bean and Saubel 1972: 19]. Spirit helpers are obtained by their shamans, called *pul* (see entry), during dreams.

Numamugu'a
Paviotso, *Basin*
The free soul, which leaves the body during a shaman's flight. Among the Paviotso, the term translates to "mind." Thus, when illness is diagnosed as soul loss, the patient is said to have "lost his mind" [Park 1938:39–40].

Nunnun letim
Huchnom, *California*
See *lamcem*.

Nutsi pilewet
Penobscot, *Canadian Eastern Woodlands*
Healers who use herbs rather than shamanistic techniques; translates to "one who cures." The last such healer, named Sockalexis, died around the turn of the twentieth century. Little is known of the activities of these individuals, except that in addition to herbs, they used fetishes, called *madaodo*, that strengthened both the healer and his herbs [Speck 1919:260].

Nyagwékya
Cayuga, *Northeast*
The Bear Society healing ceremony, which is performed only by members of the society. See *eyond-wanshgwut* for details.

Nyavedhi sumach
Mojave, *Southwest*
Also: *Nyevedhi sumatc* [Stewart 1974:5]. A particular type of healer called the ghost doctor; the literal translation is "dream of the old dead people

in the family." He treats people who are ill because of dreams of or encounters with old dead people. Such dreams make people crazy and cause them to cry—this is often called ghost sickness. People afflicted with ghost sickness are afraid of the dark, experience frequent nightmares, cry for long periods of time, and have trouble sleeping.

"If you see a ghost out somewhere, it don't kill you, but it knocks you down, and you'll be bleeding all over. You won't get up at all; you'll be paralyzed there until morning. But the 'devil man,' the ghost doctor, knows what happened. There use to be a lot of them around. He doctors him; he sings and bathes him with cold water" [Stewart 1974:6].

Shamans who have the power to treat this illness wear feathers in their hair and paint themselves with a little red paint. During the healing ceremony, conducted at night, they use owl feathers in the doctoring [Stewart 1970:19]. These specialists also treat illnesses caused by breaking funeral taboos. For more details on Mojave shamanism, see *kwathidhe*.

Nynymbi
Shoshoni, *Basin*
Evil dwarf spirits that carry bows and arrows. "They shoot arrows into the lone traveler so that the latter falls from his or her horse with a hemorrhage in the lungs. This is a supernatural explanation for the many cases of tuberculosis among the Shoshoni" [Hultkrantz 1987:48].

Object intrusion

One of the major causes of human illness from the Native American shaman's point of view. It is a concept found among all North American cultures, with the exception of certain Eskimo tribes, who believe that soul loss is the major source of illness [Ackerknecht 1942]. A harmful object is magically shot usually by a sorcerer into the body of the victim, causing illness. It is the task of the shaman to locate this object and remove it. These mystical objects can take any form; indeed, they take an array of forms that differ from shaman to shaman—even within the same tribe. Common items are stones, shells, and insects, but what is sucked from the patient's body may be as amorphous as black slime or blood. Thus, the forms taken by these items reveal nothing about the core nature of shamanism.

O'Connor, Pedro

Miwok, *California*

Known as "Petelo," O'Connor was one of the most famous Northern Miwok shamans between 1910 and his death in 1942. He was well known throughout the Northern, Central, and Southern Miwok areas. He cured through the use of singing, sucking, herbs, and prayers but was also suspected of being a poison doctor (sorcerer). He had a cocoon tied to a stick that hung on the rear wall of his house. When he was going to be called upon to doctor, this cocoon began to rattle of its own accord. "O'Connor is remembered as curing ailments that ranged from eating too much fruit, to bad joints, to life-threatening illnesses. He was known to have great powers" [Bates 1992:104].

Odas

Lenni Lenape, *Northeast*

The Unami (branch of the Lenni Lenape, also called Delaware) term for Doll Being. For details, see *nanitis*.

Odenigûn

Ojibwa, *Canadian Eastern Woodlands*

Deemed by Densmore [1910:96] to be "one of the most powerful medicine-men on the White Earth reservation" at the turn of the twentieth century, Odenigûn was particularly adept in knowing the medicine songs associated with rare medicines. Such songs are sung only by persons who have purchased the right to sing them from older shamans. When singing these songs, he used birch-bark scrolls on which mnemonics of the songs had been recorded.

One of his songs, entitled "Song of the Good Medicine," came from an old *mide* (*Midewiwin* shaman). The treatment, used for a disagreeable personality, was as follows:

"The old Mide took a feather, cut the quill, and put the threads (from the clothing of the patient) inside the quill with a little medicine. Then he fastened the quill together in such a way that the cut was not visible. The old Mide also gave the younger man (who had requested the healing) a feather which looked exactly like the one with the medicine in it. On his return the younger man gave his friend the feather containing the medicine and his friend placed the feather in his hair, supposing it to be an ornament. Both men wore the feathers in their hair. After a time the disposition of the elder man began to change. He grew kind and amiable toward everyone until at last he was entirely cured of all his disagreeable qualities. This was the work of the good medicine and the singing of the old Mide" [Densmore 1910: 100–101].

Odokanigan

Chippewa, *Canadian Eastern Woodlands*
The sucking instrument used by shamans during healing ceremonies to suck out or blow out the disease-causing object in the patient's body. The leg bones of geese are preferred, due to their length [Hilger 1951:88]. During the ceremony, the shaman swallows the bone and then ejects it. The following is a typical account of a woman treated for a toothache:

"He (the shaman) then covered her face with a clean cloth, sat down near her, and began to beat his drum and to sing. Then he swallowed three bones. Soon I heard a noise like a crane, and I looked out across the lake to see the bird. After a little while I heard the same sound, and I was puzzled again; but an old woman who was in the room pointed at the medicine man to let me know that it was he who was making the noise. And then I heard a noise for the third time and here he was, coughing up the other bone. He had asked for a clean saucer containing some water and in it he now had three small worms (the objects causing the toothache). [His wife added, 'Yes, that's true, and each worm was black at both ends, and about so big'—indicating their size by pressing the tip of her small finger between her two thumbnails]" [Hilger 1951:89].

Sometimes shamans would doctor without swallowing these bones, as indicated in the following blowing treatment that took place around 1913:

"During the night we heard sleigh bells; soon an Indian walked into the house. It was an old lady. She had come a long way. She told the old man that her son hadn't slept for 3 days and 3 nights; that he had been struck by a tree he was felling, and that splinters had entered his ear. The American doctor who lived right near them had been unable to remove them, and would the old man please do something for the boy. The son was brought in. The old man addressed the splinters in a speech ordering them to leave the young man's ear as Jonah had left the belly of the whale. While he beat the drum, he ordered his old woman to bring him a bundle. He carefully unwrapped this and from it took several hollow bones through which he blew into the young man's ear several times. He then asked for a dish, and presented the mother with the splinters. After this the boy fell sound asleep" [Hilger 1951:89].

Ogiwe Oäno

Seneca, *Northeast*
Chanters for the Dead Society, one of several Seneca medicine societies. The purpose of the society is to ward off possible illness caused by dreaming of the earthbound spirit of some former member, relative, or friend. During the ceremony, a shaman determines the identity of this spirit, and the participants perform a dance that dispels its influence. The head of this society is a woman [Parker 1909:178].

Ohgiwe

Onondaga, *Northeast*
The semiannual Feast of the Dead or Death Feast Ceremony. The ceremony has several objectives, one of which is to cure ghost sickness (see entry). When so conducted, it is held in the home of the patient and usually lasts half a night [Fenton and Kurath 1951:145]. The ceremony follows a well-defined pattern of song groupings, accompanied

by drumbeats on a large drum. The ceremony is primarily in the hands of women.

Ohocoka

Lakota, *Plains*

The sacred space demarcated in the *yuwipi* (see entry) ceremony [Kemnitzer 1976:267]. The term means "in the center" or "sacred place." The space is marked off on the floor of the room where the ceremony is to be conducted. It is usually an area about 10 feet square, outlined by a string of tobacco ties (see *canli wapahta*). A tin can filled with dirt is placed in each corner, and into the can is placed a 2-foot chokecherry stick; a square of colored cotton cloth containing a pinch of tobacco is tied by one corner to the top of the stick. The colors represent the four cardinal directions and are set accordingly. Other items, such as a bed of sage, a mound of mole dirt, gourd rattles, eagle feathers, and an eagle-bone whistle, are placed in the *ohocoka* according to the directions of the shaman. The shaman determines the contents and arrangement of the *ohocoka* according to the directions of his helping spirits, so each display differs slightly. The placing of the objects must be done in a sacred manner. For example, every item must be smudged off with steam, burning sage, and/or burning cedar. It usually takes two to three hours to complete the setup. If everything is not properly done, the ceremony will fail and the shaman will be punished by his helping spirits.

Ohshiekats

Keres, *Southwest*

The Sia Pueblo term for gourd rattles used during healing and other religious ceremonies [Stevenson 1894:79].

Oke

Algonquin, *Northeast*

Dialectical variant: *Okewis*. A term found in the early literature on the tribes of Virginia, generally equated with the word "devil." Jarvis [1820:94] calls it the *"Tutelary Deity,* which each Indian worships." Captain Smith reported in 1702 [in Jarvis 1820:103] that "they think that their werowances

(chiefs) and priests ... when they are dead, goe beyond the mountaines towards the setting of the sunne, and ever remaine there in forme of their *Oke.*" Most likely, this is an early term used to refer to a helping spirit, since shamans were known to call on *Oke* during their healing ceremonies.

Oki

Iroquois, *Northeast*

A spirit used to diagnose illness. This term is found in the early Jesuit records for this area [JR 1897–1905:33:193]. The *saokatas* (diagnosticians) call upon this spirit, which enters the body of the sick person and locates the disease. This spirit can appear in a dream or during a waking state but comes in a different form for each diagnostician—sometimes as an eagle, sometimes as a raven, and so forth. As such, each *saokata* probably has a secret name for his *oki,* the latter being a generic term. The forms inhabited by the *okis* are called *aaskuandi* by the Huron [JR 1897–1905:39:27, 33:213] and *otsinehketa* by the Iroquois of Six Nations [Shimony 1970:250]. Often in the Jesuit records the *okis* are also referred to as charms or fetishes. Fenton [1941:413] uses *oki* as a term for shamans among the Huron, and Pomedli [1991: 119–121] uses *oki* to mean a shaman's helping spirit as well as to mean spiritual power. Some authors equate the *okis* with *manitous* (see entry).

Okiwe Dance

Cayuga, *Northeast*

The Ghost or Dead People Dance (not to be confused with the widespread Ghost Dance revitalization movement of the nineteenth century). This is a healing ceremony to appease the spirits of the dead. Anyone may participate in its ritual. See *eyondwanshgwut* for details.

Old Man Dick

Apache, *Southwest*

A powerful Chiricahua shaman remembered in contemporary times. Opler [1946:87] reported on a seven-day healing ceremony by Old Man Dick in which the house shook so hard "they thought the roof was coming off."

Old Pierre
Coast Salish, *Northwest Coast*
A shaman from the Katzie village on the Fraser River (25 miles from Vancouver) who was about 75 years old when interviewed in 1936 by anthropologist Diamond Jenness. He received his healing powers in a vision at the age of 14, which he recounted as follows:

"But when winter came again I resumed my fasting; I roamed the woods, bathed in its icy pools, rubbed myself with the boughs of evergreen trees, ate nothing, but drank water copiously and gave it up again. After each bath I prayed to Him Who Dwells Above, and I danced until I fell to the ground exhausted, then at night I slept on beds of branches or in the hollow of some tree. . . . Four winters I endured this penance. Then at last my mind and body became really clean. My eyes were opened, and I beheld the whole universe.

"I had been dancing and had fallen to the ground exhausted. As I lay there, sleeping, I heard a medicine-man singing far, far away, and my mind traveled toward the voice. . . . And I prayed constantly to Him Who Dwells Above, asking for power to heal the sick. . . .

"I reached the place where the medicine-man was singing, a house unlike any that I had ever seen before. He who was behind me whispered: 'Go inside. This is he for whom you are seeking, the true medicine-man for whom you have undergone penance all these years.'

"I entered. The medicine-man was kneeling on the floor, and beside him was his water, in some mystic vessel that was neither a dish nor a basket. He turned and looked at me. 'Poor boy,' he said. 'So you have come at last. Kneel down beside me.'

"I knelt beside him. In front of us appeared every sickness that afflicts mankind, concentrated in a single human being. 'Wash your hands and wrists in this water.' I washed them. He grasped them in his own and massaged them, giving them power. 'Now lay your hands on that sickness and remove it.'

"I laid my hands to the patient and cupped his sickness out with them. He rose to his feet, cured. 'That is how you shall remove every sickness. You shall chant the song that you have heard me sing and cup out the sickness with your hands. Now go.'

"My mind returned to my body and I awoke, but now in my hands and wrists I felt power. I rose up and danced until I fell exhausted again and my mind left me once more. Now I travelled to a huge tree—the father of all trees, invisible to mortal eyes; and always behind me moved the same being as before, though I could not see him. As I stood before the mighty trunk, he said: 'Listen. The tree will speak to you.'

"For a long time I stood there waiting. Finally the tree spoke; 'O poor boy. No living soul has ever seen me before. Here I stand, watching all the trees and all the people throughout this world, and no one knows me. One power, and one only, I shall grant you. When you are treating the sick, you shall see over the whole world; when the mind of your patient is lost, you shall see and recapture it. Remain here for a while till someone comes with a noise like the rushing of a great wind—someone who always rests on top of this tree. Do not look until I bid you.'

"I waited. There came a sound as of a great wind at the top of the tree. 'Now look,' said the tree. I looked. On its summit stood a great white horse. Its hoofs were red, and two persons sat on its back. 'That horse flies all over the world,' said the tree. 'I shall not give you its power, for you would not live long.'

"My mind returned to my body; I awoke and bathed again in the pool at my side. After my bath I drank copiously of its water, and tickled my throat with a twig of maple. Then I prayed to Him Who Dwells Above, and I danced till I fell to the ground and lost consciousness. My mind travelled forth again over a beautiful prairie until something tripped me, something hard like a stone, and a voice said to me: 'Poor soul, go no farther. This is the leader of all things that are upon this earth. You are the first who has come here.'

"The being who had tripped me stood up and chanted a song. 'Take this stone that I use for a pillow,' he said. 'Hold it in your two hands and kneel down. For a long time I have been watching you, watching your struggles.'

"As I knelt down, holding the rock in my hands—it was different from all other rocks—the being mounted the back of my head and rubbed my jaw. 'You shall heal the sick. Place your lips to the rock and suck it. Suck it once only, but suck it hard.' I laid my lips to it and sucked. It became soft like flesh, and something—it was blood—issued from it and entered my mouth. 'Don't eject it on the ground, but swallow some of it and rub the rest on your hands.' He came down from the back of my head and took the rock from me. 'That is how you shall heal the sick. That is how you shall suck away their illness. Now go.'

"I awoke and found myself lying on the ground. Now I had power—power in my hands and wrists to draw out sickness, power in my mouth to swallow it, and power to see all over the world and recover minds that had strayed from their bodily homes. I was a medicine-man: I could heal the sick, I could banish their diseases, even as my mother had foretold me" [Old Pierre in Jenness 1955:66–67].

Shortly thereafter, he conducted his first healing on a 17-year-old girl named Mary. Jenness met Mary in 1936, when she was very old, and she confirmed the following account of her healing given here by Old Pierre:

"My mother came to me one evening and said: 'Mary is very ill from a large tumour in her side. I have tried to cure her, but without success. Did you receive power when you fasted?'

"'Yes,' I answered. 'I have power. But I do not want the people to see me the first time I use it because I may fail, and then they would laugh at me. Hang some mats around her bed and I will come.'

"I entered Mary's room unseen, and my mother set a basin of water in front of me. First I washed my hands, as I had washed them in my vision, and I chanted the song I learned at that time. Power flowed into me; I could feel it in my wrists and fingers. I laid my hands to Mary's side just where the tumour was situated, and manipulated it. Then I set my lips to the place and sucked. It palpitated, but my mouth remained empty. Drawing back, I said to my mother: 'I must go to the woods and obtain more power. Tomorrow evening I will come back.' Without food or drink, I went into the woods, although it was dark, and

as I stumbled along I prayed. . . . Finally I lay down, and as I slept my mind travelled away to the Holy One it had visited at the close of my fasting. Once again I sucked the hard stone, and once again I filled my mouth with its blood. When I awoke it was already light. I wandered throughout the day from pool to pool, bathing and rubbing myself with spruce-branches, and all the time I kept praying to Him Who Dwells Above, and to the Holy Ones who had given me power.

"At evening I returned to Mary's room, washed my hands, and chanted my song. My power flowed strong within me, and as I laid my lips to her side I knew that this time I could not fail. Once, and once only, I sucked; then the tumour suddenly collapsed, filling my mouth with its fluid, which I ejected outside the house. Then I said to my mother: 'She will recover now. But I will come again if she needs me.' They did not send for me again. She began to recover immediately, and, as you see, she is now an old woman" [Old Pierre in Jenness 1955:69].

It should be noted that this was an unusually early age for a Coast Salish shaman to begin his practice. In addition, most shamans waited several years after acquiring a helping spirit before they began to doctor.

Old Took'tok
Yuit, *Arctic Coast*
A powerful Diomede Islander shaman who was reported to have died several times. Weyer [1932: 439–440] reported on one such instance:

"Old Took'tok, an angakok (shaman) famed for his powers, returned from a hunting trip with his mind made up that he would be better off dead. So he took his gun and fired it directly at his heart. Blood spattered out all over his parka. All his strength ebbed from his body and he gradually slumped to the floor, an inert mass. After ten minutes, however, slight twitching indicated the return of life, and in a short time he was on his feet again. There was a hole through his parka over his heart and another in the back of the jacket; the skin of his chest showed only powder marks to indicate where the discharge had struck him."

Omahl
Clayoquot, *Northwest Coast*
Among this branch of the Nootka, the shaman's "strength to work and cure" [Koppert 1930:86].

Omazig
Chippewa, *Canadian Eastern Woodlands*
A *Midewiwin* (see entry) shaman around the turn of the twentieth century. The following is a rather humorous account of one of his unusual healing techniques:

"A girl was sick and was getting worse. This old speaker (Omazig) said, 'We are going to kill the cause of the disease which troubles her.' He gave no explanation of how he was going to do this. He simply said, 'In the morning you will know.' Early next morning at sunrise—it was foggy—we heard a big noise across the bay; then a gun shot. We wondered if there was some truth in what the old man had said. Someone said that the people had fashioned bulrushes into the shape of a person. Then they attributed the sickness, as it were, to the statue. The noise we heard was made by the women, who with hatchets, were attacking the statue. The old speaker had shot at it with the (shot)gun but missed it, and everybody laughed about it. The women chopped the statue into pieces. The old fellow predicted the girl would get better, and she did" [Hilger 1951:90].

Omotome
Cheyenne, *Plains*
The body soul (see entry).

Onayanakia
Zuni, *Southwest*
The Mystery Medicine order, one of three orders within the *Shiwannake* fraternity. A four-night initiation ceremony is conducted, during which healing of the sick takes place on the third and fourth nights. In November 1891, Matilda Stevenson [1904:496–497] observed such a ceremony:

"In a moment or two the director (leading shaman) dances before the altar and then proceeds to heal the sick. After sucking his first patient, who is a woman, he throws the supposed extracted material into the fire. His next subject is the akwamosi, from whose side he 'draws' an object and throws it into the fire. He afterward deposits the material supposed to come from his patients in the bowl presided over by the aged woman. For some time he practices healing alone . . . (then) a second theurgist (shaman) comes to the floor. Dipping his plumes in the medicine water, he sprinkles the choir and dances wildly before the altar, twisting and bending his body, and proceeds to practice on the patients. . . . Gradually the number of theurgists on the floor increases, leaving, however, a sufficient body to continue the song. One of the practicing theurgists is a Sia guest invited to take part in the healing. He falls on one knee before the altar, his back to it, then rises and proceeds to practice. Touching one of the women with the tips of his two eagle-wing plumes, he extends his hand and receives the stone, which he professes to draw from the body by the touch of the plumes, and holds it up to view. . . . The Sia theurgist stamps in the fire with his bare feet, and runs about with a large live coal in his hand, finally rubbing it over his nude body. The scene is dramatic when the floor becomes crowded and the theurgists, jumping about in groups in squatting positions, manipulate their eagle-wing plumes as they approach the invalids. As one touches an invalid the others of the group draw near, waving their plumes, which are usually held in the left hand during the dance or sucking, and pointing them toward the sick one. Occasionally two theurgists practice upon an invalid at the same time, the others manipulating their plumes about him."

Both nights of healing begin with male healers coming onto the floor to work on the patients present. Eventually, they are joined by the female healers. As many as 20 healers might be working at any point. Sometimes as many as four healers simultaneously perform sucking on a single patient. In addition to the items mentioned above, some shamans use crystals to divine the seat of the sickness in the patient. Most extracting of disease is done by sucking, but in some instances, only the plumes are used to draw disease to the surface, where it is snatched by the hand of the shaman.

Stones up to the size of a pigeon's egg, bits of cloth, and strings and yarn of various kinds are the most common items extracted. These items are then thrown into a special bowl, except for the first item taken out, which is normally thrown into the fire. Following the ceremony each night, the contents of this bowl are taken outside and buried.

Ondinonc
Iroquois, *Northeast*
Also: *ondinnonk* [Wallace 1970:61]. A secret desire of the soul manifested by a dream. The Iroquois believe that disease or bodily infirmity comes from three possible sources: natural accidents; object intrusion through witchcraft; and "the mind of the patient himself, which desires something, and will vex the body of the sick man until it possesses the thing required. For they think that there are in every man certain inborn desires, often unknown to themselves, upon which the happiness of individuals depends. For the purpose of ascertaining desires and innate appetites of this character, they summon soothsayers (shamans), who, as they think, have a divinely-imparted power to look into the inmost recesses of the mind. These men declare that whatever first occurs to them, or something from which they suspect some gain can be derived, is desired by the sick person. Therefore the parents, friends, and relatives of the patient do not hesitate to procure and lavish upon him whatever it may be, however expensive, a return of which is never thereafter to be sought" [Father Jouvency in Kenton 1927:1:7].

The Iroquois preceded Freud, Jung, and other Western psychologists by several centuries in understanding that the mind has a conscious and an unconscious part. In addition, they were aware of the great force exerted by unconscious desires in the development of psychosomatic illnesses. They understood that these desires were expressed in symbolic form by dreams but that the individual could not always properly interpret such dreams by himself. They also understood that the patient could be cured by fulfilling such frustrating desires, either directly or symbolically.

To treat such patients, the Iroquois developed techniques of free association to uncover the latent meaning of dreams. These most often took the form of guessing rites in which sacred games were played to discover the patient's true desires. The patient was permitted to speak only in riddles, leaving the exact determination up to the guessers. Often the desire was a mundane matter, such as desiring a particular item—a knife, a dog, and so forth—and resulted in symptomatic dreams that expressed a wish of the dreamer's soul. Sometimes, however, the patient was visited by a powerful spirit who had a message for him or for the community at large. These were visitation dreams, which were sometimes "personality transformation dreams, in which the longings, doubts, and conflicts of the dreamer were suddenly and radically resolved; the dreamer emerged from his vision with a new sense of dignity, a new capacity for playing a hitherto difficult role, and a new feeling of health and well being" [Wallace 1958:245].

In all cases, the cure was to grant the patient his hidden desires. The Jesuit missionaries lived in mortal fear of this procedure, because there was always the potential for someone to dream that the Iroquois would be better off without the missionaries. Most often, the dream solution was the ritual of a particular type of ceremony, determined by the guessers.

Onetda
Iroquois, *Northeast*
The tea that cured Cartier's crew of scurvy, which eventually led to the cure for scurvy. Jacques Cartier was a French captain whose three ships became frozen fast in ice on the St. Lawrence River near the present site of Montreal during the winter of 1535–1536. By mid-March 25 crew members were dead from scurvy with little hope for the rest of the crew. A chief named Domagaia cured the crew by boiling "the juice and sappe of a certain Tree." Although Cartier did not know the ingredient, linguists determined only this century that the tea was made from pine needles of the hemlock [Parker 1928:10]. James Lind, a British naval surgeon, read Cartier's logs 200 years later and launched experiments that proved a dietary (lack of vitamin C) basis for scurvy, which was then thought to be caused by "bad air."

Ongwe shona
Iroquois, *Northeast*
According to Iroquoian cosmology, the universe is made up of two worlds—the Sky World and Earth. The beings who populate the Sky World are known as the first peoples and are called *ongwe shona*. These beings can be human as well as non-human. The "real men" who occupy this world in a material form are referred to as *ongwe honwe* [Blanchard 1982].

Only-One
Tsimshian, *Northwest Coast*
See *Qamkawl*.

Onniont
Huron, *Northeast*
The strongest charm, obtained most often in trade with the Algonquin. "They say that this *onniont* is a sort of serpent, or almost the armored fish, and that this serpent pierces everything that it meets in its way—trees, bears, and even rocks, without ever deviating from its course or being stopped by anything" [JR 1897–1905:3:213–215].

Oñnonkwat
Iroquois, *Northeast*
In earlier times, a name of the soul; later, it came to designate medicine, including those things used on account of their inherent virtue and those things used in the arts of sorcery. It comes from the archaic Huron and Onondaga verb *haqtinonk*, meaning "he begs, craves it; supplicates for it." According to Hewitt [1895:113]:

"As a noun it signifies both the thing that is the agent and the object of the begging, craving, or desiring, etc. The agent of the craving was the soul, and the cause of the begging or craving was the thing desired. Since the thing desired was sought only for the welfare and health of the body, for the curing of its ills, the soul from being regarded simply as the craver for things intended to cure finally came to be regarded as the curer as well. . . . Thus, it is found that a verb denoting simply 'to beg, crave; supplicate,' has by a normal historical linguistic development come to mean, first, the soul, and then, medicine or a curative agency."

From the word *oñnonkwat* is derived *oñnonkwatcra*, today meaning "medicine"—the substance that cures or that can cure in our sense of the word.

Ononeovätaneo
Cheyenne, *Plains*
In former times, the name of the secret society to which both male and female shamans belonged. During their ceremonies, they used a special language known only to them. As a group, they represented the spiritual powers of the seven regions of the universe [Schlesier 1987:14].

Oóshtakyòu
Clayoquot, *Northwest Coast*
Term used by this branch of the Nootka for either male or female shamans who doctor. Before undertaking a healing ceremony, the shaman first goes into the woods in secret to gain strength to work the cure. This procedure is short, sometimes lasting no more than half an hour.

When doctoring a patient, the shaman seats himself by the patient's bedside. He uses his left hand to feel the patient's body and locate the sickness while shaking a rattle in his right hand. During this procedure, he sings in subdued tones. The shaman's rattle is of special design, made by clasping together the halves of a large mussel shell that has been filled with pebbles. "In more recent times cowhorns or tin cans are used (as rattles)" [Koppert 1930:86].

When diagnosing an illness, the shaman enters into a trance, his face becoming ghostlike, and he discovers the cause—most often some foreign object in the patient's body. If the object is too big or too deeply rooted to be removed, the patient will not recover. If the object can be removed by the shaman, he may deem it necessary to make several calls on the patient before its removal. In other cases not involving object intrusion, the shaman may massage the patient's body.

To remove the disease-causing object, called *mayáthle* [Koppert 1930:87], the shaman sucks on the body where the object is located. Once removed, the object is wrapped in grass or cedar bark and properly disposed of.

Nootka female shaman.

Opagi
Lakota, *Plains*
A ritual performed to secure the services of a sha-man for a healing ceremony; translates to "he fills the pipe" [Twiss 1969:15]. The *opagi* is the first step in any Lakota healing ritual. The patient, or some-one on his behalf, approaches the shaman with a gift of tobacco. The preferred method is for the pa-tient to fill a sacred pipe and present it to the sha-man. The patient approaches the shaman, says that he has come to make a pipe presentation (i.e., a request), states the purpose behind the pipe pre-sentation, and hands the sacred pipe to the sha-man.

There is a prescribed ritual at this point for handing over the sacred pipe. The shaman extends his arms forward, parallel to the ground, with his palms upward. The patient holds the sa-cred pipe in both hands, usually with the bowl in the left hand (nearest the heart), extends his arms and touches the sacred pipe lightly onto the palms of the shaman, and then withdraws the pipe back to himself. This is done four times in succession. At the end of the fourth placement, the shaman ei-ther takes hold of the sacred pipe or not. If the sha-man takes the sacred pipe, it means that he will undertake the healing request. If he refuses to grip the pipe, it means that he refuses the request for healing.

What is important is the gift of tobacco to the shaman, not the use of the sacred pipe. An *opagi* might be as simple as a person handing a pack of cigarettes or even a couple of cigarettes to the sha-man. Although the fourfold presentation is not performed with a pack of cigarettes, the other rules are the same—taking the tobacco means ac-cepting the request, and refusing the tobacco means denying it.

A shaman usually will not accept the tobacco if he has already accepted tobacco for another heal-ing that is still pending or incomplete. That is, sha-mans do not like to "step over" or "cross" healing requests.

Opina
Lenni Lenape, *Northeast*
In the Unami dialect, any object given to a shaman by a spirit during his vision quest. Normally, the shaman swallows the object. In some cases, the shaman can cough up this object at will and then swallow it again.

Oqortoq
Netsilik Eskimo, *Arctic Coast*
A powerful shaman around the turn of the twen-tieth century. His wife was also a shaman. Manêlaq [in Rasmussen 1931:216] gives a brief ac-count of a soul-retrieval ceremony conducted on a man named Qaorssuaq:

"They held a great seance in order to call the soul back to Qaorssuaq's body. And it was not long be-fore he again saw his soul. The two shamans (Oqortoq and wife), to whom nothing was im-possible, could see it too. They uttered magic words and spoke with their helping spirits' own tongue until the soul came quite close to Qaorssuaq; then they suddenly sprang to him and began to beat him here and there on his body, the consequence being that the soul was frightened and became so scared that it slipped into Qaorssuaq's body once more. At the very same moment he was well again and I could hear him shouting and singing with joy."

Orenda
Iroquois, *Northeast*
The mystical force or potential inherent in power; that is, the magic of power. This force is inherent in all matter and spirits; it is with this force that the shaman heals. Because this force is mystical, it cannot be understood by the rational mind, al-though it can be manipulated to cause things to change or to happen. *Orenda* is an Anglicization of the various dialectical forms of this word among the Iroquois nations and has been adopted in the literature as a cross-cultural term. *Orenda* was first introduced by anthropologist J. N. B. Hewitt [1902:34–45], who defined it as "a hypo-thetical potency or potentiality to do or effect re-sults mystically."

Otkon
Iroquois, *Northeast*
Any fetish that carries supernatural power [Hultkrantz 1967a:12].

Oulsgädön
Cherokee, *Southeast*

Ritualistic term for disease. It means "that which is important" but is usually translated to "the disease present in the body" or "the intruder" [Mooney and Olbrechts 1932:14]. The reason for not using the general term for disease "is to allude to a dreaded concept by a (respectful) circumlocution, so as not to offend it, or so as not to bring about its appearance, its 'materialization,' we might say, by calling it by its common name" [Mooney and Olbrechts 1932:14]. The common term is *ouyugi* where the stem *yug* means "resentment."

Even though a disease might be present in a person's body, "it by no means follows that an illness is the instantaneous result: the disease may be present in a dormant, latent condition, and often months, or even years after the revengeful animal-ghost or spirit has 'inoculated' the person the malady may become 'virulent.' It is easy to see how powerful a means this conception must be toward consolidating the prestige of the medicine man, enabling him as it does to explain many diseases, for which there is no evident cause, by events and dreams of many months or years ago, and to explain how it is that certain acts and infractions of taboos that, according to the general belief ought to be followed by the contraction of a disease, apparently remain without any immediate results" [Mooney and Olbrechts 1932:15].

The presence of a disease does not account for all cases of sickness, however: "There are, for example, the ailments due to 'our saliva being spoiled.' The Cherokee believes that the saliva is located in the throat and that it is of capital importance in human physiology; as a matter of fact, the physiologic rôle they ascribe to the saliva would lead us to believe that they consider it as important as blood and the gall. When the saliva is 'spoiled' the patient becomes despondent, withers away, and dies.

"The most frequent causes of this state of affairs are dreams, especially the dreams caused by the ghost people, but also those caused by snakes and fish. The belief is based no doubt on the feeling of oppression and anguish that accompanies many dreams, especially those of the 'nightmare' variety" [Mooney and Olbrechts 1932:15].

Outfit doctors

General term in the anthropological literature on California for a type of shaman that impersonates certain powerful healing spirits during healing ceremonies. These shamans wear special costumes to impersonate selected healing spirits, such as Kuksu, to effect a cure. The costumes are often handed down in family lineages. Some of these shamans are sucking doctors, but others only sing and administer medicines during the healing ceremony.

Owl shamans
Kiowa, *Plains*

A class of shamans whose power comes from the owl—especially the horned owl, which is feared for its great power. Owls are believed to be souls of the dead, a reason for their frequent association with sorcery. More powerful owl shamans have the power to summon spirits and render cures. Owls are also associated with evil whirlwinds that cause paralysis when they blow over sleeping persons. Thus owl shamans are particularly adept at curing various kinds of human paralysis. Sometimes a woman has the owl power.

Their spirit-calling ceremonies resemble the Shaking Tent Ceremonies (see entry) of the Ojibwa. The shaman is placed in a small 3- to 4-foot-high tepee that has been erected within a larger tepee in which the guests and patient sit. The shaman begins by smoking his sacred pipe, accompanied by the singing of older men. Collier [1944:47] describes what happens next:

"Presently a roaring noise was heard, the large tipi was shaken and filled with wind, and then the small tipi vibrated. At this time drumming and low singing were sometimes heard coming from the small tipi. The spirit of a dead person, often a renowned warrior or a shaman, came in the form of an owl. The flapping of wings was heard outside the smokehole; then the owl entered and fluttered against the small tipi. From within the small tipi was heard the voice of the spirit asking why he had been summoned. At performances in which deer hooves and a whistle had been placed beside the firepit in advance, the spirit blew the whistle and rattled the hooves before speaking.

The shaman then smoked a pipe, offered the stem to the spirit to smoke, and put the question to him. The spirit might answer at once, or fly out of the tipi to return in a half an hour or so with the answer. The spirit spoke in a high, muffled, nasal voice, and repeated everything twice.

"At one seance, after the question had been answered, a woman spectator asked to speak to her dead brother. The owl, apparently acting as intermediary, consented and rushed from the tipi. Presently, there was a surge of wind in the tipi and the spirit of the woman's brother spoke. They carried on a brief conversation during which he mentioned that his world was a land of plenty and contentment. Then the spirit departed with the usual rush of wind."

Owl Woman
Papago, *Southwest*
A shaman who recorded some of her medicine songs for anthropologist Frances Densmore in 1921. Over the years, many spirits had visited her and imparted healing songs to her. During her treatments, she would have an assistant—usually Sivariano Garcia, also a shaman—sing the appropriate healing songs. She always began her treatments with two particular healing songs that had been given to her by the spirit of a man who had been killed near Tucson.

Oxzem
Cheyenne, *Plains*
The spirit lance or wheel lance possessed by shamans. "Attached to its shaft near the point was a small braided wheel into which a specific spirit could be called who moved the *oxzem* physically. . . . The shaft of this particular weapon is carved and arranged to present symbolically a human-like physical image that either housed a shaman's spirit helper permanently or on special occasions . . . each (lance) exemplified secret knowledge and power and was made according to the instructions of the spirits. Each represented a dangerous gift from the spirit world to its shaman keeper who alone mastered the required ritual and care" [Schlesier 1987:16–17].

Owl Woman

Oye
Maidu, *California*
Also: *oya, netdim maidu* [Loeb 1934b:159]. Term used by the Northwest Hill Maidu dreaming and singing doctors. These shamans are in special contact with spirits. From their ranks is chosen a chief shaman, called *yukbe* (see entry), who also heads their secret society. These shamans are considered to be born with their ability. During a healing, they sing their spirit-calling songs and then dream their methods of curing. Concerning them, Curtis [in Loeb 1934b:160] wrote:

"There were certain men, rarely women, who with arms, chest, and lower half of the face painted white, and with prairie-falcon feathers dangling from the arms and down the back, went about constantly singing and striking the hand with a split-elder baton painted white. All this was in response to the bidding of some spirit in a dream experience. Such persons were called oya."

Pa towa
Tewa, *Southwest*
The Fishpeople. It is a collective term that refers to all the people in the pueblo who are members of one or more of the ceremonial (secret) societies; at San Juan Pueblo, for example, there are seven such societies. All the other people in the San Juan Pueblo are called Weedpeople [Laski 1958:96].

Pagahológen
Malecite, *Canadian Eastern Woodlands*
Drum [Speck 1919:241].

Pagits
Northern Ute, *Basin*
A shaman during the first part of the twentieth century who lived on the high plateau at the base of the Uinta Mountains. He recorded nine of his healing songs for anthropologist Frances Densmore. He received his power from "a little green man who lives in the mountains and shoots arrows into those who speak unkindly of him." Pagits told Densmore that "he tells me when he has shot an arrow. Then the man sends for me and pays me to get it out" [Densmore 1952:453]. He also said that "he usually had to sing five or six times before he could extract the cause of the pain, which was sometimes an inch or two in length, red in color, and in texture like a fingernail."

Pahiuhiu
Hawaiian, *Pacific*
See *hoopiopio.*

Pakholangan
Penobscot, *Canadian Eastern Woodlands*
Drum used in healing ceremonies; literally, "that which is hollow struck with a stick." Early missionaries noted that the drum was the property of shamans. The Penobscot drum is unique in that it has a snare made of rawhide stretched across the head of the drum. This snare is a feature found on the drums of Algonquin tribes northward through Labrador. The buzzing noise made by the snare is regarded as a type of singing [Speck 1919:241] .

Pakwimpa
Tiwa, *Southwest*
At Isleta Pueblo, the sacred water contained in a special bowl that appears on nearly every ceremonial altar. The

term comes from *pa,* meaning "water," and *kwimpa,* meaning "whirling" or "bubbling" [Parsons 1932:280].

Papaicoang
Chippewa, *Canadian Eastern Woodlands*
Bloodletting, a form of treatment for disease. Persons who perform bloodletting are adepts but not necessarily shamans [Hilger 1951:88]. Bloodletting is done to remove "bad" blood.

"Incisions were made with sharp-edged flint stones *(biwanak),* with pieces of broken porcelain sharpened to an edge, or with points of knives. If the blade of a knife was used it was completely wound about with string, leaving only as much of the point exposed as was needed for the depth of the cut. The gash was made by holding the point over a vein with one hand and tapping the handle end of the knife with the other" [Hilger 1951:95].

Incisions are made in the temple for headaches and insanity, "the kind of insanity which does not make people violent and is caused by evil powers" [Hilger 1951:95]. Incisions are made at the elbow to treat strained backs or arms.

About a teaspoon of blood is extracted from the patient by placing a special horn, called *wikwacigans,* over the incision. If an incision has been made into a vein, the blood flows freely into the horn; otherwise, the shaman sucks on the horn to withdraw the blood. Following this, a poultice, chewed bark, or chewed tobacco is placed over the incision to stop the bleeding.

Papalot
Sinkaietk, *Plateau*
Term used by the Southern Okanagon of Washington for power inherited from a dead relative. This form of power is rarer than their *sumix* (see entry)—another form of power that is actively sought. In some cases, *papalot* is passed down through several generations, making these families well known for healing, although not all *papalot* is used for curing. "One who heard or saw the *papalot* in a dream for the first time should send his guardian spirit out to capture and 'tame' it. He baited it, said our informants, as one would bait a fish, and by 'easing it along' his power 'made friends' with the *papalot* and drew it within him, where it remained as his own. This baiting

process might take as long as a year" [Cline 1938:153].

Papasokwilun
Lenni Lenape, *Northeast*
The Bear Ceremony of the Unami branch of the Lenni Lenape (also called Delaware). It is conducted by the Wolf clan in a special house that is built new each time the ceremony is performed—once every two years. The ceremony house is constructed of upright poles against which brush is piled. Brush is also placed over the top of the house, which measures approximately 20 by 45 feet. To the east of this is erected a pole on which bear meat (in later times, pig meat) is hung. This ceremony is conducted to ensure good health. Women are not allowed to participate in this ceremony.

Parrish, Essie
Pomo, *California*
A sucking shaman from the Kashaya division of the Pomo who was born around 1898. Her doctoring techniques were studied in depth during the late 1950s by Robert L. Oswalt, and a film was made of one of her healing ceremonies. The following account, given by Essie in 1958, is one of the most detailed ever recorded with regard to healing:

"After I had grown up and become a mature woman—at that time I was probably about, oh, about two years of being twenty years old—my power told me this: 'You are a doctor but you are still just a young woman. You will make a pole with designs. With that you will cure people. If, however, you don't do that, if you don't make that, you will die. If you don't make that, your eyes will become blind and your ears will grow deaf, and that's how you will by lying. This is your job on earth.' I had been thinking about what I was going to do; surprisingly I had come to be like that. I know I am like that now.

"Unexpectedly another person got sick. They say he was about to die with what the white people call 'double pneumonia.' He was lying almost gone. . . . Then when I had gone there I laid my hand on him here and there. And I sucked him. Amazingly it cured him. While I am doctoring I get better and better. . . . Every time I treat people I move upward (in skill).

"After a long time—several years—it was probably twelve or thirteen years—I moved still higher. Then I noticed that I had something in my throat to suck pains out with. And my hand power, I found out about my hand power. That power is always near me. But other people can't see it; I alone can see it.

"When I sit there alongside a person, I call on Our Father. That's my power—the one I call Our Father. Then it descends, my power comes down into me. And when that sick man is lying there, I usually see it (the power). These things seem unbelievable but I, myself, I know, because it is in me. I know what I see. My power is like that. . . .

"Way inside of the sick person lying there, there is something. It is just like seeing through something—if you put tissue over something, you could see through it. That is just the way I see it inside. I see what happens there and can feel it with my hand—my middle finger is the one with the power.

"When I work with the hand power it is just like when you cast for fish and the fish tug on your bait—it feels like it would with the fish pulling on your line. That's what it is like. The pain sitting somewhere inside the person feels like it is pulling your hand towards itself—you can't miss it. It lets you touch it. I don't place my hand myself; it feels like someone—the disease—is pulling with a string. It is like what the white men call a 'magnet.' That's the way the disease in a person is—like a magnet.

"And then it touches it. And when the power touches the pain, your breath is caught—it gets so that you can't breathe. But there is no fear. It is as if your chest were paralyzed—your breath is shut off. If you should breathe while holding that pain, the disease could hide itself. As the pain quiets your breathing, you can feel that pain there, with the result that your hand can take it out. However, if the breathing were not shut off I couldn't lift out the pain.

"When I take it out you can't see it. You can't see it with your bare eyes, but I see it. Whenever I send it away, I see what the disease is. When the disease comes down into a person, which the white people talk about way differently; and we

Indians too, we shamans, explain it way differently. That disease that comes down into a person is dirty; I suppose that is what the white people call 'germs' but we Indian doctors call it 'dirty.'

"I am going to talk about my hand power some more. The palm of the hand has power. And the finger in the middle of the hand has power. That doesn't work just any time, only when I summon (power).

"When there is a sick person somewhere to be found out, the hand power can find it out. Whenever someone thinks about it from somewhere, thinks toward me, there, on the tip of my middle finger, it acts as if shot—what the white people call 'shock.' If you touch something like electricity, you will know what the shock is like; that's how it acts there on the middle finger. When they think from somewhere, it is then that the power finds out, that it gives a warning. That is when I know that someone wants me. And it always turns out to be true. That is my hand power.

"There is a lot more to that (subject of doctoring). There is a doctoring power in my throat. Here, somewhere in the throat, the power sits. When that doctoring power first came down into me, I had already had some kind of growth there for about four years. It had affected me like diphtheria. I had almost died from its constricting (the throat) from the beginning, but I knew all along that it was becoming that (power) . . . my power had told me saying, 'That is because power has entered you there.' When that happened (growth came), they called a white doctor to see me. The white doctor didn't recognize it; he told me that it was probably diphtheria. But I knew what it was. When that thing had finished growing there, I recovered.

"That felt like a tongue lying there and it first moved when I sang. I was probably that way for four years with that thing lying there. After it grew on me, my voice improved. It told me for what purpose it was developing. It told me, 'Power is developing.' Without that I couldn't suck out any diseases. Only when it had developed could I suck out pains.

"Then it gave me this staff with designs and said, 'This is your power. Those designs on there are symbols. Those are disease words.' And it spoke further saying, 'There are many rules to this. You can't treat a menstruating woman and you can't doctor in a house where someone is menstruating. (In those situations) the power will not be your friend; the power will not rise for you.' It has turned out to be true.

"When I first doctored with my throat, it was for a young woman. When I treated her and sucked the disease out, something like a bubble came up out of my throat; just as it would if you blew up a big balloon, that is how it came from my mouth. Everyone there saw it. It had become inflated quite a lot when it floated from my mouth. Everyone saw it. Like foaming soap bubbles would look, that is how it looked at the start.

"Ever since that happened I have been sucking diseases out. The disease that I suck out works like a magnet inside too (as when using hand power). On the place here where I said the power entered my throat, the disease acts as fast as electricity—it acts in a flash, like a magnet. And it shuts off the breath. When it does that, when it closes off the breath, like a magnet it comes along extremely slowly.

"However, one doesn't notice how long he holds his breath. It's like being in what the white people call a 'trance.' While the disease is coming to me, I'm in a trance. It always speaks to me saying, 'This is the way it is. It is such and such a kind of disease. This is why.'

"That disease flies and sticks to a certain place in the mouth. Our (shaman's) teeth have the power; there is something attached to our teeth. There is where the power is, on one certain tooth. There is where the disease sticks. Sometimes it flies under the tongue. When it sticks there it is extremely hard to release—it is, as I said, like a magnet. Then it dies there.

"I spit out the dead disease. Then I let it fall into my hand so that many people can see it. They always see the disease that I suck out. But that is not to be touched by anyone else—it is contagious. Whoever picks the disease up, into him it would enter. Whenever it sits in my hand, it sticks to it like a magnet. It won't fall off—even if you shake your hand it won't fall off. Even if you want to shake it loose it won't come loose.

"You can put it in something like a piece of paper or a basket. If you are going to do that, you should sing for that purpose, you should call for that purpose. Some diseases sit for a while—sit

for a few minutes—but others are fast. Some fast diseases stay just so many minutes after being put down and then disappear. . . . In those many years that I have been treating people, I have seen many different kinds of disease" [Oswalt 1964:223–231].

Passaconaway
Penobscot, *Canadian Eastern Woodlands*
A chief of the region around Pennacook in the Merrimac River Valley during the first half of the seventeenth century. He was also the most noted shaman of the region at the time.

Patumawas
Lenni Lenape, *Northeast*
Also: *Pahtumowans.* One of two terms used in the Minsi dialect of the Lenni Lenape (also called Delaware) to refer to the Great Spirit. Its literal translation is "He who is petitioned." The other term, *Ketanitowet*, means "Great Spirit" [Harrington 1921].

Pauewey
Kiowa, *Plains*
The Buffalo Society [Nye 1962:46]. Members of this society are recognized by their painted faces—red stripes that run horizontally across their mouths. Their horses are painted in a similar manner. The shamans of this society are particularly adept at treating wounds. "Sometimes, while they were treating a wounded man and singing their songs, a female voice would be heard singing. The medicine men said that this was the Buffalo Woman who had had the vision (from which their powers came)" [Nye 1962:48]. Their doctoring paraphernalia almost always includes a buffalo tail that is used on the patient.

Pauwau
Massachusets, *Northeast*
Natick shaman. Another term is *maunetu* [Speck 1919:254].

Pawakan
Plains Cree, *Plains*
Shaman's helping spirit [Mandelbaum 1940:251]. The term is related to the Lakota word *wakan*,

meaning "holy" or "mysterious." The spirit powers derived from *pawakan* are called *atayohkanak* (see entry). Such spirits are obtained most often during a vision quest and give the individual specific feats that can be accomplished under its auspices. "During a vision the soul could leave the body and travel about with the spirit helper. It was the soul that experienced all contacts with the supernatural visitor" [Mandelbaum 1940:251].

Pawcorance
Algonquian, *Northeast*
Altar stones used by the natives of Virginia. Captain Smith reported in 1702 that they were used to mark the locations of "any extraordinary accident or incounter [sic]" [Jarvis 1820:106]. Evidently, a special stone was placed at sites where one had had a spirit encounter. These stones could be found near houses, temples, or out in the woods, where "as you travell by them they will tell you the cause of their erection, wherein they instruct their children."

Pawiapap
Tiwa, *Southwest*
A Taos Pueblo shaman during the first part of the twentieth century. In Isletan, the term translates to "lake spread out," but the inhabitants at Taos referred to him as "the big erring man." He was also the chief of the three north side kivas at Taos. One informant reported that Pawiapap healed a girl with a fever by first feeling her body and then using three herbs to treat her fever—*karli* (wolf root), which is often chewed for stomach pains; *palefia* (bear root—called *pawa* at Taos); and an antiwitch root called *paköli* [Parsons 1932:244].

Paxala
Kwakiutl, *Northwest Coast*
Also: *pexala*. Plural: *pepexala* [Boas 1930]. Shaman. The term refers to both the cosmic shaman (diviner) and the curing shaman. Edmonson [1958:70] includes under this term the thrower shaman, dreamer shaman, feeler shaman, sucking shaman, and soul shaman.

Among the Kwakiutl, the traditional, personal vision quest for acquiring supernatural power was transformed to one of inheritance of power through the animals associated with one's family lineage [Goldman 1975:207]. The inheritance ritual, like the vision quest, is conducted at a known source of *nawalak* (supernatural power). One such place is at the origin of a river.

The state of being through which the shaman wields his powers—the shamanic state of consciousness—is called *paxa* by the Kwakiutl [Goldman 1975:180].

Shamanism among the Kwakiutl is a "back door" to social rank. The only means by which a commoner can become a chief is through the acquisition of *nawalak*. A slave can also become a shaman but would follow the bidding of his owner. In general, women have more *nawalak* than men. The principal source of *nawalak* is animals.

The following sketch of Kwakiutl healing was obtained from one of Boas's informants in 1897 and 1900:

"When the shaman is asked to cure a person, he goes at once and sits down at the right-hand side where the sick person lies in bed. Then he asks the sick person for the place where he feels sick. Then the sick person tells him, putting the first finger on the place where he feels the sickness. Then the shaman washes his hands in a dish containing water, which has been put down for him for sucking out the disease. After the shaman has washed his hands, he feels of the place referred to by the sick man. Then the shaman presses his first finger on the place where the sickness is, and he presses it down for a long time. As soon as he lifts his finger, he watches the place that he has pressed in. If it gets red at once, he knows that the sick one will get well. Then the shaman is glad. When the place which he has pressed in remains white and never gets red, then the shaman recognizes that the sick one can not live long after that. When it does not get red for a long time and gets red gradually, the shaman says that he will be sick for a long time. Then he sucks at the place that he has pressed in; and when he lifts his head, he watches the place where he has been sucking. And when it turns blue, he knows that the sick one will not live long. When it turns red, the shaman knows that he will lie in bed for a long time. And when the place which he has been sucking really turns blue (?) [sic], the shaman knows that he will get well quickly.

"When a sick man or woman gets well, the one who made him well never asks for pay, and generally they are not paid. When the man is poor, then he does not pay the shaman; but when the one who is cured is a chief, then he would be ashamed not to pay the shaman, because he is a chief, for he would be made fun of by his tribe if he did not pay the shaman. All the shamans act that way, and not one of them names the price to be paid by the one who is cured, for if it is a common man who is cured by the shaman, he generally pays two pairs of blankets to the shaman, but often he is not paid at all; and when (the patient) is a chief, then the chief gives as much as is proper for the greatness of his position. It depends upon his own wish how much he pays the shaman. The shaman never names the price; for the shaman does not talk about the chief if he does not pay him well, for the tribe of the chief talk about their chief when he pays little to the shaman" [Hunt in Boas 1921:1:731–732].

Pegahsoy
Yurok, *Oregon Seaboard*
A shaman that specializes in divination; referred to as a seeing, wishing, or confession doctor. In healing ceremonies, they are first called upon to determine the cause of the patient's illness. They undergo stringent training to develop their clairvoyant abilities. In cases of minor illness caused by the bad wishes of an evildoer or by breaches of taboo for which a *pahsoy* (confession) is elicited, the *pegahsoy* prays and blows away the "shadow" (thing seen) with his breath. They dance, sing, and smoke their pipes, but never suck on the patient. In serious cases, the more powerful *kegey* (see entry) are called in to perform a healing ceremony and to suck on the patient [Buckley 1992: 126–127].

Peji hota
Lakota, *Plains*
Sage, which is considered a sacred plant and appears at nearly every Lakota sacred ceremony; translates to "gray grass." "Two characteristics of sage enter into the *wakan* (holy) nature of sage. First, the aromatic quality makes it associated with purification.... The second quality, 'immortality,' has never been articulated to me as contributing to its power, nor has it been mentioned

in the literature, but Indians have remarked that sage is available all year round. Unlike other aromatic bushes sage does not die in the winter, but retains its aroma. At least one informant has said this 'makes it *wakan*'" [Kemnitzer 1970:65].

Besides being burned to produce a purifying smoke, sage is used in many other ways. For example, a stem of sage is placed behind the right ear during the *yuwipi* ceremony so that the "spirits will know you." It can also be used for "errors," as evidenced by the following account:

"At one point in laying out the long string of *canali wapahta* (tobacco offerings/ties; see entry) that encloses the sacred place, the string became snarled and the helper could not untangle it. The shaman threw him a piece of sage, and told him to place the sprig on the snarl, and it would be all right" [Kemnitzer 1970:65].

Peju'da wintca'cta
Assiniboin, *Plains*
Practitioners of herbal medicine. Their herbal remedies are handed down from generation to generation and are kept extremely secret. Lowie [1909:43] reports that they "would not doctor gratuitously even in the most serious cases," but their fees were dependent on a successful cure.

Pejuta wicasa
Lakota, *Plains*
Also: *pezihuta wicasta* [Riggs 1893:215]; *pezhuta wicasha* [Walker 1926:199]; *pezuta wichasha, pezuta wapiya* [Dorsey 1894:495]. Those who limit their practice of healing to the use of herbs rather than the calling forth of spirits. The term translates to "herb man." Females are called *pejuta winyela*, meaning "herb woman." Although these persons are akin to druggists, they are still considered to be holy people among the Lakota.

Peléyc
Nez Perce, *Plateau*
Shamans who are sorcerers. Walker [1970:267] translates it as "hidden sorcerers." Sorcerers use mechanical as well as psychic means to attack their victims. For instance, "some sorcerers killed wounded persons by obtaining a rag soaked in menstrual discharge from a shamaness and placing it in the victim's bed" [Walker 1970:274]. Some-

times, special herbs are used. Walking in a person's footsteps while speaking maledictions also works. Even a glance from a powerful shaman is sufficient to cause harm. Most of these activities are learned from the shaman's helping spirit. Some animals known to carry this evil power are the rattlesnake, blue grouse, and badger.

Petewaruxti
Blackfoot, *Plains*
A shaman during the first part of the nineteenth century. His name translates to "Wonderful One." He was a sucking shaman, and the following is a brief account of one of his healing ceremonies:

"The patient was a woman who had been sick for some time and finally startled her family by remaining unconscious for twenty-four hours. It was then that Petewaruxti was called in. While his assistant rolled the water drum, the shaman sat silently by the patient for a long time. At last he moved, put his mouth to her head and began to suck. He sucked for a long time, until he seemed suddenly thrust away from the patient. When he finally regained his balance he spit a stone out of his mouth. Then he and his assistant carried her down to a brook which ran through the village. There they held the woman under water until she began to struggle. When they released her, she walked home, a well woman" [Stone 1932:99].

In another case, Petewaruxti diagnosed a woman's illness as being a case of possession by a horse spirit. To cure her, he "mixed mud with stallion's urine and covered her body with it and put a streak of paste over her forehead and nostrils. Then he took from his medicine bag a quirt made of downy feathers. With this he whipped her until she suddenly began to neigh like a horse. In a few days she was entirely well" [Stone 1932:99].

Pexala
Kwakiutl, *Northwest Coast*
See *paxala*.

Peyotism
See *Native American Church*.

Phylactery
A technical term that refers to small pieces of buckskin or other material upon which medicine

(power) symbols are drawn. The item is worn by the person who wishes to receive its powers. These items differ from an amulet or talisman in that they are kept concealed from the scrutiny of the profane. Often, other medicine is wrapped in them to augment the potential. Bourke [1892: 592] observed several of them among the Apache after convincing them that he also held powerful medicine. One of them consisted of a piece of buckskin into which had been placed a bag of pollen. Inside the pollen bag was a quartz crystal and four feathers of eagle down. This phylactery contained not only the power of the pollen, eagle, and quartz but also power from the black bear, white bear, yellow bear, and yellow snake, according to Bourke's informant.

Pilotois
Huron, Algonquin, Montagnais, *Northeast*
Shamans [Lambert 1956].

P'inan
Tewa, *Southwest*
The presence of supernatural power. Translates to "to be magical."

Pinji gosan
Ojibwa, *Canadian Eastern Woodlands*
Shaman's medicine bag [Hoffman 1891].

Pipe
See *sacred pipe*.

Pitauniwanha
Caddo, *Plains*
Shaman's helping spirit; translates to "to have power from" [Parsons 1941:34]. Most often, the shaman's spirit is an animal spirit such as beaver, buffalo, panther, or bear. When performing their ceremonies, shamans often take on the characteristics of this animal familiar. For example: "Once while Wing was curing a girl, White Moon looked into the tipi and saw Wing acting like a mad buffalo. There was a buffalo tail which seemed to be swishing about of itself" [Parsons 1941:35].

Pitcitcihtcikan
Plains Cree, *Plains*
A foreign object in the body that causes illness; translates to "something moving" [Mandelbaum 1940:254]. To effect a cure, the shaman removes

the object, most often by sucking on the patient's body.

P'iva
Tewa, *Southwest*
The ceremonial healing and blessing by a medicine man. See *Ke* for details.

Pivat
Cahuilla, *California Peninsula*
Tobacco, among the Desert Cahuilla. It is used as a medicine in healing ceremonies, where it is referred to as "breath of the Creator" [Modesto and Mount 1980:78].

Place-of-Getting-Rich
Kwakiutl, *Northwest Coast*
A shaman who specialized in treating sickness due to soul loss. He lived in the village of Koskimo around the turn of the twentieth century. The following is a brief account of him given by Great-Mountain:

"When our bird (soul) flies away from a man here, then our bodies are not strong. It is just all the time as though we were sleepy. The man just goes down in weakness without cause, for he is not hungry and, therefore, he is lean. Also, he does not feel any sickness in his body. Then he asks the soul-catching shaman, Place-of-Getting-Rich, to feel of him and then Place-of-Getting-Rich feels of the place where our soul is sitting as we are men, on each side of our necks. Then the shaman says that the soul has flown away. Then the man who has no soul just prays the shaman to try to get the bird (soul). And when evening comes, then the one who has no bird calls his numaym and all go into this house. When they are all inside then the shaman is called. Evidently at that time he catches the bird, as he comes walking along to the house in which the whole numaym is inside. When the shaman goes in he never sings his sacred songs after the manner of the shamans of the Nakwaxdaxu, when they try to catch a soul, for they sing their sacred songs as they are searching for it. The shaman just stands inside of the doorway. Then he speaks and says, 'Truly, by good luck I found this bird of our friend here, for I bring it now, as I caught it,' says he, as he comes walking and squeezing it in his right hand. Then he presses

with his right hand as he spreads it open on the right hand side of the neck of the man. Then four times he blows on it. This is referred to by the shamans as blowing the bird into (the body). Now it is finished after this" [Great Mountain in Boas 1930:22].

Plenty Fingers
Crow, *Plains*
A powerful shaman during the latter part of the nineteenth century. He could foretell the future, materialize food in times of hunger, and heal. He also carried a bulletproof medicine but was eventually killed by a bullet in the forehead. Lowie [1922:351] provides a short account of one of his healing ceremonies:

"When he came, he bade the other people go outside. Then he was heard singing a bear song. He sucked something out of the patient's skull and something out of his neck and chest. While before the man had barely been able to breathe, he now began to talk and look about and was well. Then Plenty-fingers stuck one finger into the ground, sang a song and pulled out a wild turnip, which he gave the man to eat. He told the people to bring him a plum branch, planted it in front of him, covered himself and the branch with a blanket, and began to growl like a bear. When the blanket was removed, there were plums on the limb, and he fed them to the sick man. Similarly he produced cherries and plums for him. He also stuck his fingers into the ground and pulled out wild carrots for the people he doctored."

Plenty Wolf
Lakota, *Plains*
An Oglala shaman who lived on the Pine Ridge Reservation in South Dakota. One of his *yuwipi* (see entry) ceremonies was observed by physician Robert Ruby [1966] around 1954.

Plummer, Rosie
Paviotso, *Basin*
A shaman who was born around 1880 and lived on the Walker River Reservation. She received her power around 1928 in dreams of her father, who had also been a shaman and had died about 1910. His power came from the rattlesnake, as did Rosie's. The rattlesnake came to her in dreams

three or four times before she believed that she was to become a healer. The snake told her to get eagle feathers, white paint, and wild tobacco to use in healing. The snake also gave her songs to sing during her healing ceremonies. In 1933 she was still learning new songs from the snake and being taught how to heal through this spirit helper [Park 1934:101].

P'o kwin sananwe
Tewa, *Southwest*
The holy medicine water bowl that is central to any healing ceremony. Translates as po, "water"; kwin, "lake"; sananwe, "bowl" [Laski 1958:165]. All ceremonial leaders and medicine men have such bowls, and they are used in all ceremonies—not just healing ceremonies. The water that goes into the bowl must be taken from a stream, river, lake, irrigation ditch, that is, from aboveground; it cannot come from a well, because water from beneath the ground cannot be made holy. The water, once purified, is placed into the ceramic water bowl. These bowls vary in size, but all have a rim that is cut in one to four, cloud-shaped designs. Usually these bowls are not painted.

During a healing ceremony, the *Ke* (Bear shaman; see entry) places the medicine water bowl in the middle of a corn-painting altar that has been placed in the center of the floor. It symbolizes the lakes where the kachina dwell, that is, the waters that are the source of life. When the *Ke* is about to fall into a trance, or when he has difficulty sucking out the disease object from his patient, a *Ke* woman might help him by dipping an eagle feather into the holy water and brushing the shaman's back with it. If the illness has been caused by a sorcerer, the *Ke* peers into the water in the bowl to determine the name of the culprit. At the end of the healing ceremony, the *Ke* passes the bowl first to the patient and then to the other guests, all of whom take a sip of the holy water.

Pohari
Northern Paiute, *Basin*
Shaman. In this culture, shamans receive their curing power through dreams in which a spirit comes to them. The spirit gives the shaman a song and specific instructions for dealing with its power. The shaman uses this spirit for both diag-

nosing and curing the patient. A shaman is paid a fee for his diagnosis of a patient, somewhere between $20 and $50 in the 1930s. Payment is also made to him at the end of a healing ceremony. Healing takes the form of sucking, except in cases of soul loss, when the shaman retrieves the errant soul and returns it to the patient's body [Stewart 1956].

Poínaba
Paviotso, *Basin*
A shaman's special assistant, called the talker. During a healing ceremony, he sits to the left of the shaman and repeats in a clear and loud voice the mumbling, broken phrases uttered by the shaman. He also follows the songs that the shaman sings, repeating the words loudly to enable the spectators to follow them easily and join in the singing. Such singing lasts throughout the night. In the last century, only men served in this capacity, but today, women also serve as interpreters. They are paid a fee for their service, as is the shaman [Park 1938:50].

Another type of assistant is known as the dancer. See *wütádu* for details.

Po'i-uhane
Hawaiian, *Pacific*
A special type of shaman, sometimes referred to as a diviner or fortune-teller, who is able to see the souls of living persons. These shamans are capable of catching a person's soul and imprisoning it in a water calabash, or catching it with their hands and squeezing it to death. In the former case, the shaman usually blackmails the person for the release of his captured soul; in the latter case, the victim becomes listless and soon dies.

Pokunt
Shoshoni, *Basin*
The mystical potency or potentiality to do or effect results. It is the Shoshoni equivalent of the Anglicized Iroquois term *orenda* (see entry).

Pora
Paiute, *Basin*
A crooked rod that is carried by a Chemehuevi shaman and is an insignia of his office [Miller 1983:339].

Poshayanki

Zuni, *Southwest*

The culture hero that is the head of their medicine societies. He lives east of Zuni in the Sandia Mountains [Hultkrantz 1987:95].

Pöshikö

Tiwa, *Southwest*

At Isleta Pueblo, a medicine crystal used by shamans. The healers use such a crystal in their diagnosis of a patient. If the patient is thought to be the victim of sorcery, the crystal is used to find the perpetrator. These crystals are also used for other divination purposes [Parsons 1932:285].

Powagan

Otchipwe, *Canadian Eastern Woodlands*

Also: *pawagane*. A shaman's helping spirit [Cooper 1936:8]. Shamans obtain their spirit helpers through 10-day vision quests conducted in isolated areas. Sometimes the quester places himself in a tree; sometimes he stays on the ground. The quest is usually conducted during the springtime.

Powell, John Wesley

John Powell was born in Mt. Morris, New York, on 24 March 1834. Following the Civil War, in which he lost his right arm at the battle of Shiloh, he explored the Colorado River canyons, where he did sporadic fieldwork among the Shoshoni, Ute, and Paiute. He was a founder of the Smithsonian's Bureau of American Ethnology, which he headed from 1879 to 1902. During his tenure at the bureau, he concentrated much of his effort on linguistics, producing a linguistic map of North America in 1891. He died in Haven, Maine, on 23 September 1902.

Powwowing

A nineteenth-century term used to refer to the Native American method of healing and treating the sick [Riggs 1893:214].

Poxpoxumelh

Sinkaietk, *Plateau*

One of three classes of shamanic curing specialists among the Southern Okanagon of Washington. Literally, the term means "blowing all the while" and refers to those shamans who cure by blowing on the patient. Shamans can be either men or women, although men outnumber women. Most shamans have acquired guardian spirits with which to cure. For example, a shaman with spider power can heal spider bites. In fact, a shaman with spider power can see a spider bite, even through clothing, without being told that it is there.

"Sometimes a shaman dreamed that a certain person was sick. On awaking he sang for a while and then went to the prospective patient and offered to cure him. He sometimes had to travel a long distance to his case. . . . If the cure was successful, he received a small gift; if not, he gained nothing . . . a shaman who refused to attend patients because of malice might, after due warning, be killed by the 'chiefs and the people.' They clubbed him to death, hanged him, cut his throat, or bound him, weighted him with rocks and drowned him. Arrows were not used for this purpose because many shamans were immune to them" [Cline 1938 163].

Blowing, massage, and sucking are the usual means of healing. The word *poxpoxumelh* for a curing shaman refers to the understanding that he can, by blowing on or toward the patient, either expel the source of the illness or project into the patient the latter's lost soul, also a source of illness. Sick people are heavy, but when shamans blow on them, they become as light as a feather. This blowing is often combined with manipulation or massage. When a sorcerer has blown a magical dart into his victim, the shaman employed for the cure blows the dart out of the patient, catches it between his hands, plunges it into water to cool it, and shows it to the people present.

Primary-process thinking

A psychological theory that attempts to explain shamanic activity as the ability to make unconventional combinations. It is hypothesized that in order to activate this process of primary-process thinking, the shaman uses different trance-induction techniques. Through auditory stimulation, such as drumming and rattling, and through the motor movements of dancing, all in increasing intensity, the shaman, usually with the assistance of other ritual participants and singers, journeys in search of knowledge. In trance, the shaman is hypothetically deprived of his usual critical

Anthropologist John Powell meets with Ute Chief Tau-gu in 1871. Powell was the first director of the Smithsonian's Bureau of American Ethnology.

powers, such that a flow of inner pictures creates a remarkable cerebral activity; combinations rush forth over a register of stored impressions that the shaman is not generally conscious of, where life is experienced in a flash of seconds, and where he makes combinations in a manner that comes close to what we call creativity. It is in such a state that the shaman finds the solutions needed, the knowledge to solve the problems he is addressing on the outside. Journeying along a course of visual images and intuitions, the shaman combines them at lightning speed, accepting and discarding such combinations until the solution is found [Nordland 1967].

The theory assumes the existence of "a register of stored impressions" as "inner pictures" but fails to account for how these impressions can give the exact locations of lost objects, and other such "solutions" common to shamanic abilities.

Psychopomp

A term sometimes found in the anthropological literature to refer to shamans. It is used when the shaman is seen as a "guide of souls" [Hultkrantz 1967a:133].

Puaxantï

Southern Paiute, *Basin*

Dialectical variants: *buaxantï, buxantï*. Generic term for shamans [Kelly 1939:151]. Most shamans, however, are named according to the supernatural source of their power. For example, there is the *tïmpi puaxantï* (rock shaman), *kwampï puaxantï* (spider shaman), *ubuaxantï* (arrow shaman), and *toxwa buaxantï* (rattlesnake shaman). Both men and women conduct healing ceremonies, but most shamans are male; the men are usually old, but some are young, and the women are always older. Most unusual is the fact that women, at least those in the Moapa band, are permitted to heal during menstruation, according to informants. This has not been verified through observation.

Power comes to shamans through power dreams. Although such dreams might begin in childhood, doctoring abilities are not used until adulthood. Sometimes "a novice dreamed repeatedly of an animal with which he struggled until he overcame it. This animal gave him his power and taught him to sing, dance, and suck. If he did

not want to become a shaman, he could reject his dream by arising before dawn and blowing (presumably the spirit) toward the sunrise" [Kelly 1939:160]. A shaman often acquires several spirit helpers through dreaming, thus extending his repertoire of healing abilities. The spirit gives the shaman one or more songs that become generally known, so that persons attending a treatment can join in the singing of them. The novice is also instructed in sucking and dancing. There is no variation in their basic dancing, which consists of a simple stamping backward and forward from the prone body of the patient. A spirit might impose a certain rule on the dancing, however, such as one shaman who always danced with a hand clapped to his ear.

According to Kelly [1939:152]:

"A shaman asked to treat did not leave his camp before the arrival of his familiar (helping spirit). By pressing the body of the patient with his hands he located the seat of the ailment. Staff in hand, he danced back and forth; he sang, accompanied by the gathering; and he sucked, lying on his back with the sick person face down upon him, usually across his chest. From the breast or ailing part he removed a small foreign body: a pebble, a length of twine, a piece of meat, a worm, or the like. . . . This he displayed, then swallowed. Informants say that the actual sucking was always done by the familiar spirit, lodged in the doctor's throat.

"In extreme illnesses, when the shaman doubted his ability to cure, he inserted his spirit helper into the body of the sick person. Removing the familiar from his own mouth, he held it between his palms and, singing and blowing, put it into the breast of the patient. Here it remained for a day or a night, then left of its own accord."

Variations on this general procedure occur. For instance, one shaman whose helping spirit was a wolf used an eagle-feather fan with which he scattered ashes on his patients. In another case, "a snake shaman touched his cane to the breast of a (snake bite) victim, and upon removing it, displayed a small rattlesnake on the tip. This he deposited on a near-by stone, from which it soon disappeared. With the removal of the snake, the swelling began to subside. The doctor then sucked, not from the bite but from the chest and stomach, either blood or yellow-green matter. This he sometimes swallowed, sometimes spat out" [Kelly 1939:153]. Finally, some shamans use a *pauboron* (doctor cane) made from a branch of serviceberry, knobbed on the end. The wood is heated to straighten it and then adorned with feathers. The staff itself is considered to be a doctor. "It stood up and talked, but only the doctor could hear it. It was put on top or underneath a patient to take the sickness away" [Kelly 1939:158]. It can also be used to get rid of ghosts who have caused a sickness, although sucking is the most common way of removing such a ghost. Kelly [1939:155] reports that in some cases of ghost intrusion, "when the doctor thinks that the ghost is under the patient, he stands his cane in the ground beside the sick man. This helps to pry loose the ghost. The doctor thinks (asks) that his spirit helper send the cane into the ground so as to raise the man more easily. The cane finds the ghost under the patient, and the spirit helper takes it away. Some doctors kill a ghost by spearing it to the ground with a wooden knife."

Variation also occurs among specialists. For example, the arrow shaman specializes in the treatment of arrow and gunshot wounds. Among the Moapa band, the arrow shaman does not suck on the patient but dances and sings over the patient. "If dancing did not cure, he whipped the patient with an arrow as he sang over him" [Kelly 1939:161]. In the Shivwits band, the arrow shaman dances and sucks on the patient but does not sing. In the Las Vegas band, the arrow shaman sucks the wound, dances, and sings.

Some illnesses are diagnosed as soul loss. This particular sickness is called *muxu auru xwan*, literally "soul-gone-away" [Kelly 1939:152]. "For treatment, the shaman pressed his hands on the chest of the patient and dispatched his tutelary in search of the missing soul, which was thought to have 'gone above.' . . . According to a Shivwits (band) informant, a Kaibab (band) doctor actually ran about in the hills in pursuit of the fleeing soul" [Kelly 1939:152–153].

Among the Shivwits and Gunlock bands, there are datura shamans who acquire their healing powers by drinking a solution made from the seeds and/or roots of the datura (Jimson weed) plant. These shamans are considered to be more powerful than ordinary shamans and are called upon when others have failed. "However, the power of a shaman dependent upon Datura was said to be short-lived" [Kelly 1939:158].

Minor aliments are treated by a single shaman during the day. The treatment is usually of short duration. In more serious cases, the treatment takes place at night, usually over the course of one or two days. Grave illnesses are often treated by several shamans, and the treatment extends over several nights, often lasting until sunrise. Treatments are usually conducted in a house if the weather is cold and outside in a brush shelter if the weather permits.

Puberty quest
The basic vision quest in North America [Hultkrantz 1987:31]. Most vision quests are first undertaken at the time of puberty, although vision questing is often continued throughout one's life.

Puffo nu
Tewa, *Southwest*
Medicine man. See *Ke* for details.

Puha
Numic, *Basin*
The power and energy or supernatural force received from a helping spirit. This term or dialectical variants of it are found among the Numic-speaking people, which include the Kawaisu, Chemehuevi, Southern Paiute, Ute, Panamint, Western Shoshoni (Newe), Gosiute, Northern Shoshoni, Eastern (Wind River Comanche) Shoshoni, Northern Paiute, and Mono. The spirit usually visits the person through repeated unsolicited dreams and confers such power. Power is also obtained through vision quests at well-known power spots [Miller 1983].

The term is translated by some authors as "spirit," referring to the shaman's helping spirit. Olofson [1979:12] was told by a Northern Paiute named William Paddy that it "refers to instructions, ability, and status given to a shaman by a *tumudaini* (helping spirit; see entry), enabling him to cure." Hultkrantz [1987:51] reports that *puha* is also used to refer to a person's helping spirit among the Shoshoni. Whiting [1950:27] translates *puha* as "doctoring power" among the Harney Valley Paiutes.

Puhaga
Paiute, *Basin*

Dialectical variants: *puhükü, puhagü, punagai*. Shamans, among the Owens Valley Paiutes. Both males and females become shamans. They acquire their powers mainly through dreams of a guardian spirit, who teaches them healing songs and instructs them on the use of certain paraphernalia. This is a slow process, often taking 20 years before sufficient songs are revealed and learned. Sources of the power include mountains, springs, clouds, animals, and birds. Certain animals, such as the owl, are thought to be the bearers of evil power. A shaman often has several guardian spirits to work with when healing. Shamanic powers are not inherited, nor can they be purchased.

Whiting [1950:33] reports that among the Harney Valley Paiutes, illnesses are most often diagnosed as being caused by one of the following: sorcery, breaking a taboo of one's spirit helper, attacks from ghosts, or deterioration of the patient's blood. There are, however, many variations on this general theme. For example, one shaman sickened and died because someone intentionally broke his sacred pipe while he was doctoring.

Steward [1934:313] observed their healing ceremonies in the summer of 1928 and reported on a typical healing:

"In the evening the doctor built two fires (sometimes one) 10 to 15 feet apart, north-south, laying the patient on the ground west of these. He sang, walking between the fires, toward his power, east, then toward the patient, west, etc. Spectators might sing, but songs were difficult and changed frequently. Some doctors also shook rattles; some danced, according to their power's instructions, the steps differing. One made short jumps, his left foot forward; another hopped. From time to time, he laid hands on the patient's ailing part, or touched him with a stick. Most doctors sucked the ailing part to remove the ailment with the mouth or through a stick; one used a soapstone pipe. J. S.

(an informant) described one who sucked and vomited a pebble claimed as the ailment shot in by a witch. A woman doctoring an epileptic sucked out pebbles. . . . Some exhibited pebbles or small objects sucked out, saying, 'See, here is what made him sick.' Some blew instead of sucking. Some smoked to 'blow disease away' or for other reasons. Doctors treated all night, perhaps stopping for a midnight meal. One night usually sufficed; several might be necessary. While he was performing, people joked and encouraged him, saying, 'Where did you get that song? That is no good,' or 'I like that song. I shall learn it and sing it all the time.' A fee was $5 to $30 per night. Chalfant (an informant) said fees were returned when treatments failed, and that payment was made through a third party, lest the power be insulted."

The stick mentioned in this account is called *pahuda* and is about 3 feet in length. One shaman was seen sticking it in the ground under a patient's head. Another shaman was reported to have used a fire drill in his healing ceremonies. The point of the drill was heated on the fire and then touched to the afflicted area of the patient's body.

Sickness is often diagnosed as being caused by a sorcerer. In such cases, the shaman divines who has caused the sickness. The sorcerer is then confronted and told to remove his evil workings. In other cases, one's own bad thoughts or deeds or dreams of bad deeds cause the sickness. Shamans often use herbs, but they rub their hands over the herb before administering it to strengthen its power.

An interesting curing technique is use of ants. The patient is given live ants to swallow, which bite the lining of the stomach, the poison going to the lungs. If, when the patient vomits, the ants are alive, he will live; if they are dead, he will die.

Puhágam
Paviotso, *Basin*

Shaman. Curing is the chief function of the Paviotso shamans. Dick Mahwee, a Paviotso shaman, reported: "When shamans get power it always comes from the night. They are told to doctor only at night. This power has nothing to do with the moon or stars." To which Joe Green, another Paviotso shaman, added: "There are two nights. The second one comes behind the night that everybody sees. This second night is under the darkness. It tells the shaman where the pain is and what caused the sickness. When the second night comes it makes the shaman feel that he is a doctor. The power is in him to doctor. Only shamans can see this second night. The people can only see the darkness. They cannot see the night under it" [Park 1938:17]. The meaning of Joe Green's statement remains something of a mystery, because most shamans get their power from some animal. Joe Green's power was from the otter.

Most Paviotso shamans receive their training directly from their spirit helpers. They receive little to no instruction from older shamans, although there are exceptions. There are no formal organizations or societies of shamans. Each shaman has his own unique format for healing ceremonies. When a shaman feels that he has gained enough knowledge from his spirit helper, he begins to heal. In the beginning, he may invite an experienced shaman to attend his healing ceremony. If so, the older shaman usually begins the ceremony and then turns it over to the younger shaman to finish.

Overall, there is some similarity in their healing ceremonies. In most cases, the shaman travels to the home of the patient to conduct the healing. The only preparation made is the sweeping of the floor. Either the patient, if he is well enough, or the family decides on which shaman to call upon for the doctoring. Healing ceremonies are well attended, and everyone participates in the singing of ceremonial songs.

The renown of shamans as specialists is based entirely on success in treating certain types of afflictions. For example, only very powerful shamans can treat soul loss, and only shamans who derived their power from water-babies can treat the sickness caused by these spirit beings.

Most healing ceremonies are conducted at night. However, in some cases, such as a snakebite, the shaman may effect an immediate cure. Usually the healing ceremony is conducted for two nights, with a night of rest between the first

and second sessions. A fee is agreed upon for the shaman's services before beginning the healing ceremony. In the 1930s, a typical fee was $3 to $5. If the shaman overcharges the patient, the shaman risks becoming ill himself. At the same time, shamans are required by their spirit helpers to charge for healing ceremonies. To not charge would endanger the life of the shaman. The only exception to this rule is when the shaman treats a member of his own immediate family.

Shamans rarely refuse a request to heal, otherwise their spirit helpers would become angry, resulting in sickness to the shaman and loss of power.

When the shaman begins, he removes his shoes and seats himself beside the patient. In some cases, the shaman may have his face painted in a particular manner, wear certain feathers, or decorate his clothing in a particular way, according to instructions from his helping spirit. The patient lies on the ground with his head facing south. The spectators sit against the walls of the house. Menstruating and pregnant women are not allowed to attend.

As soon as the shaman is seated by the patient, he takes his pipe, rattle, and other paraphernalia from his medicine bundle and lays them on the ground before him. He then softly sings four or five songs. On the sixth song, he picks up his rattle and shakes it in time with the singing. The number of songs and their length vary with each shaman.

After singing for some time, the shaman gets up and walks or hops slowly around the fire in the center of the room. He always moves around the room counterclockwise. Afterward, he sits back down by the patient, smokes his sacred pipe, and passes it to the spectators, who also smoke it. The pipe is recirculated thereafter every hour or so until the healing ceremony is completed.

At this point, the shaman goes into a trance (the shamanic state of consciousness) to either diagnose or treat the illness. When the shaman uses the trance for prognostic purposes, he sees not only the cause of illness but also signs that are interpreted as omens of recovery or of death. Paviotso shaman Dick Mahwee details such omens as follows:

"I smoke before I go into the trance. While I am in the trance no one makes any noise. I go out to see what will happen to the patient. When I see a whirlwind I know that it caused the sickness. If I see the patient walking on grass and flowers it means that he will get well; he will soon be up and walking. When I see the patient among fresh flowers and he picks them it means that he will recover. If the flowers are withered or look as if the frost had killed them, I know that the patient will die. Sometimes in a trance I see the patient walking on the ground. If he leaves footprints I know that he will live, but if there are no tracks, I cannot cure him.

"When I am coming back from the trance I sing. I sing louder and louder until I am completely conscious. Then the men lift me to my feet and I go on with the doctoring" [Park 1938:54].

When the shaman returns to consciousness, if the sickness is caused by some disease object, he attempts to extract it by suction. He sucks the part of the body that his diagnosis has shown to be the seat of the pain. Usually he applies his mouth to the patient's body, but some shamans use a bone or willow tube for this purpose. While the shaman is sucking, the interpreter and spectators continue to sing until he signals for them to stop by a vigorous shake of his rattle. This process is repeated several times. When the shaman finally draws out the cause of sickness, he exhibits it to the spectators. For example, he may show a pebble, a small black lizard, an insect, or a worm. The disease object is then spit into a shallow hole dug into the earthen floor beside the shaman.

Around midnight, there is an intermission during which the participants eat food prepared by the patient's family. The basket containing the food is handed about in a counterclockwise direction. Some shamans have rules for the exact way in which the food may be eaten at this time. None should be dropped on the ground or wasted, and the unconsumed leftovers are to be carefully buried.

The shaman brings the ceremony to an end in the morning a little before daylight. The shaman then gives the family instructions for the care of the patient. He may order the patient painted with simple designs or prescribe special foods.

These prescriptions are revealed to the shaman by his helping spirit in the course of the ceremony.

When the doctoring is nearly over, some shamans tell the spectators to dance, following him counterclockwise around the fire. This lasts for 10 or 15 minutes. At the end of the dance, all must shake their clothes and blow on their arms simultaneously. This action drives away the evil spirit causing the sickness, which is still in the house.

Unlike many other Native American healing ceremonies, the sweat lodge ceremony is not associated with Paviotso healings.

Contemporary shamans rarely incorporate power displays into their ceremonies, although the older people can remember shamans who handled hot coals, put hot iron into their mouths, caused things to appear, and so forth [Park 1938: 51–58].

Puhagan
Shoshoni, *Basin*

Common visionaries or medicine men; it means "possessors of power." Both men and women can become healers, but women usually enter this profession later in life, after menopause. In former times, most shamans received their helping spirits via vision quests, but in recent times, spontaneous dreams or dreams during unconscious states brought about by exhaustion from dancing the Sun Dance are the major source of *puha* (power).

During the last century, Shoshoni shamans often diagnosed an illness as soul loss, especially when the patient's condition continued to weaken, as in a high fever or coma. To cure such illnesses, the shaman would enter into a trance and make a flight from his body to find the lost soul and return it. This form of healing is no longer present among the Shoshoni. The diagnosis of spirit or object intrusion is still present, however, and all diseases are ascribed to it [Hultkrantz 1987:77].

In contemporary healing sessions, the shaman begins by diagnosing the case. The shaman looks into the body of the patient. Some shamans close their eyes to do this; others use a black scarf held up to the patient's body, which they look through. Once the cause is determined, the shaman calls forth his helping spirit. Depending on the type of disease and on the specific healing abilities of his spirits, the shaman has recourse to several methods of removing the disease agent. Some shamans brush their patients with an eagle-wing fan. The feathers draw out the disease, and the shaman then rubs the wing on something to brush it away. During the Sun Dance, he brushes his fan against the center Sun Dance pole to get rid of the extracted disease. In some cases, he simply blows the disease away. Other shamans may use a stick, horn, or other such object to remove the disease. In some cases, a shaman sucks out the disease through his rolled-up fingers, which are placed on the body of the patient at the location of the disease object; or he may simply place his mouth at the appropriate spot and suck. Quite often, the object removed is thrown into a fire to destroy it. This object is often seen as a tiny person.

Puhagant
Shoshoni, *Basin*

Also: *puhagunt* [Edmonson 1958:69]. The medicine men of the Eastern Shoshoni, in particular the Wind River Shoshoni. Typical of Plains cultures, the men seek a guardian spirit, called *puha*, through vision questing. Those who receive a spirit that possesses curing powers are called *puhagant*. (*Puha* also translates to "supernatural power.") Not all shamans use the same form of treatment, but all sing songs. Their treatments are based on dreams or visions. They make different marks near the fireplace and perhaps stick a feather up by the mark as an altar. The shaman places a feather on the afflicted part of the patient's body and sucks at the other end, then blows away or vomits the disease. Only the shaman himself sees what is extracted. If the shaman is not successful, there is no fee. To combat measles or smallpox, they have a special ceremony called the Horn Dance *(ap nöqára)* that lasts two to three days.

In former times, vision quests were most often conducted at the site of rock drawings, which were reported to have been carved by spirits. However, this method began to fade after it became understood that the drawings were made by evil spirits. This turn of thought occurred around

the 1920s. Today, most medicine men receive their healing powers by other means, most commonly through dreaming of a spirit. Another method is through a spontaneous vision. Such visions often occur during the performance of a Sun Dance. In rare instances, they occur when one is knocked unconscious by lightning. A medicine man on his deathbed can pass his power, along with the spirit's instructions for its use, to another man. Finally, a man might inherit his father's guardian spirit after his father dies. In this case, the man would be instructed to make a new medicine bundle, because the father's bundle would have been buried with him.

Shamans are often designated according to their power, such as *timpi puhagant* (rock shaman), *ubu puhagant* (arrow shaman), *mukam puhagant* (spider shaman), *toxo puhagant* (rattlesnake shaman), *pa puhagant* (water shaman), and so forth.

Puhagumi
Northern Paiute, *Basin*

Shaman; usually ascribed to those persons who have helping spirits and are able to cure.

Puhakut
Comanche, *Plains*

Any person who has supernatural powers. The term can be applied to both shamans who heal and those who act as sorcerers [Jones 1972:2].

Puhátumadápuipi
Paviotso, *Basin*

A ceremonial stick used in the altar displays of healing ceremonies by most Paviotso shamans. The stick is between 3 and 4 feet long, usually made of willow, and often painted with red or white bands. The particular design used in the painting is revealed to the shaman by his helping spirit. This stick is used only once; a fresh one is cut for each new ceremony.

To the stick is fastened the tail feather of a bird, most often an eagle. The particular type of feather used is not an indicator of the shaman's helping spirit, which is usually an animal. Attached to the quill of the feather is a 10-inch-long piece of buckskin thong. Down is also fastened to the thong, and one or two beads of bone, shell, or stone are strung onto it close to the feathers. The thong is then tied onto the stick.

During a healing ceremony, the stick is placed into the ground near the head of the patient. A powerful shaman can cause the feather to point upward during the ceremony.

Púhigan

Malecite, Passamaquoddy, *Northeast*
See *baohigan*.

Pul

Cahuilla, *California Peninsula*
Also: *puul*. Plural: *puvalam* [Bean 1972:108]. Shaman, among the Desert Cahuilla; the term also includes sorcerers. Both males and females become shamans. They receive their powers through dreams in which they acquire spirit helpers. These revelatory dreams often begin in childhood. In fact, Hooper [1972:334] reports that "shamans can usually tell when they look at children whether they will be medicine men when they grow up or not." However, some shamans do not begin dreaming until they are in their forties.

Cahuilla shamans "employed certain 'power-enhanced' objects to cure patients. Mortars and pots of the shamans were frequently endowed with powers. . . . Other equipment having power included special rocks and wooden wands to which feathers (usually owl) and sometimes an eagle claw or a raven's wing were attached. Elaborate song and ritual accompanied cures performed by shamans as well as the use of the power-endowed objects in various ways. Among the medical treatments employed by shamans were herbal remedies, sweating, massage, prescribed dietary restrictions, and sucking and the laying on of hands" [Bean and Saubel 1972:19]. The shaman may also blow or spit over the patient. Of these treatments, sucking is used most often.

Once the shaman has located the seat of pain in the patient's body, he applies his mouth to that area and sucks on it. Usually this results in the removal of some object, which passes through the body without leaving any marks on the skin of the patient. Sometimes a liquid substance is removed from the body. Hooper [1972:335] reports one case in which the shaman sucked out not only a woman's illness but also the pills given to her by a white physician, which had not alleviated her illness.

Pula

Lusieño, *California Peninsula*
Also: *pul* [Shipek 1992:89]. Plural: *puplem*. Shaman. Most shamans receive their power from dreaming. Spirits appear in their dreams and bestow sacred healing abilities. They also bring to the shaman a song to learn that invokes their healing power. They use sacred pipes in their healing ceremonies, blowing the tobacco smoke over the patient. Often the shaman sleeps beside the sick person, waiting for a dream from the helping spirit telling him how to proceed with the healing. Water is also blown on the patient. Some shamans use pieces of crystal colored with lithia in tourmaline formations that are rubbed over the patient's body.

Shamans also perform public displays of their powers. During certain dances, they "extract something from their legs or hands or different parts of the body . . . acorns or rabbits or little snakes or frogs. Albañas's great-aunt was a shaman, and could vomit up from her mouth a small live rattle-snake" [DuBois 1908:111].

Pula also refers to sorcerers [White 1976:369]. Sorcerers use a secret song, called a *Chatish* song, to bring an abundance of rain, grass, acorns, and other necessities of life. "These songs were also sung to hurt people with sickness and death, and this particular song could kill a man at a distance of many miles. . . . The 'hechicero' had within him something which could not be seen. He would draw it out and throw it off towards the man he wished to injure. The 'hechicero stick,'—wood without stone in the end, shaped like a small straight sword,—would be used to do this. Sometimes several shamans met at a house to kill a man at a distance" [DuBois 1908:111].

Qamkawl

Tsimshian, *Northwest Coast*

A renowned shaman whose name translates to "Only-One" (*qam*, only; *kawl*, one). He belonged to the Gyilodzau division of the Tsimshian (or Tsimsyan) that lived at the village of Klarhkyaals on the Skeena River. "Many times he restored life to those who were dead, and he foretold great events. . . . Only-One's fame went to all lands, to various countries, and he became not only famous, but wealthy. He was very well liked by all except his fellow halaaits (shamans) . . . as he was helping not only the rich but also many that could not pay him, he never failed to assist any that required his help" [Barbeau 1958:77–81]. He had already died by 1954, when material was gathered on his career.

Qaumaneq

Iglulik Eskimo, *Arctic Coast*

An unusual term that refers to the transformation involved in one's becoming a shaman. It encompasses both the ecstasy and the knowledge acquired during a successful vision quest for a spirit helper. Rasmussen [1929:115] provides details of such an extraordinary experience as related to him by a shaman named Aua:

"I felt a great, inexplicable joy, a joy so powerful that I could not restrain it, but had to break into song, a mighty song, with only room for one word: joy, joy! And I had to use the full strength of my voice. And then in the midst of such a fit of mysterious and overwhelming delight I became a shaman, not knowing myself how it came about. But I was a shaman. I could see and hear in a totally different way. I had gained my *qaumanEq*, my enlightenment, the shaman-light of brain and body, and this in such a manner that it was not only I who could see through the darkness of life, but the same light also shone out from me, imperceptible to human beings, but visible to all the spirits of earth and sky and sea, and these now came to me to become my helping spirits."

Qilalik

East Greenland Eskimo, *Arctic Coast*

Among the Ammassalik of eastern Greenland, a shaman—often a woman—who can perform the *qilaneq* divination ceremony. The ceremony is used, among other things, to diagnose illness. Variations on this form of divination can be found throughout the Eskimo cultures. The term comes from *qila*, meaning "a spirit in the earth." Thus, a *qilalik* is a person who has a *qila*.

The most common form taken by this divination procedure involves the shaman tying a thong to the head or foot of the patient, who is reclining on his back on the floor. The shaman then pulls upward on the thong to test the weight of the body part. Depending on whether the body part feels heavy or light, the answer yes or no is signified to any question put to the spirit by the shaman. With regards to prognosis, in western Greenland the rule is that if the head feels light, the patient will get well; if heavy, he will die. In most cases, a heaviness is seen as indicating the affirmative. (One known exception is among the Kotzebue Sound Eskimos, where a heavy head indicates the negative.)

Among the Copper Eskimo, the shaman uses a bundled-up coat called the *krilaq* (see entry). A spirit is called forth to enter the bundle, and afterward, heaviness indicates yes and lightness indicates no to any questions put to this spirit [Weyer 1932:445].

Qopine
Winnebago, *Midwest*
The supernatural aspect of power; translates to "mysterious." It is the equivalent of the widely used concept of *orenda* (see entry) found among the Iroquois [Lowie 1922:315].

Qube
Omaha, Ponca, *Plains*
See *xube.*

Querränna Society
Keres, *Southwest*
One of several religious societies found at the Sia Pueblo. Querränna is the name of the second man created on earth in the Sia origin myth. At the end of the nineteenth century, this society was nearly extinct, having only three members left. The society possessed the use of only one medicine, known as "sé-wili, which is composed of the roots and blossoms of the six mythical medicine plants of the sun, archaic white shells and black stone beads, turkis, and a yellow stone" [Stevenson 1894:113]. Concerning the preparation and use of this medicine, it was reported:

"Women are dressed in sacred white embroidered Tusayan blankets, and they grind the medicine to a fine powder amid great ceremony. When a woman wishes to become pregnant this medicine is administered to her privately by the ho'naaite (head shaman of the society), a small quantity of the powder being put into cold water and a fetich of Quer'ränna dipped four times into the water. A dose of this medicine insures the realization of her wish; should it fail, then the woman's heart is not good. This same medicine is also administered at the ceremonials to the members of the society for the perpetuation of their race; and the ho'naaite, taking a mouthful, throws it out through his teeth to the cardinal points, that the cloud people may gather and send rain that the earth may be fruitful" [Stevenson 1894:113].

Quohahles
Pueblo, *Southwest*
A shaman who lived among the Kiowas during the latter part of the nineteenth century. He became recognized as such after warning everyone one night that the camp needed to be moved before sunrise. They complied, and at sunrise, a buffalo stampede passed over the abandoned campsite. Tahan, who went on tour around the turn of the twentieth century lecturing on Native American life, reported of this shaman:

"They saw him (Quohahles) scoop his hands full of red coals of fire and rub them over his body without injury. So he became our Medicine Man. . . .

"Once Quohahles fell into a trance in which he remained two days as one dead. When he revived he told me that his spirit had left his body and traveled great distances; that he felt neither hunger nor weariness; and that he had learned mysteries of which as yet he could not speak.

"This wonderful man possessed a working knowledge of the laws of the human mind such as I have never found in books. He could not explain how he performed his wonders, but he knew what to do in order to produce certain definite results.

"Often, for instance, during religious ceremonies, I have seen men fall to the ground in a deep sleep and become rigid and stiff, after Quohahles had waved his sacred fan of crow feathers before their faces. . . . He taught me how to cause others to see what I wished them to see" [Griffis 1915:106–110].

Radin, Paul

Paul Radin was born in Poland on 2 April 1883. He was a student of Franz Boas and received his Ph.D. in anthropology from Columbia in 1910. He was best known for his in-depth knowledge of the Winnebago of Wisconsin and Nebraska, but he also published extensively on Native American religion, literature, myth, and philosophy. Radin was never a long-term member of any academic institution, and his work is better known in Europe, where he was affiliated with many different universities as well as the Jung Institute in Zurich and the Jungian Eranos Conferences at Ascona, Switzerland. Many of his publications were in German, as he studied at the Universities of Munich and Berlin between 1905 and 1907. He eventually split with the Boas quantitative method of fieldwork and adopted the historical perspective advocated by Alfred Kroeber and others. Among his classic works are *The Autobiography of a Winnebago Indian* (1920), which dealt with peyotism, *The Winnebago Tribe* (1923), and *The Trickster* (1956). He died in New York City on 21 February 1959.

Raqnowe waqonyitan

Missouri, Oto, *Plains*

Sacred pipe [Dorsey 1894:427]. Such pipes are shamans' most sacred possessions.

Rareñdiowanen

Iroquois, *Northeast*

Shaman. Literally, "one whose *orenda* is great, powerful" [Hewitt 1902:38].

Rattles Stone Like a Bell

Mandan, *Plains*

A shaman during the mid-eighteenth century who received his doctoring powers from the crane. The following account, given by Crow Heart, is of a healing performed by Rattles Stone Like a Bell and another shaman named Cherry Necklace. The patient was a warrior who had been wounded in battle by an arrow. The arrow stuck in a bone and the shaft separated, leaving the metal arrowhead in the warrior:

"Cherry Necklace tried to get the arrowhead first. He thought he ought to put him to sleep, so he smoked his medicine roots, but the injured man was in too great pain to sleep. He thought he would try another way; he would put hot coals on his pipe stem. The bull-snake came out (of the pipe), and he asked the snake to go into the wound, but the snake's jaws were too weak to extract the point, so Cherry Necklace gave up.

"Rattles Stone Like a Bell tried. He had two dried crane heads with the lower jaws attached and a stuffed crane. He tied one of the dry heads around the patient's neck and painted his face red. He put the other crane head around his own neck and painted his own face red also. He sang his medicine song which put the wounded man to sleep. While he was singing, the crane came alive and walked around the wounded man. As he was going to sleep, he heard the crane calling 'Konix,' and the medicine man answering 'Konix' from the other side of the room. When he was asleep, the crane walked up to him, stuck his bill in the wound, using his bill as pinchers. After pulling several times, he succeeded in extracting the arrowhead. Matter and blood came out of the wound. Rattles Stone Like a Bell sent word through the village for the people to come to the river's edge and see the wounded man bathe. He led the sick man to the water, all the time singing the crane's song. They washed off the red paint and went back to the lodge. Rattles Stone Like a Bell took all the goods he had been promised, but he gave some to Cherry Necklace, who was the older man" [Crow Heart in Bowers 1950:178].

Rattlesnake shaman

Shamanic specialists who control rattlesnakes, cure their bites, and protect people from their bites. It is the most frequently mentioned specialist among the California shamans.

Red Bird
Dakota, *Plains*
A shaman from the Lake Calhoun band in Minnesota. He died in 1839. Pond [1867:57] gives the following account of a Shaking Tent Ceremony (see entry) conducted by Red Bird:

"After binding Red Bird, placing the patient beside him, and upon turning out the lights a strong wind struck the tent, and the doctor cried out, as if he were in great fear, 'Boys (spirits) come carefully, your father (Red Bird) is very weak, be careful.' But the gods did not seem to regard the admonition . . . and heaved the tent furiously. The tent seemed to be full of them and they were very talkative and rude, but their voices were so fine, so soft, that we could not comprehend their meaning. They performed the ceremony of exorcising the sick man. . . . The gods called for a pipe and smoked many pipe's-full, indicating a large number of them, but it was dark and they could not be seen. Suddenly the gods were all gone, and the doctor ordered the torches to be lighted. All expected to see him still bound, as he was thrust into the tent; but, to their surprise, he was out of the robe, and all of his fingers and toes slipped out of their fastenings, though not a single knot had been untied. The sick man began from that time to recover."

Red Sky, James
Ojibwa, *Canadian Eastern Woodlands*
The last of the *mide* (see entry) masters from western Ontario in the Lake of the Woods area. His sacred birch-bark scrolls were deposited in the Glenbow-Alberta Institute by Selwyn Dewdney.

Reichard, Gladys Amanda
Gladys Reichard was born in Bangor, Pennsylvania, on 17 July 1893. She studied under Franz Boas, receiving her Ph.D. in anthropology from Columbia University in 1923. That same year, she began fieldwork on Navajo social organization as an anthropologist at Barnard College but soon turned to a study of Navajo religion and language. Throughout her life, she continued her association with both Barnard College and the Navajo. Her ethnographic contributions were among the most detailed ever published, and her two-volume work on Navajo religion, published in 1950, is a classic study. Some of her other works include *Social Life of the Navajo Indians* (1928), *Navajo Medicine Man* (1939), and *Navaho Grammar* (1950). She died in Flagstaff, Arizona, on 25 July 1955.

Remohpoh
Yurok, *Oregon Seaboard*
The doctor dance, a ritual used in the training of shamans. The ritual is performed in the sweat house to help the new shamans learn how to control their pains—that is, their healing abilities [Keeling 1992:71].

Ren

Huron, *Northeast*

The spiritual power in an individual or a group. This is a contracted form of the widespread Iroquois term *orenda* (see entry). All shamans possess *ren*. It is related to *oki* (see entry), the spiritual power obtained from one's helping spirit. "While it may be difficult sharply to differentiate ren from oki, there are some general differences. Ren power seems to reside in and characterize institutions, ceremonies or the total character of a person. More extrinsic than oki, while suffused with oki power, ren power is more humanly organized, manipulated, less mysterious and more predictable than oki power" [Pomedli 1991:123].

Rhombus

The technical name for a bullroarer or whizzer [Stone 1932:13]. These flat boards are usually 7 to 10 inches in length and are most often in the shape of a narrow parallelogram, a narrow triangle, or an isosceles triangle. They are usually made from the wood of a tree that was struck by lightning, and they often contain symbolic designs. The boards are tied to the end of a 5- to 6-foot piece of rawhide string. When whirled about the head, they make the sound of a gust of rain-laden wind. They are often used by shamans, especially in the

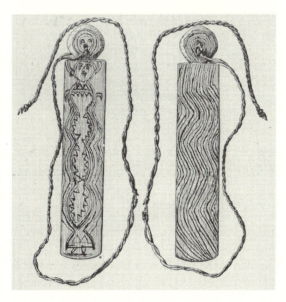

Rhombus

Southwest, for rainmaking ceremonies. However, they are also a common piece of shamanic equipment at certain healing ceremonies.

Rhythmic Sensory Stimulation

An aspect of human psychology that focuses on the effects that different rhythmic stimuli have on the body and mind. Such studies were pioneered during the 1930s. Research in this area has contributed greatly to our understanding of the various techniques used by shamans to enter into a shamanic state of consciousness (see entry).

In 1949, V. J. Walter and W. Grey Walter [1948: 82] wrote an article in which they conclude that: "Rhythmic stimulation of the organ of hearing as a whole can be accomplished only by using a sound stimulus containing components of supraliminal intensity over the whole gamut of audible frequencies—in effect a steep fronted sound such as that produced by an untuned percussion instrument . . ." such as a drum. By the early 1960s, A. Neher demonstrated that low-frequency, high-amplitude drumming elicited auditory driving responses. Neher [1962] reported that auditory responses are heightened if the main rhythm is reinforced by accompanying rhythms and by rhythmic stimulation of the tactual and kinesthetic sensory modes at the same time. Shortly thereafter, Raymond Prince [1968] conjectured that drumming was a "commonly used portal of entry into the dissociative state." In the same publication, Arnold Ludwig listed the following conditions that may produce altered states of consciousness: (1) reduction of exteroceptive stimulation and/or motor activity; (2) increase of exteroceptive stimulation, motor hyperactivity, and emotional hyperarousal; (3) focused and selective hyperalertness; (4) decreased alertness and relaxation of critical faculties; and (5) somatopsychological states such as hyperventilation, hypoxemia, dehydration, hypoglycemia, sleep deprivation, and exposure to extreme temperatures.

Such studies have demonstrated the importance of the ritual aspects of all shamanic healing ceremonies. What was once naively thought of as simply a lot of commotion can now be understood as sophisticated techniques used to alter the shaman's state of consciousness. The drumming, the singing, the dancing, the rhythms thereof, the fasting required, and so forth all contribute to the success of the shaman's entry into the shamanic state of consciousness (see entry). Thus, one or more of these aspects appear in every North American shamanic healing ceremony.

Roberts, Tudy
Shoshoni, *Basin*

A well-respected shaman during the 1940s–1960s, now deceased. He had many helping spirits, the most powerful of which was lightning. He reportedly had a precognitive ability to recognize the diseases of his patients, thus eliminating the need for an initial diagnosis. In addition to his healing abilities, he was known for his ability to forecast the weather and to lead the Sun Dance. He had also acquired invulnerability medicine, which protected him from bullets. He had the power to cure diseases such as colds, measles, and paralysis, but he never cured anyone unless he had received directions in a dream to do so. When requested to heal, he would always pray for assistance during the night, and a spirit would appear to give him instructions. For example, in undertaking a cure for measles, he dreamed about a spirit that told him to use his bull elk spirit, a medicine he had acquired during a Sun Dance. He said of this healing:

"When the sun rises in the morning I see in a [waking] vision the bull elk. It shakes me so that I see fires, I fall down and shake. Then I get up, shaking over the whole body. Then I am told what to do. I catch the measles by the palms of my hands, put it in the fire and burn it. If I don't burn it somebody else who is present will get the measles" [Hultkrantz 1992:88].

When doctoring, he would begin by calling upon the spirit that was to help him. He often used an eagle wing to draw the sickness out of the patient's body. He never overcharged a patient for a healing, and he refused to accept money as payment, but he would accept a horse or a blanket, because the spirits had told him to do so [Hultkrantz 1987:78–82].

Rogers, Will
Ojibwa, *Canadian Eastern Woodlands*

A *mide* shaman who worked closely with anthropologist Ruth Landes during the 1930s. He lived on the Cass Lake Reservation in Minnesota. His native name was Hole-in-the-Sky. Near the end of his life, he turned over his sacred Life and Ghost birch-bark scrolls and other sacred objects to Landes, who deposited them in the Milwaukee Public Museum.

Rolling Thunder
Cherokee, *Southeast*

One of the leading contemporary spokespersons for Native American shamanism and healing. Rolling Thunder resides at Carlin, Nevada, and cures patients through the use of his hands, breath, and a medicine feather. An offering of uncooked meat is used during the healing ceremony, which is placed at the foot of the patient, who sits in a chair. Rolling Thunder frequently passes over this offering with his medicine feather when working on his patients. At one point during such a ceremony, Doug Boyd [1974:88] noted that "Rolling Thunder made a sudden emphatic exhalation, leaned forward and began to sniff, but with the sound of an animal—intense and rhythmic—not the sound of a man. The loud sniffs were interspersed with quick, sharp exhalations. Once or twice the sniffing stopped and there was an eerie howling and wailing." In using his hands to doctor, Rolling Thunder first spits on one hand, holds it up, and then rubs both hands together before placing them on the body of the patient. In addition to shamanic techniques for healing, he uses plants, which he calls his "helpers."

Rupert, Henry
Washo, *Basin*

Reported by Handelman [1967:444] to be "the last shaman among the Washo Indians of western Nevada and eastern California," Henry Rupert was born of Washo parents in 1885 at Genoa, Nevada. As a child, he had a recurring dream of a bear that would come to his lean-to and stare at him. When Henry stared back at the bear, it would vanish, and then Henry would fly up in the sky toward the moon. He was also subject to spells of dizziness and fainting. At the age of seven, he had his first precognitive dream, in which he foresaw a suicide attempt by his mother. These are usually taken as early indicators of a disposition toward becoming a shaman.

Until the age of eight, he spoke only Washo. However, in 1893 he was taken to the Stewart Indian School near Carson City, where he remained for the next decade. While at Stewart, he received his first power dream at the age of 17. When he awoke from the dream, it was raining and he had a nosebleed. The nosebleed confirmed that it had been a dream that conferred power, and he interpreted the rain as meaning that water was to be his spirit power. After this dream, he aspired to become a healer, and five years later, in 1907, he hired Beleliwe (also known as Monkey Peter), a Washo shaman, to train him in the control of his powers. Under Beleliwe, he acquired his first spirit helper, which appeared as two Indian women. That same year, he performed his first healing, described by Handelman [1967:451]:

"In his first cure, Henry used techniques generally similar to those utilized by other Washo shamans. Traditional Washo curing rituals required a shaman to work for three consecutive nights from dusk to midnight, and a fourth night until dawn. In the course of the ritual, repeated every night, Henry used tobacco, water, a rattle, a whistle, and eagle feathers. He began by smoking, praying, washing the patient's face with cold water, and sprinkling all his paraphernalia with cold water. He then blew smoke on the patient and prayed to come in contact with water. A peace offering followed, in which he paid for the health of the patient by scattering gray and yellow seeds mixed with pieces of abalone shell around the body of the patient; the seeds symbolized food, and the shells symbolized money. Next he chanted, prayed, and again blew smoke on the patient and sprinkled his paraphernalia with cold water. Arising, he walked about blowing his whistle, attempting to attract the disease object or germ from the body of the patient and into his own body, whence it might be repulsed and captured by the whistle. Then he sat down again and blew a fine spray of cold water over the body of the patient. This ended the first half of the curing ritual, which was repeated each night.

"At some time during the course of the ritual, Henry would receive visions relating both to the cause of the illness and the prognosis. They usually involved either the presence or absence of water. Thus a vision of damp ground suggested that the patient was ill but would live a short while; muddy water suggested that the patient would live but would not recover completely; ice suggested that Henry must break through the ice and find water; burning sagebrush suggested that the patient would die quickly unless Henry could stamp out the fire. Over the four-night period the content of these visions, or occasionally dreams, tended to change. Thus, Henry might see a fire or a burned-over hillside on the first night, damp ground on the second, muddy water on the third, and on the fourth night a stream of clear, cold water or the Pacific Ocean rolling over the Sierra Nevada. The portent of the vision of the fourth night overrode those of the visions seen on the previous nights."

The following year, Henry acquired a second spirit helper. He was looking at the skeleton of a Hindu in the Carson City high school when the spirit of the Hindu "got on" him. This spirit demanded to be used in curing sessions, and Henry was forced to work out a reconciliation between the Hindu and the two Indian women. Afterward, Henry began his healing ceremonies by placing a handkerchief on his head to represent the Hindu turban. "He also began to place his hands on the patient's head, chest, and legs in a symbolic attempt to encompass the whole being of the patient with his power. He also began to envision himself differently while curing; while sitting by the side of the patient he saw himself as a skeleton with a turban on its head moving quickly around the body of the patient" [Handelman 1967:452].

At the age of 24, Henry performed his second healing on a man who had been diagnosed as having typhoid fever. He was called in as a last resort, the patient having been treated by both white doctors and shamans. Henry was successful in curing the man and thereafter gained renown as a shaman among the Washo. Over the years, as his fame as a healer spread, he began treating patients from the nearby Shoshoni and Northern Paiute Reservations. Eventually his patients included people from many different cultures, including Mexican, Filipino, Hawaiian, and white:

"In 1942, Henry journeyed to Sacramento to treat an old Mexican woman who had been diagnosed as having a malignant tumor of the abdomen. On the first night, Henry was unable to find water. On the second night he saw a burned-over hillside of which a section had remained untouched. On the third night he saw a small lake between two hills, and on the fourth, a stream of running water. On the morning of the fifth day the lump had disappeared from the woman's abdomen, and she later recovered completely.

". . . a Shoshoni boy from Austin, in central Nevada, was brought to Carson colony to be treated by Henry. The boy had auditory hallucinations in which he heard three men, who were following him, constantly threatening to kill him. The cause of the illness was discovered to be a tooth of a spirit which had projected into the boy's head. At the end of the curing session the boy no longer heard voices. In another case, an ex-soldier who had fought in World War II was brought to Henry with severe lacerations around his neck. This man had visual hallucinations in which two German soldiers were attempting to strangle him with barbed wire. Henry treated him successfully. In the case of a White store-keeper from Fallon, Nevada, with an apparent history of heart trouble, Henry found a butterfly in the man's chest and removed it. This man states to this day that he will not be treated by any other doctor than Henry" [Handleman 1967:456–457].

In 1942, at the age of 57, Henry finally decided to become a full-time healer. All during his life, Henry continued to increase his knowledge of healing. In 1956, at the age of 70, he acquired George, a Hawaiian spirit helper obtained through a Hawaiian shaman Henry had treated named George Robinson. This spirit manifested its powers most strongly in the vicinity of Henry's home, although the spirit lived in a volcano in Hawaii. Henry thus stopped traveling to his pa-

tients and asked that they be brought to his home. With the acquisition of George, Henry also changed his ritual procedures:

"A curing session utilizing the (new) techniques now took place in daylight, and it lasted no longer than four hours and sometimes as little as a few minutes, depending on the nature of the ailment. Henry no longer needed visions of diagnosis or prognosis, and he could also eliminate chants, the blowing of smoke and water on the patient, and the use of the whistle to capture disease objects. Instead the patient was asked the location of the pain or swelling and was seated in a chair facing west, the direction of the Hawaiian Islands. Standing behind the chair, Henry twice called upon George for help, each time placing his fingers on the patient's neck, with thumbs on spine, for about ten seconds. Then, with his hands again on the patient's neck, he called out: 'Wake up my body, wake up my nerves and circulate my blood; let my whole body be normal; let my heart beat, my speech, my eyesight, and my breathing be normal; and give me strength.' Next, standing in front of the patient, he stated: 'This person says he was sick here; he had pains here; it's not there now; it's gone.' Then he placed his hand on the 'pain spot' for some five seconds and asked the patient to take a deep breath and move his head from side to side. Usually the pain departed, but sometimes it moved to a different part of the body, in which case Henry again invoked George and repeated the procedure three or four times. Then, placing his left hand on top of the patient's head and his right hand at the patient's feet, he called to George: 'Please mend this.' Finally, he removed his hands and said: 'We will close this'" [Handelman 1967:460].

George brought new powers to Henry's healing repertoire, but not all were used by Henry. For example, he taught Henry a new way to quickly stop the bleeding in serious wounds, but Henry reported of this power: "I am kind of afraid of it; I don't have enough confidence. I have the idea it can't be done. I don't try it because I don't have enough confidence."

Sa'aba
Paviotso, *Basin*

A class of spirits from which the shaman receives his powers. In this case, the term refers to the spirits of the dead [Park 1938:15].

Sa'araws
Haida, *Northwest Coast*

Also: *ska'aga*. Plural *ska'ages*. Shamans [Barbeau 1958:3]. Translates as "medicine men." Both males and females can be shamans. During healing ceremonies, the shaman wears a special costume that includes a bark-fiber (or sometimes leather) medicine apron known (in Tsimshian) as an *ambelan*. The apron usually contains an image, below which is a row of long fringe, often with a row of rattling deer hooves. The shaman wears a carved bone piece through the septum of his nose, and bone earrings dangle from his ears. On the top of his head, he wears a headdress make of a skin that is often formed into the shape of an animal or bird. Sometimes this headdress (called a *hltelkaw*) is made of twisted red cedar that is formed into a knot on top, with a bone peg run through the knot. Also, the shaman often wears a necklace of grizzly-bear claws. The shaman sits behind a box drum and beats on it with a bone drumming stick. In his other hand is a rattle in the form of a human head, known as a spirit rattle, or the rounded box rattle, or a bone dagger. Haida carvers often portray their medicine men in argillite stone (sometimes wood) carvings, and from these carvings it is obvious that the costumes vary from shaman to shaman.

Healing ceremonies are usually attended by more than one shaman. Each shaman has at least one helping spirit acquired during a solitary vision quest in the mountains. In addition to acquiring healing songs from the spirit, the shaman usually receives some object—a carved bone, ivory, or stone—that is kept secret. This object is brought out only during a healing ceremony and is placed on the body of the patient while the shaman sings his medicine songs. Common healing spirits include the otter, the mink, the hawk, the salmon, the bullhead, the canoe, the sweat house, the moon, and the bear. Disease is most often diagnosed as evil spirits entering the body of the patient. The shaman massages the body and then sucks out the evil spirit, using his lungs to blow away the sickness.

Sacred Calf Pipe Bundle
Teton Dakota, *Plains*

The most sacred object known to the Sioux. It contains the original sacred pipe brought to them by White Buffalo Calf

Woman as a messenger from *wakan tanka* (see entry). The origin of this bundle appears to be rather recent, as determined from their winter counts—probably between 1785 and 1800 [Smith 1970]. "The Dakotas have kept a record of years from before the beginning of the ninteenth century A.D. by making a pictograph of something (memorable) which occurred during each year and naming the year for the thing which the pictograph represented, and this was called a winter count" [Walker 1982:87].

Since then, the bundle has been in the hands of various keepers. Until the tenure of Red Hair, or Old Man Elk Head, eighth keeper of the pipe bundle, the custodianship followed blood lines. Upon Red Hair's death in 1916, the bundle should have passed to his oldest son, Ernest Two Runs, also known as Ernest Eats-a-Lot and Ernest Elk Head. However, because Ernest had no children, a council on the Cheyenne River Reservation voted to pass it to his next older brother, Elias Elk Head. Instead, Martha, one of Red Hair's daughters, kept the bundle, claiming that her father had given it to her for keeping. It thus passed to the Bad Warrior family, where it remained for the next 23 years, with Martha being the first female keeper of the bundle. Upon her death in 1959, it passed to her son Ehli. It then went to Ehli's daughter Lucy, who had married into the Looking Horse family. Lucy died on 12 April 1966 and had broken tradition again by passing the bundle not to her son but to her grandson Orval, who is presently the keeper of the bundle.

The bundle contains great power, and the keepers are often fearful of it. Joe Thin Elk reported to Smith [1970:90] five reservation policemen who were sent by the reservation agent to confiscate the pipe bundle and return it to him.

"These same five returned the bundle when a great outcry was made against the agent and his actions. The policemen all met mysterious deaths within days after this incident, coming in the form of a gray mist as described in the legend of the Maiden's (White Buffalo Calf Woman) coming."

All sacred pipes used by the Sioux today are initially activated through a sacred ceremony in which a spirit comes and picks up the new pipe, taking it to this bundle. The spirit then consecrates the new pipe by touching it to the Sacred Calf Pipe Bundle, and then returns the blessed (thus activated) pipe to the ceremony. As such all the healing powers contained in any pipe are seen as coming from this original pipe.

Sacred Formula

Cherokee, *Southeast*
See *gowäli, igawésdi.*

Sacred pipe

Of all the sacred objects used in Native American healings, the sacred pipe is perhaps the most common and widespread. The pipe ritual is found in many other ceremonies as well, and it is the most widespread sacrament, along with the sweat lodge ritual, found in North America. In fact, the smoking of tobacco in any form is the most widespread religious activity among all Native Americans, including those of South America. In contemporary times, the use of the sacred pipe has spread (with the inadvertent assistance of the American Indian Movement (AIM), whose founders were mainly Lakota) to many non–Native American cultures.

In North America, the oldest known form of the pipe is tubular; the tobacco is placed in one end and inhaled from the other end. Usually the tobacco end of the pipe is slightly larger than the mouth end. Tubular pipes from the leg bones of large mammals, such as deer or antelope, were still in use on the Plains in the twentieth century. Some of the oldest pipes, found in Mummy Cave in northeastern Wyoming, are made of bone and date from around 2400 B.C. By 2000 B.C., stone tubular pipes were in use in Illinois, and by 1000 B.C., they could be found on the Columbia River in Washington. These pipes range from several inches to upwards of a foot in length.

In the Illinois-Ohio area, the tubular pipe gave way to the monitor or platform pipe by around 200 B.C. These stone pipes are usually 4 to 6 inches in length, with a flat, rectangular base and a bowl carved onto the top. Most often, the bowl is centrally located on the base platform. In other areas, such as the California coast, the tubular pipe evolved into the one-piece elbow pipe, which forms a 90-degree angle. Elbow pipes with elaborately decorated bowls were also observed being used among the Iroquoian-speaking people by early European visitors.

Thus, from the simple tube shape, the sacred pipe evolved into many different forms in many different localities. In the eastern woodlands, the simple platform pipe evolved into an elaborate effigy pipe whose bowl is in the shape of an animal, human, or spirit form—sometimes the head, and sometimes the whole body. Eventually, the Europeans also introduced a special variation of their own, used in trade, known as the tomahawk pipe; a pipe bowl is mounted opposite the tomahawk blade, and the handle is made hollow.

Other common forms that evolved were keel shapes and disc shapes. "The disc pipe, usually dated from the thirteenth through the sixteenth centuries, is found widely distributed throughout north-central North America, including the upper Mississippi, Missouri, and Ohio as well as the Lower Great Lakes drainage areas. Its use continued among the Osage and Iowa, where the pipe is found in ritual bundle complexes given up in the early Twentieth Century" [Paper 1988a:655].

Today, the most common shape is some variation of the stemmed elbow pipe, in which the bowl and stem are separate. The most common material used is the mineral catlinite, which is found in only one location in the world—along Pipestone Creek, a tributary of the Big Sioux River, in Minnesota. This location, now named Pipestone National Monument, is currently under the control of the National Park Service. However, Native Americans may go there and use the quarry. The mineral was named after painter George Catlin, who visited the quarry in September 1836 and was subsequently the first to ever write about it. Quarrying of the site probably began between 1600 and 1650. The dark red stone is symbolic of blood, most often that of ancestors or the buffalo. In former times, it was said that traditional enemies considered this site sacred and would lay down their weapons upon entering to quarry the stone.

Most contemporary pipe bearers use a mixture of tobacco made with one or more of the follow-

ing ingredients: red willow *(Salix)* "bark" (actually the layer between the outer bark and the inner wood called the cambium in botany); bearberry leaves *(Arctostaphylos uvaursi)*; sumac leaves gathered in the fall when red *(Rhus glabra)*; kinnick *(Cornus amomum)*, where the "Algonkian word, 'kinnikinnick,' is variously applied to a smoking mixture" [Paper 1988b:4]; mullein *(Verbascum)*; sage *(Artemisia)*; raspberry *(Rubus)* [Buhner 1996: 107]; and often flavored with osha *(Ligisticum porteri)* or mint. Each pipe bearer gathers and prepares his own mixture, thus it varies greatly. However, contrary to popular belief the mixtures contain no psychoactive ingredients. In fact, the method of smoking the sacred pipe is to merely puff on it and not inhale the smoke.

The bowl and stem of the pipe are usually carried in a special skin bag, often elaborately decorated, along with a tamper, the tobacco mixture, and other items. Elaborate rituals have evolved around the handling, loading, and smoking of the sacred pipe. Typically, the ritual begins with the sacred pipe being purified by smudging with sage, sweet grass, pine needles, or flat cedar. The smoke is passed over the bowl, stem, tamper, and so forth, to include all the ceremony participants. This is usually accompanied by special songs. Once the stem is connected to the bowl, the pipe is considered to be activated (the stem is often seen as male and the bowl as female). During the loading of the sacred pipe, each pinch of tobacco mixture is also smudged before being placed into the bowl, while all the participants watch in total silence. Most often, six or seven pinches of tobacco are used—representing the four cardinal directions, Heaven, Earth, and all the created.

The actual smoking of the sacred pipe is seen as an act of sending one's prayers to the Creator and as a means of communicating with the spirit world. That is, the sacred pipe is seen as a direct link between the mortal and the immortal—a sacred walkie-talkie, so to speak. As mentioned, most often the tobacco mixture is never inhaled. One simply takes several strong puffs while holding the bowl in the left hand; with the free right hand, one moves the smoke over one's head for a blessing. When finished, one often says, "All my relations," as a reminder that everything is one in the Creator. When praying with a loaded sacred pipe, one usually points the stem skyward. When blessing a person or object with the sacred pipe, one usually touches it with the stem. (For details of one pipe ceremony, see Newbery 1977.)

The actual rituals involving the use of the sacred pipe have, of course, evolved over time. So central is the use of the sacred pipe to many Native Americans that Christian missionaries have attempted to incorporate it into Christian theology. For instance, Father Paul Steinmetz, a longtime missionary among the Lakota in South Dakota, writes: "My intention was to establish the Sacred Pipe as a sacramental in Catholic ceremonies. . . . I enhanced the Sacred Pipe in the eyes of the Lakota Christian by making it a sacramental sign of Christ . . . to make it a permanent expression of Christianity" [Steinmetz 1980:178–179]. Others, such as Father William Stolzman [1989:214], contend that "active immersion in both religions (Lakota and Christianity) is a sign of more total dedication to God."

To those shamans who carry a sacred pipe, it is seen as essential for life, because through its use, one can attain those things needed to ensure life—good health, food, safety from harm, and even the control of weather. In their minds, there is nothing that cannot be attained through the proper use of the sacred pipe. It is considered to be alive, and it is treated like a loved child. It is also considered to be an instrument of mysterious power.

Säeicha
Arapaho, *Plains*
Sacred flat pipe,"looked upon by the Arapaho as an exceedingly holy object" [Carter 1938:76]. It is the source of all their medicine powers for healing, that is, the original source of supernatural powers.

This pipe is kept bundled and brought out only on special occasions. The bundle, about 2 feet long and made of buckskin, is kept cradled in a saddlebag with beaded fringe, hanging on four 5-foot poles brought together at the top so that it looks like a small tepee frame. Within this bundle, the flat pipe has several wrappings of colored felt around it. Also within this bundle are other sacred objects, such as a mud turtle shell that has been

painted red and contains items that rattle, and a grain of corn said to be placed in the bowl of the pipe.

When moved, the pipe is always carried by the official pipe keeper and is never allowed to be transported on a horse or travois. To merely open the bundle, a special ritual is enacted that requires three days and three nights to perform.

Ságodiwenha gwus
Cayuga, *Northeast*
The Dream Guessing ritual; literally, "her word (dream) taken off." This is a healing ritual in which anyone may participate. See *eyondwanshgwut* for details.

Sai'yûk Society
Makan, Clayoquot, *Northwest Coast*
One of the functions of this society is to assist in healing illnesses. Members, both men and women, go to the home of the sick individual, where they perform healing songs and dances. "The power of the *Sai'yûk* included the healing of physical ills, and it was said that they cured a cripple who had been unable to walk for at least 10 years. They came and sang for him, and he lived in excellent health to an advanced age. He was a whaler, a vocation which requires strength and endurance" [Densmore 1952:453].

Saltu
Wintun, *California*
Patwin spirit [Loeb 1934b:220].

Salye
Coast Salish, *Northwest Coast*
The Katzie term for a shaman's guardian spirit; literally, "vision" [Suttles 1955:6].

Sambo
Shasta, *California*
A shaman during the latter part of the nineteenth century who was involved in the development of the Earth Lodge cult obtained from the Wintu. He used a wand attached with fur tips and eagle wing feathers to draw out the sickness from his patients during his song and dance healing rituals. He also

sprinkled his patients with water that contained ground celery root.

Sanapia
Comanche, *Plains*
During the 1960s, Sanapia was the last remaining eagle doctor among the Comanche. She was born near Fort Sill, Oklahoma, in the spring of 1895. Both Sanapia's mother and her mother's older brother were eagle doctors. Sanapia was also a peyotist. About her eagle powers she said:

"The eagle got more power than anything living, I guess. It's got Medicine to help people get well . . . to cure them. I got power like that eagle because the eagle help me when I call on it when I doctor. . . . I can feel the eagle working in me when I doctor and try hard to get somebody well. Feels like that eagle tell me in my mind to go ahead and fix that person up . . . get him well" [Sanapia in Jones 1972:23].

Sanapia, between the ages of 14 and 17, was trained to be an eagle doctor by her mother, maternal grandmother, paternal grandfather, and maternal uncle, but most of her healing activities did not take place until after 1945, following menopause. The years in between she referred to as "the time I was roughing it out." Once she began to practice, her power dictated that she not refuse any request to perform a healing. Payment for her healings was necessary to honor her medicine, but she was never allowed to set the price; that was left to the discretion of the patient.

Part of her training involved a ritual in which her mother instilled power into Sanapia's mouth and hands:

"Sanapia's brother was told by the mother to lay a fire of pecan wood. After the wood burned to coals, the brother brought the coals to a secluded place where Sanapia and her mother waited. The mound of coals burned between them. Sanapia was cedared and fanned by her mother. . . . This blessing also included the mother's singing of her Medicine song, an action which serves to call the *puhakut's* (shaman's) power sources to his service. The mother, using her bare hand then plucked a

live coal from the mound of embers and handed it to Sanapia. . . .

"'I was sure scared then . . . almost got up and ran away. I was only a young girl at that time, you know. But, when I took them coals on my hand, inside and outside my hand I felt a chill, maybe. Oh, it was like chills in my hands. That has the meaning that power was in there . . . working in my hands. Felt like it would go up my arm even.'

"After Sanapia had taken the coal and covered her hands with the ashes, her mother began the transmission of supernatural power to Sanapia's mouth. Two eagle feathers, manipulated by the mother, were drawn across Sanapia's opened mouth four times; however, in the course of the fourth movement of the feathers, one of the feathers disappeared. At this occurrence Sanapia's mother told her that the eagle feather had entered her mouth and would dwell there for the rest of her life" [Jones 1972:32–33].

This transmission of power came in four stages during her training. The final stage was during a four-day fast. Afterward, her mother ceased doctoring. Later, when Sanapia began to doctor, she used only one calling song, which called upon the spirits of her mother and uncle to help her call the eagle for healing. She often doctored during a peyote meeting, an example of which follows:

"So that night we had a peyote meeting and the second night we had another one and the fourth night . . . the fourth she died. She just went out. She was blue . . . fingernails were blue and her lips turn blue. I told them, 'Take that drum hide out.' And they took it, rinse it out, squeeze it, and I said, 'Give it to me.' And I put it on her head. I rub her face with it, and four times I done that to her and then I sing my Medicine song. When anybody's dying and I doctor them that's the only time I sing that special song I got. So I said, 'You all carry her and put her on my bed,' and they carried her. I said, 'You all stay out there in the front room.' . . . Everybody get out. It was raining out there and the wind was howling around. I sing this song and I fan her and I doctor her . . . give her that medicine. I don't know how many times I give her that. And after awhile she open her eyes and said, 'I'm sure thirsty.' And after that she got alright" [Sanapia in Jones 1972:45].

In addition to using herbal remedies, Sanapia was a sucking doctor. For this purpose, she used the tip of a cow horn, cut 4 inches long, that had a hole drilled in the end. She would hold the tip to her mouth and place the horn against the afflicted area of the patient's body. Once she completed her sucking, she would rinse the poison from her mouth. Her mother had used kerosene for this purpose, but Sanapia opted for mouthwash, a bottle of which she always carried in her medicine case. She also used the tail feather from a golden eagle in her healings. To prevent the spread of a sickness, she used a piece of charcoal that had been placed into a water drum and used in a peyote ceremony. She drew a circle with it around the afflicted area on the patient's body. Other items included the fur of a white otter she used in doctoring infants. A piece of the fur was cut off and thrown onto a fire, and the infant was passed through the smoke from it. She also used a bone medicine known to the Comanche made from grinding bone into a powder.

Sanimuinak

East Greenland Eskimo, *Arctic Coast*
An Angmagsalik shaman who practiced during the last half of the nineteenth century. In 1884, G. Holm [1914:90–97] attended one of his shamanic rituals, conducted in the dark, and reported the following events:

"The drum now started into motion, dancing first slowly, then with ever increasing speed, and mounted slowly up to the ceiling. Now ensued a veritable pandemonium of noises, a rattling, a blustering, and a clattering, sounding now like a machine factory, now like a great winged creature. At one moment it was the angakok (shaman) one heard, succumbing to a power mightier than himself, groaning, wailing, shrieking, whining, whispering; now came the sound of spirit-voices, some deep, some feeble, others lisping or piping. At frequent intervals a harsh, demoniacal, mocking laughter made itself heard. . . . Then once more that deafening chorus of clattering, rattling and blustering noises—the drum fell to the ground

with a crash and all was still. This was the signal for the entrance of the dreaded monster, *Amortortok* . . . it has black arms and anyone whom it may happen to touch turns black and is bound to die. It walked with a heavy tread round the house and on the platform and roared out crying 'a-mo! a-mo!' All cowered into the furthest recesses of the platform for fear that the monster might touch them. It dinned in my ears and tried to tear away from me the skin on which I sat, in order to get me up in a corner with the other people, but only succeeded in tearing the skin."

Santiano

Nootka, *Northwest Coast*
Dubbed "the last great medicine man among the Makah" by Densmore [1939:286], Santiano died in 1909. In his healing ceremonies, he sang medicine songs and used a rattle made of pecten shells on a hoop of whalebone. He had several powerful *tumanos* (spirit helpers; see entry) that gave him great supernatural abilities. For instance, it was reported that he could stay under water for two hours. One informant saw him "go under water taking with him four large packing baskets which he filled with sea urchins. After a while he came up with the four baskets filled" [Densmore 1939:286].

He normally doctored alone. However, in serious cases, he would ask others to sing with him, which increased his own ability to cure. Both men and women sang, and the women clapped their hands to mark time. Crying or weeping was discouraged during the ceremony, as that tended to weaken the spirits of the patient. Sometimes only one or two songs were needed to cure the patient. In any event, however, Santiano was well known for his persistence during a treatment; he would stay with the patient, singing, for as long as it took.

He also used his spirit helpers during the ceremony. For example,

"Santiano was treating a sick boy and standing about 10 feet from the patient. He displayed his tumanos, which was a small animal, and caused it to traverse the intervening distance and disappear in(to) the body of the sick boy. The purpose was said to be that the sick boy 'might be strengthened and enabled to breathe better.' The boy recovered" [Densmore 1939:287].

Saokata
Iroquois, *Northeast*

Diagnosticians. According to the Iroquois, illnesses come from three different sources: natural causes, something needed by the soul of the patient, and sorcery. In the sixteenth and seventeenth centuries, the French Jesuits called these diagnosticians *jongleurs*, or jugglers (see entry). When people become ill, they first consult the *saokata*. Shimony [1970:240] reports that the contemporary Iroquois at Six Nations Reserve refer to these diagnosticians as *tayatowetha*, which literally means "he deliberates." The power of the *saokatas* was originally attributed to a powerful spirit name *oki* (see entry). According to the Jesuits, this spirit came in many different forms—an eagle, a raven, and so forth.

Sapir, Edward

Edward Sapir was born in Lauenberg, Germany, on 26 January 1884 and raised in New York City. He was a brilliant linguist who trained under Franz Boas at Columbia. He began his fieldwork as a graduate student in 1905 among the Wishram Chinook. In 1906, Sapir studied the now extinct Takelma in southern Oregon, and in 1907–1908, the Yana in northern California. He received his Ph.D. from Columbia in 1909 with a dissertation on Takelma grammar. Through 1910, he taught at the University of Pennsylvania, where he studied the Southern Paiute of the Basin area. From 1910 to 1925, he was chief ethnologist for the Geological Survey of Canada, where he spent his most productive years. During this period, he undertook major studies of Nootka (1910–1914), Sarcee (1922), and Kutchin (1923). His work in Canada resulted in a classification of native languages that reduced their immense diversity into six large linguistic stocks.

In 1925, he joined the anthropology department at the University of Chicago, where he became an academic figure of near-legendary proportions. During this time, he did field research with the Hupa (1927) and the Navajo (1929). In 1931, he accepted the Sterling professorship of an-

thropology and linguistics at Yale, where he remained until his death on 6 February 1939.

Many contend that Sapir was the most brilliant linguist to date to have studied Native American languages. Among Sapir's students were linguists Stanley Newman and Benjamin Lee Whorf.

Sauwel
Wintun, *California*

Special locations, often caves, that are known power spots to which shamans go to acquire supernatural powers or to receive spiritual guidance [Theodoratus and LaPena 1992:220].

Sawanikä
Zuni, *Southwest*

A term that translates to "weapons," but the abstract meaning of the word is "power," referring to the power of shamans and sorcerers [Parsons 1939:721].

Sayiws
Coast Salish, *Northwest Coast*

A headdress made of thick, long woolen strands that is worn by performers of the Spirit Dance during healing ceremonies. After it is made, it is subjected to a purification and power-charging ritual before being used. "It is purified by being passed through fire four times, and charged with power from four fully-dressed spirit dancers who dance around the smokehouse with it and present it four times to each of the four corners" [Jilek 1982b:136–137]. The term comes from *say*, meaning "wool," and *-yiw*, meaning "having contact with the supernatural."

Sbatatdaq
Coast Salish, *Northwest Coast*

Dialectical variant: *sptdaqw* (Dwamish); also *xudab*. Name of "the spirit-help which enables a man to go to the underworld" [Waterman 1930b: 553], or the special supernatural power for recovering lost souls from the underworld [Jilek 1982b:145]. *Sbatatdaq* is the Snohomish name of the one- or two-night Spirit Canoe healing ceremony (see also *Skwanilac*) conducted by most of the Salish shamans, called *duxuda'b* [Haeberlin 1918:250], living in the Puget Sound area. It is held when a person's illness is diagnosed as being caused by the loss of the patient's guardian spirit, known as *skla'letut,* or "shadow" (soul), known as *sle.* The symptoms are psychological rather than physical. However, a gradual loss of property is often diagnosed as being symptomatic of the loss of a guardian spirit or shadow.

Among the Salish, there are two types of guardian spirits—the *skla'letut* is the type obtained by most people, and the *xuda'b* is reserved for shamans. The first type confers good luck in life for hunting, fishing, gambling, property acquisition, and so forth; the second type, which comes in various forms, brings healing powers. However, only shamans who own a *sbatatdaq xuda'b* can perform this *sle/skla'letut*-seeking healing ceremony.

This healing ceremony is unusual in that the lost *skla'letut* is not captured and returned to the patient directly by the shaman. Instead, it is recaptured through a dramatization involving numerous shamans. The ceremony is performed by an even number of shamans—6, 8, 10, or 12, with 8 being the most common number used. Usually, this involves hiring shamans from other nearby nations, depending on which trails are used to travel to the land of the dead. For example, Dwamish and Suquamish *sbatatdaq* shamans would never participate in a ceremony conducted by the Snohomish, Snuqualmi, or Skokomish, although they might be in attendance.

The ceremony is usually conducted only in January (or perhaps also in December), and always at night. Because time in the land of the dead is opposite to what it is in this world, visitations to that land are during bright summer days, which is the most advantageous condition for retrieving a lost spirit. The ceremony is conducted in any house that is laid out in an east-west direction, because the land of the dead is due west. If the patient's house does not lie in such a direction, he rents one that does. The shamans all face the same direction in two parallel rows. Each shaman has a paddle-shaped cedar board that is stuck in a hole in the ground such that it stands erect. This board, called a *swan'c,* is symbolic of his experiences in the capture of his own personal *sbatatdaq* guardian spirit. Each shaman also holds a 6- to 8-foot pole that represents this spirit. During the ceremony, as the

shamans dance, they point these poles to their respective boards. The poles are also used to row the (spirit) canoe in which they journey to the land of the dead. The journey is filled with many difficulties. For example, they must cross a river that is too swift for the canoe, so they must cross it using a log that has fallen across the river. This is dramatized in the ceremony when the shamans lay their poles on the ground and walk along them. If anyone slips off of this "log," his feet swell up and he is unable to walk. Since he cannot be abandoned, the others must carry him, adding to the difficulty of an already difficult journey.

After securing the guardian spirit of the patient, the shamans return, now facing eastward. When they arrive back at the house, they sing the song of this guardian spirit, and the patient knows that they have succeeded in their quest. The patient then dances and sings this song, marking the end of the ceremony. If the sick person does not get up and dance, it means that the shamans have brought back the wrong guardian spirit. If this occurs, the shamans will not be paid for their service [Haeberlin 1918].

Sees the Living Bull
Crow, *Plains*

One of the most famous of the River Crow medicine men. His powers came after four four-day vision quests. His spirit guide wore special moccasins that he duplicated. The left moccasin was made from the head of a silver fox, and the right moccasin was made from the head of a coyote—including the ears of both animals. He wore these special moccasins when performing ceremonies. Sees the Living Bull died in 1896 at the approximate age of 98. The sacred moccasins then became the property of Gray Bull, who turned them over to the Heye Foundation in 1921. Today, they are in the National Museum of the American Indian.

Senqenim strqam
Sinkaietk, *Plateau*

The annual sing-dance of the southern Okanagon of Washington that is held during January or February. It is also called the winter dance and the medicine dance. In its later seasonal phase, it is called the Chinook Dance. The dance is generally led by a man of considerable power who has been instructed by his guardian spirits to perform this dance. A person usually performs several such dances during a lifetime.

Serrat
East Greenland Eskimo, *Arctic Coast*
See *erinaliut*.

Sgana
Haida, *Northwest Coast*
A supernatural being that possesses a shaman. During shamanic rituals, "the shaman's own identity was practically abolished. For the time he himself was the supernatural being" [Barbeau 1958:64].

Shade
Another term for "spirit" or "soul." It is rarely used by American anthropologists, but seen frequently in European ethnographies.

Shadotgea
Seneca, *Northeast*
The Eagle Society, one of several medicine societies. Its ceremony is considered one of the most powerful, and its members have the most potent charms known. One gains membership into the society only through dreams or through having been doctored by the society for an illness. The ritual itself is composed of 10 songs and a dance. The dance is performed by four selected members, who assume a squatting posture and imitate the motions of the eagle. The dance requires a tremendous amount of physical exertion. Each dancer holds in the left hand a calumet fan, made by suspending six heron or four eagle feathers parallel and horizontally from a rod or reed. In the right hand, each holds a small gourd rattle with a wooden handle, or a small rattle made of a folded strip of hickory bark. All the participants paint a round red spot on each cheek before participating in the ceremony [Parker 1909:174–176].

Shadow
In many of the early writings on Native American healing, "shadow" is often used to refer to the human soul, especially when discussing sickness caused by soul loss.

Shagodiyoweqgowa
Seneca, *Northeast*
False faces, a type of spirit found in the Native American cultures of this geographic area [Hewitt 1918:457]. During a healing ceremony, their shamans wear wooden masks representing different false-face spirits and become the embodiment of the spirit.

Shakers
A messianic cult founded among Native Americans of the northwest coast by John Slocum, a member of the Squaxin band. In the fall of 1881, John Slocum died. As they were preparing him for burial, he resuscitated and stated that he had been to heaven and seen an angel, who had sent him back to correct his sins and lead others into a Christian way of life. He announced that a church was to be built in which he would preach about this new way of life. He told people that Indian doctors were bad and that people must give them up and be cured by prayer instead.

It was Slocum's wife, Mary, who introduced the shaking aspect into the religion. This occurred a year later in 1882, when John Slocum again became gravely ill and was near death. Mary had gone to the beach, crying, when "the power fell on her" and she started shaking. "She went back to the house and, turning to the left, circled it three times, shaking all the while. The people inside were afraid when she came in, and some of them left. She touched or brushed her brother Isaac and he started to shake; she touched his wife and a Nisqually man named Sylvester Yucton and they did the same, so that all four were shaking at the same time" [Barnett 1957:19]. John Slocum recovered, and Mary attributed his recovery to the power inherent in her shaking.

Eventually, healing rites were incorporated into the religion and were conducted in either the church or the home of the patient. The ritual has a prayer phase and a shaking phase. An account involving the treatment of a 12-year-old girl around 1900 is as follows:

"The ceremony began with the lighting of the tallow candles on the numerous crosses. The father and child were placed in the center of the room and the shakers arranged themselves in circles around them and began ringing their bells in unison. Soon they began to jump in unison with the ringing of the bells. After this had continued for some time, one after another proceeded to the child and, by feeling over its body, took out some of the *masache* (evil), which was burned over the candles. Then, in a most reverential and devout manner, they knelt around the child and most earnestly prayed for its recovery. Their prayers were intermingled with responsive exercises in which they all fervently took part" [Barnett 1957: 258].

By the time the religion was incorporated in 1910, Mud Bay Louis, who was the real leader of the religion and the first bishop of the Shaker Church, had formalized the healing ritual.

"He stipulated that upon entering a house or a church the 'workers' must go around the room to touch hands with everybody and then divide themselves so that the women took seats on the south side of the building and the men opposite them. The sick person was to be placed in the center of the room and he or his relatives must ask for help. Thereupon the Shakers were to take their positions in ranks facing the east (prayer table), with the men on one side and the women on the other. Standing thus, anyone could pray or sing as the spirit moved him until all had finished. At the bell signal three tramping circuits of the room were to be made, at the end of which the men and women disengaged themselves from the procession so that they formed two parallel lines or arcs of a circle across the hall from each other. While the stamping and bell ringing continued without cessation this formation was to dissolve gradually as the power took possession of individuals and they began to mill indiscriminately around the patient. Finally, after all the shaking was over, the two lines were to re-form and the ceremony concluded with the ritual march of the handshake" [Barnett 1957:259].

Shaking Tent Ceremony
Ojibwa, Ottawa, Cree, Saulteaux (Northern Algonquian), Mistassini, Naskapi-Montagnais, Menomini (Central Algonquin), *Northeastern Woodlands Great Lakes*; Blackfoot (Blood and Peigan),

Gros Ventre, Sarsi, Kiowa, Cheyenne, Plains Cree, Dakota, Mandan, Assiniboin, *Plains*

The Shaking Tent Rite or Ceremony is one of the most widely distributed shamanic complexes in North America. Listed above are but a few of the many different nations that adopted this ritual approach to the spirit world. It is found across North America, in one form or another, from eastern Washington to Labrador. Its origin predates the coming of Columbus. Thus it is one of the earliest shamanic ceremonies to be observed in North America. It was described by Samuel de Champlain among the Algonquin as early as 1609 [Biggar 1925]. However, the first person to study this ceremony in any depth was Father LeJeune in 1634 [JR 1897–1905]. His account is also believed to be the earliest eyewitness account of a Native American spirit-calling ceremony [Lambert 1956]. The first picture of the actual conjuring lodge used in this ceremony did not appear until the 1860s, in the works of Schoolcraft. This ritual appears by various names in the literature, such as "Spirit Wigwam" [Burgesse 1944].

Among the Ojibwa, the shaman, often referred to as a conjurer in the older literature, is called a *djessakid*. The *djessakid* learns his skills from his *manito*, or helping spirit, rather than inheriting the ritual from his relatives. Thus, he cannot sell or transfer his ability to others. When someone acquires a vision that gives the power to perform this ceremony, it is not put into practice immediately. Hallowell [1942] reports that some youths waited until the same vision had appeared to them four times before they began to perform this rite. The performance requires a great deal of personal skill and power on the part of the shaman to include physical strength and maturity. In fact, the ritual is so powerful that children are not allowed to attend, and shamans use it sparingly because it drains one's personal power. In addition to divining the causes of and required cures for illnesses, this ceremony is performed for many other reasons, such as foretelling the future, locating game, finding lost objects, obtaining information on the movement of enemies during war, and calling the spirits of deceased individuals. The ceremony can even be used to call in the free soul of a sorcerer to force the sorcerer to cease evil activities, such as causing sickness [Vecsey 1983:104].

A lodge constructed for a Shaking Tent Ceremony at Lac Courte Oreille, Wisconsin, in 1899. The ceremony was performed to find disease causes and cures, as well as for such purposes as foretelling the future or calling the spirits of deceased individuals.

The ceremony is usually performed in the dark, but there are recorded instances of its being performed during the day. The *djessakid* begins by attending a sweat lodge (also called a sweat bath) ceremony to purify and strengthen himself. Afterward, his assistants construct the tent. The construction differs from shaman to shaman, depending on the instructions he has received in his visions. Most often, the structure consists of 5 to 10 freshly cut tent poles approximately 10 to 12 feet in length. Coleman [1937] reports that among the northern Ojibwa, the number of poles represents the degree of the shaman's abilities, or "steps to the Great Spirit." The poles are placed in the ground in a circle about 4 feet in diameter, bent outward in the middle and brought together at the top, and bound laterally by ropes. The poles are then covered with skins or bark, leaving about a 1-foot-diameter opening at the top for the ingress and egress of helping spirits. The floor of the lodge is usually covered in boughs, and medicine rattles are hung from the poles.

As the ceremony begins, the shaman approaches the tent, singing to his *manitos* that they should enter as he enters. Often the shaman is bound tightly with a rope beforehand and then placed in the lodge. Once the shaman enters the lodge, his *manitos* enter. This is evidenced by the lodge shaking violently, hence the name of the ceremony. In fact, from the time the shaman enters the lodge, it is seldom still [Hallowell 1942]. In this way, the audience knows when the helping spirits are present. Members of the audience then ask questions of the spirits and receive answers (via the shaman, who is by this time in a deep trance). The spirit voices heard give advice, reveal secrets, and perform other required tasks. The most common *manito* to appear during this particular ceremony is Turtle (*Mikenak* or *Michika),* whose distinctive voice resembles Donald Duck's. All the spirit voices coming from the lodge are distinguishable from the voice of the shaman, and the participants are able to recognize which spirits are present by their distinctive voices.

Quite often, the *djessakid* performs special tricks to show his power and increase his reputation and prestige in the local community. These abilities demonstrate the actual presence of the *manitos* as well as the shaman's control over them.

Although these powers are well known to Native American communities, early settlers tended to disregard them, saying that they were the work of charlatans. One such incident was reported to the Anthropological Society of Washington by a U.S. Army officer named Col. Garrick Mallery. Years later Hoffman [1891:276–277] quoted part of Mallery's report:

"Paul Beaulieu, an Ojibwa of mixed blood, present interpreter at White Earth Agency, Minnesota gave me his experience with a Jessakkid, at Leech Lake, Minnesota, about the year 1858. The reports of his wonderful performances had reached the agency, and as Beaulieu had no faith in jugglers, he offered to wager $100, a large sum, then and there, against goods of equal value, that the juggler could not perform satisfactorily one of the tricks of his repertoire to be selected by him (Beaulieu) in the presence of himself and a committee of his friends.

"A committee of twelve was selected to see that no communication was possible between the Jessakkid and confederates. These were reliable people, one of them the Episcopal clergyman of the reservation. The spectators were several hundred in number, but they stood off, not being allowed to approach.

"The Jessakkid then removed his clothing, until nothing remained but the breech-cloth. Beaulieu took a rope (selected by himself for the purpose) and first tied and knotted one end about the juggler's ankles; his knees were then securely tied together, next the wrists, after which the arms were passed over the knees and a billet of wood passed through under the knees, thus securing and keeping the arms down motionless. The rope was then passed around the neck, again, and again, each time tied and knotted, so as to bring the face down upon the knees. A flat river-stone, of black color—which was the Jessakkid's manido or amulet—was left lying upon his thighs.

"The Jessakkid was then carried to the lodge and placed inside upon a mat on the ground, and the flap covering was restored so as to completely hide him from view.

"Immediately loud, thumping noises were heard, and the framework began to sway from side to side with great violence; whereupon the clergyman remarked that this was the work of the Evil One and 'it was no place for him,' so he left and did not see the end. After a few minutes of violent movements and swaying of the lodge accompanied by loud inarticulate noises, the motions gradually ceased when the voice of the juggler was heard, telling Beaulieu to go to the house of a friend, near by, and get the rope. Now, Beaulieu, suspecting some joke was to be played upon him, directed the committee to be very careful not to permit any one to approach while he went for the rope, which he found at the place indicated, still tied exactly as he had placed it about the neck and extremities of the Jessakkid. He immediately returned, laid it down before the spectators, and requested of the Jessakkid to be allowed to look at him, which was granted, but with the understanding that Beaulieu was not to touch him.

"When the covering was pulled aside, the Jessakkid sat within the lodge, contentedly smoking his pipe, with no other object in sight than the black stone manido. Beaulieu paid his wager of $100."

As this ceremony spread to other tribes, variations on the central theme of the ritual took place. For example, among the Gros Ventre, the spirits most often speak in a whistling talk [Cooper 1944], although they are also heard speaking in normal voices. Among the Peigan, the shaman is wrapped in a moose hide and hides behind a curtain at one end of a large lodge rather than being placed in a small, specially built lodge. Among the Crow, Gros Ventre, and Blackfoot-Blood, the rituals are most often performed by female shamans, but among the Eastern Cree and Ojibwa, women rarely perform this ceremony.

Shamanic state of consciousness

A term coined by anthropologist Michael Harner to refer to the particular state of consciousness that a shaman must attain to be able to communicate with his or any spirits. "The shamanic state of consciousness (SSC) is the very essence of shamanism, and critical to the premise that the shaman is the past and present master of the imagination as healer" [Achterberg 1987:108].

Among European scholars, there is a tendency to differentiate between a shaman and a medicine man: a shaman uses ecstatic trance (i.e., an altered state of consciousness), and a medicine man does not. Thus, the word "medicine," as used in Europe, is closer to the Latin meaning of the word, "physician's art," whereas in North America, it is used to mean "supernatural power."

Some scholars object to the use of this term, opting to define shamanic abilities/activities as the products of several different levels/states of consciousness. For example, some shamans remember their trance possessions, while others do not.

Shaxöa
Tiwa, Southwest
The Isleta Pueblo word for witches. Witches or sorcerers are believed to be a major source of illness. A sorcerer causes an illness by "shooting" some object into the body of his victim. The healer must remove the object or find the sorcerer and force him to remove it. Parsons [1932:339–340] provides a partial account of one such healing:

"The chief (shaman) stands in front of the large altar blade showing his crystal to the assistants who stand in a half circle facing him. As they look into the crystal they see through all the world, whence wind or rain will come, and on what day, what sickness may be imminent, how long the sickness will last, and how to get rid of it. . . . Now the chief starts to call the witch who is the cause of the sickness and who is in hiding at the ends of the world. The chief calls him by singing his song. Every time he sings the witch's song the witch draws closer to town. Some of the assistants together with the war chief and kumpa go out to search for the witch while the chief sits near the Mothers, singing to help those who have gone on the witch quest. These spread out in a circle, as on any hunt, and close in on the witch who is so afraid of kumpa 'he does not even move.' The men seize him to take to their ceremonial house.

"Sometimes the witch is so strong they can not move him, and they tell the war chief to shoot him with his bow and arrow. He will shoot him through the body. His power thus broken, they carry him in. Everybody looks at him and spits on him. They place him near the meal basket of the altar. The chief tells those present what bad things the witch has been doing, sending sickness, starving the animals, etc. The chief will ask the witch if he is going to stop his bad ways. He will say yes, he will, and that he will keep back the bad and suffer it himself. The chief takes the blade from the altar and sticks it into the body of the witch, killing him. Two assistants carry him out and burn him on a pile of wood, i.e., burn his body, his spirit (power, *nate*) leaves the village to die outside. . . . The chief addresses those present, telling them not to worry or think about it any more. The sickness is gone. If they go on thinking about it the sickness will linger. The sooner they forget it, the sooner it will go."

Sheride
Keres, *Southwest*

The Laguna Pueblo name of Juan Rey, who was an Ant doctor and a stick swallower during the first quarter of the twentieth century. He moved to Isleta Pueblo, where his powers became well known. In 1923, he moved to Sandia Pueblo, and died the following year.

Shihio
Tiwa, *Southwest*

At Isleta Pueblo, the special stones used in the sweat bath; translates to "eye stones." The stones are heated and brought into the lodge, and water is poured over them. The sweat bath is used, among other things, to treat paralysis. The shaman sits in the lodge with his patient and sings his healing songs. In one such ceremony, the shaman is reported to have sung three songs [Parsons 1932:242].

Shikani Society
Pueblo, *Southwest*

One of the medicine societies at Laguna used for healing. For details of a ritual, see *Giwire*.

Shilup
Choctaw, *Southeast*

Ghost; the aspect of a person that travels to the land of the dead after death. "To see a ghost, is regarded as a certain precursor of death. When a sick person sees one, he despairs at once of recovery, and his doctor ceases to make any further effort for his restoration. Moreover it is customary

for the doctor, when he see his patient will die, in order to save his own reputation to give out that he has seen a ghost, and therefore his recovery is impossible. To dream of seeing a ghost is also ominous of sickness and death. . . . The nightmare is supposed to be occasioned by some restless shilup having come for the person subject to it, and it is believed that the only way to give relief is to frighten him away by some kind of incantation" [Wright in Swanton 1931:217].

Shiwanna
Keres, *Southwest*

One of four medicine societies at Acoma Pueblo, translated as the Thundercloud Society. The chief purpose of this society is to treat persons who have been shocked by lightning and to set broken bones. The members also treat those who have "a bad smell from the stomach" [White 1932:107].

Shumaikoli Society
Tewa, *Southwest*

A medicine society of the western Tewa that is called upon to perform healing ceremonies [Parsons 1939:Table 3:860].

Shunad
Tiwa, *Southwest*

A general purification held in the spring for the residents of Isleta Pueblo [Parsons 1939:Table 3:860].

Sia'ticum
Papago, *Southwest*

Diagnostician. When a person becomes ill, he first consults a *sia'ticum*, who determines the nature and cause of the illness and then refers the patient to a shaman who knows the proper songs for curing that illness.

Síatcokam
Pima, *Southwest*
See *Mákai*.

Sila
Eskimo, *Arctic Coast*

Dialectical variants: *hila, hla, shla, sla, tla*. There is considerable variation in the literature as to the exact meaning of this word, which, given the breadth of its use, is to be expected. As a noun, it can mean the world, the universe; nature, the natural order; common sense, reason; consciousness; the air, the wind(s), the weather; and the place or space outside, the open sky [Petersen 1966–1967: 262]. However, Williamson [1974:22] defines *sila* as "the life-giving element, which enfolds all the world and invests all living organisms, and without which there can be no life." As such, *Sila* is the Life-Giving Spirit, which has led many to translate the term as Supreme Being. "To characterize Sila as a supreme being is, however, inaccurate. If we ignore, as a secondary development, Sila's subordination to the Sea-woman in the central region, Sila may be described as the supreme being of the physical universe; but the Inuit also conceive of two further dimensions of existence" [Merkur 1983:36]. One is the supercelestial realm ruled by Moon Owner, and the other is the underworld ruled by Sea-woman. The three deities rule independently of one another.

"The idea of Sila as a cosmic breath-soul has general distribution, but in the heartland of the cult of the Sea-woman, Sila has been replaced by the Sea-woman with respect to the traditional observances and their enforcements. . . . The idea of Sila may be related to the masculine conception of the sun among the south Alaskan Inuit. A relation to the sun is also found in west-central Canada, and in the widespread notion in common speech and in ritual, that the sun's motion from left to right proceeds 'according to sila'" [Merkur 1985: 36].

Sitac
Nootsack, *Northwest Coast*
Soul; in this case, the body soul (see entry), which is related to soul-loss illnesses. Only shamans can see this soul. It is described as being a tiny doll in the image of its owner [Amoss 1978:44–45].

Siyotanka
Teton Sioux, *Plains*
Dialectical variant: *coyatanka* (Dakota) [Williamson 1970:259]. Whistle. These whistles are most often made from the wing bones of an eagle. They are used by shamans during healing ceremonies, the Sun Dance, and other such rituals.

Skaaga
Haida, *Northwest Coast*
Plural: *skaages*. Medicine man [Barbeau 1958:3]. *Skaraws* is another term for shaman.

Skaquis
Dwamish, *Northwest Coast*
Female shaman [Dorsey 1902]. Subsequently, T. T. Waterman [1930a:305] was unable to verify this term.

Skinaway, Tom
Ojibwa, *Canadian Eastern Woodlands*
Reported to be the last medicine man among the Ojibwa living at Mille Lacs, Minnesota.

Sklaletut
Dwamish, *Northwest Coast*
A person's spirit power [Waterman 1930b:555]. See *sbtatdaq*.

Skoyo Chaiän
Keres, *Southwest*
The Sia Peublo term for the Giant Society, one of several religious fraternities among these people. Although the primary responsibility and function of this society is the calling forth of rain for crops, the members also have certain medicine powers and associated rituals used in curing the sick.

Native American healing ceremonies reached their epitome of social organization among the cultures of the Southwest. There, shamans involved in healing are well organized into tight-knit, secret fraternities consisting of several degrees or orders of ability. The actual healing of a patient is conducted by shamans of the highest order, who are supported in song and ritual by the other members of the society. These healing ceremonies are characterized by great attention to detail and long duration, usually lasting from 4 to 10 days. For the most part, these rituals have not been observed by Westerners, mainly because of their secret nature.

The Sia doctors use two main forms of healing. One type of healing is the brushing type, in which the disease-causing agents are brought to the surface of the patient's body, and then ritually

Medicine men practice a healing cure inside a kiva in New Mexico's Sia pueblo in 1890. During the Sia new year in December, all Sia societies hold ceremonies that last four days and four nights to heal those that are ill in the pueblo.

brushed away with straws and feathers by the shaman. (Female members of the Giant Society do not participate in such healing ceremonies.) The other general type of healing found among the Sia religious societies is that of the sucking shaman (see entry). There is a detailed observation of a four-day brushing ceremony conducted for a sick Sia boy by the Giant Society, and it is included here

in its entirety to give readers an accurate view of the intricacies involved.

"During the afternoon a sand-painting was made in the east end of the room (on the floor); *yaya* (spirit fetishes; see entry) and stone fetiches were grouped upon the painting; a medicine bowl was placed before the yaya; bear-leg skins were deposited on either side of the fetiches and a white embroidered sacred Tusayan blanket was folded and laid by the bear-leg skins south of the painting. The five male members of the medicine division of the society had refreshments served early in the evening by the female members, and after supper the ti'ämoni (Sia pueblo governor), who is a member of the medicine division, placed a bowl of stewed meat and a basket of bread near the (sand) painting; the remainder of the food was stored in the northwest corner of the room for future consumption.

"The five men formed in line back of the fetiches, the ho'naaite (head shaman of the society) being the central figure; they had scarcely taken their seats, however, before the ti'ämoni brought a vase of water and a gourd from the west end of the room and set it before the sand-painting and returned to his seat; the ho'naaite, advancing, dipped six gourdfuls of water, emptying each one into the medicine bowl.

"The ho'naaite then passing to the north side of the painting stooped with bended knees, holding in his left hand two eagle plumes, and repeated a low prayer; then, taking a small piece of the bread, he dipped it into the stew and scattered it before the fetiches; and, taking more bread and a bit of the meat, he left the ceremonial chamber and threw the food as an offering to the animals of the cardinal points. The ti'ämoni then returned the bowl of meat and basket of bread to the far end of the room. Upon the return of the ho'naaite his vicar spread the Tusayan blanket upon the floor, some 5 feet in front of the painting. He next sprinkled a line of meal from the edge of the blanket nearest the painting to the bear fetich, which stood foremost on the painting; thence across the blanket and along the floor to the entrance on the south side and near the west end of the chamber; again, beginning at the center of the blanket he sprinkled a line of meal across the blanket to the south edge, and beginning again at the center he sprinkled a line of meal to the north edge and continued this line to the north wall. Then beginning at the line ending at the south of the blanket, he ran it out to the south wall (these four lines being symbolic of the four winds), and placed the bowl of meal in front of the painting and north of the line of meal. The meal having become somewhat exhausted, the pottery meal bowl was replaced by an Apache basket, containing a quantity of fresh meal, ground by a woman in an adjoining room, where a portion of the family had already retired. The basket of meal was received from the woman by the ti'ämoni, who stood to her left side while she ground the corn in the ordinary family mill. The remainder of the contents of the pottery meal bowl being deemed sufficient in quantity to lend a sacred character to the freshly ground meal. The ho'naaite then fastened about his neck a string of bears' claws with a small reed whistle, having two soft white eagle plumes tied to the end, attached midway, which he took from a pile of bear-leg skins, having first waved the necklace around the white bear fetich, which stood to the front of the painting. Each member of the society then put on a similar necklace; two of the members fastened amulets around their upper right arms and two around their left arms. The ho'naaite rolled his blanket in a wad and sat upon it. The other members made similar cushions. The ti'ämoni, whose seat was at the south end of the line, crossed to the north side of the room, and taking a bit of red pigment rubbed it across his face and returned to his seat, each member rubbing a bit of galena across the forehead, across the face below the eyes, and about the lower part of the face. The paint was scarcely perceptible. It was put on to insure the singing of the song correctly. The ti'ämoni again crossed the room, and taking from the north ledge a bunch of corn husks, he handed them to the man who sat next to him, who was careful to manipulate them under his blanket, drawn around him. The writer thinks that they were made into funnels, in which he placed tiny pebbles from ant hills. The vice-ho'naaite (vicar), at the north end of the line, left the room, and during his absence the ho'naaite, taking a bunch of straws which lay by the bear-leg skins, divided it into five parts, giving a portion to each one present. He reserved a share for the absent member, who returned in a short time, bearing the sick child in his arms, being careful to walk on the line of meal; he set the child upon a low stool placed on the broad band of embroidery of the blanket. The man then handed the basket of meal to the child, who, obeying the instructions of the vice-ho'naaite, took a pinch and threw it toward the altar with a few words of prayer to Ko'pishtaia (the cloud, lightning, thunder, rainbow peoples, and certain animals). The vicar then returned to his seat, and the members, with eagle plumes and straws in their left hands and rattles in their right, began the ritual; they were nine minutes singing the first stanza, which was sung slowly and in very low tones, and at its close each one drew a breath from the eagle plumes and straws. The second stanza was sung louder and faster. The monotony of the song was broken by an occasional animal-like call, which was a request to the cougar of the north to give them power over the angry ants (cause of the sickness). The child was afflicted with a severe sore throat, caused by ants having entered his body when he was in the act of micturition upon their house, and ascending they located in his throat. After the second stanza the ho'naaite blew first on the right side of the child, then on his back, his left side, and his breast; the other members continuing the song to the accompaniment of the rattle. When he took his seat, the ti'ämoni and the man who sat next to him each drew a breath from their eagle plumes and straws, and dipping them into the medicine water, each one extended his plumes to the child, who drew a breath from them. The two men then resumed their seats. The ho'naaite, again dipping his plumes in the medicine water, passed the ends through the ti'ämoni's mouth, and afterwards through the mouth of each member, the plumes being dipped each time into the bowl of medicine water. The men were occupied a few moments in drawing something from several of the bear-leg skins. All except the ho'naaite gathered around the altar, dancing and gesticulating in excessive excitement and blowing upon the whistles suspended from their necklaces. They constantly dipped their eagle plumes into the medicine water, throwing their arms vehemently about, sprinkling the altar and touching the animal fetiches with their plumes, and then placing the plumes to the mouths, absorbing from them the sacred breath of the animal. The ho'naaite with bowed head continued his invocations to the cougar of the north, seemingly unconscious of all that was going on about him. After maneuvering before the altar, the four men performed similar extravagances about the child, one of the men standing him in the center of the blanket, careful to place the boy's feet in diagonal angles formed by the meal lines. Then the four left the room, carrying with them the material taken from the bear-leg skins. The ho'naaite did not cease shaking the rattle and singing during the absence of the four, who visited the house of the sick boy to purify it. Upon returning to the ceremonial room they threw their arms aloft, waving their plumes above them and then about the child, singing and growling, after which they resumed their seats in line with the ho'naaite, and joined him in the song to the accompaniment of rattles. After a few moments these four men and the ho'naaite surrounded the boy; the ho'naaite standing at the northeast corner of the blanket, and the ti'ämoni at the southeast corner, while the others formed a semicircle behind the boy. They all waved plumes and straws in their left hands over the invalid boy, and passed them simultaneously down his body from head to feet, striking the plumes and straws with rattles which they held in their right hands; and as the plumes and straws were moved down the boy's body ants in any quantity were supposed to be brushed off the body, while in reality tiny pebbles were dropped upon the blanket; but the conjuration was so perfect the writer could not tell how or whence they were dropped, although she stood close to the group and under a bright light from a lamp she had placed on the wall for the purpose of disclosing every detail. The tiny nude boy standing upon the white embroidered blanket, being brushed with the many eagle plumes, struck with their rattle by five beautifully formed Indians, was the most pleasing scene of this dramatic ceremonial. The brushing of the child with the plumes was repeated six times, and he was then backed off the blanket over the line of meal and set upon the stool, which had been removed from the blanket, and was afterward given a pinch of meal and told to stand and look at the ants which had been extracted from his body, and to sprinkle the meal upon them. After this sprinkling he resumed his seat upon the stool. The ho'naaite stooped with bended knees at the northeast corner of the blanket and whispered a prayer and sprinkled the blanket. Each member with eagle plumes sprinkled the blanket with meal and carefully brushed together all the material which had fallen on the floor instead of the blanket, after which the ti'ämoni gathered the corners together, waved it over the child's head, and left the room with it. All sat perfectly quiet, holding their rattles, eagle plumes, and straws in their right hands during the absence of the ti'ämoni. Upon his return he waved the folded blanket twice toward the group of fetiches and toward himself, then passed it twice around the child's head, and finally laid it upon the pile of bear-leg skins at the south side of the painting. The child, who was ill and burning with fever, was led by the vice ho'naaite to the fetiches, which he sprinkled with meal, and was carried from the chamber and through an outer room to his mother at the entrance.

"The ho'naaite is not supposed to leave the ceremonial chamber throughout the four days and nights, as he must guard the animal fetiches and medicine. The other members are also supposed to spend much of the day and all of the night in watching the fetiches; but the writer is of the opinion that they all go to sleep after the feast, which is enjoyed as soon as the child leaves the chamber.

"The only variation in the ceremonial on the second night was that the vicar dipped the bit of bread into the bowl of stew and scattered it to the animal fetiches, having previously lifted ashes from the fireplace and sprinkled the altar with them by striking the plume held in the left hand on the under side with the plume held in the right; then holding the plumes between his hands he repeated a long and scarcely audible prayer. After scattering the food to the animal fetiches, he dipped a piece of bread into the stew, left the house and threw the food to the cardinal points, as the ho'naaite had done the previous night, and, returning, removed the bowl of stew and basket of bread to the northwest corner of the room. He then swept the floor with his two eagle plumes, beginning some 18 inches in front of the altar (the line of meal remaining perfect to this point) to the point where the blanket was to be placed, and

then laid the blanket and made the meal lines, the change in the drawing of these lines being that the line was begun at the line of meal which extended in front of the altar and ran over the blanket to the entrance of the room; then beginning in the center of the blanket, the line was extended across to the north wall. The writer mentions this deviation in the drawing of the meal lines, though she believes it was a mere matter of taste on the part of the worker. Instead of the vice ho'naaite receiving the child at the outer entrance, the man who sat between him and the ho'naaite brought the child into the room, and he was led out by the ti'ämoni. Upon this occasion, and on the third and fourth nights, the child walked into and out of the room, an indication that he was in better physical condition than on the first night of the ceremony. The songs on the second night were addressed to the bear of the west instead of the cougar of the north. The child did not seem to move a muscle throughout the ceremony, except when he stepped to his position on the blanket.

"The scenes on the third and fourth nights were coincident with those of the second, with a few variations. The man who sat between ho'naaite and his vicar dipped the ashes with his plumes and sprinkled the altar, and, returning to his seat, the vicar laid the blanket and sprinkled the meal lines in the same manner as on the previous night; he also procured the child. When dancing before the altar two men wore bear-leg skins on their left arms, and two others wore them on their right arms. It was noticed that the skins were drawn over the arms upon which the amulets were worn. Their dancing and incantations were even more turbulent and more weird than on the two former nights.

"The songs of the third night were addressed to the badger of the south and on the fourth to the wolf of the east" [Stevenson 1894:97–101].

Skudilitc
Dwamish, *Northwest Coast*
Among this branch of the Coast Salish, the painted power boards used in performing the Spirit Canoe healing ceremony. "Power entered these things during certain ceremonies, and they dragged people about, causing them to quiver

and shake" [Waterman 1930a:302]. Waterman also uses this term for the spirit power that enters such planks. See *skwanilac* for details.

Skull Bundle
Crow, *Plains*
The most sacred medicine bundle assembled by the Crow.

Skwanilac
Coast Salish, *Northwest Coast*
A shamanic healing ritual that has become part of the annual Spirit Dance ceremonial in the Upper Stalo region. The ritual "is a vestige of the ancient psychodramatic enactment of a collective shamanic boat journey to the land of the dead" [Jilek 1982b:145]. This ceremony includes a group psychotherapeutic approach in which the shaman asks the participants to "render active assistance through mental concentration on the patient in order to 'help him'" [Jilek 1982b:90–91].

The ceremony includes the use of two power boards, called *skudilitc* (see entry), or power sticks that have the capacity to heal. The power sticks are loop-shaped pieces of naturally twisted cedar branches or bark, wrapped with scarlet cloth. The power boards are rectangular cedar boards, approximately 30 by 45 centimeters (12 by 18 inches), with slots cut into them by which they are held. Sometimes they are carved or painted with a face or a skeletal figure. When painted, they are usually black and white or black and red. Jilek [1982b:140–141] witnessed their use in a healing ceremony and reported:

"The Indian Doctor in charge was assisted by other ritualists, by two groups of four ceremonial 'workers,' and by drummers and singers. Each instrument (board) was carried by a pair of husky 'workers' holding on to it with one hand and to a companion's belt with the other. The paraphernalia (boards) were 'warmed up' at the bonfires in the smokehouse and 'fed' by women, who threw pieces of smoked salmon and poured a little water into the flames. One after another, the paraphernalia were carried around the smokehouse hall, facing the audience while people stood up in reverence. The instruments would then 'smell the ground' and seemed to be magnetically attracted

to each other, defying the workers' efforts to keep them apart. Rushing together and sweeping up high, the powerful tools would drag their guardians with them in a wild chase around the hall until their master, the Indian Doctor, intervened. Only he had the power to slow down and separate the unruly instruments. This procedure was repeated several times. The *skwanilac* ran wild and the strong workers, in spite of desperate attempts to tame the instruments, were pulled around the hall, into each corner, out of the door and in again, lifted up and lowered to the ground in undulant movements. Again and again the power-charged instruments would pull together and had to be separated and pacified by the Indian Doctor who occasionally 'blew power' into his hands before touching them. From time to time, he held them close to his ears, listened attentively, and nodded his head. The instruments would then move around slowly, 'smelling' and 'searching,' while the people watched in suspense. The *skwanilac*, just like the spirit dancer, is 'blind' and yet seeing. The eyes painted on the power boards appear blind and the twisted power sticks are 'blindfolded' by red cloth wrapped around them, and yet these paraphernalia point at and single out persons in the audience for recognition, reprimand, or treatment. In the *skwanilac* curing rite, a sick person singled out by the paraphernalia would be quickly surrounded by relatives and friends. The power-laden tools would move up and down on all sides of the trembling patient, stroking him in gentle passes, and emanating their healing power while the Indian Doctor chants his (healing) songs. At the end, with all drums beating, the *skwanilac*, in a final display of power, would chase its keepers four times around the smokehouse hall with such speed that the excited audience perceived them all as flying."

Slalakum
Coast Salish, *Northwest Coast*
See *sxwlaem*.

Sle
Dwamish, *Northwest Coast*
A person's shadow or soul. Soul loss is often the diagnosis for a sickness, and in such cases, shamans are called on to perform the Spirit Canoe

healing ceremony (see *skwanilac*) to retrieve the lost soul.

Slippery Eyes
Crow, *Plains*
One of the foremost shamans during the latter part of the nineteenth century. During his vision quest, he was visited by the snake beings. His face had been dreadfully scarred by smallpox, and during his vision, the snakes "treated his deeply pitted face so that only a few pox marks showed" [Wildschut 1975:137]. In addition, a "real human being was then carried into the tipi (he entered during his vision) on a stretcher made of buffalo hide. He was ill, and was placed in front of Slippery Eyes. Then some real snakes came forward and began to doctor this sick person, showing Slippery Eyes how to proceed. When these snakes had finished doctoring, the man stood up, stretched, combed his hair, and walked out of the tipi a well man" [Wildschut 1975:137].

When Slippery Eyes returned from his vision quest, he made a snake medicine bundle containing three snake effigies that he used in doctoring his patients. Eventually the medicine bundle was obtained by Wildschut, after passing to three other individuals, and he described the contents as follows:

"The one at the bottom represents the snake chief. This effigy is of buckskin, 31" long. It is painted yellow with black eyes, mouth and stripes on its body. Two short cords strung with blue and red seed beads represent fangs, and actual rattlesnake rattles are tied to the tail of this effigy. The image is stuffed with some semi-hard material, possibly pine needles. Attached to the head of this snake is an eagle bone whistle 7" long, to which is tied a small skin packet of medicine which is decorated with green and white seed beads.

"The other two snake effigies in this bundle are symbols of the servants of the snake chief. They are the ones who carried out the directions of the snake chief in doctoring patients. The smaller of these is of stuffed buckskin, 24 1/2" long, and painted black with black beaded eyes sewn to its head. The third effigy is made of a long strip of otter skin, 1" wide, and painted red on the skin side. To this is sewn a bulbous snakehead of stuffed

buckskin with two red lines painted on the top of it. Two elk teeth and a brass bell are tied to the tail of this image. The otter skin appears in this bundle because the otter is regarded as the chief of the water animals. Water (the sacred spring—where he received his vision) cannot be included in the bundle, so its power is represented by this otter skin. The small bell symbolizes a rattlesnake's rattle. The two elk teeth represent property to be acquired by the owner through the successful use of this medicine.

"In the ceremony of doctoring with this medicine the patient was led to water, where real snakes were thought to assist in bringing the sick person back to health. While walking behind the patient Slippery Eyes blew the whistle in this bundle to call these snakes to his assistance" [Wildschut 1975:138].

Slocum, John
Squaxin, *Northwest Coast*
Founder of the Indian Shaker Church. In the fall of 1881, he died, and his friends were called to make preparations for his funeral. During the wake and before his coffin arrived, Slocum revived in front of his mourners. He told them that he had died and left his body but had been sent back to right his sins and to lead other sinners into living a Christian life. See *Shakers* for details.

Smatnatc
Lummi, *Northwest Coast*
Among this branch of the Coast Salish, the Spirit Canoe healing ceremony. See *sbatatdaq* for details.

Smith, Jake
Shasta, *California*
One of the dreamer shamans among the Shasta. He built a dance house on Moffett Creek near Fort Jones, where he conducted the dream dances of the Earth Lodge cult, an offshoot of the Ghost Dance, that he had learned from the Wintus. He doctored by rubbing his hands all over the patient and blowing water on the patient from his mouth.

Smitinak
Klallam, *Northwest Coast*
Also: *smetnaq*. Among this branch of the Coast Salish, the Spirit Canoe healing ceremony. See *sbatatdaq* for details.

Smokehouse

Sweat lodge; an alternative term found infrequently in the literature.

Smoking Pipe

See *sacred pipe.*

Sogonebuu

Paviotso, *Basin*

An emergency doctoring treatment which lasts for about three hours [Park 1938:48].

Sokadisiu

Northern Algonquin, *Canadian Eastern Woodlands*

Someone with supernatural power or mind power, as distinct from physical strength. This power is used by shamans to heal, among other applications [Cooper 1934:38].

Sokosa

Miwok, *California*

Central Miwok term for a special rattle used in healing ceremonies. It consists of cocoon shells filled with small quartz pebbles and has been described as follows:

"Four cocoons of the Pandora Moth, large and of a lustrous, natural, silvery color are tied to a stick, supposed to be Seringa [sic]. The cocoon rattle which Lemme [sic] made for me (for $1.50) was trimmed with eagle down and feathers from the side of the eagle tied on (glued underneath) with narrow leather thongs. Had a leather loop as a handle and four single strips of skin as decorations from which hung two eagle feathers and two tiny white pigeon feathers. . . . Cocoons are gathered on the sunny side of the slope on the Cyanothus [sic] bush. . . . In Medicine work, the rattle was shaken steadily in an upright position while the singing and circling of the stick was in progress. . . . At the same time the rattle is shaken while held upright, the 'stick' is waved over the person lying ill. The healing stick or whatever it is called is about 16 inches long, has a small cross piece, possibly two short branches, near the tip is decorated with a flicker feather and has a horse hair extending from the end. If the hair sticks out straight from the stick after the song, the person will not get well; if it droops down, then the per-

son is going to get well" [Cummins in Bates 1992:115].

Somlohólxaes

Takelma, *Oregon Seaboard*

A type of shaman endowed with supernatural powers and the ability to call upon powerful helping spirits. Among the Takelma, more powerful shamans are known as the *goyò* (see entry). The *somlohólxaes* differs from the *goyò* in that he cannot "shoot" disease into another person, nor can he "catch" the pain of the patient (i.e., suck out a disease-causing object). He does not dance during a healing or require the use of singers, as does the *goyò*. Instead of sucking on the patient with his mouth, this type of shaman sits himself beside the patient, "rubbing the part affected by the malady and singing his medicine-song" [Sapir 1907:44]. These two types of shamans have entirely different spirits as supernatural helpers and thus different medicine songs. For the *somlohólxaes*, the most powerful spirits are the chicken hawk, the sparrow hawk, the acorn woman, and a number of local mountain spirits such as Old Rock Woman. These shamans also use herbal remedies.

Song

The use of song is found in nearly every known healing tradition in North America. Human singing and the coming and going of spirit helpers seem to go hand in hand. However, there is tremendous diversity among the songs of North American healing traditions. Therefore, it must be understood that although generalizations can be made, there are always exceptions.

"Primitive" healing is thought by many to be characterized by affirmation. Healing songs among shamans are an exception to this notion. Rarely does one find in the words of their healing songs affirmations for the patient. There are no "you'll get better" or "you'll be healed" words to be found. For the most part, their songs are words being sent to their helping spirits, who respond accordingly. They are usually sung in a sacred and secret language that is not understood by most of those attending the ceremony; it is understood only by shamans. Thus, one aspect of healing songs is that they provide the shaman with a per-

Three men drum and sing during a medicine dance at Glacier National Park, Montana, in the early twentieth century. Almost every Native American healing tradition involves the use of song to invoke healing power.

sonal language of communication with his or her helping spirits.

Frances Densmore, the greatest student and scholar of Native American music, noted some of the overall musical characteristics of shamanic singing. She found that most of the songs, over 80 percent, are characterized by an irregularity of accent (change of rhythm) in the melody. "Sometimes this takes the form of unexpected interruptions of a steady rhythm and sometimes there is a peculiar rhythmic pattern throughout the melody," she reported. When the songs are transcribed into musical notation, this translates into frequent changes of measure lengths.

Another feature of shamanic singing is the trance-inducing tone (monotonous versus sing-

ing with expression) used by the shaman. Since the shaman's words are not comprehended by the patient or the ceremony participants, they become more attentive to the rhythmic pattern of the song and the tone of the shaman. Together, these work (somewhat like the chanting of Eastern mantras) to focus and quiet their minds. Of course, the shaman also uses this monotone, among other ritual techniques, to aid in his or her necessary shift to the shamanic state of consciousness (see entry).

Densmore also noted that healing songs are generally sung at a slow tempo. Most of the time, the drum or other accompaniment plays in unison with the singing, but in about a third of the songs, it plays at a different tempo. A slow tempo creates a more relaxed atmosphere for the participants, and the coincidence of voice and accompaniment does not seem to be necessary to create the sacred space in which the shaman conducts healings; that is, they need not work in unison. When there is accompaniment, the shaman usually uses the rattle.

Sorcerer

An evil-doing shaman who uses his power to bring harm to others; witch.

Soul loss

The technical term for a diagnosis of illness caused by the loss of the animating soul of the patient. The diagnosis can be made either by the sick person or by a shaman. The concept of soul loss is widespread in North America. It is the most common diagnosis of illness in the Far North among the Eskimo and among the cultures of the Northwest down to California, where its prevalence ebbs as one goes farther south. It is also found frequently among the Central Algonquin of the Great Lakes area and among the Northern Plateau cultures. It is not a common diagnosis among the cultures of the Southeast and Southwest and is rarely found among the Plains cultures.

Soul loss should not be confused with the wanderings of the soul in dream journeys or visions. "Only when the dreamer finds that his soul has disappeared or strayed to a place whence it cannot by itself return—e.g., the realm of the dead—may we speak of soul loss" [Hultkrantz 1953:448]. The diagnosis of soul loss often goes hand in hand with the diagnosis of object intrusion, an even more common cause of illness. In these latter cases, a person's illness may be caused by the fact that in addition to losing his own soul, he has become the host of an unwanted spirit.

In most cases of soul loss, the soul departs before death; in rarer cases, it is actually seen departing [Olson 1936:162; Gifford 1933:304]. Of course, it must be remembered that in many instances, the body is considered to have more than one soul, such as the ego soul, shadow soul, and dream soul (also called the free soul). When the body soul is lost, for example, it is evidenced by the patient being unconscious and lifeless. Children and old people are usually considered to

have the frailest souls and therefore are more susceptible to soul loss. Such loosely attached souls may easily be drawn to the land of the dead or may easily attach themselves to other persons or be lost as one makes one's way through unknown terrain. In addition, a soul may be lost as a result of a severe blow to the body, it may be driven out by its owner or by some psychic or emotional shock, or it may even leave of its own accord. Finally, it may be stolen by a sorcerer.

In most cases of soul loss, the soul heads for the land of the dead. In these cases, the shaman must make a journey toward that realm and fight off hostile forces to bring the soul back to the patient. The closer the soul journeys to the land of the dead, the less likely it is that the patient will recover. The longer the soul has been out of the body, the closer it gets to the point of no return. That point is generally reached when the soul has traveled too far down the road toward the land of the dead, crossed the river of death, or actually arrived in the land of the dead.

Soul loss for an individual is usually evidenced by a deterioration in health and strength. At the other extreme are persons who do not even know that their souls have left. For example, Underhill [1945:198] reports that during the Spirit Canoe journeys of Dwamish shamans to the land of the dead, "members of the audience might be surprised to learn that their own souls had strayed away without their knowledge." In other cases, soul loss manifests as a loss of consciousness, fainting fits, seizures, and feverishness. Among the cultures of the Northwest, a gradual loss of one's personal property can be attributed to soul loss. However, regardless of the physical manifestations that occur, the prognosis is always the same: unless the soul is returned to the body, death will ensue. The exception to this rule is when the body is seen as having more than one type of soul, as mentioned above.

Sóxwá

Tewa, *Southwest*

The ceremonial smoking of tobacco. The word literally means any moisture in the air, such as dewdrops, rain clouds, fog, and so forth. The tobacco used is homegrown, and it is wrapped in dried corn husks for smoking. Only the men smoke these ceremonial cigarettes. Each man puffs on the cigarette, raises his eyes upward, and says the Smoke Prayer. Normally, ceremonial cigarettes are rolled just before being smoked, but for use in healing ceremonies, they are rolled in advance.

Spadak
Puyallup-Nisqually, *Northwest Coast*
Among this branch of the Coast Salish, the Spirit Canoe healing ceremony. See *sbatatdaq* for details.

Speck, Frank G.
Frank Speck was born in New York City on 8 November 1881. He began his training in anthropology under Franz Boas at Columbia University in 1904. In 1907, he accepted a research fellowship with the University of Pennsylvania and began fieldwork with the Yuchi in Oklahoma. He received his Ph.D. from Columbia in 1908 and remained a professor of anthropology at Pennsylvania for the rest of his life, where he was department chairman for most of his career. Most of his fieldwork was conducted throughout eastern North America, where he became most knowledgeable about the Algonquin peoples, whom he endeared more than his colleagues, students, or fellow Philadelphians. During the 1930s, he was more likely to be found attending Native American religious ceremonies than socializing with Western friends. In 1931, he began a lengthy association with the Cayuga members of the Sour Springs Long House, which resulted in his classic study *Midwinter Rites of the Cayuga Long House* in 1949. All his fieldwork was meticulous and highly detailed, resulting in such classics as *Beothuk and Micmac* (1922), *Naskapi: The Savage Hunters of the Labrador Peninsula* (1935), and *Penobscot Man: The Life History of a Forest Tribe in Maine* (1940). He died in Philadelphia on 6 February 1950.

Spirit Lodge
The term used by Hultkrantz [1967b] and a few other scholars to refer to shamanistic séances in North America. In particular, the Spirit Lodge "is a Plains application of the Algonkian ceremony of the Shaking Tent" [Hultkrantz 1992:96]. (See *Shaking Tent Ceremony* for details.) According to this concept, the Spirit Lodge is a variety of shamanism characterized by its divining functions. Ab-

sent from this ceremony is the healing aspect—or at least it is principally absent. The Spirit Lodge includes all the variations on the Ojibwa Shaking Tent Ceremony. For example, included in the Spirit Lodge complex is the *yuwipi* (see entry) ceremony among the Oglala Sioux, in which a conjuring tent is not used. Spirit Lodge is not an often used concept with regard to studies on North American shamanism, because séances are usually not limited to divining, as the users of this concept would have one believe. For example, the *yuwipi* ceremony is frequently used for healing.

Spirit Possession
Possession is the temporary embodiment of an influence or spirit alien to the subject. With regard to Native American healing, there are two basic forms of possession—possession, or spirit intrusion, as the cause of disease; and possession of the shaman by one of his helping spirits. In the latter case, a spirit or other supernatural power enters the body of the shaman and controls, to a greater or lesser degree, his words and actions. This is a voluntary act on the part of the shaman, who ritually calls forth the spirit to take possession of him. Some scholars consider it to be possession only when an unfamiliar voice speaks from the shaman, whereas others include cases of physical manifestations, such as hysterical shrieking, violent body and facial contortions, frenzied actions, and trancelike states. In the case of voices, the voice often speaks in a language that is unintelligible to those present, including the shaman.

Shamanic possession occurs generally among the Eskimo. The shaman usually assumes the characteristics of the spirit that is possessing him, both in speech and in action. For instance, if the helping spirit is an animal, the cries of this animal are heard from the shaman and the shaman imitates its movements.

Shamanic possession is also found among most of the cultures along the Northwest coast, where it is most highly developed among the Tlingit. The Tlingit shaman has several helping spirits, for each of which there is a special carved mask. When the shaman puts on a mask, he becomes possessed by its spirit, and the words that come from his mouth are from that spirit. By changing the mask, the shaman can be possessed by another spirit.

Tlingit shamans wear several carved masks, each of which represent a specific helping spirit. The headdress pictured here was worn with a miniature face, carved in the center and perched on the shaman's brow, symbolizing one of the helping spirits.

This spirit possession always comes at a certain point in the ceremony when the shaman suddenly stops dancing, fixes his gaze on the upper side of the drum, and begins to cry loudly.

Farther south on the Northwest coast, shamanic possession is less frequent, and the possession rites of the secret societies become prominent, especially among the Kwakiutl. Among the Coast and Puget Sound Salish, novices and members of secret societies undergo possession during rites.

Among the Yurok and other cultures in northwestern California and in southwestern Oregon, there is a specialized type of possession in which the possessing spirit is referred to as a "pain." Kroeber [1925:3], in describing the Yurok, states: "Shamanistic power resides in the control of 'pains,' small animate, nonanimal and nonhuman in shape, which on the one hand cause illness by entering the bodies of men, and on the other, endow the shaman with power when he brings them to reside within himself."

Shamanic possession is found throughout the California cultures, with the bear spirit being one of the most frequent and powerful spirits used in healing. Among the Sinkyone, the possessing spirit is believed to be a permanent resident within the shaman's body, having been there since the shaman acquired his power.

Possession during healing is common among the shamans of the Plateau region. One of the most common possession spirits in this area is the bluejay. Also, many shamans in this area report that their possessing spirits reside in the heart or chest area during possession.

Shamanic possession appears to be unknown in the Basin area, except for the Shivwits Paiute, located in the extreme southern part of the area.

In the Southwest, shamanic possession is less frequent than in areas to the north. For example, several Yuman-speaking cultures have possessions, but others do not. Also, among the Apache, only the Chiricahua (or Huachuca) are known to experience possession. The hand-trembling ceremony among the Navajo appears to be a specialized form of possession in which the shaking of the hand is attributed to a spirit that has entered the hand. This ceremony is a diagnostic ritual in which the Gila monster spirit controls the hand trembling. During this ritual, the shaman goes into a trance and the spirit reveals to him the nature of the disease and the appropriate cure.

Among the Pueblo, the kachinas are possessed by the spirits of the masks they wear, such that they become the embodiment of those spirits. Among the San Felip, the bear spirit enters the shaman, who emulates the actions of the bear.

There are few known instances of shamanic possession in the eastern United States, partly because of the lack of ethnographic information for that area. However, possession is found among the Natchez, whose shamans use a rattle to bring forth the possession. It also appears among the Creek and possibly among the Eastern Siouans. Among the Lenape, shamans wear a mask and bearskin, which enables possession by a spirit. The Iroquois also have possession, especially among the members of the false-face societies. The Menomini have at least one form of possession that occurs during the Private Memorial Ceremony, conducted for a person one year after death. At this time, the spirit of the deceased enters the shaman's body and speaks to the audience.

In the Plains area, shamanic possession is found among the Dakota; the spirits of the red hawk, woodpecker, rattlesnake, and grizzly bear are among the more common ones. Possession is also found among the Mandan, Hidatsa, Wind River Shoshoni, and Crow. However, among the Crow, the possession is permanent rather than temporary.

In the Subarctic area, shamanic possession is quite common. It is found among the Western Dènè, Koyukon of Alaska, Tena, Eyak, Tanaina, Tahltan, Carrier, Naskapi, and Babine. Among the Eastern Cree and Northern Saulteaux, an insane person is regarded as being possessed. This most likely refers to cases of spirit intrusion.

(For details on the above, see Stewart 1946.)

Sptdaqw
Dwamish, *Northwest Coast*
Among this branch of the Coast Salish, the Spirit Canoe healing ceremony. See *sbatatdaq* for details.

Sqalálitut
Puyallup-Nisqually, *Northwest Coast*
Among this branch of the Coast Salish, power. Although this term is linguistically related to *sqalátut*, the word for "dream," power comes to individuals through a trance during a vision quest

rather than in a dream. Powers are most often associated with birds, animals, or inanimate objects in nature, and there are many different kinds of power. For example, *tiótlbax* "was the strongest and most desirable of wealth powers" [Smith 1940:59], and *tusátlad* was an "eating power" that shamans used to win property duels based on food consumption.

SSC
See *shamanic state of consciousness.*

Steed, Jesse
Lakota, *Plains*
A *yuwipi* (see entry) shaman who practiced during the mid-twentieth century on the Pine Ridge and Rosebud Reservations in South Dakota.

Stevens, Johnny
South Alaska Eskimo, *Arctic Coast*
An Ugalakmiut shaman who lived in the village of Eyak along the Copper River delta near the entrance of Prince William Sound during the first part of the twentieth century. (In the literature, these people are often referred to as the Eyak Indians.) He was an informant to Kaj Birket-Smith but told him little of his own shamanic practice. Another informant named Galushia provided some accounts of Johnny Stevens. Most of the Eskimo believed that Johnny Stevens had acquired his healing powers from a shaman named Chitina Joe after the latter's death. Chitina Joe willed his power to Johnny Stevens "in the shape of a beer glass, a feather, and a Y-shaped alder twig," all items formerly used by Chitina Joe in his healing ceremonies [Birket-Smith and Laguna 1938].

Stiffarm
Gros Ventre, *Plains*
A shaman around the turn of the twentieth century who got his doctoring power from the weasel. "Stiffarm had a weasel skin to live by, and to do his doctoring with. He had as his helper a big weasel, the larger of the two weasels" [The Boy in Cooper 1957:346]. Stiffarm also had some power concerning children, for which he wore a bracelet with two little dolls suspended from it—one on each side.

The following account of Stiffarm's use of his weasel power was given to Thomas Main by a Gros Ventre named Brocky:

"Stiffarm was doctoring a sick woman. He had a weasel skin. This he placed on the ground and covered with a black handkerchief. Then he took away the handkerchief and there was a live weasel. The weasel ran to the woman, bored its way half way into the woman's stomach, and came out with half of its body bloody and with something in its mouth. This object was taken by Stiffarm and shown to all present as the cause of the illness, and was then thrown into the fire outside the lodge. Then the weasel was covered with the handkerchief, the handkerchief was next taken away, and there was only the weasel skin" [Main in Cooper 1957:346].

This type of healing ceremony, in which the shaman animates the skin of the animal from which he received his doctoring powers, is common among Plains cultures. In such cases, it is the shaman's helping spirit who directly doctors the patient.

Stlalcopschudoptch
Dwamish, *Northwest Coast*
Among this branch of the Coast Salish, the painted cedar planks used during their Spirit Canoe healing ceremonies [Waterman 1930a: 299]. The cedar planks are cut into a standard shape, although the form differs among the Dwamish, Squamish, and Snohomish people of this area. Once shaped, the planks are painted according to the spirit helper of the shaman using them.

For Dwamish planks, the top is bent over to form a snoutlike projection called the *zedis*. Each side of the snout is painted with teeth, called *sedls*, and, in some cases, a line is drawn between the teeth to represent the tongue, called *tlalap*. Below this is painted a circle (sometime two circles) to represent the eye, called *kalob*, of the spirit helper. In the center of the board is painted an effigy of the spirit helper of the shaman, called *bakob*, which translates to "traveler." "It is this supernatural helper which actually makes the journey to the underworld; the shaman meanwhile 'acting out' the part in the dance-house, sharing in the perils of the journey, or the evil consequences of it" [Waterman 1930a:300]. Surrounding the central figure are painted dots that represent the songs revealed to the shaman by his spirit helper. "Every type of guardian-spirit was addicted to songs of a definite and recognized pattern, so that a bystander could recognize what type of guardian-spirit a man had, merely by hearing him sing" [Waterman 1930a: 300]. Around the edge of the plank is painted a black border called *ecwauq*, meaning "container of power."

Stleabats
Dwamish, *Northwest Coast*
Sucking doctor [Waterman 1930a:305–306]. "Shamans who assume the power of curing disease by sucking accompany their dancing by certain gestures. They first put one forearm across the forehead while with the opposite hand they rub the thigh or hip, alternating as they dance" [Waterman 1930a:307].

Stomach kneaders
Although usually not considered to be power objects, stomach kneaders are often used to treat indigestion and stomachaches. Most often they are made of wood. The wide end of the kneader is pushed against the stomach and moved in an upward direction.

Suchuma
Central Miwok, *California*
Nature spirits [Bates 1992:98].

Sucking shaman
A general anthropological term for those shamans who cure by sucking on the patient to remove an intruded object that is the cause of the illness. Most often, they place their mouths directly on the patient. Others use hollow bones, reeds, horns, or other such tubes. Such healers are usually found in those societies where curing is performed by a single shaman rather than by a group effort, although there are exceptions. Sucking shamans are considered to be an ancient institution among hunting and gathering societies, as opposed to agricultural societies. The concept of object intrusion is probably of Old World Paleolithic origin and seems to be the oldest of all disease theories. It is most prevalent in western North America,

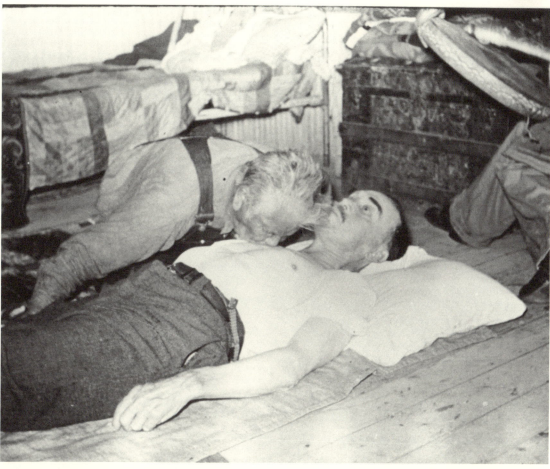

A Chippewa sucking doctor treats a patient with the use of his *odokanigan,* a tool utilized to blow or suck out disease-causing object(s).

particularly among the nations of the Great Basin and the Plateau of California. (See *Parrish, Essie* for details.)

The sucking process can be detrimental to the shaman, as evidenced in the following account given to Leslie White by a Pueblo informant from Acoma:

"A medicine man had been curing a patient; he had been sucking things from his body. When he tried to vomit them out he could not do it. He tried and tried. 'You could see he was in great pain. He broke out all over in a sweat, and he began to writhe in agony.' One of the other medicine men came over to help him. He laid the sick doctor over on his back. Then he picked up a big flint knife and cut him open (cutting a median line down his tho-

rax and abdomen). 'When he cut him open you could see his heart and stomach and everything.' The doctor looked inside the body and took out a big ball of cactus thorns, which he threw into the refuse bowl. Then the doctor closed the great incision. He rubbed the flint over it, clapped his hands, and blew on it, and it was just like it was before; you would not know that he had been cut open. Finally the doctor who had swallowed the thorns got up and staggered over to the altar" [White 1932:123].

The literature abounds with the notion that sucking shamans always conceal on their persons the objects that are extracted from patients. However, sometime between 1830 and 1850, Edwin Denig, who was married to an Assiniboin woman, had the rare opportunity to verify a sucking shaman's abilities:

"We must, at the risk of not being believed, state that on two particular occasions, and before witnesses, we have examined the divining man's mouth, hands, and all his person, which was entirely naked, with the view of discovering where these worms, snakes, etc., were hidden, and that these examinations were made without any previous intimations to him who, never having been subject to examinations of the kind by Indians, was completely unprepared for the trial, yet he acquiesced cheerfully, afterwards continued his performance, and repeated it in our presence, drawing and spitting out large worms, clots of blood, tufts of hair, skin, etc., too large to be easily secreted, and leaving no visible mark on the patient's body" [Denig 1930:424].

Sudatory

Used in some of the early literature on Native America to refer to the sweat lodges found in almost all cultures across the continent. Other terms include sweat house and steam bath. Healing ceremonies for the sick are often conducted in a sweat lodge, and some contemporary shamans, such as the Lakota Archie Fire Lame Deer, restrict their healing ceremonies only to sweat lodges.

Sulia
Coast Salish, *Northwest Coast*
A powerful dream in which a shaman has a vision of spirits and receives supernatural power via a spirit song that is taught to him. It comes from the verb *ulia,* meaning "to dream." According to Jilek [1982a:331]:

"In the initiation procedures practiced today, the time-consuming traditional quest for a tutelary spirit has become merged, under acculturative pressures, with the initiation into Spirit dancing. Thus, while in bygone days spirit power was obtained in an individual quest and later manifested and tamed in the initiation, it is today acquired by, and in, the initiation process, which also constitutes the sole therapy for spirit illness.

"A strict initiatory regime is continued until the candidates 'find their song and dance,' when the guardian spirit ... appears to the initiates and bestows upon them the gift of individual spirit power, song, and dance.

"The 'finding of the spirit song' marks the initiates' rebirth and their 'return from the dead': after a gestation period of at least four days the 'baby' cries out its newfound song, accompanied by the drumming and singing of the attendants. The initiate is then 'run' through the woods, bathed in the smokehouse, and submerged four times in an ice-cold mountain stream, a procedure intended to 'bring the baby fully back to life.' Shamanic power is instilled in the novice by the initiating ritualist who blows his power-charged breath into the 'newborn baby'" [Jilek 1982a:330].

Among the Upper Stalo, this term also refers both to one's guardian spirit and to the experience of an encounter with one's guardian spirit [Jilek 1982b:31].

Sulik müko
Miwok, *California*
Among the Northern Sierra and Plains Miwok, a bear doctor.

Sumatc
Mojave, *Southwest*
Dream power [Devereux 1961:162]. Among Mojave shamans, the ability to cure comes mainly through revelatory dreams.

Sumix
Sinkaietk, *Plateau*
Among the Southern Okanagon of Washington, power. The source of *sumix* is one's guardian spirits, which usually take human form but can also come in animal form. Every normal woman and man possesses *sumix* to some extent. The greater one's personal *sumix,* the more successful one is considered within the society. As in many other Native American societies, the Okanagon have special winter ceremonies in which individuals are encouraged to publicly display their powers. "To perform at the winter dance without giving blankets or other things to the audience would make one's power angry. The (guardian) spirit might command a girl to dance and give blankets

to the people even though she had none to give, and if her relatives did not provide them for this purpose she would die. When the girl was afflicted with power from the dead, her affectionate father or uncle helped by cutting a cow's throat and letting the blood flow on the snow, to propitiate the power and save the life of the girl" [Cline 1938:137]. Those who never receive *sumix* from a guardian spirit are seen as shiftless and lazy adults who lack concentration. Another type of power, *papalot* (see entry), can be obtained from a deceased relative.

Surrel, William
Shoshoni, *Basin*
A medicine man among the Eastern or Plains Shoshoni around the turn of the twentieth century. His real name was *Mutöingaip*, which translates to "Noseholes." He was known to have successfully cured many people. Another medicine man reported of Noseholes that he "used to hold a mirror behind his client's back, with the glass part directed to the back. He looked into the mirror, and if he did not find any faults in the back, he held the mirror in front of the client's chest, which he examined in the same way" [Hultkrantz 1986:40].

He is also remembered for having considerable influence among his people. Historically, the Wind River people had used a particular area in which there were many ancient rock drawings as a vision quest site. Noseholes had a vision in which an otter spirit, considered powerful among his people, told him that the drawings on the rocks had been made by evil spirits. Afterward, beginning in the 1920s, vision questing began to fade as the main method of acquiring a guardian spirit. (For more details, see *puhagant*.)

Sutuky yomta
Patwin, *California*
See *yomta*.

Swádas
Skokomish, *Northwest Coast*
A class of guardian spirits that confer power to shamans. Other Skokomish might have guardian spirits, but not ones that enable them to become shamans. The same spirit can grant different

powers to different people. For instance, a guardian spirit such as the cougar can grant ordinary powers—gambling or hunting powers—to one person and grant shamanic powers to another person. Different spirits can also grant the same power. Only a very small group of very potent spirits grants nothing but shamanic power. These latter are referred to by the Skokomish as head doctor powers or chief doctor powers. The most powerful shamans have a variety of guardian spirits. Their power can be used to cause illness as well as to cure it. The word for curing power is *syuwadab*.

Swanaskxw
Tsimshian, *Northwest Coast*
Shaman. Among the Tsimshian, all persons—men and women—who can alter their state of consciousness to contact power are known as *halait* (see entry). Those *halait* who acquire the power to heal are called *halaidm swanaskxw*. The power to heal is considered to be the most important power. Generally, the *swanaskxw* is more independent and individualistic than other *halait*. Anyone can become a *swanaskxw*, including those who do not wish to become one. Novices usually encounter a spirit via a vision, trance, or dream. These initial experiences "varied from a chance encounter which had slight emotional consequences to highly charged experiences from which the victim never completely recovered. The subject was sometimes described as passing into a coma in which the heart beat and breathing were so imperceptible that observers believed him dead. Others went into a convulsive state resembling epilepsy and frothed at the mouth. Shamans sometimes struggled desperately in this manner with their spirit assailants. The encounter left the initiate exhausted physically and mentally. Only with the assistance of other shamans could he get control of the spirit aides he had received, and thereby avert death" [Garfield 1951:40].

One can also become a shaman through less dramatic means. Ultimately, however, one must learn by oneself, because there is no formal shamanic training tradition among the Tsimshian calling for specific practices or the acquisition of specific spirit helpers. From other shamans, one can learn certain healing ritual power displays, such as knife swallowing or walking on coals, but the ability to control spirits must be learned directly from personal experience. The necessity for control is reflected in the trance states of advanced healers, in which the *swanaskxw* displays more control of bodily movement and retains more memory of the trance than do other *halait*. These trance states are induced via drumming, singing, dancing, and other such natural techniques; no hallucinogenic substances are used. The necessity to learn from one's own personal experience is further reflected in the wide variety of behavior, paraphernalia, and techniques used by the *swanaskxw*. Some conformities do exist. For example, most shamans do not cut their hair, most use eagle feather fans in their healing ceremonies, and most use eagle down and red ocher [Guédon 1984:196].

Spirit helpers, *naxnoq*, come in many forms—animals, supernatural beings, ghosts, astronomical bodies, and objects. The novice's initial encounter with a spirit helper usually involves some form of death and revitalization that takes place in a big house full of *naxnoq*, at different locations—at the bottom of the sea, in a cave, in the depths of the earth, inside a mountain, and so forth. Franz Boas recorded such an event experienced by two hunters who became shamans:

"He is initiated in the bottom of the great Lake of the Beginning, near Parry Town. In the lake he finds a large house, and a fire burning in it. There are four flashes of lightning accompanied by thunder-claps. Next a Grizzly Bear appears, who is transformed into a carved box; then, a Thunderbird, who, at his own request, is put into the box and becomes a drum, the red ocher on the drum being the lightning; next a being called Living Ice, which is the hail; and finally a large animal called Mouth At Each End, and a Codfish, appear. All these are put into the box, and the Grizzly Bear gives the shaman his name, Mouth At Each End. He has then obtained shamanistic powers. This man's brother is waiting for him on the banks of the lake. He dies there of starvation, is eaten by martens, until only the bones are left. The shaman restores him to life by rubbing earth with his hands over the bones, by putting in new sinews made of roots, and rubbing moss over the whole.

Then his brother revives, and becomes a shaman, who is called Devoured By Martens. The martens that have eaten him are put into his body, and he receives a vessel of blood, which is to be his supernatural power" [Boas 1916:862].

As indicated in this account, each shaman is given a specific name by his or her spirit helper. They use these names only when healing; otherwise, they use their lineage names and titles. When a shaman first contacts a spirit helper, he is given a sacred object, called an *atiasxw*, to recall his spirit during healings. The *atiasxw* can be either a mental or a physical object. One of the more well-known of such objects is the soul-catcher, which is a carved hollow bone with plugs of red cedar bark at each end. Each shaman has at least one main *atiasxw* that is used in healing, and most have several of them at their disposal, each representing a different spirit helper. The *atiasxw* is an extremely important part of the shaman's life, and if he loses it, he loses the ability to heal.

When a *swanaskxw* is called upon to cure a person, he can use an old *atiasxw* and song or dream of a new one. An experienced *swanaskxw* often has several *atiasxw* and a series of songs that can be used for healing. In some cases, the *atiasxw* is transferred from one shaman to another. Shamans operate as individuals, in the sense that there is no formal society, but they can heal either individually or in a group. In communal healings, there is a main healer, and others in attendance do not contribute unless asked to do so by the main healer.

The form taken by any healing ritual depends on the diagnosis of the patient's illness. Some of the possible diagnoses listed by Guédon [1984: 197] include:

1. "Some power may be active within the client and wanting to be expressed or manifested or allowed out in some way.
2. The soul has been swallowed by a shaman and must be found, pulled out, strengthened, and given back to the patient.
3. Some evil object, or some disease has introduced itself or been introduced in the sick person's body and must be taken out of the body.

4. Some evil influence is being produced by witchcraft which poisons and weakens the victim; such influence is to be identified and removed.

5. The soul is wandering away from the body and must be called back.

6. The patient has somehow stepped outside of the human world; the patient's soul has been scared away; or is being affected or attracted by animals, fish (salmon), or other nonhuman entities."

For an example of a Tsmshian healing ceremony see *halait*.

Swanassu
Gitksan, *Northwest Coast*
Dialectical variant: *swanasku*. Medicine man. The term was obtained from Isaac Tens, a shaman, in 1920. At that time, he was an old member of the Gitenmaks tribe of the Gitksan (variants: Gitins, Gituns, Gyitins, Kitans). The term appears to apply to a stage in the training and development of a shaman, as evidenced in the following passage quoted from Tens:

"One day a year later (after his first vision), my father summoned the halaait (medicine-men) in the village to come down and act over me. The first thing they did was to sedarhguaetu (to strengthen me), that is, they raised me from my couch and walked me round the room. Then I was really strengthened. To pay for their services my father distributed a great amount of property to all those who had assembled there to witness the event.

"That was the time when I became a swanassu (medicine-man). This was the fasting period, when one aspires to become a halaait. I had to have dreams before being able to act. This period lasted a year, in reclusion at my father's house, out of touch with other folk excepting the four attendants" [Tens in Barbeau 1958:42].

Halaait often treat a patient as a group, several of them being present during a healing. Each *halaait* owns 15 to 20 healing songs. The fee for their services depends on the wealth of the family requesting the healing. A standard fee is 10 blankets, but it could be as little as one blanket. If the patient does not recover, there is no fee. Shamans rarely refuse a request for healing, lest they be suspected of causing the illness.

Swanton, John Reed
John Swanton was born in Gardiner, Maine, on 19 February 1873. He received his Ph.D. from Yale in 1900, although he spent his last two years of graduate work studying under Franz Boas at Columbia University. After completing some fieldwork on Vancouver Island, mainly among the Haida and Tlingit, he joined the Bureau of American Ethnology at the Smithsonian, where he remained through the end of World War II. His work focused mainly on the historical migrations of Native Americans in the southeasteren United States. He also collected a basic lexicon of Muskogean and Tunica and classified North American kinship systems. His major works include *Indian Tribes of the Lower Mississippi Valley and Adjacent Coast of the Gulf of Mexico* (1905), *Source Material on the History and Ethnology of Caddo Indians* (1942), and *Indians of the Southeastern United States* (1952). He died in Newton, Massachusetts, on 2 May 1958.

Swaxtiutid
Dwamish, *Northwest Coast*
A class of supernatural beings, earth beings, that live in the ground; translates to "earths." Another term, *swawatiutid*, meaning "little earths," is also used for these spirit beings [Waterman 1930a: 306].

These earth beings are about the size of small children, and "they dance about in wild and lonely places" [Waterman 1930b:535]. Their home is often in a spring or a pond. Such spirits are obtained by shamans who fast in the woods. The potential shaman approaches a pond over which the trees bend and drinks from the water. If the quest is successful, an earth being "takes his wind," leaving the novice unconscious, at which time the spirit teaches the novice medicine songs. Once such a spirit is caught, the shaman carves its likeness into a 3- to 4 1/2-foot pole, which is planted in the ground.

Sweat Lodge Ceremony
The sweat lodge ceremony is the most widespread form of purification in North America. It

A Native American emerges from a sweat lodge in 1939. Constructed of bent withes and covered in either animal skins or blankets, the sweat lodge is used as a place for singing sacred songs and praying.

appears in nearly every nation, with the exception of those in the Southwest. The lodges come in many different forms and sizes, but they normally hold 10 to 15 people comfortably. The basic procedure is to heat rocks on a fire and then bring them into the lodge, where water is then poured over them. The ceremony leader is usually the one who pours the water. Most often, these lodges are built to be light-tight, so that the participants are in total darkness. Sacred songs are sung, prayers are recited, and spirits are called into the lodge—all to facilitate the purification of the participants. During the ceremony, the door is opened, usually four times, to bring in additional hot stones and to give the participants a moment's relief. However, the intensity of the heat helps the participants bring their minds to a single point of focus and will, which aids the process of purification.

Swimmer
Cherokee, *Southeast*

A nineteenth-century shaman whose Cherokee name was Ayûnini ("Swimmer"). During the summer of 1887, he was visited by anthropologist James Mooney, who obtained from Swimmer "a small day-book of about 240 pages, procured originally from a white man, and was about half-filled with writing in the Cherokee characters (i.e. Sequoyan syllabary)" [Mooney 1891:312]. The book contained prayers, songs, prescriptions, charms, making constant use of words derived from *wúu-sot*, 'to blow.'"

Sxet

Lummi, *Northwest Coast*

A harmful spirit sent by a sorcerer into the body of a victim that causes illness [Stern 1934:75]. Illnesses are often diagnosed as being caused by a *sxet*. The shaman removes the *sxet* by sucking on the patient's body. "Some suck out the illness by placing the mouth directly against the patient's body; others use cupped hands" [Stern 1934:80]. One shaman was observed to use a cattail stalk to suck through. See *cxwneam* for additional details.

Sxwlaem

Coast Salish, *Northwest Coast*

Dialectical variant: *sxwalem* (Upper Stalo branch) [Duff 1952:98]. Shamans who travel to the land of the dead in search of lost souls; that is, shamans who conduct the Spirit Canoe healing ceremony. The name is derived from *sxwwaliaem*, meaning "searcher of souls," and *sxwalam*, meaning "on one's course of travel" [Jilek 1982b:145]. See *sbatatdaq* for details.

Training for shamans usually begins in early childhood, with children beginning overnight vigils around the age of 12 and taking progressively longer trips each time. "Coming to a lake, a stream, a waterfall, he would stay for several days, fasting the whole time. He would make himself thoroughly clean by chewing laxative bark and by tickling his throat with a stick to induce vomiting, by sweating in the sweat-house, by frequent bathing and swimming, and by rubbing his body with boughs. All night long he would sing and dance. He would sleep only when exhausted, and then try to dream of the power he wanted" [Duff 1952:98]. When the quest is finally successful, a guardian spirit appears (usually in human guise), gives the novice instructions, reveals its true identity (usually an animal), and then departs. The appearance can be made by either a *sulia*, a spirit being from the spirit world, or a *slalakum*, a supernatural creature that inhabits the natural world. In some cases, a boy receives supernatural power directly from a powerful shaman who "blows" the power into the boy.

Swimmer, a Cherokee shaman.

and so forth, known as formulas (*gowäli*; see entry), used by Cherokee shamans. There were 137 formulas in all, many of them medicinal prescriptions. The book became known as the Swimmer manuscript, and Swimmer assisted Mooney in its translation. The book mysteriously disappeared from the Smithsonian around the turn of the twentieth century.

Swúsos ó'odham

Pima, *Southwest*

Curer; the literal meaning is "blower man," indicating the importance of breath in shamanic healing techniques. According to Bahr [1977:n.1:31] "one cannot talk in Piman about curing without

When a shaman doctors, he calls his curing spirit by singing its spirit song. The shaman's power is usually related in some way to the form of the spirit. For example, "the sucker and the leech gave the power to cure by sucking" [Duff 1952:100]. The shaman often makes his helping spirit appear during the healing ceremony as well. According to one account: "Ten or fifteen men were sitting in a square, drumming on boards. The *sxwlaem* was dancing, jumping over the sick man. Then he took off his shirt, hung it on the tent ridgepole, and blew on it. It turned into an owl. I got scared and left" [A. J. in Duff 1952:101].

For sickness caused by soul loss, "the doctor comes, puts a basket on his head (in order to see the lost soul). He has a bunch singing and drumming while he goes and gets (the soul). He brings it back in his cupped hands. He has a mouthful of water, and blows the water through his hands into the person's head. It carries the (lost) soul right in" [E. L. in Duff 1952:112]. However, blowing on the patient is not limited to cases of soul loss. A. J. also reported to Duff [1952:113] that shamans "blow on the part of your body where you are sick. They blow their power into you, and it chases the sickness away. They wear a buckskin cap down over their eyes, and sing and dance."

For illness caused by object intrusion, the cure is to suck the object from the patient. For example:

"Then the old man (shaman) sucked on my back. He kept sucking out blood and spitting it into a basin until it was almost full. This didn't hurt or leave any mark on the skin. I guess those things were alive, because they kept moving around from one side of my back to the other, and that hurt. Then I could feel them start to come out. He sucked three things out (without breaking the skin). The first two were little balls covered with black blood, about three-eighths of an inch in diameter. He held these down on a block of wood and got my sister to cut them into slices and burn them. He said that if they got away from him, they would disappear and fly back to their owner. The third thing was a piece of thread about 6 inches long. I guess that is what was used to tie that thing up with" [E. L. in Duff 1952:113].

Sucking was also used to cure other ailments. "A young girl got a sharp hook-ended grass-seed caught in her throat. The old man sucked it out through her neck. A Katz man had his chest crushed in a logging accident during the construction of the Canadian Pacific Railway and was 'filling up with blood.' The old shaman sucked all the blood out of his chest and cured him" [E. L. in Duff 1952:113].

For the Katzie branch of the Coast Salish, Suttles [1955:6] gives the term *sxwneem* for a shaman. Furthermore, one "must distinguish the *sxwneem* (shaman), whose power is derived from a special type of spirit vision, and the *slthithe*, or *syewinmet*, whose power is derived from his knowledge of *syewin* (prayer)" [Suttles 1955:6]. This latter type of shaman is often referred to as a priest or ritualist.

Syawan
Coast Salish, *Northwest Coast*
Eastern dialect: *syiwil*. Spirit illness or power sickness, referring to a class of illnesses caused by spirits. For example, depression from alcohol or drug abuse is usually diagnosed as *syawan*. Other symptoms include restlessness, fainting spells, uncontrollable crying, heavy breathing, sighing, and moaning. The cure for any *syawan* is the performance of the Spirit Dance.

A typical case history of *syawan* is reported by Jilek [1981:166]:

"The story of a middle-aged son of a respected Salish chief serves as an illustrative case study. Under acculturative influences, this man rebelled against traditional authority in his teens, and left his father's home for what then appeared to him as a freer life with social and drinking habits in sharp contrast with the austere ways of his parents. He was fairly successful as a logger, but unhappy in successive unions with non-Indian spouses. As the years passed he felt increasingly depressed, sensing the alienation from his people. In spite of his avowed indifference toward native traditions, he visited a spirit dance while on a brief visit home. From then on, the sound of deerskin drums followed him every night; he heard them even in the solitude of the forest. Nostalgia overwhelmed him; he knew he had contracted 'spirit illness' and would have to obey the call of his guardian spirit. He tried to resist but became severely depressed, resorting to excessive drinking for several weeks, becoming unconscious frequently. Waking from an alcoholic coma one day, he suddenly felt that he would surely die unless he returned to the ways of his ancestors. He approached his family and the ritualists for spirit-dance initiation, but they referred him to medical care in view of his poor physical condition and nervous exhaustion. While on the psychiatric ward in the general hospital, he maintained close contact with kinspeople and ritualists. As soon as his condition permitted, the patient was discharged to undergo the full initiation procedure. When in the presence of his proud father he displayed his newly acquired spirit power for the first time, the patient called upon his physician and psychiatrist to act as ritual witnesses. He has remained an active participant in the ceremonial which helped him to overcome anomic depression and symptomatic alcoholism."

Syawan also "denotes the spiritual powers acquired by individuals in a prescribed way, and manifested in the spirit ceremonial through specific song, dance, face painting, and other attributes displayed during the so-called *sya'wan* season. In this sense, and in contemporary usage, *sya'wan* refers to the spiritual essence of the whole ceremonial and comprises more than the individual dancer's songs" [Jilek 1982b:49].

Syòwae
Nootsack, *Northwest Coast*
A supernatural ability to see into the future or to see what is going on at a distance, or a person who has this power. Most *syòwae* are women, and their power is not usually associated with a spirit helper. Such persons cannot alter the course of

events but can only report on what they see [Amoss 1978:16].

Syòwan
Nootsack, *Northwest Coast*
Helping spirit; also, "the song and dance performed during the winter ceremonials" [Amoss 1978:49]. A less frequently used term with the same meaning is *sàliya*, which can also refer to the visions of nonshamans [Amoss 1978:64]. *Syòwan* are described as liking the daylight, so shamans usually obtain such spirit helpers early in the morning on their vision quests. Such quests are most often conducted at known power spots where other shamans are known to have obtained their helping spirits. Once obtained, the shaman must learn to control his *syòwan* so that it will take possession of him at the proper time and place. This is done through songs that come with the power. Most difficult to control are the spirits that are powerful enough to cure and kill. The major responsibility towards one's *syòwan* is "to give it adequate expression by dancing at winter ceremonials. The dancer must also be punctilious in observing the style of face painting prescribed by his spirit and wearing the special costume suggested in the vision" [Amoss 1978:61]. Because the bond between a spirit helper and a person becomes stronger over time, it also becomes more dangerous to anger one's *syòwan*, because its departure will certainly result in sickness if not death. Thus, most people see the life of a *syòwan* person as a difficult one.

Syuwadad
Skokomish, *Northwest Coast*
Curing power. *Syuwadad* is given to a shaman by a guardian spirit. The term is derived from *yuwadab* (see entry).

T

Taachi
Apache, *Southwest*
Sweat lodge. Apache shamans make frequent use of the sweat lodge to contact their helping spirits [Bourke 1892:462]. Attending the sweat lodge is also a required part of treatment if the patient is physically able to do so [Bourke 1892:455].

Taarteq
East Greenland Eskimo, *Arctic Coast*
Also: *taartat, tarta, tartok.* Among the Eskimo of East Greenland, the shaman's helping spirit. It comes from *taq,* meaning "human being," and translates to "its human being." Such a spirit may be the spirit of a dead shaman or the spirit of an animal that has changed into a man [Birket-Smith 1924:441]. Most often they are creatures that live unnoticed in the neighborhood of the settlements under the earth, under the beach rocks, or inland. Only the shaman can see them and speak to them, using the sacred language of the spirits [Thalbitzer 1928:374]. With regard to healing, Holm [1914:97] reports that when a shaman "has performed his arts in order to heal a sick person, an indispensable condition for the success of the cure is that it shall be paid for. It is the *tartok,* however, and not the angakok (shaman) that is paid for its trouble. . . . The payment is, of course, proportioned to the circumstances of the sick person."

Tadi nyac
Cayuga, *Northeast*
The Tug-of-War or Pulling ritual used for healing; literally, "they (both sides) grab the stick." Anyone may participate in the ritual. See *eyondwanshgwut* for details.

Take
Salina, *California*
Shamans [Mason 1912:183]. Female shamans are unknown in this culture. "When called to treat a patient, the doctor made a cut, generally on the arm or at the point of pain, with a flint. He sucked at the cut and drew out small sticks or stones or other small objects which were supposed to be the cause of the complaint. In the case of wounds he chewed an herb and spit it on the hurt. Dancing and singing are said to have been also practiced as means of cure" [Mason 1912:184].

Taköonin
Pueblo, *Southwest*
Shamans who are stick swallowers. *Takö* is the shuttle used in weaving, and *taköonin* refers to a special stick swallowed

by some shamans during their ceremonies [Parsons 1932:267].

Tam Apö

Shoshoni, *Basin*

The name of the Creator among the Wind River branch of the Eastern or Plains Shoshoni. It translates to "our father" [Hultkrantz 1986:43].

Tamanoas

Puget Sound Salish, *Northwest Coast*

Also: *tamahnous.* Chinook jargon for the widespread concept of *orenda* (see entry), a magical power that permeates the universe. This supernatural power resides in all objects in nature and in spirits [Radin 1914:345]. Waterman [1930b:557] reports that the word is "applied to supernatural beings, 'medicines,' and ceremonial objects in general." About this term, Myron Eells reports:

"It is derived from a word in the old Chinook language, *it-a-mah-na-was*. In general, it means anything supernatural either among good or bad spirits. . . . The word is used as a noun, adjective, and verb. As a noun, tamahnous is the spirit or supernatural being in the other world, which has an influence over man, as his guardian spirit or the spirit which makes him sick or kills him; also the act of invoking the good ones and driving away the bad ones, so that a great tamahnous is often spoken of, meaning a great gathering of people who are performing their incantations. As an adjective, it qualifies and defines certain persons and things, so that a tamahnous man is one who, by his incantations, can influence the spirits—a medicine man; a tamahnous stick, or stone, or painting, is one in which the spirits are believed to dwell, or which is sometimes used in performing their incantations. It is likewise a verb, and 'to tamahnous' is to perform the incantations necessary to influence these spirits. In some cases it is done mainly by the medicine men, but in others by any one" [Eells in Castile 1985:361].

The most powerful *tamanoas* is that used to cure the sick. The other two forms of *tamanoas* are called black *tamanoas* and red *tamanoas* [Castile 1985:395]. Waterman [1930b:558–560] provides the following sketch of a healing ceremony using black *tamanoas:*

"Shamans who undertook this ceremony selected a certain boy, very often, I am told, a boy who refused to 'believe' his elders. One of the 'doctors' took some water into his mouth, blew it into his hands, 'twisted' it, and 'struck' the boy with it. This knocked the lad insensible. They then 'put him away' somewhere for five days. Meanwhile, the shamans assembled in a house, gathered the people, and had long performances, singing spirit-songs and preparing for the climax. The songs used at this time were utterly different from those of any other ceremony.

"The performers, including usually a number of women, formed a circle around the fire, six or eight of them bearing wooden rattles. It was absolutely necessary for the face to be blackened (with charcoal), if one wished to get the 'power.' The women were obliged to wear the hair hanging loose and decorated with duck-feathers; also, they fasted for several days before the ceremony. Blood was often visible about the mouth and on the chests of the dancers, though uninitiated people did not know whence it came. One man who acted as leader started the songs, accompanied by the rattles. Later on, these rattles were passed about the circle to other performers. There is one special song which causes the people to be 'crazy' or possessed *(q^{ε}li'Exs)*. When that occurred, they would dash at the fire and scatter it about. These ceremonies started early each evening and terminated about midnight. When at the close of the observances the boy is produced, the shamans gather around him. They have wooden rattles made of maple or alder, called *xwuba'otcid*, representing the grouse. Shaking these rattles, they dance around him, which brings him out of his stupor. On coming into consciousness he vomits a quantity of 'blood' and begins to act very violently. He cannot speak, and his eyes are staring. He wishes to throw himself into the water, or, if he sees a fire burning, he dashes at it and attempts to claw it around. The shamans tie a strap around him, and two of them hold him, and move him about, dancing. . . .

"The remainder of the ceremonials seem to be intended to bring the candidate back to normal.

One of my informants, Burnt Charley, who had acted as a leader in this rite, spoke of a tossing performance, in which the candidate was lifted by six men, who, after singing, tossed him into the air. The first time, they caught him; the second time, he landed on his feet and dashed away. Bystanders made an effort to seize and hold the trailing ropes fastened to his waist, always without success, and the candidate disappeared. He ran to a certain secret place, guided by the 'power,' and took a bath. On returning to the village, he sang his songs, and was met by the people and escorted to another house, where he was 'fixed up.' Shredded cedar-bark, dyed red with alder, was tied around his head, and two ironwood wands were thrust under the head-band standing vertically. These wands, called *skeátctid*, served as head-scratchers. The candidate did not dare touch his head with his fingers. When I inquired whether the candidates wore any special clothes, my informant replied that they did not wear any at all. The candidate continued to fast for a period of days, meanwhile taking daily baths at his secret place. The other performers bathed daily near the village."

Myron Eells witnessed a healing ceremony in October 1876 and reported the following:

"The patient was a woman of perhaps fifty years. . . . At times she could not see, she would know almost nothing, and could not tell where she was sick, and they were tamahnousing to find what was the difficulty, and when they had learned this they would send and obtain the right kind of medicine. They say that they often do tamahnous, first in order to learn what is the difficulty and afterwards to cure.

"Having asked permission, I went in and took my seat, as directed, behind the doctor, so that he was between me and the patient. The house was about twenty feet square, a summer house, built on the gravelly beach of the Skokomish River. There were about fifteen persons in the house, both men and women, all of whom while the doctor was performing beat with small sticks on larger ones and sang in regular time. I was in one corner of the house, the patient (female) in the opposite corner facing me, sitting up and held by

another woman. There were two fires near the middle, and the doctor was between them on his knees on the gravel. He was stripped to the waist, having only pantaloons and boots on, and faced the woman, having his hair tied in a knot over his forehead. He had a small tub of water near the woman. As he began he almost lay down on the gravel and sang and kept swinging his head up and down, constantly singing, while the other Indians joined in the singing for about twelve minutes, when he began to vomit violently over himself and the ground. . . . Then came a rest of a few minutes, when he rested and washed himself off. But soon all began again, when he worked up to the woman and, as near as I could see placed his mouth on her chest or shoulders and sucked very strongly and then blew out of his mouth with all his force, making a great noise, sometimes blowing into the water in the tub, and sometimes blowing into the air, always remaining on his knees. This was kept up about fifteen minutes longer, when I left during another respite. But this was neither the beginning nor the end of the tamahnous. Sometimes they kept it up for most of the day and night or longer" [Castile 1985:413–414].

Tamoémli
Washo, *Basin*
Dream doctor; shamans who have obtained healing powers via a dream. Most dream doctors are men, but women also become healers, usually at an advanced age.

Most healing ceremonies last four nights. They are of the sucking variety, in which the shaman sucks on the afflicted area of the body to remove an object causing the illness. "He would spit out objects, the last one expectorated being the pathogenic agent. Putting it on his palm, he would look at it, as would his spectators. Sometimes it was a bug. The shaman put hot ashes on his hand, rubbed them on the bug, killed it, and threw it away. The patient would get better and possibly in a week feel as well as ever" [Lowie 1939:319].

Tamyush
Luiseño, *California Peninsula*
Sacred stone bowls used in ceremonies. They are treated as persons [White 1976:364, 368].

T'ànwen

Tewa, *Southwest*

Illness; also, bad luck, evil, weariness. Illness is believed to be caused by evil spirits or witches, who project foreign, disease-causing objects into the body. The cure requires a sucking shaman to remove the object.

Tao

Caddo, *Plains*

Beaver doctor [Parsons 1941:34]. See *konah* for additional details.

Tarrak

Eskimo, *Arctic Coast*

See *torngak*.

Tartok

East Greenland Eskimo, *Arctic Coast*

Angmagsalik shaman's helping spirit. Most *angakut* (shamans) have an *amortortok* as their *tartok*. This particular spirit being comes during the shaman's rituals and acts as a kind of oracle, bringing news from far distances and answering questions laid before it. It has black arms and is dangerous to approach. In fact, if it touches a person, that person will turn black and die. Every *angakok* (shaman) also has his *tornarsuk* and *aperketek*, who act as his spirits. *Tornarsuk* is as long as a big seal but much thicker in proportion. His head and back paws resemble those of the seal, and his forepaws are as long as a man's arm but thicker and ending in fins. *Aperketek* is about 4 feet long and black and has nippers in his head. Both of these beings reside in the sea. During the shaman's ceremonies, *tornarsuk* answers questions addressed to it, and *aperketek* acts as a mediator between the shaman and his *tornarsuk:* he receives the shaman's questions and states them to *tornarsuk*, and then obtains replies from *tornarsuk*. Thus, shamans have several *tartoks*.

Shamanic rituals are generally held only during winter and in the dark. Before the ritual begins, the shaman's arms are bound tightly behind his back. Often his head is also tied down between his legs. A thong is tied tightly around his head, which allows him to see clearly in the pitch dark.

Once the shaman is so tied, the lamps are extinguished. His *tartok* picks up a drumstick and drums while dancing around the head of the shaman. The drum is a circular wooden frame over which a bearskin or sealskin has been stretched. A rawhide handle is attached to the side. The drum is always moistened before using to give it a more beautiful ring. It is played by striking the stick against the edge of the wooden frame versus striking the stretched skin as is done in most other cultures. Sometimes the shaman is not tied, in which case he also beats time to the drum on a piece of bearded-sealskin held in his hand. The *tartoks* cannot be seen, but they can be heard. There is seldom more than one present at any one time. The *tartok* speaks through the shaman in a strange language. Sometimes, when there is a bit of light, the participants can see the drum dancing about the head of the shaman.

William Thalbitzer observed one such ceremony near the end of the nineteenth century and reported:

"The spirits were immediately summoned with the cries: 'Goi! goi goi goi!'—proceeding now from one voice, now from several, now from one part of the house, now from another. All the while the angakok kept puffing and groaning and heaving heavy sighs. All at once the dry skin before the entrance began to rattle, as if caught by a rushing wind. The drum now started into motion, dancing first slowly, then with ever increasing speed, and mounted slowly up to the ceiling. Now ensued a veritable pandemonium of noises, a rattling, a blustering, and a clattering, reminding one at one moment of a machine-factory at work, at another of the puffing of engines, and now seeming to proceed from a number of great winged creatures. In the midst of this hideous din the platform and window-sill would ever and anon shake. At one moment it was the angakok one heard, succumbing to a power mightier than himself, groaning, wailing, shrieking, whining, whispering; now came the sound of spirit-voices, some deep, some feeble, others lisping or piping. At frequent intervals a harsh, demoniacal, mocking laughter made itself heard. The voices seemed to proceed now from above; now from under the ground, now from one end of the house, now from the other, now from outside the house, now from the passage-way" [Thalbitzer 1914:91–92].

Tawashichunpi
Lakota, *Plains*
Shamans' guardian spirits [Dorsey 1894:475]. Spirit helpers are usually acquired through vision questing and often confer healing powers on the recipient shaman. Most often they come in the form of an animal, but the most powerful spirits are the Thunder Beings.

Tayatowetha
Iroquois, *Northeast*
See *saokata*.

Tchi can ama
Atsugewi, *California*
The phrase used by one Atsuge informant to refer to their doctors. He reported: "In our history, there were two doctors. One was called *tchi can ama*. That was the name of the best doctor. He was a good doctor, and he was the first one. The second doctor was Coyote *(mache da)*. These two were the best doctors. These two had different ways of curing, but they cured sick people just the same" [Grant in Park 1986:39]. See *betsaki* for details.

Tchissakiwinini
Ojibwa, *Canadian Eastern Woodlands*
Also: *tcisaki* [Grim 1983:113]. One of the four classes of Ojibwa healers, according to Vizenor [1981:81]. Ojibwa shamans are classified according to the different techniques used in healing and divining, and *tchissakiwinini* are the medicine men who perform the Shaking Tent Ceremony (see entry). They are primarily diviner shamans. The etymology of the word is unknown.

Tcikamitc sumatc
Mojave, *Southwest*
A specialist shaman who is an adept clairvoyant and diviner and has mastered ture spirit possession. According to Stewart [1974:9] a Mojave informant told him:

"They build kind of a hut of bent-over willow branches. The *tcikamitc* goes behind it, and they pour sand in his mouth. His spirit comes out. There are about four or five people in that hut waiting for what they are going to ask him. They say a 'road' comes in. Next a roadrunner comes in and makes a noise. They ask him if he can see anything around the world, and he tells what he can see, like the 'fly-by-nights' (the Whites) were gonna come and take everything away. The spirit of the mountain, *Avikwame*, got in there too, and talked through his mouth. It said just a few words, then would be gone. The spirit of *Avikwame* talks through his mouth, and tells when the enemy is coming, or anything you want to find out, like if you lost something or someone, and what kind of weather it's gonna be. The people have to shake sand out of him later. He could find out where the enemy was, and if the enemy was coming. That's why the Mojaves weren't attacked. They put dirt in his mouth when he's unconscious, and the spirits come and talk through his mouth and give information. When they put sand in his mouth, he *dies* with it, and comes back to life later when they shake the sand out. That's his power. They don't live to be old, though."

Te Ithaethema
Omaha, Ponca, *Plains*
The Buffalo Society or "order of Buffalo shamans" [Dorsey 1894:392]. Members of this society have had visions of the buffalo and use buffalo songs when healing the sick. The healing shamans of this society are primarily surgeons. Among the Omaha and the Iowa, the only surgeons are the buffalo shamans [Dorsey 1894:429].

Teckwine
Zuni, *Southwest*
Altar; from *teckwi*, meaning "sacred" or "taboo," and literally means "sacred thing." The altars of the medicine societies consist of painted slat altars (a sort of reredos) upon which are placed stone images of the Beast Priests, tutelary gods of the medicine society, and *miwe* (amulets), among the more specialized items [Bunzel 1932:491]. Their altars are always erected on the side of the room away from the door and are called "the valuable place."

Outsiders are not allowed in the altar room, nor are they ever allowed to touch any of the altar items.

Teipalai
Diegueño, *California Peninsula*
A shaman who lived at Manzanita in southern California around the turn of the twentieth century. He was a specialist in rattlesnake medicine and was called by the Kumeyaay (the Diegueño's preferred term for themselves) a *wikwisiyai*. Spier [1923:313] was told by his informant McCarty of the following incident during one of McCarty's visits with Teipalai and his two sons:

"'There goes an old man with a basket on his head (he meant a snake).' His son said, 'You lie; there is nothing there. We are going to look.' Teipalai said, 'All right; go and see. Go close to the bush by the draw.' They went where he directed them and saw a snake. They were frightened; one ran off, the other ran back. This man was owner of the snakes and could cure their bite. He was a snake. He could talk with them. A snake would come to him to say that he was going to borrow something. He really meant he was going to bite someone. But Teipalai would say, 'No, you will put me to a lot of work,' i.e. to cure the patient."

Tekohanna
Zuni, *Southwest*
Blessing; translates to "white day" or "light" [Parsons 1939:489].

Telbut
Wailaki, *California*
A large Kato bullroarer used to simulate the noise of thunder. It is used in healing ceremonies to cure fright sickness, caused by dreams of or encounters with spirit beings. The Kato have a special verb designating the act of seeing a harmful spirit: *gusan*, "to see bad luck" [Loeb 1934a:37, 40].

Telogel
Yurok, *Oregon Seaboard*
Disease; translates to "pain." Healing involves having this pain removed by a *kegey* (see entry),

who is a sucking doctor. The *telogel* is a manifestation of power. Thus, in removing it, the shaman acquires power over it and adds it to her own inventory of powers. "Doctors were ranked in terms of the numbers and strength of the *telogel* and other powers they controlled" [Buckley 1992:140].

Temnepa
Coast Miwok, *California*
Sucking doctor; also referred to as *wakilapi*. These shamans undergo formal training by older shamans before becoming practitioners. In cases of serious illness, they call upon the Kuksu society (see guksu ceremony) to perform a four-day healing dance ceremony. Among the southern Coast Miwok, the sucking doctor is called *wenenapi* [Loeb 1934a:114].

Tens, Issac
Tsimshian, *Northwest Coast*
An old Gitksan man when interviewed in 1920, Issac Tens was then a renowned shaman. He described his first healing of a woman who had been unsuccessfully treated by other shamans as follows:

"So I went into her house and instructed the people there to light a fire first. As I began to sing over her (he eventually had three groups of healing songs for a total of twenty-three healing songs), many people around me were hitting sticks on boards and beating skin drums for me. My canoe came to me in a dream, and there were many people sitting in it. The canoe itself was the Otter (*watserh*). The woman whom I was doctoring sat with the others inside this Otter canoe. By that time, about twenty other *halaaits* (shamans) were present in the house. To them I explained what my vision was, and asked, 'What shall I do? There the woman is sitting in the canoe, and the canoe is the Otter.'

"They answered, 'Try to pull her out.'

"I told them, 'Spread the fire out, into two parts, and make a pathway between them.' I walked up and down this path four times, while the other *halaaits* kept singing until they were very tired. Then I went over to the couch on which the sick woman was lying. There was a great up-heaval in the singing and the clapping of drums and the sticks on the boards. I placed my hand on her stomach and moved round her couch, all the while trying to draw the canoe out of her. I man-aged to pull it up very close to the surface of her chest. I grasped it, drew it out, and put it in my own bosom. This I did.

"Two days later, the woman rose out of bed; she was cured. My prestige as a *halaait* gained greatly" [Tens in Barbeau 1958:47–48].

Teomul
Micmac, *Canadian Eastern Woodlands*
See *tiómel*.

Tepe'muésuki
Washo, *Basin*
The sucking process used by a shaman to remove a disease-causing object from the body [Lowie 1939:319].

Tewebatsigan
Montagnais, *Canadian Eastern Woodlands*
Dialectical variant: *tawabatsigan* (Michikamau). A Naskapi twirling buzzer, or bullroarer (see entry), that calls the winds. It is made of a single caribou astragalus attached by sinew to the two sticks serving as grips [Speck 1935:196].

Tewehigan
Montagnais, *Canadian Eastern Woodlands*
Naskapi drum; it comes from the stem *twew-*, as-sociated with the idea of magic and sound. Sha-mans treat their drums as living beings. As one informant stated, "It can speak to him who un-derstands its language when it is beaten. It talks, but all do not understand. When it is beaten by one whose soul is strong, it reveals what is going to happen. Sometimes during sleep the drum will address itself to the soul of a man and urge him to rouse himself and consult its meaning by attack-ing it with his drumstick. Whereupon it utters forth its message, to be grasped, if possible, by the imagination of the operator" [Speck 1935:171–172].

Such drums are also capable of sending mes-sages to distant parts—to other shamans and even to animals.

This is also the term for drum among the Mon-tagnais [Speck 1919:241].

Tewusu
Zuni, *Southwest*
Any action involved with acquiring help from the spirits—from the simple gesture of offering corn-meal to the more elaborate ceremonies. All the rit-ual curing activities of shamans fall under this term.

Teyewa
Cahuilla, *California Peninsula*
Shaman's helping spirit [Bean 1972:109]. Spirit helpers are obtained through a series of power dreams in which the *teyewa* instructs the novice shaman in song, dance, and healing techniques. The *teyewa* resides in the shaman's body. "Repre-sented by an animate or inanimate object, such as a lizard, snake, seed, or cactus thorn, it communi-cated with the *puul* [shaman; see *pul*] and was em-ployed in the performance of acts demonstrating supernatural power. The *teyewa* was treated with extreme care and respect by the *puul* and his fam-ily" [Bean 1972:109–110].

Thauwithok sumatc
Mojave, *Southwest*
A shaman who specializes in treating hunters who have broken the taboo of not eating the meat of the game they have killed. "He will get sleep-ing sickness and sleep until he dies, unless the doctor treats him by throwing him in the river and bathing him four times" [Stewart 1974:11].

Théwatshi
Ponca, *Plains*
The Buffalo Doctor Society. Its members are sha-mans who acquired their healing power from the buffalo. They deal primarily with wounds, mostly from warfare. Howard [1965:117] reports that they were the Ponca surgeons. "If a man were wounded the buffalo doctors got together and squirted water on the wound. They would dance

in the imitation of the buffalo, wearing robes, buffalo horn caps, and tails. They painted only with clay which is the buffalo's pigment. They painted only the upper or lower halves of their faces. The buffalo dancers were very *waxúbe* or powerful" [Skinner in Howard 1965:118–119].

Thilyamo sumatc
Mojave, *Southwest*
A specialist shaman called the fly doctor. He treats wounds, both animal and human, so that they do not become infected by screwworms from blow-flies. Also, he "was reputed besides to be able to raise a cloud of dust or a cold wind" [Stewart 1974:10].

Tiger, Susie
Seminole, *Southeast*
A shaman in the northern or Cow Creek band of Seminole who recorded five of her healing songs for Frances Densmore. "These included songs for lumbago, for a sick baby, for bringing a child into the world, a song addressed to the 'white sun-lady,' and a song addressed to the dying in which she besought the spirit to turn back before reaching nine different places in the journey" [Densmore 1952:445–446].

Tingavish
Cahuilla, *California Peninsula*
Doctors [Bean and Saubel 1972:19]. Most of them are women renowned for their curing abilities. Unlike shamans, they do not use sacred powers but limit their practice to the use of herbal remedies. Plants are gathered mostly between April and November. "Not only were ritual restrictions imposed by Cahuilla leaders on who could gather plants and when they could be gathered, but regular 'taxes' were levied against those with excessive reserves so that all community needs could be met as they arose" [Bean and Saubel 1972:21]. In addition, each family usually owns the right to gather in specific areas.

Tinun
Tolowa, *Oregon Seaboard*
Doctors [Drucker 1937:258].

Tiómel
Micmac, *Canadian Eastern Woodlands*
Also: *teomul*. Shaman's helping spirit. *Ntióm* translates as "my helping spirit," whereas *utiómel* translates as "his helping spirit." The stem without its pronominal and intervocalic elements is simply -*iom* [Speck 1919:254].

Tirára
Pawnee, *Plains*
Supernatural powers [Alexander 1910:44].

Tiwét
Nez Perce, *Plateau*
Shaman. Walker [1967:75] reports the following account of a healing (necessitated by sorcery) given to him by an informant in 1963:

"There was this young Flathead man over here. He had gotten some horses at Umatilla and stopped here on the way home, and while he was here one of his horses happened to bump into Poor Coyote. When he did, it made Poor Coyote mad, and he shot (*qetí·wit*) at him. That boy went home, but the further he went, the sicker he got. When he got home they called in the doctor (M.D.), but he couldn't do anything. The longer he was there the sicker he got. They decided to call in the *tiwé·t* (shaman). He called other *titwé·t*, and they began working on him. One wasn't strong enough to get Poor Coyote. They had a hell of a time getting him out. You could see how he was fighting by the way they moved their hands around. He didn't want to die. They were fighting him all over the place, but they finally got him. Then they heard him speaking Nez Perce. None of them could understand it but one *tiwé·t* (came there) who could, and he told them that was what he was talking. When they told the boy about bumping into the old man, the boy remembered it. He hadn't meant to do it. Those *titwé·t* told the people they weren't killers, they were healers. You know if you start killing people you'll lose your power. They asked the people what they wanted to do with Poor Coyote, and they said to kill him. They cut him in two. Poor Coyote was going out to the barn to feed his horses, but he never made it. He fell flat, dead."

Tixyi
Biloxi, Ofo, *Southeast*
Medicine [Dorsey and Swanton 1912:221].

Tjui
Wintun, *California*
The Patwin cause of illness, called pain. To effect a cure, a shaman has to locate the pain and then remove it by sucking on the patient.

Tlakwilex xalaspuxem
Sinkaietk, *Plateau*
One of three classes of shamanic curing specialists among the southern Okanagon of Washington. This class of shamans cures by blowing and manipulation. Often the blowing includes the use of tobacco smoke from a sacred pipe. The shamans wear no special clothing during their healing ceremonies. In serious cases, several shamans cooperate to effect the cure. Dance rituals by the shaman are also a routine part of curing. According to Cline [1938:163–164]:

"Blowing was often combined with manipulation or massage. Fly power enabled its possessor to cure scrofula by blowing on the afflicted part and subsequently extracting the 'worm' by the motion of his hands. This was done also for toothache. . . . To restore the soul to a person who had lost it by foolishly touching the central dance post, a shaman drew the soul out of the post, probably by manipulation, rubbed it once or twice between his hands, and blew it back into the patient's body.

"A cure involving both manipulation and blowing was described as follows by Cecile. The doctor first sang for about ten minutes, presumably his power song. Then he worked his hands over the reclining patient from feet to head and grasped the sickness over the head in both hands. One or two bystanders seized him 'to prevent him from dying or being carried away by the strength of the medicine,' and plunged his hands, which still held the sickness, into a vessel of water. When the sickness had become quiet, the doctor took his hands out of the water and 'threw away' the sickness by blowing on it. He repeated this process four times, twice working his hands up from the patient's feet and twice down from the head."

Tlakwilex xalslapem
Sinkaietk, *Plateau*
One of three classes of shamanic curing specialists among the southern Okanagon. This class of shamans uses sucking techniques to perform their healings. They are recognized by a tattooed line running from each corner of the mouth down each side of the chin. Often they have blood-sucking guardian spirits, such as the mosquito and the horsefly. According to Cline [1938:164]:

"The shaman sometimes sucked the patient's blood between his (cupped?) hands placed over the heart or over the afflicted member. After the treatment he deposited the blood or other cause of trouble in a vessel of water where it would cool down and become quiet, and where people could see it. No visible break remained in the patient's skin as a result of the sucking. Among ailments cured in this way were wounds and hemorrhage, appendicitis, a fish bone in the throat, blood-poisoning, toothache, and extreme grief."

Tlequiltc
Salish, *Northwest Coast*
Shaman.

Tlogwe
Kwakiutl, *Northwest Coast*
The gifts bestowed by the spirits on individuals; general term for the specific forms in which power manifests; translates to "coming down the beach," a reference to the *tlogwe* indicating that they come down from the primordial world. A *tlogwe* is the specific form taken by *nawalak* (see entry) supernatural power. One informant translated *tlogwe* as "treasures." In some cases, the *tlogwe* is an object such as a pole, house post, or mask; in other cases, it is a certain ritual privilege. Most often the *tlogwe* is inherited through family lineage [Goldman 1975:26–27].

Tlu qali
Makah, *Northwest Coast*
See *klukwalle*.

Crow shamans performing a tobacco planting ceremony in a dance tepee on 4 July 1895.

Toalache
Yokuts, *California*
The Jimson weed ceremony among the southern Yokuts, used to initiate young men into the tribe. They make a tea from the roots of the Jimson weed *(Datura meteloide)*, and while under the influence of the plant, they pass on their oral history to initiates.

Tobacco Offerings/Ties
See *canli wapahta*.

Tobacco Planters
Crow, *Plains*
Shamans. Among the Crow, those persons who follow the ancestral ritual of planting tobacco are "endowed with supernatural powers, to bring rain, avert pestilence, control the wind, conquer disease, make the buffalo come near their camp, and increase the number of all kinds of game; that they can in fact bring about any event not dependent upon ordinary human possibility" [Denig 1933:59].

Tomanawis
Chinook jargon, *Oregon Seaboard/Northwest Coast*
In Chinook jargon—a trade language spoken by many different nations on the West Coast—the mysterious power that pervades the universe. It is analogous to the more widely used *orenda* (see entry) [Reagan 1937:7].

Toneakoy
Kiowa, *Plains*
A shaman during the late nineteenth century. His special medicine came from the turtle—Toneakoy

means "Snap Turtle." He also obtained other medicines during his vision quest, when he was taken into an underwater lodge filled with underwater creatures. An informant provides this description:

"So Docti [Toneakoy's nickname] went around the circle (in the underwater lodge) and asked each one (of the spirits present) for a piece of his medicine. In this way he not only got bewitch medicine but medicine to make bewitch fail—unbewitch medicine. He also got medicine to cure sickness and still other medicine to give success with women. Any kind of medicine—he has it.

"When Docti went to cure a sick man he would sit on the foot of the sick man's bed and sing and shake his rattle. The sick man liked to hear that; it made him feel good. Then Docti would give him something to swallow—I don't know what. In his medicine pouch he had different things, one medicine for stomach hurt, other medicine for other trouble. He also slapped the sick person gently with a fan made of five or six eagle feathers. Sometimes he sucked the sore place, or scratched it with a flint knife. Then he sucked out the blood, and with it the sickness, which he spat out on the ground. At other times he only sang and danced a little. Or he blew on the sickness, and the man got well and paid him for it" [Iseeo in Nye 1962: 258].

According to another informant:

"Once a small child named Clyde Koko fell sick with a high fever. Tone-a-koy lifted the boy in his arms and walked into the deep blue pool now called Heyl's Hole, above Medicine Bluffs. He kept the child under water for an hour. When he finally came up, with Clyde sleeping peacefully in his arms, the fever was gone" [Hunting Horse in Nye 1962:259].

Tonneraouanount
Iroquois, *Northeast*
A shaman who was recorded by Father LeJeune in 1637. LeJeune witnessed a sweat lodge ceremony in which Tonneraouanount diagnosed an illness by addressing the devil. He noted that the shaman

used tobacco as an offering by throwing it over the hot stones.

Tornaq
Eskimo, *Arctic Coast*
See *torngak*.

Tornarssuit
Eskimo, *Arctic Coast*
See *tornguang*.

Torngak
Labrador Eskimo, *Arctic Coast*
Shaman's helping spirit; translates to "spirit." Labrador area shamans are unusual in that they usually acquire only a single spirit helper, unlike other Eskimo shamans, who often have 50 or more helping spirits [Hawkes 1916:181].

The *torngak* is one of two types of spirits used by shamans; the other is the *inua* (see entry). The *torngak* is a metaphysical being. It differs from the *inua* in that it does not dwell in any physical body. In some cases, these spirits are conceived as the earthbound ghosts of animals or humans. In others cases, they are wholly mythic beings or indeterminate shapes, some of which take fiery forms. All forms are susceptible to coming under the control of a shaman and performing as the shaman's helper. They can even be bound to physical objects and, as such, become amulets that even laypeople can employ [Merkur 1985:226–227].

The Iglulik, West Greenland Eskimo [Birket-Smith 1924:453], and other Inuit form is *tornaq*; plural form, *tornat*.

Torngevok
Labrador Eskimo, *Arctic Coast*
Shaman; translates to "one who has a spirit helper." See *angakoq* for details.

Tornguang
Polar Eskimo, *Arctic Coast*
Shaman's guardian spirit, from which the shaman directly or indirectly receives his powers [Rasmussen 1908:134]. In addition, according to Weyer [1932:427], the "ministering spirits of the

angakok (shaman) among the Polar Eskimos are called *tornarssuit* and spoken of as invisible beings attached to localities or objects and exercising powers for evil."

Tornrak
Copper Eskimo, *Arctic Coast*

Plural: *tornrait*. Dialectical equivalents: *tornait, torngrat, tartat, tungat, tornarsuk*. Shaman's helping spirit. These spirits are differentiated from those that are the shades of men and animals, the latter being termed *tarrait* (singular: *tarrak*) [Jenness 1922:186]. *Tornrait* "never had a normal life like human beings, though they are semi-human in their form. . . . At times some little peculiarity in their appearance distinguishes them from human beings, for example, extraordinarily long hair; but they can change their forms and appear or disappear at will" [Jenness 1922:186].

A shaman who owns a tornrak may sell it to another individual, male or female. However, "all that the owner can impart is his good-will, and a knowledge of how to approach and summon the particular spirit that he has sold; the rest depends on the spirit itself. The aspirant must go out to some lonely place and summon the spirit, which may or may not appear. Sometimes, however, a spirit will come to a man without being invoked, and tell him that henceforth it will accompany him everywhere and place its powers at his disposal" [Jenness 1922:191]. For example, this happened to an old man named Ilatsiak who was out alone fishing for tomcod. A spirit appeared as a young man and "caught a tom-cod and made him (Ilatsiak) eat it, and the eating of this fish gave him magical power. The spirit accompanied him back to his camp, conversing with him, and giving him various injunctions; thus he was forbidden to eat the intestines of any animal, only the meat and the fat. The spirit disappeared as soon as they reached the camp" [Jenness 1922:191–192].

Shamans usually have more than one helping spirit, and, as a rule, they are nameless. For example, Uloksak, one of the most renowned shamans at the turn of the twentieth century, had for his spirits a white man, a polar bear, a wolf, and a dog. Their attachment to the shaman is voluntary; they abandon him at will, especially if he breaks one of

their taboos. Also, "a shaman will often change his form, and take on that of the animal by which he is possessed, or will assume at least some of its characteristic" [Jenness 1922:193]. For instance, a shaman named Makettak "would bend down to the floor of the dance-house, resting his hands on the ground. Slowly his hands would change into polar bear's feet, then his arms become legs, and finally his whole body and head would assume the shape of the bear" [Jenness 1922:193]. Although such transformations are not the rule, all shamans become possessed by their helping spirits, and they have no recall of their shamanic rituals.

In Greenland, the *tornait* are spirits of all kinds that become shamans' helpers. In Alaska, the term "applies to Beings that are not souls of visible things but have strange forms of their own. Often the word is used particularly for the Beings that are evil and harmful if not treated just right, for example, Half-people (as if split lengthwise) and thirsty little dried-up Wandereres and mountain Giants. They are races or groups which some Eskimos think are controlled by chief spirits. In Alaska and the Central Region, they may or may not be shamans' supernatural helpers, and they are not the only familiar spirits of shamans, who may have animal spirit-helpers as well" [Lantis 1950:322].

In the region of Coronation Gulf, the shaman's helping spirit is referred to as either *tornrak* or *tupilek*, usually the former; the latter may be a borrowed word [Stefansson 1914:368].

Totam
Ojibwa, *Canadian Eastern Woodlands*

Term used during the late eighteenth century by J. Long, a merchant who lived among the Ojibwa, for a person's helping spirit. He wrote: "One part of the religious superstition of the Savages, consists in each of them having his *totam*, or favourite spirit, which he believes watches over him. This *totam* they conceive assumes the shape of some beast or other, and therefore they never kill, hunt, or eat the animal whose form they think this *totam* bears" [Long in Hultkrantz 1967a:66]. It is from Long's account that the word "totemism" is derived. However, Hultkrantz [1967a:67] points out that "the word *totam*, usually rendered *ototeman* in the Ojibwa language, probably refers to a kinship group or lineage."

Toyide
Tiwa, *Southwest*

Isleta Pueblo word for medicine man. The shamans in this culture belong to one of several medicine societies. They work both as individuals and in group healing ceremonies. The following account is a typical cure performed by an individual. It involves a man named Juan who became ill because he had burned an anthill. He called for the Ant Father shaman to perform a cure on him. The shaman came to Juan's house and performed his healing ceremony on him for four consecutive nights. Juan was required to remove his clothes and put on a breechclout. Then:

"The (Ant) Father went and spat of the root (*li-fiewah*) in each corner of the house and then on Juan. He asked for some ashes from the fireplace. (He would not take them from the stove, so we had to build a fire in the fireplace to get the ashes.) He rubbed the ashes on Juan's body. Then he made a circle of ashes on the sheepskin, singing all the time. With his feathers he brushed the ground

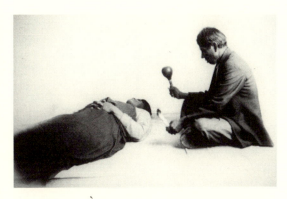

Joée Panco, a Papago shaman, holds a deer tail in his left hand while inducing a trancelike state through chanting and by the rhythmic movement of his rattle. The altered state of consciousness allows Panco to activate his healing power for the patient.

outside of the ash circle, and tapped one feather against the other, the feathers at right angles to each other. Three times he did this. This rite of brushing he repeated on each side of Juan, the third time turning away from him to tap the feathers. Grasping the feathers by the tips and butts he breathed from them, turned toward the east and forcibly breathed out. Now he wiped Juan down with cotton, and as he brushed him with the feathers, the ants fell from Juan's body into the circle of ashes on the sheepskin Juan was standing on. The Father told Juan to step off, cover himself with a blanket and sit down. Then the Father sprinkled ashes on the ants, then pollen, then meal, then bread crumbs, feeding them.

"Now the Father went up to Juan, held him by the head and sucked something from it. As he did this he fell down, as if faint. Juan was frightened, he bent and rubbed the Father and stood him up. The Father tottered. Then he spat out of his mouth all the pebbles and sand he had sucked from Juan's head. The room was full of dust. Three times the Father spewed these out from his mouth. He brushed up the pebbles, sweeping them on to the sheepskin where the ants remained, unable to leave the circle of ashes. The Father asked for some tobacco which he carried out together with the sheepskin of ants and pebbles, beyond the village. On his return he told Juan to dress. Five times he waved his feathers in front of Juan and then up and down, giving him breath. (It is down and up when you take breath out.)

"Four nights this ceremony was performed. Juan got well, but as his eyes had been eaten by the ants, he can not see clearly" [Parsons 1932: 444].

Trance

In psychological terms, a trance is a shift in one's psychic state that results in an altered state of consciousness. Contemporary psychologists have identified at least 20 different altered states of consciousness, some of which have been observed to be utilized by Native American healers. Not all Native American healers use an altered state of consciousness in their curing, but shamans who use their abilities to heal do, by definition, enter into an altered state of consciousness. Shamans were recognized by Eliade [1964] as entering into an ecstatic state of consciousness, in contrast to an enstasis or samadi, a state which is achieved through such techniques as yogic meditation. In many cases, the shaman becomes possessed by his helping spirit during trance. In other cases, the shaman enters into a visionary type trance to communicate with his helping spirits.

Bourguignon [1979:257–265] assigns the spirit-possession trance to agricultural societies; it is typically performed by women before public audiences, and the period of trance is usually forgotten by the possessed person. Possession trances can be either voluntary or involuntary. The possession trance of shamans is of the voluntary type, in which the trance is started and ended at will, whereas the possession trance of the patient, when it occurs, is of the involuntary type [Peters and Price-Williams 1983:16].

The visionary trance is usually associated with males in hunting and gathering societies, and the trance is most often remembered by the shaman. In some cases, this trance is induced through the use of psychoactive plants, such as the use of datura (Jimson weed) among the shamans of the Southwest.

In all cases, shamans have initiatory experiences into the art of shamanism that are psychotherapeutic and lead to self-control of altered states of consciousness [Peters 1982; Meyerhoff 1976]. The only differences found among Native American healers are cultural differences regarding the methods of induction of the respective trance states, the cultural influence on content and value, and the community goal of the practice.

Trance induction

The methods by which a shaman achieves a trance state. The most common method of trance induction is the use of a drum or other percussion instrument. For example, among the cultures of the Northwest coast, a wooden plank is often beat on to produce a rhythmic sound that aids in trance induction. In many cultures, a hand rattle is used for the same purpose. All such techniques involve the rhythmic stimulation (see *rhythmic sensory stimulation*) of the central nervous system, which is known to aid one's ability to enter a trance state of consciousness.

Trehero, John
Shoshoni, *Basin*

A shaman who used primarily his hands to doctor patients. However, he was also a sucking doctor and would spit into a vessel what he had sucked from the patient's body. The disease (object) was then placed into a fire. He received his initial power as a shaman through a dream at a known power spot that contained many ancient rock drawings. He dreamed of a snake and a bear, which gave him the power to cure snakebites and to kill people with bear medicine.

Here is a rare account of an ethnographer being treated by a traditional healer—in this case, John Trehero. The patient is Åke Hultkrantz, a world-renowned Swedish scholar, often cited as the father of Native American comparative religious studies. This incident probably took place around 1948, during one of Hultkrantz's several visits to the Wind River Reservation of the Eastern Shoshoni during the 1940s and 1950s. He writes:

"Twice I was myself exposed to this kind of curing. In both cases John Trehero was my medicine man. On one occasion I complained about pains in my cheek—I had an infection in the left oral cavity. John lifted his hand, pointed it at my cheek, and regarded it with a resolute determination. Then he quickly lowered his hand and touched my cheek. He held it there some seconds, and then, swift as lightning, he drew it back again. It was my impression that he had mobilized a great amount of psychic energy.

"On the other occasion Trehero cured rheumatism in my left shoulder. First he used some peacock feathers that I had given him, laying them against my shoulder. Then he removed them, put his right hand on my shoulder, and ordered me to put mine on top of his. Thereafter he removed his hand and put it on top of mine. Suddenly he quickly withdrew it and asked me if I had felt the power enter me. He wanted me to feel his power, so he extended the palm of his hand and asked me to put my finger in its center. I did so and felt the quick pulse. That, declared John Trehero, was the power. Later he told me that while curing me he had seen the beaver. It was with the beaver's power that he had healed me. The effects of the cure? Well, for some four years I was without rheumatic pains" [Hultkrantz 1992:91].

Tripne
Yokuts, *California*
An advanced class of male healers who practice some form of shamanism. The term *tripne* also means "supernatural." Most often, their shamanism takes the form of a sucking ceremony in which the shaman uses a hollow tube—usually made of stone, but sometimes made of an elder limb— about 6 inches long with a 3/4-inch hole through the center. This tube is placed over the affected area, and the shaman sucks out an object—a lizard tail still twitching, a stone projectile point, and so forth—said to be causing the ailment. The shaman spits the object from his mouth and shows it to all present. Other treatments are also used, such as bloodletting and sacred songs. Also reported is pounding and hammering the patient during the treatment. For the most part, these shamans are feared and are called on only as a last resort [Latta 1949].

Trudum
Yokuts, *California*
Snake doctors, or the shamans who conduct the Yokuts Rattlesnake Dance each spring. The ceremony is designed to prevent snakebites during the coming summer.

Tsatsawâ'a
Gros Ventres, *Plains*
One of two classes of spirit beings. These spirit helpers are ghosts of deceased persons. One usually acquires such a spirit by keeping in one's possession something from the deceased person rather than by performing any ritual action. Other terms are used for ghosts in general, whereas this one refers only to helper ghosts. These spirits most often make their presence known through sounds such as whistling, knocking, and so forth. Cooper [1944:66] relates the following amusing story of what happened to a young man who decided to test a *tsatsawâ'a:*

"When the ghost helper came and the noise was heard, the young man, who was sitting near the door in the darkness where no one else could see he was exposed, pushed his breechclout aside and exposed his genitals, saying to himself: 'If this is really a ghost, he will see me and do something about it.' All of a sudden the young man let out a yell as if hit by someone, and ran out of the lodge. 'You had better run. What is being done here is the real thing,' said the ghost to the young fellow, and added to the crowd: 'I hit that young fellow's genitals sharply with a stick, that is why he dashed out of the lodge.' They then asked the young man: 'Is that what happened?' And he replied: 'Yes. He hit me good and hard there,' and he became a believer."

Tsekteya
Yurok, *Oregon Seaboard*
Also: *tsekwel.* Stone seats or stone chairs used by shamans during their vision quests for spirit helpers. They consist of semicircular walls of stones piled 3 or 4 feet high and built at known power spots high in the mountains [Keeling 1992:295].

Tse'makwin
Zuni, *Southwest*
Soul. It comes from the root verb *tse'ma,* meaning to "think" or "ponder." According to Bunzel [1932:481], the Zuni see the soul as aspects of the head, heart, and breath. The head is the source of one's skill and intelligence, and the heart is the source of emotions and profound thoughts. More important, however, is the breath, which is the symbol of life. It is through breath that one communicates with the spirits and receives power therefrom. It is breath that empowers the sacred essence of prayer; for that reason, at the end of every prayer, the Zuni inhale strongly rather than say "amen."

Tshi'saqka
Menomini, *Midwest*
A class of shamans recognized by Hoffman [1896] as the juggler class. This class performs the Shaking Tent Ceremony (see entry) in a structure (called the *tshi'saqkan*) similar to that of the Ojibwa.

Tsiahk
Nootka, *Northwest Coast*
Among the Makah branch, the ritual of the *Tsayeq* Society, a secret medicine society. The Makah believe in a supernatural being that often appears to sick persons, promising relief of their illness if the ceremonies he prescribes are well performed by this society. Before the actual healing begins, the patient is initiated into the secret mysteries of the society in a three-day initiation ceremony. This is followed by a public healing ceremony conducted both in the ceremonial house and outdoors. One informant provides this description:

"The outdoor performance consists of a procession which moves from the lodge to the beach; the principal actor or conductor being at the head, followed by all the males in single file, the last one being the doctor (distinguished by red stripes of paint covering his body). Immediately behind the doctor the patient follows, supported on each side by a female assistant. The females close up the procession. All parties, male and female, have their hands raised as high as their faces, and the motion of the procession is a sort of shuffling dance. They move in a circle which gradually closes around the patient, who, with the novitiate, is left seated on the ground in the centre; songs with choruses by the whole of the spectators, drumming, shaking rattles, and the firing of guns wind up the performance, and all retire to the lodge, where dancing and singing are kept up for several days" [Swan in Boas 1897:643–644].

Tsiditindi
Apache, *Southwest*
Bullroarer (see entry), a device used by shamans for rainmaking. The Apache make them from the wood of a fir or pine tree that has been struck by lightning [Bourke 1892:478].

Tsikili
Cherokee, *Southeast*
Translates to "hooting owl," but because owls are considered ill omens, the term also means witches. Witches are the most dreaded cause of human disease. They are described as follows:

"A witch is held to be a human being, male or female, who is a 'powerful wizard' such as a medicine man may become who has 'got the utmost,' but the semantic, and especially the emotional value given to the word, always conveys concepts expressing baseness, meanness, slyness, an activity of an insidious, nefarious, deleterious nature. . . .

"Moreover, whatever the witch can steal of the life, and therefore of the vital principle, of the animus, the power, the 'orenda' of his victim, he adds to his own, and this is the reason why witches are always hovering about the sick, the feeble, the moribund people; invisible as they can make themselves, they put their mouths over those of the victims, and steal their breath; according to some informants 'because they like the taste of sick people's breath; it is so sweet'(!); according to others, because stealing their breath comes to the same as securing for themselves the victim's vitality, which they add to their own. At the time the moribund expires, especially, the witch is careful not to miss the chance" [Mooney and Olbrechts 1932:29–30].

Advanced witches are capable of transforming into other shapes and traveling through the air at night to their victims. One method of protecting a sick person from witches is to place pinches of crushed tobacco on a small pile of ashes taken from the fire hearth. As the tobacco catches fire, the direction of the ashes indicates the location of a witch. "If the dust alights on the center of the ashes it is a sign that the witch is right overhead, and should the tobacco, as it drops on the center, take fire with a crack or a burst, it shows that the witch has already entered the room. In this case the burst will cause the death of the witch within four days, if she is one of the kind that has fasted for four days to attain her occult power; within seven days if she is one of the kind that 'has got the utmost'" [Mooney and Olbrechts 1932:31].

A more drastic method is to shoot the witch. A certain medicine plant has to be mixed with the gunpowder, and a hair taken from the crown of the head has to be wound around the bullet. In order to be able to see the witch in the first place, one also has to fast for seven days and drink an infusion of the root by which witches commonly obtain their powers.

Tsiniiakoianorenhseraten
Iroquois, *Northeast*
A contemporary synonym used by the Iroquois at Kahnawake for *kahsatsenhsera* (see entry), which means the power inherent in nature.

Tso lagayv li
Cherokee, *Southeast*
Tobacco *(Nicotiana rustica)*; translates to "tobacco, ancient." Unlike most Native Americans, the Cherokee believe that tobacco per se has no inherent power. Thus, before it can be used in a healing ceremony, it has to be "remade," a ritual for imbuing it with power. "The principal factor in 'remaking' tobacco is the saying (or thinking) or singing of a text over it; for this transfers the creative thought to the inert herb. The potential power of the tobacco, already magical now that it has been endowed with the generative force of the human mind, can be enhanced by strengthening measures that are not absolutely necessary for the accomplishment of the purpose for which the tobacco was 'remade,' but which do serve to achieve the desired end more quickly" [Kilpatrick 1967b: 9]. These texts are usually repeated four times in succession, or they may be repeated on four occasions during the day or said once on four consecutive days. The shaman usually holds the tobacco in his left hand and faces east while reciting them. The best time to remake tobacco is at dawn. Once empowered, the sacred tobacco must be kept from

the presence of pregnant and menstruating women and from corpses or anyone who has been in recent contact with a corpse.

Tsondacoüanné
Huron, *Northeast*
A shaman who became prominent during the 1630s. According to Fenton [1941:414], his name still persists in the everyday language: "my informants identify it with their term for the individual who sponsors a medicine feast."

Tsotibenén
Yuchi, *Southeast*
The Medicine Drinking Ceremony [Speck 1909: 136], which is performed when sickness, or trouble in general, threatens the community. Everyone is required to attend the ceremony, which begins at sunset. The Warrior Society ensures that none of the ritual rules are broken. For instance, no one is allowed to sleep during the ceremony. The ritual consists of everyone drinking an emetic until they vomit. The "medicine" is ingested several times over the course of the night, and during the intervals of fresh preparation, the remainder of the community dances together. The ceremony concludes at sunrise.

Tsukamxowi
Pomo, *California*
Sucking doctors among the Southeastern Pomo. They acquire their healing powers through a vision of a helping spirit [Loeb 1934a:126].

Tu udum
Yokuts, *California*
Snake shaman [Edmonson 1958:70].

Tudáb
Puyallup-Nisqually, *Northwest Coast*
Among this branch of the Coast Salish, a shaman or the class of power held by shamans. When a shaman has good *tudáb*, he uses it to cure sickness; when he has mean *tudáb*, he uses it for sorcery or to steal power from other shamans. Shamans are

highly competitive within this culture. Their other class of power is *sqalálitut* (see entry).

Both warriors and shamans obtain *tudáb*. For instance, a warrior has the "ability to cure his own wounds, a curing power not in the possession of shamans" [Smith 1940:62]. One warrior was known to have fog power. He could call forth fog within 10 minutes to hide himself from his enemies. Another warrior had seal power that enabled him to "walk or run along the bottom of the river just as he could on land" [Smith 1940:65].

Shamans who heal conduct their healing ceremonies either upon invitation from the patient's relatives or because their power informs them that someone is sick and needs to be cured. If the shaman does not follow his power and inform the patient of his need for a healing ceremony, the shaman risks becoming ill himself:

"This happened generally to younger men, who had not yet established reputations and who might not have been previously aware that they had a shaman power. Because of the compulsion engendered by the possibility of his own illness the shaman dared not turn his back upon the opportunity of curing. The treatment in such cases was of the very simplest, involving a motion or two with the hands as in other shaman curing or a single, unaccompanied song. There need be no people present beyond the patient and the shaman. The ills cured were apt to be minor. Cures of this type formed a sort of trial period during which the shaman tested his power and the society formed its tentative judgment as to his prowess" [Smith 1940:75–76].

Exceptional men establish healing reputations during their thirties, and few begin healing after the age of 50. Thus, a shaman's prime is usually between 40 and 60 years of age. After that, a shaman's power becomes sluggish, and his reputation as a healer declines. Those who begin to heal after the age of 50 usually have established reputations for other shamanistic powers and do not go through the normal trial period of a beginning healer. During a new shaman's trial period, no payments are made for healing ceremonies. Once his reputation is established, however, payment is made in the form of gifts, usually before he cures but after he diagnoses the patient. Shamans never become rich men; that is reserved for the nobility.

Healing ceremonies are most often conducted indoors at night. Others can attend the ceremony besides the patient, usually the patient's relatives. The shaman begins by calling on his power through his medicine songs to aid him in diagnosing the patient. Often the shaman conducting the diagnosis is not the one who cures, depending on the outcome of the diagnosis. That is, a shaman might diagnose an illness for which he has no power to cure. In difficult cases, a shaman might call upon another shaman to assist him in the cure. Most often, the illness is diagnosed as being caused by another shaman (sorcerer). In such cases, the attending shaman captures the power sent into the patient in his own hands and then asks the audience what is to be done with it:

"If the power was to be sent back (to the culprit), the shaman held his hands, in which the power was imprisoned, before his mouth, opened a small crack at the thumbs, blew noisily into the crack and at the same time opened the outer edge of his hands 'like a door.' With the breath his hands were flung apart, outward and upward in the direction which the power was to take. If the power was to be killed, the shaman clenched his hands and placed one fist above the other. During this shift great caution was taken not to allow the power to escape. The fingers of the right hand closed upon it where it lay in the hollow between the palms and this hand, closed, was slowly slid upward until it lay above the other. As it moved it was kept tight against the left hand, the fingers of which closed together as soon as was possible. The power was not held in both fists. To cripple it, the shaman twisted his hands one above the other 'like wringing,' and then threw it from him with a sudden gesture, in which the hands opened and separated, starting from chest height and moving upward. To kill it, the shaman held it tightly while another man passed a knife between the two fists, cutting it in two. In this case the shaman threw the power from him by flinging his arms to the side and opening his hands so that the severed portions flew in opposite directions. . . . In cases of indecision the shaman wrapped the power in cedar bark and laid it to one side, guarded by his own power, until the question was settled. It had to be settled before the end of the curing session, *i.e.* morning.... During the diagnosis and capture the shaman himself, although he could see the power, was ignorant as to its identity. As soon as he removed it and had it in his hands, however, he could recognize the power and automatically, the individual with whom it was connected. His answer, then, came in the form of the name of the man to whom the penalty would accrue if the decision were to kill the power" [Smith 1940:80–81].

If the shaman is not successful in removing the foreign power lodged in the patient, the patient is doomed to die. In such rare cases, the attending shaman would often "bind the patient with cattail fiber twine and hold the power within the patient so that it could not escape victorious. When the power was disposed of with the dead patient the contact between the dead and the guilty was so strong that death followed soon after. This was a means of identification of the power as well, the likely person who died first being obviously killed by the process" [Smith 1940:82].

Other diagnoses call for other forms of treatment. Persons showing signs of torpor or weakness are usually diagnosed as suffering from soul loss. In such cases, the shaman "sent his power along the paths which had been traveled by the patient during the last few days until the lost soul was encountered. His power brought the soul back and he replaced it in the patient, who was immediately cured" [Smith 1940:87]. Some illnesses, such as consumption and tuberculosis, are often treated by sucking. In this case, the substance removed is either blood or a "'whitish slime' and the diseases were those in which either of these was thought to have been involved, mainly blood clots and infections. It was always that portion of the body which was diagnosed as the seat of the trouble to which the sucking was applied" [Smith 1940:87]. When sucking is applied to aid in the capture of an intrusive power, no substance of any kind is produced. During a sucking treatment, the shaman might suck on the patient 5 to 10 times. In difficult cases, the treatment might occur over several nights. When sucking on the patient, the shaman "generally bit into the patient leaving his or her tooth marks plainly visible on the skin.... Between each sucking the mouth was carefully rinsed with clear water"

[Smith 1940:88]. In contrast to other healing ceremonies, sucking cures usually last only about one hour. Such healings are usually conducted by a single shaman without the help of assisting singers.

Smith [1940:88–89] relates one unusual healing ceremony:

"The only instance of the removal of any solid object from the body during a shaman cure occurred in what was considered a phenomenon by itself. This was *tsalé*, 'wilting as a plant wilts,' called in English 'shooting bone.'

"A man (sorcerer) with a power enabling him to perform the act cupped his hands in the position used to hold a gun and his power enabled him to drive into a living object a force which there assumed the form of a sharp bone. The sender used no magical techniques. It was a plain power performance. The victim did not sicken but suffered either a sudden or gradual cessation of motor ability. The shaman who restored well-being did not suck but performed the usual singing cure. He produced from the body of the victim a sharpened deer bone or ironwood needle. The sender could not, as in usual power killing, be killed himself by the curing shaman through any treatment applied to what was withdrawn from the victim. If the bone were left in, the victim would eventually die."

Tûkte
North Alaska Eskimo, *Arctic Coast*
The term used by shamans in the vicinity of Point Hope, Alaska, to refer to themselves in conversation [Murdoch 1892:431].

Tumanos
Makah, *Northwest Coast*
Shaman's spirit helper [Densmore 1939:31], the most powerful of which is the thunderbird. Densmore, who claimed that this term has no English equivalent, also assigns to it the meaning "medicine" or "medicine power."

Tumudaini
Northern Paiute, *Basin*
Shaman's helping spirit. These spirits usually come in animal form, and a shaman generally has

Sacred stone owned by Brave Buffalo. Shamans wear such a *tunkan,* which contains healing power, in a pouch around the neck. Sometimes a shaman's spirit places the *tunkan* inside the body.

several spirit helpers. Spirits are obtained most frequently through special power dreams called *nossii* (see entry).

Tungat
North Alaska Eskimo, *Arctic Coast*
Also: *tuaña* [Murdoch 1892:431]. Plural: *tungai.* Among the Tikerarmiut of the village of Tikera (also written Tigara) at Point Hope and by other Eskimo in the Bering Strait area, spirits that are in the service of shamans. The word *gilya* is used also to refer to such spirits. The first missionaries translated *tungat* as "devil," causing its meaning to remain blurred over the years. Nevertheless, *tungai* are spirit beings who might be the spirits or souls of dead men or animals or simply beings of the air or the ground who have no connection with actual men and animals.

Not all spirits are helping spirits. The spirit of a dead person is called *inyusuq,* and the spirit of the shaman that leaves his body to travel is called *ilitkosaq.*

Once a shaman acquires a *tungat,* he carves a wooden mask to represent the spirit. The masks are usually normal or slightly distorted human faces, given the understanding that animals may appear at times in a human face. Thus, human-faced masks are said to represent the caribou people, the whale people, and so forth [Rainey 1947: 274–275].

Tunghak
Alaska Eskimo, *Arctic Coast*
Shaman; translates to "one who is furnished with a helping spirit." Equivalent words for shaman found in other Inuit dialects in the Bering Sea area

are *tunghalik* and *tunralik*. On the north Alaskan coast, it is *tunerak*, and some Copper bands use the dialectical variant *tonngag* [Merkur 1985:411].

Tunghalik
West Alaska Eskimo, *Arctic Coast*
Among the Unalit and along the adjacent Bering Sea coast, shaman. It translates to "possessor of *tun-ghät*," meaning the wandering souls of men and animals. These shamans wear masks representing their helping spirits during healing ceremonies [Nelson 1899:427].

Tuníku'hu
Paviotso, *Basin*
A doctoring ceremony; translates to "singing." This was the orthodox form of doctoring. The ceremony was held at night. See *puhágam* for details [Park 1938:48].

Tunkan
Lakota, *Plains*
Also: *toonkan*. Small round power stones used by shamans. The word is probably a contraction of the Lakota *Tunkashila*, meaning "grandfather," a term often used when addressing the Creator. In the Lakota language, any stone is called *inyan*, so these stones are also referred to as *inyan wakan*, or "holy stone." *Tunkans* are acquired through ceremony from the spirits and contain great powers for healing and protection. Some shamans have these stones placed into their bodies by the spirits, and others carry them in small pouches worn around their necks. Crazy Horse is said to have worn such a stone that protected him and his horse from enemy bullets. In some cases, the stone may be relatively large. For example, Godfrey Chipps, a *yuwipi* (see entry) shaman, uses a stone on his altar that is about 1 1/2 inches in diameter. These stones are considered to be alive and therefore must be fed and cared for in a sacred manner. A *tunkan* may also be formed by lightning and later found and used. For example, Brave Buffalo reported:

"It is significant that these stones are not found buried in the earth, but are on the top of high buttes. They are round, like the sun and moon, and we know that all things which are round are related to each other. Things which are alike in their nature grow to look like each other, and these stones have lain there a long time, looking at the sun. Many pebbles and stones have been shaped in the current of a stream, but these stones were found far from the water and have been exposed only to the sun and the wind. The earth contains many thousand such stones hidden beneath its surface. The thunderbird is said to be related to these stones and when a man or an animal is to be punished, the thunderbird strikes the person, and if it were possible to follow the course of the lightning, one of these stones would be found embedded in the earth. Some believe that these stones descend with the lightning, but I believe they are on the ground and are projected downward by the bolt. In all my life I have been faithful to the sacred stones. I have lived according to their requirements, and they have helped me in all my troubles. I have tried to qualify myself as well as possible to handle these sacred stones, yet I know that I am not worthy to speak to Wankan tanka. I make my request of the stones and they are my intercessors" [Brave Buffalo in Densmore 1918:208].

During a healing ceremony, the shaman rolls a *tunkan* around on the patient's body to locate the sickness. Often the patient is allowed to hold the *tunkan* in his mouth, as this produces an internal effect. In addition, during a healing ceremony, "the stones, flying through the air in the darkened tent, sometimes strike those who have refused to believe in them" [Densmore 1918:205].

Lynd, calling it a "stone god," reports [in Dorsey 1894:447] that the *tunkan* is painted red, but this is more than likely an individual preference. He also reports that they are "about the size of a human head." Riggs reports [in Dorsey 1894:447] that the *tunkan* "is the symbol of the greatest force or power in the dry land. And these came to be the most common objects of worship." Riggs describes them as large boulders painted red and green.

Tunraq
Netsilik Eskimo, *Arctic Coast*
Shaman's helping spirit. This is considered to be the most powerful class of helping spirits among these Labrador Eskimos. It is reported that

advanced shamans can get their *tunraqs* to kill seals in the open sea and then bring them ashore. They are also used to locate game [Balikci 1963:386].

Tupiliq
Netsilik Eskimo, *Arctic Coast*
Equivalent: *tupilek*. A type of evil spirit that causes human sickness. It is said to be round in shape and filled with blood under considerable pressure. In a typical healing ceremony, the shaman wages a fight with the *tupiliqs* and kills as many as he can with his knife. If the patient dies, it is said that the *tupiliqs* were too numerous.

Turtle
Cheyenne, *Plains*
A shaman who recorded some of his healing songs for anthropologist Frances Densmore. He learned his medicine songs from a shaman named Dragging Otter, who had, in turn, received them from an older shaman. Turtle had only one medicine song that he acquired directly from the spirits himself, from a buffalo spirit. He used this song when the spirit of a sick person was in danger of departing. He told Densmore that when he sang this song, a young buffalo stood in the way and tried to keep the spirit from going away. After singing his song for a sick person, he always made a violent blowing sound in imitation of a buffalo.

Tutelary
Term used infrequently in the anthropological literature to refer to a shaman's helping spirit or guardian spirit.

Tuuhikya
Hopi, *Southwest*
A "true healer," with a special ability for healing beyond that of ordinary healers. For the most part, they are elders, corresponding to the Hopi notion that "a man cannot begin to work as a *tuuhikya* until he has gray in his hair" [Grant 1982:299]. These shamans are required to respond to requests for healing without payment.

Personal illnesses are first submitted to ritual diagnosis. This is usually done in two sessions—one for the diagnostic ritual, and one to obtain the results. Normally, the shaman examines the patient by looking into a crystal, where he sees what

the problem is. Illness is generally attributed to some form of emotional imbalance, but a final diagnosis might not be made until a number of therapeutic approaches have been tried.

In observing their healing rituals, Grant [1982: 302] notes that a shaman's treatment might differ according to the ethnic background of the patient. For example, with white patients, the healer never prays loud enough to be heard and tells them to take herbs at mealtimes or to "do this two or three times a day." With Hopi patients, the shaman prays openly and clearly and gives instructions in multiples of four, using the position of the sun as a time designator. With Navajo patients, his prayers are audible but muttered, so as not to be understandable. He uses more ritual with Navajo patients than with white or Hopi patients.

The overall procedure usually involves the following steps: history taking, physical examination via crystal, prayers, discussion of the diagnosis, stories about former clients who had the same problem, and prescription of treatment regimens. The treatment for natural diseases is usually herbal teas prepared in a ritual manner. Unnatural diseases—those ailments arising from unnatural causes—require more powerful treatments. Such treatments involve "bathing" in cedar smoke, the use of special prayer feathers, and the taking of herbs that have a religious as well as a medicinal use. At the conclusion of treatment, patients are usually given advice on how to alter their lifestyles to prevent future recurrences.

Tzidaltai
Apache, *Southwest*
Wooden amulets worn about the neck that resemble small bullroarers 3 to 4 inches long. These amulets are prayed to for supernatural help. For example, they are used to locate lost or stolen horses and to determine the right direction of travel when lost. In a *tzidaltai*, the figure is drawn in yellow except for the three snake heads, *a*, *b*, and *c*, which are black with white eyes. Flat pearl buttons are attached at *m* and *k*. On each side of the amulet, small eagle-down feathers are attached. The symbolism includes the rain cloud, the serpent lightning, the rainbow, raindrops, and the cross of the four winds.

Uctaqyu
Nootka, *Northwest Coast*
The leading shaman who is the most important member of the secret society called *tsayeg* [Boas 1987:642]. See *tsikili* for a *tsayeq* ritual.

Udkukut
Yokuts, *California*
People hired by the shaman to help perform his ceremonies. They not only sing and dance but also act like clowns during the ceremony, doing everything wrong.

Ukémawas
Menomini, *Midwest*
A magical red powder that is placed inside a plume of dyed feathers and worn by an officer during the *Metewen* (Medicine Lodge; see entry) ceremonies. The wearer can then read the hearts of the members. "It enables this officer to see who in the medicine-lodge have done or contemplate wrong, so that they may be ejected" [Skinner 1920:172].

Ulanigvgv
Cherokee, *Southeast*
This term approximates the notion of shamanic power but is used in a much broader sense. For example, it can be the power derived from lightning as well as spirit beings in the form of animals, ghosts, plants, objects, and so forth. The eastern Cherokee use the term in connection with concepts such as black power or Indian power. It can also refer to power used for evil.

This power is accumulated by those individuals who, over the course of their lives, pay close attention to ritual detail, accumulate knowledge, and lead moral lives. Absent from the Cherokee is the notion, found in so many other Native American cultures, whereby an individual establishes a lifetime, personal relationship with a powerful helping spirit. "In fact, the whole idea of dramatic individual religious experience and altered states of consciousness as a route to personal power seems foreign to the controlled and pragmatic Cherokee orientation toward life" [Fogelson 1977:187].

Power is not believed to be permanent within an individual, and those who heal have to rejuvenate their powers "via autumnal baths in a flowing river whose waters contained medicinal properties imparted by falling leaves" [Folgelson 1977:187]. Sorcerers renew their power by taking the lives of others. One of the Cherokee power objects is a sacred quartz crystal, called *ulunsata*, which is used for divination. The power of this crystal has to be renewed by periodically feeding it a few drops of human or animal blood, or misfortune will befall its caretaker.

If a person has power, he never proclaims or brags of it. This stands in contrast to the often public power rituals of other Native American shamans. A Cherokee shaman consents only to *try* to help the patient and never claims that he can cure the patient.

Umaah
Yurok, *Oregon Seaboard*
Sorcerer. Sorcerers cause illness by "shooting" magical objects, called *umaah* or *umaa* ("pain"), into the body of a victim [Keeling 1992:70]. The resultant disease is called *telogel* (see entry), which translates to "pain." To cure such victims, one calls in a *kegey* (see entry), who is a sucking doctor. "When a doctor sucks out an *uma'a* pain she holds it between her hands, closes her eyes, chants 'ahokahokahok' and then begins to sing. Then the pain flies upward, spirals in the air, and suddenly flies in a beeline to where it came from, leaving a trail of fire, by which the doctor can tell from whom it was sent. Usually she does not tell, for fear that the *uma'a* will be sent back into herself" [Spott and Kroeber 1942:167–168].

Underhill, Ruth
Ruth Underhill was born in Ossining, New York, on 22 August 1883. Following a 20-year career in social work, she enrolled in Columbia University in 1930, beginning a 50-year career in anthropology. Her initial fieldwork was among the Tohono O'odam (Papago), which resulted in her classic work *Autobiography of a Papago Woman* in 1936—the first published life history of a southwestern Native American woman. Underhill spent most of her academic career at the University of Denver but traveled for 13 years, mainly during the 1930s, as a consultant for the Bureau of Indian Affairs, for which she published many works. Most of her fieldwork was conducted in the Southwest. Among her best-known works are *Singing for Power* (1938), *Papago Indian Religion* (1939), and *The Navajos* (1956). She died in Denver, Colorado, on 14 August 1984.

Unihipili
Hawaiian, *Pacific*
A helping spirit that is a former relative of a sorcerer. Sorcerers have many different evil spirits that they call upon, and in some cases, they use their deceased relatives by keeping the bones of that relative. The *unihipili* are very demanding, as helping spirits go, and have to be fed every day. If the sorcerer misses a single day of propitiation, the evil powers of this spirit turn on him.

Ûntali
Cherokee, *Southeast*
An animal ghost; the spirit of any animal. Both animal and human ghosts are sources of sickness; the latter, called *asgina*, most often cause psychopathic illnesses. Almost all sickness is attributed to either a specific animal spirit or a human spirit. "Rheumatism and dysentery, swelling in the cheek, and violent headaches may all be caused in different patients by one and the same animal ghost, e.g., a deer's. On the other hand, several different kinds of animal ghosts may all manifest their ill will and take vengeance on the human race by inflicting one and the same disease, as rheumatism which can be caused by the measuring worm, rabbit, or the buffalo" [Mooney and Olbrechts 1932:28].

Utem letimk
Yuki, *California*
Fright doctor among the Huchnom branch of Yuki. Both men and women can become such healers. They make an image of the thing, usually a harmful spirit, that has frightened their patient. Showing this image to the patient during the healing ceremony restores the patient to health.

Uwámu
Kutenai, *Plateau*
Shaman [Turney-High 1941:176]. Shamans receive their power through vision questing, which often begins by the age of seven. Both males and females can acquire powers, which are bestowed at the discretion of the spirits. When the spirit appears to the novice, it usually first comes in the

form of a human and then reveals its true form, usually that of an animal or a bird. Following instructions received in a vision quest, a shaman prepares a medicine bundle to house the items he is to use in manifesting his powers. These bundles are normally buried with the shaman at the time of death. Young shamans are considered to be charged with more power than older shamans, because power diminishes with use. However, a shaman's power can be increased by the acquisition of new spirits. When a shaman loses a patient, his powers are considered to be weak, and his reputation diminishes.

The most powerful shamans are the blanket shamans, those who go behind the blanket. They are the ones usually called upon to heal the sick. This form of shamanizing is known as *kumnakànikitnámu* [Turney-High 1941:176], and its ritual bears many similarities to the widespread Shaking Tent Ceremony (see entry). The general pattern of this ritual is as follows:

"The lodge is set up in either a tipi or a modern house. A rope is tied from one lodge pole, skipping the second, and made fast to the third, just high enough to be above the shaman's head when he retires behind the blanket. If a modern dwelling is used, a corner of a room is roped off to provide the hidden space.

"A blanket is hung so as to curtain off a space from the people's view. A string of deer hoof rattles is then hung down the middle of the blanket from a cord. . . .

"The shaman enters the lodge and strips to the breech clout. He has purified himself beforetime. . . . He proceeds to paint his face according to his (spirit) instructions. He then sits on the floor with his back to the blanket facing the people. A long, light ruffle is beaten on the drum either by the shaman or a delegated assistant. The shaman sings the song of the spirit invoked and blows long blasts on his (bone) whistle. When he thinks (knows) that a spirit has come behind the blanket, he retires there himself. It is not hard to know that the spirits have come. One can hear them walking on the roof. Furthermore, the blanket begins to shake, sometimes violently, so that the rattles are sounded.

"The shaman emerges from behind the blanket and shows that his thumbs have been tied behind his back. Sometimes the spirit completely hog-ties him, so that he must roll out. At other times, in order to test his powers, he has someone bind and tie him as firmly as possible before the people's eyes. He then rolls behind the blanket and in about two seconds comes out entirely free. The spirit almost always prefers to tie the shaman, so that he rolls out in order to have someone put his bone whistle in his mouth. He then retires behind the blanket to whistle until several spirits come in. In the meantime the people keep the song going. One can hear the shaman talking to the spirits, imitating their twittering, and can hear the spirits respond.

"The shaman comes from behind the partition to be untied and to smoke several times, the specific number varying with the individual. (For example, one shaman always went behind the blanket and came back four times.)

"Generally but not always the shaman has a rope tied around his waist. Retiring behind the blanket, he throws the free end of the rope over it so the people may see it. Soon they observe that the rope has lost all tension, since it has cut the shaman in two. They hear his two halves hit the floor.

"As many as four spirits might attend the seance. Owl is especially sought. It is he who shakes the blanket. The audience changes the song and drum rhythm with the arrival of each new spirit.

"The Owls then pick up the shaman and fly a long way off with him, where they deposit him and return. There is now presumably no human agent behind the blanket, yet it shakes and voices issue forth. More and more spirits flock in, if the seance is a success. It is useless to tell the number of Kutenai who claim to have seen the blanket raised and have seen absolutely nothing behind it to produce the voices. Such a contention is all but universal.

"When this stage of the seance is reached, the people bring their pipes to the blanket to pray. An official sits on the left side of the blanket's face to light the pipes for the people. He hands a pipe back of the blanket, where a spirit takes it and smokes. After the spirit has blown a few puffs, he hands the pipe back over the top where it is received by the owner. The supernatural who has smoked then advises his client. It is often very hard to understand the spirits. . . . Often they speak in an archaic Kutenaian which is not understood today. Sometimes . . . a second shaman must be asked for the interpretation. Ordinarily, however, they only speak softly, so that the official just mentioned is just a man with keen ears who can hear their remarks and relay them to the client.

"When the seance is over, the supernaturals bring the shaman back, and he rolls or walks from behind the blanket in a befuddled condition. He smokes and soon recovers" [Turney-High 1941: 174–176].

Visual mental imagery

There are few ethnographic accounts that give specific details about the training of shamans. Thus, little is known regarding this aspect of shamanism. However, recent studies tend to confirm the notion that one of the central goals of shamanic training involves the novice's development of visual mental imagery skills. This training appears to proceed in a two-phase fashion:

"First, the neophyte shaman is trained to increase the *vividness* of his visual mental imagery through various psychological and physiological techniques. The purpose is to block out the noise produced by the external stimuli of perception and to attend to internal imagery processes, thus bringing them more clearly into focus . . . to induce a cognitive figure-ground reversal by increasing the vividness of mental imagery until it is attended to as primary experience (figure) and diminishing the vividness of precepts until they are attended to as secondary experience (ground). Once the novice shaman can report more vivid imagery experiences, a second phase of shamanic mental imagery training is aimed at increasing the *controlledness* of the experienced visual imagery contents, actively engaging and manipulating the visionary phenomena. These two phases are not necessarily discrete; increase in control over visual mental imagery may be sought concurrently with an increase in its vividness" [Noll 1985:445–446].

Although visualization is the basic and minimum sensory experience of the shamanic journey, all the other sensory experiences—hearing, smell, taste, and touch—also commonly come into play. The essential, however, is imagery, and it is virtually impossible to experience the shamanic journey and most of shamanic practice without the ability to visualize [Harner in Noll 1985:452].

Vonhäom

Cheyenne, *Plains*

Sweat lodge. The term comes from *vonä* or *vonhä*, meaning "to lose by heat," and *om*, meaning "lodge" [Schlesier 1987:63]. "When it is employed in healing disease the thought is that the power of the spirits, not the steam, will expel the sickness" [Curtis in Schlesier 1987:65]. The emphasis on the use of the sweat lodge in healing appears to be a rather recent innovation among the Cheyenne.

Wabani

Keres, *Southwest*

Acoma Pueblo term for prayer feather bundles. Among other things, the *wabani* are used in making formal requests to the head of a medicine society to procure a healing ceremony. See *hictiani* for details.

Wabeno

Menomini, *Midwest;* Ojibwa, *Canadian Eastern Woodlands*

Also: *wabunoh, waabano, wâbeno, wabano.* Shamans associated with the *Wabeno* complex, a religious revitalization movement that began around 1796. Ojibwa shamans are given different names according to the different techniques they use to heal or divine. The *wabenos* "showed their powers by juggling and fire displays, by taking coals and red hot stones in their hands or mouth. Some plunged their hands into boiling grease or water, or tore off their burned flesh with their teeth while singing and dancing. Others breathed fire through reeds in their mouth" [Vecsey 1983:191]. *Wabeno* translates to "red dawn sky" [Grim 1983:113] and is indicative of the symbolic color of fire and the fact that dance rites continue throughout the night until dawn. The tutelary spirit of these shamans is the Sun or Morning Star. Thus, their powers include a special association with and immunity to fire, evidenced by their ability to hold hot coals in their hands and mouths during rituals. Cooper [1936:26] reports that the shaman first chews "a certain medicine, *wabanowask,*" which he spits on his hands to protect him from the fire.

Hoffman [1896:151] notes the *wabeno* among the Menomini and reports that at night these shamans may be seen flying along in the shape of a ball of fire or a pair of fiery sparks. Like their Ojibwa counterparts (see *Waubunowin*), these shamans often take the form of animals such as fox, bear, owl, and bat. The fox forms are known by the flame of fire that comes out of their mouths every time they bark. The following incident, demonstrating these shamans' ability to handle fire, was reported by Hoffman [1896:152] and witnessed by a large number of people:

"Two small wigwams were erected, about 50 paces from each other, and after the *wâ'beno* had crawled into one of them his disparagers built around each of the structures a continuous heap of brush and firewood, which was then kindled. When the blaze was at its height all became hushed for a moment. Presently the *wâ'beno* called to the crowd that he had transferred himself to the other wigwam, and immediately, to their profound astonishment, crawled forth therefrom unharmed."

In addition to conducting healings, these shamans locate game for hunters and make charms, such as love powder, which the Menomini term *takosa'wos*. This powder, composed of vermilion and mica laminæ, is ground very fine and then placed in a thimble that is worn around the neck.

The drums used by the *wabeno* "almost always had a human figure on them to indicate that the (eastern?) spirit had visited the owner in a vision and offered him protection" [Vennum 1982:184].

Wabinu
Montagnais, *Canadian Eastern Woodlands*
Literally, "seeing man." Speck [1919:254] uses this term to mean shaman but notes that the *wabinu* "is generally a member of a specific grade of shamans among the Central Algonkian who possess the graded Medicine Lodge (Midewin)."

Wacickani
Ponca, *Plains*
Also: *Waxobi Watugari.* The Pebble Society, which is thought to be a derivative of the Ojibwa Medicine Lodge Society (see *Midewiwin*). This society has long been extinct, and very little is known of its activity. Instead of shooting cowrie shells, as is done in most of these societies, they used small pebbles. The main function of the society was conducting healing ceremonies in which the pebbles would be rubbed on the patient to effect a cure [Skinner 1920:306–308].

Wacucke
Iowa, *Plains*
A magical cowrie shell, called a medicine arrow, that is shot into members of the *Mankánye Waci* (Medicine Dance) society and is also used in healing ceremonies. See *migis* for details.

Wadákati
Paviotso, *Basin*
A bowl-shaped basket containing pebbles or beads that is used as a rattle during a healing ceremony. See *puhágam* for details.

Wagmuha
Lakota, *Plains*
Dialectical variant: *wamnuha* (Dakota). The rattle used by shamans in healing ceremonies [Dens-

more 1918:252]. The shaman or the shaman's helping spirit chooses the type of rattle used. Most often they are made from either a gourd or rawhide. When rawhide is used, the skin is sewn together to form a bulb shape and then soaked in water, packed tightly with sand, and allowed to dry. In both cases, a wooden handle is attached. Great care is taken when selecting the number and type of stones to be placed inside the rattle.

Wahconwechasta
Assiniboin, *Plains*
Shaman. The Assiniboin call shamans "diving men" [Denig 1930:422]. To secure the healing services of a shaman, gifts are sent to him, such as a horse or a gun. There is no set fee, the payment being based on the wealth of the patient's family. The shaman goes to the lodge of the patient, accompanied by five or six singers who use drums, bells, and rattles. The shaman dresses only in a breechcloth and has no special doctoring outfit.

During his healing ritual, the shaman sings his medicine songs while using a drum and a rattle. Most illnesses are diagnosed as object intrusion, and the shaman sucks with his mouth on the patient's body several times until an object such as wolf hair, a bug, or a small snake is removed. In some cases, the upper 3 inches of a buffalo horn is used in sucking out the object. The large end of the horn is placed against the patient's body, and the shaman sucks through the smaller end until the object is removed. This process may be repeated several times, resulting in more than one object being extracted from the patient. During the extraction, the shaman is in a trance and often emulates his animal helping spirit. During some treatments, the patient is also given a concoction of powdered roots or other ingredients to drink. The treatment can last from two to three hours or for an entire night. In serious cases, the shaman doctors over a period of several days.

Concerning the use of herbs for doctoring, Denig [1930:425–426] reports:

"They have no medicine except some roots, some of which are known to be good for the bite of the rattlesnake, frozen parts, and inflammatory wounds. The principal of these is the black root, called by them the comb root. . . . It is chewed and applied in a raw state with a bandage to the part affected. We can bear witness to the efficacy of this root in the cure of the bite of the rattlesnake or in alleviating the pain and reducing the tension and inflammation of frozen parts, gunshot wounds, etc. It has a slightly pungent taste resembling black pepper, and produces a great deal of saliva while chewing it. Its virtues are known to all the tribes with which we are acquainted, and it is often used with success."

Denig [1930:426] also reports an unusual treatment for hydrophobia, although he never witnessed such a treatment:

"Indians are often bitten by mad wolves, yet they never die from the disease if operated upon. After

A gourd rattle used by shamans in healing ceremonies.

it is known that the patient has hydrophobia, the symptoms of which they are well acquainted with, and has had a fit or two, he is sewed up in a fresh rawhide of a buffalo. With two cords attached to the head and foot of the bale the man is swung backward and forward through a hot fire until the skin is burnt to cinders and the patient is burned and suffocated. He is brought to the brink of the grave by the operation; taken out in a state of profuse perspiration and plunged into cold water; and if he survives the treatment the disease disappears."

Wahuprin
Iowa, Oto, Missouri, *Plains*
Mysterious. This term is applied only to a person, such as a shaman, or to an animal [Dorsey 1894:367]. When referring to an inanimate object, the term is *waqonyitan*.

Waititcani
Zuni, *Southwest*
The sacred medicine bowl used during the healing ceremonies of Zuni medicine societies. It contains an herb and water mixture that is given to the patient to drink. The bowls have four terraced sides and are black and white in color. Bears, snakes, lions, lightning, and cloud symbols are painted on these special bowls.

The medicine men gather most of their herbs from Mount Taylor, some 20 miles north of Zuni. They walk there, taking several days to gather the necessary herbs. At the summit of the mountain they deposit prayer sticks and perform other rituals required when gathering medicinal herbs [White 1932:110].

Wakan
Lakota, *Plains*
Power; sometimes translated to "mysterious," "wonderful," "incomprehensible," or "holy" (by missionaries) [Dorsey 1894:366]. Because *wakan* cannot be comprehended, it is impossible to completely control it. Anything *wakan* is something that is hard to understand. The *wakan* of a warrior is evidenced by his physical prowess in warfare and his immunity to injury, whereas the *wakan* of a shaman refers to his spiritual abilities. *Wakan*

can therefore be acquired by individuals, and it can be used for either good or evil. *Wakan* is an expression of numinousness—that which can be felt but not conceptualized. It is the Lakota equivalent of *orenda* (see entry).

Wakan tanka
Lakota, *Plains*
Literally, "great mysterious (one)"; it formerly referred to the Thunder Beings [Dorsey 1894:366]. During the nineteenth century, however, missionaries began using *wakan tanka* to mean the Creator, and today, it translates to "great mystery" and has come to mean the ultimate reality. *Wakan tanka* can appear as different persons, such as White Buffalo Calf Woman (see *Sacred Calf Pipe Bundle*) or Inktomi, the Spider spirit. The term itself is genderless and can be singular or plural. During contemporary prayer one often hears the term *Tunkashila*, meaning "Grandfather," being used to address the Creator, although *wakan tanka* is just as acceptable. In any healing ceremony, it is ultimately *wakan tanka* who is the source of healing. (For a clarification of Lakota ultimate reality, see Bunge 1987.)

The shamans have a secret system known as *tobtob kin* (the four times four) that is used for understanding the great mystery. Because only shamans know the secret, most people identify *wakan tanka* with the sun. This four times four system "is an all-inclusive classification of the universe based on the distribution and function of power in the universe. Those who are at the source of it and who can transmit it are *wakan tanka*" [DeMallie and Lavenda 1977:155]. *Wakan tanka* can also be interpreted as "the power of the universe" and implies a singularity at the core.

As stated above, the development of the term *wakan tanka* came with the advent of Christianity among the Sioux. In fact, Riggs [1880:266] himself a ninteenth-century missionary to the Santee (Dakota), states that "we simply *claimed our own*, in using Wah-kon-ton-ka for God." Prior to that, the general name for all the powerful spirits (called "gods" by the Christians) was *taku wakan*, that is, that which is *wakan* ("holy"), a general term including all that is wonderful, incomprehensible, and supernatural. *Taku wakan* literally means "something mysterious" and is usually translated to "someone mysterious" or "holy being" [Dorsey 1894:366]. A shaman or medicine man was a *wakan*-man. The Sioux did not have the concept of a single supreme god until contact with the Europeans [Pond 1867:33–34].

Wakan tcañkara
Winnebago, *Midwest*
Shaman. Literally "mysterious man" [Dorsey 1894:367].

Wakan Wacipi
Dakota, *Plains*
The Medicine Dance among the Wahpeton. Literally, "Holy Dance." It is a variant of the Grand Medicine Society Ceremony (see *Midewiwin*) of the Ojibwa. It was last performed in the 1860s. Variations on this ceremony include the use of double-pointed oblong objects that appear to be cut from yellow or white shell and are used as medicine arrows (made from cowrie shells in other nations) and tiny magic bows and arrows that are used to shoot "offenders or their images in the lodge to punish them for their transgressions" [Skinner 1920:265–266]. Their lodge differs in that it is open at the top.

Wakan yan
Lakota, *Plains*
Also: *wakan han* [Densmore 1918:245]. The "highest type of medicine-men" [Densmore 1918:245], known today as *yuwipi* (see entry) men; translates to "sacredly" or "mysteriously" [Buechel 1970:526].

These shamans possess at least one *tunkan* (see entry), a sacred stone used in healing and other shamanic activities, such as locating lost articles. Brave Buffalo [in Densmore 1918:208] reports that "in my dream one of these small round stones appeared to me and told me that the maker of all was Wakan tanka (Creator), and that in order to honor him I must honor his works in nature. The stone said that by my search I had shown myself worthy of supernatural help. It said that if I were curing a sick person I might ask assistance, and that all the forces of nature would help me work a cure." Lone Man [in Densmore 1918:214] reports that a "medicine-man also told me that the sacred stone may appear in the form of a person who talks and sings many wonderful (medicine) songs."

Wakanda
Ponca, Omaha, Kansa *Plains*
Dialectical variant: *wakanta* (Osage, Iowa, Oto, Missouri). Generally, superhuman beings or powers; however, a Ponca shaman, Cramped Hand, told Dorsey [1894:366]: "I am a Wakanda." The term is used in the same sense as the Lakota *wakan* (see entry); formerly, it also referred to the Thunder Beings. Gilmore [1977:3] gives the term *wakandagi* as meaning "something supernatural."

Wakandagi waganxe
Kansa, *Plains*
Mysterious feats display by shamans. *Wakandagi* translates to "something supernatural," "mysterious" [Dorsey 1894:367].

Wakandja
Winnebago, *Midwest*
Although the term means "thunderbird," it is also identical in meaning to the Omaha *wakonda* (see entry). Because *wakandja* is not related to the Winnebago word for thunder, Paul Radin suggests that it originally meant "he who is sacred" [Radin 1923:282].

Wakantcañkara
Winnebago, *Midwest*
Shaman [Dorsey 1894:367]; translates to "mysterious man."

Wakawanx
Winnebago, *Midwest*
Witch [Dorsey 1894:367]. Witches are frequently diagnosed as being the cause of a sickness.

Wakilapi
Coast Miwok, *California*
See *temnepa*.

Wakinyan
Lakota, *Plains*
The powerful Thunder Beings, translated by Riggs [1880:267] as the great "Thunder Bird" and by Walker [1917:83] as the "Winged God." Of the *wakinyan*, Lame Deer [1972:241] says: "If the

thunder-beings want to put their power on earth, among the people, they send a dream to a man, a vision about thunder and lightning. By this dream they appoint him to work his power for them in a human way." Although the power of the *wakinyan* is considered to be good, they represent a fear-inducing and dangerous aspect of *wakan tanka* (see entry). Shamans who receive their power from the Thunder Beings are considered to be among the most powerful of the Lakota shamans. Symbols of the *wakinyan* are often seen painted on tepees, shields, and sometimes bodies. See also *Heyóka*.

Wakonda
Omaha, Osage, *Plains*
The Omaha counterpart of the Lakota/Dakota term *wakan tanka* (see entry). *Wakonda* is the mysterious life power that permeates all natural forms and forces. "This power is seen as akin to human consciousness itself. *Wakonda* symbolized the integrity of the universe, a universe in which man was a small part, dependent, as was the entirety of the universe, on the power that animated it. This power of *wakonda* was not conceived of as a neutral force, but was invested with a moral quality. Truthfulness, pity, and compassion were attributed to *wakonda*, so that the will of *wakonda* was not to be altered or questioned, and an individual was to obtain favors, as in the Dakota case, by humble supplication" [DeMallie and Lavenda 1977:159].
    Among the Osage, *wakonda* is also used as a designation for shamans. *Wakonda* is also the Omaha and Osage equivalent for *orenda* (see entry).

Wakondagi
Osage, *Plains*
Shaman; one who communicates with spirits. It is also used to refer to anything held sacred or holy [La Flesche 1932:194].

Walimitca
Coast Miwok, *California*
Outfit doctors; from the root *wali-*, meaning "doctor." These shamans undergo training by older shamans before they begin to practice healing. The outfit doctor always visits the patient first to diagnose the illness. Some of these shamans are also sucking shamans. In cases of serious illness,

the outfit doctor requests that the patient be treated by the Kuksu society, which then conducts a four-day healing dance ceremony [Loeb 1934a: 114].

Wapiye
Lakota, *Plains*
Also: *wapiya* [Densmore 1918:245]. One of several terms applied to shamans; the literal translation is "to make fortunate." According to Riggs [1893: 214], the shaman's skill and applied power are called *wapiyapi*, meaning "renewing" or "fixing over." Buechel [1970:548], however, translates *wapiyapi* to "conjuring." Usually, *wapiye* means anyone who heals, but those who know only a few herbs and do not use supernatural powers are called *pejuta wicasa* (see entry).

When a person seeks to be healed by a *wapiye*, he presents the shaman with tobacco—usually by filling a sacred pipe and taking it to the *wapiye*. However, a person can also present a pack of cigarettes, a bag of pipe tobacco, or the like. If the *wapiye* accepts the tobacco, it means that he is committed to helping the person.

The *wapiye* uses supernatural means to find medicinal herbs. When a diagnosis calls for a plant that is unknown to the *wapiye*, he searches for it in the dark by supernatural means. First, his helping spirits tell the *wapiye* to go to a certain area on the reservation where the herb grows. Once there, he is usually led to the specific place by tiny flashing lights (the spirits), which come to rest over the sought-after herb. One *yuwipi* man reported that his "white root" medicine initially glowed in the dark, and that was how he first knew which one to pick. Once the herb is found, a tobacco offering is made to the plant before taking it.

Following the acquisition of the needed herb, some *wapiye* simply administer the herb; others use the herb in conjunction with spirit helpers. Those shamans who do not use spirit helpers in their healing ceremonies are usually referred to as *pejuta wicasa*, meaning "medicine man." Those shamans who call in spirit helpers during their healing are usually called *wicasa wakan*, meaning "holy man." In this latter category are also the *yuwipi* men, who have mastered the ritual of the *yuwipi* (see entry) ceremony.

A typical healing ceremony is as follows:

"When he (the shaman) entered my lodge (tipi) he seated himself back of the fire. After a time he came and sat by my head, looking me over. He then took up a lock of hair on my forehead and tied a wisp of grass around it, letting the rest of my hair hang loose. Then he had me placed so that I lay facing the east and he began his preparations for the treatment. Opening a bundle (medicine bag), he took from it a whistle (*śi'yotaŋka*), a small drum (*ćaŋ'ćeǵa*), and a rattle (*wagmu'ha*) which he used in beating the drum. He also took out a black cloth, which he tied over his eyes. Then he dropped on one knee, facing me, holding the drum in his right hand and the rattle in his left hand. Beating the drum rapidly with the rattle, he said; 'Young man, try to remember what I tell you. You shall see the power from which I have the right to cure sicknesses, and this power shall be used on you this day.' Then he told the dream by which he received his power as a medicine-man. When he rose to his feet I noticed that a horse's tail hung at his side, being fastened to his belt. Standing, he offered his drum to the cardinal points, then beat it as hard as he could, sometimes louder, sometimes softer. A wooden bowl which he carried was placed next to my head. Then he came toward me, still beating his drum. As he came near me his breath was so forcible it seemed as if it would blow me before it. Just before he reached me, and while blowing his breath so strongly, he struck his body on the right side and on the left side. He was still telling his dream and singing, but when he paused for an instant I could hear the sound of a red hawk; some who were there even said they could see the head of a red hawk coming out of his mouth. He bent over me and I expected that he would suck the poison from my body with his mouth, but instead I felt the beak of a bird over the place where the pain was. It penetrated so far that I could feel the feathers of the bird. The medicine-man kept perfectly still for a time; then he got up with a jerk to signify that he had gotten out the trouble. Still it was the beak of a bird which I felt. A boy stood near, holding a filled pipe. It was soon apparent that the medicine-man had swallowed the poison. He took four whiffs of the pipe. Then he must get rid of the poison. This part of the performance was marked by great activity and pounding of the drum. At times he kicked the bare ground in his effort to get rid of the poison; he paced back and forth, stamped his feet, and used both rattle and drum. Finally he ejected the poison into the wooden bowl. Then he told the people that he had sucked out all the poison, that none remained in my body, and that I would recover.

"Opening his medicine bag, he took out some herbs and placed them in a cup of cold water. He stirred it up and told me to drink it and to repeat the dose next morning, and that in less than ten days I would be well. I did as he told me, and in about 10 days I was entirely well" [Use-as-a-Shield in Densmore 1918:247–248].

Waqonyitan
Iowa, Oto, Missouri, *Plains*
Mysterious; the term is applied to inanimate objects [Dorsey 1894:367]. When referring to a person or animal, the term is *wahuprin*.

Warukana
Winnebago, *Midwest*
Translates to "exerting one's powers" [Radin 1923:254]. The following account, given by an unknown shaman, is an example of *warukana* as it applies to healing:

"My ability to spit water upon the people whom I am treating I received from an eel, from the chief among the eels, one who lives in the center and in the deepest part of the ocean. He is absolutely white and he is the one who blessed me. Whenever I spit water it is inexhaustible, because it comes from him, the eel.

"Then I came to this earth again (after my vision). They, the spirits, all gave me advice before I left them. When I came upon this earth I entered a lodge and there I was born again. As I said, I thought that I was entering a lodge, but in reality I was entering my mother's womb. Even in my prenatal existence, I never lost consciousness. Then I grew up and fasted again and again, and all those spirits who had blessed me before sent me their blessings again. I can dictate to all the spirits that exist. Whatever I say will come to pass. The tobacco you (the patients) offer me is not to be used by myself. It is really intended for the spirits.

"Spirits, a person is sick and he offers me tobacco. I am on earth to accept it and to try to cure him.

"You will live (this is addressed to the patient), so help yourself as much as you can and try to make yourself strong. Now as I offer this tobacco to the spirits you must listen and if you know that I am telling the truth, you will be strengthened by it."

(What follows is the shaman's offering of tobacco to the spirits.)

"*Han ho!* Here is the tobacco, Fire. You promised me that if I offered you tobacco you would grant me whatever request I made. Now I am placing tobacco on your head as you told me to, when I fasted for four days and you blessed me. I am sending you the plea of a human being who is ill. He wishes to live. This tobacco is for you and I pray that the one who is ill be restored to health within four days.

"To you too, Buffalo, I offer tobacco. A person who is ill is offering tobacco to you and asking you to restore him to health. So add that power which I obtained from you at the time I fasted for six days and you sent your spirits after me who took me to your lodge which lies in the center of this earth and which is absolutely white. There you blessed me, you Buffaloes, of four different colors (symbols of the four directions). Those blessings that you bestowed upon me then, I ask of you now. The power of breathing (on the patient) with which you blessed me, I am in need of now. Add your power to mine, as you promised. The people have given me plenty of tobacco for you.

"To you, Grizzly-bear, I also offered tobacco (during a vision quest). At a place called Pointed Hill lives a spirit who is in charge of a ceremonial lodge and to this all the other grizzly-bears belong. You all blessed me and you said that I would be able to kill whomsoever I wished, and that at the same time I would be able to restore any person to life. Now, I have a chance to enable a person to live and I wish to aid him. So here is some tobacco for you. You took my spirit to your home after I had fasted for ten days and you blessed me there. The powers with which you blessed me there I ask of you now. Here is some tobacco, grandfathers, that the people are offering to you.

"To you, the Chief of the Eels, you who live in the center of the ocean, I offer tobacco. You blessed me after I had fasted for eight days. With your power of breathing and with your inexhaustible supply of water, you blessed me. You told me that I could use my blessing whenever I tried to cure a patient. You told me that I could use all the water in the ocean, and you blessed me with all the things that are in the water. A person has come to me and asked me for life; and as I wish him to live, I am addressing you. When I spit upon the patient may the power of my saliva be the same as yours. Therefore I offer you tobacco; here it is.

"To you, the Turtle, you who are in charge of a shaman lodge, you who blessed me after I fasted seven days and carried my spirit to your home, where I found many birds of prey (literally, birds with sharp claws). There you blessed me and you told me that should, at any time, any human being have a pain I would be able to drive it out of him. For that reason you called me One-who-drives-out-pains. Now before me is a person with a bad pain and I wish to take it out of him. That is what the spirits told me when they blessed me, before I came down to earth. Therefore I am going to heal him. Here is the tobacco.

"To you, who are in charge of the snake lodge, you who are perfectly white, Rattlesnake, I pray. You blessed me with your rattles to wrap around my gourd and you told me after I had fasted for four days that you could help me. You said that I would never fail in anything that I attempted. So now, when I offer you tobacco and shake my gourd, may my patient live and may life (an additional number of years) be opened to him. That is what you promised me, grandfather.

"I greet you, too, Night Spirits. You blessed me after I had fasted for nine days, and you took my spirit to your village which lies in the east, where you gave me your flutes which you told me were holy. You made my flute holy likewise. For these I ask you now, for you know that I am speaking the truth. A sick person has come to me and has asked me to cure him; and because I want him to live I am speaking to you. You promised to accept my tobacco at all times; here it is.

"To you, Disease-giver, I offer tobacco. After I had fasted two days you let me know that you were the one who gives diseases and that if I desired to heal anyone it would be easy for me to do so were I blessed by you. So, Disease-giver, I am offering you tobacco, and I ask that this sick person who has come to me be restored to health again as you promised when you bestowed your blessing upon me.

"To you, Thunderbirds, I offer tobacco too. When you blessed me you said that you would help me whenever I needed you. A person has come to me and asked me to cure him, and as I want him to live, I wish to remind you of your promise. Grandfathers, here is some tobacco.

"To you, the Sun, I offer tobacco too; here it is. You blessed me after I had fasted for five days and you told me that you would come to my aid whenever I had something difficult to do. Now, someone has come to me and pleaded for life, and he has brought good offerings of tobacco to me because he knows that you have blessed me.

"To you, grandmother, the Moon, I also offer tobacco. You blessed me and said that whenever I needed your power you would aid me. A person has come to me and asked for life, and I therefore call upon you to help me with your power as you promised. Grandmother, here is some tobacco.

"To you, grandmother, the Earth, I too offer tobacco. You blessed me and promised to help me whenever I needed you. You said that I could use all the best herbs that grow upon you, and that I would always be able to effect cures with them. Those herbs I ask of you now, and I ask you to help me cure this sick person. Make my medicine powerful, grandmother.

"To you, Chief of the Spirits, I offer tobacco. You who blessed me and said that you would help me. I offer you tobacco and ask you to let this sick person live, and if his spirit is about to depart, I ask you to prevent it.

"I offer tobacco to all of you who have blessed me.

"Then the shaman blew upon his flute, breathed upon the sick man and sang four times (his medicine songs). Then he walked around the lodge and spat water upon the patient. After this he sang four times and stopped. The spirits would now let him know whether the patient was to live or die.

"In this manner a shaman treats his patients for four days, and after that takes his offerings and goes away. If the sick person happens to recover, the shaman would tell him that he would never be sick again" [Radin 1923:272–275].

Waruksti
Pawnee, *Plains*
The Skiri term for power [Murie 1981:44]. It is the equivalent of the Lakota *wakan* and the Iroquois *orenda.*

Wasáse
Cayuga, *Northeast*
The War Dance healing ceremony. It is performed in connection with the Thunder Rite, and anyone may participate in the ritual. See *eyondwanshgwut* for details.

Washington, Mrs.
Northern Ute, *Basin*
A shaman who was interviewed by anthropologist Frances Densmore. "Mrs. Washington gave no material remedies, for she claimed to have supernatural power. Her specialty was the treatment of illnesses caused by an evil influence proceeding from some person (sorcery). She recorded six of her songs and said that she usually sang them when the sun was at a height corresponding to its position at about 10 o'clock on a summer morning" [Densmore 1952:446].

Washíshka-athè
Ponca, *Plains*
The Medicine Lodge Ceremony; translates to "white-shell-owners" [Howard 1965:119], a reference to the medicine arrows or medicine projectiles used during the ceremony. As such, the *Washíshka-athè* is the Ponca equivalent of the Ojibwa *Midewiwin* (Grand Medicine Society; see entry). The Medicine Lodge, a shamans' organization, is the largest and most important Ponca medicine society.

Prior to the twentieth century, cowrie shells (*Cyprea moneta*) were used as the medicine arrows. However, over time, other items also came into use, including rooster spurs, fishbones, and mescal beans. Also, a small, round stone is often used, leading to the organization being referred to as the Pebble Society. As in the Ojibwa ceremony, the medicine arrows are shot with medicine "bows," which are the decorated skins of small animals, such as mink, otter, or weasel. The Ponca also occasionally use other items for these bows, such as an eagle's wing. In one known account, a black handkerchief was used by a shaman. These medicine bows serve as the badges of membership in the society.

The following is an account of a Medicine Lodge Society healing ceremony. It was conducted in 1910 to heal a young boy named Henry Le Roy who had become sick due to an encounter with *Gisná* (the water monster):

"Shaky and three other doctors came (to Henry's house) and put on their dance (healing ceremony). They had my brother stand naked in the center while they danced around him. They asked my brother what the Gisná had told him when it shot him with its tail. My brother said, 'It told me I was to be a doctor.'

"The first doctor danced around my brother. He suddenly stopped dancing right in front of my brother and took a big black water beetle from my brother's chest. This was part of what the Gisná had put there. I saw this bug myself as it was crawling away. Then the second medicine man danced around my brother. He took some green moss from the joints of my brother's arms and legs. He piled this moss on the floor. The Gisná had put this there too. Then the third medicine man danced around my brother. He found some of the round stones that we call 'marbles' in my brother's hands. All of this stuff had been shot into my brother by the water monster.

"Then Shaky came out to the middle of the floor. He asked each of the others if they had taken out everything they could find. 'Try again, and see if you can find anything else,' he said to them. Each of them tried again, but each found him empty. Then Shaky, the head doctor, said, 'There is something else. I will try to get it out. If I can't get it out it will kill him.' He went around and around my brother, without saying a word. Finally he stopped. 'There is something else! He is standing on them!' He had my brother move each of his feet. From under each one he took a human eyeball.

"'Now he is cleaned out!' said the doctors. Then Shaky said, 'Don't take it all away from him.

We must leave him some power to protect himself.' So the doctor who had taken the marbles from my brother's hands gave him back one of these. After that he was considered a member of the Medicine Lodge Society, and was respected for having water-monster power" [Howard 1965:120–121].

Waterman, Thomas Talbot

Thomas Waterman was born in Hamilton, Missouri, on 25 April 1885. He entered the University of California to pursue a career as an Episcopal priest but soon became attracted to anthropology. He became Alfred Kroeber's protégé and remained at Berkeley until 1921, becoming an associate professor of anthropology. During this time, his fieldwork focused mostly on ethnographic and linguistic details, especially among the Yurok and Tolowa of northwestern California. However, he is best remembered for his association with Ishi, the Yana man who lived at the Museum of Anthropology from 1911 to 1916 as "the last remaining Indian in America." Waterman also taught at the University of Washington from 1918 to 1920. During this time, he did important work on the Native Americans of Puget Sound and the Makah. After leaving Berkeley in 1921, he joined the Heye Foundation in New York City. His tenure was short-lived there, and his career fell into unproductive disarray. Most of his last decade was spent in Hawaii, and he died in Honolulu on 6 January 1936. Among his major works are *The Yana Indians* (1918), *Yurok Geography* (1920), and *American Indian Life* (1922).

Waubunoh

Ojibway, *Canadian Eastern Woodlands*
See *wabeno*.

Waubunowin

Ojibwa, *Canadian Eastern Woodlands*
A dark society that is purported to be dedicated to sorcery; from the Ojibwa word *waubunoh*, meaning "dawn." Its power is equal to that of the Third Order of the *Midewiwin* (see entry). Some claim that it originated years ago when some members of the Third Order were inspired by evil and broke away on their own. Its members are still feared to this day. They often practice medical magic, especially the exorcism of evil spirits that cause disease [Johnston 1982; Hoffman 1891].

Waunyapi

Lakota, *Plains*
Also: *waunyanpi* [Walker 1926:199]. The personal objects a shaman uses in setting up his altar display for a healing ceremony. The term translates to "offerings." They symbolize certain aspects of his power, and their proper placement calls his helping spirits to a ceremony. They consist of such items as eagle plumes and feathers, gourds, eagle-bone whistles, and so forth.

One common item is the prayer stick. It is usually made from the sprout of a wild plum or chokecherry tree. Anyone who desires to have his prayers placed into a ceremony can make one. The prayer stick is usually assembled in solitude while the individual offers prayers to the spirits. The sprout is cut 20 to 30 inches long, and the outer bark is peeled off; often the stick is painted. Fastened near the top of the stick is an offering to the spirits—usually a pinch of tobacco wrapped in a 3-inch-square piece of cotton cloth. In former times, other items were tied to the top of the stick, such as medicine, food, a bit of hair, or colored feathers. These prayer sticks are displayed as part of the ceremonial altar set up for a healing ceremony. They are made to stand upright in the display by placing the bottom end into the ground or into a can of dirt.

Wawa

Keres, *Southwest*
The general term at Acoma Pueblo for medicinal herbs; translates simply to "medicine" [White 1932:110].

Waxobi Watugari

Ponca, *Plains*
See *Wacickani*.

Waxopini

Winnebago, *Midwest*
According to Radin [1923:282], this is the only word for "spirit" among the Winnebago.

Waxopini xedera
Winnebago, *Midwest*
Translates to "great spirit"; also called Earth-maker. The term corresponds to the Dakota *wakan tanka* and the Omaha *wakonda*. However, unlike these two, the Winnebago developed the concept into a personified creator god, probably an influence from Christianity.

Waxúbe
Ponca, *Plains*
Also: *waxube, waqube.* A shaman's supernatural power [Howard 1965:120]. Shamans obtain their power through either vision quests or training by a recognized shaman. Dorsey [1894:367], however, translates this term as "mysterious" and reports that it is applied only to inanimate objects.

Wayan
Ojibwa, *Canadian Eastern Woodlands*
A container made from animal hide to hold the sacred objects used by shamans; a type of medicine bundle. It is also referred to by the Ojibwa as a *mide migis* sack. For its ceremonial use see *migis.*

Wazethe
Ponca, Omaha, *Plains*
Also: *wazathe* [Gilmore 1977:3]. Shamans who doctor [Dorsey 1894:417]. During their healing ceremonies, they locate the *nie* (pain) in the patient's body that is causing the illness and remove it by sucking on the afflicted area.

Welewkushkush
Washo, *Basin*
A shaman who was a well-known healer during the nineteenth century. He was born around 1810–1820 and practiced in the area of Genoa, Nevada, a few miles south of Carson City. He conducted his healing ceremonies in a lean-to. One aspect of his ceremonies included dancing around in the lean-to fire and emerging unharmed. One of his better remembered power feats was to walk under the waters of Lake Tahoe without drowning. His nephew (his wife's sister's son) was Henry Rupert, who was reported to be the last shaman among the Washo.

We'mawe
Zuni, *Southwest*
Also: *we'ma a'ciwani.* The Beast Gods, the most dangerous and violent gods in the Zuni pantheon. According to Bunzel [1932:528–529]:

"They are the priests of long life (onaya·nakä a·'ci'wan·i, literally road fulfilling priests). They are the givers of medicine, not only medicinal plants, but the magic power to make them effective. They are the source also of black magic or witchcraft. Their leaders are associated with the six directions as follows: north, Mountain Lion; west, Bear; south, Badger; east, Wolf; above, Knife-wing; below, Gopher (some accounts have Eagle, above and Shrew, below). Of all, the most powerful is the Bear. He is compelled through impersonation at curing ceremonies. The symbol of his personality is the bear paws which are drawn over the hands and have the same properties as the (Kachina) masks of the gods. The worship of the beast gods is conducted by 12 societies or fraternities. Membership in these societies is voluntary and is open alike to males and females. All offices are held by men, and only they have the ultimate magical powers—the powers of impersonating the bear, the use of the crystal, the power to remove sickness by sucking, and the use of magical songs. Some knowledge of therapeutic plants is hereditary in certain matrilineal families. Except for midwifery, which is practiced independently, all medical practice is in the hands of these societies. They are, in fact, medical guilds, closed corporations which guard their secrets jealously. The combined body of esoteric knowledge and ritual held by these groups is enormous, and this is genuinely esoteric. . . . No knowledge is more closely guarded than this.

"Each society in addition to practicing general medicine has a specialty—one cures sore throat, another epilepsy, another has efficacious medicine for delayed parturition, yet another cures bullet wounds, and so forth.

"Initiation into the societies is a precaution taken to save one's life. If a person is desperately ill he is given by his relatives to one of the medicine societies. (In less serious cases an individual medicine man is called.) The officials of the society come in a body to cure him. They bring with them all their ceremonial paraphernalia and lend the whole force of their ritual toward defeating the disease. If the patient recovers he is not necessarily cured. He has been granted a respite, and until he fulfills his pledge and receives a new heart and places himself under the direct protection of the Beast Gods through joining the society which cured him, his life is in jeopardy. Since initiation involves one in great expense, frequently many years elapse before it is completed."

As long as 20 years can elapse before the person is initiated. At the initiation, the former patient receives a "new heart" and is also given a new name to symbolize the new life he will lead as a member of the society. However, this name is rarely used thereafter.

There is a convening of all these medicine societies each year during the winter solstice ceremonies. On the tenth day following the solstice, the members all come together in the evening to begin a four-day retreat. Four days later, on the last night of the gathering, all the society members, male and female, come together in full ritual regalia, including body and face painting. In addition to the members, all those in the pueblo who are very sick attend for a curing. Around midnight, a fresh altar is set up. During this time, individual members of the society are allowed to demonstrate their medicine powers through demonstrations of fire eating and the like. Afterward, the Beast Gods are called into the ceremony through drumming, rattles, and dancing. Finally, only the oldest and most powerful medicine men, the ones who have the power to impersonate the bear, take control of the ceremony. Entering into trance states, they begin to gaze into their sacred crystals to find and diagnose the illnesses present among the visitors. "When they see sickness in anyone they draw from his body the foreign substance that has caused it. Dust, stones, bits of calico, feathers, fur or the entrails of animals are extracted from the mouth and other parts of the bodies of patients. Each article as it is extracted is exhibited to the company and dropped into a bowl to be disposed of the following day. . . . It is general knowledge that these 'cures'

are accomplished by sleight-of-hand. . . . The act itself is but a symbol of the relationship with the supernaturals (the Beast Gods). The efficacy lies not in the performance of the act itself but in the god-given power to perform it" [Bunzel 1932: 532].

Throughout the night, the most powerful shamans respond to invitations—offerings of cornmeal—to visit individual homes, where they also conduct healings. The ceremony ends at dawn with a sacred feast.

Other meetings of these societies are held only for the purpose of attending to serious individual illnesses. These ceremonies are held in secret; the only people in attendance are the officers of the society, those shamans with the specific medicine powers needed for the particular case at hand, and the patient. Basically, the same procedures used in the public healing ceremonies are followed. The shaman diagnoses the illness through the use of a crystal. If the diagnosis is witchcraft, the Bow Priests are summoned to extract a confession from the accused, which breaks the power of the illness. However, in most cases, a harmful object is located and extracted from the patient's body. Some shamans ingest psychoactive plants during these ceremonies to help them diagnose an illness.

Wenenapi
Coast Miwok, *California*
See *temnepa*.

Weppah
Southern Miwok, *California*
Amulet. "Southern Miwok people wore roots of an unidentified rare plant on string necklaces to protect themselves from sickness" [Bates 1992: 98].

Wes comi
Atsugewi, *California*
A shaman's power quest or vision quest, undertaken to procure helping spirits. Power quests usually take place at locations of known power, most often a particular lake. During the quest, the novice often swims underwater in search of a sa-

cred object; if one is found, it is accompanied by the appearance of spirits that give the shaman power songs [Park 1986:6]. See *betsaki* for details.

Wesatwas Gatcikwai

Cayuga, *Northeast*

The Football Rite used for healing; literally, "kicking game." Anyone may participate in the ritual. See *eyondwanshgwut* for details.

Wewacpe

Omaha, *Plains*

A series of precisely memorized prayers. The Omaha use the *wewacpe* to put their people in proper relation with *wakonda*. Each clan or lineage is responsible for some specific portion of ritual prayer. These prayer rituals are used by the Omaha "to open a way between the people and the mysterious *Wakonda;* therefore they had to be accurately given in order that the path might be straight for the return of the desired benefit" [Fletcher and La Flesche 1911:596]. Often the desired benefit is some form of individual healing.

Wéyekin

Nez Perce, *Plateau*

Both the shaman's helping spirit and the ability derived from such a spirit through vision quest, inheritance, or an unsolicited visitation from a power-bearing spirit [Walker 1970:269].

White Weasel

Gros Ventre, *Plains*

A sucking shaman who practiced during the early twentieth century. The following is an account of a woman who suffered neck pains for several months and called upon White Weasel after getting no relief from other doctors:

"Once I hooked up the wagon and went for wood. We were living at the time down the Milk River Valley (in Montana). While getting the wood, all of a sudden I was struck with a sharp pain in the back of my neck. It was like a sharp pinch. . . .

"This was a little before the Fourth of July and I went to the celebration suffering with that pain in the neck. After that they began to call all kinds

of Indian doctors for me—Stiffarm, Bill Jones, Ragged Robe. Each pulled (sucked) out something, a piece of skin or something. And they had to give a lot of things away to each doctor. But none of them did me any good.

"We were living close to a friend who told me: 'The only one who can cure you is my brother (White Weasel).' So I called him and they gave him a lot of things—about seven big things, including horses. He is the one who cured me. He pulled out a little animal from himself. That was his medicine. He showed it to the people present and its tail just shook. Then he doctored me by sucking on my cheek and on the nape of my neck. He extracted from me a fingernail. It was all green, it had been there so long. I had not called White Weasel until the fall. . . .

"White Weasel said that it was not a spirit that had shot me (with the fingernail) but that it had been done by somebody living although he did not mention the person's name. I never knew who did it" [Singer in Cooper 1957:344–345].

Whizzer

See *rhombus.*

Wicahmunga

Lakota, *Plains*

A shaman who practices sorcery, that is, uses his powers to harm others.

Wicasa wakan

Lakota, *Plains*

Literally "holy men"; used to refer to shamans because they are the persons who control the power of *wakan tanka* (see entry). "The *wicasa wakan* seeks solitude where he can meditate and feel the earth move and talk to the plants and hear their answers. As Lame Deer says, something flows into him, and something from him, and what he sees with his eyes closed is what matters" [Erdoes 1973:30].

Wikwisiyai

Diegueño, *California Peninsula*

Rattlesnake shaman. See *Teipalai* for an example.

Williams, Duke
Skokomish, *Northwest Coast*
See *Xelxalelkt*.

Willier, Russell
Woods Cree, *Canadian Eastern Woodlands*
See *Mehkwasskwan*.

Wilson, Charles
Yuma, *Southwest*
A leading shaman during the early twentieth century. One of his medicines was the treatment of gunshot wounds, for which he used four healing songs. "Each song has a special purpose. With the singing of the first song he expects the patient to regain consciousness. With the second he calls upon a small insect that lives in the water and is believed to have power over the fluids of the body; the purpose is to check the hemorrhage. The third mentions a lively insect, and with this song Wilson expects the patient to regain the power of motion. The fourth mentions a certain kind of buzzard that has white bars on its wings and flies so high that it cannot be seen by man. Wilson said, 'Each of these insects does his best, but it is the buzzard whose great power gives the final impetus and cures the sick man'" [Densmore 1952: 452].

Wilson, Jack
Paiute, *Basin*
See *Wovoka*.

Windigo
Also: *weendigo*
Ojibwa, *Canadian Eastern Woodlands*
A giant spirit who takes delight in eating human flesh. Shamans who acquire the powers of darkness through evil spirits such as *Missabe* are said to become *windigos*. This transformation can be so subtle that the shaman does not know it has happened until he eats raw meat or tastes blood. Women can also be *windigos*.

Wintca'cta wakan'
Assiniboin, *Plains*
Shamans who use spirit helpers to heal their patients; translates to "holy man." They are sought in the most serious cases of illness.

In addition to treating patients individually, these powerful shamans sometimes put several tents together to form a large lodge in which they heal all comers. Lowie [1910:45] provides one such account:

"On one occasion a woman with a crooked neck came in to be treated. She was laid on blankets near the fireplace. Four shamans stood around her. There were many men to sing and drum. These began to chant, beating their hand-drums. One shaman had a large knife. He made a feint at the woman's neck. As soon as he pulled back his knife, all the spectators shouted, 'Ho, ho, ho, ho!' this being a wish for success. The other three practitioners examined the neck. One of them prophesied as to the issue of the operation. A fire was built on one side of the lodge. After the third song, the operator wetted the edge of the knife with his lips, heated it at the fire, and then brought it down to the woman's neck. There was a general whoop. He began to cut. The blood came gushing forth. Then he removed the knife, having almost completely severed the patient's neck. The doctors raised the woman, made her stand up, turned her head backwards, walked her once around the lodge, and then laid her down at the former place. One of them left the tent, and brought back a bunch of sage-brush. The operator rubbed it around her neck, and handed it to the second shaman, who did the same and passed it to the third colleague. After the fourth shaman had gone through the same operation, the patient was made to sit up and was as well as ever. No trace of blood was visible. She danced around the circle once, then she went home."

Wisábaya
Paviotso, *Basin*
Rattle, such as that used by a shaman in doctoring patients. There are two kinds of shaman's rattles covered by this term. One is a jingling deer hooflet type. Fifty or more deer claws are used, depending on the number available; some rattles may contain only 15. A hole is made in the tip of each hooflet, and a short piece of buckskin thong is knotted at one end and put through the hole from the inside. The hooflet is then fastened by the thong to a willow or greasewood handle. The

claws dangle in a bunch an inch or two from the handle, which is usually 8 to 10 inches long.

The other rattle is made from the dried skin of a deer's ear, which is tanned and soaked in water, and the two edges are sewn together. It is then packed with sand to form a rounded shape and allowed to dry. When the sand is removed, an 8-inch handle of greasewood or willow is put through holes made in the center of the two pieces of skin. The handle projects an inch or less on one side of the rattle. It is fastened firmly in place with sinew. Small pebbles, usually gathered on an anthill, are put into the rattle, and the opening is closed.

Which type of rattle to use is determined by the shaman's power [Park 1938:33–34].

Wissler, Clark

Clark Wissler was born on a farm near Cambridge City, Indiana, on 18 September 1870. He received a Ph.D. in psychology from Columbia University in 1901. Although the Anthropology Department at Columbia was part of the Psychology Department until 1902 (when it became a separate department), Wissler took only three anthropology courses during his last year of graduate school, all taught by Franz Boas. Following his graduation, however, he eagerly pursued a career in anthropology, beginning at the American Museum of Natural History as an assistant to Boas. He remained at the museum until 1924, by which time he had long been the chairman of the Department of Anthropology. Under Boas, he did extensive fieldwork in the Plains area and came to know the Blackfoot well; they were the subject of his major works. Most of his Native American material was published before 1924, when he became a professor of anthropology at Yale University, where he remained until his retirement in 1940. There his interests turned to theoretical matters, and he was the first anthropologist to define culture as learned behavior and to describe it as a complex of ideas. He was also the innovator of the culture area concept in anthropology. He died in New York City on 25 August 1947.

Witapanóxwe

Delaware, *Northeast*

Translates to "Walks with Daylight"; it is the Delaware (or Lenni Lenape) name for James C.

Webber, who, during the late 1920s and early 1930s, cooperated with the University of Pennsylvania in recording his extensive traditional medicine practice. He describes his visionary experiences through which he obtained his healing powers as follows:

"'I was delirious the greater part of the time for seven days. . . . It was at this time a vision came to me and accompanied me around the world. At times it seemed as though we were not on earth. This man spoke the Delaware language and he showed me many of the Indian ceremonies, some of which I had never seen or heard before. He showed me men and women who had departed this life many years before, and told me their names. . . . It was here that I fully realized that the teachings of my mother had been so deeply impressed on my mind. This experience turned me back to the Delaware Big House.

"'So it happened that years later . . . these same strange visions came and spoke to me from mid-sky and gave me a song. They seemed to be four in number and were not earthly persons, but belonged to the sky. It was then they came to tell me what my mission on earth was to be. Since everyone has a purpose in life, mine was to heal the sick. . . . I am confident that my dream-vision power will bring me success throughout life since the Creator does not abandon his children to whom He had entrusted such gifts. By this I have learned to work out my own salvation, knowing that the Indian wholly depends upon the talent allotted to him by the Creator. These experiences fully qualify me to lead in the Big House if I choose to do so. My brothers do not know this but they suspect that I have a vision to relate. Some day they may have the pleasure of hearing it when the opportunity offers'" [Witapanóxwe in Tantaquidgeon 1942:6–7].

In addition to healing powers obtained through his dream visions, Witapanóxwe was an adept herbalist. He was taught the traditional art of compounding and administering herbal remedies by his mother, herself a recognized herbalist and elder. In gathering a plant to be used in healing, a special procedure was followed:

"After coming upon the first plant of the variety required, he does not gather it but performs a ritual to appease the Spirit of the plant. A small hole is dug towards the east near its base and a small quantity of native tobacco *(Nicotiana rustica)* placed within. The herbalist then lights his pipe and smokes, meanwhile making the following appeal to the Creator and to the Spiritual forces which govern vegetation. The songs and properties are regarded as personal property and the accompanying medicine-gather prayer of Witapanóxwe is regarded as typical:

"'Grandfather, I come now for medical treatment. Your grandson (name of patient) needs your aid. He is giving you a smoke-offering here of tobacco. He implores you that he will get well because he, your child, is pitiful. And I myself earnestly pray that you take pity on him the sick one, I wish for him to get well forever of that which is causing pain in his body. For with you alone rests the spiritual power sufficient to bless anyone with, and hear now him our Grandfather tobacco, I beg of him that he will help me when we plead with earnest heart that you will take pity on your grandchild and that you will accept this appeal. I am thankful Grandfather, also Creator, that you grant our appeal this day for all that we ask. I am thankful, Grandfather. That is enough for this time.'" [Witapanóxwe in Tantaquidgeon 1942:8–9].

Witcasta wakan
Dakota, *Plains*

The term for shaman among the Canadian Dakota residing at Portage la Prairie and Griswold, Manitoba. Most of these shamans claim that before they were born they were with the *wakia* (Thunderers), traveling around with every thunderstorm looking for a place on earth to be born. Some report that they are warned that if they are born among the whites and do not do the *wakia*'s bidding, they will be killed by the vengeful *wakia*. Thus, they seek to be born among their own people so that they can follow the commands of the *wakia*. The *wakia* give such a person a sign when it is time to start his career as a shaman. When the sign comes, the shaman announces to all his people the messages given to him by the *wakia* before his birth.

In contrast to most shamans, who acquire their powers from helping spirits after birth, these shamans are imbued with power from the onset by the *wakia*. However, throughout life, they may acquire power from other *wakan* (holy) beings (spirits) such as the stone, spider, buffalo, turtle, and so forth. "In general, medicine powers acquired in the orthodox manner before birth remain with one during the greater portion of one's life and these are the most common, whereas those acquired from specific *wakan* beings such as we have mentioned, are specific and occasional" [Wallis 1919:325].

There is one account of a shaman receiving his curing abilities from the *wakia* during a Sun Dance around 1901. This man had a dream that he was to perform the Sun Dance. He then pledged to dance for two days and two nights and predicted that on the last night he would be visited by the *wakia*:

"They began the singing and he danced the first night. Early in the morning, he went to the ceremonial ground, dancing there all day and all night. The second day, at the time mentioned, there was a big thunderstorm. He stopped, took the sweat bath, and invited all of the men in the tipi to smoke with him. All went in and smoked with him. He said he had not given the sun dance because he wished to fight or to steal horses (as was often done), but was going to take care of all the children (meaning the sick ones in the camp), so that as long as he lived they should have plenty of meat; every man who went to hunt would obtain what he desired. After that he was one of the ablest medicine men in treating the sick" [unidentified informant in Wallis 1919:337].

Witceawa
Wailaki, *California*
Spirit. Spirits come to the Wailaki most often in unsolicited dreams [Loeb 1934a:76–77].

Wo
Tewa, *Southwest*
Medicinal herbs.

Wogey
Yurok, *Oregon Seaboard*
A class of spirit beings; the immortal beings who lived in the area before the Yurok came to live there. Among the Hupa, they are known as *kixunai;* the Karok refer to them as *ikhareyev* [Keeling 1992:19]. Often described as small human beings, these spirits took refuge in trees, rocks, springs, and other places upon the arrival of the Yurok. Their special gift to humans was that of healing. They are said to have "originated nearly every form of medicine making" [Keeling 1992:56].

Wonoyekw
Yurok, *Oregon Seaboard*
The trance states attained by *kegeyowor* (shamans; see *kegey*) during their rituals and vision quests; translates to "up in the middle of the sky." Most Yurok shamans are women [Buckley 1992:150].

A healer and holy man, Wovoka's 1889 vision led him to revive the Ghost Dance.

Wopila Ceremony
Lakota, *Plains*
A thank-you ceremony conducted after a healing ceremony in which the person treated gives thanks to the spirits and all the participants, including the shaman, for their assistance. Often the *wopila* is attached to the end of a healing ceremony such as the *yuwipi* (see entry). It always includes a feast. Any food may be served, but some shamans require more traditional foods such as pounded dry meat, corn, fried bread (fry bread), and a wild fruit pudding *(wojapi)* usually made from chokecherries. In cases of serious illness, a young puppy is sacrificed and made into a dog-meat soup that is served at the *wopila*. During the ceremony, the spirit of the puppy travels to seek the aid of other spirits in effecting a cure.

Wot
Wallawalla, *Plateau*
The traditional vision quest performed by Wanapam shamans seeking spirit helpers. They are solitary quests undertaken in the nearby mountains [Ruby and Brown 1989:20]. Relander [1956:41] translates this term to "spirit helper."

Wovoka
Paiute, *Basin*
Wovoka was born around 1856–1858 near Walker River in Mason Valley, Nevada. Later, he acquired the English name Jack Wilson. His father was a known "dreamer" who had supernatural powers. Around the mid-1880s, Wovoka became an active healer and weather prophet. On 1 January 1889, during a solar eclipse of the sun, Wovoka had a great vision, which caused him to found the Ghost Dance movement of the 1890s. He became a leading prophet and performed many miracles. His father had followed the teachings of one of the founding prophets of the initial 1870s Ghost Dance, so Wovoka was well versed in the dance. Many knew of him simply as the prophet from Walker Lake. His fame spread rapidly, and within two years he had spread his teachings to the Bannock, Shoshoni, Arapaho, Crow, Cheyenne, Caddo, Pawnee, Kiowa, Comanche, Hualapai,

and Sioux. It was among the Minneconjou Sioux, who had gathered to perform the dance, that the massacre of Wounded Knee (inappropriately termed "The Last Indian War") occurred on 29 December 1890, effectively ending the Ghost Dance movement for all nations.

Thereafter, Wovoka continued to serve his people as a holy man and a healer. He was best known for his ability to heal gunshot wounds. He died on 20 September 1932 [Moses 1985].

Wúsosig
Pima, *Southwest*

Cure; the literal meaning is "the blowing." It comes from the Pima verb *wúsot*, "to blow," which refers to animate blowing only [Bahr 1977].

Wütádu
Paviotso, *Basin*

A shaman's assistant known as the dancer. The dancer is always a woman who is said to be virtuous; she may be either single or married. During healing ceremonies, she carries a bowl-shaped basket, called a *wadákati*, that contains pebbles or beads. This basket is jerked up and down in time to the dance step in front of the patient's body. Also, the dancer follows the shaman at a distance of 4 to 5 feet when he gets up and dances around the fire in a counterclockwise direction. She is paid for her services. Not all shamans employ dancers [Park 1938:51].

Another type of ceremonial assistant is the interpreter or talker. See *poínaba* for details.

Xàexae
Nootsack, *Northwest Coast*
This term, which also appears in other closely related Salish languages, "refers not only to the supernatural itself but also to the distinguishing characteristics of the relationship between the everyday world and the supernatural" [Amoss 1978:42].

Xapáaliia
Crow, *Plains*
Objects that are imbued with sacred power or medicine [Frey 1987:61], including all the items contained in a shaman's medicine bag, such as sacred stones, eagle feathers, otter skins, and other such items used in doctoring the ill. Objects obtained from spirits during vision quests are also included in this category. All such objects serve as a channel through which power flows.

Xatáùl
Navajo, *Southwest*
Chant; used to refer only to those ceremonies in which songs are accompanied by rattles [Haile 1938:639]. In actual usage, the term is usually translated to "way." Thus, the Night chant is usually referred to as Nightway, the Enemy chant as Enemyway, and so forth. Within a single chantway ritual there may be a series of songs that constitutes a smaller ritual. For example, most of the chantways follow a general pattern that includes "its evil or misfortune–way" and "its blessingway." These two parts graphically illustrate the entire process of restoration. In the misfortune part, the ceremonial recalls what the patient can expect if the hold of the disease-causing factor is not released. In the blessing part, the patient is assured that this hold has been removed and that the disease-causing factor has no more claims upon the patient.

In holyway ritual, which most chantways observe, it appears sufficient to designate a set of songs as the misfortune part or way. The same may be done in chantways observing the ghostway ritual, so that the ghostway misfortune part really refers to this particular set of songs in that ritual. In either ritual, the blessing part must follow, because this set of songs is usually borrowed from Blessingway. If the songs are borrowed from this rite, they are also made to correct omissions and errors made during the course of a ceremonial and thus render it effective. If Blessingway songs have not been employed in the blessing part of the ceremonial, they must be added, either immediately after the close of a ceremonial or sometime later. This ensures correction of any errors or omissions. This rite, therefore, is in supreme control of every chantway and ceremonial. It does not call upon a chantway ceremonial for correction but corrects itself in Blessingway's blessing part, a special set of songs set apart for that purpose [Haile 1938: 650–651].

Xelxalelkt
Twana, *Northwest Coast*
A powerful shaman from the Skokomish branch who died about 1920. His English name was Duke Williams. His power came from the cougar, a powerful healing spirit, and also from a fiery-eyed, shape-changing, powerful spirit called *áyahos.*

Xi
Biloxi, Ofo, *Southeast*
The supernatural aspect of power; translates to "mysterious." It is the equivalent of the widely used concept of *orenda* (see entry) found among the Iroquois [Dorsey and Swanton 1912:221].

Hastin-Acani-Badanie, a medicine man from St. Michaels, Arizona, administers a female shooting chant to a mother and baby for better health. Xatáùl is used to refer only to those ceremonies in which the songs are accompanied by rattles.

Xlubak yomta
Miwok, *California*
See *yomta*.

Xop
Winnebago, *Midwest*
The awe-inspiring quality of the sacred; corresponds to the Omaha word *xube* (see entry). It is what German theologian Rudolf Otto termed the "numinous," the *mysterium tremendum et fascinans*, which is the emotional, ineffable basis for religion.

Winnebago shamans are often seen as the reincarnation of powerful shamans who received permission from the grandfathers to return to earth and be reborn. Such a shaman, "having entered into direct communication with spirits who control power, receives some of that power for himself. Just as the spirits are able to cure, to take life, and to give it, so, too, can the new shaman. When he returns to earth, we note something that serves to focus our understanding of the Winnebago notion of power. The shaman acts as a *conduit* for the power. He is a mediator between the world of the spirits and the world of men, and it is through him that those who are in great need of blessing—the sick—receive it" [DeMallie and Lavenda 1977: 163].

Xqpini
Mandan, *Plains*
The supernatural aspect of power; translates to "mysterious." It is the equivalent of the widely used concept of *orenda* (see entry) found among the Iroquois.

Xube
Ponca, Omaha, *Plains*
Also: *xúbe* [Howard 1965:99]; *qube* [Lowie 1922: 315]; *qúbe* [Dorsey 1890:468]. The manifestation of supernatural power, or mysteriousness, in objects. From this concept comes the words *uqube*, the power of animate objects, and *waqube*, the power of inanimate objects [Dorsey 1894:367], such as the feathers used in peyote rituals.

Xube is used in various ways. It can mean supernatural power, a helping spirit, or a shaman. "*Xúbe* could also be bought and sold in the form of medicine packets" [Howard 1965:99].

Xudab
Coast Salish, *Northwest Coast*
H. K. Haeberlin [1918] defines this term as "the spirit-power which enables a man to become a shaman and visit the underworld" [Waterman 1930a:304]. Waterman [1930a:305], however, translates it to "spirit-helper," meaning also the spirit help that enables a shaman to go to the underworld in the Spirit Canoe Ceremony. Waterman [1930b:553] also equates this term with Haeberlin's *sbatatdaq* (see entry).

Xupá
Hidatsa, *Plains*
Also: *hopá*. The supernatural aspect of power. Translates to "to be mysterious; sacred; to have curative powers; to possess a charm; incomprehensible; spiritual. Same as Dakota *wakan* (see entry), but signifies also the power of curing diseases" [Matthews 1877:149]. It is the equivalent of the widely used concept of *orenda* (see entry) found among the Iroquois. This term also appears as *maxupá*. The initial *ma* in Hidatsa is the generic nominal prefix. The noun is rendered as "medicine, charm, spell." As such, *xp* is the consonantal complex to be used for comparative purposes [Lowie 1922:315].

Yabaicini
Keres, *Southwest*

At Acoma Pueblo, the altar that is set up during the curing ceremonies of the Fire and Flint medicine societies. Among the eastern Keres, however, this word refers to the sand-painting that the medicine societies outline on the floor during their healing ceremonies [White 1932:109].

Yáika
Paviotso, *Basin*

The shamanic state of consciousness or trance that a shaman enters into during a healing ceremony [Park 1938:53].

Yamomk
Mojave, *Southwest*

Translates to "insanity"; associated with a speech disturbance called *yavook*, which one informant described as "they talk, but do not know what they are talking about" [Devereux 1961:33]. In cases of serious mental disorders, one requests a healing from a shaman, and the patient is "treated in the usual shamanistic way: by singing songs or, if the traditional songs are no longer remembered, by reciting the appropriate portion of the Creation myth; by massage; by blowing upon the patient; by the use of saliva; by food taboos and baths; and by other magical means" [Devereux 1961:34].

Yantcha
Wallawalla, *Plateau*

Describes "a leader with strong spiritual qualifications" [Ruby and Brown 1989:19]. It is a Wanapam term that is used for both diviners and shamans.

Yapota
Zuni, *Southwest*

See *mile*.

Yatckinolos
Wailaki, *California*

Healing as performed by the *nachulna*, a class of Kato shamans that treats severe cases of illness by impersonating certain powerful spirit beings; translates to "bring-him-down."

Yaya
Keres, *Southwest*

A type of fetish used at Sia Pueblo during healing and other ceremonies. *Yaya* translates to "mother"; the proper name of the fetish is *Iärriko* [Stevenson 1894:40]. It is "an ear of corn which may be any color but must be symmetrically perfect, and not a grain must be missing. Eagle and parrot plumes are placed in pyramidal form around the corn. In order that the center feathers may be sufficiently long they are each attached to a very delicate splint. The base of this pyramid is formed of splints woven together with native cotton cord and ornamented at the top with shells and precious beads. A pad of native cotton is attached to the lower end of the corn. When the ya'ya is completed there is no evidence of the corn, which is renewed every four years when the old corn is planted.... The I'ärriko is the Sia's supreme idol" [Stevenson 1894:40].

The *yaya* are made only by shamans, who follow a prescribed ritual in their assembly. They are a common feature in the various altar displays of the different religious societies. "The ya'ya are placed immediately in front of the altar upon a parallelogram of meal, which is always drawn at the base of the altars, and is emblematic of seats for the ya'ya" [Stevenson 1894:76]. Each *yaya* is considered to be a sacred item and normally has great intrinsic value, mainly because of the parrot feathers, which must be obtained in trade from Mexico.

When stored, the "ya'ya are (individually) wrapped first with a piece of soft cloth, then with buckskin, and finally with another cloth; slender splints are placed around this outer covering and a long buckskin string secures the packages" [Stevenson 1894:76].

Yehasuri
Catawba, *Southeast*

Leprechaunlike spirits that are referred to as "wild Indians." They are said to live in the ground in the woods. They have a propensity for kidnapping children, but they also play other tricks, such as coming and touching a baby's drying clothes during the night. For this reason, women rarely leave their laundry out on the clothesline to dry overnight. Another common trick is to plait the mane or tail of a horse. In rare instances, these spirits are said to teach one to doctor [Blumer 1985].

Yei
Navajo, *Southwest*

The holy people, a class of spirits ritually used in Navajo ceremonies. They appear both as costumed dancers, who embody the *yei*, and as figures drawn in sandpaintings. According to Toelken [1989:69]:

"During a healing ritual, for example, the patient is caused to walk around on the delicate sand painting of the *yei*, and through ritual is closely identified with each one and with the world of reality they live in. Psychologically, the patient is taken from his own context, the interior of his own hogan usually, and is described as standing on patterns, ledges, floating through the air with jewels, and other kinds of suggestive actions which bring the person simultaneously into two dimensions: this world and the 'other world' interpenetrate and reciprocate at the point of the ritual. The patient is made whole, it is hoped, partly by the application of medicines, and partly by the forced realization of a deeper relationship between the person and sacred forces than might be evident in everyday life."

Yek
Tlingit, *Northwest Coast*

Shamans' helping spirits. They most often appear in human or animal form and live in the surrounding forests, mountains, and water. *Yek* decorate all sorts of shamanic paraphernalia, such as masks, rattles, and charms. Because the *yek* have supernatural power, they enhance the spiritual potency of the objects on which they appear. This display of supernatural art ensures the success of the shaman's therapeutic rituals [Jonaitis 1983:43]. During the healing ceremony, the shaman normally becomes possessed by his helping spirit and takes on its personality.

The two most powerful animal helpers are the land otter and the octopus, or devilfish. Land otters appear more frequently on shamanic paraphernalia than any other animal. When a person dies by drowning, he doesn't really die but turns into a land otter that becomes a werewolflike creature bent on drowning other humans. These *yek* cause storms, avalanches, and the falling of trees in the natural world, and skin diseases, mental illnesses, and death among humans.

During a healing ceremony, the shaman's different *yek* are each represented by a carved mask. The shaman calls on the appropriate *yek* by putting on the corresponding mask. Throughout a ceremony, many different masks may be used, each calling forth a different power controlled by the shaman. Only shamans are allowed to wear such masks.

Swanton [1908:451] takes a slightly broader view of this term, stating that it is "a name which

A shaman acquires power when wearing a sacred, carved mask. Pictured here is a small mask that barely covers the face; it is painted blue with thin red stripes running across the planes of the face.

is affixed to any specific personal manifestation of spiritual power."

Yellow Bear
Hopi, *Southwest*
A shaman who lived during the latter part of the nineteenth century. Following is a partial account of one of his healing ceremonies conducted in 1894 and reported by the patient:

"He then drew from his pouch an irregular shaped lump of quartz crystal, about the size of a walnut, retaining it in his hand. 'Now,' said he to me, 'take off your shirt and sit up and I will try to see what makes you ill.' Taking the crystal between finger and thumb, sometimes one hand sometimes the other, he placed it close to his eye and looked intently at me. Then he would hold the

The ivory figure depicts a shaman as indicated by the long braided hair and crown. In his arms and between his legs the shaman holds an octopus, a spirit helper.

crystal at arm's length toward me. Then he would bend over so as to bring the crystal close to me, and thus he swayed back and forth, in silence, occasionally making passes with his arms to and fro and toward me, for about four or five minutes. Suddenly he reached over me and pressed the crystal against my right breast, and just upon the region of a quite severe pain, which I had probably described to him, but whether or not, he located the seat of the pain exactly.

"He at once put the crystal in his pouch without a word, and told me to lie down again, and, after I had done so, he took up the pretty green knife (a three-inch, laurel-leaf-shaped, pale green stone) and began sawing the skin up and down, i.e. lengthwise, over the spot where he had set the crystal. It was a mere scarification, just enough to draw blood, which, being effected, he put the knife back in his pouch and sipped a little of the charm water (water into which an herb had been sprinkled). He then bent over me, and, placing his lips against the wound, he exhaled twice upon it, and the effect was to send an icy chill through me from head to foot. After each exhalation he raised himself on his knees and breathed ostentatiously away from me; he again bent over me, and, placing his lips again on the wound, he inhaled twice, no marked sensation following these inhalations. But after the second time he carried my left hand to his mouth, and spat into my palm an abominable-looking, arrow-shaped, headless sort of a centipede. It was about an inch and a quarter long; it was of a dark-brown color and seemed to be covered with a viscid substance; it had no head that I could make out, but its legs certainly moved, and it seemed to be a living insect. 'This,' said Yellow Bear, 'is the sorcerer's arrow.'

"Yellow Bear only permitted me to look at it briefly because it must instantly be carried forth to the cliff edge and there exorcised. On coming in again, he made me drink part of the charm water. . . . He then munched between his teeth the dried roots of herbs, spitting them into a bowl of cold water, and the compound was very fragrant, and somewhat mucilaginous. This he told me to drink from time to time for four days, which I did, and I really received much benefit, but whether

from the cold infusion or the scarification, I am still in doubt; at any rate, the pain in my chest ceased from that day" [Parsons 1939:717–718].

Yenaldlosi
Navajo, *Southwest*
Witches who travel at great speeds during the night in the form of animals, called were-animals. The tracks left by were-animals are generally larger than those of the real animal being guised. Kluckhohn [1944:26] found this word to be one of the most common colloquial terms for witch.

Yia kwiyó
Tewa, *Southwest*
The sacred Cornmother who gives power to the Bears (*Ke;* see entry), the shamans who specialize in healing. Each Bear has to have his own *yia kwiyó*, or he cannot become a healer. The sacred Cornmother is symbolized by a perfect ear of white corn that is decorated with strings of turquoise and soft eagle feathers. This ear of corn is treated in a sacred manner as a living entity—it is "fed" with white cornmeal, it is prayed to, and so forth. When it is not in use, it is kept in a reed container in the shaman's medicine bundle.

Yoi wai quiolit
Pomo, *California*
Outfit doctors. Southeastern Pomo term that translates to "rattle with doctor." Most of these shamans inherit their outfits through the family lineage [Loeb 1934a:126].

Yomi
Maidu, *California*
Sucking doctor. The root *yom-* signifies a healer among the Maidu and Wintun [Loeb 1934a:8]. According to one informant:

"The more orthodox way of becoming a shaman (*yomi*) was by meeting the semifabulous red-headed bird moloko (condor), which is said to be of the size and appearance of a turkey, and to live in the water. . . . The next autumn the man related his experience to the shaman who had saved him (from the moloko) and the latter said, 'I think we shall have to doctor you.' Messengers were sent to the medicine men of other villages, and on the appointed night they met in a house. The people attended. Each medicine man had a cocoon rattle which he struck against the left hand while all sang, assisted by some of the young men, who sang and struck two clam shells together. After a while they danced round the fire, and the novice danced in his place between two shamans, each of whom held one of his arms. Later in the night one of the old medicine men sucked blood from the novice's forehead.

"The ceremony continued five nights, and during the time neither the novice, nor the medicine men, nor the young men who assisted in the singing, ate anything except acorn mush, pinole, and bread. At some time during the course of the ceremony one of the old shamans 'shot' a recent initiate. The two stood on opposite sides of the fire, crouching, facing each other, and singing. The young man slowly crept toward the fire. Suddenly he fell backward. The old shaman had shot him with his 'poison,' that is, with the disease which he could magically project through space and into the body of his victims. He lay there feigning death for a time, then rose and pretended to vomit up something of the appearance of an elongated pebble. Sometimes he could not bring it up and the old man then sucked it out" [Curtis in Loeb 1934b:160].

This shooting of the novice shaman as a death and resurrection initiation bears a striking resemblance to the *Midewiwin* (see entry) cult of the central Algonquin and southern Siouan cultures. In the Maidu case, the novice is considered a sucking doctor only if he can spit up the pain that was shot into him. If the pain has to be sucked out, the young man is rejected for the profession.

Either a man or a woman can become a *yomi*. Usually, they acquire only a single helping spirit, frequently that of the rattlesnake. From then on, they are not allowed to eat the flesh of whatever animal spirit aided them. Sucking doctors wear porcupine quills in their noses. Among the novices at Chico, these quills are inserted into their noses during initiation. If they can remove the quills without help, they become *yomi*.

During a healing ceremony, the *yomi* eats no salt or meat. He wears a hairnet with various kinds of feathers in it. Objects that are sucked from the patient's body are either burned or buried. At the end of the healing, the *yomi* "smokes" the patient using his stone pipe. He is paid for his services only if the patient recovers [Loeb 1934b:160–162].

Among the Yuba River Maidu, the term *yom* is used for the sucking doctor; among the Sacramento Maidu, the term is *yomuse*. "The yom diagnosed by feeling, putting hot ashes on the patient's hands and feeling out the location of the disease. Then the 'pain' was sucked out" [Loeb 1934b:180]. According to Loeb, the *yom* "was definitely not in contact with the spirit world and had no guardian spirit." He was born with his abilities, which were revealed later on in life. A *yom* can also be an *oye* (singing doctor), the latter being in possession of a helping spirit. However, a woman cannot become an *oye*, because women cannot control spirits [Loeb 1934b:180]. They do, however, become sucking doctors.

Yomta
Pomo, Miwok, Maidu, Wintu, *California*

All kinds of doctoring, whether dancing, singing, or sucking. The word *yomta* also indicates a member of the secret Kuksu cult among the Coast Central Pomo, and the head of this secret society among the Eastern Pomo. The root *yom* signifies a doctor among the Maidu and Wintu [Loeb 1934a:8].

Among the Lake Miwok, sucking doctors are called *Xlubak yomta* and singing doctors are called *momai yomta*. The singing doctor among these people acquires his medicine and healing songs from his father or grandfather [Loeb 1934a:121]. Among the Patwin, male sucking doctors are called *eye yomta*, and the females are *sutuku yomta*.

Yomto
Wappo, *California*

Shaman. Among the Wappo, the sucking doctor is called *yomto komutco*, and the dream doctor is called *yomto hintcome*. For healing purposes, the dream doctor usually diagnoses the patient first. He usually sings and gives medicines to the patient. Dream doctors obtain their powers by dreaming of a spirit, which then becomes the source of their healing abilities. Sucking doctors, in contrast, obtain their power from a spirit who appears during a vision while awake. When this spirit appears, if the person begins to bleed from the mouth and nose, it is taken as a sign that this person is to become a sucking doctor. Both men and women become sucking doctors [Loeb 1934a:108].

Youlápxda
Takelma, *Oregon Seaboard*
Shaman's helping spirit, which, as a rule, is an animal spirit or natural objects and forces [Sapir 1907:41]. See *goyò* for details.

Yukbe
Maidu, *California*
The chief doctor among the Northwest Hill Maidu. He is the head of the *yeponi* (members of their secret society) and is chosen from the ranks of the *oye* (dream doctors; see entry). He has a small ceremonial house of his own and uses an interpreter, called *peheipe*, during his rituals to translate the special spirit language he uses. These shamans speak to their spirits rather than being possessed by the spirits and having the spirits speak through them. They use tobacco smoke in calling forth their spirits. Singers are also used, and during the ritual, they beat on baskets with their hands while singing. In addition to questioning their spirits concerning illnesses, these shamans ask questions about warfare, hunting, and other concerns.

The *yukbe* rule the village in conjunction with an elected elder, who is also a *yeponi* but not a shaman. The *yukbe* is never a sucking doctor. He obtains his powers through dreams [Loeb 1934b: 163].

Among the Yuba River Maidu, the *yukbe* is called *kakinpe*. His function is the same as that among the Northwest Hill Maidu, except that he lives in the community ceremonial house rather

than having his own. Of his activities, Loeb [1934b:181] reports:

"The medium shook his cocoon rattle (sokot) and sang for about an hour. Then one spirit after another arrived, climbed the center pole, and, from the top, spoke to the doctor telling him how to doctor, whether certain sick people would survive and giving information about things happening at a distance. Sometimes one of these spirits doctored a sick person present without the doctor laying hands on the invalid. The spirit cured by singing and rattling from his position on top of the pole."

Yuko
Caddo, *Plains*
Also: *yuku, yoko*. Wound doctor [Parsons 1941:34]. See *konah* for details.

Yuwadab
Twana, *Northwest Coast*
The healing activity of a Skokomish shaman. The derivative *syuwadab* means "power for curing." This power comes to the shaman through either inheritance or vision questing, the latter being the most common. In the case of inheritance, the power is always inherited from a kinsman. Usually the recipient falls ill, and the services of another shaman are required to control the new power, which is considered potentially harmful on one's first encounter with it. According to Elmendorf [1970:155]:

"At times a spirit granting shaman power appeared to a human seeker under fearsome aspects: rushing down a mountain gully on a bloody freshet, roaring and wallowing in a pool of bloody froth, rushing through the night with blazing eyes and fangs agape, etc. If the seeker showed fear at such an apparition, particularly if he fled from it, the rejected spirit might blast . . . him with projected shaman power. This produced a condition . . . in which the seeker either succumbed on the spot, or after his return home went into convulsions and died with contorted limbs, unless a treating shaman could be summoned quickly."

Power received in a vision quest is, therefore, power directly imbued into the individual's body. There are accounts among the Skokomish of shamans who return from their vision quests with this newly acquired power and break rocks or twist the limbs of trees simply by gazing at them, exerting a force called by them the "magical power of eye."

Yuwipi
Lakota, *Plains*

The most powerful healing ceremony currently conducted by Lakota shamans; translates to "they wrap him up." It is performed only by advanced shamans. The ceremony is a derivation of the Shaking Tent Ceremony (see entry). It is usually conducted in one room of a house that has been totally darkened. The shaman's hands are bound together behind his back, and he is then enveloped in a blanket, usually a star quilt, that is tied round and round so that he looks like a mummy. The shaman is then laid face down on a bed of fresh sage (in winter, stored sage is used). During the ceremony, the spirits free the shaman from his bonds.

When the spirits are called forth by the shaman, they appear in the darkened room as tiny flashes of blue light. Often one can hear an eagle flying about the room or feel its wings, as well as hear rattles flying about and an eagle-bone whistle being blown. Sometimes the rattles hit the floor or ceiling violently sending off flashes of bluish light as they land. Thus, this is a tumultuous ceremony, and first-time participants are often scared by all the spirit activity going on. For example, the spirits break any glass or other reflective surface in the room, so participants must remove eyeglasses if they are wearing them. Exposed glassware is protected from breakage by placing sage on it.

At one point in the ceremony, the person being healed must stand and state what is needed from the spirits—that is, why the spirits have been called forth. The spirits then proceed to doctor the person by touching him or her. Depending on the seriousness of the illness, up to four nights of doctoring are needed.

In addition to healing, the *yuwipi* ceremony is used for many other purposes, such as finding lost objects or persons, calling forth the spirits of deceased relatives, and predicting the future.

The earliest known "*yuwipi*" man is Old Man Chips (see Horn Chips).

Zemaheonevsz

Cheyenne, *Plains*

Plural: *zemaheonevesso*. Shaman; translates to "the mysterious one" [Schlesier 1987:14]. Another term is *maheonhetan* (see entry), which refers to shamans who have also served as priests in one of the great ceremonials.

Zhiishiigwan

Ojibwa, *Canadian Eastern Woodlands*

Rattle. It comes from *zhiishiigwag*, meaning "rattlesnake." One of the more interesting forms of rattle is the doctor's rattle—a small, double-headed drum containing buckshot [Vennum 1982:37]. Such rattles, imbued with supernatural power, are used by shamans during their healing ceremonies.

This term was adopted by the French early on to refer to any Native American rattle. For instance, "Maximilian Neuwied refers to the Assiniboin rattle as 'schischikue,' and Catlin sketched two Siouan rawhide rattles that he calls 'She-she-quois'" [Vennum 1982:37].

Bibliography

Aberle, David F.
1966 "Religio-Magical Phenomena and Power, Prediction, and Control." *Southwestern Journal of Anthropology* 22(3):221–230.

Achterberg, Jeanne
1987 "The Shaman: Master Healer in the Imaginary Realm. " In *Shamanism: An Expanded View of Reality*, edited by Shirley Nicholson. 103–124. Wheaton, IL: Theosophical Publishing House.

Ackerknecht, Erwin H.
1942 "Problems of Primitive Medicine." *Bulletin of the History of Medicine* 11(5):503–521.

Aitken, Larry P., and Edwin W. Haller
1990 *Two Cultures Meet: Pathways for American Indians to Medicine.* Duluth: University of Minnesota Press.

Alexander, Hartley B.
1910 *The Religious Spirit of the American Indian.* Chicago: Open Court Publishing Company.

Alexander, W. D.
1899 *A Brief History of the Hawaiian People.* New York: American Book Company.

Allen, Marion V.
1982 *The Yana: An Indian Story.* Redding, CA: CP Printing and Publishing.

Almstedt, Ruth Farrell
1977 *Diegueño Curing Practices.* San Diego Museum Papers no. 10. San Diego, CA: San Diego Museum of Man.

Amoss, Pamela
1978 *Coast Salish Spirit Dancing: The Survival of an Ancient Religion.* Seattle: University of Washington Press.

Bahr, Donald
1977 "Breath in Shamanic Curing." In *Flowers of the Wind*, edited by Thomas C. Blackburn. 29–40. Socorro, NM: Ballena Press.

Balikci, Asen
1963 "Shamanistic Behavior among the Netsilik Eskimos." *Southwestern Journal of Anthropology* 19:380–396.

Barbeau, Marius
1958 *Medicine Men on the North Pacific Coast.* Ottawa: National Museum of Canada.

Barnett, H. G.
1957 *Indian Shakers: A Messianic Cult of the Pacific Northwest.* Carbondale: Southern Illinois University Press.

Barrett, S. A.
1911 "The Dream Dance of the Chippewa and Menominee Indians of Northern Wisconsin." *Bulletin of the Public Museum of the City of Milwaukee*, vol. 1, art. IV, 251–406.
1917a "Ceremonies of the Pomo Indians." *University of California Publications in American Archaeology and Ethnology* 12(10):307–441.
1917b "Pomo Bear Doctors." *University of California Publications in American Archaeology and Ethnology* 12(11):443–465.

Bates, Craig D.
1992 "Sierra Miwok Shamans, 1900–1990." In *California Indian Shamanism*, edited by Lowell John Bean. 97–115. Menlo Park, CA: Ballena Press.

Bean, Lowell J.
1972 *Mukat's People: The Cahuilla Indians of Southern California.* Berkeley: University of California Press.
1976 "California Indian Shamanism and Folk Curing." In *American Folk Medicine: A Symposium*, edited by Wayland D. Hand. 107–123. Berkeley: University of California Press.

Bean, Lowell J., and Katherine S. Saubel
1972 *Temalpaka: Cahuilla Indian Knowledge and Usage of Plants.* Banning, CA: Malki Museum.

Beck, Peggy V., and Anna L. Walters
1977 *The Sacred: Ways of Knowledge, Sources of Life.* Tsaile, AZ: Navajo Community College Press.

Biggar, H. P., ed.
1925 *The Works of Samuel de Champlain.* Toronto, Canada: The Champlain Society.

Birket-Smith, Kaj
1924 "Ethnography of the Egedesminde District." *Meddelelser om Grønland* 66:1–484.
1953 *The Chugach Eskimo.* Nationalmuseets Skrifter, Etnografisk Roekke, VI. København, Denmark: Nationalmuseets Publikationsfond.

Birket-Smith, Kaj, and Frederica de Laguna
1938 *The Eyak Indians of the Copper River Delta, Alaska.* Det Kgl. Danske Videnskabernes Selskab. Copenhagen, Denmark: Levin and Munksgaard.

Black, Mary B.
1977 "Ojibwa Power Belief System." In *The Anthropology of Power,* edited by Raymond D. Fogelson and Richard N. Adams. 141–151. New York: Academic Press.

Black Elk, Wallace and William S. Lyon
1990 *Black Elk: The Sacred Ways of a Lakota.* San Francisco: HarperCollins Publishers.

Blanchard, David
1982 "Who or What's a Witch? Iroquois Persons of Power." *American Indian Quarterly* 6(3, 4):218–237.

Blish, Helen H.
1926 "Ethical Conceptions of the Oglala Dakota." *University Studies* 26(3,4):79–123. University of Nebraska.
1934 "The Ceremony of the Sacred Bow of the Oglala Dakota." *American Anthropologist* 36:180–187.

Blumensohn, Jules
1933 "The Fast among North American Indians." *American Anthropologist* 35:451–462.

Blumer, Thomas J.
1985 "Wild Indians and the Devil: The Contemporary Catawba Indian Spirit World." *American Indian Quarterly* 9(2):149–168.

Boas, Franz
1897 "The Social Organization and the Secret Societies of the Kwakiutl Indians." In *Smithsonian Institution, Annual Report for the year ending 30 June 1895.* 311–738.
1916 "Tsimshian Mythology." In *Thirty-first Annual Report of the Bureau of American Ethnology.* 29–1037.
1918 *Kutenai Tales.* Bureau of American Ethnology, Bulletin 59.
1921 "Ethnology of the Kwakiutl." In *Thirty-fifth Annual Report of the Bureau of American Ethnology,* Part 1. 43–794.
1930 *The Religion of the Kwakiutl Indians, Parts 1 and 2.* Columbia University Contributions to Anthropology. New York: Columbia University Press.

Bolton, Herbert Eugene
1987 *The Hasinais: Southern Caddoans as Seen by the Earliest Europeans.* Norman: University of Oklahoma Press.

Boscana, Geronimo (Fray)
1970 "Chinigchinich: An Historical Account of the Origin, Customs, and Traditions of the Indians of Alta-California." In *Life in California,* edited by Alfred Robinson. 1–116. Santa Barbara, CA: Peregrine Publishers.

Bourguignon, E.
1979 *Psychological Anthropology: An Introduction to Human Nature and Cultural Differences.* New York: Holt, Rinehart and Winston.

Bourke, John G.
1892 "The Medicine-Men of the Apache." In *Ninth Annual Report of the Bureau of Ethnology.* 451–603.

Bowers, Alfred W.
1950 *Mandan Social and Ceremonial Organization.* Chicago: University of Chicago Press.
1965 *Hidatsa Social and Ceremonial Organization.* Bureau of American Ethnology, Bulletin 194.

Boyd, Doug
1974 *Rolling Thunder: A Personal Exploration into the Secret Healing Powers of an American Indian Medicine Man.* New York: Random House.
1994 *Mad Bear: Spirit, Healing, and the Sacred in the Life of a Native American Medicine Man.* New York: Simon and Schuster.

Broadbent, Sylvia M.
1964 *The Southern Sierra Miwok Language.* University of California Publications in Linguistics, no. 38.

Brodzky, Anne Trueblood, Rose Dansewich, and Nick Johnson (eds.)
1977 *Stones, Bones and Skin: Ritual and Shamanic Art.* Ontario, Canada: Society for Art Publications.

Brown, Joseph Epes
1977   "The Immediacy of Mythological Message: Native American Traditions." In *Native Religious Traditions*, edited by Earle H. Waugh and K. Dad Prithipaul. 101–116. Waterloo, Ontario: Wilfrid Laurier University Press.
1992   *Animals of the Soul: Sacred Animals of the Oglala Sioux*. Rockport, MA: Element.

Buckley, Thomas
1992   "Yurok Doctors and the Concept of 'Shamanism.'" In *California Indian Shamanism*, edited by Lowell John Bean. 117–161. Menlo Park, CA: Ballena Press.

Buechel, Rev. Eugene
1970   *Lakota-English Dictionary*. Pine Ridge, SD: Red Cloud Indian School.

Buhner, Stephen Harrod
1996 *Sacred Plant Medicine: Explorations in the Practice of Indigenous Herbalism*. Boulder: Roberts Rinehart Publishers.

Bunge, Robert
1987   "Concept of Ultimate Reality and Meaning of the Teton Sioux." *Ultimate Reality and Meaning* 10(2):83–100.

Bunzel, Ruth L.
1932   "Introduction to Zuñi Ceremonialism." In *Forty-seventh Annual Report of the Bureau of American Ethnology*. 467–544.

Burgesse, J. Allan
1944   "The Spirit Wigwam as Described by Tommie Moar, Pointe Bleue." *Primitive Man* 17(3-4):50–53.

Bushnell, David I. Jr.
1909   *The Choctaw of Bayou Lacomb, St. Tammany Parish, Louisiana*. Bureau of American Ethnology, Bulletin 48.

Capron, Louis
1953   "The Medicine Bundles of the Florida Seminole and the Green Corn Dance." In *Anthropological Papers, Numbers 33–42*, 159–210. Bureau of American Ethnology, Bulletin 151.

Carter, John G.
1938   "The Northern Arapaho Flat Pipe and the Ceremony of Covering the Pipe." In *Anthropological Papers, Numbers 1–6*, 69–102. Bureau of American Ethnology, Bulletin 119.

Casagrande, Joseph B.
1956   "The Ojibwa's Psychic Universe." *Tomorrow* 4(3):33–40.
1960   "John Mink, Ojibwa Informant." In *In the Company of Man*, edited by Joseph B. Casagrande. 467–488. New York: Harper and Brothers.

Castile, George Pierre
1985   *The Indians of Puget Sound: The Notebooks of Myron Eells*. Seattle: University of Washington Press.

Charlevoix, Pierre de
1761   *Journal of a Voyage to North-America*, 2 vols. London (reprinted 1966). Ann Arbor, MI: University Microfilms.

Clifton, James A.
1977   *The Prairie People: Continuity and Change in Potawatomi Indian Culture 1665–1965*. Lawrence: Regents Press of Kansas.

Cline, Walter
1938   "Religion and World View." In *The Sinkaietk or Southern Okanagon of Washington*, edited by Leslie Spier. 131–182. General Series in Anthropology, no. 6, Contributions from the Laboratory of Anthropology, 2. Menasha, WI: George Banta Publishing.

Coleman, Sister Bernard
1937 "The Religion of the Ojibwa of Northern Minnesota." *Primitive Man* 10(3, 4):33–57.

Collier, Donald
1944   "Conjuring among the Kiowa." *Primitive Man* 17(3, 4):45–49.

Cooper, John M.
1934   *The Northern Algonquian Supreme Being*. Anthropological Series no. 2. Washington, DC: Catholic University of America.
1936   *Notes on the Ethnology of the Otchipwe of Lake of the Woods and Rainy Lake*. Anthropological Series no. 3. Washington, DC: Catholic University of America.
1944   "The Shaking Tent Rite among Plains and Forest Algonquians." *Primitive Man* 17:60–84.
1957   *The Gros Ventres of Montana. Part II: Religion and Ritual*. Anthropological Series no. 16. Washington, DC: Catholic University of America Press.

Curtin, L. S. M.
1949   *By the Prophet of the Earth*. Santa Fe, NM: San Vicente Foundation.

Cushing, Frank Hamilton
1974   *Zuni Breadstuff.* Indian Notes and Mono-graphs, vol. 8 (reprint edition). New York: Museum of the American Indian, Heye Foundation.

DeMallie, Raymond J.
1984   *The Sixth Grandfather: Black Elk's Teachings Given to John G. Neihardt.* Lincoln: University of Nebraska Press.

DeMallie, Raymond J. Jr., and Robert H. Lavenda
1977   "*Wakan*: Plains Siouan Concepts of Power." In *The Anthropology of Power*, edited by Raymond D. Fogelson and Richard N. Adams. 153–165. New York: Academic Press.

Denig, Edwin Thompson
1930   "Indian Tribes of the Upper Missouri." In *Forty-sixth Annual Report of the Bureau of American Ethnology.* 375–628.
1933   "Of the Crow Nation." In *Anthropological Papers, Numbers 33–42,* 1–74. Bureau of American Ethnology, Bulletin 151.

Densmore, Frances
1910   *Chippewa Music.* Bureau of American Ethnology, Bulletin 45.
1918   *Teton Sioux Music.* Bureau of American Ethnology, Bulletin 61.
1939   *Nootka and Quileute Music.* Bureau of American Ethnology, Bulletin 124.
1952   "The Use of Music in the Treatment of the Sick by American Indians." In *Annual Report of the Smithsonian Institution Annual Report for 1952.* 439–458.

Devereux, George
1961   *Mohave Ethnopsychiatry and Suicide: The Psychiatric Knowledge and the Psychic Disturbances of an Indian Tribe.* Bureau of American Ethnology, Bulletin 175.

Dorsey, George
1902   "The Dwamish Indian spirit and its use." In *Free Museum of Science and Art,* Bulletin 3. 229–238. Philadelphia: University of Pennsylvania.

Dorsey, James Owen
1890   *The Ǫegiha Language.* Contributitions to North American Ethnology, vol. 6. Washington, DC: Department of the Interior.
1894   "A Study of Siouan Cults." In *Eleventh Annual Report of the Bureau of Ethnology.* 351–544.

Dorsey, James O., and John R. Swanton
1912   *A Dictionary of the Biloxi and Ofo Languages.* Bureau of American Ethnology, Bulletin 47.

Draper, Wm. R.
1946   *Indian Dances, Medicine Men, and Prophets.* Girard, KS: Haldeman-Julius Publications.

Drucker, Philip
1937   "The Tolowa and Their Southwest Oregon Kin." *University of California Publications in American Archaeology and Ethnology* 36(4):221–300.

DuBois, Constance Goddard
1908   "The Religion of the Luiseño Indians of Southern California." *University of California Publications in American Archaeology and Ethnology* 8(3):69–186.

Duff, Wilson
1952   *The Upper Stalo Indians of the Fraser Valley, British Columbia.* Anthropology in British Columbia, Memoir no. 1. Victoria: British Columbia Provincial Museum.

Edmonson, Munro S.
1958   *Status Terminology and the Social Structure of North American Indians.* Seattle: University of Washington Press.

Eliade, Mircea
1964   *Shamanism: Archaic Techniques of Ecstasy.* Bollingen Series 76. New York: Pantheon Books.

Elmendorf, William M.
1970   "Skokomish Sorcery, Ethics, and Society." In *Systems of North American Witchcraft*, edited by Deward E. Walker, Jr. 147–182. Moscow: University of Idaho.

Engelhardt, Fr. Zephyrin
1920   *San Diego Mission.* San Francisco: James Company.

Erdoes, Richard
1973   "My Travels with Medicine Man John Lame Deer." *Smithsonian* (May), 30–37.

Fairbanks, Charles H.
1979   "The Function of Black Drink among the Creeks." In *Black Drink*, edited by Charles M. Hudson. 120–149. Athens: University of Georgia Press.

Fenton, William N.
1941   "Masked Medicine Societies of the Iroquois." In *Smithsonian Institution Annual Report for 1940.* 397–429 and 25 plates.
1953   *The Iroquois Eagle Dance an Offshoot of the Calumet Dance.* Bureau of American Ethnology, Bulletin 156.

Fenton, William N., and Gertrude P. Kurath
1951   "The Feast of the Dead, or Ghost Dance at Six Nations Reserve, Canada." In *Symposium on Local Diversity in Iroquois Culture*. 139–180. Bureau of American Ethnology, Bulletin 149.

Feraca, Stephen E.
1963   *Wakinyan: Contemporary Teton Dakota Religion.* Museum of the Plains Indian, Studies in Plains Anthropology and History, Number 2. Browning, MT: Bureau of Indian Affairs.

Fletcher, Alice C., and Francis La Flesche
1911   "The Omaha Tribe." In *Twenty-seventh Annual Report of the Bureau of American Ethnology*. 27:17–672.

Fogelson, Raymond D.
1977   "Cherokee Notions of Power." In *The Anthropology of Power,* edited by Raymond D. Fogelson and Richard N. Adams. 185–194. New York: Academic Press.

Forde, C. Daryll
1931   "Ethnography of the Yuma Indians." *University of California Publications in American Archaeology and Ethnology* 28:83–278.

Frey, Rodney
1987   *The World of the Crow Indians.* Norman: University of Oklahoma Press.

Frisbie, Charlotte J.
1987   *Navajo Medicine Bundles or Jish: Acquisition, Transmission, and Disposition in the Past and Present.* Albuquerque: University of New Mexico Press.

Gardner, David
1973   *Choctaw-English Dictionary.* Oklahoma City: Oklahoma City Indian Calendar.

Garfield, V. E. et al.
1951   "The Tsimshian: their arts and music." In *American Ethnological Society,* Publication 18, 1–302.

Gifford, E. W.
1926a   "Clear Lake Pomo Society." *University of California Publications in American Archaeology and Ethnology* 18(3):287–390.
1926b   "Miwok Cults." *University of California Publications in American Archaeology and Ethnology* 18(3): 391–408.
1932   "The Southeastern Yavapai." *University of California Publications in American Archaeology and Ethnology* 29(3):177–252.

1933   "The Cocopa." *University of California Publications in American Archaeology and Ethnology* 31(5): 257–334.

Gill, Sam D.
1983   *Native American Traditions: Sources and Interpretations.* Belmont, CA: Wadsworth Publishing.
1987   *Native American Religious Action: A Performance Approach to Religion.* Columbia: University of South Carolina Press.

Gilmore, M. R.
1919   "Uses of Plants by Indians of the Missouri River Region." In *Thirty-third Annual Report of the Bureau of American Ethnology*. 43–154. (Pages in text refer to University of Nebraska reprint.)
1977   *Uses of Plants by Indians of the Missouri River Region.* Lincoln: University of Nebraska Press.

Goldman, Irving
1975   *The Mouth of Heaven: An Introduction to Kwakiutl Religious Thought.* New York: John Wiley and Sons.

Goodwin, Grenville
1938   "White Mountain Apache Religion." *American Anthropologist* 40:24–37.

Grant, Richard Earl
1982   "Tuuhikya: The Hopi Healer." *American Indian Quarterly* 6(3, 4):291–304.

Griffis, Joseph K.
1915   *Tahan: Out of Savagery into Civilization.* New York: George H. Doran.

Grim, John A.
1983   *The Shaman: Patterns of Siberian and Ojibway Healing.* Norman: University of Oklahoma Press.

Grinnell, George Bird
1923   *The Cheyenne Indians.* 2 vols. New Haven, CT: Yale University Press.

Guédon, Marie-Francoise
1984   "Tsimshian Shamanic Images." In *The Tsimshian,* edited by Margaret Seguin. 174–211. Vancouver: University of British Columbia Press.

Haeberlin, Herman K.
1918   "SBeTeTDA'Q, a Shamanistic Performance of the Coast Salish." *American Anthropologist* 20(3):249–257.

Hagar, Stansbury
1896   "Micmac Magic and Medicine." *Journal of American Folk-Lore* 9(34):170–177.

Haile, Bernard
1938   "Navaho Chantways and Ceremonials." *American Anthropologist* 40:639–652.

Hallowell, A. Irving
1942   *The Role of Conjuring in Saulteaux Society.* Publications of the Philadelphia Anthropological Society, 2.

Handelman, Don
1967   "The Development of a Washo Shaman." *Ethnology* 6(4):444–464.

Handy, E. S. Craighill, et al.
1974   *Ancient Hawaiian Civilization.* Rutland, VT: Charles E. Tuttle.

Harrington, M. R.
1921   *Religion and Ceremonies of the Lenape.* Indian Notes and Monographs, Heye Foundation. New York: Museum of the American Indian.

Hawkes, Ernest W.
1916   *The Labrador Eskimo.* Memoir 91, The Geological Survey of Canada, Anthropological Series no. 14.

Heusch, L. de
1962   "Cultes de Possession et Religions: Initiatiques de Salut en Afrique." In *Annales du Centre d'Etudes des Religions.* Brussels, Belgium: Université Libre de Bruxelles, Institut de Sociologie.

Hewitt, J. N. B.
1895   The Iroquoian Concept of the Soul." *Journal of American Folklore* 8(28):107–116.
1902   "Orenda and a Definition of Religion." *American Anthropologist* 4(3):33–45.
1918   "Seneca Fiction, Legends, and Myths. Part I." In *Thirty-Second Annual Report of the Bureau of American Ethnology.* 39–819.

Hilger, Sister M. Inez
1951   *Chippewa Child Life and Its Cultural Background.* Bureau of American Ethnology, Bulletin 146.

Hodge, Frederick Webb
1907   *Handbook of American Indians North of Mexico, Parts 1 and 2.* Bureau of American Ethnology, Bulletin 30.

Hoebel, E. Adamson
1935   "The Sun Dance of the Hekandika Shoshone." *American Anthropologist* 37(4):570–581.

Hoffman, W. J.
1888   "Pictography and Shamanistic Rites of the Ojibwa." *American Anthropologist* 1:209–229.
1891   "The Mide'wiwin or 'Grand Medicine Society' of the Ojibwa." In *Seventh Annual Report of the Bureau of Ethnology.* 143–300.
1896   "The Menomini Indians." In *Fourteenth Annual Report of the Bureau of Ethnology.* 3–328.

Holm, G.
1914   "Ethnological Sketch of the Angmagsalik Eskimo." *Meddelelser om Grønland* 39(1):1–147.

Holt, Catharine
1946   "Shasta Ethnography." *Anthropological Records* 3(4):299–349. Berkley: University of California Press.

Hooper, Lucile
1972   *The Cahuilla Indians.* Ramona, CA: Ballena Press.

Howard, James H.
1954   "The Dakota Heyóka Cult." *Scientific Monthly* 78:254–258.
1965   *The Ponca Tribe.* Bureau of American Ethnology, Bulletin 195.
1981   *Shawnee! The Ceremonialism of a Native Indian Tribe and Its Cultural Background.* Athens: Ohio University Press.

Hudson, Charles M.
1979   *Black Drink: A Native American Tea.* Athens: University of Georgia Press.

Hultkrantz, Åke
1953   *Conceptions of the Soul among North American Indians.* Stockholm: Ethnographical Museum of Sweden.
1967a   *The Religions of the American Indians.* Berkeley: University of California Press.
1967b   "Spirit Lodge, a North American Shamanistic Séance." In *Studies in Shamanism,* edited by Carl-Martin Edsman. 33–68. Stockholm: Almqvist and Wiksell.
1973   *Prairie and Plains Indians.* Leiden, Netherlands: E. J. Brill.
1983   "Water Spirits: The Elders of the Fish in Aboriginal North America." *American Indian Quarterly* 7(3):3–22.

1986 "The Peril of Visions: Changes of Vision Patterns among the Wind River Shoshoni." *History of Religions* 26(1):34–46.
1987 *Native Religions of North America.* San Francisco: Harper and Row.
1992 *Shamanic Healing and Ritual Drama: Health and Medicine in Native North American Religious Traditions.* New York: Crossroads.

Hurt, Wesley R.
1960 "A Yuwipi Ceremony at Pine Ridge." *Plains Anthropologist* 5(10):48–52.

Jarvis, Samuel Farmar
1820 *A Discourse on the Religion of the Indian Tribes of North America.* New York: C. S. Van Winkle.

Jenness, Diamond
1922 "The Life of the Copper Eskimos." *Report of the Canadian Arctic Expedition, 1913–18,* vol. 12.
1943 "The Carrier Indians of the Bulkley River: Their Social and Religious Life." In *Anthrological Papers, Numbers 19–26,* 469–586. Bureau of American Ethnology, Bulletin 133.
1955 *The Faith of a Coast Salish Indian.* Anthropology in British Columbia, Memoir no. 3. Victoria: British Columbia Provincial Museum.
1963 *The Indians of Canada* (sixth edition). National Museum of Canada, Bulletin 65, Anthropological Series No. 15.

Jilek, Wolfgang G.
1981 "Anomic Depression, Alcoholism and a Culture-Congenial Indian Response." *Journal of Studies on Alcoholism,* Suppl. 9:159–170.
1982a "Altered States of Consciousness in North American Indian Ceremonials." *Ethos* 10(4):326–343.
1982b *Indian Healing: Shamanic Ceremonialism in the Pacific Northwest Today.* Surrey, Canada: Hancock House Publishers.

Johnson, Frederick
1943 "Notes on Micmac Shamanism." *Primitive Man* 16(3, 4):53–80.

Johnston, Basil
1982 *Ojibway Ceremonies.* Toronto: McClelland and Stewart.

Jonaitis, Aldona
1983 "Liminality and Incorporation in the Art of the Tlingit Shaman." *American Indian Quarterly* 7(3):41–68.

Jones, David E.
1972 *Sanapia: Comanche Medicine Woman.* New York: Holt, Rinehart and Winston.

Jones, Peter
1861 *History of the Ojebway Indians.* London: A. W. Bennett.

JR
1897–1905 *The Jesuit Relations and Allied Documents, Travels and Explorations of the Jesuit Missionaries in New France, 1610–1791,* edited by Reuben Gold Thwaites. 76 vols. Cleveland, OH: Burrows Brothers.

Keeling, Richard
1992 *Cry for Luck: Sacred Song and Speech among the Yurok, Hupa, and Karok Indians of Northwestern California.* Berkeley: University of California Press.

Kelly, Isabel T.
1939 *Southern Paiute Shamanism.* University of California Anthropological Records, vol. 2, no. 4. Berkeley: University of California Press.

Kemnitzer, Luis S.
1969 "Yuwipi." *Pine Ridge Research Bulletin* 10:26–33.
1970 "The Cultural Provenience of Objects Used in Yuwipi: A Modern Teton Dakota Healing Ritual." *Ethnos* 35:40–75.
1976 "Structure, Content, and Cultural Meaning of Yuwipi: A Modern Lakota Healing Ritual." *American Ethnologist* 3(1):261–280.

Kenton, Edna
1927 *The Indians of North America.* 2 vols. New York: Harcourt, Brace.

Kilpatrick, Jack Frederick, and Anna Gritts Kilpatrick
1965 *Walk in Your Soul: Love Incantations of the Oklahoma Cherokees.* Dallas, TX: Southern Methodist University Press.
1967a "Muskogean Charm Songs among the Oklahoma Cherokees." *Smithsonian Contributions to Anthropology* 2(3):29–40.
1967b *Run toward the Nightland: Magic of the Oklahoma Cherokees.* Dallas, TX: Southern Methodist University Press.
1970 "Notebook of a Cherokee Shaman." *Smithsonian Contributions to Anthropology* 2(6):83–125.

Kluckhohn, Clyde
1944 *Navaho Witchcraft.* Boston: Beacon Press.

Kniffen, Fred, Gordon MacGregor, Robert McKennan, Scudder Mekeel, and Maurice Mook
1935   *Walapai Ethnography.* Memoirs of the American Anthropological Society, no. 42.

Koppert, Vincent A.
1930   *Contributions to Clayoquot Ethnology.* Anthropological Series no. 1. Washington, DC: Catholic University of America.

Kroeber, A. L.
1907   "The Arapaho. Part IV. Religion." *Bulletin of the American Museum of Natural History* 28(4):279–454.
1925   *Handbook of the Indians of California.* Bureau of American Ethnology, Bulletin 78.
1940   "Psychosis or Social Sanction." *Character and Personality* 8(3):204–215.

La Flesche, Francis
1905   *Who Was the Medicine Man?* Hampton, VA: Hampton Institute Press.
1921   "The Osage Tribe." In *Thirty-sixth Annual Report of the Bureau of American Ethnology.* 37–604.
1932   *A Dictionary of the Osage Language.* Bureau of American Ethnology, Bulletin 109.

Lafitau, Joseph
1974   *Manners and Customs of the American Indian as Compared with the Customs of Primitive Times*, edited by William Fenton. Toronto: Champlain Society.

Lahontan, Baron
1703   *New Voyages to North-America*, vol. 2. London. (Edited and reissued by Reuben Gold Thwaites, 2 vols., in 1905.)

Lambert, R. S.
1956   "The Shaking Tent." *Tomorrow* 4(3):113–129.

Lame Deer, John Fire, and Richard Erdoes
1972   *Lame Deer: Seeker of Visions.* New York: Simon and Schuster.

Landes, Ruth
1968   *Ojibwa Religion and the Midéwiwin.* Madison: The University of Wisconsin Press.

Lantis, Margaret
1950   "The Religion of the Eskimos." In *Forgotten Religions*, edited by Vergilius Ferm. 311–339. New York: Philosophical Library.

Laski, Vera
1958   *Seeking Life.* Philadelphia: American Folklore Society.

Latta, Frank
1949   *Handbook of the Yokuts Indians.* Oildale, CA: Bear State Books.

Leeuw, G. van der
1933   *Phänomenologie der Religion.* Tübingen: J. C. B. Mohr (Paul Siebeck).

Lewis, I. M.
1971   *Ecstatic Religion: An Anthropological Study of Spirit Possession and Shamanism.* Harmondsworth, UK: Penguin.

Lewis, T. H.
1980a   "The Changing Practice of the Oglala Medicine Man." *Plains Anthropologist* 25(89):265–267.
1980b   "A Sioux Medicine Man Describes His Own Illness and Approaching Death." *Annals of Internal Medicine* 92:417–418.
1981   "Phallic Masks and Fear of Sexuality." *Journal of Operational Psychiatry* 12(2):100–104.

Loeb, E. M.
1929   "Shaman and Seer." *American Anthropologist* 31:60–84.
1934a   "The Western Kuksu Cult." *University of California Publications in American Archaeology and Ethnology* 23(1):1–138.
1934b   "The Eastern Kuksu Cult." *University of California Publications in American Archaeology and Ethnology* 23(2):139–232.

Lowie, Robert H.
1910   "The Assiniboine." *Anthropological Papers of the American Museum of Natural History* 4(1):1–270.
1922   "The Religion of the Crow Indians." *Anthropological Papers of the American Museum of Natural History* 25(2):309–444.
1924   "Notes on Shoshonean Ethnography." *Anthropological Papers of the American Museum of Natural History* 20(3):185–314.
1935   *The Crow Indians.* New York: Farrar and Rinehart.
1939   "Ethnographic Notes on the Washo." *University of California Publications in American Archaeology and Ethnology* 36(5):301–352.

Ludwig, Arnold G.
1968   "Altered States of Conscious." In *Trance and Possession States*, edited by Raymond Prince. 69–95.

Montreal: R. M. Bucke Memorial Society, McGill University.

Lyon, William S.
1996   "Back from the Edge of Chaos: A Psychotherapeutic Use of the Lakota Yuwipi." *Shaman's Drum* 40:50–65.

McAllister, J. Gilbert
1970   "Dävéko: Kiowa-Apache Medicine Man." *Bulletin of the Texas Memorial Museum* 17:29–62.

McIlwraith, Thomas Forsyth
1948   *The Bella Coola Indians. Vol. 1.* Toronto: University of Toronto Press.

Mandelbaum, David G.
1940   "The Plains Cree." *Anthropological Papers of the American Museum of Natural History* 37(2):155–316.

Mason, J. Alden
1912   "The Ethnology of the Salinan Indians." *University of California Publications in American Archaeology and Ethnology* 10(4):97–240.

Matthews, Washington
1877   "Ethnography and Philology of the Hidatsa Indians." In *Miscellaneous Publications, United States Geological and Geographical Survey,* no. 7, 1–239.

Merkur, Daniel
1983   "Breath-Soul and Wind Owner: The Many and the One in Inuit Religion." *American Indian Quarterly* 7(3):23–39.
1985   *Becoming Half Hidden: Shamanism and Initiation among the Inuit.* Stockholm: Almqvist and Wiksell International.
1990   "Metaphysical Idealism in Inuit Shamanism." In *Religion in Native North America,* edited by Christopher Vecsey. 49–63. Moscow: University of Idaho Press.

Merrill, William L.
1979   "The Beloved Tree: *Ilex vomitoria* among the Indians of the Southeast and Adjacent Regions." In *Black Drink,* edited by Charles M. Hudson. 40–82. Athens: University of Georgia Press.

Meyerhoff, Barbara G.
1976   "Shamanic Equilibrium: Balance and Mediation in Known and Unknown Worlds." In *American Folk Medicine: A Symposium,* edited by W. D. Hand. 99–108. Berkeley: University of California Press.

Michelson, Truman
1921   *The Owl Sacred Pack of the Fox Indians.* Bureau of American Ethnology, Bulletin 72.
1930   *Contributions to Fox Ethnology—II.* Bureau of American Ethnology, Bulletin 95.

Miller, Jay
1983   "Numic Religion: An Overview of Power in the Great Basin of North America." *Anthropos* 78: 337–354.

Modesto, Ruby, and Guy Mount
1980   *Not for Innocent Ears: Spiritual Traditions of a Desert Cahuilla Medicine Woman.* Arcata, CA: Sweetlight Books.

Mooney, James
1891   "'The Sacred Formulas of the Cherokees." In *Seventh Annual Report of the Bureau of Ethnology.* 301–397.
1896   "The Ghost-Dance Religion and the Sioux Outbreak of 1890." In *Fourteenth Annual Report of the Bureau of Ethnology.* 641–1136.

Mooney, James, and Frans M. Olbrechts
1932   *The Swimmer Manuscript: Cherokee Sacred Formulas and Medicinal Prescriptions.* Bureau of American Ethnology, Bulletin 99.

Moses, L. G.
1985   "'The Father Tells Me So!' Wovoka: The Ghost Dance Prophet." *American Indian Quarterly* 9(3): 335–351.

Murdoch, John
1892   "Ethnological Results of the Point Barrow Expedition." In *Ninth Annual Report of the Bureau of Ethnology.* 3–441.

Murdock, George Peter, and Timothy J. O'Leary
1975   *Ethnographic Bibliography of North America.* New Haven, CT: Human Relations Area Files Press.

Murie, James R.
1981   *Ceremonies of the Pawnee.* Smithsonian Contributions to Anthropology, no. 27, parts 1 and 2. Washington, DC: Smithsonian Institution Press.

Needham, Rodney
1967   "Percussion and Transition." *Man* 2:606–614. (Reprinted 1972 in *Reader in Comparative Religion,* edited by William A. Lessa and Evon Z. Vogt, 391–398. New York: Harper & Row, Publishers)

Neher, A.
1962   "A Physiological Explanation of Unusual Behavior in Ceremonies Involving Drums." *Human Biology* 34:151–160.

Nelson, Edward W.
1899   "The Eskimo about Bering Strait." In *Eighteenth Annual Report of the Bureau of American Ethnology.* 3–518.

Newbery, J. W. E.
1977   "The Universe at Prayer." In *Native Religious Traditions,* edited by Earle H. Waugh and K. Dad Prithipaul. 165–179. Waterloo, Ontario: Wilfrid Laurier University Press.

Newkumet, Vynola Beaver and Howard L. Meredith
1988   *Hasinai: A Traditional History of the Caddo Confederacy.* College Station: Texas A & M University Press.

Noll, Richard
1985   "Mental Imagery Cultivation as a Cultural Phenomenon: The Role of Visions in Shamanism." *Current Anthropology* 4(26):443–461.

Nordland, Odd
1967   "Shamanism as an Experiencing of 'the Unreal.'" In *Studies in Shamanism,* edited by Carl-Martin Edsman. 166–185. Stockholm: Almqvist and Wiksell.

Nye, Wilbur Sturtevant
1962   *Bad Medicine and Good: Tales of the Kiowas.* Norman: University of Oklahoma Press.

Olofson, Harold
1979   "Northern Paiute Shamanism Revisited." *Anthropos* 74(2):11–24.

Olson, Ronald L.
1936   "The Quinault Indians." *University of Washington Publications in Anthropology* 6:1–190.

Opler, Morris Edward
1935   "The Concept of Supernatural Power among the Chiricahua and Mescalero Apaches." *American Anthropologist* 37(1):65–70.
1941   *An Apache Life-Way.* Chicago: University of Chicago Press.
1946   "Chiricahua Apache Material Relating to Sorcery." *Primitive Man* 19(3, 4):81–92.

Oswalt, Robert L.
1964   *Kashaya Texts.* Berkeley: University of California Press.

Paper, Jordan
1980   "From Shaman to Mystic in Ojibwa Religion." *Sciences Religieuses/Studies in Religion* 9(2): 185–199.
1983   "The Post-Contact Origin of an American Indian High God: The Suppression of Feminine Spirituality." *American Indian Quarterly* 7(4):1–24.
1988a   "The Sacred Pipe: The Historical Context of Contemporary Pan-Indian Religion." *Journal of the American Academy of Religion* 56(4):643–665.
1988b   *Offering Smoke: The Sacred Pipe and Native American Religion.* Moscow: University of Idaho Press.

Park, Susan
1986   *Samson Grant, Atsuge Shaman.* Occasional Papers of the Redding Museum, no. 3. Redding, CA: Press Room, Inc.

Park, Willard Z.
1934   "Paviotso Shamanism." *American Anthropologist* 36:98–113.
1938   *Shamanism in Western North America.* Northwestern University Studies in the Social Sciences no. 2. Menasha, WI: George Banta Publishing.

Parker, Arthur C.
1909   "Secret Medicine Societies of the Seneca." *American Anthropologist* 11(2):161–185.
1923   *Seneca Myths and Folk Tales.* Buffalo, NY: Buffalo Historical Society.
1928   "Indian Medicine and Medicine Men." In *Thirty-sixth Annual Archaeological Report.* 9–17. Appendix to the Report of the Minister of Education, Ontario. Toronto: Printer to the King's Most Excellent Majesty.

Parsons, Elsie Clews
1932   "Isleta, New Mexico." In *Forty-seventh Annual Report of the Bureau of American Ethnology.* 193–466.
1939   *Pueblo Indian Religion.* Chicago: University of Chicago Press.
1941   *Notes on the Caddo.* Memoirs of the American Anthropological Association, no. 57.

Peters, Larry G.
1982   "Trance, Initiation, and Psychotherapy in Tamang Shamanism." *American Ethnologist* 9:21–46.

Peters, Larry G., and Douglas Price-Williams
1980   "Towards an Experiential Analysis of Shamanism." *American Ethnologist* 7(3):397–413.
1983   "A Phenomenological Overview of Trance." *Transcultural Psychiatric Research Review* 20(1):5–39.

Petersen, Robert
1966–1967 "Burial-Forms and Death Cult among the Eskimos." *Folk* 8–9:259–280.

Pomedli, Michael M.
1991 *Ethnophilosophical and Ethnolinguistic Perspectives on the Huron Indian Soul.* Lewiston, NY: Edwin Mellen Press.

Pond, G. H.
1867 "Dakota Superstitions." *Collections of the Minnesota Historical Society* 2(3):32–62.

Porterfield, Amanda
1984 "Native American Shamanism and the American Mind-Cure Movement: A Comparative Study of Religious Healing." *Horizons* 11(2):276–289.

Powers, Stephen
1877 *Tribes of California.* Contributions to North American Ethnology, Volume 3. Washington, DC: Government Printing Office.

Preston, Richard J.
1975 *Cree Narrative: Expressing the personal meaning of events.* National Museum of Man Mercury Series. Canadian Ethnology Service Paper No. 30.

Prince, Raymond
1968 "Can the EEG Be Used in the Study of Possession States?" In *Trance and Possession States,* edited by Raymond Prince. Montreal: R. M. Bucke Memorial Society, McGill University.
1982 "Shamans and Endorphins: Hypotheses for a Synthesis." *Ethos* 10(4):409–423.

Radin, Paul
1914 "Religion of the North American Indians." *Journal of American Folk-Lore* 27(106):335–373.
1923 "The Winnebago Tribe." In *Thirty-seventh Annual Report of the Bureau of American Ethnology.* 35–560.

Rainey, Froelich G.
1947 "The Whale Hunters of Tigara." *Anthropological Papers of the American Museum of Natural History* 41(2):229–283.

Raitt, Thomas M.
1987 "The Ritual Meaning of Corn Pollen among the Navajo Indians." *Religious Studies* 23:523–530.

Rasmussen, Knud
1908 *The People of the Polar North.* Philadelphia: J. B. Lippincott Co.

1929 "Intellectual Culture of the Iglulik Eskimos." In *Report of the Fifth Thule Expedition, 1921–24,* vol. 7, no. 1. Copenhagen: Gyldendalske Borhandel, Nordisk Forlag.
1931 "The Netsilik Eskimos: Social Life and Spiritual Culture." In *Report of the Fifth Thule Expedition 1921–24,* vol. 8, nos. 1 and 2. Copenhagen: Gyldendalske Borhandel, Nordisk Forlag.

Regan, Albert B.
1937 "Some Notes on the Religion of the Indians." *Utah Academy of Sciences, Arts, and Letters* 14:1–15.

Reichard, Gladys A.
1944 *Prayer: The Compulsive Word.* Monographs of the American Ethnological Society, no. 7. New York: J. J. Augustin Publisher.

Reinhard, J.
1976 "Shamanism and Spirit Possession: The Definition Problem." In *Spirit Possession in the Nepal Himalayas,* edited by R. K. Jones. 12–23. New Delhi, India: Vikas Publishing House.

Relander, Click
1956 *Drummer and Dreamers.* Caldwell, ID: Caxton Printers.

Riggs, Stephen R.
1880 "The Theology of the Sioux." *American Antiquarian* 2(4):265–270.
1893 *Dakota Grammer, Texts, and Ethnology.* Contributions to North American Ethnology, vol. 9. Washington, DC: Department of the Interior.

Robbins, Wilfred William, John Peabody Harrington, and Barbara Freire-Marreco
1916 *Ethnobotany of the Tewa Indians.* Bureau of American Ethnology, Bulletin 55.

Rogers, Spencer L., and Lorraine Evernham
1983 "Shamanistic Healing among the Diegueño Indians of Southern California." In *The Anthropology of Medicine: From Culture to Method,* edited by Lola Romanucci-Ross, Daniel E. Moerman, and Laurence R. Tancredi. 103–118. New York: Praeger Publishers.

Ruby, Robert H.
1966 "Yuwipi: Ancient Rite of the Sioux." *Montana, the Magazine of Western History* 16(4):74–79.

Ruby, Robert H., and John A. Brown
1989 *Dreamer-Prophets of the Columbia Plateau.* Norman: University of Oklahoma Press.

Sapir, Edward
1907   "Religious Ideas of the Takelma Indians of Southwestern Oregon." *Journal of American Folklore* 20(76):33–49.
1909   *Takelma Texts.* University of Pennsylvania, Museum Anthropological Publications, vol. 2, no. 1. Philadelphia: University Museum.

Sapir, Edward, and Leslie Spier
1943   "Notes on the Culture of the Yana." *Anthropological Records* 3(3). 239–297. Berkeley: University of California Press.

Schaeffer, Claude E.
1965   "The Kutenai Female Berdache: Courier, Guide, Prophetess, and Warrior." *Ethnohistory* 12(3): 193– 239.
1969   *Blackfoot Shaking Tent.* Occasional Paper no. 5. Calgary, Alberta: Glenbow-Alberta Institute.

Schlesier, Karl H.
1987   *The Wolves of Heaven: Cheyenne Shamanism, Ceremonies, and Prehistoric Origins.* Norman: University of Oklahoma Press.

Schoolcraft, Henry Rowe
1857   *History of the Indian Tribes of the United States, Part IV.* Philadelphia: J. B. Lippincott and Co.

Schultes, Richard Evans
1938   "The Appeal of Peyote *(Lophophora williamsii)* as a Medicine." *American Anthropologist* 40(4):698–715.

Shepherd, Alice
1992   "Notes on the Wintu Shamanic Jargon." In *California Indian Shamanism,* edited by Lowell John Bean. 185–210. Menlo Park, CA: Ballena Press.

Shimony, Anne-Marie
1970   "Iroquois Witchcraft at Six Nations." In *Systems of North American Witchcraft and Sorcery,* edited by Deward E. Walker, Jr. 239–267. Moscow: University of Idaho Press.

Shipek, Florence
1992   "The Shaman: Priest, Doctor, Scientist." In *California Indian Shamanism,* edited by Lowell John Bean. 89–96. Menlo Park, CA: Ballena Press.

Skinner, Alanson
1916   "Political and Ceremonial Organization of the Plains-Ojibway." *Anthropological Papers of the American Museum of Natural History* 11:475–511.

1919a   "The Sun Dance of the Plains-Cree." *Anthropological Papers of the American Museum of Natural History* 16(4):287–293.
1919b   "The Sun Dance of the Plains-Ojibway." *Anthropological Papers of the American Museum of Natural History* 16(4):311–315.
1920   "Medicine Ceremony of the Menomini, Iowa, and Wahpeton Dakota, with Notes on the Ceremony among the Ponca, Bungi, Ojibwa, and Potawatomi." *Indian Notes and Monographs,* vol. 4.
1925a   "Tree-Dweller Bundle of the Wahpeton Dakota." *Indian Notes* 2(1):66–73.
1925b   "Some Seneca Masks and Their Uses." *Indian Notes* 2(3):191–207.

Slotkin, J. S.
1957   *The Menomini Powwow.* Milwaukee Public Museum Publications in Anthropology, no. 4:26. Milwaukee, WI: Milwaukee Public Museum.
1958   "The Peyote Way." In *Reader in Comparative Religion: An Anthropological Approach,* edited by William A. Lessa and Evon Z. Vogt. 519–522. New York: Harper and Row.

Smith, J. L.
1970   "The Sacred Calf Pipe Bundle: Its Effect on the Present Teton Dakota." *Plains Anthropologist* 15:87–93.

Smith, Marian W.
1940   *The Puyallup-Nisqually.* New York: Columbia University Press.

Speck, Frank G.
1909   *Ethnology of the Yuchi Indians.* University of Pennsylvania, Anthropological Publications of the University Museum, vol. 1, no. 1.
1919   "Penobscot Shamanism." *Memoirs of the American Anthropological Association* 6(4):238–298.
1935   *Naskapi: The Savage Hunters of the Labrador Peninsula.* Norman: University of Oklahoma Press.
1949   *Midwinter Rites of the Cayuga Long House.* Philadelphia: University of Pennsylvania Press.

Spenser, Robert F.
1959   *The North Alaskan Eskimo: A Study in Ecology and Society.* Bureau of American Ethnology, Bulletin 171.

Spier, Leslie
1923   "Southern Diegueño Customs." *University of California Publications in American Archaeology and Ethnology* 20:297–369.
1928   "Havasupai Ethnography." *Anthropological Papers of the American Museum of Natural History* 29(3):83-392.

1938 *The Sinkaietk or Southern Okanagon of Washington.* General Series in Anthropology, no. 6. Contributions from the Laboratory of Anthropology, 2. Menasha, WI: George Banta Publishing.

Spindler, George D.
1955 *Sociocultural and Psychological Processes in Menomini Acculturation.* University of California Publications in Culture and Society, vol. 5. Berkeley: University of California Press.

Spindler, Louise
1970 "Menomini Witchcraft." In *Systems of North American Witchcraft and Sorcery,* edited by Deward E. Walker, Jr. 183–220. Moscow: University of Idaho Press.

Spott, Robert, and Alfred L. Kroeber
1942 "Yurok Narratives." *University of California Publications in American Archeology and Ethnology* 35(9):143–256.

Springer, James Warren
1981 "An Ethnohistoric Study of the Smoking Complex in Eastern North America." *Ethnohistory* 28:217–235.

Stefánsson, Vilhjálmur
1914 "The Stefansson-Anderson Arctic Expedition of the American Museum: Preliminary Ethnological Report." *Anthropological Papers of the American Museum of Natural History* 14(1):1–396.

Steinmetz, Paul B.
1980 *Pipe, Bible, and Peyote among the Oglala Lakota.* Knoxville: University of Tennessee Press.

Stern, Bernhard J.
1934 *The Lummi Indians of Northwest Washington.* New York: Columbia University Press.

Stevenson, Matilda Coxe
1894 "The Sia." In *Eleventh Annual Report of the Bureau of Ethnology.* 3–157.
1904 "The Zuñi Indians." In *Twenty-third Annual Report of the Bureau of American Ethnology.* 3–634.

Steward, Julian H.
1934 "Ethnography of the Owens Valley Paiute." *University of California Publications in American Archaeology and Ethnology* 23(3):233–350.

Stewart, Kenneth M.
1946 "Spirit Possession in Native America." *Southwestern Journal of Anthropology* 2(3):323–339.

1970 "Mojave Indian Shamanism." *Masterkey* 44(1):15–24.
1974 "Mojave Shamanistic Specialists." *Masterkey* 48(1):4–13.

Stewart, Omer C.
1956 "Three Gods for Joe." *Tomorrow* 4(3):71–76.
1987 *Peyote Religion: A History.* Norman: University of Oklahoma Press.

Stolzman, William
1989 *The Pipe and Christ.* Chamberlain, SD: Tipi Press.

Stone, Eric
1932 *Medicine among the American Indians.* Clio Medica, no. 7. New York: Paul B. Hoeber.

Strong, William Duncan
1929 "Aboriginal Society in Southern California." *University of California Publications in American Archaeology and Ethnology* 26:1–358.

Sturtevant, William C.
1960 "A Seminole Medicine Maker." In *In the Company of Man,* edited by Joseph B. Casagrande. 506–532. New York: Harper and Brothers.

Suttles, Wayne
1955 *Katzie Ethnographic Notes.* Anthropology in British Columbia, Memoir no. 2. Victoria: British Columbia Provincial Museum.

Swanton, John R.
1908 "Social Conditions, Beliefs, and Linguistic Relationship of the Tlingit Indians." In *Twenty-sixth Annual Report of the Bureau of American Ethnology.* 391–485.
1931 *Source Material for the Social and Ceremonial Life of the Choctaw Indians.* Bureau of American Ethnology, Bulletin 103.

Tantaquidgeon, Gladys
1942 *A Study of Delaware Indian Medicine Practice and Folk Beliefs.* Harrisburg, PA: Pennsylvania Historical Commission.

Thalbitzer, William
1914 *The Ammassalik Eskimo: Contributions to the Ethnology of the East Greenland Natives, First Part.* Copenhagen: Bianco Luno.
1928 "Die Kultischen Gottheiten der Eskimos." *Archiv für Religionswissenschaft* 26:364–430.

Theodoratus, Dorothea J., and Frank LaPena
1992   "Wintu Sacred Geography." In *California Indian Shamanism*, edited by Lowell John Bean. 211–225. Menlo Park, CA: Ballena Press.

Titiev, Mischa
1956   "Shamans, Witches and Chiefs among the Hopi." *Tomorrow* 4(3):51–56.

Toelken, Barre
1989   "The Demands of Harmony." In *I Became Part of It: Sacred Dimensions in Native American Life*, edited by D. M. Dooling and Paul Jordan-Smith. 58–71. New York: Parabola Books.

Tukummiq and Tom Lowenstein
1992   *The Things that Were Said of Them: Shaman Stories and Oral Histories of the Tikigaq People Told by Asatchaq*. Berkeley: University of California Press.

Turner, Lucien M.
1894   "Ethnology of the Ungava District, Hudson Bay Territory." In *Eleventh Annual Report of the Bureau of Ethnology*. 159–350.

Turney-High, Harry Holbert
1941   *Ethnography of the Kutenai*. Memoirs of the American Anthropological Association, no. 56. Menasha, WI: George Banta Publishing Company.

Twiss, Gayla
1969   "The Role of the Pipe in Dakota Religion." *Pine Ridge Research Bulletin* 10:7–19.

Underhill, Ruth
1945   *Indians of the Pacific Northwest*. Washington, DC: Department of the Interior.
1946   *Papago Indian Religion*. New York: Columbia University Press.
1965   *Red Man's Religion: Beliefs and Practices of the Indians North of Mexico*. Chicago: University of Chicago Press.

Vecsey, Christopher
1983   *Traditional Ojibwa Religions and Its Historical Changes*. Philadelphia: American Philosophical Society.

Vennum, Thomas Jr.
1982   *The Ojibwa Dance Drum: Its History and Construction*. Smithsonian Folklife Studies, no. 2. Washington, DC: Smithsonian Institution Press.

Vizenor, Gerald
1981   *Summer in the Spring*. Minneapolis, MN: Nodin Press.

Vogel, Virgil J.
1970   *American Indian Medicine*. Norman: University of Oklahoma Press.

Walker, Deward E. Jr.
1967   "Nez Perce Sorcery." *Ethnology* 6(1):66–96.
1970   "Sorcery among the Nez Perces." In *Systems of North American Witchcraft and Sorcery*, edited by Deward E. Walker, Jr. 267–295. Moscow: University of Idaho Press.

Walker, James R.
1917   "The Sun Dance and Other Ceremonies of the Oglala Division of the Teton Dakota." *Anthropological Papers of the American Museum of Natural History* 16(2): 52–221.
1926   "Dakota Offering Sticks." *Indian Notes* 3(3): 199–200.
1982   *Lakota Society*, edited by Raymond J. De Mallio. Lincoln: University of Nebraska Press.

Wallace, Anthony F. C.
1958   "Dreams and the Wishes of the Soul: A Type of Psychoanalytic Theory among the Seventeenth Century Iroquois." *American Anthropologist* 60:234–248.
1970   *The Death and Rebirth of the Seneca*. New York: Alfred A. Knopf.

Wallace, Ernest, and E. Adamson Hoebel
1952   *The Comanches: Lords of the South Plains*. Norman: University of Oklahoma Press.

Wallis, W. D.
1919   "The Sun Dance of the Canadian Dakota." *Anthropological Papers of the American Museum of Natural History* 16(4):317–380.

Walter, V. J., and W. Grey Walter
1949   "The Central Effects of Rhythmic Sensory Stimulation." *Electroencephalography and Clinical Neurophysiology* 1(1):57–86.

Waterman, T. T.
1910   "The Religious Practices of the Diegueño Indians." *University of California Publications in American Archaeology and Ethnology* 8(6):271–358.
1930a   "The Paraphernalia of the Duwamish 'Spirit-Canoe' Ceremony." *Indian Notes* 7(3):295–312.
1930b   "The Paraphernalia of the Duwamish 'Spirit-Canoe' Ceremony." *Indian Notes* 7(4):535–561.

Weyer, Edward Moffat
1932   *The Eskimos: Their Environment and Folkways.* New Haven, CT: Yale University Press.

White, Leslie A.
1932   "The Acoma Indians." In *Forty-seventh Annual Report of the Bureau of American Ethnology.* 17–192.

White, Raymond
1976   "Religion and Its Role among the Luiseño." In *Native Californians: A Theoretical Retrospective*, edited by Lowell J. Bean and Thomas C. Blackburn. 355–377. Ramona, CA: Ballena Press.

Whiting, Beatrice Blyth
1950   *Paiute Sorcery.* Viking Fund Publications in Anthropology, no. 15. New York: Viking Fund.

Wildschut, William
1975   *Crow Indian Medicine Bundles.* Contributions from the Museum of the American Indian, Heye Foundation, vol. 17.

Wilken, G. A.
1887   "Het Shamanisme bij de volken van den Indischen Archipel," *Bijdragen tot de Taal-Land-en Volkenkunde* xxxvi:427–497.)

Williamson, John P.
1970   *An English-Dakota Dictionary.* Minneapolis: Ross & Haines, Inc.

Williamson, Robert G.
1974   *Eskimo Underground: Socio-Cultural Change in the Central Canadian Arctic.* Uppsala, Sweden: Almqvist and Wiksell.

Wolf, Fred Alan
1991   *The Eagle's Quest: A Physicist's Search for Truth in the Heart of the Shamanic World.* New York: Summit Books.

Wyman, Leland C.
1970   *Blessingway.* Tuscon: University of Arazona Press.

Young, David, Grant Ingram, and Lise Swartz
1989   *Cry of the Eagle: Encounters with a Cree Healer.* Toronto: University of Toronto Press.

Zimmerly, David W.
1969   "On Being an Ascetic: Personal Document of a Sioux Medicine Man." *Pine Ridge Research Bulletin* 10:46–70.

Ethnobotany Bibliography

The following list of references is provided for readers who are interested in the medicinal plant usage of Native Americans in North America. For further references, consult the bibliographies of the works listed here. Also, most field ethnographies contain a short section on medicinal plant use.

Barrows, David Prescott
1967   *The Ethnobotany of the Coahuilla Indians of Southern California.* Banning, CA: Malki Museum Press.

Bean, Lowell John, and Katherine Siva Saubel
1972   *Temalpakh: Cahuilla Indian Knowledge and Usage of Plants.* Banning, CA: Malki Museum, Inc.

Bigelow, Jacob
1817–1820   *American Medical Botany, Being a Collection of the Native Medicinal Plants of the United States.* Boston: Cummings & Hilliard.

Brooks, Harlow
1929   "The Medicine of the American Indian." *Bulletin of the New York Academy of Medicine* 5(6): 509–537.

Buhner, Stephen Harrod
1996   *Sacred Plant Medicine: Explorations in the Practice of Indigenous Herbalism.* Boulder, CO: Roberts Rinehart Publishers.

Castetter, Edward F. and Ruth M. Underhill
1935   "The Ethnobiology of the Papago Indians." *The University of New Mexico Bulletin, Biological Series* 4(3):3–84.

Chesnut, V. K.
1902   *Plants Used by the Indians of Mendocino County, California.*   Contributions U. S. National Herbarium, Vol. VII, No. 3.

Culley, John
1936   "The California Indians: Their Medical Practices and Their Drugs."   *Journal of the American Pharmaceutical Association* 25(4):332–339.

Curtin, L. S. M.
1949   *By the Prophet of the Earth.*   Santa Fe, NM: San Vicente Foundation, Inc.
1957   *Some Plants Used by the Yuki Indians of Round Valley, Northern California.*   Los Angeles: Southwest Museum.
1965   *Healing Herbs of the Upper Rio Grande.*   Los Angeles: Southwest Museum.

Densmore, Frances
1928   "Uses of Plants by the Chippewa Indians." In *Forty-fourth Annual Report of the Bureau of American Ethnology.* 275–397.

Gilmore, Melvin Randolph
1919   "Uses of plants by the Indians of the Missouri River region."   In *Thirty-third Annual Report of the Bureau of American Ethnology.* 43–154.

Greenlee, Robert F.
1944   "Medicine and Curing Practices of the Modern Florida Seminoles."   *American Anthropologist* 46(3):317–328.

Grinnell, George Bird
1905   "Some   Cheyenne   Plant   Medicines." *American Anthropologist* 7(1):37–43.

Hamel, Paul B. and Mary U. Chiltosdey
1975   *Cherokee Plants: Their Uses—A 400 Year History.* Asheville, NC: Hickory Printing.

Hellson, John C. and Morgan Gadd
1974   *Ethnobotany of the Blackfoot Indians.* Ottawa: National Canadian Ethnology Service, Museums of Canada. Mercury Series, Paper No. 19.

Hutchens, Alma R.
1969   *Indian Herbalogy of North America.* Windsor, Ontario: Merco.

Keewaydinoquay
1978   *Puhpohwee for the People: A Narrative Account of Some Uses of Fungi Among the Ahnishinaubeg.*

Cambridge, MA: Botanical Museum of Harvard University.

Mahr, August C.
1951   "Materia Medica and Therapy among the North American Forest Indians."   *Ohio State Archaeological and Historical Quarterly* 40(4):331–354.

Moerman, Daniel E.
1986   *Medicinal Plants of Native America.* University of Michigan Museum of Anthropology, Research Reports in Ethnobotany, Vol. 1, Contribution 2.

Mooney, James
1891   "The Sacred Formulas of the Cherokees."   In *Seventh Annual Report of the Bureau of Ethnology.* 301–397.

Mooney, James (edited by Frans M. Olbrechts)
1932   *The Swimmer manuscript: Cherokee Sacred Formulas and Medicinal Prescriptions.* Bureau of American Ethnology, Bulletin 99.

Murphey, Edith Van Allen
1959   *Indian Uses of Native Plants.* Fort Bragg, CA: Mendocino County Historical Society.

Palmer, Edward
1878   "Plants Used by the Indians of the United States."   *American Naturalist* 12: 593-606 and 646–655.

Porcher, Francis P.
1849   "Report on the Indigenous Medical Plants of South Carolina."   *Transactions of the American Medical Association* 2:677–862.

Robbins, Wilfred William, John Peabody Harrington, and Barbara Freire-Marreco
1914   *Ethnobotany of the Tewa Indians.* Bureau of American Ethnology, Bulletin 55.

Scully, Virginia
1970   *A Treasury of American Indian Herbs: Their Lore and Their Use for Food, Drugs, and Medicine.* New York: Bonanza Books.

Smith, Huron H.
1933   *Ethnobotany of the Forest Potawatomi Indians.* Bulletin of the Public Museum, Vol. VII, No. 1, Milwaukee.
1923   *Ethnobotany of the Menomini Indians.* Bulletin of the Public Museum, Vol. IV, No. 1, Milwaukee.

1928   *Ethnobotany of the Meskwaki Indians.* Bulletin of the Public Museum, Vol. IV, No. 2, Milwaukee.

1932   *Ethnobotany of the Ojibwe Indians.* Bulletin of the Public Museum, Vol. IV, No. 3, Milwaukee.

Speck, Frank G.
1937   "Catawba Medicines and Curative Practices." *Publications of the Philadelphia Anthropological Society* 1:179–198.

1941   "A List of Plant Curatives Obtained from the Houma Indians of Louisiana." *Primitive Man 14:49–73.*

Stevenson, Matilda Coxe
1915   "Ethnobotany of the Zuñi Indians." In *Thirty-third Annual Report of the Bureau of American Ethnology.* 31–102.

Stone, Eric
1932   *Medicine Among the American Indians.* New York: Paul B. Hoeber, Inc.

Swanton, John R.
1928   "Religious Beliefs and Medical Practices of the Creek Indians." In *Forty-second Annual Report of the Bureau of American Ethnology.* 473–672.

Tantaquidgeon, Gladys
1942   *A Study of Delaware Indian Medicine Practice and Folk Beliefs.* Harrisburg, PA: Pennsylvania Historial Commission.

Teit, James A. (edited by Elsie Viault Steedman)
1930   "Ethnobotany of the Thompson Indians of British Columbia." In *Forty-fifth Annual Report of the Bureau of American Ethnology.* 441–522.

Vogel, Virgil J.
1970   *American Indian Medicine.* Norman: University of Oklahoma Press.

Whiting, Alfred F.
1939   *Ethnobotany of the Hopi Indians.* Bulletin No. 15. Flagstaff, AZ: Museum of Northern Arizona.

Williams, Stephen W.
1849   "Report on the Indigenous Medical Botany of Massachusetts." *Transactions of the American Medical Association* 2: 863–927.

Wyman, Leland C. and Stuart K. Harris
1941   *Navajo Indian Medical Ethnobotany.* University of New Mexico Bulletin No. 366. Albuquerque: University of New Mexico Press.

Youngken, Heber W.
1924–1925   "Drugs of the North American Indians." *American Journal of Pharmacy* 96: 485–502; 97: 158–185 and 257–271.

Illustration Credits

19	Plate XIV from the *Eleventh Annual Report of the Bureau of Ethnology*, 1894.
30	National Anthropological Archives 81-2130, Smithsonian Institution.
33	National Anthropological Archives 57569, Smithsonian Institution
34	National Anthropological Archives 3303-C, Smithsonian Institution.
37	National Anthropological Archives 3360-C, Smithsonian Institution.
46	Figure 39 from *Indian Notes*, 2(1), 1925.
48	National Museum of American Art 1985.66.161, Washington, D.C./Art Resource, New York.
50	Corbis-Bettmann.
53	©Martha Cooper/Peter Arnold, Inc.
60	National Anthropological Archives 568A, Smithsonian Institution.
62	Plate VIII from the *Ninth Annual Report of the Bureau of Ethnology*, 1892.
68	National Anthropological Archives 3377-C-22, Smithsonian Institution.
72	National Anthropological Archives 2657, Smithsonian Institution.
80	American Museum of Natural History 13561, New York.
81	Milwaukee Public Museum 202819.
83	National Anthropological Archives 55300, Smithsonian Institution.
87	National Anthropological Archives 55298, Smithsonian Institution.
94	Colorado Historical Society.
99	The Seattle Art Museum, gift of John H. Hauberg.
103	Plate XII from the *Eleventh Annual Report of the Bureau of Ethnology*, 1894.
111	©Martha Cooper/Peter Arnold, Inc.
118(t)	Figure 24 from the *Eleventh Annual Report of the Bureau of Ethnology*, pp. 159-350.
118(b)	Figure 436 from the *Ninth Annual Report of the Bureau of Ethnology*, 1892.
123	National Anthropological Archives 452, Smithsonian Institution.
163	National Anthropological Archives 720-D-6, Smithsonian Institution.
169	National Anthropological Archives 77-2861, Smithsonian Institution.
172	American Museum of Natural History 38475, New York.
173	Corbis-Bettmann.
175	Plate CI in the *Twenty Third Annual Report, Bureau of American Ethnology*, 1904.
189	American Museum of Natural History 43481, New York.
190	©Walter H. Hodge/Peter Arnold, Inc.
207	Special Collections Division, University of Washington Libraries, NA#472.
210	National Anthropological Archives 2777, Smithsonian Institution.
221	Corbis-Bettmann
233	Figure 431 from the *Ninth Annual Report of the Bureau of Ethnology*, 1892.
247	National Anthropological Archives 476-A-13, Smithsonian Institution.
252	National Anthropological Archives 2189, Smithsonian Institution.
259	Corbis-Bettmann.
262	Photo #118405 by H. S. Rice. American Museum of Natural History, New York.
265	Milwaukee Public Museum 9530.
270	UPI/Corbis-Bettmann
271	National Anthropological Archives 1008, Smithsonian Institution.
284	National Anthropological Archives 3434, Smithsonian Institution.

Index

Aaskouandy, 3
Áata, 3
Aatirh, 3
Aaum sumatc, 3
Abenaki, 26
Achomawi, 57
Acoma Flint Society, 105–106
Acoma Pueblo, 127, 185
Adälön, 4
Adanöwiski, 4–5
Ádantí, 5–6
Adelaghadhíya, 6
Adliz aze, 6
Aenichit, 6–7
Agotkon, 7
Aguain, 7
Ahma Humare, 7
Ahutru, 8
Ai sumatc, 8
Aixagidalagilis, 8–10
Aiyakokiyiu, 10
Aiyicks, 10
Ajasowin, 10
Akaka, 10
Akbaalía, 10, 27–29
Akbaria, 10
Akeutit, 10–11
Akicita, 11
Akme, 11
Akua, 11
Akuwacdiu, 11, 28
Akúwecdìu, 11
Alaska Eskimo, 294–295
Algonquian, 164, 201, 215, 217. *See also* Northern
    Algonquian
Alikchi, 11
Alini, 11
"All my relations," 178
Altars, 11–12, 18, 160, 279–280, 325
    snake society, 19f.
Ambelan, 12
American culture, xxxvii
American Indian Life, 312
American Museum of Natural History, 36
Amnaa, 12
Amulets, 99f., 175–176, 296, 314

Anáájí, 12
Anaana, 12
Anaidjuq, 13
Anakua, 13
Angakoq, 13–15
Angatkok, 15–16
Angatkungaruk, 16
Angelica, 16
Angmagsalik, 21
Ant doctors, 250
Ant Father Ceremony. *See* Toyide
Antelope Shaman. *See* Deer shamans
Antuw, 16
Aoutmoin, 16
Apache, 47, 61, 68, 107, 118, 129, 151–152, 165, 186,
    201, 275, 290, 296
Aperfat, 16
Aperksaq, 16
Apo leo, 16
Apuluq, 16–17
Arapaho, 31, 240
Arctic Coast, 10, 13–17, 20, 21, 51–52, 70–71, 113,
    114–115, 116, 117–118, 127, 129–130, 135, 139,
    202, 208, 229–230, 242, 250–251, 263, 275, 278,
    285, 293, 295
Arctic shamanism, 17
Arnägneq, 17
Arrow wound doctors, 118
Arrows, 195
Artgeist, 17
Asatchaq, 17
Asgina, 17
Assiniboin, 216, 304–305, 316
Atayohknak, 17–18
Ätchin, 18
Atci sumatc, 18
Atcigamultin, 18
Atiasxw, 18–20
Atsugewi, 30–31, 85, 92–93, 157, 165–166, 279,
    314–315
Aua, 20
Aumakuas, 20
Autmoin, 20
Autobiography of a Papago Woman, 298
The Autobiography of a Winnebago Indian, 231
Ave sumatc, 20–21

Avgo, 21
Avi sumatc, 21
Awahokshu, 21
Awonawilona, 21–22
Awusua, 22
Axèki, 22
Axikiye, 22
Ayañkxiyan, 22
Ayelkwi, 22–23
Ayikcomí, 23
Ayûnini. *See* Swimmer

Baaheamaequa, 25
Baaxpàak, 25
Baaxpée. *See* Maxpe
Bacóritsi'tse, 25
Bad Bad Bull, 25–26
Bàkumbírio, 26
Baltadak, 26
Baohigan, 26
Barbeau, Marius, 26
Basamacha, 26–27
Basbatadaq, 27
Bashiammisheek, 25
Basin, 52, 65–66, 93–94, 152, 155, 158, 165, 179,
    180, 183–184, 185–186, 187, 192, 196, 197, 211,
    218, 219, 222–228, 234–236, 237, 258, 267, 276,
    277, 281, 288–289, 293–294, 304, 311, 313,
    316–317, 325
Baskets, 304
Batse maxpe, 10, 27–29
Batsirápe, 29
Beads, 4
Bear Butte. *See* Mato tipi
Bear doctors, 29, 86–87, 166, 266
Bear, Tom, 30
Bear Butte, South Dakota, 166
Bear Ceremony, 212
Bear Doctor Society, 166–167
Bear shamans, 130–132, 195
Bear Society, 194, 197
Beast gods, 30, 313–314
Beaulieu, Paul, 248
Beaver doctors, 278
Becenti, Ernest C., 53
Bella Coola, 141–143
Beothuk and Micmac, 261
Berdache, 30
Betil, 30
Betsaki, 30–31
Beuski, 31
Beynon, William, 196

Biisänoxu, 31
Bilisshíissanne, 31
Billie, Josie, 31–32, 42
Biloxi, 22, 283, 322
Biricísande, 32
Birket-Smith, Kaj, 32, 263
Black drink, 32–33, 33f.
Black Eagle. *See* Blue Back, Walter
Black Elk. *See* Black Elk, Sr., Nicholas
Black Elk, Sr., Nicholas, 34–36
Black Elk, Wallace, xv, xxxvii
Black Fox. *See* Inâli
Black Road, 36
Black Wolf, 36
Blackfoot, 10, 90, 217
Blanket shamans, 299
Blankets, 183
Blessings, 105, 280
Blood tribe, 38–39
Bloodletting, 212
"Blow it away," 187
Blowing, 220, 271
Blue Back, Walter, 36
Boas, Franz, 36–37, 192, 196, 231, 232, 261, 317
Bob-Tailed Wolf, 37
Body soul, 37, 180, 204, 251
Bone doctors, 116
Bone-setting, xiii
Booöinwadagan. *See* Buówinudi
Booöwinode. *See* Buówinudi
Bourke, John, 186
Bowls, 219, 277, 305
Boyd, Doug, 157, 234
Braided Tail Bundle, 37
Brave Buffalo, 37–38
Breath soul, 38
Buaxantï. *See* Puaxantï
Buckley, Raymond, 104–105
Buffalo Chip Woman, 38–39
Buffalo Doctors, 102, 281
Buffalo Society, 212, 279
Bull Lodge, 39–40
Bull-All-the-Time, 40–41
Bulletproof medicine, 41–42
Bullroarers, 42, 231, 231f., 278, 279, 287
Bundles, 177, 301, 311. *See also* Ceremonial bun-
    dles; Medicine bundles; Sacred Calf Pipe
    Bundle
Buówin, 42
Buówinudi, 42
Burn doctor, 3
Busk Ceremony, 42

Buxantï. *See* Puaxantï
Buyabu'ú, 42–43

Caddo, 7, 57, 137, 217, 278, 330
Cadekwcrache kaihweyoni, 45
Cahuilla, 12, 159, 197, 218, 228, 281, 282
California, 8, 11, 12, 16, 22, 30–31, 51, 57, 58, 64, 71,
        85, 86–87, 92–93, 95, 99, 104, 106, 107, 110–112,
        114, 122–124, 129, 130, 133–134, 135, 137,
        138–139, 140, 141, 143, 149–150, 154–155, 157,
        158, 162, 165–167, 172–173, 179–180, 184–185,
        193, 197, 210, 212–214, 240–241, 243, 257, 258,
        264–266, 275, 279, 280, 283, 284, 289, 291, 297,
        298, 307–308, 314–315, 318, 325, 328–329,
        329–330
California Peninsula, 22–23, 95, 144, 145–146, 159,
        179–180, 197, 218, 228, 277, 280, 281, 282, 315
Calkins, Hiram, 47
Calumet, 45
Can hotidan, 45
Canadian Eastern Woodlands, 6, 10, 16, 20, 26, 42,
        52, 59–60, 64, 87, 88, 121–122, 122, 129, 134,
        135–136, 140, 144, 157–158, 158, 165, 166, 168,
        170–171, 171, 173, 174, 175, 176–177, 178, 179,
        185, 192, 194, 194–195, 197–198, 201–202, 209,
        210, 212, 215, 220, 232, 234, 251, 258, 277, 281,
        282, 286–287, 303–304, 304, 312, 313, 316,
        333
Cangcega, 45
Canli wapahta, 46
Cantojuha, 46
Caribou Eskimo, 114–115
Carrier, 61–63, 129, 146–148
Cartier, Jacques, 205
Cass, Lewis, xxxvii, 177
Catawba, 326
Catches, Pete, 46
Catlin, George, 47
    paintings by, 48f.
Cattail pollen, 107
Cayuga, 45, 60, 64, 86, 99, 102, 130, 194, 197, 201,
        240, 275, 311, 315
    curing rites, 71–73
    False Face, 72f.
    healing rites, 73–77
    restricted medicine societies, 73–75
    unrestricted societies, 75–77
Cecene. *See* Keteu
Cedar planks, 264
Central Miwok, 107, 264
Ceremonial bundles, 162
Ceseko, 47

Chalchihuitl, 47
Chantways, 12, 47–49, 321–322
Chanunpa, 49
Charisma, 49
Charlevoix, 20
Charms, 3, 192, 206
Cherokee, 4, 6, 17, 57, 60, 64–65, 85, 86, 91–92, 114,
        115, 116–117, 130, 135, 185, 206, 234, 270–271,
        290–291, 297
    healing system, 4–5
Cherry Necklace, 49–51, 231–232
Cheyenne, 37, 70, 71, 103, 104, 108, 158, 159, 181,
        185, 195, 204, 206, 210, 296, 301, 333
Chgalyic, 51
Childbirth specialists, 167
Children's doctors, 118
Chinook jargon, 284
Chipewyan, 117, 186
Chipmunk healing ceremony, 194
Chippewa, 10, 52, 158, 200, 204, 212
Chipps, Ellis, 110
Chipps, Godfrey, 110
Chips, Charles. *See* Horn Chips
Chiricahua, 70
Chitina Joe, 51–52, 263
Choctaw, 11, 108, 109–110, 183, 185, 250
Chugach, 16–17
Cicigwan, 52
Cicigwun, 52
Cigigwan, 52
Clayoquot, 6–7, 204, 206, 240
Cleansing and purification rituals, 192, 250
Club wounds, 8
Coast Miwok, 154, 278, 305–306
Coast Salish, 68, 143–144, 202–203, 240, 243, 256,
        266, 270–271, 323. *See also* Puget Sound
        Salish
Coast Yuki, 104
Coffee Charlie, 52
Comanche, 158, 225, 241–242
Coming Daylight, 67
Common Faces, 52–53
Conjurati, 53
Conjuring, 53
Conjuring complex, 53
Conna. *See* Konah
Contraries, 104–105, 108
Copper Eskimo, 10–11, 15, 70, 118, 286
Corn flour, 107
Corn pollen, 53–54
Cornmeal, 54, 140
Cornmother, 328

Corpse poison, 5–6
Cowrie shells, 138, 304
Coyote doctors, 157
Coyote Woman, 54–55
Crazy Horse, 41
Creator, 276, 306. *See also* Great Spirit
Crow, 10, 11, 22, 25, 26, 27–29, 31, 32, 37, 40–41,
    57–58, 115–116, 167–168, 180, 218, 244, 256,
    257, 321
Crow Heart, 231
Crystals, 157, 220
Culture areas, xvii
Culture hero, 220
Cupping instrument, 55
Cures, 106, 320
Curtis, Natalie, 55
Cushing, Frank Hamilton, 55
Cusiyaes. *See* Kwisiyai
Cuwaha, 55–56
Cxwneam, 56

Dadahnesesgi, 57
Daitino, 57
Dakota, 45, 69–70, 104–105, 232, 306, 318. *See also*
    Teton Dakota
Damaagome, 57
Dances, 107, 179
Dancing doctors, 129, 184, 329
Dapic, 57–58
Dark Dance Ceremony, 58
Dark Dance Society, 64
Dasan, 58
Dävéko, 58–59, 60f.
Dawando, 59
Day, David, 59
Dead People Dance, 201
Dead Society, 200
Dean, Peter, 116
Death Feast Ceremony, 200–201
Debwawendûnk, 59–60
Deer shamans, 60
Degiyagon oäno, 60
Dek Setskéha, 60
Delaware, 172, 317–318
Densmore, Frances, 210, 211, 259–260, 295, 311
Desires, 205
Deswadenyationdottu, 60
Devil Dance Ceremony, 130
Dewanondiissondaikta. *See* Dark Dance Ceremony
Diagnosis and diagnosticians, 128, 201, 243, 250
    ceremonies, 68
Didahnvwisgi, 60
Didanöwiski. *See* Adanöwiski

Diegueño, 95, 141, 144, 145–146, 280, 315–316
Disease, 7, 60–61, 146, 209, 280. *See also* Illness
Disease-Giver, 61
Dismemberment, 61
Divination, 139, 190, 229–230
Diyi, 61
    medicine shirt, 62f.
Diyinne, 61–63
Diyunanda kwa, 64
Diyúsodáyego, 64
Dja minawan, 64
Djasakid. *See* Jessakkid
Djesikiwinini, 64
Djessakid. *See* Jessakkid
Djigamágan, 64
Djutidro, 64
Doctor Charley, 64
Doctor dance, 232
Doctor Mink, 64–65
Doctors, 11, 61, 71, 282
Dodd, Bobby, 65–66
Dog Doctors, 103
Doha, 66
Dokulungkili, 66
Doll Beings, 186, 199
Dolls, 118
Domagaia, 205
Dorsey, George Amos, 66
Dorsey, James Owen, 66
Dorsey, Willie, 66–67
Dragging Otter, 296
Dream doctors, 158, 185, 210, 277, 329–330
Dream Guessing ritual, 240
Dream soul. *See* Free soul
Dreamers, 99
Dreaming, 102
Dreams, 192, 196–197, 266
    power, 266
Dream-sickness, 129–130
Drops in the Fire, 67
Drums, 45, 64, 67–68, 172, 179, 211, 281, 285
Dúajida, 68
Duhisa, 68
Duklij, 68
Duride, 68
Duxuda'b, 68
Dwamish, 30, 251, 255–256, 256–257, 263, 264
Dyaguna gaut, 68–69

Eagle Dance, 85–86
    Society, 130
Eagle doctors, 179–180, 241–242
Eagle Shield, 69–70

Eagle Society, 245
East Greenland Eskimo, 116, 229–230, 242, 275, 278
Eastern Cree, 144, 178
Ecstasy, 70
Eehyom, 70
Eells, Myron, 277
Effigies, 135, 196
Elik, 70
Emergency treatment, 258
Emetic rite, 12
Endorphins, 70
Enemyway, 12
Enti, 70
Entry format, xvii
Erinaliut, 70–71
Eskimo, 13–16, 71, 117–118, 250–251. *See also*
    Alaska Eskimo; Caribou Eskimo; Copper
    Eskimo; East Greenland Eskimo; Iglulik
    Eskimo; Iñupiaq Eskimo; Labrador Eskimo;
    Mackenzie-Yukon Eskimo; Netsilik Eskimo;
    North Alaska Eskimo; Polar Eskimo; South
    Alaska Eskimo; Tikerarmiut; West Alaska
    Eskimo
Estufa. *See* Kiva
Etien, 71
Etowe, 71
Evilway, 12
Ewil letimk, 71
Exhastoz, 71
Eye yomta. *See* Yomta
Eyondwanshgwut, 71–77

False Faces, 72f., 81f., 245 *See also* Masks
    medicine water, 196
False-Face Society, 79–82, 80f.
Familiar, 82
Fasting, 31, 82
Feathers, 107, 186–187, 303. *See also* Plumes
Fetishes, 71, 109, 113, 114, 208, 325–326
Fire Lame Deer, John, 105
Fire Society, 99
Fire-eaters, 130
Fish doctors, 18
Fishpeople, 211. *See also* Pa towa
Fletcher, Alice Cunningham, 82, 83f.
Flint Society, 82
Flounder, Fanny, 82–83
Football Rite, 315
Four Bears, 51
Fox, 162, 177–178, 191–192
Free soul, 84, 104, 192, 197
Frenzy witchcraft, 5, 6
Fright doctors, 298

Gahoya, 85
Gahuni manuscript, 85
Gajisashono, 85
Galaxy Fraternity, 193
Galushia, 263
Ganegwäe, 85–86
Garcia, Sivariano, 210
Gatci kwae, 86
Gatgwanasti manuscript, 86
Gauk burakal, 86–87
Gebegabau, 87
Geesick, John Ka Ka, 87
Gemiwûnac, 87
Ghost Dance, 87. *See also* Wovoka
The Ghost Dance: Origins of Religion, 149
Ghost Midewiwin, 88
Ghost sickness, 88, 197–198, 200
Ghosts, 17, 87, 110–112, 118, 165–166, 250, 298
Ghostway, 12
Giant Society, 251–255
Gicelemûkaong, 88
Gilya. *See* Tungat
Gínap, 88
Gisamá, 88
Githie, 88–89
Githiye, 89
Gitksan, 3, 99, 155, 186, 269
Giving-Potlatches-in-the-World, 98
Giwire, 89–90
Glacier Bull, 90
Goda'ensiyus'ta'kwa, 90
Goes Back, 90–91
Good Bear, 54–55
Good Horse, 46
Good Lance, Frank, 46, 91
Good Singer, 91
Gowäli, 91–92
Goyò, 92
Grand Medicine Society/Lodge/Ceremony. *See*
    Midewiwin
Grant, Samson, 92–93
Great Bird-medicine, 194–195
Great God Society, 137
Great Lakes, 47
Great Spirit, 88, 133, 214, 313. *See also* Creator;
    Manitou; Wise One Above
Green, Joe (Northern Paiute), 93–94
Green, Joe (Paviotso), 225
Grizzly-Bear Dance, 94–95
Gros Ventre, 25–26, 39–40, 67, 90–91, 152–154,
    187–189, 263–264, 289, 315
Guardian spirits. *See* Helping spirits
Guisiyag, 95

Guksu Ceremony, 95
Guy, Sarah, 7

Hächamoni, 97, 103f.
Hadaho, 98
Hadigadjisashooh, 98–99
Hadntin. *See* Hoddentin
Hadrauta, 99
Hai detoi, 99
Haida, 237, 245, 251
Hakan, 99
Halaait, 99
Halaidm swanaskxw, 99
Halait, 99–101
Haldawit, 101–102
Hanaitus, 102
Hanbloglaka, 102
Hanmdepi, 102
Hánwahe waci, 102
Harav heya, 102
Hatcamuni, 102–103
Hatcok sumatc, 103
Havasupai, 88, 89
Hawaiian, 11, 12, 16, 20, 109, 127–129, 135, 140,
    219, 298
Hawaiian shamans, 128
    power, 118
    societies, 191, 240
    and spirituality, xiii
Hayoka. *See* Heyóka
Headdresses, 243
Head-lifting divination technique, 139
Healers, 103, 185
Healing, 104, 155, 165, 218, 220, 255–256, 325,
    330–331
    artificial western distinction between rational
        and irrational therapies, xiii
    ceremonies, 182–183, 185, 331
Heammawihio, 103
Heliga, 103
Helika, 103
Helping spirits, 16, 57, 107, 115–116, 117–118, 164,
    177, 185, 186, 192, 192–193, 196, 197, 201,
    214–215, 217, 220, 223–224, 240, 243–244, 267,
    273, 275, 278, 279, 281, 282, 285, 293, 295–296,
    298, 315, 323, 326–327
Hemaneh, 104
Hematasooma, 104
Hen fó, 104
Herbalists and herbalism, xiii–xiv, 4, 23, 165, 170,
    171, 194–195, 216, 312, 318
Herrotume, 104
Hetimwok, 104

Hexing, 116
Heyóka, 104–105
Hianyi, 105
Hictiani, 105–106
Hidatsa, 49–51, 109, 158, 173, 323
Higilak, 15
Hila. *See* Sila
Hilleeshwa, 106
Hilotca kaiyan, 106
Hilyulit, 106
Hinawa, 107
Hishämi, 107
Hithoitcimai sumatc, 107
Hithorau sumatc, 107
Hiwarau sumatc, 107
Hiweyi, 107
Hiweylak sumatc, 107
Hobbomock, 107
Hochinagen, 107
Hoddentin, 107
Hodrauta, 99
Hoffman, Walter James, xxxvii
Hohnuhka, 108
Hokshu, 108
Holhkunna, 108
Holkkunda, 108
Holy Dance, Robert, 108
Honaaite, 108–109
Honani, 109
Hoopiopio, 109
Hopá, 109
Hopaii, 109–110
Hopi, 68, 189–190, 293–294, 325–326
Horn Chips, 110
Hotcine gada, 110
Howlish Watkonot, 110
Hózhó, 110
Huapsi, 110
Hulkilal, 110–112
Hultkrantz, Åke, 17
Hunka, 112
Hupa, 136
Huron, 206, 217, 233, 291
Husikpe, 112
Husk-Faces Society, 85, 98–99, 112

Iariko, 113
Ibrukaon, 113
Ibrukok, 113
Ickade, 113
Idiaxílalit, 113–114
Idos oäno, 114
Ie yomta, 114

Iemaparu, 114
Igawésdi, 114
Igjugarjuk, 114–115
Iglulik Eskimo, 13, 16, 20, 229
Igv nedhi, 115
Iikhááh, 115
Iilápxe, 115–116
Ikhareyev. *See* Wogey
Iksivalitaq, 116
Ilisiniq, 116
Ilisitsut, 116
Ilitkosaq, 116
Illness, 278
    cause of, 280. *See also* Disease; Spirit illness
Ilyesa sumatc, 116
Imitative shamanism, 116
Inâli, 116–117
Inâli manuscript, 116–117
Incantations, 10–11
*Indian Tribes of the Lower Mississippi Valley and
    Adjacent Coast of the Gulf of Mexico*, 269
The Indians' Book, 55
Indians of the Southeastern United States, 269
Inikagapi, 117
Inipi, 117
Initiatory sickness, 117
Inkoze, 117
Insanity, 325
Insect medicine, 31
Inua, 117–118
Inugwak, 118
Inuit. *See* Eskimo
Iñupiaq Eskimo, 17
Inviter-Woman, 8
Inyan wakan. *See* Tunkan
Inyuin tarrak, 118
Iowa, 102, 165, 304, 305, 309
Ipa sumach, 118
Iroquois, 3, 7, 52–53, 79–82, 85–86, 112, 127, 157,
    201, 205, 206, 208, 231, 243, 285, 291
Itcuthau sumatc, 118
Ithaethe, 119
Izzekloth, 119

Jackson, Jimmy, 121
Jeesuhkon. *See* Jessakkid
Jenness, Diamond, 15, 202
Jessakkid, 121–122, 123f., 246–249
Jimson weed, 141
    ceremony, 284
Jish, 122
John-Paul, 122
Jones, Flora, 122–124

Jossakeed. *See* Jessakkid
Juggler, 124–125

Kabina, 127
Kachina. *See* Koko
Kaetcine, 127
Kagske, 127
Kahsatsenhsera, 127
Kahuna, 127
Kahuna anaana, 128
Kahuna ha ha, 128
Kahuna hoonoho, 128
Kahuna hoonohonoho, 128
Kahuna kahea, 128
Kahuna lapaau, 128–129
Kahuna lomilomi, 129
Kakini, 129
Kakinpe. *See* Yukbe
Kalalik, 129
Kalangi, 129
Kalullim, 129
Kamantocit, 129
Kan, 129
Kangalik, 129–130
Kanhyae, 130
Kanine, Jim. *See* Howlish Watkonot
Kanouga, 130
Kanrugwae, 130
Kansa, 194, 307
Kapay. *See* Kuwi
Karok, 116, 143
Katagara, 130
Kato, 51
Katsa tala, 130
Ke, 130–132
Kegey, 132–133
Kein, 133
Keres, 18, 82, 89–90, 97, 99, 102–103, 104, 105–106,
    107, 108–109, 113, 127, 159, 185, 201, 230, 250,
    251–255, 303, 312, 325–326
Ketaltnes, 133
Ketanitowet, 133
Ketcima Netowani, 132
Keteu, 134
Keyugak, 134
Khichikouai, 134–135
Khmungha, 135
Kichil woknam, 135
Kickapoo, 177
Kikituk, 135
Kilokilo uhane, 135
Kilpatrick, Jack Frederick, 135
Kiowa, 66, 209–210, 214, 284–285

Kiowa-Apache, 58–59
Kitche Manitou, 135–136
Kiva, 136, 252f.
Kixunai. *See* Wogey
Klallam, 257
Kluckhohn, Clyde Kay Maben, 136
Klukwalle, 136
Kohota, 136–137
Kohuyoli, 137
Koiahpe. *See* Koyabi
Kokkothlanna, 137
Koko, 137
Konah, 137–138
Konäpämik, 138
Koo bakiyahale, 138
Koo detul, 138
Koyabi, 138–139
Krilaq, 139
Kroeber, Alfred Louis, 93, 139–140, 228
Ktahándo, 140
Kuksu. *See* Guksu Ceremony
     Cult
Kúlañ o'odham, 140
Kúlañmada. *See* Dúajida
Kulkuli, 140
Kumnakàniktnámu. *See* Uwámu
Kuni Ceremony, 140–141
Kunque, 141
Kununxäs. *See* Atcigamultin
Kuseyaay. *See* Kwisiyai
Kusi, 141
Kusiut, 141–143
Kutenai, 11, 196, 298–300
Kuwi, 143
Kwacmin, 143–144
Kwaipai, 144
Kwakiutl, 8–10, 98, 103, 149, 155, 161–162, 192,
     215–216, 218
Kwashapshigan, 144
Kwashaptum, 144
Kwathidhe, 144–145
Kwaxot. *See* Kohota
Kwisiyai, 145–146
Kyan, 146
Kyanyuantan, 146–148

La Barre, Weston, 149
La Flesche, Francis, 82, 149, 180
Labrador Eskimo, 118, 285
Lagekwa, 149
Lainaitelge, 149–150
Lakota, 11, 36, 37–38, 45, 46, 49, 59, 91, 102,
     104–105, 108, 117, 135, 154, 155, 160, 166, 178,
     201, 208, 216, 218, 263, 279, 295, 304, 305–306,
     306–307, 308–309, 312, 315, 331
Lakota Night Cult. *See* Yuwipi
Lamcem, 150
Lamshimi, 150
Landes, Ruth, 234
Languages, xviii
Larsen, Nils, 128
Le Clair, John, 150–151
Le Clercq, Chretien, 197
Legerdemain, 151
LeJeune, Father, 134–135
Lenni Lenape, 18, 88, 133, 164, 178, 179, 186, 199,
     208, 212, 214
Lescarbot, Marc, 16
Life soul. *See* Body soul
Lifietoynin, 151
Lifiewah, 151
Liföla, 151
Lightning shaman, 151–152
Little Dickey, 152
Little Man, 152–154
Little Warrior, 154
Little Water Society, 64, 154
Liwa wenenapi, 154–155
Loeb, E. M., 172–173
Lohau sumatc, 155
Lokoala, 155
Long, J., 286
Looks Twice, Willie, 155
Lopez, Walter, 155
Lowanpi, 155
Luirh, 155
Luiseño, 22–23, 197, 277
Lummi, 56, 257, 271
Lusiaño, 226
Lycanthropy, 155

Macaiyoyo, 157
Mache da, 157
Mackenzie Eskimo, 134
Mackenzie-Yukon, 61, 70–71, 117, 129, 146, 186
Mad bear, 157
Madatcan, 157–158
Madockawando, 158
Madodoson, 158
Madstone, 158
Madu, 158
Maheonhetan, 158
Mahopá, 158
Mahwee, Dick, 158, 224–226
Maickuriwapai, 159
Maidu, 129, 140, 210, 328–329, 330

Maiswat, 159
Maiyun, 159
Makah, 136, 293
Mákai, 160
Makakagapi, 160
Makan, 240
Makan athinma, 161
Making-Alive, 161–162
Malecite, 211, 228
Mali Yomta, 162
Mamaqa, 162
Mana, 22–23
Mandan, 54–55, 231–232, 321
Mani micami, 162
Manitou, 132, 136, 164. *See also* Great Spirit
Manitowak, 164
Manitowi, 164
Manitowuk, 164
Mankan, 164
Mankani, 164–165
Mankánye Waci, 165
Mantu, 165
Maps, xviii
Maraidi, 165
Masked-Dancer Ceremony, 165
Maskiki, 165
Maskikiwinini, 165
Masks, 122, 262f., 327. *See also* False Faces
Massachuset, 107, 214
Massage, xiii, 5, 129
Masta, 165–166
Masters, 127–129
Mataka libu, 165
Matakanto, 165
Matcupeik, 165. *See* Kwathidhe
Matkothau sumatc, 165
Matnonaltcigan, 165, 166
Mato tipi, 166
Mato wapiye, 166
Matógaxe, 166–167
Matovara sumatc, 167
Mattahando, 167
Matu, 167
Maunetu, 167
Maxpe, 167–168
Maxupá. *See* Xupá
Mayáthle. *See* Oóshtakyòu
Meda, 168
Medassoguneb, 168
Medéoulino, 168
Mede'wegan, 168
Medicine, 106, 164, 165, 168, 206, 282
   preventive, 110

Medicine aprons, 12
Medicine bags, 138, 217
   contents, 197
Medicine bone, 158
Medicine bundles, 37, 122, 162, 163f., 256
Medicine cords, 118f., 119
Medicine Dance, 306
Medicine Dance Ceremony, 165
Medicine Drinking Ceremony, 291
Medicine Lodge Ceremony, 311–312
Medicine Lodge Society, 172, 173, 174
Medicine men and women, 48f., 53, 165, 168, 184,
      185, 223, 226–227, 251, 267, 269, 287, 306–307
   Havasupai, 88
   Lakota, 154
   Ojibwa, 251, 279
   Shoshoni, 226–227, 267
   Takelma, 92
   See also Adanöwiski; Shamans
Medicine Men's Society, 102
Medicine pipe, 168
Medicine societies, 127, 250
Mednanenwek, 170
Meges, 170
Megise, 170
Mehkwasskwan, 170–171
Membertou, 171
Men of Mystery, 171
Menomini, 47, 138, 172, 177, 178–179, 193, 290, 297,
      303–304
Mescal-bean doctors, 57
Meskwoh, 171
Metèolinu, 171
Meteu, 172
Metewen, 172
Metock, Tony, 172–173
Micami. *See* Mani micami
Michelsen, Truman, 180
Micmac, 16, 20, 42, 64, 88, 171, 180, 197, 281
Midahopa, 173
Mide, 173
Midemegis, 174
Midewigun, 174
Midewiwin, 170, 174, 204, 304
   lodge, 172, 173f.
Midwest, 61, 94–95, 112, 132, 138, 162, 164–165,
      172, 177, 178–179, 191–192, 230, 290, 297,
      303–304, 306, 307, 309–311, 312, 313, 323
Midwinter Ceremony, 45
Midwinter Rites of the Cayuga Long House, 261
Migis, 175
Mile, 175–176, 175f.
Mink, John, 176–177

Miqkä′no, 177
Mishaami, 177
Misinghâlikun, 178
Missouri, 231, 305, 309
Mistabeo, 178
Mistapeo, 178
Mitakuye oyasin, 178
Mitä′kwe, 178
Mitäwäpe, 178–179
Mitäwin. *See* Metewen
Mitchell, Tom, 179
Mitigwakik, 179
Mitten, Peter, 157
Miwachi. *See* Mile
Miwe, 179
Miwok, 11, 112, 129, 138–139, 199, 258, 266, 329. *See also* Central Miwok; Coast Miwok; Southern Miwok
Mizinkintika, 179
Modesto, Ruby, 179–180
Mohegan, 180
Moigú, 180
Mojave, 3, 7, 8, 18, 20–21, 102, 103, 107, 116, 118, 136–137, 144–145, 155, 166, 167, 197–198, 266, 279, 281, 325
Moli, 180
Momai yomta. *See* Yomta
Montagnais, 52, 129, 134–135, 157–158, 166, 171, 178, 194, 217, 281, 304
Mo′o dedu, 180
Mooney, James, 4, 64, 85, 114, 116, 180, 270
Mosona, 180
M′teoulinak, 180
Mud Bay Louis, 246
Múdu, 180
Mugwa, 180
Muskrat, 180
Mutöingaip. *See* Surrel, William
Mxeeom, 181
Mystery, xiii, 305, 309
  and observation and experience, xiv
Mystery Medicine order, 204–205

Na lakofichi, 183
Naarhin, 183
Nabu′u, 183–184
Nachulna, 184–185
Nàe, 185
Nahneetis. *See* Nanitis
Nahullo, 185
Naicdia, 185
Naitulgai, 185

Naiyu sumatc. *See* Kwathidhe
Nana ishtohoollo, 185
Nanandawi, 185
Nanandawiiwe wanini, 185
Nanasuigaint, 185–186
Nanitis, 186
Nantadotash, 186
Nantena, 186
Narhnorh, 186
Nashie, 186–187
Naskapi: The Savage Hunters of the Labrador Peninsula, 261
Nassassukwi, 187
Nätanhehi, 187–189
Natick, 167
Native American Church, 155, 189–191. *See also* Peyote
Native American culture, xxxvii
Native American languages, xviii
Natoi, 191
Natugwä, 191–192
Natutshikan, 192
Naualak, 192
Navaho grammar, 232
Navajo, 5–6, 12, 47–49, 53–54, 110, 115, 122, 193, 321–322, 326, 328
  ideal of beauty, harmony, and well-being, 110
Navajo Medicine Man, 232
The Navajos, 298
Navochiwa, 192
Navuzieip, 192
Nawalak, 192–193
N′dilni′h, 193
Neher, A., 233
Neihardt, John, 34
Ne′moak, 193
Netdim maidu. *See* Oye
Netsilik Eskimo, 13, 16, 17, 116, 127, 139, 208, 295–296
Newekwe, 193–194
Nexnox, 194
Nez Perce, 216–217, 282, 315
Ngak saga nii, 194
Niagwai Oäno, 194
Nibikiwinini, 194
Nictut, 194
Nightway, 50f.
Níka qùwe, 194
Nika wakandagi, 194
Nikahnegaah, 194–195
Nilkin. *See* Diyinne
Nimahenan, 195

Niniba, 195
Nipikakaka, 196
Nisimàtozom. *See* Mxeeom
Nisimon, 196
Noho'o, 196
Nomyoh, 196
Nonhonzhinga, 196
Nooks, 196
Nootka, 242–243, 290, 297
Nootsack, 251, 273, 321
North Alaska Eskimo, 135, 293
Northeast, 3, 7, 18, 45, 52–53, 58, 59, 60, 64, 68,
    71–77, 79–82, 85, 86, 88, 90, 98–99, 102, 107,
    110, 112, 114, 127, 130, 133, 154, 157, 164, 167,
    172, 178, 179, 180, 185, 186, 194–195, 197, 199,
    200, 201, 205, 206, 208, 212, 214, 215, 217, 228,
    231, 233, 240, 243, 245, 275, 285, 291, 311, 315,
    317–318
Northern Algonquian, 258
Northern Paiute, 65–66, 93–94, 165, 183–184,
    196–197, 219, 227, 293–294
Northern Ute, 211, 311
Northern Yuki, 135
Northwest Coast, 3, 6–7, 8–10, 12, 18–20, 26, 27, 30,
    56, 64, 68, 98, 99–102, 103, 110, 136, 141–143,
    143–144, 149, 150–151, 155, 161–162, 183, 186,
    192–193, 194, 202–203, 206, 215–216, 217, 218,
    229, 237, 240, 242–243, 243–244, 251, 255–256,
    256–257, 261, 263, 264, 266, 267–269, 271–273,
    276–277, 280–281, 283, 284, 290, 291–293, 297,
    316, 321, 322, 323, 326–327, 330–331
Noseholes. *See* Surrel, William
Nossii, 196–197
Noth, 197
Noxkwasagi, 197
Ntiómel, 197
Nukatem, 197
Numamugu'a, 197
Nunnun letim. *See* Lamcem
Nutsi pilewet, 197
Nyagwékya, 197
Nyavedhi sumach, 197–198
Nynymbi, 198

Object intrusion, 199
Objects, 18–19, 217–218, 312, 321
Obsidian ceremony, 135
O'Connor, Pedro, 199
Odas, 199
Odenigûn, 199–200
Odokanigan, 200
Offerings, 97

Ofo, 22, 283, 322
Ogiwe Oäno, 200
Ohgiwe, 200–201
Ohocoka, 201
Ohshiekats, 201
Ojibwa, 6, 59–60, 87, 88, 104–105, 121–122, 135–136,
    165, 168, 173–175, 176–177, 179, 185, 199–200,
    217, 232, 234, 251, 279, 286–287, 302–303, 312,
    313, 316, 333
Oke, 201
Oki, 201
Okiwe Dance, 201
Olbrechts, Frans, 64–65
Old Man Chips, 331. *See also* Horn Chips
Old Man Dick, 201
Old Pierre, 202–203
Old Took'tok, 203
Omaha, 113, 119, 161, 194, 279, 307, 315, 323
The Omaha Tribe, 149
Omahl, 204
Omazig, 204
Omotome, 204
Onayanakia, 204–205
Ondinonc, 205
Onetda, 205
Ongwe shona, 206
Only-One. *See* Qamkawl
Onniont, 206
Oññonkwat, 206
Onondaga, 200
Ononeovätaneo, 206
Oóshtakyòu, 206
Opagi, 208
Opina, 208
Oqortoq, 208
Oregon Seaboard, 82–83, 92, 113–114, 116, 132–133,
    136, 171, 216, 232, 258, 280, 284, 289, 298, 319
Orenda, 208, 231, 233, 276, 284, 322
Osage, 195, 307
Oswalt, Robert L., 212
Otchipwe, 52, 64, 165, 194, 220
Otkon, 208
Oto, 231, 305, 309
Otter Ceremony, 18
Otto, Rudolf, 323
Oulsgädön, 209
Outfit doctors, 58, 64, 106, 209, 307–308, 328
Owl sacred pack, 162, 163f.
Owl Shamans, 207–208
Owl Woman, 210, 210f.
Oxzem, 210
Oye, 210

Pa towa, 211

Pacific, 11, 12, 16, 20, 109, 127–129, 135, 140, 219, 298

Paddy, William, 65, 66

Pagaholágen, 211

Pagits, 211

Pahiuhiu. *See* Hoopiopio

Paiute, 219, 224, 319–320. *See also* Northern Paiute; Southern Paiute

Pakholangan, 211

Pakwimpa, 211–212

Panco, Joée, 287f.

Papago, 3, 159–160, 210, 250

Papago Indian Religion, 298

Papaicoang, 212

Papalot, 212

Papasokwilun, 212

Park, Susan, 93

Parrish, Essie, 212–214

Passaconaway, 214

Passamaquoddy, 228

Patumawas, 214

Pauewey, 214

Pauwau, 214

Paviotso, 52, 152, 158, 179, 197, 218–219, 224–226, 227–228, 237, 258, 295, 304, 316–317, 320, 325

Pawakan, 214–215

Pawcorance, 215

Pawiapap, 215

Pawnee, 21, 108, 282, 311

Paxala, 215–216

Pebble Society, 304

Pegahsoy, 216

Peigan, 30

Peji hota, 216

Peju'da wintca'cta, 216

Pejuta wicasa, 216

Peléyc, 216–217

Penobscot, 26, 140, 158, 166, 167, 168, 180, 197, 211, 214

Penobscot Man: the Life History of a Forest Tribe in Maine, 261

Petehe. *See* Horn Chips

Petelo. *See* O'Connor, Pedro

Petewaruxti, 217

Pexala. *See* Paxala

Peyote, 112, 180, 189–191, 190f., 231
     ceremony, 189f.
     See also Native American Church

The Peyote Cult, 149

Phylactery, 217

Physical procedures, 115

Pilotois, 217

Pima, 68, 140, 160, 250, 271, 320

P'inan, 217

Pinji gosan, 217

Pipe. *See* Sacred pipes

Pitauniwanha, 217

Pitcitcihtcikan, 217–218

P'iva, 218

Pivat, 218

Place-of-Getting-Rich, 218

Plains, 7, 10, 11, 17–18, 21, 22, 25, 26, 27, 29, 30, 31, 32, 34–36, 37–41, 45, 46, 49–51, 54–55, 57–59, 66, 67, 69–70, 71, 90–91, 102, 103, 104–105, 108, 109, 110, 113, 115–116, 117, 119, 135, 137–138, 150, 152–154, 155, 158, 159, 160, 161, 165, 166–168, 173, 178, 180, 181, 185, 187–189, 194, 195, 196, 201, 204, 206, 208, 209–210, 214–215, 216, 217–218, 227, 230, 231–232, 237–238, 240, 241–242, 244, 251, 256, 257, 263–264, 278, 279, 281–282, 284–285, 289, 295, 296, 301, 304–307, 308–309, 311–312, 313, 315, 316, 318, 319, 321, 323, 330, 331, 333

Plains Cree, 17–18, 104–105, 214–215, 217–218

Plants, 16. *See also* Herbalists and Herbalism

Plateau, 11, 110, 196, 212, 216–217, 220, 244–245, 266–267, 282, 298–300, 315, 319, 325

Plenty Fingers, 218

Plenty Wolf, 218

Plumes, 104, 159. *See also* Feathers

Plummer, Rosie, 218–219

P'o kwin sananwe, 219

Pohari, 219

Poínaba, 219

Po'i-uhane, 219

Poison, 85. *See also* Corpse poison

Pokunt, 219

Polar Eskimo, 285–286

Police societies, 11

Pomo, 58, 64, 86–87, 95, 99, 130, 138, 158, 166, 167, 212–214, 291, 328, 329. *See also* Southeastern Pomo; Southern Pomo

Ponca, 36, 104–105, 113, 119, 161, 166–167, 194, 279, 281–282, 304, 307, 311–312, 313, 323

Pora, 219

Poshayanki, 220

Pöshikö, 220

Potawatomi, 164

Powagan, 220

Powder, 297

Powell, John Wesley, 55, 220, 221f.

Power boards, 255–256

Power spots, 243

Powers, 17–18, 22–23, 31, 42, 71, 103, 113, 127, 140, 165, 166, 167, 168, 180, 192, 193, 212, 217, 219,

233, 243, 258, 263–264, 266, 273, 276–277, 282, 284, 291, 297–298, 305–306, 307, 311, 313
exerting one's, 309–311
harmful aspect, 70
healing, 118
mystical force of, 208
supernatural aspect of, 230
See also Orenda
Powwowing, 220
Poxpoxumelh, 220
Prayer sticks. See Sticks
Prayers, 315
Primary-process thinking, 220–222
Prince, Raymond, 233
Psoriasis, 170
Psychopomp, 222
Puaxantï, 222–223
Puberty quest, 223
Pueblo, 54, 136, 141, 230, 250, 275
Puffo nu, 223
Puget Sound Salish, 276. See also Coast Salish
Puha, 223–224
Puhaga, 224
Puhágam, 224–226
Puhagan, 226–227
Puhagant, 227
Puhagumi, 227
Puhakut, 227
Puhátumadápuipi, 227
Púhigan. See Baohigan
Pul, 228
Pula, 228
Purification. See Cleansing and purification rituals
Puyallup-Nisqually, 150–151, 261, 263, 291–293

Qamkawl, 229
Qaumaneq, 229
Qilalik, 229–230
Qopine, 230
Quapaw, 194
Qube. See Xube
Querränna Society, 230
Quohahles, 230

Radin, Paul, 231
Raqnowe waqonyitan, 231
Rareñdiowanen, 231
Rattles, 201, 258, 288, 304, 305f., 316–317, 333
Rattles Stone Like a Bell, 231–232
Rattlesnake shamans, 232, 315
Red Bird, 232

Red cedar, 173
  bark, 149
  collar, 155
Red Sky, James, 232
Reichard, Gladys Amanda, 232
Remohpoh, 232
Ren, 233
Representative objects, 3
Rey, Juan, 250
Rhombus, 233, 233f.
Rhythmic sensory stimulation, 233–234
Rituals, 281, 290. See also Cleansing and purification rituals
Roberts, Harry, 83
Roberts, Tudy, 234
Rock wounds, 21
Rocks. See Stones
Rods, 219
Rogers, Will, 234
Rolling Thunder, 234
Roosevelt, Theodore, 55
Root doctors and medicine men, 151, 161
Rupert, Henry, 234–236

Sa'aba, 237
Sa'araws, 237
Sacks, 313
Sacred Calf Pipe Bundle, 237–238
Sacred formula, 114. See also Gowäli; Igawésdi
Sacred pipes, 45, 49, 140, 170, 195, 231, 238–240
  substances smoked, 239
Sacred stones. See Stones
Säeicha, 240
Sage, 216
Ságodiwenha gwus, 240
Sai'yûk Society, 240
Saltu, 240
Salye, 240
Sambo, 240
Sanapia, 241–242
Sand paintings, 19f., 111f., 115
Sanimuinak, 242
Santiano, 242
Saokata, 243
Sapir, Edward, 243
Sauk, 177
Sauwel, 243
Sawanikä, 243
Sayiws, 243
Sbatatdaq, 243–244, 257
Scalpers, 21
Science, 36
Scratching instrument, 130

Scurvy, 205
Seeing, 13
Seers, 196, 273
Sees the Living Bull, 244
Seminole, 10, 23, 31, 42, 106, 282
Sending-Away Ceremony, 3
Seneca, 58, 59, 60, 85, 90, 98–99, 107, 110, 114, 154,
    194–195, 197, 200, 245
Senqenim strqam, 244
Serrat. *See* Erinaliut
Sgana, 245
Shade, 245
Shadotgea, 245
Shadow, 245
Shagodiyoweqgowa, 245
Shakers, 245–246
Shaking Tent Ceremony, 38, 47, 53, 64, 122,
    134–135, 144, 246–249, 247f., 261, 290, 333. *See
    also* Aiyakokiyiu
Shamanic state of consciousness, 249
Shamanism
    Arctic, 17
Shamans, xiv–xv
    Alaska Eskimo, 293
    Algonquin, 217
    Angmagsalik, 21
    Apache, 61, 151–152, 186, 201
    Assiniboin, 304–305, 316
    assistants to, 219, 295–296, 320
    Atsugewi, 30–31, 92–93, 279
    Bear, 130–132, 194
    Bella Coola, 141–143
    Biloxi, 22
    Blackfoot, 90, 217
    Caddo, 137–138
    Cahuilla, 179–180, 228
    Carrier, 61–62, 146–148
    Cherokee, 64–65, 234
    Cherokee formulas, 91–92, 116–117
    Cheyenne, 37, 70, 158, 204, 296, 333
    Chipewyan, 117
    Chippewa, 204
    Choctaw, 108, 109–110
    Chugach, 16–17
    Clayoquot, 6–7, 206
    Coast Miwok, 154–155
    Coast Salish, 68, 150–151, 202–203, 271–272, 283
    Comanche, 227, 241–242
    Copper Eskimo, 70
    Crow, 40–41, 57–58, 180, 218, 244, 256, 257, 284
    Dakota, 69–70, 232, 318
    deer, 60
    Diegueño, 144, 145–146, 280

Dwamish, 251
East Greenland Eskimo, 229–230, 242
Eskimo, 13–16, 51–52, 113, 114–115, 116
Gitksan, 99
Gros Ventre, 25–26, 39–40, 67, 90–91, 152–154,
    187–189, 263–264, 315
Haida, 237
Havasupai, 89
Hawaiian, 127, 128–129, 135, 219
Hidatsa, 49–51
Hopi, 296, 327–328
Huron, 217, 288
imitative shamanism, 116
Iroquois, 157, 231
Kansa, 194
Karok, 133, 143
Keres, 89–90
Kiowa, 284–285
Kiowa-Apache, 58–59
Kutenai, 196, 298–300
Kwakiutl, 8–10, 98, 161–162, 215–216, 218
Labrador Eskimo, 285
Lakota, 36, 37–38, 46, 59, 91, 108, 110, 155, 208,
    218, 263, 308–309, 315
Lummi, 56
Lusiaño, 228
Maidu, 210
Mandan, 169f., 231–232
Massachusets, 214
Menomini, 178–179, 193, 290, 303–304
Micmac, 42, 88, 171
Miwok, 11, 112, 138–139, 199
Mohegan, 180
Mojave, 20, 102, 107, 116, 136, 144–145, 155, 166,
    197–198, 279, 281
Montagnais, 129, 171, 217, 304
Natick, 167
Navajo, 53f., 111f.
Netsilik Eskimo, 208
Nez Perce, 216–217, 282
Nootka, 207f., 242
North Alaska Eskimo, 294
Northern Paiute, 65–66, 93–94, 219, 227
Northern Ute, 211
objects given to during vision quest, 208
offerings, 97
Ojibwa, 59–60, 87, 121–122, 168, 173, 174, 175,
    176–177, 199–200, 232, 234, 303–304, 316
Omaha, 194, 313
Osage, 307
Otchipwe, 64
owl, 209
Paiute, 224

Papago, 159–160, 210
Paviotso, 152, 158, 179, 218–219, 224–226
Peigan, 30
Penobscot, 158, 167, 168, 214
Pima, 140, 160
Pomo, 138, 212–214
Ponca, 36, 194, 313
Pueblo, 230
Puyallup-Nisqually, 150–151, 291–293
Quapaw, 194
ritual for securing services of, 208
Salina, 275
Seminole, 282
Seneca, 107
Shasta, 240–241, 257
Shoshoni, 234
Sinkaietk, 220, 283
snake, 232, 291
South Alaska Eskimo, 129, 263
Southern Paiute, 222–223
specializing in venomous bites, 20–21
Takelma, 258
Tewa, 130–132
Tiwa, 215
transvestite, 30, 104
Tsimshian, 99–101, 196, 229, 267–269, 280–281
Twana, 64, 322
Ute, 155
Wailaki, 71
Walapai, 88–89
Wallawalla, 325
Wappo, 329–330
Wasco, 113–114
Washo, 234–236, 277, 313
West Alaska Eskimo, 129, 293
Winnebago, 164–165, 306, 309–311
Wintu, 122–124
Woods Cree, 170–171
Yana, 143
Yavapai, 26–27
Yokuts, 16
Yuit, 203
Yuki, 150, 172–173, 298
Yuma, 316
Yurok, 82–83, 132–133, 216
See also Medicine men and women
Shasta, 22, 240–241, 257
Shaughnessy, Florence, 83
Shawnee, 177
Shaxöa, 249
Shells, 138, 170, 174, 175, 304
Sheride, 250
Shihio, 250

Shikani Society, 250
Shilup, 250
Shiwanna, 250
Shoshoni, 179, 185–186, 187, 192, 198, 219, 226–227, 234, 267, 276, 288–289
Shumaikoli Society, 250
Shunad, 250
Sia Pueblo, 251–255, 252f.
Sia'ticum, 250
Síatcokam. See Mákai
Sila, 250–251
Sing-dance, 244–245
Singing doctors, 129, 149–150, 162, 180, 184–185, 210, 329
ceremony, 295
Singing for Power, 298
Sinkaietk, 212, 220, 244–245, 266–267, 283
Sitac, 251
Siyotanka, 251
Skaaga, 251
Skagit, 26
Skaquis, 251
Skinaway, Tom, 251
Sklaletut, 251
Skokomish, 267, 273
Skoyo Chaiän, 251–255
Skudilitc, 255–256
Skull Bundle, 256
Skwanilac, 256
Sky World beings, 206
Slalakum. See Sxwlaem
Sle, 256–257
Slippery Eyes, 257
Slocum, John, 245–246, 257
Slocum, Mary, 245–246
Smatnatc, 257
Smith, Jake, 257
Smith, Marion, 150
Smitinak, 257
Smokehouse, 258
Smoking materials, 239. See also Tobacco
Smoking pipe. See Sacred pipes
Snake shamans, 291
Snake society, 19f.
Snowhouses, 127
Snow-Snake Healing Ceremony, 64
Social Life of the Navajo Indians, 232
Society of Mystic Animals, 114
Society of Otters, 59
Sogonebuu, 258
Sokadisiu, 258
Sokosa, 258
Somlohólxaes, 258

Song, 258–260, 259f.

Sorcerers, 7, 101–102, 116, 128, 135, 216–217, 260, 298, 315

   evil, 12, 57

   See also Witches

Sorcery, 5, 6, 68, 109

   causing victim to lose ability to speak, 16

Soul loss, 260, 271–272

Souls, 117–118, 205, 206, 256–257, 289. *See also* Body soul; Breath soul; Free soul; Shade; Shadow

Source Material on the History and Ethnology of Caddo Indians, 269

South Alaska Eskimo, 51–52, 129, 263

Southeast, 4, 6, 10, 11, 17, 22, 23, 31, 32, 42, 57, 60, 64–65, 85, 86, 91, 92, 106, 108, 109–110, 114, 115, 116–117, 130, 183, 185, 209, 234, 250, 270–271, 282, 290–291, 297–298, 322, 326

Southeastern Pomo, 137

Southern Miwok, 314

Southern Paiute, 222–223

Southern Pomo, 106, 180

Southwest, 3, 5–6, 7, 8, 10, 12, 16, 18, 20–22, 26–27, 30, 42–43, 47–49, 53–54, 55–56, 61, 66, 68, 70, 71, 82, 88–90, 97, 99, 102–103, 104, 105–106, 107, 108–109, 110, 113, 114, 115, 116, 118, 119, 122, 127, 129, 130–132, 136–137, 140, 141, 144–145, 151–152, 155, 157, 159–160, 165, 166, 167, 175–176, 179, 180, 185, 186–187, 191, 192, 193–194, 197–198, 201, 204–205, 210, 211–212, 215, 217, 218, 219, 220, 223, 230, 243, 249–250, 251–255, 260–261, 266, 271, 275–276, 278, 279–280, 281, 282, 287, 289, 290, 296, 303, 305, 312, 313–314, 316, 318, 320, 321–322, 325–326, 327–328

Sóxwá, 260–261

Spadak, 261

Speck, Frank G., 167, 261

Spells, 70–71

Spirit Canoe healing ceremony, 255–257, 261, 263, 264, 271

Spirit Dance, 143, 243, 256

Spirit illness, 271

Spirit lance, 210

Spirit Lodge, 261. *See also* Midewiwin

Spirit Lodge Ceremony, 181. *See also* Midewiwin

Spirit Possession, 261–263

Spirit powers, 17–18, 251

Spirits, 6, 11, 20, 61, 110, 116, 129, 134, 146, 159, 162, 164, 178, 185, 186, 194, 196, 237, 240, 264, 271, 293–294, 295–296, 313, 318, 319, 326–327

   calling, 11–12

   healing, 30

   obtaining gifts from, 155, 283

   sea people, 30

   species-specific, 17

   Zuni, 21–22

   See also Helping spirits

Spirituality, xiii

Sptdaqw, 263

Sqalálitut, 263

Staffs, 104

Steed, Jesse, 263

Steinmetz, Paul, 240

Stevens, Johnny, 52, 263

Stewart, Omer, 155

Sticks, 99, 102–103, 103f., 113, 127, 133, 143–144, 186–187, 227–228

   swallowers, 275–276

Stiffarm, 263–264

Stlalcopschudoptch, 264

Stleabats, 264

Stolzman, William, 240

Stomach kneaders, 264

Stone seats, 289

Stones, 25, 215, 250, 294f., 295

Striking Stick Dance, 130

Suchuma, 264

Sucking doctors, 28, 38, 59, 71, 90, 104, 114, 122, 123f., 129, 133, 134, 150, 155, 158, 167, 172–173, 180, 184, 194, 203, 212–214, 242, 264–266, 265f., 272, 280, 281, 291, 315, 328–329

   devices used, 55, 200

   object removed by, 138

   process used, 281

Sucking shamans. *See* Sucking doctors

Sudatory, 266

Sulia, 266

Sulik müko, 266

Sumatc, 266

Sumix, 266–267

Supernatural, 322

   aspect of powers, 230, 322, 323

   beings, 22, 45, 46f., 243–244, 269, 307, 319

Surrel, William, 267

Sutuky yomta. *See* Yomta

Swádas, 267

Swanaskxw, 267–269

Swanassu, 269

Swanton, John Reed, 269

Swaxtiutid, 269

Sweat lodge, 22, 117, 157–158, 258, 266, 275, 301

   ceremony, 269–270, 270f.

Swimmer, 4, 270–271, 271f.

Swúsos ó'odham, 271

Sxet, 271

Sxwlaem, 271–272
Syawan, 272–273
Syòwae, 273
Syòwan, 273
Syuwadad, 273

Taachi, 275
Taarteq, 275
Tadi nyac, 275
Take, 275
Takelma, 92, 258
Taköonin, 275–276
Tam Apö, 276
Tamanoas, 276–277
Tamoémli, 277
Tamyush, 277
T'ànwen, 278
Tao, 278
Tarrak. See Torngak
Tartok, 278–279
Tau-gu, 221f.
Tawashichunpi, 279
Tayatowetha. See Saokata
Tchi can ama, 279
Tchissakiwinini, 279
Tcikamitc sumatc, 279
Tciplitcu, 107
Te Ithaethema, 279
Teckwine, 279–280
Teipalai, 280
Tekohanna, 280
Telbut, 280
Telogel, 280
Temnepa, 280
Tens, Issac, 280–281
Teomul. See Tiómel
Tepe'muésuki, 281
Teton Dakota, 237–238. See also Dakota
Teton Sioux, 251
Tewa, 42–43, 66, 104, 130–132, 211, 217, 218, 219,
    249–250, 260–261, 278, 318, 328
Tewebatsigan, 281
Tewehigan, 281
Tewusu, 281
Teyewa, 281
Thalbitzer, William, 278
Thank-you ceremony, 319
Thauwithok sumatc, 281
Théwatshi, 281–282
Thilyamo sumatc, 282
Thorns, 151
Thunderbird, 307
Thundercloud Society, 250

Tiger, Susie, 282
Tikerarmiut, 113, 116
Tingavish, 282
Tinun, 282
Tiómel, 282
Tirára, 282
Tiwa, 16, 68, 114, 151, 186–187, 191, 211–212, 215,
    220, 249–250, 287
Tiwét, 282
Tixyi, 283
Tjui, 283
Tlakwilex xalaspuxem, 283
Tlakwilex Xalslapem, 283
Tlequiltc, 283
Tlingit, 326–327
Tlogwe, 283
Tlu qali. See Klukwalle
Toalache, 284
Tobacco, 218, 239, 260–261, 291
    offerings, 46
Tobacco Planters, 284
Tolowa, 282
Tomanawis, 284
Toneakoy, 284–285
Tonneraouanount, 285
Tornaq. See Torngak
Tornarssuit. See Tornguang
Torngak, 285
Torngevok, 285
Tornguang, 285–286
Tornrak, 286
Totam, 286–287
Toyide, 287
Trance, 70, 128, 287, 319, 325
    induction, 287f., 288
Transvestite shamans, 30, 104
Treatment, 22
Tree dwellers, 45, 46f.
Trehero, John, 288
Tribes, xvii
The Trickster, 231
Tripne, 289
Trudum, 289
Tsatsawâ'a, 289
Tsekteya, 289
Tse'makwin, 289
Tshi'saqka, 290
Tsiahk, 290
Tsiditindi, 290
Tsikili, 290–291
Tsimshian, 12, 18, 99–102, 194, 196, 229, 267–269,
    280–281
    amulet, 99f.

Tsiniiakoianorenhseraten, 291
Tso lagayv li, 291
Tsondacoüanné, 291
Tsotibenén, 291
Tsukamxowi, 291
Tu udum, 291
Tudáb, 291–293
Tug-of-War, 275
Tûkte, 293
Tumanos, 293
Tumudaini, 293–294
Tungat, 294
Tunghak, 294–295
Tunghalik, 295
Tuníku'hu, 295
Tunkan, 295
Tunraq, 295–296
Tupiliq, 296
Turtle, 176, 296
Tutelary, 296
Tuuhikya, 296
Twana, 27, 64, 322, 330–331
Tzidaltai, 296

Uctaqyu, 297
Udkukut, 297
Ukémawas, 297
Ulanigvgv, 297–298
Umaah, 298
Underhill, Ruth, 298
Unihipili, 298
Ûntali, 298
User's guide, xvii–xviii
Ute, 155
Utem letimk, 298
Uwámu, 298–300

Vision quest, 32, 223, 314–315, 319
   shaman's transformation in, 229
Visionaries, 226–227
Visions, 25, 191–192
Visual mental imagery, 301
Vonhäom, 301

Wabani, 303
Wabeno, 303–304
Wabinu, 304
Wacickani, 304
Wacucke, 304
Wadákati, 304
Wagmuha, 304
Wahconwechasta, 304–305
Wahuprin, 305

Wailaki, 71, 134, 149–150, 184–185, 280, 318, 325
Waititcani, 305
Wakan, 305–306
Wakan tanka, 306
Wakan tcañkara, 306
Wakan Wacipi, 306
Wakan yan, 306–307
Wakanda, 307
Wakandagi waganxe, 307
Wakandja, 307
Wakantcañkara, 307
Wakawanx, 307
Wakilapi. See Temnepa
Wakinyan, 307
Wakonda, 307
Wakondagi, 307
Walapai, 88–89
Walimitca, 307–308
Wallawalla, 110, 319, 325
Walter, V. J., 233
Walter, W. Grey, 233
Wapiye, 308–309
Wappo, 329–330
Waqonyitan, 309
War Dance, 311
Warukana, 309–311
Waruksti, 311
Wasáse, 311
Wasco, 113–114
Washington, Mrs., 311
Washíshka-athè, 311–312
Washo, 234–236, 281, 313
Water, 211–212
Waterman, Thomas Talbot, 312
Waubunowin, 312
Waunyapi, 312
Wawa, 312
Waxobi Watugari. See Wacickani
Waxopini, 312
Waxopini xedera, 313
Waxúbe, 313
Wayan, 313
Wazethe, 313
Webber, James C., 317–318
Welewkushkush, 313
We'mawe, 313–314
Wenenapi. See Temnepa
Weppah, 314
Wes comi, 314–315
Wesatwas Gatcikwai, 315
West Alaska Eskimo, 129, 295
Wewacpe, 315
Wéyekin, 315

Whistles, 130, 166, 251
White, Leslie, 265
White Buffalo Calf Woman, 237–238
White Buffalo Society, 68
White Weasel, 315
Whizzer. *See* Rhombus
Wicahmunga, 315
Wicasa wakan, 315
Wikwisiyai, 315–316
William, Henry, 152
Williams, Duke. *See* Xelxalelkt
Williams, Suzie, 11
Williams, Tom, 11
Willier, Russell, 170–171
Wilson, Charles, 316
Wilson, Jack. *See* Wovoka
Wilson, Robert, 196
Windigop, 316
Winnebago, 61, 94–95, 112, 164–165, 230, 306, 307,
    309–311, 312, 313, 323
The Winnebago Tribe, 231
Wintca'cta wakan', 316
Wintu, 329
Wintun, 162, 196, 240, 243, 283
Wiping off, 55–56
Wisábaya, 316
Wise One Above, 103
Wish power, 166
Wissler, Clark, 317
Witapanóxwe, 317–318
Witcasta wakan, 318
Witceawa, 318
Witchcraft, 5–6, 108
Witches, 5–6, 68, 135, 249–250, 290–291, 307, 328.
    See also Sorcerers
Wizardry, 5, 6
Wo, 318
Wogey, 319
Wolves
    turning into, 155
    wolf ritual, 136
Woman, 26
Wonoyekw, 319
Woods Cree, 170–171
Wopila Ceremony, 319
Wot, 319
Wound doctors, 11, 28, 57–58, 330
Wovoka, 87, 319, 319f.
Wúsosig, 320
Wütádu, 320

Xàexae, 321
Xapáaliia, 28–29, 321

Xatáùl, 321–322
Xelxalelkt, 322
Xi, 322
Xlubak yomta. *See* Yomta
Xop, 323
Xqpini, 323
Xube, 323
Xudab, 323
Xupá, 323

Yabaicini, 325
Yáika, 325
Yamomk, 325
Yana, 143
The Yana Indians, 312
Yantcha, 325
Yapota. *See* Mile
Yatckinolos, 325
Yavapai, 10, 26
Yavook, 325
Yaya, 325–326
Yehasuri, 326
Yei, 326
Yek, 326–327
Yellow Bear, 327–328
Yenaldlosi, 328
Yia kwiyó, 328
Yoi wai quiolit, 328
Yokuts, 8, 16, 196, 289, 291, 297
Yomi, 328–329
Yomta, 329
Yomto, 329–330
Youlápxda, 330
Young, David, 170–171
Yuchi, 291
Yuit, 203
Yukbe, 210, 330
Yuki, 71, 106, 110–112, 150, 172–173, 180, 298
Yuko, 330
Yuma, 316
Yurok, 82–83, 132–133, 171, 216, 232, 280, 289,
    298
Yurok Geography, 312
Yuwadab, 330
Yuwipi, 11, 102, 201, 263, 306, 331

Zemaheonevsz, 333
Zhiishiigwan, 333
Zuni, 21–22, 30, 55–56, 71, 107, 127, 137, 157,
    175–176, 180, 193–194, 204–205, 220, 243,
    279–280, 281, 289, 305, 313–314
    curing society chief, 180